Yale Russian and East European Studies, 12

Plan and Market

Economic Reform in Eastern Europe

edited and with an introduction

by Morris Bornstein

New Haven and London, Yale University Press

1973

Designed by John O. C. McCrillis
and set in Times Roman type.
Printed in the United States of America by
The Murray Printing Company
Forge Village, Massachusetts.

Published in Great Britain, Europe, and Africa by
Yale University Press, Ltd., London.
Distributed in Canada by McGill-Queen's University
Press, Montreal; in Latin America by Kaiman & Polon,
Inc., New York City; in Australasia and Southeast
Asia by John Wiley & Sons Australasia Pty. Ltd.,
Sydney; in India by UBS Publishers' Distributors Pvt.,
Ltd., Delhi; in Japan by John Weatherhill, Inc., Tokyo.

Contents

Preface

This book is concerned with why and how economic systems change, how such change can be measured and evaluated, and its consequences, as illustrated by recent experience in Eastern Europe. The authors identify problems, explore alternative approaches to them, and examine possible solutions. Although the papers cover various topics, they all blend theoretical analysis and empirical observation, and consider the political and social as well as economic aspects of system change. The subjects included were chosen to illuminate exciting key issues in the field, rather than to provide encyclopedic coverage of the evolution of the many aspects of economic reform in each country in the area. Although such comprehensive studies are useful reference works, they usually become out-of-date rather quickly and sometimes make dull reading.

For this project, the Comparative Economics Program at the University of Michigan assembled a team of specialists with rare language talents, technical skills, and institutional knowledge. The papers are based on detailed field research, where this was feasible, supported by the Program. Draft versions of the papers were discussed intensively at a three-day working conference in November 1970 cosponsored by the Program and the Center for Russian and East European Studies at the University of Michigan. The papers were subsequently revised for publication in this volume in light of the discussion at the conference.

The authors are grateful for the suggestions and advice of the discussants at the conference: Abram Bergson, Harvard University; Keith Bush, University of Munich; Z. M. Fallenbuchl, University of Windsor; Gregory Grossman, University of California (Berkeley); Michael Kaser, Oxford University; Peter Knirsch, Free University of Berlin; Andrzej Korbonski, University of California (Los Angeles) and the Ford Foundation; Rikard Lang, Ekonomski Institut (Zagreb); Bedřich Levčík, United Nations Economic Commission for Europe; Támas Nagy, Institute of Economics of the Hungarian Academy of Sciences; Alec Nove, University of Glasgow; Richard D. Portes, Princeton University; Jan Vanek, International Labor Office; and Jaroslav Vanek, Cornell University. Thanks are also due Robert F. Dernberger, Alexander Eckstein, Alfred G. Meyer, and Colleen Glazer of the University of Michigan for their assistance in connection with the conference. Finally, we owe a special debt of gratitude to Nancy Nimitz of the RAND Corporation, who kindly revised the paper by Jerzy F. Karcz after his untimely death.

This volume is the second in a series resulting from research conferences conducted by the Comparative Economics Program at the University of Michigan. The first volume, edited by Alexander Eckstein and published by the University of California Press in 1971, is *Comparison of Economic Systems: Theoretical and Methodological Approaches*.

The Comparative Economics Program is financed by a grant from the Ford Foundation, whose support and encouragement are gratefully acknowledged.

M.B.

1

Introduction

MORRIS BORNSTEIN

An economic system may be viewed as the set of arrangements by which the community determines what shall be produced ("the bill of goods"); how it shall be produced, including the institutions and instruments to be used and the pattern of resource allocation; and how the resulting personal income and claims to goods and services shall be distributed (and re-distributed) among households. Three main groups of factors influence economic systems and cause them to change: the level of economic develop-ment, social and cultural factors, and the "environment."[1]

The level of economic development can be measured and compared by various indicators, including the level of per capita income, the rate of growth of per capita income, the share of investment in GNP, the share of primary, secondary, and tertiary activities in total employment or GNP, etc. Whichever measures are used, it is clear that economic growth alters the size and structure of the economy and that these changes in turn can lead to modifications in the economic system.

Many aspects of society and culture influence the economic system. One is social stratification, based on race, occupation, income, wealth, or other factors. In addition, the customs, traditions, values, and beliefs of society shape the economic system, one of its institutions. Especially important is ideology—a set of ideas and values guiding individuals (and organizations composed of them) in interpreting their environment, choosing goals in regard to maintaining or changing the environment, and selecting the means to achieve these goals. Ideology affects the economic system in various ways: it influences both the ends and the means of the system, and it may maintain or alter the system.

Finally, an economic system operates in an "environment" which affects not only its performance but also the system itself. The "natural" environ-ment of an economic system includes such elements as the size, location, and

1. Cf. Morris Bornstein, "The Comparison of Economic Systems: An Integration," in *Comparison of Economic Systems: Theoretical and Methodological Approaches*, ed. Alexander Eckstein (Berkeley: University of California Press, 1971), pp. 339–55.

natural resource endowment of the economy. These features influence the nature of the economic system through their effect on the level and character of economic development and on ideology and other aspects of culture. Another aspect of "environment" is contact with other economic systems, which is a source of transmission of ideology and of information about alternative arrangements and their results.

Beginning around 1960, the economic systems of Eastern Europe have experienced changes originating in all three of these factors. In some cases, these changes have cumulated into what may be considered "major" or "minor" economic reforms. However, the pattern and the process have varied significantly among countries. The papers in this volume analyze the reasons for change, its forms, its development, and its results. They explore a wide range of issues of great significance in system design, including the following:

1. The appropriate combination of centralization and decentralization in economic organization and decision making, including the nature and status of the firm
2. The objectives and methods of economic planning
3. The extent, character, and role of competition, in both its economic and its sociopolitical aspects
4. The power of prices and money to allocate resources, and thus the role of monetary and fiscal policies and instruments
5. Performance indicators and incentives for managers and workers, with their broad social and ideological implications for income distribution
6. The mechanisms to generate technological progress
7. Property rights over the use of the means of production and the income they generate, including the possibility of "industrial democracy" through "workers' self-management"

To introduce the ten studies which follow, section I of this chapter provides a general summary of the causes and characteristics of economic reform in Eastern Europe. Section II then discusses how some of the principal issues in system design and system change illustrated by the reforms are analyzed in the remaining chapters of the book.

I. Main Features of Economic Reforms in Eastern Europe

The economic reforms represent a retreat from the traditional "command economy" model of comprehensive central planning and administrative control established in the USSR in the 1930s and introduced into East

Germany, Poland, Czechoslovakia, Hungary, Bulgaria, Romania, Yugoslavia, and Albania after World War II. The reform movement can therefore best be understood by considering the nature and results of this traditional model, the pressures for change, the sources of resistance to change, and the main features common to the reforms in most of these countries.

The Traditional Soviet Model

The chief features of the traditional model included the following: (1) All significant means of production outside agriculture were nationalized. (2) In agriculture, the dominant pattern was collectivization, involving nominally cooperative ownership under close state control. However, the collectivization drive was abandoned in Yugoslavia in 1953 and in Poland in 1956. (3) The hierarchical system of economic organization had several important characteristics: Decision making was concentrated near the top. The different levels bargained about production assignments and the allocation of resources to meet them. Interenterprise relationships were determined "vertically" through the respective administrative hierarchies, rather than "horizontally" through the market. (4) Production and its disposition were planned in detail in physical units. (5) To enforce these ambitious plans, the means of production were rationed—materials by administrative orders, and labor by controls over the size (and sometimes the distribution) of wage expenditures.

In turn, (6) prices were administratively set and infrequently changed. Industrial wholesale prices were fixed on a cost-plus basis, with the aim of enabling most branches of industry to earn revenues sufficient to cover current (but not also capital) expenditures and show a small profit. Retail prices, including a large element of excise taxes, were supposedly set near market-clearing levels, but they were often too low, as shown by persistent shortages. Agricultural procurement prices were low relative to retail prices for the same commodities and to prices for industrial inputs into agriculture, and various controls were needed to enforce procurement quotas. (7) Money was "passive," at least in the production sector: the flow of funds was adjusted by taxes and credit to implement the allocation of resources and goods previously made in physical terms. (8) Managerial and worker incentives stressed the fulfillment and overfulfillment of quantitative production targets. Finally, (9) foreign economic relations were conducted by special export-import corporations; producing enterprises had no direct contacts with foreign customers or suppliers, and their interest in foreign trade was weak.

This model was originally applied in the Soviet Union in the 1930s to achieve rapid industrialization and military power in a large but relatively backward country with considerable supplies of unskilled labor and extensive natural resources. The aim was to secure rapid growth and drastic structural change, despite considerable economic and social costs, through the comprehensive mobilization of labor and capital under centralized administrative direction. However, it was much less relevant to the circumstances of the much smaller East European countries in the late 1940s—and even to those of the Soviet Union itself by the 1950s.

At the end of World War II, Czechoslovakia and East Germany were already highly industrialized by European standards. They had little surplus agricultural labor which could be shifted to industry, and their population was accustomed to central European, not Soviet, living standards. Poland (in its postwar boundaries) and Hungary were less industrialized, but still more advanced than the Balkan countries, which did have large underutilized agricultural labor forces. More important, all of these countries are much smaller than the Soviet Union and lack both its varied resource endowment and its potential market for large-scale production. Therefore, they are inherently much more dependent on foreign trade. Hence, the Soviet pattern of rapid development of heavy industry (for which some of the East European countries lacked even the basic resources), at the expense of international specialization based on comparative advantage, did not fit the circumstances and needs of the smaller East European countries.

The harmful consequences of the imposition of the traditional Soviet model became evident relatively soon and sharply in the more developed countries of the area, such as East Germany, Poland, Czechoslovakia, and Hungary, although later and less acutely in the less advanced countries, such as Romania and Bulgaria. Overcentralization of decision making, excessively detailed planning and rigid materials allocation procedures, the suppression of local initiative, unsound price structures, and overambitious targets led to waste and inefficiency. Shortages of both producer and consumer goods were chronic, while stocks of unwanted goods accumulated. Lacking adequate material inputs and incentives, the agricultural sector performed especially poorly. The low quality and technological lag of manufactured goods limited the possibilities for sale both within CEMA (the East European trade bloc) and on the world market. Despite continuing high rates of investment, the accustomed high growth rates of national product and labor productivity began to decline by the late 1950s or early 1960s, depending upon the country.

In the unique case of Yugoslavia, the abandonment of the traditional Soviet system began much earlier, in 1952. The result was a search for a new kind of socialist economy and society—still in progress—based on workers' management of enterprises and progressively diminishing central regulation of the economy.

Pressures for Reform[2]

By the early 1960s, a growing number of economists had begun to perceive and express the need for economic reform as part of a shift from a more centralized economic system in the "extensive" phase of economic development to a less centralized system in the "intensive" phase. This formulation was politically convenient because it enabled them to argue the need for change without as such condemning the traditional system, with which the Communist party leadership was so intimately involved. Instead, it was argued that different conditions called for a different system of economic planning and management.

In the "extensive" phase, it was asserted, the chief aims of "economic construction" were to alter the structure of the economy drastically and rapidly—to industrialize, to urbanize, to adjust to changes in territory which resulted from World War II, to reshape foreign economic relations, to develop backward regions. The methods were socialization of the means of production, a sharp increase in the rate of investment, rapid expansion of the industrial labor force, and revision of the presocialist income distribution. In contrast, in the "intensive" phase, the emphasis is no longer on rapid structural change, but rather on smaller, marginal changes in the composition of output, technology, etc. With a slowdown in the rate of growth of the labor force, capital deepening rather than capital widening is stressed. In the consumer goods sector, there has been a shift from a sellers' market toward a buyers' market for some goods, as a result of the rise in living standards and the availability of stocks.

Thus, the economic system must be modified to deal with the new conditions of the "intensive" phase. More decisions should be made at lower levels and on technical-economic rather than political grounds. However, to be sound, these decentralized decisions must be guided by more rational prices and by more appropriate performance indicators. Product mix and product characteristics should respond more closely to customer demand— for consumer goods as well as producer goods, and especially for exports. The coercion and ideological appeals used to mobilize resources in the extensive phase must be replaced by more emphasis on incentives to promote the efficient production of the correct output. Finally, a new approach to foreign trade is required, since it represents simultaneously a way to obtain economies of scale beyond the capacity of the domestic market, a means of competition to discipline highly-concentrated domestic industry, and a source of innovation in products and technology.

2. A number of the points which follow are discussed in another context in my "East European Economic Reforms and the Convergence of Economic Systems," *Jahrbuch der Wirtschaft Osteuropas* [Yearbook of East European Economics], vol. 2 (Munich: Günter Olzog Verlag, 1971), pp. 257–62.

Discussion of the need for reform and of specific reform proposals was aided by political destalinization after 1956, which permitted freer discussion of new ideas in the economic sphere and the inflow of information from abroad. The latter brought both greater awareness of economic growth and living standards in Western Europe, and greater understanding of the operation of regulated market economies, in contrast to the "anarchic" capitalist economies depicted in orthodox Marxian writings. Thus, what was previously considered an issue of principle—e.g. central formulation of detailed enterprise production plans—became a matter of technique, to be evaluated on its merits. Similarly, economists in Communist countries began to use techniques, such as mathematical programming and econometrics, previously condemned as "bourgeois." As a result, it became possible to propose "mixed" economic models in which the central authorities could continue to control the main lines of economic development (including income distribution and foreign trade) through macroeconomic planning and monetary-fiscal measures, while permitting more enterprise autonomy in microeconomic decisions in response to market forces.

Resistance to Reform

Nevertheless, the political leadership was slow to recognize both the need for change and the form it should take. In the first place, it was reluctant to believe that the system itself, rather than the incompetence of individual officials, was responsible. In some cases, shortcomings in the statistical system failed to disclose the facts and causes of declining economic performance promptly and accurately. Reform was also opposed on ideological and philosophical grounds: Reliance on the market is inconceivable in a socialist planned economy, because socialism is more than simply public ownership of the (principal) means of production. It requires central planning of investment, output, prices, and distribution. Capital and land charges, production for profit, and emphasis on material incentives are incompatible with socialism. The official ideology of the "solidary society" denies any conflict between group interests, whereas reform proposals recognize the separate interests of firms, workers, and consumers, and recommend the market as the mechanism for reconciling these interests.[3]

Reforms are also opposed on more pragmatic grounds. (1) Some fear reform will mean loss of central (Party) control over the main directions of economic development. Whereas central planning can assure the priority development of sectors important to the national welfare, decentralized decision-making by autonomous enterprises in response to market forces

3. Cf. Gregory Grossman, "The Solidary Society: A Philosophical Issue in Communist Economic Reforms," in *Essays in Socialism and Planning in Honor of Carl Landauer*, ed. Gregory Grossman (Englewood Cliffs, N.J.: Prentice-Hall, 1970), pp. 184–211.

can lead to the diversion of resources from investment and military programs to consumption. (2) Because centrally planned economies typically operate under conditions of repressed inflation and administrative allocation (rather than price rationing) of many goods, more influence for market forces can bring open inflation, which would in turn affect the distribution of income and popular attitudes toward the regime. (3) At the same time, unemployment may occur or increase as enterprises lay off excess workers in response to a shift from output maximization to profit maximization, to more autonomy in the use of wage funds, or to the curtailment of budget subsidies. (4) Furthermore, reducing the artificial separation between the domestic economy and foreign trade, hitherto provided by the buffer of foreign trade corporations, would make it impossible for many enterprises to produce for export without large subsidies. In short, some opposition to reform is based on an assessment of the risk and uncertainty attached to both the benefits and costs of reform, including the problems involved in transition from the old system to a new one.

Reforms are also resisted on more personal grounds by various interest groups. The Party apparatus and ministerial and financial bureaucracy believe they will lose power as enterprises are given more freedom to make decisions in response to market forces, in place of the traditional system of joint supervision of enterprises by higher administrative agencies and by parallel Party organizations. Although reforms promise to enhance the authority of enterprise management, the reaction of managers depends both on the type of reform and on the kind of manager. Probably virtually all managers favor mild, limited reforms which offer more freedom over the use of the enterprise's resources (e.g. the wage fund and the labor force) and retention of a larger share of profit at the disposal of the enterprise for bonuses, employee housing, and expansion of productive facilities. However, many managers who have been successful under the traditional system are not enthusiastic about more comprehensive reforms which call for them to become independent, cost-conscious, innovation-minded entrepreneurs selling products in a competitive buyers' market—in short, to become "businessmen" instead of production engineers.

Workers, in turn, are concerned about the impact on their real incomes of changes in wages and prices associated with reform. New incentive schemes may increase the money incomes of managerial and technical personnel and more-skilled workers relative to less-skilled workers. It is widely feared that retail prices may be increased, because the rationalization of the wholesale-price structure will affect the general level of wholesale and then retail prices; because emphasis on cost consciousness and profitability may lead to reduction or elimination of subsidies for some consumer goods and services, especially housing; and because higher agricultural procurement prices to stimulate farm output would have to be covered by correspondingly higher retail food prices. Also, the curtailment of unprofitable production and greater freedom for managers over the enterprise wage fund and labor force may lead to at least frictional and perhaps even structural unemployment, despite a national macroeconomic policy of full employment.

Finally, economic reforms are opposed on the ground that liberalization in the economic sphere may spread, threatening the paramount role of the Communist party in national life. Freer discussion of alternatives in the economic sphere might lead to demands for open discussion of cultural, social, and even political issues. Economic reforms imply some diffusion of power, first to enterprise management, but subsequently to the population through reliance on the market for guidance on the composition of at least part of the national output. It is feared that professionals in other fields may also seek greater autonomy.

Chief Aspects of Reforms

The struggle between proreform and antireform forces has produced different reform models or blueprints in the various East European countries. Nevertheless, some of the chief features of the reforms common to several, if not all, of the countries can be noted briefly.

One general feature is a somewhat greater role for market forces. However, even the most far-reaching reform proposals assume a continued basic commitment to socialism (and thus the retention of public ownership and limitations on inequality in the distribution of income and wealth). They also hold that the market mechanism is complementary to, not inconsistent with, a considerable measure of central planning. The latter should determine the "main proportions" of the economy: the shares in national product of investment, collective consumption (including military programs), and individual consumption; the rate of growth of the economy and of its different sectors, industrial branches, and regions; and income policies. The market mechanism, on the other hand, would be used primarily to achieve greater efficiency and flexibility in the use of resources.

Thus, the aim is to adapt production more closely to demand, through the greater use of financial indicators such as sales, profits, or profitability (usually in relation to capital) to evaluate enterprise performance—instead of gross or net output or cost reduction, as under the traditional system. In turn, managerial incentives schemes have been revised to relate bonuses to the new indicators, and managerial and worker bonuses are to be paid from profits. "Economic effectiveness" and "economic accountability" are to be stressed, and subsidies reduced. Greater use is to be made of indirect financial "levers" such as prices, taxes, and credit, in place of detailed output assignments and input authorizations enforced by central allocation of supplies.

In turn, enterprises are to receive greater autonomy in preparing and executing plans as the number of enterprise targets fixed by higher authorities is reduced; at the extreme (in Hungary), enterprises receive no plans from higher agencies. Administrative rationing of producer goods is to be replaced at least in part by wholesale trade through direct contacts between enterprises and their suppliers and customers.

However, in some countries devolution of authority to enterprises is limited by the creation of "associations" (or "directorates" or "centrals") which, depending upon the country, control the activities of their member enterprises in some or all of the following aspects: production plans, assignment of customers, pricing, allocation of investment, and research and development. The powers and behavior of the association thus determine the extent to which "decentralization" of authority to the enterprise occurs and whether the enterprise or the association effectively becomes the socialist counterpart of the autonomous profit-seeking capitalist corporation.

In regard to investment, a greater share of total financing is to come from self-finance of enterprises (from depreciation allowances and retained earnings) as well as from repayable bank credits, rather than from free budget grants. Enterprises are supposed to have more authority over investment projects, but all major investments will still be decided and chiefly financed centrally. Moreover, the availability of materials, equipment, and labor—depending on the scope of central control and the level of aggregate demand—will determine the extent to which enterprise and bank funds can in fact be used for decentralized investments.

Reform of producer goods prices from the traditional system of cost-plus nonscarcity prices is obviously essential to any decentralization, in order to provide appropriate signals for enterprise decision-making in a market framework. In this respect, progress has been limited by fears about the big changes in real and financial relationships which would be generated by a substantial increase in the general price level and a radical revision in the relative price structure. In the Soviet Union and East Germany, for example, the new prices include capital charges and eliminate or reduce losses and subsidies, but they are not scarcity prices which would permit the abolition of administrative rationing of producer goods. However, both the Hungarian reform and the Czech model aim at a partial shift toward more flexible prices eventually approaching market-clearing levels, through the creation of a three-category system including centrally set "fixed" prices, "controlled" prices set by enterprises within limits specified by the central authorities, and "free" prices set by enterprises in response to market conditions.

Finally, in foreign trade, only in Hungary are enterprises to have significantly greater autonomy in making export and import decisions and establishing direct contacts with foreign firms, although such powers for associations are included in the Bulgarian, Romanian, East German, and Czech reforms.

Not only the reform blueprints but also the actual implementation of reforms—in terms of extent, timing, speed, and reversibility—vary by country. In Albania, reforms are negligible. The Soviet Union, Poland, East Germany, Romania, and Bulgaria have made only limited changes in their economic systems. They have reduced the number of plan targets for enterprises and have given managers more autonomy over the use of inputs (especially labor) to meet them. Also, sales, profit, and profitability have become more important performance indicators, to which incentives are related, and profit is a major source of incentive funds.

In Hungary a "guided market" system has been introduced. The central fixing of enterprise targets has been abolished, and the allocation of materials largely terminated. Profit-seeking enterprises choose their inputs and outputs and suppliers and customers. Planning is chiefly macroeconomic, with greater use than before of monetary and fiscal instruments to affect the general level of activity and also to guide enterprise decisions in the market. These were also the main lines of the aborted Czech reform.

Yugoslavia still represents the extreme in various respects. The scope of central planning has been steadily curtailed since 1952. It may now best be compared with French-style "indicative" planning, although current moves toward greater regional autonomy would abridge the role of the central authorities further. Most distinctive is the syndicalist aspect. Worker-managed enterprises pursue profit in an imperfect market, subject to controls—originating in stabilization measures rather than in comprehensive planning—over prices and the use of foreign exchange.

The diversity in blueprints for, and implementation of, economic reforms stems from differences among these countries in the nature and severity of the problems leading to reforms, as well as from differences in national policymakers' responses to similar problems. The variety of reforms in turn raises the interesting question of the extent to which reform proposals and measures in one country have affected those in other countries. Unfortunately, partly because economic reform issues are debated and resolved inside the Communist party leadership, it is not possible to draw firm conclusions about the interaction among the various reforms. However, some inferences and conjectures can be made. For example, Leon Smolinski has argued that Yugoslav, Polish, and Hungarian economists probably influenced Soviet economic thought and methodology, particularly in regard to mathematical methods such as input-output and linear programming, but that there is little evidence of East European influences on Soviet economic policy, especially economic reforms.[4] In turn, the less innovative Soviet reforms have not inspired important new ideas in Eastern Europe. Rather, because of the political dominance of the Soviet Union, the conservatism of its reform imposes constraints on reforms in other countries in the area.[5]

II. Issues in System Design and System Change

As the preceding survey shows, economic reforms in Eastern Europe involve a wide spectrum of issues and problems, some relatively technical and others of the broadest social significance. They range from the principles of price formation to property rights and income distribution. A number of these issues are analyzed from both theoretical and empirical standpoints in the following chapters.

Strategy of Reform

Chapters 2 and 3 consider the possibilities and problems of reform from the viewpoint of the top political leaders, who must make the ultimate decisions about what kind of reforms, if any, to undertake.

In chapter 2, Thomas A. Marschak explores how reform-minded economists and political leaders can formulate a strategy to decide how, how far, and how fast to reform the economic system. Their goal would be a strategy which specifies a sequence of reform measures which will (in the policy-makers' opinion) increase welfare—as measured by such performance indicators as growth of GNP, the level and composition of consumption (seen as the final objective of economic activity), various aspects of efficiency, and so forth.

4. "East European Influences on Soviet Economic Thought and Reforms," Indiana University International Development Research Center, Working Paper No. 6 (September 1971), revised version of a paper presented at the University of Michigan Conference on the Influence of Eastern Europe and the Western Territories of the USSR on Soviet Society, May 14–15, 1970.

5. The Soviet reform is not treated separately in this book. It is among the less innovative reforms and less illuminating in regard to system change. Also, it has been widely discussed. See, for example, Eugene Zaleski, *Planning Reforms in the Soviet Union, 1962–1966* (Chapel Hill, N.C.: University of North Carolina Press, 1967); George R. Feiwel, *The Soviet Quest for Economic Efficiency: Issues, Controversies, and Reforms* (New York: Frederick A. Praeger, 1967); Robert W. Campbell, "Economic Reforms in the U.S.S.R.," *American Economic Review* 58, no. 2 (May 1968): 547–58; Gertrude E. Schroeder, "Soviet Economic 'Reforms': A Study in Contradiction," *Soviet Studies* 20, no. 1 (July 1968): 1–21; Michael Ellman, "Economic Reform in the Soviet Union," *Planning* (London) 35, no. 509 (April 1969): 283–371; Karl W. Ryavec, "Soviet Industrial Managers, Their Superiors, and the Economic Reform," *Soviet Studies* 21, no. 2 (October 1969): 208–28; Keith Bush, "The Implementation of the Soviet Economic Reform," *Osteuropa Wirtschaft* 15, no. 2 (June 1970): 68–90, and no. 3 (October 1970): 190–98; and Gertrude E. Schroeder, "Soviet Economic Reform at an Impasse," *Problems of Communism* 20, no. 4 (July–August 1971): 36–46.

Marschak uses the tools of modern decision theory and information theory to define and relate the elements of such a strategy. They include the organization of the economy; its supplies of capital and labor; its "environment" of natural resources, climate, technology, and political constraints; its "policy vector" (how the organization uses its resources in its environment); and the indicators by which its performance is evaluated. Since most reform proposals involve "decentralization," Marschak analyzes two alternative approaches to the issue of centralization versus decentralization: the "authority" approach and the "information" approach. From these viewpoints, he evaluates proposals for decentralization, including the classic Lange–Lerner model of market socialism.

In view of the uncertainty both about the outcome of new arrangements and about the problems of transition from one scheme to another, Marschak stresses the need for a cautious "pragmatic" approach. However, both small and large steps have their pitfalls. On the one hand, small steps seem attractive because bigger steps are more complex and difficult to implement and appear to involve greater uncertainties and risk. On the other hand, the results of small steps may be quite different from the results of a complete reform mechanism in operation. Moreover, small, incomplete measures may worsen performance by introducing or aggravating inconsistencies—for example, if enterprises are given more authority over the determination of outputs and inputs without corresponding changes in the price system and in performance indicators and incentives. Thus Marschak finds no simple, generally applicable strategies for reform. Instead, they must be tailored to the particular case.

In chapter 3, John Michael Montias analyzes in detail one of the problems of economic reform identified by Marschak: to what extent and how can the top planners delegate authority to lower levels and still get results which they consider satisfactory? To examine this question, Montias visualizes the economy as a hierarchy of tiers, in which decisions about various activities are made at the highest tier and then disaggregated and parceled out to functionaries at each successively lower tier. These activities—all of which are subject to some decentralization—include choosing production levels, transferring goods from one unit to another, investment choices, research and development decisions, price setting, determining the use of labor and the corresponding wage rates, apportionment of net revenue among and within units, regulating the flow of information, and creating or dissolving organizations.

Montias then traces the effects of delegating authority over the first two of these activities, production and transfer, to lower levels, particularly to enterprise managers. Through a set-theoretic model of a three-tier hierarchy, he examines alternative decentralizing measures in order to determine which of the "attainable" set of outputs and allocations that can be generated by decision making at lower tiers will be "acceptable" or even "preferred" from the standpoint of higher tiers.

Montias considers the problems of consistency and aggregation in planning, incentives to managers to comply with rather than violate plans, and the critical role of prices in securing decentralized decision-making which will be acceptable to the higher tiers being asked to surrender authority. His rigorous analysis shows that, unless incentive and price systems are properly aligned, limited devolution of authority over production decisions to enterprises may bring benefits from better use of information but is likely to generate bills of net outputs which will not be acceptable to higher authorities.

Concentration and Devolution

These issues are pursued further in the light of East German experience by Michael Keren in chapter 4. If reforms are to entail some devolution of authority from central planners to lower tiers operating in response to profit criteria and market signals, what should be the organizational structure of these markets? What is the appropriate unit for autonomous decentralized decision-making—the enterprise or a grouping of enterprises in "associations" of some type? If profit maximization is adopted as the managerial decision criterion, will this lead to problems of monopolistic or oligopolistic abuse of market power?

Keren shows that two sets of considerations affect the optimal number of producing units in a market economy. First, from the standpoint of potential output, if economies of scale are available, production should be concentrated in a smaller number of units. Second, the fewer the enterprises, the more likely is the abuse of monopoly power and the poorer the actual, as distinct from the potential, performance. However, in a centrally administered economy, there is no similar link between large numbers of enterprises and a better exploitation of potential. All other factors being equal, the number of enterprises should be smaller ("concentration" should be greater) in a centralized economy than in a market socialist economy. With this conceptual framework, Keren then analyzes the "reformed centralism" introduced in East Germany in 1963–64 under the rather misleading name of the "New Economic System," noting the differences from the market socialist reform in Hungary.

The East German reform kept the allocation hierarchy intact but tried to make meaningful changes in its mode of operation. The aim was to free the higher echelons of decisions on detail without eliminating their authority over those details. At the same time, the concentration drive to create bigger and fewer enterprises not only continued but accelerated. Enterprises were concentrated in profit-seeking industrial administrations or lower-level "combinates" grouping enterprises on horizontal, vertical, or locational lines, but detailed information on their activities continued to flow upward. Keren analyzes the changes in the planning process, performance indicators and incentives, and price system. How can the centralized allocation of supplies operate along with an incentive system which encourages enterprises to produce what is profitable rather than their assigned outputs? Keren finds the answer lies in a scheme of contracts to enforce these production assignments, plus the willingness of top authorities to permit the economy to operate with enough slack to make plans for production and supply attainable.

As in East Germany, there was a comprehensive industrial reorganization in Hungary (in 1962–63), with the twin aims of cutting production costs and simplifying supply planning. Firms were combined into big enterprises directly under ministries, or into trusts operating on a profit principle. Thus the "New Economic Mechanism" introduced in 1968 (analyzed in detail by Bela Balassa in chapter 10) began with a highly concentrated market structure. However, in contrast to East Germany, the Hungarian reform eliminated current production assignments and materials allocations, and some prices were set free. The Hungarian authorities are well aware of the monopoly problem. Many trusts have been abolished, although looser forms of association are authorized (under close ministerial control) to enable enterprises to act jointly in research, purchasing, and sales. But two main forces for competition—free entry of new firms and the possibility of imports —are limited in the Hungarian case.

In regard to the analysis of decentralization by Marschak and Montias in chapters 2 and 3, Keren finds that in East Germany there has been decentralization in the "authority" but not the "information" dimension, while in Hungary there has been significant decentralization in both respects.

Foreign Trade

Particularly in Hungary, East Germany, and other more developed countries of the area, a major reason for economic reform is the need to increase competitiveness in foreign trade. Chapter 5, by Alan A. Brown and Paul Marer, considers the role of foreign trade in the East European reforms, both as a cause for reform and as an important dimension of the reform model.

First, Brown and Marer compare the relationship between foreign trade difficulties and economic reforms in the more versus the less developed countries in Eastern Europe. Over the last 20 years trade in the region has grown faster than domestic production, not so much as a result of planned development as of a rise in unintended imports and the corresponding exports to pay for them. Expanding trade flows were concentrated in the

Eastern trading area's sheltered market, where (as in each of the domestic sellers' markets) outdated producer goods and inferior consumer goods could be sold. But absence of competition, parallel industrial development strategies, and slow technical progress created problems for the more developed countries in the area, which export machinery and import primary products. In CEMA trade the former became "soft" goods and the latter "hard" goods. The ability of the more developed countries to shift trade toward the world market is constrained—aside from political factors discussed by R. V. Burks in chapter 11—by their inability to compete with Western manufacturers in terms of design, quality, marketing, and service. Thus, these countries seek in domestic economic reforms a way of increasing their competitiveness in world markets. In contrast, in the less developed countries of the area (such as Bulgaria, Romania, and the Soviet Union itself), there is less pressure for reform originating in foreign trade, since these countries export primary products which can be sold relatively easily both in the CEMA and the world markets.

Hence, the more developed the East European country, the greater its interest in comprehensive rather than partial reforms in foreign trade. Partial reforms include the introduction of multiple shadow exchange rates in central decision-making on foreign trade, and the award of direct trading rights to selected enterprises or associations. Comprehensive reforms involve the elimination of compulsory annual plan targets, the subordination of foreign trade enterprises to producing enterprises, and the introduction of operational exchange rates to affect enterprise decisions. Only in Yugoslavia and Hungary have such fundamental foreign trade reforms been adopted as part of the move to a market economy. However, Yugoslavia is clearly a special case in Eastern Europe: it is not a member of CEMA; it trades mainly with the West, from which it has received large amounts of aid; and it permits substantial international mobility of capital and labor. Therefore, Brown and Marer find the Hungarian case much more relevant for the rest of Eastern Europe, with which Hungary shares institutional and political constraints and heavy dependence on CEMA trading partners.

Brown and Marer then examine in detail the implications for foreign trade of the reforms introduced in Hungary in 1968 (other aspects are analyzed by Balassa in chapter 10, Marschak in chapter 2, Keren in chapter 4, and Jerzy F. Karcz in chapter 6). Brown and Marer discuss changes in the planning of foreign trade, the relationship between producing and foreign trade enterprises, the price system, and exchange rates. They devote special attention to the problem of "dual exchange rates" for trade with CEMA and with the West, and its implications for continued regulation of foreign trade by the Hungarian central authorities, in contrast to their diminishing intervention in the domestic economy. Brown and Marer show that decentralized decision-making in foreign trade is incompatible with the existing CEMA trade mechanism of fixed prices, commodity bilateralism, and inconvertible currencies. Thus, as a logical counterpart to its domestic economic reform, Hungary has urged a step-by-step transition to multi-lateral trade and payments within CEMA.

Agriculture

Just as domestic economic reforms offer lessons and precedents for inter-national reforms, so the less heralded agricultural reforms in Eastern Europe have important implications for the more widely studied industrial reforms. As Jerzy F. Karcz shows in chapter 6, "Agricultural Reform in Eastern Europe," agricultural reforms had already begun in the 1950s, and new important measures were enacted as recently as 1970. He stresses that the East European countries vary from each other in agricultural organization, problems, and reforms much more than in the industrial sphere, because of differences in climate, levels of development, and Party-peasant relation-ships. Thus, the Polish and Yugoslav experiences with agricultural reform are drastically different despite the fact that since the mid-1950s over 80 per-cent of agricultural land has been owned and farmed by individual peasants in both countries.

Karcz begins by examining the characteristics of "command farming" and the lasting problems it created. The activities of farms were closely regulated through excessively detailed planning and tight procurement controls to enforce unfavorable prices. The structures of prices, output, investment, machinery supply, and land use were all distorted, and acute manpower problems developed, especially on weaker farms. As a result, farm productivity, output, and incomes were low. Farmers turned to private household plots. Domestic food supplies lagged in the face of a high income elasticity of demand for food on the part of the urban population. The gap could not be covered by imports either from other East European countries (for lack of surpluses) or from the West (for lack of hard currency).

These problems make the achievement of greater efficiency in farm pro-duction imperative in Eastern Europe. Karcz analyzes three types of reform measures, broadly parallel to those proposed in the industrial sector. First, reforms of planning and administration seek to give farm management greater authority over their enterprises. In some countries, control has been transferred from the ministry of agriculture to unions or associations of farms hierarchically and physically closer to farms and more sympathetic to their needs. In addition, the number of products subject to compulsory procure-ment quotas has been reduced, and the farms' ability to bargain with procurement agencies has been strengthened by various measures. Second, procurement prices have been raised, but sometimes there have been offsetting increases in prices of off-farm inputs, and the level of profitability of many important products is still low. Third, since the mid-1950s the differential between farm and non-farm earnings has been narrowed sharply in most of these countries, although income from household plots remains an important element. Here also first Yugoslavia and then Hungary have offered assistance and incentives to private agriculture to expand output and thus raise living standards and popular morale. The most recent reform measures introduced in Yugoslavia in 1965 aim to raise farm prices, output, investment, exports, and incomes, primarily through market instruments of economic regulation. However, Karcz shows, the results have been disappointing, as in other aspects of the Yugoslav reform.

Karcz concludes that some issues of economic reform are the same in agriculture as in industry, while others differ. In both, reforms seek to increase efficiency by decentralizing authority to enterprises and by strengthening incentives. In the case of agriculture, however, there are special problems of overcoming previous neglect in the allocation of investment, the loss of manpower to industry, and high-level attitudes toward the peasantry.

Workers' Management

Yugoslavia pioneered sweeping economic reforms early in the 1950s, a decade before the reform movement burgeoned elsewhere in Eastern Europe. The Yugoslav reforms included decollectivization of agriculture, a more tolerant attitude toward small private enterprise in trade and handicrafts, progressive diminution of the scope and intensity of economic planning, genuine enterprise autonomy in free (if imperfect) markets, and—most noteworthy—control of enterprises by their workers. Of these innovations, marketization of enterprise relations and curtailment of central planning have been most widely accepted elsewhere in the area, although so far only Hungary has also introduced a genuine socialist market economy. But the distinctive Yugoslav institution of workers' management has not been adopted elsewhere. Not only does it imply great independence for enterprises in determining output, prices, customer and supplier relations, and the disposition of enterprise profits; it also has far-reaching ideological, political, and social implications.

What is worker's self-management and how does it really operate in Yugoslavia? What are the consequences for the behavior of Yugoslav firms and the performance of the economy? These questions are explored, respectively, in chapter 7, "The Yugoslav Self-Managed Enterprise: A Systemic Approach," by Egon Neuberger and Estelle James, and chapter 8, "The Banking System and the Investment Behavior of the Yugoslav Firm," by Svetozar Pejovich.

As a framework for their analysis of the Yugoslav firm, Neuberger and James develop a model of the economic system consisting of organizations composed of decision-making members or "actors." Variables in the model include (1) constraints on flows of resources and information, (2) the actors and their respective objective functions, and (3) the distribution of decision-making power and information. Neuberger and James then apply this model to the Yugoslav self-managed enterprise.

First, they analyze the founding of the enterprise, the assignment of entrepreneurial responsibility to the labor factor rather than capital, the property rights of workers, their attitudes toward investment and risk, and the implications of these factors for cost accounting, incentives, and labor mobility. Next, the authors examine the various objectives of the members of the enterprise, including maximizing individual income over time, stability of employment, joint consumption of enterprise housing and recreational facilities, and participatory democracy. Third, Neuberger and James study the distribution of decision-making power among various self-management organs and between workers and managers. Finally, they consider the influence on self-management of two special characteristics of Yugoslav society: egalitarianism and the nationality problem. Neuberger and James conclude that, although self-management may be attractive from the sociopolitical viewpoint, its merits as an economic system are open to question.

In chapter 8, Pejovich pursues the evaluation of the economic aspects of self-management by analyzing the scheme of property rights and its consequences for unemployment, inflation, and enterprise liquidity. He first examines briefly the evolution of the Yugoslav economic system since World War II, tracing the changes in central planning, the attempt to regulate the economy by monetary and fiscal measures, and the growing power of the enterprise over the distribution of its resources.

To analyze the investment behavior of the Yugoslav firm, Pejovich uses a model illustrating the behavioral effects of property rights structures on the share of enterprise income voluntarily devoted to investment. He shows that in Yugoslavia less is devoted to investment instead of current consumption than would be the case if capital goods were privately owned. The precise distribution of profits between reinvestment and current bonuses will depend on the compromise reached among the different objective functions of the various members of the firm, as previously explained by Neuberger and James.

Because the property rights structure constrains the voluntary allocation of enterprise income to investment, the banking system has an especially important role in financing growth. Pejovich explains the evolution of the banking system and the significant change in its role under the 1965 reform.

The banking system can raise the rate of investment above what enterprises would make voluntarily, but it thereby encourages further the allocation of profits to wage supplements, contributes to inflationary pressure, and creates a serious liquidity problem for Yugoslav firms. Thus, Pejovich concludes, the operation of market forces in Yugoslavia leads to different results than in Western market economies because of the different property rights structure on which the worker-managed firm rests.

The Reversibility of Reform: The Czechoslovak Experience

Czechoslovakia is the only East European country besides Yugoslavia in which the reform movement encompassed broad politicosocial aspects beyond the modification of the "economic mechanism." The scope and content of reforms in Czechoslovakia led to the Soviet invasion in 1968, which stalled, then reversed, the drive for reform. In chapter 9, "Planning and the Market in the Czechoslovak Reform," Václav Holešovský considers the extent to which the Czech reforms have survived Soviet opposition.

First Holešovský summarizes the main features of the Czech economic reform program introduced in 1967. The reform was conceived as a succession of measures, subject to review and correction, leading ultimately to a combination of central macroeconomic planning and enterprise autonomy in microeconomic decisions. Holešovský discusses the status of the enterprise, the determination of output by firms, the use of taxes as a method of central regulation, the rationalization of the price system, and investment finance and criteria. He analyzes some of the inherent deficiencies of the reform, and the problems caused both by the measures themselves and by the sequence of their introduction.

Next Holešovský shows how the reform movement gained momentum and went beyond the confines of the official program. Three striking developments arose spontaneously "from below." One was the attempt to vest control of the newly autonomous enterprises in workers' councils, along Yugoslav lines. The second was the effort of managerial interests to strengthen enterprise autonomy by transforming industrial "associations" from administrative supervisory organs to voluntary bodies performing functions assigned by enterprises. The third was the emergence of authentic trade unionism to represent the interests of workers, rather than those of the state.

Holešovský explains how the reform movement continued for some months after the Soviet invasion, until the leadership of the Czech Communist Party was changed. Then various aspects of the reform were successively abridged: targets were reimposed on enterprises, wage controls were restored, and prices were frozen. But there has not been a complete return to the traditional model which existed before the reform. Instead, as in 1965–66, there is again a search by the authorities for a new combination of command and the market, somewhere between the old system and the reform model.

Managerial Market Socialism: The "New Economic Mechanism" in Hungary

Only Hungary has followed Yugoslavia along the road to market social-ism, although without the syndicalist aspect of workers' management. Instead, firms are run by state-appointed managers. Different aspects of the Hungarian reform are analyzed in several chapters of this book: its basic strategy by Marschak in chapter 2; industrial organization by Keren in chapter 4; foreign trade by Brown and Marer in chapter 5; and agriculture by Karcz in chapter 6. In chapter 10, Bela Balassa provides a comprehensive survey and evaluation of the reform. He appropriately examines the reform from the viewpoint of the firm, since the fundamental changes in the nature and role of the firm best illustrate and epitomize the reform. Balassa begins by contrasting the situation of the firm under the traditional system and under the "New Economic Mechanism" (so labeled to assert the technical, non-political character of the reform). He then discusses the operation of the firm and the economy under the new system in regard to three crucial aspects: short-term decision-making, investment decisions, and foreign trade.

To analyze decisions on current production, Balassa considers three central questions. Is the incentive system conducive to the maximization of profit? Do managers consider profit maximization their main objective? Is profit maximization by the firm in the interest of the economy as a whole? The first two issues require close study of taxation and bonus schemes as well as the attitudes of managers as reported in sample surveys. The third involves the nature of the price system, the extent of competition, and limitations on the firm's autonomy by both government agencies and non-governmental organizations such as trade unions and the Communist party.

Balassa next examines the extent to which investment decisions have been transferred to the firm, how investments are financed, and investment criteria. He then turns to foreign trade, discussing the old system's inadequate export incentives for both producing and trading firms. He notes the main features and shortcomings of the new scheme, which involves separate foreign exchange conversion ratios for ruble and dollar trade, tariffs, and subsidies.

Yet Balassa concludes that the balance sheet of the "New Economic Mechanism" is basically positive. Most central directives have been abol-ished. Domestic prices increasingly reflect relative scarcities and are in-creasingly linked to foreign prices. Firms now emphasize profit rather than output. But imperfect competition causes the interests of the firm to diverge from those of the economy, leading some to advocate more state inter-vention while others favor greater domestic and foreign competition. Thus, although Hungary has clearly opted for market socialism, as in Yugoslavia the economic system is still evolving and the final form is by no means certain.

Economics versus Politics

All of the authors explicitly recognize and discuss to some extent the sociopolitical aspects of economic reform. However, it is the specific task of R. V. Burks in chapter 11 to analyze the domestic and international political implications of economic reform in Eastern Europe.

Domestically, Burks notes, a striking feature of reforms is that they stem from a fundamental change in the relationship between the rulers and the ruled. In the Stalinist era, Communist leaders largely regarded their populations as resources to be mobilized in the national interest; the relationship was one of command and control. After the death of Stalin, the attention of East European regimes turned from mobilization of resources to increasing the efficiency of their use. The regimes began to rely more on motivation and cooperation, using incentives and market coordination instead of administrative directives.

Burks stresses, however, the political costs of a true shift to the market economy. It would undermine the "solidary conception of society," hitherto a cornerstone of the official ideology. As Marxists, the East European leaders believe that a change in the "substructure" of economic organization inevitably will result in profound changes in the political "superstructure." Thus, competition in the market for goods may be accompanied by competition in the market for ideas, as the rest of the intelligentsia seeks its counterpart of the autonomy newly granted to managers.

Economic reform in Eastern Europe also has far-reaching implications for international politics. Burks discusses the desire of the smaller countries to reduce their dependence on the Soviet Union, how large-scale credits from the West could help them modernize their economies, and the interest of West Germany in providing such aid as part of its *Neue Ostpolitik*. He notes the lesson of the Yugoslav experience: the introduction of market socialism and economic modernization were accompanied by a shift of trade to the West and the receipt of substantial aid from the West.

However, the dominant political factor in East European reforms is the attitude of the Soviet leadership toward reforms—in the USSR itself, in other East European countries, and in CEMA trading arrangements. Burks analyzes how marketization in the Soviet Union could affect the Soviet economy, polity, and society. He suggests possible parallels to the Yugoslav experience, for example in the nationality problem (discussed by Neuberger and James in chapter 7). Burks concludes that continuation of the traditional centrally planned economy is a prime element both in the Soviet Communist party's control of the Soviet Union and in its hegemony over the smaller East European countries. Thus, the progress of reform throughout the area depends on developments in the Soviet Union. The present Soviet leadership is reluctant to take clear-cut steps toward marketization. How much bolder the next group of leaders will be, only the future can reveal.

The fundamental pressures for reform in Eastern Europe continue and cumulate. But the implications of reform are far-reaching, involving crucial economic, social, and domestic and international political issues. Hence, the progress of reform is slow, irregular, and sometimes reversible. The further evolution of economic reform in the East European countries will therefore be observed with great interest not only within the area but outside it as well. The studies in this volume seek to provide background, tools, and insights for the analysis of these systemic changes and their consequences in the years ahead.

2

Decentralizing the Command Economy:
The Study of a Pragmatic Strategy for Reformers

THOMAS A. MARSCHAK

A task of stupefying complexity faces the reformers of an economy who want to replace an inherited mechanism for allocating resources by another one and who want their performance as reformers to be creditable. There is virtually no area of economic theory and no technique of economic measurement that does not present itself as a candidate for a useful role in the task. Where theory or technique are helpful in guiding the reform, the economist has a rare sensation of concrete justification; where they are not, a tantalizing gap beckons to be filled. One thread tying together the present survey is precisely the taking of a modest inventory of the relevancies and the gaps.

We take, that is to say, a normative view, and imagine the reformers to seek a successful strategy for economic reform. They start with an economy labeled "command" and search out a path toward another type of economy, generally labeled "decentralized." They cannot make the transition all at once because administrative rearrangements and the learning of new roles and responses takes time and because too rapid change is harmfully disruptive. But even if they could easily make an instantaneous transition they would not wish to, since knowledge of the comparative properties of the many alternative forms which the decentralized economy could take is so exceedingly incomplete. The reformers would therefore want, even if they were not forced, to pursue the reform "sequentially," learning more and more, as they proceed, about the properties of alternative patterns of decentralization and responding to this accumulating knowledge by making further changes in the economic mechanism. Their responses will use, in addition to the newly accumulated knowledge, whatever general findings of economic theory and measurement appear helpful.

It would, however, be useless dreaming to talk seriously of an "optimal" strategy for economic reformers in the precise meaning of that term developed in current decision theory. A strategy, in decision theory, instructs

I am grateful to Jaroslav Vanek, who served as discussant of the paper, for useful comments.

a decision maker how to respond to changing information—information generated partly by "Nature" and partly by his own previous responses. A strategy is optimal if, when compared to any other, it achieves a not lower expected value of the discounted sum of the stream of net benefits, measured in some appropriate way, which result from Nature's choices and from the responses selected by the strategy. The expectation is to be taken with respect to the probability law governing the successive choices of Nature, a probability law expressing the decision maker's own beliefs.

For the concept of optimal strategy to have meaning, the decision makers must know everything, at the time the strategy is chosen, except the future choices of Nature; they must know, in particular, the benefits that would result at an instant of time if they made a particular response and Nature's choice had a particular value.

Now, in the reformers' case such knowledge is highly imperfect, just as is the knowledge of future choices of Nature. (Nature chooses magnitudes beyond the reformers' control—technological discoveries, weather, political changes, developments in other countries, and so on.) Though the reformers may know very well how to measure (from observations) the benefits actually enjoyed by the economy during any past period they do not know, for any *given* sequence of Nature's choices and any *given* sequence of future decisions by themselves, what the stream of these benefits will be. Their ignorance is due, in essence, to the difficulties of computing that stream of benefits; it is ignorance that would vanish for someone with gigantic computing and information-gathering capacity. It is *not* the ignorance due to an unpredictable Nature, and it cannot therefore be legitimately expressed in a probability distribution.[1]

To formulate a true optimality in the behavior of reformers who have limited information-gathering and computing capacity seems therefore not to be conceptually possible. We must be content with a description of a "satisfactory" strategy. This will have to be a subjective description and will depend for its appeal on a consensus by the practitioners of economic reform. We shall try to sketch here the main elements of a proposed satisfactory or "pragmatic" strategy, to develop some concepts needed in the description, to identify the existing theoretical and empirical findings that might defend the strategy, and to point to open theoretical and empirical questions whose resolution would make the evaluation and the conduct of the strategy far more precise. Toward the end we shall briefly examine some aspects of the Hungarian reform in an attempt to view it as the application of a pragmatic strategy.

1. For discussion of this point, see R. Radner, "Competitive Equilibrium under Uncertainty," *Econometrica* 36, no. 1 (January 1968): 31–58; and L. J. Savage, *Foundations of Statistics* (New York: John Wiley and Sons, 1954), p. 7.

I. The Skeleton of a Pragmatic Strategy

A brief exercise in the formal statement of a strategy is useful to help clarify and unify the discussion that follows. The elements in terms of which a strategy can be formally defined are a collection of magnitudes, each taking a value at successive discrete points of time t. The elements are as follows:

1. R_t, the *structure* of the economy being reformed, as it stands at time t; alternative terms might be the "organization of the economy" or the "state of the reform." The structure is specified by a choice of values for each of the variables under the reformers' control.

2. S_t, the *state* of the economy at time t, aside from its organizational aspects; the vector S_t includes, as in growth models, the stock of productive capital, disaggregated as desired. It also describes the labor force and its composition, as well as the bureaucracy and equipment whose function is to operate the·economic mechanism specified by R_t.

3. P_t, the value of the *policy vector* at time t. Its components are the current-policy variables which always have to be set, no matter what the state of the reform; they may, in principle, be set by "policy makers," a group of agents distinct from the reformers. The vector expresses, very roughly speaking, the manner in which the economic mechanism, in its current state, is being "used." Governmental investment decisions are, of course, a major part of P_t, but it also includes decisions about changes in the size and quality of the mechanism-operating bureaucracy.

4. E_t, the economy's *environment* at time t. Its components are beyond the control of reformers or policy makers. They are chosen by Nature and their path follows a probability law.

5. Ω_t, a vector, determined by a relation

$$\Omega_t = w(E_t, S_t, P_t, R_t),$$

whose components determine the *welfare* experienced by the economy at time t. The vector specifies final consumption, suitably disaggregated; in the extreme, it specifies the consumption of every good by every individual. The relation w generalizes the relationships often expressed (in growth models, for example) by an economy-wide production function.

6. π_t, a vector of *performance indicators*, determined by a relation

$$\pi_t = q(E_t, S_t, P_t, R_t).$$

The indicators are observable by the reformers and the policy makers. For generality, π_t may include a summary of performance indicators of previous periods. In general the complete descriptions of S_t, E_t, and Ω_t are *not* directly observable; given the limited information-gathering capacity of reformers and policy makers, π_t yields the most nearly complete description of this triple available.

Now, given the current environment E_t, a probability law F specifies the conditional probabilities (as perceived by the reformers) of alternative values of the subsequent environment E_{t+1}. Given the current triple (R_t, S_t, P_t), next period's state S_t is determined by a relation

$$S_{t+1} = v(R_t, S_t, P_t).$$

The relation expresses, among other things, the fact that the additions to current capital stock dictated or guided by current policy P_t determine next period's capital stock.[2]

The reformers and policy makers seek a *strategy* specifying, at each of a sequence of time points t, the further reforms to be initiated—and hence the next economic structure or "state of the reform," R_{t+1}—and the policy of the next period, P_{t+1}. Both decisions can be based only on the current information available, namely, the performance indicators π_t; the strategy, in other words, consists of a pair of relations

$$R_{t+1} = g(\pi_t, t)$$
$$P_{t+1} = h(\pi_t, t),$$

where, for generality, the two response rules are allowed to change with time. Given an initial description of the economy,

$$(R_0, S_0, P_0, E_0),$$

the strategy (g, h) and the probability law F imply together a probability distribution on the possible sequences

$$\{(R_t, S_t, P_t, E_t, \pi_t)\}$$

which can occur and hence on the possible sequences $\{\Omega_t\}$ of the welfare determinants.

The strategy (g, h) is good if it implies a high expected value of the discounted sum of the successive values taken by a *reformers' and policy makers'* utility function u, defined on alternative values of the vector Ω_t. The discount rate used, and the form of the function u itself, express reformers' and policy makers' preferences with respect to present versus future welfare, consumption of one final commodity versus another, consumption by one

2. The environment E_t could be included as an additional argument of v—e.g., the current environment may affect the actual addition to capital stock achieved by a given policy of intended investment.

group of consumers versus another, and high expected value of consumption but high variance of consumption versus low expected value and low variance.

In the extreme, the performance indicators would be a full description of the economy at t—that is, π_t would comprise the entire quintuple $(S_t, R_t, P_t, E_t, \Omega_t)$. Even if such full observation were feasible, the complex relation between current reforms and policies and subsequent values of the welfare determinants would be unknown, or if known then not computable by reformers and policy makers of limited computing power. A truly "optimal" strategy (g, h)—a strategy maximizing the expected discounted sum just described when π_t is a complete description—is unobtainable and so is a strategy which is optimal *given* the constraint that the reformers' current knowledge of the economy and its welfare is incomplete and must be summarized by a particular incomplete performance-indicator vector π_t. Moreover, as argued in the introductory section of this chapter, it appears conceptually not possible to enlarge the optimal-strategy concept so that among those performance-indicator vectors and those responses to them which are consistent with a given fixed information-gathering and computing capacity (suitably measured) the "best" ones are chosen.

The pragmatic reformers (and policy makers) must content themselves with very incomplete information about the relation w and possibly the relation q as well. This information will suggest promising ways of responding to the current values of the performance indicators. Experience and various pieces of empirical and theoretical knowledge may strengthen confidence in the strategy (g, h) so contrived, but no feasible calculation can reveal its distance from a truly optimal strategy.

We now consider, in more concrete terms, the strategy elements we have introduced and such information about the relations determining a strategy's outcome as the reformers may hope to acquire.

II. The Reformers' and Policy Makers' Utility Functions

A great deal of literature has assumed a "planners'" utility function and a respectably large body of discussion[3] has stressed the unreality of such an assumption. The latter discussion applies as well to our reformers.

Note that a special utility function would be that appropriate to reformers who have no aim in mind except to come close to the ideal allocative efficiency of the textbooks. Such reformers have no distributive preferences

3. E.g., A Zauberman, *Aspects of Planometrics* (New Haven: Yale University Press, 1967), chap. 16; J. Drewnowski, "The Economic Theory of Socialism: A Suggestion for Reconsideration," *Journal of Political Economy* 69, no. 4 (August 1961): 341–54; P. C. Roberts, "Drewnowski's Economic Theory of Socialism," *Journal of Political Economy* 76, no. 4, pt. 1 (July–August 1968): 645–50.

and are willing to accept the distribution of final (consumption) goods which are determined by initial factor endowments and by the course of reform, policy, and environment. They do not feel that some efficient (Pareto-optimal) bundle of final consumptions is more in the public (or the political powers') interest than another. For such reformers, the utility function on the economy's bundle of final consumptions, labeled according to households, has the value one if the bundle is Pareto optimal and zero if it is not.

To formulate a utility function may be difficult, and to compute its value for contemplated alternatives is even more so. Nevertheless, reformers (and the associated policy makers) wish their preferences—or at least those which they consult in reaching decisions—to meet, at the minimum, a transitivity requirement: if some contemplated value of W_t, the vector of welfare determinants, is judged superior to another, W_t', and W_t' is superior to W_t'', then W_t ought to be judged superior to W_t''.

A less modest requirement is that the choices of welfare determinants which the reformers *believe* they are making when they choose current additions to the reform satisfy a revealed preference axiom. If they believe that of two alternative, contemplated feasible new reforms the first would lead to a certain stream of future welfare determinants and the second to another stream, and if the first reform is chosen, then the first stream is revealed preferred to the second. This preference should not be contradicted by any future choice among the same two welfare streams (or rather among reforms leading to them).[4] A stronger form of the requirement is that if stream 1 is revealed preferred to stream 2, and stream 2 is revealed preferred to stream 3, then if stream 1 and stream 3 are ever encountered together in the choices faced by the reformers, stream 3 must not be revealed preferred to stream 1.

If the reformers exhibit conformity with such revealed-preference constraints then their behavior is at least *consistent* with the existence of a complete utility function and with the ranking of reforms according to the expectation of the discounted sum of the values taken by the function. Checking that revealed preference conditions do not appear to be violated is a relatively simple matter if only a small number of possible new reforms are contemplated by the reformers at any one time.

In any case, a pragmatic strategy requires a far less onerous cataloguing than true optimality. True optimality would require a complete and transitive ordering of all streams of welfare determinants, an ordering representable, moreover, by a utility function from which preferences between alternative probability mixtures of possible streams can be deduced.

4. More accurately, a new reform implies a probability distribution over alternative future streams of welfare determinants, and the relevant probability distributions must satisfy the revealed-preference axiom.

Typically, simple statements about certain of the performance indicators themselves will serve as a sufficient expression of preferences. The classically satisfied ex post remarks of planners—that such and such an indicator has risen in the period under review as compared with the previous period—can surely be expected to be heard again from reformers. It can be interpreted to imply that whenever one of the performance indicators has risen and none has fallen the welfare determinants in the period in question have improved. When some have risen and some have fallen, the ex post judgment whether improvement has occurred may be difficult. But the strategy may well rarely require the reformers to choose between two alternative new reforms when these seem likely to lead to performance-indicator vectors neither of which dominates the other.

III. THE PERFORMANCE INDICATORS

We retain the assumption that the future stream of final consumptions is the very complicated magnitude in which the reformers and associated policy makers are ultimately interested. The performance indicators used are those which seem likely to have a roughly decipherable bearing on the stream of final consumptions.

Of course, it is possible that the reformers have clearly in mind a "direction" in which the reform is moving, can measure in some satisfactory way the "distance traveled" along this direction, and have such deep faith in the desirability of the chosen direction, as it affects future final consumption streams, that they can dispense with all performance indicators except the "distance traveled" itself.

Some notions of direction and distance may be useful simplifications in formulating a strategy, a question we explore in the next section. But it seems most unlikely that the reformers' faith in their own intuition would be deep enough to make more conventional performance indicators unneeded. We now consider the main classes of indicators.

National ("Social") Product and Its Rate of Growth

These have historically been the most popular indicators for the limited evaluation of past reforms which has so far occurred[5] as well as the evaluation of performance of economies of fixed structure. A high rate of growth of national product over a short number of years has been taken as a signal that the economy is on a path which, over a long future period, is a desirable

5. See, e.g., B. Horvat, *Towards a Theory of Planned Economy* (Belgrade: Yugoslav Institute of Economic Research, 1964), p. 181; B. Balassa and T. Bertrand, "Growth Performance of East European Economies and Comparable Western European Countries," *American Economic Review*, 60, no. 2 (May 1970): 314–20.

path; desirability is to be measured, presumably, by the sum of the discounted values of an appropriate function of annual final consumption.

Without an implicit appeal to a final-consumption path (to a utility function on alternative final consumptions and to a discount rate), national product and its growth are too aggregative as performance indicators to have much significance: national product is composed of consumption goods and investment goods, but the latter make no welfare contribution in themselves, only as a potential source of future consumption goods. A high current growth rate may be undesirable for some utility functions and discount rates: it may be achieved by too high a rate of capital formation. It has been the function of models of optimal growth, incorporating neoclassical aggregate production functions, to clarify, under simple assumptions, the properties of an investment policy which gives the amount of the economy's current product to be invested and achieves a path desirable in the above sense. Under some assumptions on the production function and the utility function the optimal policy in the model has certain simple properties,[6] and these may conceivably serve as a guide to aggregate planning in an economy of constant structure with little environmental change (i.e. little uncertainty).

It may be that an extremely simple deterministic version of the model outlined in section I, with the policy vector P_t confined to aggregate investment and the reform variable R_t having one dimension, would also yield simple properties of an optimal reform-and-policy strategy when the only performance indicators used are national product and its rate of growth. That would, in any case, be a logical starting place for theorizing about strategy, once a one-dimensional reform variable has been defined—the subject of section IV below.

Economy-wide Efficiency Indicators

The performance of the economy is affected not only by the capital and labor currently available for use but also by the efficiency with which they are used. The reform will generally help to determine both.

A good pragmatic strategy will require indicators which focus specifically on efficiency. The leading family of such indicators, in the present state of economists' techniques, are estimated production functions. An economy-wide production function could be estimated from time series on capital, labor, and output in the years since the start of the reform.

In a typical year the reformers' econometricians would try to explain the observed series up to the present by a production function shifting through time, part of the shift to be explained by "technical change" and part by the course of the reform. Such a production function might be of Cobb–Douglas

6. See, e.g., T. C. Koopmans, "Objectives, Constraints, and Outcomes in Optimal Growth Models," *Econometrica* 35, no. 1 (January 1967): 1–5.

type and in its most naïve form would be written

$$Y_t = K_t^\alpha L_t^\beta \, e^{\lambda r_t + \mu_t},$$

where K_t, L_t, Y_t are capital stock, labor force, and product in year t; r_t is some index of the scope of the reform at time t; λ measures the shift in production efficiency due to changes in the scope of the reform; and μ measures the (residual) shift due to "technical change."

A reasonable measure r_t may be very difficult to obtain, and one might, therefore, try other variants of the above relation. First, one might be content with estimating the impact of the reform on efficiency during a previous intensive period of organizational change, in each year of which the scope of the reform was greatly enlarged. This would be appropriate if the reform were currently quiescent for several years following the period of intensive reform, which lasted, say, T years. Then the term r_t in the above relation simply becomes equal to zero before the period of intensive reform; equal to $1, 3, \ldots, T$ during the first, second, third, ..., Tth years of the period; and equal to T for the years following the period. The estimated relation would enter the reformers' strategy when they are to decide whether to revive the reform and pursue it further following the quiescent period.

Second, one may suppose that all "technical" (nonorganizational) change affecting the efficiency of the economy's production is of the "embodied" type: technical improvement has its effect only through the use of newer machines which, by virtue of their newness, incorporate the improvements. Then K_t is replaced, for example, by a weighted sum of capital stocks of different "vintages," the term μ_t is deleted, and r_t becomes t. The relation between product, age-differentiated capital stock, and labor shifts at the rate implied by μ, but the shift is now entirely due to the progress of the reform.

Note that the more years elapse, the more confidently can the reformers use the shift of the production function as an efficiency-change indicator, to which the strategy is to respond: more years mean more observations and hence more confidence in the estimated parameters. It may well be, however, that such confidence is most needed at the early stages of the reform when it is least available. The difficulty can be alleviated to some extent by supplementing time-series estimation with cross-section estimation, in which separate observations are made on firms or industries in each year, a production function (and its shift) for the typical firm or industry is estimated, and an economy-wide production function is then obtained, if desired, by aggregation of the separate production functions.[7]

7. One recently completed study of the Czech and Polish economies deals with all the above production-function variants, and others, and estimates them using both time-series and cross-section data. See O. Kýn and L. Kýnova, "Aggregate Production Functions for Czechoslovakia and Poland," mimeographed (Berkeley, 1970), abstract in *Econometrica* 30, no. 4 (July 1971): 365.

Other efficiency indicators include economy-wide data on unsold stocks, waiting periods for delivery, and inventory-output ratios. Their interpretation, however, raises complex questions which existing allocation theories have only begun to treat. In the first place, surpluses and shortages can, after all, be avoided, by setting absurdly low or high prices. In the second place, efficient resource allocation over time in an uncertain world, in which each unit in the economy has limited information about the others and limited computing power may, even with the best of allocation mechanisms, *require* a steady level of unsold stocks and of unfilled orders as well. Thus too low levels of unfilled orders may, in some allocation mechanisms, signal inefficiency (for example, risks of stock-out are avoided but at too high a cost in resources).

Disaggregated Growth and Efficiency Indicators

The aspects of performance measured for the whole economy by the indicators just described can also be measured for sectors of the economy. Output and its rate of growth can be measured, for example, for particular industries in which the reform has been particularly intense. At the industry level, however, such gross indicators are unlikely to be helpful, since they take no account of the inputs used. More refined indicators are value added per man-hour or, preferably, the coefficients and the shifts of an industry production function, in which industry output is related to capital, labor, *and* materials used.

If the reform is an attempt to construct a thoroughgoing market mechanism with prices fulfilling their ideal role as marginal-social-productivity signals, then enterprise profits, or enterprise return on capital, may be treated as an indicator by which to judge the progress of the reform. The reformers, in other words, as well as the enterprise managers themselves, should carefully observe profit which, ideally, serves as an index of efficiency.[8] But the reformers must guard against a potentially dangerous circularity: if the purpose of the reform is, in part, to *make* profits an appropriate signal for managers (leading them to contract or expand their operations), then profits may be a misleading indicator for the reformers until the reform is complete. Before then, taking high profits in some industry as a sign that the reform is particularly successful ("productive") there and should therefore be intensified in that industry (by further freeing of its price and output decisions, for example) may be a highly premature inference and may lead to a further departure of observed prices and profits from their desired values as "correct" allocative signals.

8. In an extreme version of a market mechanism, of course, increased entrepreneurial (managerial) efficiency would be reflected in an increased "price" of the efficient entrepreneur (manager), who would be mobile and could be bid away by other enterprises; his price would rise to the point at which his enterprise's profits become zero.

Indicators Bearing on the Resources Devoted to Operation of the Reformed Allocation Mechanism

The reformers and associated policy makers must be concerned, as we shall emphasize in section v below, with the resources to be devoted to the chosen resource-allocating mechanism itself—the central economic bureaucracy and the administrative staffs of enterprises, and the communication and computing equipment at the disposal of both. They will decide on the central bureaucracy's facilities and, if they do not directly choose the enterprises' facilities, they will at least wish to monitor the enterprises' own decisions in this regard. Consequently, indicators reflecting the judiciousness of the resources devoted to operating the mechanism will be sought.

Size of the various administrative staffs is the simplest such indicator. More sophisticated ones would include magnitudes like "administrative man-hours per ton of steel produced" and, ultimately, production functions in which the labor and capital devoted to operation of the mechanism is distinguished from other labor and capital, so that its productivity can be estimated and crude guesses can be made as to whether it is currently too high or too low.

The Ultimate Indicator: The Final Consumption Path Itself

If we suppose that the reformers' ultimate interest is in the consumption path followed by the economy over a long period extending well into the future, then the previous indicators are its surrogates or predictors, using some theory suggesting the way in which they affect the consumption path. On the other hand, direct observation is possible on the current steps taken by the economy along the consumption path—the first few steps in the path of ultimate interest. These limited direct observations serve as indicators, possibly in the aggregated form of expenditures by sample households, total output of key consumption goods, measures of income equality, and so forth.

IV. CHARACTERIZING THE REFORM COMPACTLY AND MEASURING ITS SCOPE

The Disorder of Economic Reform

Measuring in some way the level or scope of the reform, or at least characterizing it in an orderly fashion—that is really the heart of the matter for reformers who want to formulate a strategy which, however crudely, guides their decisions. Without doing so the catalogue of possibilities for reform appears as an endless jumble. It includes:

—permitting the setting of prices by enterprises,[9] subject to varying

9. "Enterprises" is meant to have a broad definition; it includes agencies which provide public goods.

constraints, e.g. upper and lower limits, constraints on frequency of price changes, review of pricing decisions to detect undesired "monopolistic" pricing.

—permitting enterprise production decisions, subject to varying constraints: upper limits on amounts of certain raw materials used, foreign exchange or imported commodities used, labor recruited from other regions; lower limits on quantities of certain outputs produced; the explicit directive that profit, or another criterion, be used to rank alternative production possibilities.

—permitting enterprise investment decisions, subject to varying constraints: credit rationing, central review of investment proposals, with varying scope and stringency of the criteria used.

—permitting the distribution of enterprise profits to be determined by enterprises, subject to varying constraints: taxes (to be paid by the enterprise) in all their variety; limitations on the proportion of profit to be distributed and the proportion to be devoted to investment or to collective purchases of services and facilities for workers.

—varying the charges made, to be paid to a central authority, for enterprise use of existing capital.

—varying the scope of workers' influence on enterprise decisions.

—varying the conditions to be met for the establishment of a new enterprise and the dissolution of an existing one.

—varying the prevailing combinations of all the above alternatives from industry to industry, enterprise to enterprise, and region to region.

In Search of "Decentralization": The Traditional Approach

One approach to ordering this chaos has so far overwhelmingly predominated: to let the terms "decentralized" and "centralized" denote opposite ends of a spectrum along which the current organization of the economy can be placed; to characterize the direction in which an economic reform moves, in the whole economy or in a particular part of it, as the direction of "more centralization" or "more decentralization"; and to make and act upon broad conjectures about the expected changes in the performance of the economy as it moves in one direction or the other under certain general conditions on the complexity of the economy, the way its performance is measured (i.e. the reformers' preferences), and the economy's environment.

Central to this tradition, without a doubt, has been the crown jewel of Western economic thought—the invisible hand of the "price" or "market" mechanism, and its miraculous achievements in an ideal economy. Virtually all theoretical discussion (with perhaps the very recent exception to be discussed below) of economic decentralization and its merits and limitations has, whether explicitly admitted or not, taken this ageless model as its starting point. Whatever we decide that "decentralized" means, the ideal market mechanism must turn out to be decentralized. And whatever propositions we ultimately verify about the net performance of alternative mechanisms for resource allocation—"net" in the sense that the resources required to run the mechanism are subtracted—surely we will be astounded if any other mechanism turns out to be superior to the price mechanism in the ideal or "classical" economies in which it works best. Even for economies more realistic than the ideal ones it is a powerful model, and enormous effort is devoted to discussions of how to patch up the mechanism so that it functions well in nonideal economies—those with nonconvexities, externalities, limited information, uncertainty, and an infinite future.

The classic debates of the 1930s on the possibility of socialism took the same starting point and, in fact, did not really get beyond a general consensus that a market mechanism, real or imitated, held out the only hope.

From these debates, in turn, has sprung a vigorous stream, still flowing, of proposed "decentralized" processes. A stimulus to the more recent contributions—unexpected at the time of the debates and later—has been the literature of programming, where an algorithm often turns out to have an interpretation as a decentralized resource-allocating process for a hypothetical economy. Each of the processes proposed has elements of the original Lange–Lerner schemes produced by the debates of the 1930s.

In each of them a sequence of information exchanges occurs between a "center" and outlying agents, often called "managers," each associated with some production facility; the messages exchanged vary, but in the typical process the messages flowing in one of the directions have an interpretation as "prices." Each process achieves, in its equilibrium state, a task confronting the economy: the maximization of a planners' utility function or the achievement of a Pareto-optimal resource allocation given an initial distribution of primary resources. Many of the processes converge, in some precise sense, to their equilibria. All of them are claimed, by virtue of their "decentralized" properties, to perform the task achieved at equilibrium in an *informationally* attractive way, and, in some cases, in a way compatible with the individual incentives of the participants. In the most recent, and quite ingenious, additions to this bulky catalogue of "decentralized" processes, increasing returns, a condition previously largely excluded, are shown to be compatible with convergence to at least local solutions to the economy's task.[10]

10. M. Aoki, "An Investment Planning Process for an Economy with Increasing Returns," and G. M. Heal, "Planning, Prices, and Increasing Returns," both in *Review of Economic Studies* 38, no. 115 (July 1971).

All of these proposed processes have been studiously ignored, it appears, by recent practitioners of economic reform—a remarkable phenomenon, to which we return in section v. Nevertheless, the tradition in which the "decentralized" processes are developed flourishes and has, as we have seen, deep and ancient roots. It is not surprising, therefore, that the main attempts to make "decentralization" precise are related to the tradition. These attempts ask, essentially, "What do the proponents of 'decentralized' processes have in mind when they so label the process; what properties might one associate with this term, in a precise manner, so that these properties agree with informal usage of the term and so that they may exhibit, in a rigorous analysis, the advantages of better information and incentive that intuition claims for them?"

Motivated thus, it is natural to take as the main primitive terms of a proposed definition the terms "message," "response," and possibly "action"; to take "adjustment processes," or simply "processes," as the objects to be modified by the terms "decentralized," "centralized," and, if possible, "more decentralized than"; and to give first priority to the informational aspects of "decentralization" as the word appears to be used in the adjustment-process literature.

In Search of "Decentralization": The "Authority" Approach

What is the alternative? Koopmans and Montias[11] have very recently provided us with a partial answer. In this approach one takes as a primitive concept the relation between individuals in which one is "in authority over" another "with respect to a particular activity." Using this primitive relation one can then develop the notion of a "hierarchy" and its "tiers." A "more decentralized" economy then becomes one in which more "decisions" (another primitive term) are made at lower tiers.[12]

Though "in authority over" may be taken as a primitive, one would nevertheless like to recognize the relation when one sees it; or, more accurately, one would wish that a clear consensus of observers might agree on it. One obvious guide to its recognition is the presence of some sort of sanction. A is in authority over B with respect to an activity if B's decision with regard to the activity is to meet a constraint imposed by A; should his decision fail to meet the constraint B will suffer some sort of unpleasant sanction, imposed by A or by some other agent in the economy.

---

11. "On the Description and Comparison of Economic Systems," in *Comparison of Economic Systems: Theoretical and Methodological Approaches*, ed. Alexander Eckstein (Berkeley: University of California Press, 1971), pp. 42–48.

12. The preceding is a quick and oversimplified extract from the paper of Koopmans and Montias, which contains many other concepts.

Consider now the manager of an enterprise and a central agency. Suppose that in one mode of organizing the economy the center gives the manager detailed instructions as to the enterprise's monthly production plan. If the manager fails to obey the instructions he suffers a severe sanction. Clearly, it appears, the center is in authority over the manager with respect to the enterprise's production.

Now the economy is reorganized. Market prices appear and the central agency still operates for some purposes but withdraws from the scene as far as current production is concerned. The manager is now responsible to a workers' council (a group of stockholders would serve to illustrate the point just as well). His function is to choose each month a production plan which uses the existing plant and work force to achieve maximum profit if he can, or at least "reasonably high" profit if he cannot. If he is believed consistently to fail at this task, the council dismisses him—another unpleasant sanction. Now, virtually all observers would agree, it is the council that is in authority over the manager. If the reorganization is a decentralizing one then in some appropriate sense the manager has more scope for action in avoiding the new sanctions than in avoiding the old ones.

But how is the increase in scope to be measured? Is the number of production plans consistent with the avoiding of sanctions really an appropriate measure? True, in the example, sanctions are avoided by following a single command—one plan only—before the reorganization and by all production plans achieving "reasonably high" profit—many plans—after the reorganization. Suppose, however, we slightly perturb the example and say that to avoid sanctions the command before the reorganization must be "reasonably closely" followed. Then we must compare two sets of many plans each, where, quite possibly, many plans are in one set but not in the other. Or, more drastically, we could change the example further by imagining that the manager is in charge of a classic convex, nonpolyhedral set of production possibilities and that the council insists on true profit maximization, so that there is a unique production plan which avoids sanctions after the reorganization. Has the reorganization then been "centralizing" rather than "decentralizing"?

But, it could be argued, there is a simple way to avoid this difficulty. Let the "enterprise" replace the "manager" in the analysis. Before the reorganization, the enterprise includes both workers and manager, but its actions are in fact chosen by the manager, subject to whatever constraints those in authority over the enterprise impose. After the reorganization the actions are chosen by manager and workers (via their council) together and we need not be concerned with whatever internal arrangements the two parts of the enterprise may have made with each other. Then the center is in authority over the enterprise before the reorganization—we need only adopt the convention that if the center's sanctions are unpleasant for part of the enterprise (the manager) we consider them to be unpleasant for the enterprise as a whole. After the reorganization no one, it appears, is in authority over the enterprise; therefore, it has unlimited scope in choosing its actions and the reorganization is unambiguously a decentralizing one.

Is this an appealing abstraction from reality, however? Surely, in fact, no enterprise, no matter what the mode of economic organization, can deliberately bankrupt itself without feeling some sanctions imposed by some agents in the rest of the economy—if nothing else the wrath of irate wives, or mothers-in-law, or creditors of those whose income is affected.

Moreover, when one examines the proposed resource allocation schemes which so many economists have confidently labeled "decentralized," one finds this confidence rudely shattered if one applies a test for decentralization based on the authority concept, where the presence of sanctions is the observer's clue to the authority relationship. A scheme of the classic Lange–Lerner type does not appear as clearly more decentralized than a command scheme.[13]

Now suppose that, in view of these difficulties, the attempt to use sanctions to identify authority is abandoned. A promising candidate for a new identifying technique requires introducing the concept of "message" and is as follows: A is in authority over B with respect to some activity if the messages A sends to B contain virtually complete information about the actions B is subsequently observed to take with respect to that activity. If, after a reorganization, the messages A sends to B about each activity now contain less complete information about the actions B takes with respect to that activity, then the reorganization is decentralizing. Moreover, one might be able, in this approach, to use as a more elaborate primitive the term "the degree of authority which A holds over B with respect to an activity," a higher degree being recognizable by the greater information about B's observed actions in the message he previously receives from A. A decentralizing reorganization is then one in which A has a lower degree of authority over B with respect to each activity, A has authority of given degree over B with respect to fewer activities, or both.

In this approach to identifying the authority relationship, however, we

13. Note that in a Lange–Lerner scheme the central price-setting agency is in authority over the managers with respect to their production decisions, but the managers also appear to be in authority over the central agency (with respect to its price changes, which must have a sign opposite to that of excess demand). Similarly, one has the example given by Herbert Simon (in *Administrative Behavior* [New York: Macmillan, 1961], p. 138) when he discusses the difficulty of identifying the authority relationship: the dispatcher who mans the radio transmitter and receiver at police headquarters, though possibly a very "low-ranking" functionary, appears to be in authority over the officers to whom he relays information about the locations where they are needed; they suffer sanctions if they disobey his instructions.

are forced back to informational concepts, and the question then arises whether one cannot dispense with the authority relationship altogether in satisfyingly defining decentralizing changes.[14] Does the authority concept really add anything useful in the pursuit of such a definition? We will not attempt to answer that question here, or to choose between the two suggested methods of identifying the authority relationship.

In Search of "Decentralization": A New Informational Definition

Instead we now consider an informational decentralization concept in which the authority relation does not explicitly play a role. It has its own difficulties when one starts applying it to complex reality; the choice between it and abstractions based on the authority concept—if indeed it is a choice and not a synthesis that has to be made—must await much further experience with both theoretical and empirical applications.

In the approach we now suggest, "centralized," "decentralized," and "more decentralized than" will be applied to *processes*. A process is used by an *organization* of *n members*, e.g. an economy composed of enterprise managers, households, and government policy makers and other government agencies; if the organization is an economy undergoing reform, then it is its process which the reformers are engaged in modifying. The organization faces an *environment* which changes in accordance with a probability law and over which the organization has no control. We consider a sequence of points of time one unit apart. If the environment changes it does so only at those points of time (it may stay unchanged for several successive time points). At time t (and until time $t + 1$), the current environment is E_t, a vector.[15]

The process specifies how, at time t, each member of the organization observes some part of E_t; sends messages to other members; revises the information he has stored, in accordance with his new observations on the environment and messages he has newly received from other members; and, using his most recently stored information, revises the *actions* which he currently has in force. In general, the information currently stored by all members (which includes their current actions), and the current environment, together determine some sort of "welfare," "benefit," or, as we shall now call it, *payoff*, received by the organization.

14. See L. Hurwicz, "Centralization and Decentralization in Economic Processes," in *Comparison of Economic Systems*, ed. Eckstein, pp. 79–102, for an attempt to develop the hierarchy concept in an essentially informational manner.

15. The time points t in the present discussion are not to be confused with the reformers' decision points t, discussed in section I. The objects among which the reformers choose are processes. Most of the successive points of time through which the operation of a chosen process passes may, in particular, lie between the reformers' successive decision points.

To define the process formally[16] we assign to member i a number, say $k^i > 2$, of *slots*. Each slot stores some piece of information, and its contents are updated at each time t; the contents of member i's rth slot at time t is denoted $s_r^i(t)$. Now member i's first slot *always* contains his observations on the current environment E_t; and his second slot *always* contains information specifying the value of his current action (and therefore may as well be *called* his current action), which will be in force from t to $t + 1$.

Thus

$$\{s_1^i(1), s_1^i(2), s_1^i(3), \ldots\}$$

is the sequence of the ith member's observations on the environment sequence

$$\{E_1, E_2, \ldots\},$$

and

$$\{s_2^i(1), s_2^i(2), s_2^i(3), \ldots\}$$

is the sequence of the ith member's actions, the tth one prevailing while the tth environment, E_t, prevails. The remaining slots contain other information ultimately useful for the future choice of actions by all the members.[17]

The process consists of n functions

$$f^1, \ldots, f^n,$$

one for each member. The typical one, f^i, is defined on the current contents of all the k^i slots of member i, *and* the messages he received at the previous time point. Given these arguments, the function f^i yields the new contents of all member i's slots *and* the messages sent by i at time t, denoted $m^i(t)$. The *message vector* $m^i(t)$ has components

$$m_1^i(t), \ldots, m_n^i(t),$$

16. Here we loosely adapt the main concepts of the theory of sequential machines.

17. If the organization is an economy and a given member is the manager of an enterprise, then his action slot specifies his current operating and investment decisions; other slots specify his current stock of equipment (which depends in part on his last period's investment action). His environment slot specifies the current state of his technology (his production possibilities). Then the environment sequence and the sequence of actions taken by all members (including the government policy makers mentioned in section I), together with the successive contents of all members' other slots, determine the economy's successive capital stocks (or its successive *states*, to use the more general term of the introductory section), the production decisions of enterprises, and the stream of final consumptions (welfare determinants). A stream of values of a given reformers' utility function is therefore also determined. If the "actions" are not detailed operating plans but (as they may be in some processes) merely amounts of factors to be used, then that information, together with the production-possibilities information in the environment slot, and the capital-stock information in the remaining slots, may determine (via an enterprise production function) the enterprise's current input–output combination. In either case, full generality requires that we let slots other than the current action and environment slots influence the relevant current payoff.

where $m_j^i(t)$, denotes the message sent by i to j between t and $t + 1$. The message $m_j^i(t)$ is itself a vector; each of its components is a symbol of a fixed *alphabet,* and the alphabet includes a "null" symbol which, whether alone or accompanied by other components, conveys no information. A message vector $m_j^i(t)$ may have any number of components; it may in particular consist of the null symbol alone, which then means "no message." The message $m_i^i(t)$ is always such a null message, but in addition many other messages $m_j^i(t)$, with $i \neq j$, may be null messages as well.

In summary, then, we have, letting $s^i(t)$ denote $[s_1^i(t), \ldots, s_{k_i}^i(t)]$,

$$[s^i(t), m^i(t)] = f^i[s^i(t - 1), m^i(t - 1)].$$

Once we specify an *initial situation*—that is, an initial slot content $[s^1(0), \ldots, s^n(0)]$, initial messages $[m^1(0), \ldots, m^n(0)]$, and an initial environment E_0—then the functions f^i, together with Nature's choice of the subsequent environment sequence $\{E_1, E_2, \ldots\}$, completely determine[18] all that goes on within the organization at the time points $1, 2, 3, \ldots$ —the actions taken, messages sent, and information stored.

The above concept of process appears broad enough to include any of the adjustment processes proposed by economists. There may be one member who plays the role of a "center," but there need not be. The members may be grouped, in some fashion, into "divisions," or into tiers of a hierarchy.[19]

The organization may be a firm or a planning agency, and the process may be a well-studied algorithm which achieves a high value of some many-valued payoff function. Or it may be a whole economy whose members comprise enterprises, households, and governmental units, with actions of some enterprises including the product prices they choose and the actions of households including the consumptions they choose.

If there are indeed price-making enterprises, the responses defining the process are probably difficult to write down, and in modeling them in a process one may have a number of choices, the path defined by each variant being as yet quite unstudied. But even in this complex case, both the complex

18. The way in which the ith member responds to a *given* previous slot-content and given previously received messages may or may not change over time. If it does change, that is formally expressed by simply letting one of the slots store the index (t) of the current period.

19. Thus, for example, one might say that members 1 to m ($m < n$) belong to one tier and $m + 1$ to a second, "higher" tier if (1) each of the members 1 to m receives messages from one or more of the members $m + 1$ to n; (2) the current action of each of members 1 to m (his second slot) is sensitive (as revealed in the function f^i) to these previous messages and only to those messages; and (3) the messages sent by members $m + 1$ to n are sensitive to the content of their environment slots, so that members $m + 1$ to n cannot be mere passive robots (falsely appearing to be "superiors"), whose "instructions" to the lower tier are themselves determined only by the messages previously received from the lower tiers.

reality and a simplified model are, in principle, a set of functions $f^1, \ldots, f^n$—a process.

Finally, one does *not* need to introduce, as a sort of dangling addendum to the formal specification of the members' responses, some way of getting from "paper" to "physical" actions; other approaches have required such an addendum.[20] The current physical actions are always specified in the second slot, and they may be accompanied by "paper" specifications or preliminary "paper" proposals (stored in some other slot) for future actions —next period's or still further ahead. Any relation between physical and paper specifications—any combination of the "tatonnement" and "non-tatonnement" properties—is permitted.

The proposed formulation is, then, highly versatile. Its versatility might, indeed, be expected to make difficult a reasonable definition of decentralized and centralized processes. Instead a definition is immediately possible and so, moreover, is a definition of "more centralized than" ("less decentralized than").

To define these terms, we imagine an observer totally outside the organization. He knows the functions f^i. *If* he were to observe the environment sequence, he could then, in principle, reconstruct the entire sequence of slot contents generated by the process. He does *not*, however, observe the environment sequence; he *does* observe the sequence of messages exchanged. Then the process is the more centralized, roughly speaking, the more accurately the observer can reconstruct the sequence of actions taken (and the other slots as well), given only his observations of the messages exchanged and his knowledge of the functions f^i, but excluding from consideration any "superfluous" message components, which have no effect on their receiver's subsequent actions. If these "effective" messages are very rich in information about the aspects of the environment which ultimately determine, via the process, the actions taken and the payoffs generated, then the payoff is highly centralized:[21] if we imagine the outside observer becoming a "center" (an $(n + 1)$-st member) then the information transmission performed by the process is sufficiently voluminous and sufficiently relevant so that he could guess confidently at the actions actually taken by members 1 to n. He could then issue instructions specifying these actions, thereby transforming the original process into a "command" process which achieves roughly the same sequence of actions. Of course if the process already is a command

20. The "outcome rule" in L. Hurwicz, "Optimality and Informational Efficiency in Resource Allocation Processes," in *Mathematical Methods in the Social Sciences*, ed. Arrow, Karlin, and Suppes (Stanford: Stanford University Press, 1959), pp. 27–46; the "arrangement" in T. Marschak, "Computation in Organizations: the Comparison of Price Mechanisms and Other Adjustment Processes," in *Decision and Organization*, ed. C. B. McGuire and R. Radner (Amsterdam: North-Holland Publishing Co., 1972), pp. 237–82.

21. One might prefer the term "centralizable."

process, then the $(n + 1)$-st member merely needs to observe and duplicate the messages sent by the already existing center.

Formally, the definition comes in several variants. To state them more compactly, let f, $m(t)$, $s(t)$, $s_j(t)$ denote the appropriate n-tuples: f denotes $(f^1, f^2, \ldots, f^n)$; $m(t)$ denotes $(m^1(t), \ldots, m^n(t))$; $s(t)$ denotes $(s^1(t), \ldots, s^n(t))$; $s_j(t)$ denotes $(s_j^i(t), \ldots, s_j^n(t))$. Further, for a given initial situation $(E_0, s(0),$ $m(0))$, we shall call a component of a message $m_j^i(t)$, say the vth component, *superfluous* for the process f if the following is true: let $\bar{m}(t)$ denote the n-tuple obtained from $m(t)$ when the vth component of $m_j^i(t)$ is made the null symbol, the rest of the entire message n-tuple remaining intact. Then for all environment sequences which start with E_0, the action sequence following t (the sequence $\{s_2(t + 1), s_2(t + 2), \ldots\}$) which would be generated if the response functions f were applied to $\bar{m}(t)$ instead of $m(t)$ is the same as the original action sequence. For a given process f and a given initial situation we let the symbol $\bar{m}(t)$ denote, in fact, the message n-tuple obtained from $m(t)$ by making superfluous components equal to the null symbol. We shall speak of the sequence $\bar{m}(1)$, $\bar{m}(2)$, ... as the *effective message sequence* for f given an initial situation. We then have

DEFINITION—FIRST (WEAK) VARIANT. *The process f' is at least as central-ized as the process f'' if for every initial situation $(E_0, s(0), m(0))$, and every subsequent effective message sequence $\{\bar{m}(1), \bar{m}(2), \bar{m}(3), \ldots\}$, any action (second-slot) sequence $\{s_2(1), s_2(2), \ldots\}$ consistent with[22] that initial situation, that effective message sequence, and the response functions f' is also consistent with the same initial situation, the same effective message sequence and the response functions f''. The process f' is more centralized than f'' if f' is at least as centralized as f'' and it is not true that f'' is at least as centralized as f'. A process f is totally decentralized if the set of action sequences consistent with the initial situation, the effective message sequence, and the response function f is the set of all possible action sequences. The process f is totally centralized if the set of action sequences consistent with these three elements is always (for all environment sequences beginning with the given E_0) composed of one element, namely, the action sequence which actually occurs.*

Several remarks about this definition[23] are in order. First, the exclusion

22. An action sequence is consistent with an initial situation $(E_0, s(0), m(0))$, an effective message sequence $m(1)$, $m(2)$, ..., and response rules f, if there exists some environment sequence beginning with E_0, for which, given $[s(0), m(0)]$, f would generate *both* that effective message sequence and the given action sequence.

23. This definition owes much to discussions with A. Camacho and has some similarity to definitions proposed by him in "Centralization and Decentralization of Decision-Making Mechanisms: A General Model," prepared for the Second World Congress of the Econometric Society, September 1970.

of superfluous messages from those the "outside observer" takes into account is intended to exclude as highly centralized processes those in which a great deal of highly detailed information is exchanged but this information is simply stored away and not acted upon. (Income tax returns, for example, may be sent to a central member—the government—and may contain highly detailed information, much of which never affects the government's actions.) Unless we exclude such superfluous transmissions the definition might judge a process to be highly "centralized" which predominant usage would not call so.

Second, the above variant is weak, since it provides only a partial ordering: f' is more centralized than f'' if the set of all action sequences which the outside observer knows to be consistent with the effective message sequence observed and with f'' *contains* the set which he knows to be consistent with the same message sequence and with f'. But it may be that the first set overlaps with, but does not contain, the second.

Third, the above variant seems a clear improvement over previous attempts to capture the "privacy" property which most of the classic literature (notably the socialism debates of the 1930s) gropingly identified as the principal mark of decentralization. In this tradition one examines the information stored by member i in his environment slot, following an initial environment E_0. Given $(E_0, s(0), m(0))$ the functions f imply what is in that slot at $t = 1, 2, \ldots$. If the contents of i's environment slot always coincide with member i's "natural" observation on the environment (to be defined separately), then the process exhibits the privacy property. Classic examples of a member's "natural" observation are his production-possibility set if i is a manager, his preferences and endowment if i is a consumer. The difficulty is that even if member i stores nothing about the environment except such "natural" information he can indirectly *deduce* (if he wishes) some aspects of other members' natural observations: he knows that the messages he receives as the process unfolds are inconsistent with certain values of the others' natural observations. Thus real privacy is something of a chimera.

Finally, if we turn briefly to the authority concept, much of the popular idea that decentralization means more decisions left to "lower" tiers seems captured in the definition. If a center delegates to outlying members more of the decisions about the actions which those members take, then the messages the center sends will contain fewer clues about the actions, and the outside observer's best guesses about what the actions will be are far less accurate.

In constructing a second, stronger variant, wherein "more centralized than" becomes a complete ordering relation, there are a number of choices. One needs some appropriate measure of "closeness" between two action sequences. A natural measure is the expected summed discounted payoff (averaging over the possible environment sequences) yielded by the two action sequences or, more generally, by the entire sequence of slot-content vectors[24] $\{s(1), s(2), \ldots\}$.

We can now, accordingly, imagine that the outside observer, knowing at each time t the observed effective message sequence thus far, the functions defining the process, the initial situation and the probability law governing the environment sequence—but *not* that sequence itself—tries to duplicate the achievements of the process and carefully chooses a sequence of slot-content vectors $s(t)$ for the organization, the tth one to be chosen prior to the tth environment. His "best" sequence of choices achieves a value of the summed discounted payoff as close as possible, on the average, to the summed discounted payoff actually yielded by the vectors which the process in fact generates. This gives us our strong variant.

DEFINITION—SECOND (STRONG) VARIANT.[25] *The process f' is more centralized than the process f'' if, given an initial situation $(E_0, m(0), s(0))$, the smallest attainable difference between the expected discounted summed payoff yielded by f' and the expected discounted summed payoff yielded by n-tuples $s(t)$ chosen (by an outside observer who knows f' and the initial situation but not the subsequent environment sequence) in response to the effective message sequence generated by f' is smaller than the corresponding difference for f''.*

Applications of the definition. We conclude our discussion of decentralization with some brief examples of the application of the suggested definition to the choices faced by reformers.[26]

24. Recall that when the organization is an economy some slots specifying the economy's current "state" (e.g. capital stock) and current payoff (e.g. national product) may depend on the "state" as well as on the current actions (e.g. investment and production decisions).

25. Note that we could, if desired, restate the first (weak) variant so that it also deals with the sequences $s(t)$ of all slots rather than the action (second-slot) sequences. But nothing important would appear to be gained by doing so. In the strong variant we must do so since we must allow current payoff to depend in general on the current content of certain slots, in addition to the action slot.

26. One not completely facetious application pertains to a remark made by P. Wiles at a previous conference: The U.S. economy is surely the most centralized in the world, since each entrepreneur begins his day with the *Wall Street Journal*, to whose numbers and reports he appears to be a slave. His Soviet counterpart receives only infrequent, and probably briefer, communications from Gosplan.

Our definition takes care of the paradox. Reading of the *Wall Street Journal* may indeed be ritually followed by the entrepreneur's daily decisions but an outside observer, seeing only the *Journal* and knowing nothing about the entrepreneur's own particular environment, could say little about the entrepreneur's daily decisions. On the other hand, knowing the entire compendium of Gosplan directives the observer could make accurate statements about a particular manager's decisions.

First, suppose the reformers start from a command economy with production decisions centrally made: technological information is gathered at the center and the main production decisions of enterprises are computed at the center and sent to enterprise managers as instructions. Now the reformers wish, cautiously, to take successive steps in the direction of "decentralization." At each step they are to choose, for example, between the industries of the economy, to decide in which one next to delegate the production decisions to managers. They want an industry for which the delegation makes neither a "very small" further move in the decentralized direction nor a "very large" one. Following the above definitions in a very rough fashion, as a guide, they would probably not choose an industry with intensive connections (massive buying and selling relations) to many other industries, nor one which is virtually detached. For in the former case an outside observer, deprived of knowledge of the industry's production decisions, finds his knowledge of the actions taken by all enterprises in the economy greatly diminished and in the latter case hardly diminished at all.

Suppose next that the reformers are to choose between delegation to all enterprises of current production decisions on the one hand and investment decisions on the other. Of the two alternatives, the delegation of investment decisions appears to be the smaller step toward decentralization, in the sense of the strong definition, with payoff taken to be, say, national product. Knowing the investment decisions and an initial environment (which includes initial enterprise capital stocks and production possibilities), the outside observer can make a good estimate of the current enterprise production possibilities and capital stocks and hence can make a good guess at the production frontier of each enterprise. If the process is one in which each enterprise chooses always a point on its frontier, then he knows a large set of points which include the enterprise production decisions actually made. But the alternative is to know these decisions exactly, and they are likely to closely determine current payoff (national product).

As a third example, consider the delegation of price setting. Suppose the reformers are to replace the prices of a command economy (designed merely, say, to balance the money flows associated with a planned material balance) by a new price-setting scheme. They are to choose between central price adjusting in the Lange–Lerner style, on the one hand, and enterprise price making on the other. Which choice is a greater move toward decentralization? One cannot answer until the second alternative is expressed as precisely (using the "process" terminology) as the first. This is a matter we turn to in the next section. We only point out here that "more decentralized" cannot be meaningfully used in this particular context until the enterprise price-making alternative is more closely studied.

We have seen that while the word "decentralized" is so vigorously and frequently invoked in a desperate attempt to compactly characterize the alternative steps in a reform, doing so consistently is fraught with difficulties. A reasonable definition of "more centralized than" seems possible, but its application is often difficult. Is the compactness sought in fact worthwhile? Or is it better to talk of the steps in a reform in a far more complex manner? The answer cannot be given until many more efforts have been made at theories and measurements which relate degrees of decentralization to the performance of processes.

V. The Reformers' Decisions and Their Effect: Selected Topics

We keep open, then, the question of the ultimate form which the reformers' decision variable—R_t in the framework of section I—will take. We conclude our survey of present knowledge about the elements of a pragmatic reformers' strategy by looking briefly at what can be said or learned, and what appears to be currently thought, about the effect on economic performance of three major decisions confronting the reformers: who sets prices, who makes investment decisions, and what resources are to be used in operating the chosen allocation mechanism.[27]

The Setting of Prices: Theoretical Issues

Economists must face a remarkable fact. The practitioners of economic reform in socialist countries, attempting to decentralize a command economy, have rejected any idea of adapting in some practical way the classic proposals for a socialist economy in the Western literature. The scheme of Lange and Lerner, with market-clearing price setting by a central agency and profit-maximizing production decisions by managers, and the many later schemes which are its offspring, appear to be treated with amusement, disdain, or total neglect. What the reformers specify instead is that, subject to varying constraints, a great many product prices are to be set by the producing enterprises themselves, even though the economies in question are small, often with very few producers of each product.

This is a double embarrassment for Western economic theorists. Not only is their "accepted" solution to the question of price formation neglected but the solution proposed instead is one on which Western theory is extremely murky indeed. The needed theory is, in effect, one of an economy with oligopolistic pricing under various institutional constraints and in the presence of the "competition" presented by the world market, which may provide an external source or destination for the oligopolistically priced product.

27. For the formal statement of a strategy one may, as in section I, prefer to think of the last as a decision of policy makers, reformers being confined to the choice of the allocation mechanism itself.

It does not help matters to say that the Western theory, in its nonsocialist version, deals with an atomistic market as an extreme and that its conclusion remains roughly true as long as there are "enough" firms in each industry. The fact is that the crucial assumption of the theory is that enterprises take prices as given and that they indeed do so (however few of them there may be in each industry) in the Lange–Lerner scheme. But when enterprise price-setting is permitted, then "taking prices as given" must be carefully explained and justified—if prices are "taken" *someone* must still "make" them.

Let us first deal briefly with the world-market complication, for, important as it may be in some economies, it obscures the really puzzling issue. Ideally, the external world market would indeed play the role of a central price setter, beyond the enterprise's control. This would be so if foreign exchange—an input of importing enterprises and an output of exporting enterprises—were freely sold to domestic enterprises and households and freely bought from them by an agency which always sets a market-clearing domestic price for foreign exchange. Assume enterprises to be profit seekers. Then no enterprise would set the price of its product above the world price of its product as expressed in the domestic currency via the current market-clearing domestic price of foreign exchange. If it did so its customers—households or other enterprises—would purchase the product externally. No enterprise would set its price below the world price: it would make higher profits by exporting at the world price. If an enterprise could not cover its costs when it sold at the world price then it would cease production of the product in question.

Inevitably, reality strongly violates this ideal in a number of ways. A particular domestic product may simply not appear on the world market. There may be a great discrepancy between the buying and selling prices of a product on the world market since selling externally may involve major extra "selling costs." At a given moment, importing or exporting of a particular commodity may be possible only as a result of special bilateral agreements with another country, quite possibly made for political reasons, involving an exchange against specific other commodities. Even a small economy's export or import of a sufficiently specialized commodity may affect the world price, so that it cannot be taken as given. Above all, there is most unlikely, except under the most sweeping reforms, to be anything like freely purchasable and salable foreign exchange, with a domestic price flexibly finding its market-clearing level. Instead, the central government is most likely to ration foreign exchange, giving priority to purposes it favors, a priority which is likely not to coincide with enterprises' profitability criteria.

It is very difficult to analyze the effects of enterprise price-making when the world market's policing role is such a complex variant of the simple ideal.

To make a start it would be useful to imagine the economy to be isolated from the rest of the world. One strongly suspects that contemporary reformers would even then favor enterprise price-making over adaptation of the Lange–Lerner scheme—that the basic intuitive reasons for the preference have nothing to do with the world market. What are these intuitive reasons? We conjecture that there are four main ones.

First, the informational requirements of central price-adjusting are imagined to be too severe. When enterprises make prices, they need, it is thought, only knowledge of their own demand curves and technologies—"private" knowledge which they naturally possess. The enterprises clear their own markets, in effect, and with little effort do the work the central price setter would have to do; he must, after all, take very frequent readings on the excess demand for very many commodities and this will require new devices, never used by any economy before, for quickly measuring and reporting unsold stocks and unfilled orders.

Second, there is great mistrust of the dynamic properties of a central price-adjustment scheme. The theoretical literature only proves global convergence to the market-clearing prices associated with enterprise profit maximization under classic conditions on the enterprise production possibility sets and also (1) on the planners' (or reformers') utility function to whose maximum the scheme is to converge, or (2) on consumers' preferences if the scheme is to converge not to the maximum of a planners' utility function but rather to the competitive equilibrium determined by consumers' initial resource endowments.

These conditions may be violated. Increasing returns (nonconvexities) in the enterprises' production-possibility sets are an important violation and, as we noted above, recent literature does suggest schemes, roughly of Lange–Lerner type, which, in the presence of increasing returns, converge to the nearest local maximum of a planners' utility function. But these schemes do not allow discrimination among the alternative local maxima (equilibrium positions), some of which may be superior to others.

Even if convergence is not a worry, far more complex properties of the scheme certainly are. The reason is that equilibrium is not likely ever to be reached. The environmental conditions determining the current excess demand functions are likely to change rapidly and the price-adjustment procedure will, in effect, be started and restarted in response to these shifts.

The convergence literature assumes that production possibilities and the ultimate determinants of demand (e.g. consumer preferences) stay the same as the scheme generates its prices and associated production decisions, but it does not tell us about the scheme's dynamic properties when these basic elements of the environment change and, moreover, change randomly. It does not tell us, to use the terminology of the preceding section, about the expected summed discounted payoff yielded by the action sequence which the scheme generates when the environment changes according to some probability law.

One might suggest avoiding this problem by adopting a strictly "non-tatonnement" version of a Lange–Lerner scheme; the procedure starts afresh at the beginning of each month and enterprises and households in the current month's operation of the process use the production possibilities and preferences *as they were at the beginning of the month* in computing their responses to the month's successively announced prices. These responses, moreover, are merely "paper" responses (or intentions) and the prices merely "paper" prices.

Only when the month's operation of the procedure has been declared complete do the last announced prices become the prices at which transactions actually occur and the productions and consumptions associated with these terminal prices become those actually physically occurring. Those terminal prices and decisions then remain in force until the end of the month, when the procedure begins again.

In this version, however, the reformers must decide (or have a mechanism for deciding) how many rounds (iterations) of the procedure to engage in each month, what initial prices to use at the start of the month, and what prices to have in force (with their associated responses) while operation of the procedures is going on. These matters have been considered for abstractions of the Lange–Lerner process,[28] but the results are far from being practical guides to reformers, to say the least.

Third in the reasons for rejecting the Lange–Lerner scheme is suspicion of the incentive properties of the scheme. In feeling such suspicion the contemporary socialist reformers curiously share a common view with the antisocialist participants in the debates of the 1930s, for it was on the grounds that managers would lack the incentive to follow Lange's rules that they mainly rejected his solution. The view is, perhaps, that depriving enterprises of the control of prices, leaving them only production decisions, hinders their initiative and their sense of experiencing rewards and penalties as clear consequences of their decisions: today's production decisions have a remote effect on profits actually received when the price-adjustment process reaches equilibrium.

A fourth reason for rejecting schemes of the Lange type lies in fundamental questions, notably raised in recent writings of J. Kornai,[29] about whether prices can realistically serve as the crucial resource-allocating signals. Might it really be that within broad limits the buying decisions of households and

28. See Marschak, "Computation in Organizations."
29. J. Kornai, *Anti-Equilibrium* (Amsterdam: North-Holland Publishing Co., 1972).

enterprises are sensitive not to prices but to the waiting time required for delivery or more generally to the time and effort currently required to find a given commodity?

Western economists would, of course, be inclined to put the matter as follows: In principle every commodity could be labeled with its delivery time and place *and* with the effort required to arrange for its delivery at that time and place. In principle each such labeling defines a distinct commodity and in principle each such distinct commodity could have a price, set by a market-clearing agency. But the staggering number of distinct commodities required make this a practical impossibility. Hence some sort of balance is struck between the costs of price-setting and the inefficiences due to omitting many of the possible prices; such inefficiencies include the existence of queues, with some households or enterprises willing, but unable, to pay others for a place in the front of the queue. In the absence of prices for places in the queue its length is indeed a signal to which prospective joiners of the queue respond, but it is a signal to be examined *in addition to* the price for the commodity being delivered at the front of the queue; it does not *supplant* that price.

Whether this Western way of putting the difficulty captures the point being made one cannot yet say. One must await the development of a much more articulated theory of resource allocation for economies in which many of the prices possible in principle do not in fact exist.

These, then, are four lines of objection to the adaptation of schemes of the Lange–Lerner variety. Against these objections must be put a massive objection to enterprise price-making in a closed economy: unrealistic as the accepted theory of resource allocation in an economy of price-taking firms may be we have *no* theory—only the beginnings of some suggestions—about the allocation of resources in an economy of price-making firms. The first theoretical task in this direction—development of a true general-equilibrium theory when the economy contains price-making firms (and perhaps a price-taking sector as well)—is currently under study.

The suggestions which have substance and promise in this task are those in which the essential game-theoretic nature of the problem is brought out and dealt with and is not hidden (as it is, for example, in attempts to make rigorous, but essentially preserve, the Chamberlinian framework). One must choose first of all, between a cooperative and a noncooperative approach: may enterprises talk to each other and jointly decide on price and output decisions or are there institutional barriers (e.g. laws) to such communication? In the cooperative case, current work concentrates on exchange economies in which there are no separate "enterprises" or "consumers" but only agents with fixed initial resource endowments. Agents can form coalitions, a coalition may make exchanges, if it wishes, with those outside the coalitions, and a coalition may divide up among its members the proceeds of such exchanges (or the coalition's initial endowment if it makes no outside exchanges) in whatever manner its members agree upon.

The core of such an economy can be studied: the set of allocations of the economy's initial total endowment each of which no group of agents has the desire and the ability to "block" by forming a coalition and sharing the coalition's endowments in a manner that makes these agents better off. The core then identifies the set of exchanges which are "robust" against the freest bargaining and coalition formation. Under classic conditions on the agents' preferences the core contains any competitive equilibrium; if the agents, in a precise sense, are "many" and "small" the core contains nothing else. In very recent developments[30] this result is preserved even when a few agents are big (each of them owns a nonnegligible part of the economy's total resources). There is a hint in this unexpected result that when enterprises are finally brought into the analysis, the presence of oligopolistic ("nonatomic") enterprises may still allow the core to contain Pareto optima (and perhaps nothing else); conceivably, then, only Pareto optima are stable against free bargaining and coalition formation among enterprises. But this is pure speculation at present.

If one takes the noncooperative approach, which may be institutionally sounder, other worlds open up. Assume that price-making enterprises seek high profits. Then the most tradition-bound view would be that the economy's price-making firms grope for an equilibrium of the type described by Cournot and, in more general fashion, by Nash. If the economy is in a general equilibrium of this type then all markets are cleared and at the same time, given the prices chosen by every price-making enterprise but one, the remaining one has no incentive to change its price. If it did so and all other enterprises responded by making no change at all in their prices, it would find itself, after all effects of the change had worked themselves out, with less profit than before. Such equilibria can in fact be studied,[31] and it is not at all clear that no such equilibrium could ever be Pareto-optimal.

There are two difficulties with this approach—an approach traditional in spirit but only recently seriously studied—to characterizing the stable resource allocations in an economy with price-making, profit-seeking, non-

30. B. Shitovitz, "Oligopoly in Markets with a Continuum of Traders," Research Memorandum no. 47, Research Program in Game Theory and Mathematical Economics, Department of Mathematics, Hebrew University, Jerusalem, July 1969; J. Drèze, J. Gabszewicz, D. Schmeidler, and K. Vind, "Cores and Prices in an Exchange Economy with an Atomless Sector," Discussion Paper no. 7023, Center for Operations Research and Economics, Louvain University, 1970.

31. T. Negishi, "Monopolistic Competition and General Equilibrium," *Review of Economic Studies* 28, no. 3 (1961): 196–201; K. J. Arrow and F. Hahn, *General Competitive Analysis* (San Francisco: Holden-Day Co., 1972), chap. 6.

cooperative enterprises. In the first place, the conditions (on the economy's technology and its consumers' tastes) under which such an equilibrium can be shown to exist are very complex and very stringent; under very reasonable conditions it may not exist at all. In the second place, equilibria of this type have a very vulnerable property: each price-making enterprise finds it reasonable to remain at its equilibrium price provided that if it "experimentally" deviates from this price it finds that it does not dislodge other enterprises from their prices. But why should this be—why should other enterprises not respond to such experimental deviations with changes of their own?

These difficulties lead one to new approaches to the characterization of noncooperative equilibria. In one recent approach[32] one lets each enterprise respond to a deviation from the existing situation by one enterprise and regards the response consisting of no change at all to be very special and generally "unreasonable." One requires, in fact, that the response rule followed by each enterprise in responding to a deviation from the existing situation by one of them satisfy a certain intrinsic "reasonableness" property, violated by the response consisting of no change at all and by many other simple response rules. Equilibria are then situations which are *stable* for each enterprise with respect to such "reasonable" response rules: no enterprise wants to deviate from the situation because the responses of the others would make it sorry it did so (would leave it with lower profit).[33]

This concept of equilibrium opens a new institutional possibility, quite possibly of interest to a reforming economy: it may be possible to stabilize a particular n-tuple of price and output choices by the economy's n price-making enterprises, an n-tuple that is desirable from a reformers' viewpoint. This would be done by institutionalizing a response pattern, with the response functions satisfying the reasonableness requirement, with respect to which the desired n-tuple, or equally good ones, are the only choices stable for all enterprises. It may even be the case that the response rules which perform this trick are fairly simple ones, rules like those which tell enterprises

32. T. Marschak and R. Selten, "General Equilibrium with a Monopolistic Sector: a Non-cooperative Approach," Technical Report No. 4, Collaborative Research on Economic Systems and Organizations, Center for Research in Management Science, Berkeley, 1970.

33. An n-tuple of response rules specifies for the ith enterprise (out of the n in the economy) the new choices it makes given an existing n-tuple of choices and a deviation from it by some enterprise $j \neq i$. A reasonable n-tuple of response rules for the n enterprises has two properties: (1) given an n-tuple of choices stable for enterprise i, any deviation by some enterprise $j \neq i$ leads to a new n-tuple which is again stable for i; (2) at least one n-tuple of choices is stable for all enterprises. If the n-tuple of response rules has these properties (is "rationality-preserving"), then it also has the property that no enterprise i wants to violate its rule, following a deviation by $j \neq i$ from a point stable for i, if i knows that all other enterprises $k \neq i$ and $\neq j$ are obeying theirs. Details are given in Marschak and Selten.

selling a close substitute to a deviating enterprise's product to respond to the deviation by undercutting the deviator's new price. Such simple rules would be informationally "cheap," since they require each enterprise only to observe deviations, not to have any knowledge of other enterprises' demand curves or technologies.

To summarize: Obviously there is a great deal of theory to be constructed —in particular, the above suggestions leave open the question of what *process* leads to an equilibrium of the type proposed—but the behavior of price-making, profit-seeking enterprises may yet turn out to be compatible, given a proper institutional framework, with the aims of reformers.

The Setting of Prices: The Hungarian Case

In the current stage of the Hungarian reform, the adjustment of centrally set prices (or maximum prices) does *not* follow a systematic procedure that could reasonably be called a loose adaptation of the classic Lange–Lerner procedure. The price office does not change the initial (1 January 1968) prices unless it feels certain distinct pressures; it clearly does *not* make any routine attempt to collect current excess demand data (unsold stocks and unfilled orders) for long lists of commodities.

Typically, since the start of the reform, it has revised a price upward when enterprises producing the good in question strongly argued that given their current input prices (which may be other centrally set or constrained prices, or free prices, or import prices) the costs of meeting current demand cannot be covered. The proposed increase may not be permitted (or may be accompanied by appropriate compensating subsidies) if it would go against social policy (basic consumer goods) or foreign trade policy (key exports). The costs to be covered by the increase may include the costs of expanding current capacity; if a central price rise occurs it is, in fact, likely to be justified primarily as a stimulus to needed capacity expansion. The notion of a central price rise as a means of drying up current excess demand, or a means of allocating a scarce commodity to those who want it most, is not a popular one.

It is true that in the first few months following the reform there was very high excess demand for many commodities, probably due to a feeling on the part of many buyers that many of the new prices were "too good to be true," would not last very long, and would lead to shortages as enterprises hoarded supplies against expected future shortages. This temporary situation was dealt with (the Council of Ministers taking a role) by temporary directed cuts in the initial buying orders of a number of enterprises, not by price rises. After a while a belief in the general stability of most relative prices was thought to have spread and many of the excess demands subsided.

Again, a lowering of a fixed or maximum price, or selling below the maximum price (both relatively rare events) has occurred when foreign competition has provided a cheaper source of the commodity in question, or when newly constructed facilities have permitted lower production costs; it has not occurred as a systematic response to unsold stocks.

As for the free-price sector, which is hoped eventually to become the dominant one, a good example of its proper functioning is considered to be the pricing of certain consumer goods, such as items of clothing, in which lowering of prices at both retail and manufacturing levels to dispose of unpopular stocks is gradually becoming routine.

The oligopolistic pricing issue, discussed above as a theoretical mystery which a far-reaching switch to enterprise pricing must face, has not seemed to cause serious worry so far. The main free-price industries either contain more than one major domestic enterprise or else have some world-market competition. It appears to be accepted in principle that input constraints must be lightened where they interfere with the world market's competitive effect on a potential domestic monopoly. Further steps in the reform are expected to insure such selective lightening and to respond in other ways (not yet well formulated) to the observed oligopolistic behavior of domestic enterprises.

The Delegation of Investment Decisions

We argued in section IV that according to the proposed (strong) definition of "more centralized than" the shifting of investment decisions about the expansion or modernization of enterprises from a central authority to enterprise managers is probably a smaller step towards total decentralization than is the same shift with respect to current production decisions. Practitioners of economic reform, however, appear to be more hesitant to perform the smaller step than the larger one: "decentralizing" of the investment decisions comes last and is likely to be very incomplete, the center retaining at least some control over which enterprise obtains credit for what purpose. Moreover, in established private-ownership economies such as the French, sophisticated "planning" mechanisms are designed to encourage consistency of both private and public-sector investment with certain national goals, and credit rationing may again serve as an instrument for some central control over the direction of enterprise investment.

What theoretical (or empirical) insights lead to the conviction that investment decisions ought not to be left, unguided, to enterprises? We consider several.

Externalities. One has first an appeal to a hoary, popular, and compelling general conjecture which is also, however, an extremely complex and badly understood one: "When externalities are very great, decentralization works less well than when they are not; hence, the appropriate degree of centralization may be a high one." In the case of enterprise investment decisions the externalities in question might include the impact which each large investment decision has on the total volume of investment and, hence, on the macroeconomic consequences of the volume of investment. The externalities also include the public-goods character of some enterprise's outputs and the classic externalities (pollution, etc.) which expansion of some enterprises carries with it. The latter externalities may also characterize the production decisions of such enterprises, but production decisions are less "lumpy" and far more easily reversible than investment decisions.

Can the pervasive general conjecture be given a clear formulation and can it then be supported? Adopting the general formulation of section IV, let a payoff function be defined at any instant of time on the prevailing environment, the prevailing actions of the economy's agents, and the prevailing "state" of the economy.[34] Then the extent of externalities in the economy may be viewed as a property of the payoff function: externalities (or "interactions") are great if a small change in a typical agent's action has a large effect on the change in payoff associated with slightly altering another typical agent's actions. (If payoff is $w(a^1, \ldots, a^n, X)$ with a^i denoting member i's action and X denoting state and environment together, and if this is a function possessing second derivatives, then externalities are large if for each X, $|\partial^2 W/\partial a^i \partial a^j|$ is large for the typical pair i, j, with $i \neq j$.) The conjecture could then be put: given two processes and two payoff functions the performance of the more centralized process (as measured by expected summed discounted payoff) exceeds that of the less centralized one more when the payoff function is the one with great externalities than when the payoff function is the one with small externalities.

Put in this form, the conjecture is just beginning to be explored (for very simple processes and payoff functions) and the very few results available are mixed in their support of the conjecture.[35]

The popular acceptance of the conjecture does not, of course, rest on such a very general formulation but probably stems from what is known about a specific process, namely, the price mechanism. The principal sufficient condition for the achievement of Pareto optimality by a competitive equilibrium is the absence of externalities in the following sense: each enterprise has production possibilities, and each consumer endowments and preferences, unaffected by the productions and consumptions chosen by the other members of the economy. It does not follow that Pareto optimality can never be achieved by a competitive equilibrium when such externalities do occur, only that the situation is then indeterminate. Nevertheless, current theoretical

34. The contents of slots other than the first and second.

35. R. Radner, "The Evaluation of Information in Organizations," *Proceedings of the Fourth Berkeley Symposium on Probability and Statistics* (Berkeley: University of California Press, 1961), 1: 491–530; Marschak, "Computation in Organizations."

efforts are directed at enlarging the scope of the price mechanism (by introducing prices for individual consumption of public goods and for certain kinds of polluting effects, for example) so that an equilibrium may still imply optimality.[36] The price mechanism's difficulties in dealing with externalities do not mean that no other highly decentralized process could avoid such difficulties. But, so far, theory has not suggested one.

Shortcomings of multiperiod models as guides to decentralized mechanisms for investment decisions. Investment is best studied in a dynamic economy-wide model, most satisfyingly, for current theorists, a model with an infinite number of time periods. Recent theory has yielded results about efficient paths of capital accumulation in such models, even results for multisectoral models in which separate investment decisions are to be made for each of many sectors;[37] an individual enterprise may, in fact, be a sector in such models. It is shown, moreover,[38] that under classic conditions on the economy, and some additional ones, there are associated with an efficient sequence of investment decisions a sequence of prices, one for each commodity (including investment goods) at each point of time, and an accompanying interest rate as well. These have the property that each investment decision in the sequence is, in fact, a present-value-maximizing decision. The difficulty is, however, that the sequence of prices which must be consulted in order to compute the present value of alternative investments is an infinite sequence, and it is very hard to imagine a price-setting agency computing such a sequence in a manner analogous to the computing of the Lange–Lerner price-setting agency.

One can abandon the infinite-period property and can imagine the economy to disappear after a finite number of time periods. In that case, a purely static model suffices in principle. Once again, each physical commodity, labeled with the date at which it appears, becomes a distinct commodity with a price of its own. The prices of competitive equilibrium, computed once and for all (by a Lange–Lerner process, for example), induce enterprise profit-maximizing responses which, under classic conditions, solve the economy's problem. Each enterprise chooses, once and for all, in response to the announced prices, a profit-maximizing production plan governing its behavior for the future finite life of the economy. Borrowing, with repayment x periods from now at some interest rate, in order to buy equipment now, is included in such a plan: formally it means that a machine in the present period is an input and the interest, expressed in terms of some arbitrary

36. See, e.g., D. Foley, "Resource Allocation and the Public Sector," *Yale Economic Essays* 7 (Spring 1967): 43–98.

37. E.g., R. Radner, "Optimal Growth in a Linear-Logarithmic Economy," *International Economic Review* 7, no. 1 (February 1966): 1–33.

38. See papers in *Review of Economic Studies* 34 (1), no. 97 (January 1967).

commodity delivered x periods from now, is a further input. The product stream obtained from the machine is a bundle of dated outputs.

Such a static decentralized finite-period scheme is, of course, not to be taken seriously because of the enormous number of commodities and prices required. Debts in terms of money and interest rates for the use of money may be introduced to cut down the number of prices required. Even then the informational burden imposed on both enterprises and price-and-interest-rate setter, if the markets for loans of all possible lengths up to the terminal point are to be properly cleared, is immense. At best, therefore, the limited information-processing capacity with which members of the economy are endowed (even allowing for its mechanical augmentation) means that equilibrium achieves something falling short of Pareto optimality. Existing theory does not tell us what this penalty is, or how to estimate it knowing the information-processing capacities, or how to measure these capacities, or the net benefit due to augmenting these capacities at some cost in resources.

All the difficulties just described arise in a world of perfect certainty, in fact one in which production possibilities and tastes display classic properties. Both the static finite-period or the dynamic infinite-period models are even less well developed as guides to the decentralization of investment decisions when uncertainty is introduced.

Lumpiness and irreversibility of investment decisions. These two properties are strong additional reasons for hesitancy in delegating investment decisions. Whatever the defects of a centralized scheme for determining the volume and composition of the economy's investment, at least only one agency has control over the scheme and can modify it if it appears to perform badly. Too much seems at stake, and the consequences of investment mistakes must be lived with too long, to trust the matter to many separate agents, to the self-policing induced by profits or other incentives, and to the imperfect controls a weakened central agency can impose.

The Choice of Resources Placed at the Disposal of the Resource-Allocating Mechanism

This is a fundamental decision, though often overlooked, which must accompany the steps of a reform. Suppose the starting point of the reform is a thoroughgoing command mechanism which collects detailed technological data from enterprises, possibly demand curves or other preference data from consumers, and then digests this information in order finally to issue production instructions to enterprises. This mechanism can itself be given a very costly or a cheap bureaucracy and associated information-processing equipment. The instructions generated, for a given length of time spent on the generating, will differ in quality, as measured by some *net* payoff function, in which the resources required for operating the mechanism are subtracted.

Suppose the terminal stage of the reform were a thoroughgoing Lange–Lerner scheme. As emphasized at the beginning of this section, one would probably not operate such a scheme by letting it reflect rapid changes in enterprises' environments: its performance would be too hard to predict. Instead each enterprise would take periodic observations on the environment and the iterative scheme would be operated afresh, "on paper," for some finite number of iterations following each such observation point, the enterprises imagining their environments to remain unchanged (which might be roughly the case) during the operation. Following the terminal iteration, the terminally computed production plans will remain in force at least until the next observations on the environment.

Again, a crucial question is what information-processing resources are placed at the disposal of price-setting agency and enterprises as they repeatedly operate the scheme. The choice will determine, again, the quality of the production plans generated for alternative time periods spent on each operation of the scheme. Generally, more expensive information-processing facilities (human and mechanical) mean that more iterations can be completed in a given time period; the terminal actions obtained at the end of the period are therefore better ones.

Suppose the terminal stage of the reform is not a Lange–Lerner scheme but an economy of price-making enterprises, empowered also to make virtually all other decisions, with a minimal governmental role confined to macroeconomic policy instruments and possibly to influencing enterprise decisions where certain externalities are very severe. Then the task of operating the allocation mechanism falls largely on the enterprises themselves. The reformers (or policy makers) may not decide on the resources enterprises devote to this task but they ought to worry about whether enterprises will automatically, following the incentives which the mechanism provides, devote a desirable amount of resources to it. It may be, for example, that the price equilibrium toward which the price-making enterprises drift is of an excessively primitive type because each avoids (given its too-small information-processing capacity) complex computations about the others' reactions; a less primitive type of equilibrium might be more desirable from the reformers' point of view.

Whatever the terminal stage, a decentralizing reform will, in its intermediate phases, preserve a role for the center, and the resources placed at the center's disposal in fulfilling that role will influence the performance of the entire mechanism at that stage of the reform.

That there should be theory relevant to the subtle choice of resources for resource allocation is possibly a novel proposal. Without it the reformers or policy makers can only be intuitive or casually empirical in making this choice.

VI. CONCLUDING REMARKS: A PRAGMATIC STRATEGY IN THE PRESENT STATE OF KNOWLEDGE

We have surveyed, incompletely and unevenly, the main elements of the strategy sketched in section I: the performance indicators, the compact characterization of a direction in which a reform moves, some specific choices which reformers confront, and the state of general knowledge or conjecture about the consequences of these choices.

The state of general knowledge is impressive for its gaps. It seems abundantly clear that reformers at present can do no better than to adopt the following sort of pragmatic strategy: to divide the reform into a few major areas of decision (including the three treated in the section just concluded); to abandon hope, for the present, that compact characterizations like "size of the next step toward decentralization" can be made useful; to identify performance indicators which seem reasonably likely to be relevant, in view of the reformers' broadly stated aims, to each area of decision in each stage of the reform; and to choose, at each stage, that alternative in each area of decision which, when its counterpart was chosen in previous stages, was followed by good values, or at least not by bad values, of the relevant performance indicators. When, moreover, the chosen magnitude of the reform's changes in previous stages appears too great—when they seem to induce temporary disturbances such as a speculative inflation in anticipation of price changes—then the reform has subsequently to proceed at a slower pace.

The strategy described is vague, but its pragmatic character precludes more precision, though examples can help give it concreteness. It does not escape the fundamental dilemma of reform: small steps ought to be taken because one is ignorant about the effect of large steps and does not want to risk them, but the performance of small steps—the only reliable empirical information one has—may be a highly misleading clue to the performance of the final allocation mechanism, obtained when the reform is complete. It may well be, in short, that small changes are worse than none.

Let us consider a few specific examples. Let the delegation of production decisions, but not price decisions, to enterprises who are to maximize profits constitute one stage of the reform. Let this stage further consist of substages in which the delegation of decisions is extended to one industry after another. The relevant performance indicators are then measures of efficiency change for the industries affected. Specifically, the output and input combinations which are chosen by the "liberated" enterprises may be outrageous from the global standpoint of a totally liberated (and well-functioning) economy, because of the distorted input and output prices these enterprises are given. But each enterprise may display an improvement in the use made of the physical inputs actually selected (an upward shift in a production function). In the pre-"liberation" stage the enterprises had been hampered, say, by precise (but poor) instructions about the input mix to be used and even about the precise mix of production processes which each enterprise was to use to produce a specified output mixture.

Next suppose, in a subsequent stage, that price as well as production decisions are delegated to enterprises, but investment decisions are not. Suppose final consumptions are the reformers' ultimate concern. Then performance measures are relevant which bear on the economy's ability to generate desirable final consumptions, given its current, centrally determined, capacities. If the delegation of decisions has spread across all industries, customary aggregate production functions and their shifts are relevant indicators. If the delegation has been extended to only one industry at a time, queues and surpluses in each such industry might be argued to be relevant indicators—"good" pricing tending to eliminate them—as well as industry-wide efficiency indicators.

Other indicators possibly relevant to other reformers' decisions were discussed briefly in section II, as were some of those decisions themselves. Once the reform is terminated, and is to be evaluated ex post, as a whole, sweeping aggregate performance indicators such as before-and-after growth rates and economy-wide production functions come into play.

Turning briefly from hypothetical reforms to the Hungarian case, it may appear at first glance that the reform deliberately violated a pragmatic but cautious and sequential strategy, for what strikes one immediately is how large the initial leap was. On 1 January 1968, all at once, the scope of enterprise decisions increased drastically and the scope of ministerial and Planning Office decisions correspondingly decreased. In the case of commodities sold by enterprises to enterprises, prices are allowed to be freely set by the selling enterprises for commodities amounting to roughly 30 percent of the volume (measured in value, at the new prices) of such intermediate commodities. (For some of these commodities the freedom is ineffective since ceilings are placed on their prices when they reach the retail stage.) For commodities sold directly to consumers a roughly comparable proportion is freely priced. The remaining commodities have either a centrally set price or a centrally set maximum price (almost always the price actually used); the maximum price is a new one, often very different from the prereform price and intended to reflect average production cost. Drastic changes also occurred, all at once, with respect to enterprise investment decisions, the use of profits for management and worker bonuses, and the availability of foreign exchange for imports. We are not concerned here with the details.[39]

39. See the paper by B. Balassa in the present volume.

One's first impression as to the size of the initial leap and the finality of the resulting initial state of the reform must be tempered in two respects. First, the reform was preceded by an extremely lengthy and detailed series of "paper" experiments, in which many units of the economy participated. Many of the nonfree prices effective on 1 January 1968, for example, were based on previously collected enterprise data concerning production costs of the commodities in question. An iterative "paper" process of a sort had been operated, in other words, so as to yield initial nonfree prices which were at least likely to be consistent in the sense of covering costs. It was not left to subsequent stages of the actual reform to generate such consistency.

It may be, in fact, that a detailed study of the pre-1968 preparations would permit the following interpretation: with respect to pricing as well as other aspects the 1 January 1968 reform was obtained, in effect, by applying some strategy to *estimated* performance indicators for that hypothetical economy which would result from the "paper" reforms proposed in the final stage of the pre-1968 preparations, the estimates being based on "paper" responses of various sectors of the economy to the proposals; each of the prior stages in the preparation itself represented a similar application of a strategy and each yielded *small* changes in the proposed reform.

Secondly, while the step taken on 1 January 1968 may have been a large one, it was surely not the terminal one. Even official statements strongly imply that enlarging the number of commodities whose prices are free, resetting many fixed prices, and further lifting of constraints on enterprise investment and import-export decisions will occur at appropriate times to come.[40]

The natural formal occasion for specifying the next steps in the reform will be the approval of the forthcoming 1971–75 Five-Year Plan. In particular, specific steps are expected liberalizing import restrictions and allowing wider use of profits to supplement wages. In official parlance the plan provides the "framework" within which the new mechanism operates,[41] and a new plan is the opportunity for revising the framework.

The performance indicators by which the reform is already officially judged, and which will presumably be used in choosing future steps, include[42] productivity measures (especially with respect to agriculture); aggregate output increases in principle sectors,[43] growth of real national product; and real wages.

40. *Vingt questions—vingt réponses: Les expériences de la réforme du mécanisme de l'économie en Hongrie, une interview de M. Rezső Nyers, secrétaire du Comité Central du Parti Socialiste Ouvrier Hongrois* (Budapest: Pannonia, 1970).

41. Ibid., p. 16.

42. Ibid., pp. 5–14.

43. The rate of growth of industrial production, lower in 1968 than in 1966 and 1967, is judged to be as intended, since more resources were expected to flow to consumer-goods production after the reform. See ibid., p. 7.

Some central direction of enterprises' current production decisions remains in reserve to cope with unusual and temporary situations, due to the working of the mechanism or to external disturbances, for which price measures alone are not adequate. Prior to the winter of 1969, for example, the workings of the new mechanism had led to a massive change from coal heating of homes to oil and gas heating, with the resultant closing of some coal fields. The winter proved unexpectedly cold and long, the world price of coal unexpectedly high, and scheduled crude oil imports insufficient. Domestic wood-fuel stocks were low due to a low price and a high tax on stocks the previous summer. Faced with these converging circumstances, the central authorities, including the Materials and Price Board, took matters in hand. They revived previously canceled coal import orders, commandeered the needed transport, and revived (partly by special overhead-tax exemptions) some coal production previously abandoned as unprofitable. To prevent a repetition of the crisis in the following year, coal prices were subsequently raised—to stimulate coal production as well as to accelerate the shift to oil and gas.

The Materials and Price Board also performs, fairly routinely, certain "wheel-oiling" functions. For example, enterprises unable to find critical imports because the suppliers are exporting nearly the entire supply may report this fact, and appropriate temporary directives may be issued to provide relief.

To summarize, what one finds in the Hungarian case appears to be an experimental mix of reluctantly changing central prices, with changes largely designed to affect long-term profitability in a desired direction, not to correct short-term excess demand; free prices in a somewhat detached part of the economy whose price-making behavior has not yet stabilized; and occasional recourse to temporary administrative reallocation. What proportions the mix will take in the future is, of course, very hard to predict; the reformers' continuing application of a pragmatic strategy will determine it.

If the reforms completed ever numbered more than a very few, then retrospective experience, systematically organized, could give some general empirical support to the superiority of a particular pragmatic strategy. In the meantime, theory has cut out for it, as we have tried to show, a large number of tasks of clarification and of conjecture verifying. It is to be hoped that the stimuli that the puzzles posed by ongoing reforms provide for these tasks do not disappear from the scene. With luck they may multiply.

3

A Framework for Theoretical Analysis of Economic Reforms in Soviet-type Economies

JOHN MICHAEL MONTIAS

The bulk of this paper is devoted to the analysis of a simplified model of plan implementation in a "centralized" and in a "reformed" economy. The producers in this hypothetical economy are organized as a single, all-encompassing hierarchy. In the centralized system, basic production and allocation decisions are made in the highest tier and then disaggregated and parceled out to functionaries at each successively lower tier. The model aims at tracing the effects on the operation of the economy during the plan period of delegating production and allocation decisions to functionaries in lower tiers, including especially the managers of subhierarchies called "enterprises."

To set the scene for the main problem, I offer a few suggestions on how the facts and data in the record of a reform might be organized for quantitative or qualitative analysis. By introducing a few facts (or alleged facts) about one specific reform—the Czechoslovak reform of 1958–60—I hope to dispel the impression, which may well arise from reading the main part of the paper, that I am completely oblivious to the reality of economic reforms in Communist countries.

I. Reforms and Their Outcomes

What is meant by the "effects of a reform"? What variables would have to be traced or allowed for in order to single out the impact of the reforms on the outcomes in which one or more observers happen to be interested? How can the outcomes under the old system be compared with the outcomes under the new? In this part of the paper, I attempt to give as precise as possible an

I am grateful to Edward Ames, Abram Bergson, Morris Bornstein, John Broome, Michael Keren, Mohammed Ali Khan, Tjalling C. Koopmans, Janos Kornai, Frederic L. Pryor, Salim Rashid, and Martin Weitzman for their detailed and perceptive comments, which helped me significantly in my revisions. Mohammed Ali Khan also collaborated in writing appendix B.

answer to these methodological questions, in part with the help of terms and definitions set forth in Koopmans and Montias.[1]

The grand relationships we should like to know and understand with regard to a system change, such as an economic reform, may be written in the form of the following equation:

$$O_t = f(e_t, s_t, p_{s_t})$$

where O_t is a vector of outcomes observed in period t (t may stand for any period preceding or following the introduction of the reforms), e_t is the environment of the period, s_t is the set of system rules and current patterns of interaction and organization of the period, and p_{s_t} is the policy or set of policies, available under that system, which were actually put into effect during the period considered.

Let us consider these variables in detail for a change observed over two periods—before and after the reforms were introduced.

The list of relevant outcomes,[2] which depends on the preferences or interests of the person making the comparison, may include flow variables such as national income or the consumption of foodstuffs, per capita averages in these variables, or even higher moments in their distribution over the population or selected groups in the population, stock variables such as the level of inventories or the capital stock at the end of the period, ratios such as the "rate of accumulation to national income" (to the extent that it is not already accounted for in the other outcomes), irksome effects of economic behavior, such as pollution or the destruction of national scenery, or even system traits, such as "centralization" or "autonomy of enterprise managers." For some observers within the system another outcome that may matter is the position in the various hierarchies operating under the system of selected groups in the population as well as the chances of access to these positions (holding constant the incomes and other benefits already expressed in other outcomes).

Environment comprises both "initial conditions"—the levels of all stocks at the beginning of the period, including capital, population, and the technologies and other forms of knowledge held in participants' memories, libraries, and other stores of information—and the "states of nature" affecting outcomes during the period under consideration. To these states of nature belong all actions affecting outcomes that originate outside the system and are not a response to actions taken by participants within the system.

1. See T. C. Koopmans and J. M. Montias, "On the Description and Comparison of Economic Systems," in *Comparison of Economic Systems: Theoretical and Methodological Approaches*, ed. Alexander Eckstein (Berkeley: University of California Press, 1971), pp. 38–41 and 64–70.

2. For a detailed but nonexhaustive list of possibly desired or odious outcomes, see Koopmans and Montias, pp. 42–48.

The type of economic reform we shall be examining in the second part of this paper rules out any basic overhaul of the organizational structure of the system: the complete hierarchy, which embraces all participants in the system from the plant or collective farm to the Politbureau, remains in existence during the reform period, at least for certain activities, including the appointment and promotion of its own higher-tier personnel.

In the course of a reform, the "system directors"—high functionaries of the Communist party and/or the central administration—change the rules and procedures governing decisions at various tiers in the economy. These changes have the effect of reapportioning the responsibility for making certain types of decisions, generally from members placed in higher tiers to members in lower tiers. This "delegation" of responsibility to members in lower tiers may be specific and formal—as where an enterprise is allowed to undertake a type of investment that was formerly "centralized"—or merely de facto—as where a restraint is removed on the assortment of output an enterprise was formerly enjoined to produce.

Several of the activities in the following list, which may either be planned for later execution or scheduled for immediate action, are normally delegated to members in lower tiers in the course of a reform:

1. Choosing production levels for goods and services within the responsibility of a member of the hierarchy
2. Transferring a good or a batch of goods in the custody of one group of hierarchy members to the custody of another (in the same or in different tiers)
3. Making investment decisions
4. Making research and development decisions
5. Price setting
6. Determining how much labor will be employed, in what skill categories, and at what wage and salary rates
7. Apportioning the payoff of an organization within the hierarchy between emoluments to its members, additions to reserves and investment funds, and (at higher levels) taxes and other remittances to financial organs (which are also in the complete hierarchy)
8. Determining what information will be transferred from one organization in the hierarchy to another
9. Creating new or winding up old organizations

A *decentralizing measure* denotes the delegation or devolution of the responsibility for one or more of these activities from a superior (superordinate) in the complete hierarchy to a subordinate. The reverse operation —where responsibility for an activity is shifted from a lower to a higher tier in the hierarchy—is evidently a *centralizing measure*. A given measure may be decentralizing vis-à-vis one pair of tiers and centralizing vis-à-vis another pair. Take as an example the seventh, or payoff-sharing, activity.[3] Suppose that, before the reform, the third tier in the complete hierarchy—say, a *glavk* or chief administration—used to set the actual amounts enterprises had to pay into a bonus fund. After the reform, the *percentage* of profits going into this fund is fixed by the second tier (e.g. a ministry). The measure is then decentralizing with respect to tiers three and four and centralizing with respect to tiers two and three.

A *reform* may, and usually does, encompass both centralizing and decentralizing measures. When plants that were formerly organized as enterprises on *khozraschet* (cost accounting) are amalgamated with other plants to form new, consolidated enterprises, some of the responsibilities for detailed output-setting, transfer, and investment decisions may be taken away from the plant and vested in the larger enterprise, which, on the other hand, may be given wider autonomy with regard to these activities than the old enterprises enjoyed.

This ambiguity notwithstanding, I believe that it makes sense to say, as one usually does, that the system has undergone "decentralization" if decentralizing measures have been taken with respect to the "enterprise," whether or not the same production capacities are designated by this term before and after the reform. The analysis in part II will focus on the delegation of production and transfer decisions.

To control for the effect on outcomes of various policies available under the system, it would be most convenient if a single center empowered to make policy decisions could be identified for each system. Unfortunately, the fiction of a single policy maker, while it might give satisfactory analytical results for a highly centralized and well coordinated system, is unlikely to do so for one where key decisions affecting economic life are delegated to several organs that do not fully coordinate their respective policies. I have in mind, for example, the possibility that in a more or less decentralized system the investment policy of the Planning Commission might not be harmonized with the financial policy of the National Bank. In a simple comparison of pre- and post-reform outcomes for a single country, it is hardly possible, in any case, to control for the differential impact of policies. But in statistical comparisons pooling data for a number of different countries that have undergone reform—an exercise that would hold out better prospects for isolating system from environment and policy effects—it would be essential, particularly if the sample of countries were small, to state with precision the set of relevant decision makers and the domain within which each was empowered to make his decisions.

3. This example was suggested to me by Michael Keren.

How shall the vectors of outcomes for the pre- and post-reform periods be compared? Is a gain of five points in the relative income earned by the lowest decile of income recipients, together with a two-point decline in the yearly rate of growth of industrial output, a net plus or minus for the reform? This depends of course on the preferences or norms that are considered relevant to the comparison, whether those of decision makers in the system or of observer(s) evaluating the reform from outside the system. To express these potentially divergent preferences, we postulate for each observer (or "comparor" in the case of observers outside the system) a "norm function" for combining the outcomes in the two periods. Odious as such comparisons may seem to outsiders, for individuals pent up in the system, and particularly for those in a position to affect the direction and the pace of the reforms, overall comparisons are virtually unavoidable. It matters a good deal whether party leaders who value central controls for political reasons are willing to give other outcomes that are likely to be positively affected by reforms sufficient weight to offset their propensity for centralization. For, in compensation for partial loss of central controls, they may demand more improvement in efficiency and living standards than the new system is capable of delivering, at least in the short run, and, if they do not get or perceive these positive results, they will soon move to reimpose a tighter hold on their subordinates in the hierarchy.

A few qualitative observations culled from the first Czechoslovak experiment with reforms introduced in the years 1958 to 1960 may illustrate the general approach described in this section.

The available data may be grouped in three periods: 1956–57, the "pre-reform" period; 1958–60, a "transition period"; and 1961–63, the "reform" period. The quantifiable outcomes for the first two periods must have seemed quite satisfactory to Czech political leaders, who may be presumed to place a significant weight on the yearly growth of national income and industrial output and the "rate of accumulation" (averaging 6–7 percent, 10–11 percent, and 18–20 percent, respectively, according to official statistics).[4] For the third period, on the basis of the same criteria, the outcomes were mixed: good in 1961, fair-to-poor in 1962, and very poor in 1963 when national income and industrial output both declined, while the rate of accumulation fell from 21.8 percent in 1961 to 15.2 percent in 1963. Personal consumption per capita also rose much more rapidly in the first two periods

4. For observers within the system, official statistics, irrespective of their methodological shortcomings, may be quite appropriate, since these are the indicators they will be aware of and that they will use in evaluating results. The data cited are from *Statisticka Ročenka ČSSR* (Statistical Yearbook, Czechoslovak Socialist Republic), 1966, pp. 128, 194. "National Income Distributed" is measured in constant prices of 1955 until 1960 and of 1960 until 1963. The output of industry is based on "gross value" at constant prices.

than in the third, but, at least according to the official data, it did not retrogress, even in the crisis year of 1963.[5]

The environment was more favorable to the growth of industry and of national income as a whole in the first two periods than in the third: (1) climactic conditions seem to have been poorer than average in 1961–63; (2) the growth of the capital stock in industry, which was largely determined by the level and the gestation period of investments in previous years, was slower in 1961–63 than in 1956–60; (3) external conditions affecting Czechoslovakia's foreign trade deteriorated in the third period, owing in part to the collapse of exports of capital goods to Communist China (a change originating entirely outside the economic system).

The decentralizing measures introduced in the course of the reforms affected the making of production decisions, custody and transfer of producer goods, investments, and research and development. The delegation of these responsibilities was made not to the managers of enterprises existing in 1956–57 but to larger aggregates also called "national enterprises." Price-setting for both producer and consumer goods remained within the jurisdiction of central organs. The enterprise managers were given new incentives to volunteer higher levels of plan targets. Higher enterprise profits and labor-productivity increases were also given more weight in the new bonuses that management could strive for.

Investment policy in the years 1958–61 had a major impact on outcomes but one that is exceedingly difficult to separate from the influence of other factors. For one thing it appears that the decisions taken by the highest authorities, who were more or less identical in all three periods considered, were governed by preferences that did not undergo basic change in the course of the reforms. The idea that the "extensive growth" of industry propelled by vast investments and a high labor intake should give way to "intensive growth" through the renewal of machinery and equipment in existing plants and to the introduction of superior technology—an essential component of reforms throughout Eastern Europe in the mid- and late 1960s—had not yet permeated the thinking of high-level Party functionaries. Thus a high weight was still implicitly assigned to all the indicators of extensive growth such as the rate of increase of industrial gross output and the number of investment projects launched. It was assumed, as it had traditionally been in Communist ideology, that high industrial growth, accompanied by satisfactory conditions in agriculture, transportation, and trade, would guarantee rising levels of personal consumption as well as other desired outcomes.

One may legitimately ask, however, whether the ambitious yearly and long-term targets centrally imposed on enterprises in the years 1958–61 and the

5. Ibid., p. 129.

extraordinary proliferation of investments in "centralized projects"—financed from the central budget—competing for resources with the self-financed demands of enterprises for decentralized projects were the proper means to adopt even in the pursuit of extensive growth. The partially decentralized system could not withstand another turn of the pressure screw. The decline in centralized coordination, which might otherwise have been compensated by the benefits of greater managerial initiative and closer interfirm contacts, created conditions of chaos. To meet an acute balance of payments crisis, which was brought on in good part by excessive tension in the plans, the economic *apparat*, in 1962 and 1963, had to resort to hastily improvised measures, including the forced export of capital goods originally earmarked for domestic investment. The centrally issued commands through which these improvisations were carried out spelled the effective end of the reforms, which were officially abandoned a few months later.

The most influential members of the Party's Politbureau, including President Novotny, declared that the reforms were to blame for the intolerable relaxation of discipline which had left the economy in shambles. The proponents of decentralization argued that the reforms had not gone far enough and, in any event, that they had been undermined by ill-conceived central policies.

Although the actual differential effect of environment, system, and policies on the assumed outcomes probably cannot be ascertained from the study of a single system change, it should be kept in mind that important participants in the system, whose ideas helped determine whether or not the reforms were to be expanded or curtailed, thought they understood the direction and perhaps even the extent of the causal relations involved. In investigating the record of any reform in a Soviet-type economic system, it would be a mistake to dismiss these "subjective factors." The intellectual climate, the state of official ideology, as well as the writings of those who sought to revise it influenced the Communist élite to varying degrees.

One must study this background thoroughly if one wishes to understand how various groups of system participants perceive changes in the system and how they comprehend and evaluate their effects.

II. A MODEL FOR ANALYZING THE EFFECTS ON PRODUCTION ACTIVITIES OF CHANGES IN SYSTEM RULES

Our basic model is that of the operation of a centralized Soviet-type economy after the promulgation of the yearly plan. Once we have explained how this simplified system works, we shall examine the effects of delegating input and output decisions to lower-level functionaries in the complete hierarchy (see above, pp. 67–68). In part III, the model will be reduced to three tiers and a particular type of decentralizing measure will be investigated ("decentralization via aggregation"). This greater degree of specificity will allow us to draw logical inferences—on the basis of certain more or less plausible assumptions—and to support more solidly based conclusions than the broad speculations in this present section.

II.1. Description of the Centralized (Prereform) System

The analysis will be based on an economy described as follows:

1. All participants in the system engage in consumption, in production activities, or both. When they engage in a production activity—either in direct contact with means of production or acting as supervisors—they operate within the complete hierarchy defined over all production activities.[6]

2. Consumers (i.e. participants engaging in consumption activities) sell their labor to and buy goods from the complete hierarchy at prices set by officials in the hierarchy's highest tier.

3. If member a supervises member b of the complete hierarchy for activity j, a supervises b for all activities in which b is engaged. In other words, there is a single chain of supervision for the entire personnel of the complete hierarchy. In particular, a subordinate receives orders from the same supervisor for production activities, transfers of custody, and financial transactions.

4. Within each hierarchic chain descending from the head of the hierarchy (say, the politbureau) to the lowest worker, there is a node below and including which all members belong to a subordinate hierarchy called an *enterprise*. The member corresponding to this node is the enterprise manager (or its management board if leadership is "collegiate").

5. All enterprises are in the same tier, i.e., they are related to the head of the complete hierarchy by chains of supervision with the same number of nodes.

6. When a good is transferred from the custody of a member in one enterprise to a member in another, the selling enterprise's monetary assets are

---

6. As in Koopmans and Montias, pp. 68–70, a supervision relation between two members of an organization is defined with respect to a specific activity. The complete hierarchy for an activity includes all the members of the organization that are involved in the supervision relation for that activity, whether as supervisor or as supervisee. The complete hierarchy for the organization is the union of the complete hierarchies for all the individual activities in which the organization may be engaged. In most Soviet-type economies, there is a subhierarchy subordinate to the first tier and organized along regional lines, which administers "local industry." This subhierarchy may be fitted without strain in the present, very general, organizational model. However, the special problems that this would give rise to, particularly in connection with the decentralization of production decisions, will not be dealt with in this paper.

increased to the extent of the quantity sold multiplied by its transfer price.

7. Transfer prices for all goods and services are set at the highest tier. There is a unique ex-factory price for each identical good or service.[7]

8. The payoff for enterprise managers consists in some linear function of the inputs transferred from and the outputs transferred to that hierarchy valued at "incentive prices," which may be, but are not necessarily, "transfer prices."[8] (Output-bonus schemes and profit incentives are both compatible with this definition of the payoff.) All such transfers are supposed to take place within the "plan period" (see no. 11, below).

9. A transfer of custody for a good may only be decided upon by a member of the hierarchy who is superior to both the enterprise in whose custody the good is presently held and the enterprise to which it is transferred.

10. All goods transferred to producers are strictly rationed. An enterprise can only obtain an extra allotment by appealing to a superior common to it and to the enterprise(s) capable of supplying the desired product.

11. A plan—a vector of inputs and outputs for the year, corresponding to an appropriate nomenclature—is *addressed* by a superior to the head of each hierarchy (below the head of the complete hierarchy). Assumptions about these plans will be made in the course of the analysis.

12. In the prereform system, the communication of information takes place exclusively along hierarchic lines. Thus two members, neither of which is superior to the other, can only communicate with each other via a common superior.

13. Each member of the complete hierarchy makes observations upon his environment and receives information from his superiors and/or his subordinates. The information communicated to a superior by his subordinates is always at least as aggregated as that contained in their information sets.[9]

14. A significant cost is incurred each time an allocation decision by the enterprise is altered as a result of interference by a superior. This cost, which may take the form of a loss in output for given inputs or a distortion of the desired output mix, is due to the disruption of the production process in the (sub)hierarchy corresponding to a production plant.

7. This is one point where the model diverges most flagrantly from the reality of Soviet-type economies—where goods may have different "plan" and "transfer" prices. In part III of the paper, we shall introduce "aggregation prices," which may differ from transfer prices.

8. In reality, incentives may be geared to "plan" prices differing from transfer prices (e.g., in schemes rewarding managers for exceeding gross-output targets).

9. See J. Marschak, "Problems in Information Economics," in *Management Controls: New Directions in Basic Research*, ed. Charles P. Bonini et al. (New York: McGraw-Hill, 1964). See also the illuminating discussion in Roy Radner's "Competitive Equilibrium under Uncertainty," *Econometrica* 36, no. 1 (1968): 37–38.

II.2. Production Sets[10]

We plan to analyze the consistency problem in the simplest possible general-equilibrium setting. Our purpose here is twofold: (1) for our subsequent discussion of efficient allocations we need to define *attainable sets* for (sub)hierarchies or for entire tiers, and, to construct these sets, we must consider all the economy-wide constraints that codetermine them; and (2) the analysis of excess demand in consumers' and producers' markets can most conveniently be imbedded in a general-equilibrium framework. (This will not be undertaken in the present paper but is suggested as a topic for further research.)

The time dimension for all the definitions that follow is the plan year. All quantities are defined as yearly rates and the distinction between an intermediate and a capital good depends on whether or not it is to be used up by a producer during the course of the plan year. However, the environment of the system need not be assumed to remain unchanged during the year. Different "states of nature" may occur. The production sets which will presently be defined will then presumably differ for each state of nature affecting a plant's or a farm's operation. While the state that will occur at a given time is likely to be uncertain at any previous time, we may still ask how such production units would behave if such and such a state were to prevail for a long enough period of time to allow the heads of these units to adjust their production decisions to this particular environment. We do take it for granted that the environment changes slowly enough, or at least that the impact of such changes as occur is small enough, to justify this assumption.

We shall distinguish conceptually between two types of information losses as one moves from lower to higher tiers. The first is due to the coarsening of the production nomenclature. Accordingly, we postulate the existence of L^s goods and services in the nomenclature of tier s, a number no larger (normally smaller) than L^{s+1}, the nomenclature for the tier below s.[11] The second is due to the increasingly crude representation by superiors of the production possibilities of subordinate plants. The crudeness of representation is partly the result of aggregation and partly of the lack of information available to superiors or the receipt of distorted information from subordinates.

We associate with each (sub)hierarchy k in tier s a production set ^sY_k, the set of all production activities for transforming inputs into outputs "available" to k or at least to its subordinate plants. By a process being "available" at the level of the plant, I mean that its management, under typical conditions,

---

10. The reader unfamiliar with general equilibrium notation may find it useful to read this section in conjunction with the first two sections of appendix A.

11. For a more formal presentation, see p. 85.

would stand a good chance of obtaining the process outputs from the specified inputs if this process were the only one, or one of the few, that it planned to operate during the year.[12] The existence of $^s Y_k$ neither implies that all processes have been "explored"[13] by the management nor that the plant could shift from one process to the other without cost. Indeed, costs of shifting from one production plan to the other in the course of the year play at least a supporting role in our subsequent analysis. If k stands higher in the hierarchy than the head of a plant, then its production set represents the sum of the production sets of its subordinate plants[14] expressed in the coarser nomenclature (or "language") of this superior. (This aggregation process will be described in detail at a later point.) The superior has only a general idea of the production set for his hierarchy, which represents the sum of the production sets of all subordinate plants.[15]

The elements of a production vector $^s y_k$ in $^s Y_k$ are positive if they represent quantities of outputs and negative if they represent quantities of inputs. A production vector in $^s Y_k$ is said to be *feasible*.

The total production set $^s Y$ equals $\sum_{k=1}^{K_s} {}^s Y_k$, where K_s is the number of hierarchies with heads in tier s.. The positive elements in vector $^s y$ in $^s Y$ represents the *net outputs* of the complete hierarchy in the nomenclature of tier s. We also define production sets such as $^s Y^h$, obtained as the sum of the production sets of members of the (sub)hierarchy in tier s headed by supervisor h. Vectors in such sets, unlike those in $^s Y$, may include intermediate goods, destined for "productive consumption" during the plan year.

The summing of production sets is only appropriate if there are no interdependencies in the *techniques* of production between the units whose sets are summed. I assume that these interdependencies can be neglected.

We now introduce the set U, which represents the set of possible consumption vectors of the head of the complete hierarchy. The elements of a vector u in U are the amounts of final goods of the system that are not delivered to consumers (including newly produced capital goods, additions

12. By this definition, I try to meet some of the objections raised against the concept of production sets by Richard R. Nelson and S. G. Winter ("Production Theory, Learning Processes, and Dynamic Competition," unpublished paper, 1970).

13. The term is due to Janos Kornai, *Anti-equilibrium: On Economic Systems Theory and the Tasks of Research* (Amsterdam: North-Holland Publishing Co., 1971), pp. 105–06.

14. On summing production sets, see appendix A.

15. The production set for a hierarchy as defined above differs significantly from the "planners' estimate of the production set (of subordinates)" in Martin Weitzman's "Iterative Multilevel Planning with Production Targets," *Econometrica* 38, no. 1 (January 1970): 54. The definition I have adopted allows me to concentrate on the "objective" requirements for consistency at any tier of the hierarchy, which would not be possible if the higher-tier production sets were only subjective representations of the production sets at the plant level.

to inventories, goods exported, armaments, and other public goods). The vectors in U contain only nonnegative elements. Since all nonnegative u are possible, U equals the positive orthant.

The consumption set X_i consists of all consumption vectors x_i that are *possible* for consumer i, in the sense that if he were to consume the goods and services listed in x_i, he would be capable of rendering the labor services listed in this vector. Quantities of goods and services consumed in x_i are preceded by a positive sign, of services rendered by a negative sign. The total consumption set X equals $\sum_{i=1}^{m} X_i$.

Finally, we introduce the set Ω containing vectors denoted ω (one for each distinct state of nature). This set represents resources available from nature and all the stocks (inventories and capital goods) that can be run down during the course of the plan period. The fixed capital goods and equipment attached to a particular hierarchy make up a subvector of ω.[16]

Given a state of nature $\bar{\omega}^s$, an attainable allocation for tier s is a triple of vectors x^s, u^s, y^s, such that:

$$x^s + u^s - y^s \leq \bar{\omega}^s, \tag{1}$$

where x^s is in X^s, u^s is in U^s, y^s is in Y^s, $\bar{\omega}^s$ is in Ω (all these vectors having the same list of elements), and the "no-larger-than" sign implies the assumption that excess supplies of all goods are freely disposable.

The set of all attainable triples (x^s, u^s, y^s) is denoted ^sA. The attainable production set $^s\hat{Y}$ is defined as the set of all production vectors ^sy occurring in a triple $(^sx, ^su, ^sy)$ belonging to ^sA. Every production vector ^sy is the sum of K_s production vectors ^sy_k. The attainable set for a (sub)hierarchy k, denoted $^s\hat{Y}_k$, is the set of all production vectors $^s\hat{y}_k$ occurring in a K_s-tuple $(^s\hat{y}_1, \ldots, ^s\hat{y}_k, \ldots, ^s\hat{y}_{K_s})$ belonging to $^s\hat{Y}$.

The fully constrained set of (sub)hierarchy k (a subset of $^s\hat{Y}_k$) is the set of all feasible production vectors compatible with the labor, material, and capital constraints to which k is actually subject, where these constraints may be determined by capacity (e.g. fixed capital installed), allotments (in the case of materials allotted to k by superiors), or maximum quota (e.g. on hiring of labor). This set is denoted $^s\hat{\hat{Y}}_k$. (A fuller definition of these sets is given in section III.1.)

For all organizations standing higher in the complete hierarchy than the plant, attainable and fully constrained sets are defined *objectively*, in the sense that they represent the entire subset of feasible outputs subject to economy-wide or specific constraints rather than their superiors' subjective

---

16. Primary resources other than plant capacity are supplied by specialized producers, with or without the aid of inputs, within the limits set by ω.

representations of these sum-sets. The vectors in these sets, however, are expressed in the coarser nomenclature of the corresponding tier.

Each consumer decides what labor services to offer to the hierarchy on the basis of the goods allotted to him or which he can obtain from the consumers' market in quantities limited by his budget constraint. The negative elements in vector x^s, corresponding to the aggregates of these services supplied, thus depend on the positive elements in the vector that correspond to the goods offered for distribution to the consumer, as well as on the preference orderings of the individual consumer in question. In the simplified model, developed in part III, we shall assume that these freely offered services are available in fixed supplies to each (sub)hierarchy during the plan year.

II.3. Acceptable Sets

Each supervisor h in the hierarchy is said to have an *acceptable set* (A.S.)[17] representing all the possible combinations of his subordinates' production vectors that he will "accept," in the sense that he will not interfere with his supervisees' production and transfer decisions if the combined production of subordinate plants falls in that set.[18] This set is denoted G^h. In addition, h may have a separate A.S. for each supervisee k. It may not be a matter of indifference to h, for example, whether a plan for this (sub)hierarchy has been fulfilled because every supervisee hit his targets or because some supervisee overshot his target and compensated for the shortfalls of one or more of his cosupervisees. Acceptable sets imposed on individual supervisees are denoted G_k^h. Obviously, G^h need not be identical with $\sum_{k=1}^{K_h} G_k^h$. All A.S. are assumed to have the following property: If a vector $\bar{y}^h$ is acceptable to h then any other vector $\bar{\bar{y}}^h$ (different from $\bar{y}^h$) such that all its elements are at least as great as the corresponding elements of $\bar{y}^h$ will also be acceptable to h.

We have postulated that the structure of the information available to members of the complete hierarchy at any tier s was always at least as "coarse" as that available at tier $s + 1$, the tier below s (where $s = 1, \ldots, S - 1$, and S is the total number of tiers in the complete hierarchy). A convenient way of modeling this impoverishment of the information structure is

17. This concept, together with that of an "acceptable and attainable set" (defined in the next section), was developed independently by Kornai in his *Anti-equilibrium*, pp. 95–97 and 106–07.

18. Implicit in the definition of an A.S. in the text is the notion that a supervisor is indifferent between given quantities of output produced in different subordinated plants (or between given quantities of the same inputs employed in different plants). Ignoring the effects of production decisions on the individual plant's inventory levels may, however, jeopardize future production, especially if the costs of transferring inputs from one plant to the other are appreciable. A dynamic theory would have to take this point into account, possibly by including in the A.S. of each supervisor the inventory levels of supervised (sub)hierarchies.

to assume that the information obtained by the head h of a (sub)hierarchy in s on a production or consumption vector in $s + 1$ is aggregated from the elements of this vector and transformed into a vector of smaller dimension (if coarsening actually occurs). A plausible way of modeling this transformation is to assume the mapping to be linear. Thus we postulate the existence of an aggregation matrix Λ^s for each tier s (except the last), possessing a larger number of columns than rows, that will map vectors such as $^{s+1}y_k$ in $^{s+1}Y_k$ or $^{s+1}x_k$ in $^{s+1}X_k$ into smaller-dimensional vectors ^sy_k and ^sx_k.

Consider all the points in the nomenclature of tier $s + 1$ that map into the A.S. of a supervisor h in s. These points generate a *finer acceptable set* (F.S.) for the supervisees of h in tier $s + 1$. Increasingly fine sets can be defined in the same manner for each successively lower tier. The F.S. for the lowest tier S contains all the points acceptable to h in s in terms of the nomenclature of S.

The A.S. of a subordinate hierarchy k, however, cannot be translated mechanically from the acceptable sets of its superiors. What the head of k expects from his subordinates will depend in part on what he thinks his superiors expect from his (sub)hierarchy. It will depend also on the interests he may be pursuing, which may or may not be congruent with the desires of superiors. This relationship will be considered in greater detail in connection with our study of incentives.

II.4. Attainable and Acceptable Production Sets

A key role in the subsequent analysis is played by "attainable-and-acceptable production sets" (A.A.S.). The A.A.S. of (sub)hierarchy k supervised by h is the intersection of its fully constrained production set with h's A.S. for k. It is denoted E_k^h. The head's A.S. and A.A.S. are written without subscripts or superscripts. Thus:

$$E = \hat{\hat{Y}} \cap G.$$

Consider now the hierarchy in tier s headed by h in tier $s - 1$. We may write:

$$E^h = {}^s\hat{\hat{Y}}^h \cap {}^{s-1}G^h$$

where $^s\hat{\hat{Y}}^h$ is the fully constrained production set of the hierarchy supervised by h.

In diagram 3.1, the fully constrained production set of the plants supervised by h has been drawn for *given levels* of inputs supplied by other supervisors in tier $s - 1$. (We may assume, for example, that the levels of inputs supplied correspond to the planned allotments—*nariady* in Soviet practice—approved by one of h's superiors.) The area marked $^{s-1}G^h$ is the acceptable

Diagram 3.1

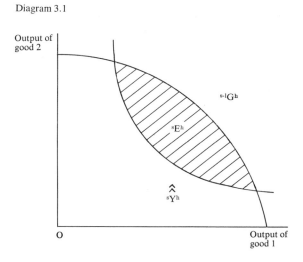

set of h. The A.A.S. of the plants subordinate to h is the intersection of these two sets, the shaded area marked $^sE^h$.

A vector in $^sE^h$ is not necessarily "attainable and acceptable" from the viewpoint of h's superiors, and in particular of the head of the complete hierarchy. If h along with l and m are supervised by r, then their combined production vector, expressed in the nomenclature of tier $s - 2$, must belong to r's A.A.S. if r is not to interfere in its subordinates' affairs. Similarly, if there are K_s (sub)hierarchies in tier s, then ^sy_k must belong to the set of K_s-tuples of vectors, each in its own attainable set, that map into a point in G, the A.S. of the head.

II.5. Plans

A plan for a (sub)hierarchy k in tier s supervised by h is a vector $^sP_k^h$ of output targets and input quotas assigned by h to that hierarchy. The plan for all hierarchies in tier s under the same supervisor h is denoted P_h^s. It is equal to $\sum_{k=1}^{K_h} {}^sP_k^h$, where K_h is the number of hierarchies supervised by h.

We shall not concern ourselves here with the techniques used by the staff organs attached to the first tier for attaining consistency between net and gross outputs or between gross outputs and production capacities as they may be estimated in the highest tier. We shall merely assume that there are *some* combinations of attainable tier 2 outputs that will be acceptable in tier 1. If the targeted outputs are attainable, they will be accepted. But if they are not, there are some other combinations that will satisfy the head without prompting him to interfere in the production and transfer decisions of subordinates.

If we now descend from the first tier, a basic question in the implementation stage of the yearly plans is whether $\sum_{k=1}^{K_h} {}^sP_k^h$ belongs to ${}^{s-1}E^h$ ($s = 1, \ldots, S$; $h = 1, \ldots, H_{S-1}$), that is whether the sum of plans assigned by any supervisor in the complete hierarchy to his supervisees belongs to his "attainable and acceptable set."

Since the production set $\hat{\hat{Y}}_h$ is constrained not only by the fixed factors assigned to the producers under h but also by the material inputs allotted to h by his supervisor in tier $s - 2$, the attainability of plans in any tier evidently hinges on the attainability of plans in higher tiers.

There are two distinct reasons why the sum of the plans of the supervisees of h may not belong to h's A.A.S., even though it may be taken for granted that this sum will be contained in his acceptable set.

1. E^h may be empty, due to the lack of realism of h's acceptable set, which may in turn be derived from unrealistic A.S. at higher levels, and/or to the failure of other hierarchies to deliver material inputs in the desired qualities and quantities.

2. The plans for $k = 1, \ldots, K_h$ may be inefficient, and a reallocation of available material inputs among them, the assignment of a different output mix to at least some of them, or a combination of both types of measures might make it possible for them collectively to attain a vector in ${}^{s-1}E^h$.

The equilibrium problem in central planning may be posed as follows. Is there a set of plans, one for each supervisee of h (where h may be any hierarchy included in the complete hierarchy), such that the production vectors selected by these supervisees, in response to these plans and/or in the pursuit of their own objectives, will sum up to a total production vector in the acceptable set of h?

Our study of this adjustment process, in section II.6, will only enable us to affirm the existence of equilibrium so defined in a special case.[19]

Another important problem consists in finding such an equilibrium if it exists. What information must be collected by superiors to set equilibrium plans? How can incentives to subordinates be shaped or reshaped to help

---

19. The requirement that the total production vector be in the A.S. of h is quite stringent and rules out the mechanical use of fixed-point theorems to demonstrate the existence of a plan that can be exactly fulfilled. Edward Ames in his interesting and imaginative paper on general equilibrium in a centrally planned economy imposes no such conditions on the nature of the equilibrium solution and is therefore able to state that there must exist a plan that will be exactly fulfilled; see "The Structure of General Equilibrium in a Planned Economy in *Jahrbuch der Wirtschaft Osteuropas*, ed. H. W. Gottinger, vol 1 (Munich: Günter Olzog Verlag, 1970), p. 26.

solve the problem? These questions, to which I have no ready answers, lie, for the most part, outside the purview of this paper.

When plans are *taut*, we mean that they can be fulfilled only under better-than-average circumstances, that is, under favorable "states of nature."[20] The idea behind taut plans is that subordinates will respond to the challenge by exerting special efforts toward their fulfillment. "Pressure" on the other hand may be taken to refer to the frequency and importance of changes in production orders decreed by supervisors in response to the unsatisfactory performance of their subordinate plants.

Tautness and pressure usually go together, but this need not be the case. In a low-pressure system, supervisors may accept output combinations falling significantly short of the targets set for their hierarchy, especially if these targets were unrealistic to begin with, as long as they anticipate that their superiors will also tolerate the shortfall.

The decision on the part of a supervisor to apply pressure on subordinates will depend in part on the losses, measured in output forgone or additional inputs required, that will have to be sustained each time a production schedule is altered (either because a change in the output-mix has been ordered or because a reallocation of available inputs has made it necessary). The cost of disturbing the "tranquility" of plants is presumably an increasing function of the complexity of production processes, which in turn is associated positively with the economy's level of development.

II.6. Incentives

The manager of an enterprise or a plant rewarded according to an incentive scheme that is not very strongly tied to plan fulfillment is likely to make production decisions at variance with these plans. According to a plausible model of managerial behavior, the decision whether or not to violate a plan that could be fulfilled will depend on the net gain a manager expects to derive from this violation (compared to a compliance policy), on the chances of retaliation by his supervisor (who might cut his bonuses if his actions jeopardize the activity of the entire hierarchy subordinate to him), and on his aversion to any such retaliatory moves. Whatever the model employed, it is reasonable to postulate the existence of a certain zone within which a manager would choose to conform to plan, or at least produce within the set that he believes would be acceptable to his superiors, even in the face of a larger putative gain elsewhere. This compliance zone would presumably be larger, the greater the loss due to the disruption of production scheduling when interference from above did occur.

20. For models of the tautness phenomenon, see Holland Hunter, "Optimum Tautness in Developmental Planning," *Economic Development and Cultural Change* 9 (July 1961): 561–73; and Michael Keren, "Central Allocation of Resources under Uncertainty" (Ph.D. diss., Yale University, 1968), appendix B.

Diagram 3.2 illustrates the effect of incentives on consistency, where the fully constrained set of a (sub)hierarchy is defined on the assumption that it will actually receive its planned quotas of materials. It represents a particular set of attainable outputs of goods 1 and 2 for (sub)hierarchy k in tier s constrained by the labor services, fixed capacities, and planned allotments of

Diagram 3.2

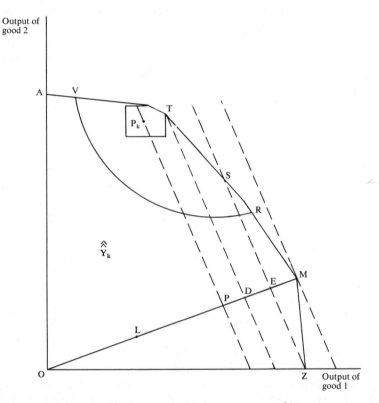

materials assigned to it by its supervisor in tier $s - 1$.[21] It is assumed, to simplify the exposition, that the head of k has full and accurate information on k's production set.

Two sets of mutually compatible outputs will be represented, based on alternative definitions of consistency, which hinge on the range of choice

21. There will clearly be a different projection of $\hat{\hat{Y}}_k$ on the first quadrant for each level of input of labor and primary sources available from nature. It is assumed here that these inputs are fixed according to some attainable allocation, and that neither the total supplies of labor resources nor their distribution among producers will be affected by the decisions considered in this analysis.

postulated for all other heads of (sub)hierarchies with whom k interacts. We will assume here that supervisor h is willing to accept any production program in k's set as long as the sum of the programs submitted by k and the other K_{h-1} supervisees falls into his A.S.

In diagram 3.2, the boundary of k's strictly constrained production set is the line going through A, T, M, and Z. The broken straight line through M is the highest attainable representative of a family of parallel payoff lines with slope corresponding to the price weights in k's payoff function. Distances marked out on the line OM are meant to represent the various possible values attained by k's payoff function. OL, for instance, is the reduced payoff that would result from interference by one of k's superiors.[22]

The area in k's fully constrained set with lower bound VR represents (E_k^h), the projection on k's space of the A.A.S. for the supervisees of h, where every vector in this A.A.S. is of dimension $K_h \times n_s$ (K_h being the number of supervisees of h and n_s being the number of goods in the nomenclature of the enterprise tier). Production in this set by all hierarchies in tier s is a *necessary* condition for the aggregate net outputs of all goods to be satisfactory from the viewpoint of the head of the complete hierarchy.

The square around the plan P_k assigned by h to k is a zone of safety where no interference is guaranteed as long as all the (sub)hierarchies supervised by h manage to produce in this zone.[23]

It is evident that point M is *not* optimal for k. Because it is outside (E_k^h), production at this point makes it impossible for the enterprises or plants supervised by h to produce an acceptable combination of output vectors. Interference by h leads to a reduced payoff of OL, smaller than OP, the payoff that would result from exact plan fulfillment.

If the management of h tried to produce at T and succeeded, it would earn a payoff OD with virtually no risk of interference. An interesting question is whether it would pay to try for point S with payoff OE with *some* risk of ending up at OL in case the production vector corresponding to point OE, when combined with the $(K_h - 1)$ production vectors selected by fellow-supervisees, did *not* fall into h's A.S.[24] Whether k would wish to incur this risk would in part depend on how well k had estimated the extent of plan fulfillment in the rest of the "sector" supervised by h.

22. The strong assumption underlying this representation is that the loss due to interference does not depend on the particular transgression observed by a superior. This loss is assumed to be the same whether enterprise k must rework its entire production schedule or make a slight alteration in its output mix.

23. To rule out the possibility of interference by h's superiors, we may assume that if all the producers in tier s produce within their corresponding square, there will be no interference by any superior in the hierarchy.

24. Point S, for example, might not be in the set $\hat{E}_h^D$ defined in section III.4.

84   JOHN MICHAEL MONTIAS

Given the (subjective) probability P_r of interference if k were to produce at S, this production vector would only be selected if:

$$P_r(OL) + (1 - P_r)(OE) \leq OD$$

where OD corresponds to the virtually certain payoff of producing at T, OL is the reduced payoff resulting from interference, and OE is the payoff that would be obtained from producing at S in the absence of interference.[25]

III. A THREE-TIER MODEL

III.1. Introduction

In part III the framework of part II, above, is simplified in a number of ways. In particular, it is assumed that each enterprise k *must* produce in the acceptable set of its supervisor (a "ministry"). A model is constructed which attempts to reason out the production decisions of payoff-maximizing enterprises before and after the reform and to determine under what conditions the production bundles jointly produced by all enterprises in the complete hierarchy will be acceptable to its head.

Section III.2 describes the allocation process and shows, with greater precision than in part II, how the fully constrained production sets of enterprises are generated.

In section III.3 the postreform acceptable set of a ministry for each of its enterprises is derived from the prereform A.S. by aggregation. It is assumed that, after the reform, a ministry will accept any production program worth at least as much at aggregation prices as *some* program that happened to be acceptable before the reform. A theorem is then stated and proved which specifies under what conditions an enterprise maximizing its payoff, subject to the requirement that it produce in its ministry's acceptable set (before and after the reform), will increase its payoff as a result of the reform (in the absence of any change in allotments of centrally rationed materials, in prices, or in incentive schemes, consequent upon the reform).

Section III.4 analyzes the relation between the bonus-maximizing programs of individual enterprises and the head's acceptable set. It is shown that if the sum of the enterprise payoffs exceeds the sum of the maximum possible payoffs that each enterprise could obtain, subject to the constraint of having to produce within a set derived by decomposition from the head's A.S., the resulting joint program will be unacceptable to the head.

Section III.5 takes as its starting point a situation where the postreform program produced by all enterprises simultaneously was unacceptable to the head and traces the possible effects on the enterprises' production

25. It is assumed, of course, that the head of k is either indifferent or averse to risk. A risk-prone head might select point S even if its expected payoff were lower than OD.

decisions and on the joint program of all enterprises of an expansion in the fully constrained production sets of enterprises due to an improvement in the allocation process. The conclusion reached is that if enterprises are allowed to exert influence over the materials-allocation process to obtain relatively larger allotments of the materials that would make the greatest contribution to increasing the value of their payoff, the expansion of the enterprises' production frontiers will not help the system to generate a joint program acceptable to the head.

III.2. The Distribution System

To simplify the exposition and to attain more readily intelligible results, we now reduce our complete hierarchy to three tiers, described with the aid of the following notation. There are K enterprises headed by managers in the third tier, H ministries headed by ministers in the second, and a single head for the complete hierarchy in the first. The minister heading ministry h supervises K_h enterprises.

As a further simplification of the framework of part II, we posit that the prereform nomenclature of the top tiers is the same as that of the second tier. There are n_3 commodities in the nomenclature of tier 3 and n_2 in tiers 1 and 2, where $n_2 < n_3$.

Let λ stand for a vector of price-weights, one for each of the n_3 commodities in the nomenclature of tier 3. The elements of λ may be ordinary prices or "quasi prices" used to aggregate commodities by tonnage or by some proxy for value (e.g. yarn count, calorific content, etc.). The vector λ is partitioned into n_2 subvectors $\lambda_1, \ldots, \lambda_i, \ldots, \lambda_{n_2}$. Call Λ the bloc-diagonal matrix of n_2 rows, with the subvectors λ_1 to λ_{n_2} appearing in the diagonal and zero's elsewhere.

For any vector of resource endowments $^3\omega_k$ or of production ^3y_k, we may write:

$$^2y_k = \Lambda\,^3y_k; \qquad ^2\omega_k = \Lambda\,^3\omega_k$$

where the superscript on the left-hand side of the vector, here as in all other instances, denotes the nomenclature of the vector, or set of vectors, to which the superscript is attached.

We denote by $^3v_k^h$ a vector of allotments of centrally rationed materials by ministry h to enterprise k in the nomenclature of the latter.

The attainable set for the economy, denoted $\hat{Y}$ in the nomenclature of tier 1, is defined in precisely the same way as in our more general model.

For the sake of simplification, I shall assume that labor can be treated as a fixed exogenous factor for each enterprise. This implies that the supply of labor is not responsive to changes in the availability of consumer goods. If we posit that all exogenous factors are in the custody of individual enterprises, then, as a result of this simplification, we may assert that any net-output vector for the complete hierarchy satisfying all the exogenous-factor and technological constraints to which enterprises are subject is attainable.

We now proceed to construct the fully constrained sets ${}^3\hat{\hat{Y}}_k$ and ${}^3\hat{\hat{Y}}^h$ in the nomenclature of tier 3.

The head of the complete hierarchy, with the aid of material balances, input-output tables, or any other computational aids at its disposal, sets allotments of all allocable materials for its H ministries which it considers sufficient to support an acceptable bill of final demand. An allocation to ministry h is a vector ${}^1v_h$, made up of n_1 goods, corresponding to the nomenclature of the head. (If a material is not allotted to the ministry in question, then a zero appears for that element in ${}^1v_h$ in the nomenclature of the head.) Each ministry subdivides its allotments among the enterprises it supervises according to this same nomenclature. Enterprise k under h is scheduled to receive a bill of allotments denoted ${}^2v_k^h$, a vector of n_2 $(=n_1)$ dimensions corresponding to the nomenclature of tiers 1 and 2. Allotment vectors are made up of nonpositive elements in accord with our sign convention for inputs. Therefore, this suballocation satisfies the relation:

$$\sum_{k=1}^{K_h} {}^2v_k^h = {}^2v_h^1 \quad (h = 1, \ldots, H).$$

We postulate the existence of a "marketing organization" in each ministry with exclusive responsibility ("gestion") for "balancing" and allocating goods predominantly produced by enterprises subordinate to its ministry within the aggregated quotas set by the head. In particular, the marketing organization is charged with the disaggregation of allotments of the commodities for which it has exclusive responsibility. If an allotment of commodity i in the list of n_2 commodities in tier 2 is allotted to enterprise k, then the marketing organization of the ministry responsible for the production of that commodity disaggregates this allotment in such a way that:

$$\sum_{j=1}^{n_2^i} \lambda_{ij} \, {}^3v_{kj}^h = {}^2v_{ki}^h \quad (i = 1, \ldots, n_2)$$

where λ_{ij} is the price weight of the jth commodity in row i of matrix Λ, ${}^3v_{kj}^h$ is the allotment of the jth commodity in the vector of allotments by h to k expressed in the nomenclature of tier 3 and ${}^2v_{ki}^h$ is the allotment of the ith commodity in the vector of allotments expressed in the nomenclature of tier 2, and n_2^i is the number of elements in the ith subvector of λ. In matrix form the above relation may be written:

$$\Lambda \, {}^3v_k^h = {}^2v_k^h$$

There will generally be more than one vector of allotments $^3v_k^h$ that will satisfy the above relation. It is understood that the marketing organization will try to match the total allotments of any disaggregated commodity j against the total expected supply of j that will be produced by enterprises of the ministry in the plan period, but we will not specify any process of interaction between the enterprises in the ministry and its marketing organization for achieving this consistency.

To complete the description of the information network of the complete hierarchy, however, we stipulate that the marketing organization collects data on the inventories of all disaggregated commodities in its charge and, if there is a discrepancy between the rate of production of any commodity j and its rate of consumption on the basis of the allotments that have been distributed to the enterprises consuming j, it notifies the head that the current joint production program cannot be sustained. At this point, the process breaks down, just as if the joint outputs themselves had been unacceptable to the head.

When we shall write that a production program is acceptable to the head, we shall always imply that the allotments of materials expressed in the nomenclature of tier 3 can be sustained from current production without any undesirable decline in inventories. In other words, when the necessary condition for acceptability to the head has been satisfied (that a joint program fit into its acceptable set), it will be taken that the other condition for sufficiency—satisfactory levels of inventories for all goods in the detailed nomenclature of the lowest tier—is also satisfied (although we will not examine the precise process whereby this second condition gets to be fulfilled).

The description of the allocation-disaggregation process above is adequate for the purpose of this model, which essentially takes the vectors of allotments $^3v_k^h$ as given. If these vectors have not been set properly, then the chances that enterprises will produce acceptable output programs will be reduced. All that is required is that the first two tiers set allotments to enterprises "as best they can" so that at least one production vector $^2\hat{\hat{y}}_k$ will be acceptable to its ministry and at least one production vector $^1\hat{\hat{y}}^h$ will be acceptable to the head (for all k and all h).

We now denote by $^3\omega_k$ the (nonpositive) vector of exogenous factors, including labor, available to enterprise k; by $^3y_k^-$, the vector of centrally allocated material inputs consumed by k; and by $^3y_k^+$ the vector of outputs produced by k. To be precise, $^3y_k^- \equiv \min(^3y_k, 0)$ and $^3y_k^+ \equiv \max(^3y_k, 0)$, where min and max are taken one component at a time.

The fully constrained set $^3\hat{Y}_k$ is the set of vectors ^3y_k in $^3\hat{Y}_k$ such that:

$$^3y_k^- \geq {}^3v_k^h + {}^3\omega_k.$$

The net outputs $^3\hat{\hat{y}}_h$ produceable by ministry h are equal to:

$$\sum_{k=1}^{K_h} (^3\hat{\hat{y}}_k^+ + {}^3v_k^h) \quad (h = 1, \ldots, H)$$

where $^3\hat{\hat{y}}_k^+$ is a vector of positive elements in a vector $^3\hat{\hat{y}}_k$ in $^3\hat{\hat{Y}}_k$. By summing the net outputs $^3\hat{\hat{y}}_h$ over all H ministries, we obtain a vector of net outputs $^3\hat{\hat{y}}$ for the complete hierarchy.

We assume that goods available as positive net outputs may be traded abroad for imports.

If the allotments $^3v_k^h$ are not fully consumed by enterprise k, materials left over are added to inventory for use in subsequent periods.

Suppose that $^3\hat{\hat{y}}$ contained negative elements corresponding to currently allocated materials. In case inventories of the goods produced in negative quantities are available, these may be scaled down or imports of these goods may be stepped up; but, if such solutions are unfeasible or unacceptable to the head, the latter may either interfere in subordinates' production decisions to cause them to improve their output-mix or he may order allotments to be shifted among ministries (or directly among enterprises) so as to induce them to produce an acceptable mix. Changes in prices or in incentives that might be introduced to bring about such an improvement will not be considered in this paper, which is limited to decentralizing measures concerning output and allocation decisions.

Given the exogenous constraints limiting the output of every enterprise, it is evident that $^3\hat{\hat{Y}}_k$, $^3\hat{\hat{Y}}^h$ and $^3\hat{\hat{Y}}$ are all bounded from above. We shall also assume that every $^3\hat{\hat{Y}}_k$ is closed. $^3\hat{\hat{Y}}^h$ and $^3\hat{\hat{Y}}$ are then compact (closed and bounded) as the sum of a finite number of compact sets. If the production sets ^3Y_k are assumed to be convex, subsets of ^3Y_k satisfying the constraints $^3v_k^h$ as well as the exogenous constraints on k must also be convex (as the intersection of convex sets). Thus every set $^3\hat{Y}_k$ is convex. Furthermore, $^3\hat{\hat{Y}}^h$ and $^3\hat{\hat{Y}}$ are convex as the sums of convex sets.

We recall that the matrix Λ maps vectors ^3y_k in the sets $^3\hat{\hat{Y}}_k$ from n_3-dimensional to n_2-dimensional space. Since this mapping is single valued, the image $^2\hat{\hat{Y}}_k$ of any compact set $^3\hat{\hat{Y}}_k$ is also compact. Since the mapping is linear, the image $^2\hat{\hat{Y}}_k$ of any convex set $^3\hat{\hat{Y}}_k$ is also convex.[26] It is therefore evident that the sets $^2\hat{\hat{Y}}_k$, $^2\hat{\hat{Y}}^h$ and $^2\hat{\hat{Y}}$ will all be convex and compact as long as $^3\hat{\hat{Y}}_k$, $^3\hat{\hat{Y}}^h$, and $^3\hat{\hat{Y}}$ have these properties.

From now on, whenever we refer to a vector or to a set of vectors, we shall have in mind vectors expressed in the nomenclature of the second tier (i.e. after aggregation by the matrix Λ), and all superscripts denoting tiers will be omitted.

26. Claude Berge, *Topological Spaces* (New York: Macmillan, 1963), pp. 69 and 143.

"Incentive prices," set by the head, are the prices that are relevant to the enterprise's payoff (e.g. the output bonuses or profit shares accruing to its managers). Every enterprise k is supposed to maximize the same payoff, a linear function of $\hat{\hat{y}}_k$ ($k = 1, \ldots, K$).

A vector π of incentive prices, for example, will consist of current transfer prices for all inputs and outputs in the enterprise's nomenclature, in case the enterprise is acting as a profit-maximizer; it will consist of "plan prices" for outputs and zeros for inputs, in case the enterprise is maximizing the value of its output at plan prices; or it will consist of current prices for outputs and for material inputs, in case the enterprise is maximizing "value added." By assuming a linear payoff function we rule out incentive systems that reward the enterprise at a higher rate for just fulfilling the plan than for overshooting its targets.

Since every set $\hat{\hat{Y}}_k$ is bounded from above and closed, the payoff function $\pi \hat{\hat{y}}_k$ on $\hat{\hat{Y}}_k$ has a maximum, denoted πy_k^*, where y_k^* is said to be a "maximizer on $\hat{\hat{Y}}_k$ for π." As there may be several such maximizers, we may refer to $y_k^*(\pi)$ as a (supply) correspondence from $\hat{\hat{Y}}_k$ to the set of production vectors y_k^*.

We recall that E_k, equal to $G_k \cap \hat{\hat{Y}}_k$, is the set of production vectors $\hat{\hat{y}}_k$ acceptable to h. The plan assigned to k, a vector denoted P_k, is contained in E_k.

We now introduce another supply correspondence $y_k^{\bar{a}}(\pi)$ for each enterprise k. This correspondence generates the set of points $y_k^{\bar{a}}$ such that:

$$\pi y_k^{\bar{a}} = \max \pi \hat{\hat{y}}_k, \quad \text{where } \hat{\hat{y}}_k \text{ is in } E_k.$$

A vector $y_k^{\bar{a}}$, in other words, is an attainable-and-acceptable program yielding the highest value of k's payoff at incentive prices π.

Our concern here will be with situations where $y_k^* \neq y_k^{\bar{a}}$. Since E_k is contained in $\hat{\hat{Y}}_k$, we must have: $\pi y_k^* > \pi y_k^{\bar{a}}$. The efficient boundaries of $\hat{\hat{Y}}_k$, $\hat{\hat{Y}}^h$, and $\hat{\hat{Y}}$ are denoted $\widehat{Y}_k$, $\widehat{Y}^h$, and $\widehat{Y}$ respectively. The efficient boundary of $\hat{\hat{Y}}$, by definition, excludes any vector $\hat{\hat{y}}$ if there exists another vector $\hat{\hat{y}}'$ in the set at least one of whose elements is larger than the corresponding element of $\hat{\hat{y}}$ and none smaller. The boundaries of $\hat{\hat{Y}}^h$ and $\hat{\hat{Y}}_k$ are similarly defined.

III.3. Aggregation and Decentralization

We shall consider the effect on the production decisions of enterprises and on the aggregate production vectors of enterprises under a ministry of the following (alternative) decentralizing measures, which may be interpreted as special cases of the delegation of production decisions.

1. Ministry h, after the reform, is willing to accept every vector $\hat{\hat{y}}_k$ belonging to a new acceptable set E_k^R containing all vectors $\hat{\hat{y}}_k$ worth at least as much at nonnegative aggregation prices (defined below) as any vector in the

prereform acceptable set E_k. (Since any vector in E_k satisfies this condition, E_k is included in E_k^R.)

2. Ministry h abolishes the plan P_k for the individual enterprise k and no longer demands that k produce in an acceptable set G_k. However, because h must still satisfy the head of the complete hierarchy, he still has an A.S. for the aggregate production vectors of the enterprises he supervises, and he will interfere in their decisions if they do not collectively produce in this set G^h.

Most of our theoretical speculations will concern the first alternative.

The basic assumption of this model is that ministry h will accept any aggregated vector, whether or not it is aggregated from a vector in G_k, provided it has the same value at aggregation prices as, and therefore cannot be distinguished by h from, some vector in G_k. If we now reintroduce our nonsatiety assumption on acceptable sets (i.e., if y' is in G_k, so is any arbitrary vector y with the property $y \geq y'$), we may infer that h will accept any aggregated vector having *at least* the same value at aggregation prices as some vector in G_k.

Consider first the most extreme aggregation that maps points of G_k from n_2-dimensional space into scalars. Given a vector of positive aggregation prices π^o, of the same dimension as the vectors in $\hat{\hat{Y}}_k$ and G_k, we first pick out a vector y_k^m minimizing $\pi^o\hat{\hat{y}}_k$ over the set of all vectors $\hat{\hat{y}}_k$ in E_k. By assumption any other vector in $\hat{\hat{Y}}_k$ (but not necessarily in E_k) *yielding at least the value* $\pi^o y_k^m$ will be acceptable after the reform (since y_k^m is in E_k). Call the set of all the vectors satisfying this condition E_k^m. Now if we were to choose any point y_k^e in E_k other than y_k^m and defined the set E_k^e of all vectors in $\hat{\hat{Y}}_k$ yielding at least the value $\pi^o y_k^e$, it is evident that every point in this set would have to be contained in E_k^m (since $\pi^o y_k^e \geq \pi^o y_k^m$). Thus E_k^m is identical with E_k^R, the union of all the sets generated by arbitrary points of E_k (as E_k^m both contains E_k^R and is contained in it). From now on, therefore, the postreform attainable-and-acceptable set E_k^R will be defined as the set of vectors $\hat{\hat{y}}_k$ satisfying the relation $\pi^o\hat{\hat{y}}_k \geq \pi^o y_k^m$, where y_k^m is any minimizer for π^o on E_k.

We next define the correspondence $y_k^o(\pi)$ generating the set of points y_k^o maximizing $\pi\hat{\hat{y}}_k$ for all y_k in E_k^R. (If y_k^o were a single point, $y_k^o(\pi)$ would be a function maximizing $\pi\hat{\hat{y}}_k$ on E_k^R.)

The following theorem, proved in appendix B, requires, among the assumptions already made, that $\hat{\hat{Y}}_k$ be convex, an assumption which, as we have already seen, will be satisfied as long as the original production set Y_k is convex.

THEOREM 1. *Provided that $\pi^o y_k^m \neq \pi^o y_k^{\bar{a}}$, and $\pi y_k^{\bar{a}} < \pi y_k^*$, there must exist a vector y_k^o such that $\pi y_k^o > \pi y_k^{\bar{a}}$.*

The outline of the proof is as follows. Since $\pi^o y_k^{\bar{a}} \neq \pi^o y_k^m$, the point $y_k^{\bar{a}}$ must be in the interior of the set E_k^R. Now any convex combination $y(\alpha)$ of $y_k^{\bar{a}}$ and

y_k^* with a weight α larger than zero attached to y_k^* must be worth more at prices π than $y_k^{\bar{a}}$, since, by assumption, $\pi y_k^* > \pi y_k^{\bar{a}}$. If we choose α small enough, $y(\alpha)$ must be in a neighborhood of $y_k^{\bar{a}}$ and hence must be contained in E_k^R (since $y_k^{\bar{a}}$ is an interior point of this set). Thus we have found at least one point in E_k^R worth more at prices π than $y_k^{\bar{a}}$. Any maximizer y_k^o on this set (for prices π) will be worth at least as much at these prices as $y(\alpha)$. Hence $\pi y_k^o > \pi y_k^{\bar{a}}$.

The interpretation of the theorem is straightforward. Provided that $y_k^{\bar{a}}$ (the most advantageous point for k formerly acceptable to h) is worth more at aggregation prices than the minimum value attained at these prices by any vector in E_k, the old A.S., there must exist a production vector y_k^o in the new A.S. that is worth more at incentive prices than $y_k^{\bar{a}}$.

That there may be no program y_k^o such that $\pi y_k^o > \pi y_k^{\bar{a}}$ when the assumption $\pi^o y_k^m \neq \pi^o y_k^{\bar{a}}$ is not satisfied will be shown in diagram 3.5 below. The interpretation of the assumption is that, to ensure the existence of a program worth more at incentive prices than $y_k^{\bar{a}}$ after the reform, there must have existed *before the reform* a program in E_k acceptable to h *worth less at aggregation prices* than $y_k^{\bar{a}}$. It may be conjectured that, for a given $\hat{\hat{Y}}_k$, the larger the difference between $\pi^o y_k^m$ and $\pi^o y_k^{\bar{a}}$, the greater will be the improvement in k's payoff resulting from the reform.

Theorem 1 is illustrated in diagram 3.3. In this diagram, as well as in all the ones that follow, the degree of aggregation represented is that corresponding to the nomenclature of ministry h *before the reform*. By means of this representational device we can trace the effect on the production decisions of enterprises of aggregation in the course of the reform.

It is evident from the diagram that there exist many points in E_k^R, such as y_k^o, that are worth more at prices π than $y_k^{\bar{a}}$.

Diagram 3.3

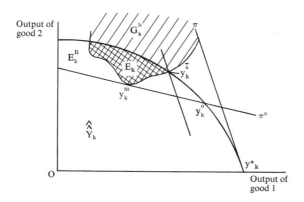

In diagram 3.4, the assertion of the theorem fails to hold because $\hat{\hat{Y}}_k$ is not convex. The convex combinations of $y_k^{\bar{a}}$ and y_k^* all lie outside $\hat{\hat{Y}}_k$. Clearly, there is no point in E_k^R (the set of points in $\hat{\hat{Y}}_k$ above the line $\pi^o y$ through y_k^m) worth more at prices π than $y_k^{\bar{a}}$.

Diagram 3.4

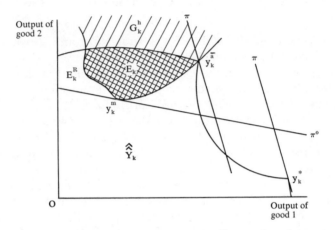

Finally, in diagram 3.5, we show a situation where, even though $\hat{\hat{Y}}_k$ is convex, the theorem fails because $\pi^o y_k^m = \pi^o y_k^{\bar{a}}$.

In this case y_k^m and $y_k^{\bar{a}}$ are identical, and there is clearly no point in E_k^R that would have a higher value at prices π than $y_k^{\bar{a}}$.

Theorem 1 may be used to analyze the effects on enterprises' production decisions of abolishing the assortment plan to which they were subject prior to the reform.

Diagram 3.5

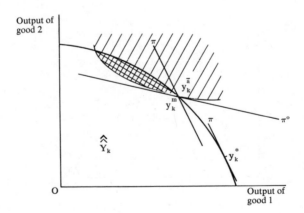

Suppose that G_k, the prereform acceptable set of h for k, consisted of all programs y_k such that $y_k \geq \alpha_k$, where α_k was a positive vector of minimum acceptable outputs (and/or maximum acceptable inputs). Let α_k be an interior point of $\hat{\hat{Y}}_k$ and $y_k^{\bar{a}}$, the maximizer for π on E_k, be such that $\pi y_k^{\bar{a}} < \pi y_k^*$. It is immediately clear that y_k^m is unique (since all elements of π^o are positive) and must be worth less at prices π^o than $y_k^{\bar{a}}$. Hence, by theorem 1, there exists a program y_k^o such that $\pi y_k^o > \pi y_k^{\bar{a}}$. This proposition is illustrated in diagram 3.6.

Diagram 3.6

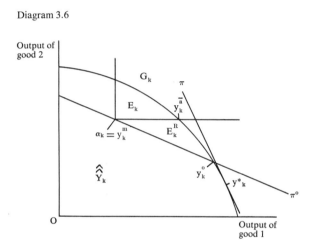

From the two-good case illustrated in diagram 3.6, it appears that, in order for $\pi^o y_k^{\bar{a}}$ to equal $\pi^o \alpha_k$, which is clearly a minimizer on E_k for π^o, the first element of π^o would have to be zero. Hence $\pi^o y_k^{\bar{a}} \neq \pi^o y_k^m$, and the theorem applies. Note also that if α_k were not an interior point and were located on the boundary of $\hat{\hat{Y}}_k$, α_k would be identical with $y_k^{\bar{a}}$ and the statement of the theorem would fail. As we shall have occasion to point out again in greater detail, the fact that $\pi^o y_k^{\bar{a}} = \pi^o y_k^m$ will necessarily cause the statement of the theorem to fail only in the case of aggregation from two goods to one. If we have three goods, the plane $\pi^o y$ through $y_k^{\bar{a}}$ (and y_k^m) will intersect with other boundary points of $\hat{\hat{Y}}_k$, which *may* be worth more at prices π than $y_k^{\bar{a}}$.

We recall the useful, harmless (and plausible) assumption that if $\hat{y}_k'$ is in E_k, then any other vector $\hat{y}_k \geq \hat{y}_k'$ will also be in E_k (the sign $\geq$ is taken to mean that the vector on the right contains no element greater than the corresponding element of the vector on the left). Its crucial implication is that every maximizer $y_k^{\bar{a}}$, $y_h^{\bar{a}}$, and $y^{\bar{a}}$ for an arbitrary positive price vector π on E_k, E^h, and E, respectively, must be on the efficiency frontier of $\hat{\hat{Y}}_k$, $\hat{Y}^h$, and $\hat{\hat{Y}}$, respectively (if this were not the case, there would clearly exist some other vector in the intersection of the A.A.S. with the corresponding efficiency frontier that would be worth more at these prices than this "maximizer").[27]

We also note that if y_k^* is a maximizer for π on E_k^R and if $\pi y_k^* > \pi y_k^o$, then y_k^o must be on the hyperplane $\pi^o y_k$ through y_k^m, so that $\pi^o y_k^o = \pi^o y_k^m$ (for a proof see appendix B).

Wherever π and π^o are such that $\pi^o y_k^m = \pi^o y_k^{\bar{a}}$, these two price systems will be said to be *counterposed*.

It is easy to show that if $\pi = \pi^o$ and $\pi y_k^* > \pi y_k^{\bar{a}}$, where $y_k^{\bar{a}}$ is again a maximizer for π on E_k, then y_k^* must be in E_k^R. This is so because $\pi^o y_k^* > \pi^o y_k^{\bar{a}} \geq \pi^o y_k^m$ and y_k^* must therefore satisfy the definition of programs $\hat{\hat{y}}_k$ in E_k^R (all programs $\hat{\hat{y}}_k$ such that $\pi^o \hat{\hat{y}}_k \geq \pi^o y_k^m$).

We now extend theorem 1 to cases where acceptable programs in a pre-reform A.S. are aggregated with the aid of an aggregation matrix. We partition the vector of aggregation prices π^o into subvectors $\pi^{1o}, \ldots, \pi^{io}, \ldots, \pi^{qo}$ and construct the following (bloc-diagonal) aggregation matrix from these subvectors:

$$
\Pi^o = \begin{bmatrix}
\pi^{1o} & & & & & & \\
& \cdot & & & & 0 & \\
& & \cdot & \cdot & & & \\
& & & \pi^{io} & & & \\
& 0 & & & \cdot & & \\
& & & & & \cdot & \\
& & & & & & \pi^{qo}
\end{bmatrix}
$$

The non-zero elements of any row of Π^o may all be equal to unity if there is aggregation by weight or by number (depending on the units of measurement of goods corresponding to these elements in $\hat{\hat{y}}_k$).

A subvector y_k^i of $\hat{\hat{y}}_k$ is the projection of $\hat{\hat{y}}_k$ to the coordinates for which π^{io} is defined.

E_k^R, the acceptable set of ministry h for k after a partial-aggregation reform, is the set of all vectors $\hat{\hat{y}}_k$ in $\hat{\hat{Y}}_k$ such that:

$$\Pi^o \hat{\hat{y}}_k \geq \Pi^o y_k^e \quad \text{for all } y_k^e \text{ in } E_k.$$

An arbitrary vector y_k^e belonging to E_k will be said to "seed" all the sets subscripted (e). (Up to the statement of the corollary below, the kth enterprise subscript will be omitted in the notation for both vectors and sets.) Thus $E_{(\bar{a})}^R$ refers to the postreform acceptable set seeded by $y^{\bar{a}}$, a given maximizer for π on E_k.

27. See remark 2 of appendix B.

We let $y^{(\bar{o})}$ stand for the program in E that seeded $E^R_{(\bar{o})}$, a postreform acceptable set containing y^o, a maximizer for π on E^R_k.

We now consider a class of vectors that are identical with each other except in the ith subspace. The *sub*script i refers to the ith subvector in an n_2-dimensional vector. As a *super*script it denotes the ith subvector by itself.

$y^{\bar{a}}_i$ is a vector, all of whose subvectors are equal to the corresponding subvectors of $y^{\bar{a}}$, except for the ith, the elements of which can assume any values compatible with $y^{\bar{a}}_i$ being in $\hat{\hat{Y}}$. The set $\hat{\hat{Y}}^{\bar{a}}_i$ contains all the vectors $y^{\bar{a}}_i$. The set $E^{\bar{a}}_i$ contains all the vectors $y^{\bar{a}}_i$ that belong to E. The sets $\hat{\hat{Y}}^{i\bar{a}}$ and $E^{i\bar{a}}$ are the projections of the sets $\hat{\hat{Y}}^{\bar{a}}_i$ and $E^{\bar{a}}_i$ on the coordinates defined by π^{io}. The set $E^{i\bar{a}R}$ contains all the vectors y^i such that

$$\pi^{io}y^i \geq \pi^{io}y^{im}, \quad \text{where } y^i \text{ is in } \hat{\hat{Y}}^{i\bar{a}}.$$

The vector y^{im} is a minimizer for π^{io} on $E^{i\bar{a}}$; the vectors y^{ia} and y^{io} are maximizers for π^i on $E^{i\bar{a}}$ and $E^{i\bar{a}R}$ respectively, where π^i is the subvector of π corresponding to π^{io} in π^o. (A vector y^{io} is not necessarily identical with the ith subvector of y^o, to which we shall never have occasion to refer.)

Sufficient conditions for generating a program $y^{o\bar{a}}_k$ in E^R_k such that $\pi y^{o\bar{a}}_k > \pi y^{\bar{a}}_k$ may be obtained most simply by restricting our attention to the set $E^R_{(\bar{a})}$, the set seeded by $y^{\bar{a}}_k$, a maximizer for π on E_k. It is evident that $E^R_{(\bar{a})}$ is included in E^R_k. The following corollary is proved in the appendix.

COROLLARY TO THEOREM 1. *If (1) at least one row of Π^o (say π^{io}) is such that $\pi^{io}y^{i\bar{a}}_k \neq \pi^{io}y^{im}_k$ and (2) $\pi^i y^{i*}_k > \pi^i y^{i\bar{a}}_k$ (where π^i is the subvector in π corresponding to π^{io} in Π^o), then there must exist a vector $y^{o\bar{a}}_k$ in E^R_k such that $\pi y^{o\bar{a}}_k > \pi y^{\bar{a}}_k$.*

It should be noted that $y^{o\bar{a}}_k$ is not necessarily identical with any maximizer y^o_k for π on E^R_k. For one thing, $E^R_{(\bar{a})}$ may not contain y^o_k. For another, even if y^o_k were in $E^R_{(\bar{a})}$, $y^{o\bar{a}}_k$ might not be a maximizer on that set.

The corollary states that if prices are not counterposed for some subspace of $\hat{Y}_k$ corresponding to a row of the aggregation matrix Π^o, when all other coordinates of y_k are set at the level of the constrained maximizer $y^{\bar{a}}_k$, there must exist some production vector $y^{o\bar{a}}_k$ worth more at prices π than $y^{\bar{a}}_k$.

If the price systems are counterposed for every subspace, a sufficient condition for increasing the payoff of k is that in some subspace i containing at least three goods, there should be a boundary point y^{io}_k of $\hat{Y}^i_k$, other than $y^{i\bar{a}}_k$, such that $\pi^{io}y^{io}_k = \pi^{io}y^{im}_k$, with the property $\pi^i y^{io}_k > \pi^i y^{i\bar{a}}_k$, where $y^{i\bar{a}}_k$ is the ith subvector in $y^{\bar{a}}_k$, the given maximizer for π on E_k.

To simplify the exposition of the problem raised by partial aggregation, I will demonstrate the above corollary in only three dimensions.

We start out with n goods and a vector $y^{\bar{a}}_k$, which maximizes $\pi \hat{y}_k$ for all $\hat{y}_k$ in E_k. As before, $\pi y^*_k > \pi y^{\bar{a}}_k$. We now write the vector $y^{\bar{a}}_k$ as $(u^a, v^a, w^a_1,$

$\ldots, w_{n-2}^a)$ and let w^a represent the subvector $(w_1^a, \ldots, w_{n-2}^a)$. The subvectors π^1 and π^{1o} consist, respectively, of incentive and aggregation prices for the first two goods the quantities of which are shown in the subvector y^1. The set $Y_k^{w^a}$ contains all vectors (u, v, w^a) in $\hat{\hat{Y}}_k$; the set $E_k^{w^a}$ contains all vectors (u, v, w^a) in E_k.

Suppose the prereform acceptable set E_k had consisted of all vectors in $\hat{\hat{Y}}_k$ whose uth coordinate was at least as large as u^a. The sets $\hat{\hat{Y}}_k$ and E_k are represented in diagram 3.7. The diagram is meant to represent a convex

Diagram 3.7

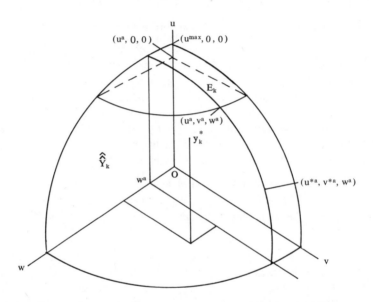

solid, such as a quarter of a spheroid object sliced into four parts by two planes perpendicular to each other. The set E_k consists of all points in $\hat{\hat{Y}}_k$ whose first coordinate is at least equal to u^a—the entire top part of the solid above the line of boundary points that includes (u^a, v^a, w^a). It is clear in this particular case that the "slice" through the solid, defined as the locus of all points whose wth coordinate equals w^a, cuts through E_k.

We now represent this slice, denoted $\hat{\hat{Y}}_k^1$, where the superscript 1 refers to the first subvector, in diagram 3.8. The minimizer for π^{1o} on E_k^1 for this cut is denoted y_k^{1m}. The line $\pi^{1o}y_k^1$ through y_k^{1m} intersects the boundary of $\hat{\hat{Y}}_k^1$ at (u^o, v^o). The postreform acceptable set consists of all programs in $\hat{\hat{Y}}_k^1$ worth at least as much at prices π^{1o} as y_k^{1m}, or all the points on or above the line $\pi^{1o}y^1$ through y_k^{1m}. It is evident that if (u^{*a}, v^{*a}), the maximizer for π^1 on $\hat{\hat{Y}}_k^1$, is not in E_k^1, there will exist some point, such as (v^o, u^o) that will be worth more at prices π^1 than (u^a, v^a). It is just as evident that the n-dimensional vector (u^o, v^o, w^a) will be worth more at prices π than (u^a, v^a, w^a), since the two vectors only differ in the first two elements, the combined value of which at π^1 is greater for the first vector than for the second.

Diagram 3.8

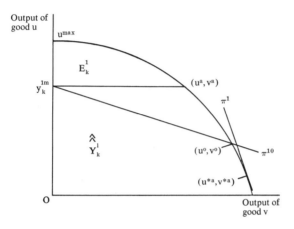

The way the problem has been set up, the price systems π^1 and π^{1o} cannot be counterposed, at least as long as the price of v is greater than zero. But this is only accidental to the definition of E_k. They could easily have been counterposed, for example, if E_k had consisted of all points above the cord drawn between $(u^{max}, 0, 0)$ and (u^a, v^a, w^a).

III.4. The Decomposition of the Head's Acceptable Set

We shall now construct acceptable sets for the head, the ministries, and the enterprises that will allow us to be more specific about the effects of decentralization measures on the mutual compatibility of production programs.

The head, it may be assumed, is not indifferent among all the programs in its acceptable set. Its preferences may be expressed in a binary relation among all possible programs: Given any two programs y_1 and y_2 (in its aggregated nomenclature), (1) y_1 is preferred to y_2, or (2) y_2 is preferred to y_1, or (3) y_1 is indifferent to y_2. This relation is assumed to be transitive and reflexive.

We also adopt the usual assumption that the set of all programs preferred to an "indifference class" (i.e. a set of programs among which the head is indifferent) is convex. Finally, we restate the assumption made earlier about all A.A.S., that if $\hat{y}'$ is in E, so is every program $\hat{y}$ such that $\hat{y} \geq \hat{y}'$.

The head's acceptable set G consists of all programs indifferent or preferred to an indifference class associated with a minimum level of satisfaction for the head. This A.S. is obviously convex, as is E, its intersection with $\hat{\hat{Y}}$.[28] We shall assume that G is closed. Since, as we have already seen, $\hat{\hat{Y}}$ is compact (closed and bounded), the set E will also be compact (as the intersection of two closed sets, one of which is bounded above and the other bounded below).

Consider a production program $\hat{y}$, in E, which, for some semipositive price vector ρ, maximizes ρy on E. (Such maximizers must exist, since, as we have just noted, E is compact.) The program $\hat{y}$ is an efficient point of $\hat{Y}$ and hence on the efficiency frontier $\hat{Y}$. The efficient set of programs in E, denoted $\hat{E}$, is defined as the intersection of E with $\hat{Y}$.

The problem is to decompose $\hat{E}$ into the ministry sets.

Consider again program $\hat{y}$ in $\hat{E}$ and the price vector ρ such that $\rho\hat{y} \geq \rho\hat{\hat{y}}$, for all $\hat{\hat{y}}$ in $\hat{\hat{Y}}$. By the construction of $\hat{\hat{Y}}$, there must exist at least one program $\hat{y}^h$ in $\hat{\hat{Y}}^h$ (for every h) such that $\sum_{h=1}^{H} \hat{y}^h = \hat{y}$. Every such program $\hat{y}^h$ will be said to belong to a set $\hat{E}_h^D$. Repeating this procedure for appropriate price vectors for every vector in $\hat{E}$, we obtain the entire set $\hat{E}_h^D$ (for every h), which we shall call "the decomposed set of the head for ministry h." By a well-known theorem relating to the maximization of a linear function on a sum of sets,[29] if the price vector ρ and the vector $\hat{y}$ in $\hat{E}$ generate $\hat{y}^h$ in $\hat{E}_h^D$, then $\rho\hat{y}^h \geq \rho y^h$ for all y^h in $\hat{E}_h^D$. It is evident that $\hat{E}_h^D$ is a subset of $\hat{Y}^h$, the set of boundary points of $\hat{\hat{Y}}^h$. By a similar construction, we derive from the set $\hat{E}_h^D$ (for every h) the decomposed sets $\hat{E}_k^D$ ($k = 1, \ldots, K_h$) for the enterprises under h.

The actual efficiency frontier of the acceptable sets of the ministries need not coincide with the decomposed sets of the head for the ministries. For one thing, a ministry will be uncertain as to precisely what combinations of ministerial programs the head will accept, and it may wish to play safe by imposing more demands on its subordinate enterprises, with respect to plan fulfillment or to other indicators, than it strictly needs to in order to satisfy the head.

Suppose, on the other hand, that at least some of the maximizers for the incentive price system π on the ministries' postreform acceptable sets for their subordinate enterprises were not contained in $\hat{E}_h^D$. For at least one well-defined class of cases, we can show that the aggregate program equal to the sum of these maximizers over all enterprises would not be acceptable (i.e. would not be in the head's acceptable set G).

28. $\hat{Y}_k$ and $\hat{\hat{Y}}_k$ are convex and hence so is $\hat{\hat{Y}}$, as the sum of a finite number of convex sets. G is convex by assumption. E is therefore convex as the intersection of two convex sets.

29. Theorem I.2 in T. C. Koopmans, *Three Essays on the State Of Economic Science* (New York: McGraw-Hill, 1957), p. 12.

Let y_k^D be a maximizer for π on $\hat{E}_k^D$ $(k = 1, \ldots, K)$ and $y^o = \sum_{k=1}^{K} y_k^o$

THEOREM 2. *If (1) E and $\hat{E}_k^D$ are compact ($k = 1, \ldots, K$), (2) $\pi y_k^o \geq \pi y_k^D$ for every k, with the strict inequality holding for at least one enterprise, (3) for any vector y, $y \geq y'$, where y' is in G, y is also in G: then y^o cannot be in G.*

Proof. By (1) there exist maximizers $y_1^D, \ldots, y_k^D, \ldots, y_K^D$ for π on $\hat{E}_1^D, \ldots, \hat{E}_k^D, \ldots, \hat{E}_K^D$ respectively. Also by (1), there exists at least one maximizer $y^{\neq}$ for π on $\hat{E}$.

Let $\hat{\hat{E}}$ be defined as $\sum_{k=1}^{K} \hat{E}_k^D$. $\hat{E}$ is a subset of $\hat{\hat{E}}$ (because [a] every vector in $\hat{E}$, by construction, is the sum of K vectors, one from each of the sets $\hat{E}_1^D, \ldots, \hat{E}_k^D, \ldots, \hat{E}_K^D$, and [b] every such aggregate of K vectors must be in $\hat{\hat{E}}$, the sum of these K sets).

The vector y^D, defined as $\sum_{k=1}^{K} y_k^D$, must be a maximizer on $\hat{\hat{E}}$ (by the theorem on the maximization of a linear function on a sum of sets).[30] Moreover, since $y^{\neq}$ is a maximizer for π on $\hat{E}$, a subset of $\hat{\hat{E}}$, $\pi y^{\neq} \leq \pi y^D$.

By (2),

$$\pi y^o = \pi \left(\sum_{k=1}^{K} y_k^o \right) > \pi \left(\sum_{k=1}^{K} y_k^D \right) = \pi y^D \geq \pi y^{\neq}.$$

Thus, $\pi y^o > \pi y^{\neq}$.

If y^o were in $\hat{E}$, $y^{\neq}$ would not be a maximizer for π on $\hat{E}$. Thus, by contradiction, y^o is not in $\hat{E}$.

It follows from assumption (3) that $\pi y \leq \pi y^{\neq}$ for all y in E. Hence, since $\pi y^o > \pi y^{\neq}$, y^o cannot be in E.

Since y^o is in $\hat{Y}$ but not in E, it cannot be in G. Q.E.D.

Theorem 2 is illustrated for two goods in diagram 3.9, in which $\hat{Y}$ is the sum of the sets $\hat{Y}_k$ and $\hat{Y}_l$, where enterprises k and l are the only enterprises producing goods 1 and 2.

The reader's attention is drawn to the fact that, even if enterprises k and l happened to consume each other's products as inputs, the set $\hat{Y}$ would not depend on the output decisions of k and l. This invariance is a straightforward consequence of the assumption made in constructing the fully constrained sets that every allocation decision with respect to material inputs was precisely fulfilled. Thus suppose that good 1 produced by enterprise l was consumed by enterprise k and compare two vectors $\bar{y}_l$ and $\bar{y}_l'$, which differ only in that $\bar{y}_l'$ contains Δy_1 less of the first good and Δy_2 more of the second. Unless other enterprises compensated for the shortfall in good 1, the

---

30. By Theorem I.1, in Koopmans, p. 12.

Diagram 3.9

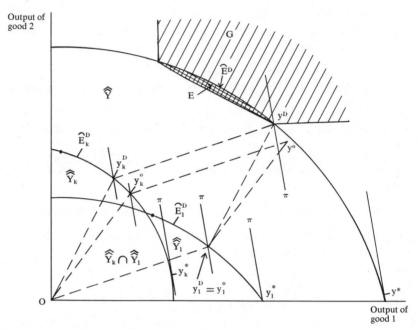

allotment to enterprise k would have to be fulfilled at the expense of net output. If the program $\bar{y}'_l$ is introduced instead of $\bar{y}_l$, all other production decisions remaining the same, the only effect will be that the net output of good 1 will be reduced by Δy_1 and the net output of good 2 will be augmented by Δy_2. If $\bar{y}$ in $\hat{\hat{Y}}$ was the sum of the actual programs $\bar{y}_k$ and $\bar{y}_l$ before the substitution of $\bar{y}'_l$, and no other changes took place, the new aggregate program would be obtained by subtracting Δy_1 from and adding Δy_2 to $\bar{y}$.

In the diagram y_k^* and y_l^* are maximizers on $\hat{\hat{Y}}_k$ and $\hat{\hat{Y}}_l$ respectively for prices π. The programs y_k^D and y_l^D are the constrained maximizers (i.e. they maximize πy_k and πy_l on $\hat{E}_k^D$ and $\hat{E}_l^D$ respectively). It is assumed that $y_l^o = y_l^D$, but $\pi y_k^o > \pi y_k^D$. The theorem says that y^o, the sum of y_k^o and y_l^o, cannot be in G.

III.5. Reallocation of Material Inputs after the Reform

So far, the allocation of materials by the head to the ministries and by the ministries to their subordinate enterprises has helped us to construct fully constrained sets that were, in the aggregate, capable of generating acceptable production programs. These allocations need not be efficient. Indeed, they will at best be efficient for only one combination of outputs. We recall that the attainable set $\hat{Y}$ contains all the programs made possible by any conceivable allocation of nonfixed inputs, first among ministries and then among enterprises. If we let y^{opt} stand for the program most preferred by the head in $\hat{Y}$, we shall assume, with some plausibility, that y^{opt} will *not* be contained in the set $\hat{Y}$ actually generated by the prereform allocation. Given the coarseness of the information available to the head, there is a strong presumption that it should be possible to redistribute materials among ministries and among enterprises in such a way as to generate aggregate production sets strictly containing the production sets resulting from the prereform allocation. In this section we shall take another look at the comparative statics of reform, this time taking into consideration the enlargement of the aggregate production set $\hat{\hat{Y}}$ made possible by a more efficient allocation of materials in the postreform period. Needless to say, the environment of the system, including the technology available to each enterprise, is meant to be the same before and after the reform.

Again we shall study the consequences of a reform that would confer greater autonomy on enterprises by allowing them to produce any program worth at least as much at aggregation prices as any formerly acceptable program (where such aggregation may be partial or complete).

We shall preserve a convenient feature of the construction of our fully constrained sets, namely that the *production decisions* of each enterprise k have no influence on the allotments of materials and other inputs of any other enterprise. This can be done in either of two ways. We may assume that the particular goods whose output will be affected by a given redistribution of inputs are all end products or that enterprises are permitted to exchange allotment quotas (i.e. claims on materials) but not the products of their own output activities. In either case, this implies that, once the new allotments have been set (by a supervisor or as the result of exchanges), alternative production decisions will affect only the levels of net outputs of goods produced in the system (or consumed by the system if these net outputs are negative).

If responsibility for the allocation of materials is at least in part delegated by the head to the ministries and, in turn, by the ministries to enterprises, we would expect that every enterprise would be in a position to "protect" its payoff, that is, to secure at least as large a payoff at incentive prices π after the reform as they did beforehand. We suppose therefore that the new frontier of the fully constrained sets of enterprises will be such as to contain the old constrained maximum $y_k^{\bar{a}}$ (the optimal point for k subject to the constraint that k must satisfy h). For at least one enterprise, say the kth, the new frontier will also contain programs worth more at prices π than $\pi y_k^{\bar{a}}$, as in diagram 3.10.

In this diagram y_k^{R*} denotes the unconstrained maximizer for k at prices π after the reform. The postreform acceptable set includes all programs worth at least as much at prices π^o as y_k^m. (The diagram, in case of partial aggregation, represents a "cut" in the subspace occupied by goods 1 and 2,

Diagram 3.10

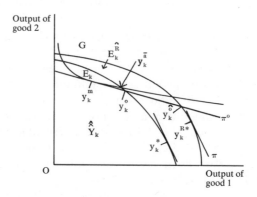

where the levels of output of all the other goods is set at $y_k^{\bar{a}}$, the constrained maximum for π on the initial acceptable set E_k.)

The problem we wish to study is this. The ministries have all introduced the same type of decentralizing measure. Each ministry h allows its subordinate enterprise k to produce any program y_k in $\hat{\hat{Y}}_k$, such that $\Pi^o y_k \geq \Pi^o y_k^e$, where Π^o is the aggregation matrix derived from the partitioning of π^o, and y_k^e is a program acceptable to h before the reform. It is assumed that $y^e \left(= \sum_{k=1}^{K} y_k^e \right)$ was acceptable to the head before the reform for *any* y_k^e in E_k.[31] The maximizers y_k^o for π on E_k^R *before the expansion of* $\hat{\hat{Y}}_k$ are such that their sum, taken over all enterprises in the hierarchy, or $\sum_{k=1}^{K} y_k^o$, is *not* acceptable to the head. (In particular, for every k, $\pi y_k^o \geq \pi y_k^D$, and $\pi y_l^o > \pi y_l^D$ for some l). We now denote by $\hat{\hat{Y}}_k^R$ the postreform fully constrained production set of k and by $E_k^{\hat{R}}$, the postreform acceptable set of ministry h for enterprise k containing all programs in $\hat{\hat{Y}}_k^R$ such that $\Pi^o y_k \geq \Pi^o y_k^e$, where y_k^e, as before, is any program in the original set E_k. The head's postreform fully constrained production set $\hat{\hat{Y}}^R$ is equal to $\sum_{k=1}^{K} \hat{\hat{Y}}_k^R$. We want to know whether it is possible for the expansion of the production sets (from $\hat{\hat{Y}}_k$ to $\hat{\hat{Y}}_k^R$ for every k) to be of such a character that the new maximizers $y_k^{\bar{o}}$ on $E_k^{\hat{R}}$ might be jointly acceptable to the head (i.e. that $\sum_{k=1}^{K} y_k^{\bar{o}}$ might be in $E^{\hat{R}}$, where $E^{\hat{R}}$ is defined as

31. If this assumption seems too strong, we may weaken it by requiring only that y_k^e belong to a subset of points in E_k with the property that $\sum_{k=1}^{K} y_k^e$ be in E. The point y_k^m would then be an element of this subset.

the intersection of G with $\hat{\hat{Y}}^R$.) The question, more broadly posed, is whether the expansion of the production sets due to a greater efficiency of allocation might offset the distortion in the product-mix due to the "pull" of incentive prices and cause joint programs to be produced that, despite this distortion, turned out to be acceptable to the head.

We again assume that $\pi y_k^* > \pi y_k^o$ for every enterprise k. (We shall come back to this strong assumption in the concluding part of this section.) Every maximizer y_k^o for π on E_k^R must then be located on the boundary of $\hat{\hat{Y}}_k$ and on a hyperplane $\pi^o \hat{y}_k$ through y_k^m. (*Mutatis mutandis* for any subspace i generated by π^{io}.)[32] The same applies of course to the maximizers y_k on $E_k^{\bar{R}}$. We may write therefore:

$$\pi^o y_k^o = \pi^o y_k^m$$

and

$$\pi^o y_k^{\bar{o}} = \pi^o y_k^m$$

Summing over all enterprises and simplifying we obtain:

$$\pi^o y^{\bar{m}} = \pi^o y^o = \pi^o y^{\bar{o}}$$

where

$$y^{\bar{m}} = \sum_{k=1}^{K} y_k^m, \quad y^o = \sum_{k=1}^{K} y_k^o, \quad \text{and } y^{\bar{o}} = \sum_{k=1}^{K} y_k^{\bar{o}}.$$

Since, by the above assumption, y_k^* and y_k^{R*} lie in one half space and y_k^o in the other half space defined by the hyperplane $\pi^o y_k$ through y_k^m, the points y^* and y^{*R}, the sum of these vectors taken over all enterprises, must lie "below" $\pi^o y$ through $y^{\bar{m}}$, if y^o lies "above" it.

For two goods and a convex preference set G for the head, the answer to the question posed is unambiguously negative. In diagram 3.11 the problem is illustrated by violating the convexity assumption on G. In this example, $y^{\bar{m}}$ is in E, as it must be by construction. It is not—and need not be—a minimizer for π^o on E. The program y^o is unacceptable, but $y^{\bar{o}}$, after the expansion of $\hat{Y}$ in the general direction of the first good, is acceptable.[33] The reason why the convexity of G would rule out this example is that all convex combinations of $y^{\bar{m}}$ and $y^{\bar{o}}$ would then have to be in G and thus y^o, which represents such a combination, would have had to be acceptable.

It is evident, even in this case, that for $y^{\bar{o}}$ to be acceptable, the head must be willing to trade off good 2 for good 1 along $\pi^o y$ through $y^{\bar{m}}$ at some point or points between y^o and $y^{\bar{o}}$ at a rate greater than that indicated by the ratio

32. On the special problems posed by partial aggregation, see below, p. 108 and appendix C.II.

33. On the implicit assumption that y^o is in $\hat{Y}$ and $y^{\bar{o}}$ in $\hat{Y}^R$, see below, pp. 105–06.

Diagram 3.11

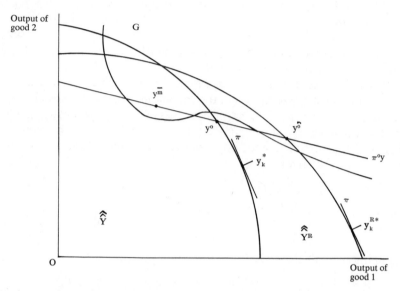

of the prices in π^o. This appears to be a generalizable condition for any goods j and j' where y is a vector of n goods ($n > 2$).

Diagram 3.12, drawn for three goods, shows how $y^{\hat{o}}$ may be in G, even though y^o was not in that set, without violating the convexity assumption for $\hat{\hat{Y}}$, $\hat{\hat{Y}}^R$, or G. All the lines drawn and all the sets enclosed by these lines are meant to be located on the plane $\pi^o y$ through $y^{\bar{m}}$, which plane is inclined

Diagram 3.12

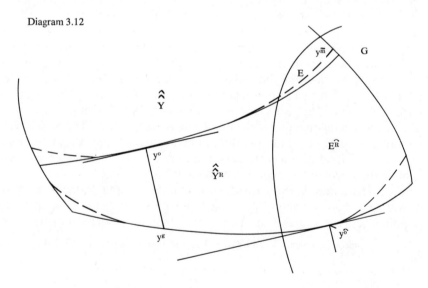

downward. The set denoted $E^{\hat{R}}$ is the intersection of $\hat{\hat{Y}}^R$ with G, or, more precisely, the subset of this intersection lying on the plane $\pi^o y$ through $y^{\bar{m}}$. (There may also be points in G below the plane.) Programs y^o and y^δ have been drawn on the boundaries of $\hat{Y}$ and $\hat{\hat{Y}}^R$ respectively. Actually, if the maximizers for π on E_k^R and $E_k^{\hat{R}}$ occur at extremal points of these sets and are such that their slopes on the plane $\pi^o y_k$ through y_k^m differ for at least one pair of enterprises, y^o will be interior to $\hat{Y}$ and y^δ to $\hat{\hat{Y}}^R$. In such a case, the arguments that follow will apply to the boundaries of $\sum\limits_{k=1}^{K} E_k^R$ and $\sum\limits_{k=1}^{K} E_k^{\hat{R}}$ respectively rather than to the boundaries of $\hat{Y}$ and $\hat{\hat{Y}}^R$. The boundary points of $\sum\limits_{k=1}^{K} E_k^R$ in the interior of $\hat{Y}$ and of $\sum\limits_{k=1}^{K} E_k^{\hat{R}}$ in the interior of $\hat{\hat{Y}}^R$ are shown as broken lines in the diagram.

In the case represented in diagram 3.12, the expansion of the production sets for the individual enterprises has made it possible for the ministries to grant greater autonomy to their enterprises (via aggregation) without jeopardizing the acceptability to the head of the hierarchy of the joint production program of the K enterprises.

The success of the reform in this case may be attributed to the favorable direction of the expansion of the fully constrained production sets of the enterprises along the planes $\pi^o y_k$ through y_k^m. It would not have occurred, had it not been for the disproportionate expansion of $\hat{Y}$ in the direction of G along $\pi^o y$ through $y^{\bar{m}}$. In particular, if the slope of the boundary of $\hat{\hat{Y}}^R$ at the point y^g where it is intersected by the directional line perpendicular to the tangent at y^o had been equal to the slope of this tangent line, then y^δ (identical with y^g) would not have been acceptable.[34] The basic proposition discussed above may be put in the form of a theorem with a trivial mathematical content.

THEOREM 3. *Assume: (1) y^δ is a maximizer for π on $\sum\limits_{k=1}^{K} E_k^{\hat{R}}$, a subset of $\hat{\hat{Y}}^R$.*

(2) $E_k^{\hat{R}}$ is compact for every k. Then a sufficient condition for y^δ to be in G is that there exists no supporting hyperplane with directional coefficients proportional to π at any point of $\sum\limits_{k=1}^{K} E_k^{\hat{R}}$ not in G.

Proof. (1) Given a maximizer for π at y^δ, there must be a supporting hyperplane with directional coefficients proportional to π at that point

---

34. If the vectors y and π^o have n elements, then the "slopes of the tangents at y^δ and y^g" become the directional coefficients of supporting hyperplanes at those points, which hyperplanes will have $n - 1$ dimensions.

(by the definition of a supporting hyperplane). (2) Hence if there exists no such supporting hyperplane at any point of $\sum_{k=1}^{K} E_k^{\hat{R}}$ not in G, there cannot be a maximizer for π on that subset of $\sum_{k=1}^{K} E_k^{\hat{R}}$. Every maximizer for π on $\sum_{k=1}^{K} E_k^{\hat{R}}$ must therefore be in G.   Q.E.D.

For the condition stated in the theorem to be necessary, it is easily seen that the set $\sum_{k=1}^{K} E_k^{\hat{R}}$ must be strictly convex (to eliminate the possibility that the set of maximizers for π on $\sum_{k=1}^{K} E_k^{\hat{R}}$ might include points in G and points not in G, in case, for example, $y^{\hat{o}}$ were located on a linear segment of the boundary of $\sum_{k=1}^{K} E_k^{\hat{R}}$).

Consider the intersection B of $\sum_{k=1}^{K} E_k^{\hat{R}}$ with the hyperplane $\pi^o y$ through $y^{\bar{m}}$ and its boundary points $\hat{B}$. By the same arguments as are used to prove corollary 1 and remark 2 to theorem 1, in appendix B, every maximizer $y^{\hat{o}}$ for π on $\sum_{k=1}^{K} E_k^{\hat{R}}$ must be in $\hat{B}$, provided $\pi y^{R*} > \pi y^{\hat{o}}$. Since $\sum_{k=1}^{K} E_k^{\hat{R}}$ is convex (as the sum of convex sets), $\hat{B}$ may (loosely) be said to have a "continuously turning tangent." Thus if y^o is a boundary point of $\sum_{k=1}^{K} E_k^{R}$ not in G and $y^{\hat{o}}$, on the boundary of $\sum_{k=1}^{K} E_k^{\hat{R}}$, is in G, we may describe the expansion of $\sum_{k=1}^{K} E_k^{R}$ to $\sum_{k=1}^{K} E_k^{\hat{R}}$ as a disproportionate outward movement of the boundary of the first set along the hyperplane $\pi^o y$ through $y^{\bar{m}}$ in the general direction of G. To the extent that the boundary points of $\sum_{k=1}^{K} E_k^{R}$ coincide with boundary points of $\hat{\hat{Y}}$ and those of $\sum_{k=1}^{K} E_k^{\hat{R}}$ coincide with boundary points of $\hat{\hat{Y}}^{\hat{R}}$, we may also think of the boundary of $\hat{\hat{Y}}$ along the hyperplane $\pi^o y$ through $y^{\bar{m}}$ expanding disproportionately in the direction of G.

These propositions suggest that the success of a reform of the type modeled may depend on the process for redistributing allotments that actually takes place after the reform. If enterprises, as we have postulated so far, exert a paramount influence in this process, we would expect that they would attempt to secure inputs that would help them increase the value of their output at incentive prices, subject to the acceptability conditions imposed on them by their ministry. It is not unreasonable to speculate that the enlargement of $\hat{\hat{Y}}_k$ (or at least of E_k^R) would proceed in the general direction along the plane $\pi^o y_k$ through y_k^m of the normals to the tangent lines at y_k^o (for every k). This would cause $\hat{\hat{Y}}$ (and/or $\sum_{k=1}^{K} E_k^R$) to expand in the direction of the normal to the tangent at y^o along $\pi^o y$ through $y^{\bar{m}}$. Barring an especially favorable extension of G in the direction of goods with high incentive prices, the result would be an unacceptable joint program. All this presupposes, of course, that enterprises sought only to satisfy their ministry (i.e., tried to produce programs in $E_k^{\bar{R}}$) and knew nothing of the preferences of the head.

But why should the preferences of the ministry and of the head differ? Suppose, for example, that the ministry of metallurgy had only been willing to accept certain combinations of output of nickel- and vanadium-alloy steels from every steel mill before the reform but now was ready to accept any combined tonnage of the two types of steel that came to at least the minimum aggregate tonnage in an acceptable combination before the reform. Why shouldn't the head go along with this greater tolerance? The answer lies at the heart of the coordination problem. If it is advantageous for the mills to produce more nickel-alloy steels at the expense of the vanadium-alloy steels, the head will find its stocks of vanadium steel diminishing as the planned allotments of this input are met. Unless the two types of steel can be exchanged abroad at a fixed rate—by exporting nickel steel and importing vanadium steel at fixed prices—the marginal utility to the head of the vanadium steel will increase relative to the marginal utility of the nickel steel—until the substitution in the output mix of the two types of steel begins to threaten the fulfillment of the allotment plans for vanadium steel, at which point further substitution will presumably become intolerable. The position of the head as coordinating center compels it to differentiate the value of a ton of two different steels depending on their relative outputs, whereas, from the ministry's perspective, they might be equally valued, irrespective of their relative outputs.

The analysis in this section suggests that *the middle tier in a three-tier hierarchy can only take decentralizing measures with respect to enterprises' production decisions such that the incentive system to which these enterprises are subject would lead them to outputs that would be jointly acceptable to the head in the absence of any gain in efficiency due to the redistribution of inputs.* This means, in effect, that the only gain to be expected from a limited reform —at least if the preferences of the head are to remain the same before and after the reform—is from the abolition of "petty tutelage," which may be defined as the restriction of enterprises to acceptable sets excluding at least some programs in $\hat{E}_k^p$ or $\hat{E}_h^p$ that would have been jointly acceptable to the head.

This broad conclusion hinges on the enlargement of the sets $\hat{Y}_k$ in conformity with the interests of enterprises. In the contrary case, if the head, in concert with the ministries and enterprises, can improve the allocation of inputs in such a way as to enlarge $\hat{Y}$ mainly in the direction of output combinations acceptable to the head, the reform would hold out brighter prospects for simultaneously increasing the payoff of enterprises and expanding output with given resources in ways agreeable to the highest authorities.

There are two problems in the analysis which may restrict the generality of these broad conclusions.

1. Whether in the case of complete or of partial aggregation, it is unrealistic to expect that the unconstrained maximizer for π on $\hat{Y}_k$ (or for π^i on $\hat{Y}_{(o)}^i$) will fall outside E_k or E_k^R (resp. E_k^i or E_k^{iR}) for every k. If, for some enterprise l, y_l^{R*} is interior to E_l^R, it will not be true that $\pi^o y^{\bar{m}} = \pi^o y^o = \pi^o y^{\bar{o}}$ (since, y_l^o, identical in this case with y_l^{R*}, will not lie on the hyperplane $\pi^o y_l$ through y_l^m). In appendix C.I, this difficulty is met by analyzing separately the effects of the reform on the enterprises whose unconstrained maximizers are acceptable (i.e. are in E_l, in E_l^R, or in both for some l) and for those where the unconstrained maximizers are worth more at prices π than any vector in the relevant acceptable sets (for which our main result applies).

2. In the case of partial aggregation, the expansion of the production sets poses a special analytical difficulty. Suppose $y_k^{(o)}$ in E_k were the program which "seeded" $E_{(o)}^R$ before the expansion of $\hat{Y}_k$ to $\hat{Y}_k^R$, where $E_{(o)}^R$ contained y_k^o, the maximizer for π on E_k^R. We cannot assert that $y_k^{(o)}$ must necessarily seed the postexpansion set $E_{(o)}^R$ containing $y_k^{\hat{o}}$, the maximizer for π on $E_k^{\hat{R}}$. If the programs $y_l^{(o)}$ and $y_l^{(\bar{o})}$ generating $E_{(o)}^R$ and $E_{(o)}^{\hat{R}}$ respectively differ for some enterprise l, then $E_{(o)}^{iR}$ need not be a subset of $E_{(o)}^{i\hat{R}}$ for any subspace i and y_l^{io} and $y_l^{i\bar{o}}$ will not be on the same hyperplane $\pi^{io} y_l^i$ through a unique subvector y_l^{im} (since the minimizer for π^{io} on $E_{(o)}^{iR}$ will not generally be identical with the minimizer for π^{io} on $E_{(o)}^{i\hat{R}}$, where $E_{(o)}^{iR}$ and $E_{(o)}^{i\hat{R}}$ refer to the ith subspaces of E_l^R and $E_l^{\hat{R}}$ generated by $y_l^{(o)}$ and $y_l^{(\bar{o})}$ respectively). This second difficulty is analyzed in appendix C.II. The idea suggested here is to consider only the sets seeded by $y_k^{(\bar{o})}$ before and after the expansion of $\hat{Y}_k$ (for every enterprise k). The additional, rather plausible, assumption is made that the sum over all enterprises of the maximizers for π on the preexpansion, postreform acceptable sets seeded by $y_k^{(\bar{o})}$ (instead of by $y_k^{(o)}$) is unacceptable to the head (just as y^o, the sum of the maximizers on E_k^R—the relevant set for each enterprise k if there had been no expansion—was held to be unacceptable to the head).

III.6. Conclusions

This is about as far as I was able to pursue the logic of the three-tier model developed in this section, based on what I took to be fairly realistic assumptions (with the possible exception of the convexity of production sets, which played a key role in a number of these speculations). Nevertheless, the model is undeniably narrower in its behavioral assumptions than the general framework for analysis sketched out in part II allowed. In particular, I assumed throughout this section that enterprises complied with the demands made on them by their superiors by always producing within their acceptable sets, in contrast to the previous section where it was argued that the decision whether or not to comply might depend on the chances of retaliation by superior authorities and on how disruptive one enterprise's noncompliance might be in terms of the aggregate performance of all the enterprises under a given supervisor.

I also omitted, for the top two tiers, to show how the autonomy conferred on enterprise managers via aggregation would fit into the information system blocked out in part II, where the decision makers in each tier communicated with their supervisors in a "coarser" (more aggregated) nomenclature than that which they used to make their production or allocation decisions. After all, reforms are grafted on to a "centralized system" in which some three to five million individual products are normally produced and sold, whereas less than a thousand items are balanced and planned at the highest level of the hierarchy. The aggregation due to reform may be thought of as an increased degree of coarsening of the production nomenclature as information is conveyed upward, compared to the prereform situation. Thus the question I have been dealing with is not whether aggregation works at all—it clearly must since neither the ministries nor the head could possibly issue detailed instructions covering three to five million goods—but whether a greater degree of aggregation is justified, in the sense that the increased autonomy thereby conferred on managers would lead to a sufficient improvement in the efficiency of allocation to offset whatever distortion in the product-mix might be induced under the influence of the incentive system.

While the analysis in this section can only allow us to draw some very tentative conclusions on this subject, it does suggest that (1) if the disparity induced by the incentive and price systems between the interests of managers and the preferences of the top planners is significant, (2) if ministries before the reform did not exercise an excessively petty tutelage over their wards, and (3) if the expansion of the production sets was not biased in the direction of output mixes acceptable to the central authorities, this greater degree of aggregation is likely to generate bills of net output that will not be acceptable after the planned allocations of intermediate goods have been met.

We may also reformulate our conclusion in Jacob Marschak's terminology.[35] A reform of the type we have been dealing with will only be successful, in the absence of changes in preferences, in the environment, and in the
price systems, if it improves on an information structure that was not "payoff relevant" to begin with—which was too "fine" for supervisors to dis-
criminate efficiently in making certain of their decisions between different
communications expressed in that nomenclature (e.g., between a message
from enterprise k notifying ministry h that its entire monthly output was
1,500 tons of vanadium-alloy steel and another message that it amounted
to 1,500 tons of nickel-alloy steel).

The overwhelming emphasis in this paper has been on the wider autonomy
that enterprises gained as a result of the willingness of their supervisors to
judge their performance in aggregated terms. This has made it possible to
get a theoretical hold on a particular variant of a larger problem at the core
of reforms: the curtailment in the detailed control of enterprises by their
hierarchic superiors. This notion, I believe, is captured by the enlargement of
the acceptable sets attributed to these superiors. There may be other ways—
other than the construction in the present model of the sets E_k^R from the
prereform E_k—to conceive this enlargement. One might, for example,
postulate that every point in E_k was interior to the postreform acceptable set.
My guess is that the conclusions of such an analysis would be similar in
import and of a lower degree of specificity than those I have drawn in this
section.

35. Jacob Marschak, "The Pay-off Relevant Description of States and Acts," *Econometrica*
31 (October 1963): 719–25.

Appendix A

Production and Consumption Sets

Consider a subhierarchy j in tier s producing some of the products in the nomenclature of s, made up of L^s products. Its production set Y_j consists of vectors in the space R^{L^s} (the L^s-dimensional space of real numbers). Each L^s-dimensional vector y_j may contain positive elements representing outputs (goods produced) and negative elements representing inputs (labor, materials, etc.). If a good or service is neither produced nor consumed in y_j, which essentially represents a *process* for transforming inputs into outputs, then zero appears in the row corresponding to that good or service. The possibility of doing nothing is always allowed for by including in Y_j a vector of zeros ("The origin is included in the set"). Y_j, in short, consists of all the processes known and available to j. It is *not* constrained in any way by the availability of factors or materials.

Let us now introduce another subhierarchy k also supervised by h.

Suppose y_j is produced by j and y_k by k. Their sum is the sum of their L^s individual elements. The accompanying diagram shows a cross-section in two-dimensional space for labor and some good 2 of the two sets. The second

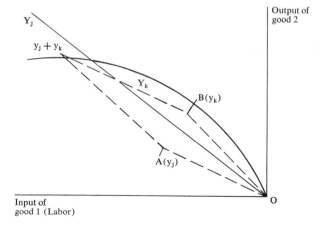

quadrant is used because labor on the horizontal axis is an input to which, by convention, we have attached a negative sign.

Y_j is a "convex cone" extending to infinity. Its upper bound is indicated by a straight line originating at 0. That this cone is convex means that (1) if y_j^1 is in Y_j then ty_j^i is also in this set, for any real number t greater or equal to zero, and (2) if y_j^1 and y_j^2 are both in the set, so is their sum $y_j^1 + y_j^2$. (In other words, the set exhibits constant returns to scale and additivity.)

Y_k is a set exhibiting diminishing returns to scale. Its upper bound is a concave line originating at 0.

The sum of y_j and y_k happens to be a point in Y_j but not in Y_k. (It is obtained by drawing lines parallel to OA and OB and finding the intersection of these lines. The construction of this parallelogram corresponds to the addition of the two vectors, coordinate by coordinate.)

Now the sum-set $Y_j + Y_k$ is the sum of *every* point in Y_j with *every* point in Y_k.

If Y_j is a convex cone (or just exhibits additivity)[36] then $Y_j + Y_j \subseteq Y_j$.

This is just another way of saying that the sum of every two points in Y_j must also be in Y_j.

Suppose Y_k were nonconvex but Y_j were a convex cone. Could $Y_j + Y_k \equiv Y$ be convex? (Convexity of Y is essential to proofs of the existence and optimal properties of general equilibrium.) The answer is yes. If $Y_k \subset Y_j$, then $Y \equiv Y_k + Y_j$ must be convex. For if Y_k is a subset of Y_j, then, by the additivity assumption on Y_j, the sum of every vector in Y_k with a vector in Y_j must belong to Y_j, which is convex. Hence $Y_k + Y_j$, or Y, must be convex.

Attainable Sets

In the following simplified model, there are three "goods": (1) labor, (2) a consumption good, and (3) an exogenous factor, which may be allocated among two plants with production sets Y_1 and Y_2. A production vector consists of a column of three elements, the first negative, the second positive, and the last negative.

There is a single consumer maximizing the simple utility function:

$$u = x_2.$$

He offers his labor services (x_1) in response to the amount supplied of x_2 according to the following equation:

$$x_1 \leq -x_2.$$

---

36. If a set Y is convex, then, for any two of its points y_1 and y_2, any convex combination $ty_1 + (1 - t)y_2$, where $0 \leq t \leq 1$, is also in Y. If additivity obtains, then if y_1 and y_2 are in Y, their sum $y_1 + y_2$ is also in Y.

The maximum amount of labor he can supply is 10 units:

$$x_1 \geq -10.$$

The production sets are these:

$$Y_1 = \{y_1 | y_1 \leq t(-\tfrac{1}{2}, 1, -1)^T ; t \geq 0\}$$

$$Y_2 = \{y_2 | y_2 \leq t(-1, 1, -\tfrac{1}{2})^T ; t \geq 0\}$$

where y_1 and y_2 are, respectively, vectors in Y_1 and Y_2 and where the superscript T (transpose) indicates that the row vector actually represents a column vector.

In other words, the first producer is limited to a convex cone by a linear technology that requires 0.5 unit of labor and 1 unit of the exogenous factor to produce one unit of the second good; the second produces according to a process that requires 1 unit of labor and 0.5 unit of the exogenous factor to produce one unit of the second good.

The resource set $\{\omega\}$ consists of the single vector $(0, 0, -10)$. (There are 10 units "from nature" of the exogenous factor, none of the other two.)

The acceptable set of the supervisor consists of all combined production vectors from the two plants such that the total output of the second good amounts to at least 12 units.

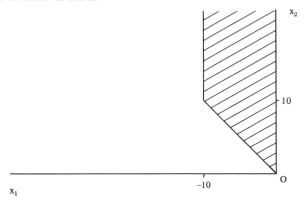

The *attainable* sets $\hat{Y}_1$ and $\hat{Y}_2$ will be determined by the amounts of labor and of the exogenous factor that can be obtained by the two producers, where these amounts add up to no more than the total labor supplied by the consumer and the amount of the exogenous factor available (10 units).

In other words:

$$\begin{bmatrix} x_1 \\ x_2 \\ 0 \end{bmatrix} - \begin{bmatrix} y_1^1 \\ y_1^2 \\ y_3^1 \end{bmatrix} - \begin{bmatrix} y_1^2 \\ y_2^2 \\ y_3^2 \end{bmatrix} \leq \begin{bmatrix} 0 \\ 0 \\ -10 \end{bmatrix}$$

where y_j^a ($a = 1, 2; j = 1, 2, 3$) is the jth element of the ath plant's production vector, which must of course be in Y^a ($a = 1, 2$). Similarly the consumption vector $(x_1, x_2, 0)$ must belong to the set shaded in in the diagram on page 113. The vector equation above corresponds to the equation on page 76 of the text except for the omission of the vector of "public goods" u.

Suppose 5 units of the exogenous factor were allotted to the first producer and 5 to the second. If these allotments were to be totally used up, the first producer would wish to employ 2.5 units of labor and the second 10 units, thus exceeding the total amount of labor available. The following allocation, however, would be an attainable allocation:

Consumer	Producer 1	Producer 2	Resources
-10	-2.5	-7.5	0
12.5	5	7.5	0
0	-5	-3.75	-10

In this allocation the exogenous factor would not be totally utilized (1.25 units left over in custody of the second producer).

Each of these vectors is then said to be in the *attainable set* of the participants. Note also that, even though the allocation of the exogenous factor is inefficient, the combined production of the second good (12.5 units) would fall in the supervisor's acceptable set.

What is the attainable allocation (i.e. the triplet of vectors) that would maximize x_2 if, instead of fixing ex ante the allocation of the exogenous factor, we considered all the possible allocations of either labor or the exogenous factor between the two producers (subject to the overall constraints on consumption and resources)? It would be approximately the following:

Consumer	Producer 1	Producer 2	Resources
-9.95	-3.35	-6.6	0
13.3	6.7	6.6	0
0	-6.7	-3.3	-10

By fully utilizing both labor and the exogenous factor a gain in consumption of 0.8 unit has been achieved.

There are many other attainable allocations, and the reader may wish to block out the entire attainable sets of the three participants.

CONSISTENCY SETS

There are J_h subhierarchies (say, 30) under supervisor h. There are all kinds of combinations of 30 production vectors, each attainable, that will sum up to an acceptable vector for h. Suppose that y_j^*—a production vector for subhierarchy j—belongs to one of these combinations, which we shall call C^*.

Unless it is teamed up with the $(J_h - 1)$ other production vectors (29 in all) that belong to C^*, there can be no assurance that the sum of the vectors will be acceptable and/or will meet all the exogenous constraints, such as the quantities of materials allotted by h to its 30 supervisees.

A simple numerical example may be of help here: h has only two supervisees or plants, both of which can produce some of product x_1 and some of x_2. Let x_1^1 and x_2^1 denote the outputs of these two products by plant 1 and x_1^2 and x_2^2 the corresponding outputs of the second plant. The A.S. of h is:

$$\{x_1, x_2 | x_1 \geq 1, x_2 \geq 1.5\}$$

In other words, the total output of x_1 must be no less than 1 unit and of x_2 no less than 1.5 units.

Each plant has a fixed capacity, which is used in making both products and each plant uses some exogenous material supplied by h.

The capacity constraints for the two plants are

(1) $\qquad\qquad 5x_1^1 + x_2^1 \leq 6 \quad$ for the first,

(2) $\qquad\qquad x_1^2 + 2x_2^2 \leq 5 \quad$ for the second.

The joint constraint for the exogenous material is

(3) $\qquad\qquad 0.1x_1^1 + 0.2x_2^1 + 0.2x_1^2 + 0.1x_2^2 \leq 1.6.$

(This implies that the material can be shifted by h from one plant to the other at will. Alternatively we could fix a certain planned allotment for each plant, but then, in order to make up a convincing example, there would have to be some consumption by each plant of at least one product of the other.)

Consider the following output vectors, where the first number in parentheses corresponds to the first product and the second number to the second:

Program 1: $(0, 6)$ for plant 1 and $(1, 2)$ for plant 2.

Program 2: $(1, 1)$ for plant 1 and $(4, 0.5)$ for plant 2.

One can verify that either program taken separately meets both capacity constraints (1) and (2) and joint constraint (3). They also satisfy h.

Hence, vector $(0, 6)$ which corresponds to y_j^* in my earlier example, belongs to a consistency set. Suppose, however, it were matched in a third program with $(4, 0.5)$, which also belongs to a consistency set. Then, substituting in the joint constraint, we would have:

$$0.1\,(0) + 0.2\,(6) + 0.2\,(4) + 0.1\,(0.5) = 2.05 > 1.6.$$

The joint constraint is no longer satisfied.

In other words, one cannot pick a vector from each plant's consistency set and expect that these vectors will be mutually consistent. In the above example, one can only be sure they will be mutually consistent if one picks vectors corresponding to the same program.

Appendix B

I. Definitions, Assumptions, Statement and Proof of Theorem 1

Let G_k, $\hat{\hat{Y}}_k$ be two closed subsets of R^n, where G_k is bounded from below and $\hat{Y}$ bounded from above.

Let $E_k = G_k \cap \hat{\hat{Y}}_k \neq \phi$.

E_k is compact (closed and bounded) as the intersection of two closed sets, one of which is bounded from above and the other bounded from below.

We now define the following supply correspondences:

(a) Unconstrained supply: $y_k^*(\pi) = \{y_k^* | \pi y_k^* = \max \pi y_k; y_k \in \hat{\hat{Y}}_k\}$,

(b) Constrained supply: $y_k^{\bar{a}}(\pi) = \{y_k^{\bar{a}} | \pi y_k^{\bar{a}} = \max \pi y_k; y_k \in E_k\}$,

(c) $y_k^m(\pi^o) = \{y_k^m | \pi^o y_k^m = \min \pi^o y_k; y_k \in E_k\}$,

(d) Constrained supply after reform: $y_k^o(\pi) = \{y_k^o | \pi y_k^o = \max \pi y_k; y_k \in E_k^R\}$,

where $E_k^R = \{\hat{y}_k | \pi^o \hat{y}_k \geq \pi^o y_k^m; \hat{y}_k \in \hat{\hat{Y}}_k\}$ and $\pi^o > 0$, $\pi > 0$, and $\pi^o \neq \pi$.

(Ordering rule for vectors $\gg$, $>$, $\geq$).

Observation 1. $\pi y_k^o \nless \pi y_k^{\bar{a}}$, since $E_k \subseteq E_k^R$.

We now strengthen the inequality.

Theorem 1. *Let (i) $\hat{\hat{Y}}_k$ be convex, (ii) $\pi^o y_k^m \neq \pi^o y_k^{\bar{a}}$, (iii) $\pi y_k^* > \pi y_k^{\bar{a}}$.*
Then $\pi y_k^o > \pi y_k^{\bar{a}}$.

Proof. Let $y(\alpha) = \alpha y_k^* + (1 - \alpha) y_k^{\bar{a}}; \alpha =]0, 1[$.
Then $y(\alpha) \in \hat{\hat{Y}}_k$ (from (i)).
Also $\pi y_k^{\bar{a}} < \pi y(\alpha) < \pi y_k^*$ (from (iii)).
Now $\pi^o y_k^{\bar{a}} > \pi^o y_k^m$ (from (ii) and the definition of y_k^m).
Therefore: $\pi^o y_k^+ > \pi^o y_k^m$, where $y_k^+ \in N(y_k^{\bar{a}}, \varepsilon)$, and $N(y_k^{\bar{a}}, \varepsilon)$ denotes an ε-distance neighborhood of $y_k^{\bar{a}}$.
For $\alpha < \varepsilon$, $y(\alpha) \in N(y_k^{\bar{a}}, \varepsilon)$.
Hence: $\pi^o y(\alpha) > \pi^o y_k^m$ and $y(\alpha) \in E_k^R$ for small α.
Thus there exists some point $y(\alpha)$ in E_k^R such that $\pi y(\alpha) > \pi y_k^{\bar{a}}$.
Since E_k^R is compact, y_k^o exists, and $\pi y_k^o \geq \pi y(\alpha) > \pi y_k^{\bar{a}}$.   Q.E.D.

Remark 1. If $\pi = \pi^o$, $y_k^* \in E_k^R$.

Proof. $\pi y_k^* > \pi y_k^m$, hence $\pi^o y_k^* > \pi^o y_k^m$. Hence, by the definition of E_k^R, $y_k^* \in E_k^R$.

116

COROLLARY 1 TO THEOREM 1. *Given assumptions* (i), (ii), *and* (iii) *of theorem 1 and the further assumption* $\pi y_k^* > \pi y_k^o$, *then:* $\pi^o y_k^o = \pi^o y_k^m$.

Proof. Suppose not: $\pi^o y_k^o > \pi^o y_k^m$.

Substitute y_k^o for $y_k^{\bar{a}}$ in the proof of theorem 1.

There must exist a point $y(\alpha)$ in E_k^R such that $\pi y(\alpha) > \pi y_k^o$. Hence y_k^o is not a maximizer on E_k^R for π. This contradiction proves the corollary.

Remark 2. Let (i) $\hat{\hat{Y}}_k$ be convex. (ii) If $y_k' \in G_k$, then $y_k \in G_k$ where $y_k \geq y_k'$. Then $y_k^{\bar{a}} \in \hat{E}_k$, where $\hat{E}_k$ is the set of boundary points of E_k.

Proof. Suppose not. Then $y_k^{\bar{a}}$ is an interior point of $\hat{\hat{Y}}_k$, and, by (ii), there exists another point $y_k^{\bar{\bar{a}}}$ in $\hat{E}_k$ such that $y_k^{\bar{\bar{a}}} \gg y_k^{\bar{a}}$ and $\pi y_k^{\bar{\bar{a}}} > \pi y_k^{\bar{a}}$. Hence $\pi y_k^{\bar{a}} \neq \max_{y_k \in E_k} \pi y_k$, a violation of the definition of $y_k^{\bar{a}}$. By the same reasoning, y_k^o is a boundary point of $\hat{\hat{Y}}_k$.

II. ADDITIONAL DEFINITIONS, STATEMENT AND PROOF OF COROLLARY 2 TO THEOREM 1

The initial assumptions are those used in theorem 1 plus assumption (ii) of remark 2.

The subscript k is omitted in identifying production programs and production sets for the kth enterprise.

Let the vector π^o be partitioned into q subvectors $\pi^{1o}, \ldots, \pi^{io}, \ldots, \pi^{qo}$ and form the aggregation matrix Π^o:

$$
\begin{bmatrix}
\pi^{1o} & & & & & & \\
 & \cdot & & & & 0 & \\
 & & \cdot & & & & \\
 & & & \pi^{io} & & & \\
 & 0 & & & \cdot & & \\
 & & & & & \cdot & \\
 & & & & & & \pi^{qo}
\end{bmatrix}
$$

For any subvector π^{io}, we may project any vector y in $\hat{\hat{Y}}$ to those coordinates for which π^{io} is defined, to get y^i ($i = 1, \ldots, q$).

A vector of constrained supply $y^{\bar{a}}$, defined as in I(b), may then be partitioned into subvectors $(y^{1\bar{a}}, y^{2\bar{a}}, \ldots, y^{i\bar{a}}, \ldots, y^{q\bar{a}})$.

Consider the set $\hat{\hat{Y}}_i^{\bar{a}}$ of vectors $y_i^{\bar{a}}$ defined as follows:

$$\hat{\hat{Y}}_i^{\bar{a}} = \{y_i^{\bar{a}} = (y^{1\bar{a}}, y^{2\bar{a}}, \ldots, y^i, \ldots, y^{q\bar{a}}) | y_i^{\bar{a}} \in \hat{\hat{Y}}_k\}.$$

Thus, every subvector but the ith in any vector $\hat{\hat{y}}_i^{\bar{a}}$ in $\hat{\hat{Y}}_i^{\bar{a}}$ is set at its level in $y^{\bar{a}}$. The elements of the ith subvector may take on any value as long as $y_i^{\bar{a}}$ is in $\hat{\hat{Y}}_k$.

We also define $E_i^{\bar{a}}$ as follows:

$$E_i^{\bar{a}} = \{y_i^{\bar{a}} = (y^{1\bar{a}}, y^{2\bar{a}}, \ldots, y^i, \ldots, y^{q\bar{a}}) | y_i^{\bar{a}} \in E_k\}.$$

By construction $\hat{\hat{Y}}_i^{\bar{a}} \subseteq \hat{\hat{Y}}$, $E_i^{\bar{a}} \subseteq E$, and $E_i^{\bar{a}} \subseteq \hat{\hat{Y}}_i^{\bar{a}}$. Also the imposition of constraints on convex $\hat{\hat{Y}}$ to generate $\hat{\hat{Y}}_i^{\bar{a}}$ implies that $Y_i^{\bar{a}}$ must also be convex (as the intersection of convex sets).

We now let $\hat{\hat{Y}}^{i\bar{a}}$ and $E^{i\bar{a}}$ be the projections of $\hat{\hat{Y}}_i^{\bar{a}}$ and $E_i^{\bar{a}}$ on the coordinates defined by π^{io}.

Let y^{i*} be a maximizer for π^i on $\hat{\hat{Y}}^{i\bar{a}}$ and y^{ia} be a maximizer for π^i on $E^{i\bar{a}}$.

It is clear that $\pi^i y^{ia} = \pi^i y^{i\bar{a}}$, where $y^{i\bar{a}}$ is the subvector of $y^{\bar{a}}$ corresponding to the coordinates of π^{io} (since $E_i^{\bar{a}} \subseteq E_k$, a maximizer for π on E must also be a maximizer for π on $E_i^{\bar{a}}$).

For the "cut" corresponding to $\hat{\hat{Y}}^{i\bar{a}}$, we now define y^{im}, $E^{i\bar{a}R}$, and y^{io}, equivalent to the definitions in I(c) and (d) for the entire set $\hat{\hat{Y}}_k$:

$$y_{(\pi)}^{im} = \{y^{im} | \pi^{io} y^{im} \leq \pi^{io} y^i ; y^i \in E_k^{i\bar{a}}\}$$

$$E_k^{i\bar{a}R} = \{y^i | \pi^{io} y^i \geq \pi^{io} y^{im} ; y^i \in Y_k^{i\bar{a}}\}$$

$$y_{(\pi)}^{io} = \{y^{io} | \pi^i y^{io} = \max \pi^i y^i ; y^i \in E_k^{i\bar{a}R}\}.$$

Note that y^{io} is not necessarily identical with the ith vector in y^o.

Finally, we define $y^{o\bar{a}}$ as the vector $(y^{1\bar{a}}, y^{2\bar{a}}, \ldots, y^{io}, \ldots, y^{q\bar{a}})$.

COROLLARY TO THEOREM 1.   *If* (i) $\pi^i y^{i*} > \pi^i y^{ia}$, (ii) $\pi^{io} y^{im} \neq \pi^{io} y^{ia}$, *then* $\pi y^{o\bar{a}} > \pi y^{\bar{a}}$.

Proof. For the sets $\hat{\hat{Y}}^{i\bar{a}}$, $E^{i\bar{a}}$, and $E^{i\bar{a}R}$, all the conditions are satisfied for theorem 1. Hence:

$$\pi^i y^{io} > \pi^i y^{ia} = \pi^i y^{i\bar{a}}.$$

It therefore follows that:

$$\pi y^{o\bar{a}} = \pi^1 y^{1\bar{a}} + \pi^2 y^{2\bar{a}} + \cdots + \pi^i y^{io} + \cdots + \pi^q y^{q\bar{a}} > \pi y^{\bar{a}}. \quad \text{Q.E.D.}$$

Appendix C

I. The analysis on pp. 104–05 rests on the strong assumption that y_k^* and y_k^{R*}, the unconstrained maximizers for π on $\hat{\hat{Y}}$ and $\hat{\hat{Y}}^R$ respectively, lie outside E_k^R and $E_k^{\hat{R}}$ for every k. Owing to this assumption, we were able to confine our analysis to points in the aggregate set on the hyperplane $\pi^o y$ through $y^{\bar{m}}$. Can this assumption be relaxed? For one subcase of this problem—where y_l^* was in E_l before the reform and $y_l^* = y_l^{R*}$—only a trivial modification of the model is required. We need only redefine $y^{\bar{m}}$, the point through which the hyperplane $\pi^o y$ must pass in the aggregate set, as $\sum_{k=1}^{K_1} y_k^m + \sum_{l=1}^{K_2} y_l^*$, $(k = 1, \ldots, K_1; l = 1, \ldots, K_2)$ where K_1 is the number of enterprises with production sets such that the unconstrained maximizer on each of these sets was not in E_k and K_2 is the number with production sets such that the unconstrained maximizers before the reform were in E_l and $y_l^* = y_l^{R*}$ ($K_1 + K_2$ being equal to K).

If y_l^{R*} differs from y_l^* for one or more enterprises in the second group, the analysis of the effects of the reform becomes more complicated. The following construction, however, may provide at least a theoretical basis for solving the problem. We first construct a set $\hat{\hat{Y}}^*$ differing from $\hat{\hat{Y}}$ only for the subset of K_l enterprises where y_l^{R*} is in E_l^R but is not on the hyperplane $\pi^o y_l$ through y_l^m. The set $\hat{\hat{Y}}^*$ equals $\sum_{k=1}^{K_k} \hat{\hat{Y}}_k + \sum_{l=1}^{K_l} \hat{\hat{Y}}_l^R$ ($K_k + K_l = K$).

Now the effects of the reform may be decomposed into two parts. First a "move" from y^{o*} (equal to $\sum_{k=1}^{K_k} y_k^o + \sum_{l=1}^{K_l} y_l^*$) to y^{oR*}, defined as $\sum_{k=1}^{K_k} y_k^o + \sum_{l=1}^{K_l} y_l^{R*}$; then another "move" from y^{oR*} to $y^{\hat{o}}$. If y^{o*} was acceptable, there is some likelihood that y^{oR*} would also be acceptable (since the distortion of the output-mix under the influence of incentive prices stopped short of the constraints imposed by the aggregation hyperplanes). The critical move will then be from y^{oR*} to $y^{\hat{o}}$, which may be analyzed as follows:

We expand $\hat{\hat{Y}}^*$ by adding all the increments (or decrements) to the sets $\hat{\hat{Y}}_k$ induced by the redistribution of inputs ($k = 1, \ldots, K_k$), and thereby generate $\hat{\hat{Y}}^R$. To trace the differential effect of reform-through-aggregation,

119

we may now confine our attention to programs on the hyperplane $\pi^o y$ passing through a new point $y^{\bar{m}*}$ in $\hat{\hat{Y}}^R$ defined as $\sum_{k=1}^{K_k} y_k^m + \sum_{l=1}^{K_l} y_l^{R*}$. The success or failure of this aspect of the reform will again turn on the "direction" of the expansion of the sets $\hat{\hat{Y}}_k$, associated with enterprises whose incentive prices induced them to distort their output-mix (at least from the prereform viewpoint of their ministry).

This rather awkward procedure for analyzing the effects of the reform may be warranted by the potential importance of this "mixed case," which is even more likely to occur if aggregation and/or incentive prices were centrally revised at the time the reform was launched. For, to the extent that this revision lessened the disparity between the interests of enterprise managers and the preferences of the head, the chances that the unconstrained maximizers of some enterprises both before and after the expansion of their production sets would be acceptable to their hierarchic superiors would be enhanced. The same remark applies to any change in the system of aggregation prices or of incentive prices that would tend to bring the two systems more closely in line with each other.

II. Suppose that $E_{(\bar{o})}^{\hat{R}}$ was seeded by $y_k^{(\bar{o})}$ and $E_{(o)}^R$ by $y_k^{(o)}$ and $y_k^{(\bar{o})} \neq y_k^{(o)}$. Consider the intersection of $E_{(\bar{o})}^R$ and $\hat{Y}_k$. This set, which we may denote $E_{(\bar{o})}^R$, will differ from $E_{(o)}^R$, seeded by $y_k^{(o)}$, since the latter is not identical with $y_k^{(\bar{o})}$. Let $y_{\bar{o}k}^o$ be a maximizer for π on $E_{(\bar{o})}^R$ and $y_{\bar{o}}^o$ be the sum of these maximizers for all K enterprises. In case the subvector $y_{\bar{o}}^{io}$, the projection of $y_{\bar{o}}^o$ for the coordinates for which π^{io} is defined, differs from y^{io}, the corresponding projection of y^o (equal to $\sum_{k=1}^K y_k^o$), then we shall assume that $y_{\bar{o}}^{io}$ is unacceptable to the head, just as y^{io} was assumed to be in the original problem (that is, both $y_{\bar{o}}^{io}$ and y^{io} are assumed to be subvectors of unacceptable programs). This assumption makes it possible to analyze the pre- and post-reform attainable-and-acceptable sets generated by the same program $y_k^{(\bar{o})}$ for every k and thus to compare $y_{\bar{o}}^{io}$ and $y^{i\bar{o}}$ on the same hyperplane $\pi^{io} y^i$ through $y^{i\bar{m}}$.

Glossary of Terms

There are H ministries under the head. A ministry is identified by the superscript h or, if necessary to simplify the notation, by the subscript h. There are K_h enterprises under ministry h and K enterprises in the complete hierarchy. An enterprise is identified by the subscript k or l.

A superscript placed before a symbol denoting a vector or a set of vectors refers to the nomenclature of the commodity list in that vector or set of vectors. Superscript 3, for example, signifies that the nomenclature in question is that of tier 3 (a list of n_3 elements).

$\hat{Y}$ — the attainable set for the complete hierarchy, given the resources available to the hierarchy.

$\hat{\hat{Y}}_k, \hat{\hat{Y}}^h, \hat{\hat{Y}}$ — fully constrained sets for k, h, and the head.

$$\hat{\hat{Y}}^h = \sum_{k=1}^{K_h} \hat{\hat{Y}}_k \quad \text{and} \quad \hat{\hat{Y}} = \sum_{h=1}^{H} \hat{\hat{Y}}^h$$

$\hat{Y}, \hat{Y}^h, \hat{Y}_k$ — efficiency frontiers of $\hat{\hat{Y}}, \hat{\hat{Y}}^h$, and $\hat{\hat{Y}}_k$.

π — a vector of incentive prices.

π^o — a vector of aggregation prices.

y_k^* — a maximizer on Y_k for prices π.

G, G^h, G_k — acceptable sets for the head, for a ministry, and for an enterprise.

E, E^h, E_k — sets of acceptable vectors in $\hat{\hat{Y}}, \hat{\hat{Y}}^h$, and $\hat{\hat{Y}}_k$ respectively.

E_h^R, E_k^R — sets of acceptable vectors in $\hat{\hat{Y}}^h$ and $\hat{\hat{Y}}_k$ after the reform.

$\hat{E}$ — the intersection of E and $\hat{Y}$.

$\hat{E}_h^D, \hat{E}_k^D$ — the decomposed sets of $\hat{E}$ for h and k.

$y_k^{\bar{a}}$ — a maximizer for π on E_k.

y_k^e — an arbitrary vector in E_k.

y_k^o — a maximizer for π on E_k^R.

y_k^D — a maximizer on $\hat{E}_k^D$ for π.

y_k^m — a minimizer for π^o on E_k.

${}^3 v_k^h$ — a vector of allotments by ministry h to enterprise k expressed in the nomenclature of tier 3.

${}^3 v_{kj}^h$ — the jth element in ${}^3 v_k^h$.

121

$^3\omega_k$ a nonnegative resource vector of n_3 elements assigned to enterprise k.

λ a vector of n_3 price-weights used to map vectors from R^{n_3} to R^{n_2}.

λ_i the ith subvector of λ ($i = 1, \ldots, n_2$).

Λ a matrix of prices or quasi prices mapping vectors in R^{n_3} into R^{n_2} ($n_2 < n_3$).

Π^o a matrix of prices or quasi prices mapping vectors in R^{n_2} into R^q ($q < n_2$).

π^{io} the ith subvector of π^o.

π^i the ith subvector of π.

Note: The subscript k is omitted in all the definitions from $y^{i\bar{a}}$ to y^{io} below.

$y^{i\bar{a}}$ the ith subvector of $y^{\bar{a}}$.

$y_i^{\bar{a}}$ a vector, all of whose subvectors are equal to the corresponding subvectors of $y^{\bar{a}}$, except for the ith, which can assume any value compatible with $y_i^{\bar{a}}$ being in $\hat{\hat{Y}}$.

$\hat{\hat{Y}}_i^{\bar{a}}$ the set of vectors $y_i^{\bar{a}}$ in $\hat{\hat{Y}}$.

$E_i^{\bar{a}}$ the set of vectors $y_i^{\bar{a}}$ in E.

$\hat{\hat{Y}}^{i\bar{a}}$ the projection of the set $\hat{\hat{Y}}_i^{\bar{a}}$ on the coordinates defined by π^{io}.

$E^{i\bar{a}}$ the projection of the set $E_i^{\bar{a}}$ on the coordinates defined by π^{io}.

y^{im} a minimizer for π^{io} on $E^{i\bar{a}}$.

y^{ia} a maximizer for π^i on $E^{i\bar{a}}$.

$E^{i\bar{a}R}$ the set of vectors y^i such that $\pi^{io}y^i \geq \pi^{io}y^{im}$ where y^i is in $Y^{i\bar{a}}$.

y^{io} a maximizer for π^i on $E^{i\bar{a}R}$.

$\hat{\hat{Y}}_k^R, \hat{\hat{Y}}^R$ fully constrained production sets after the postreform expansion.

y_k^{R*}, y^{R*} maximizers for π on $\hat{\hat{Y}}_k^R$ and $\hat{\hat{Y}}^R$.

$E_k^{\hat{R}}$ the postexpansion postreform acceptable set of h for k.

$y_k^{\hat{o}}$ a maximizer for π on $E_k^{\hat{R}}$.

$y^{\hat{o}}$ the sum of the maximizers $y_k^{\hat{o}}$ taken over all K enterprises.

$y^{\bar{m}}$ the sum of the minimizers y_k^m taken over all K enterprises.

$y^{\neq}$ a maximizer for π on $\hat{E}$.

$\hat{\hat{E}}$ $\displaystyle\sum_{k=1}^{K} \hat{E}_k^D.$

y^D $\displaystyle\sum_{k=1}^{K} y_k^D.$

4

Concentration Amid Devolution in East Germany's Reforms

MICHAEL KEREN

The 1960s ushered in two types of economic reforms in Eastern Europe. The more familiar one is the market socialist reform of Hungary and 1967–68 Czechoslovakia. The second type, the experiment in reformed centralism of the German Democratic Republic (GDR), has received much less attention in the West. Unlike the Hungarian reforms, which severed many links between the enterprise and the top of the planning beaurocracy, the New Economic System (NES) of East Germany has kept the allocation hierarchy intact but tried to introduce meaningful changes into its mode of operation. This route is much less risky for the political authorities, and this is what lends importance to the reforms: should they prove workable and seem to produce favorable results, the NES, rather than the new Hungarian mechanism, will be the blueprint which others will follow in Eastern Europe.

In common with the market-socialist reforms, the NES delegated functions to lower rungs of the hierarchy, including the enterprise; but any such delegation was clearly to be within the directions given from above. The term "market" was carefully avoided, so as not to give the impression that central direction might be eliminated from any sphere of allocation. At the same time the concentration drive—the drive to create bigger and fewer enterprises—not only continued but accelerated. In this the reformers of the NES differed radically from their Hungarian counterparts, who were concerned with the high degree of concentration of their industry.

This paper focuses on the changes in the organization of East German industry. Particular attention is paid to the problems of concentration. Is the concentration drive an aberration on the part of GDR planners? Is it

I am grateful to Bedřich Levčik, whose perceptive comments were invaluable for the revision of this paper; to Gert Leptin for detailed comments and illuminating discussions; to Kurt Erdmann, Friedrich Haffner, and Harry Trend for valuable discussions; and to the Osteuropa Institut at the Free University of Berlin, the Research Department of Radio Free Europe at Munich, and the Gesamtdeutsches Institut at Bonn for granting me access to their valuable material.

megalomania, bigness for bigness's sake? I do not think so. The optimal degree of concentration cannot be studied in vacuo, apart from the mode of operation of the resource allocation mechanism and in neglect of the particular environment in which the enterprise, or firm, functions. Part I attempts to construct a theoretical model to examine the optimal degree of concentration in different environments. Its conclusions are that there are more advantages to concentration, and fewer to dispersion, in a centralized than a decentralized economy. Microeconomic efficiency has been most widely discussed in the context of the market economy; hence the market economy serves as a yardstick for both the centralized and (to a lesser extent) the market socialist models.

The model of part I provides a convenient framework within which the reform measures are presented and evaluated in part II. Where relevant, the Hungarian experience is compared to that of the GDR.

I. THE FRAMEWORK

The model which is constructed below is designed to shed light on the problem of the optimal degree of concentration. The term "concentration," as used here, has to be elucidated first. The unit whose degree of concentration is of interest here is the enterprise, the decision-making unit which has legal custody of commodities, the lowest unit which is on *khozraschot*. Concentration on the enterprise level is clearly not the same thing as concentration on the plant level, the plant being the unit on whose level actual production takes place. The two, nonetheless, are usually related.

Next, there are various measures of concentration, and given patterns of dispersion of industry may be ranked differently by differing measures. The assumptions of the model presented below will lead to enterprises of identical size for each industry. This being so, the relevant measure of concentration here is some decreasing function of the number of enterprises. Thus the number of enterprises determines the degree of concentration.

Suppose an economy is faced with the problem of how many enterprises should be entrusted with production in a given industry. Two sets of considerations will influence the optimal number of producing units. The first relates to potential output, which is dependent on the number of units if there are economies or diseconomies of scale. The second relates to the actual use made of the potential: the fewer the enterprises in a market economy, the more likely is the abuse of monopoly power, and the poorer actual performance as against potential. These two (possibly conflicting) considerations are among those which help determine the optimum number of independent producers in an industry. This is not to say that the static number of units in an industry is the only, or even the most important, factor influencing market behavior. The dynamic aspect of the actual or potential change in the population of units—the problem of exit and entry—may be more important. But the two are closely related, and greater weight is given here to the former problem only because it is more amenable to analysis in the present context.[1]

In what follows the units comprising the economy are first presented. An analysis of the optimum number of enterprises follows, with factors determining the potential of the economy discussed first and those relevant to allocative efficiency coming next.[2] The final section discusses the combined effects of both types of factors.

I.1. The Participants

The participants[3] in our economy are producing enterprises (or firms), distributing enterprises, and a governmental hierarchy. We shall not be concerned with consumers as such; the governmental hierarchy is assumed to have desires with respect to the basket of goods which will be available for consumption (and investment) as a result of the interaction of the participants. These desires may be based on consumers' tastes, but we shall not be concerned with the relation between the two. We shall also disregard the production of public goods, particularly those self-produced by government agencies which have little similarity to enterprises (such as armies and police forces).

The links between the participants are the variables of the model. In the centralized case the enterprises are an integral part of the governmental hierarchy: they constitute its lowest tier. In the capitalist market there are no official hierarchical links between the government and the enterprises; the former guides production through rules, or laws, and taxation. Market socialism stands in between: the subordination of enterprises is restricted to a limited sphere of activities, particularly those related to capital expenditures.

The producing enterprise consists of a managing unit and one or several plants. If enterprises in all systems have access to the same technologies, there is no reason to assume different production functions for their plants.[4]

1. Cf. Aubrey Silberston, "Price Behaviour of Firms," *Economic Journal* 80, no. 319 (September 1970), particularly pp. 560–67. The neglect of the entry problem in the first version of this paper was criticized by Professor Pejovich and, indirectly, by Dr. Levčík, who has brought this article to my attention.

2. The use of the term "allocative efficiency" to describe the partial effect of market structure alone on efficiency follows H. Leibenstein, "Allocative Efficiency vs. X-Efficiency," *American Economic Review* 56, no. 3 (June 1966): 392. The problem dealt with below is, however, more akin to that treated by O. E. Williamson, "Economics as an Antitrust Defence: The Welfare Tradeoffs," *American Economic Review* 58, no. 1 (March 1968): 18.

3. This term and others in the following analysis are based on T. C. Koopmans and J. M. Montias, "On the Description and Comparison of Economic Systems," in *Comparisons of Economic Systems*, ed. A. Eckstein (Berkeley: University of California Press, 1971), pp. 27–78.

4. This point was forcefully made by Dr. Levčík and others in the discussion at the Conference.

The mode of operation of the managing unit may differ. The enterprise is assumed to be led by a manager who is motivated by some simple objective, like maximization of money income (although we are fully aware that the true facts are much more complex). The manager makes decisions on production in his enterprise on the basis of impulses received from outside; in the centralized system the impulses are plans (which he may obey or disobey) *and* prices,[5] and in the market systems they are prices or demand and supply functions. Of all the units in the economy, enterprises are most alike across the systems. They differ in their interaction with the institutional environment, but are potentially alike in their internal functioning.

What differs most in the three systems is the governmental hierarchy. The centralized hierarchy encompasses the whole economy and all participants of the system are its parts. We shall divide the hierarchy into two or three levels in this chapter: the enterprise and the top, or the enterprise, the industrial administration, and the top, where the industrial administration is the hierarchical tier which is assumed to be the immediate superior of all enterprises producing the same products. The head, the chairman of the State Planning Commission, organizes the hierarchy and draws up plans so as to produce a satisfactory bundle of goods and services. In the capitalist market economy the hierarchy will comprise a very small part of the government, meaning here perhaps some parts of the Department of Commerce and the trust busters of the Department of Justice in the United States, or parts of the Board of Trade and the Ministry of Technology in the United Kingdom. In the capitalist market economy, the head is too concerned with the production of the most satisfactory bundle of goods and services. The market-socialist regime will have a hierarchy which reaches down to the enterprise, but it will be far less ramified than its centralist counterpart.

The distributive sector has a more important role in the market economies than in the centralized system. In both it has to serve as a bridge between producer and consumer, bringing goods when and where they are needed from where they are produced. Its tasks also include dividing (or assembling) consignments from the size convenient to producers to that which consumers demand. These functions require the holding of inventories. In the capitalist market it has other important roles: it provides services of arbitrage and speculation, and financial and consumer services, which are lacking in centralized economies. In the centralized economy this function, so far as it is carried out in the official (non-*tolkatch*) market, is exercised on the instructions of the central hierarchy. It may require the availability of risk capital on short notice, and hence may be quite difficult to decentralize when credit is centralized, as in market socialism. The financial market is

5. Cf. Edward Ames, "The Structure of General Equilibrium in a Planned Economy," in *Jahrbuch der Wirtschaft Osteuropas*, ed. H. Raupach, vol. 1 (Munich: Olzog, 1970), p. 15.

quite a different creature when the rights of ownership of means of production are unlimited and can be traded. Even the intermediary role of banking is much more limited when, as in market socialism, credit is highly centralized. Furthermore, the capitalist distributor, particularly the retailer, provides many more services with the goods he sells; he brings the goods much closer to the consumer, as G. Ofer puts it in his study of Soviet services.[6] Retail trade (and banking) services may sometime come nearer the consumer in the socialist market. When this happens the weight of distribution will grow.

To sum up: when all other things are equal, a centralized economy is likely to spend a higher proportion of resources on the government hierarchy and a lower proportion on the distributive sector, than a market economy. A market-socialist economy should emerge in between.[7]

1.2. The Production Function of Plans

The government hierarchy's goal is to produce good plans with the least expenditure of resources (here assumed to consist only of labor). The activity of the hierarchy[8] consists of observing the environment, transmitting information up the hierarchy, storing it, calculating responses to external impulses, and conveying instructions down the arcs of the hierarchy.

Let us portray the hierarchy as a directed tree as in figure 4.1, in which each node represents a member, and each directed arc the line of subordination. We shall assume that messages flow in both directions through the arcs alone (this assumption is relaxed in section 1.6). The capacity of each member of the hierarchy is limited. Each computation, decision, or observation uses some part of this capacity, and each message uses some part of the capacities of both transmitter and receiver. The greater the stress on the capacity of the node, the less efficient its performance; under greater stress, messages take longer to transmit and are garbled on the way, and computations grow less exact. All other things being equal, an overloaded hierarchy will prepare a plan that is likely to lead to the production of a less satisfactory bundle of goods than one that is not working under such a stress. The workload of a planning hierarchy depends on the number and complexity of the problems it has to solve. How many problems it must solve

6. Gur Ofer, "The Service Sector in the Soviet Union" (Ph.D. diss., Harvard University, 1968).

7. Ofer's revealing study shows that the Soviet system manages to spend less labor resources on the service sector, including both government and distribution, than the market system. A partial explanation provided by him is that the Soviet system manages not to provide certain services. May it also be that bureaucratic administration of the economy is cheaper than the "invisible" hand of the market?

8. Edward Ames, *Soviet Economic Processes* (Homewood: R. D. Irwin, 1965), ch. 14, has a discussion of the work of the planning hierarchy which is, in some respects, similar to the following.

depends in part on the number of producing agencies and on the number of problems that have to be settled for each producer (that is, for each enterprise). The complexity of the problems also depends on the interrelations of the problems.

Growing pressure on the hierarchy means growing pressure on each node. This pressure can be alleviated by the creation of an intermediate tier which takes upon itself some of the decisions formerly made by a superior node. This is illustrated by figure 4.1. The original hierarchy consists of the superior, s, and subordinates a to e. A new tier, consisting of p and q is then created; p and q are subordinate to s, and each supervises some of his

Fig. 4.1.   *Left*, original hierarchy; *right*, hierarchy with additional tier

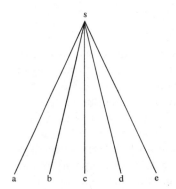 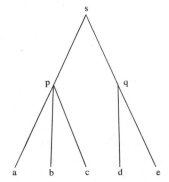

original five subordinates. The members of the new tier make some of the decisions and calculations formerly done by s himself; they also sift the information transferred to him. His workload is reduced. The costs associated with this reorganization are of two types: the direct costs of the additional resources manning the new tier, the indirect costs of more noise in the information flowing in the hierarchy, and an increasing need for coordination and supervision of the subordinates. The overall problem-solving process may be speeded up and the number of messages flowing through the arcs of the hierarchy may grow; but there may be added distortion of the information flowing up and the orders flowing down, both because of the longer line of communication and because an essential element in the devolution of authority is further aggregation and coarsening of information.[9] If our measure of the capacity of a hierarchy is its ability to produce good decisions, decisions that lead to the production of a satisfactory bundle of goods, we find that this capacity cannot be expanded without limit, using a given

9. Cf. J. M. Montias's contribution in this volume, particularly p. 74 and n. 11.

technology of administration. In other words, the marginal costs of increasing this capacity will increase rapidly, and may approach infinity at a finite capacity.

It is a consequence of the administrative production process that each problem considered by the hierarchy and each decision generated by it has a cost. This cost is not necessarily felt in terms of the increased resources required for planning but is often felt in terms of a delay in attending to other business or in attending to it less efficiently. Decisions which often receive insufficient attention relate to investment activities.

The incremental costs of any problem depend both on the problem itself—its importance, measured perhaps by the number of tiers it has to climb to be answered, and its complexity—and on the load of work all other problems impose on the hierarchy. The greater the load, the higher the incremental costs. To put it symbolically: let Q be the set of questions flowing through the hierarchy at any point of time, and $1, \ldots, q - 1 \in Q$, and let $h(q)$, $q \in Q$, measure (in a highly simplified way) the difficulty of the question, where $h(q) = h(t_q, m_q)$, and t_q measures its importance by the number of tiers, t, that q has to climb (where tiers are counted from below), and m measures its complexity (e.g. by the number of items the decisions have to include). Then $e(q)$ is the incremental costs of the qth problem, and

$$e(q) = f[h(q); h(1), \ldots, h(q - 1)],$$

where both h and f are increasing with respect to their arguments, the latter very rapidly, possibly shooting to infinity within the finite and relevant range of q.

The problems that arise in the hierarchy are bound up with the activity of enterprises. Some are not related to the number of enterprises. But some arise because production tasks have to be parceled out among enterprises, and others arise from the need to coordinate the activities of enterprises. With fewer and stronger enterprises, some of these problems might become intra-enterprise problems and be solved at the enterprise level. Thus the number of problems with which the hierarchy must deal may fall with fewer enterprises.

The difficulty of the problems depends on the method of plan construction, that is, on the level at which each detail of the plan is settled (t), and on the detail of the plan, the complexity (m) of the message conveying the plan to the enterprise. Thus the cost of planning is an increasing function of the number of enterprises, and a reduction in their number, by amalgamation, may free resources and improve the quality of the plan. A similar effect can be gained by a reduction in the detail of the plan.

The managing unit of a bigger enterprise which replaces several smaller ones will be faced with the same coordinating tasks which the extraenterprise hierarchy has faced prior to the amalgamation. It will reduce the work load of the top only if it solves some of the problems which used to go higher up (only if it reduces t). If most coordination requirements are with enterprises outside the amalgamated firm, there may be little chance to reduce the top's administrative pressure. Even when this is possible, the pressure will decrease only if the managing unit has both the capacity and the incentive to make decisions formerly made by superiors. The capacity of the amalgamated unit may be larger than that of the separate enterprises because of indivisibilities in administrative functions: the larger unit offers an opportunity for further divisions of labor. Thus there may be some economies of scale in small administrative units, at the same time that there are diseconomies in large ones. Furthermore, coordination among the enterprises may be simplified by the amalgamation; the reasons for this were dealt with thoroughly by Coase in 1937.[10] If there are also returns to scale on the plant level amalgamation may uncover them if it leads to concentrating production in fewer plants. Experience has shown that these potential savings in material and administrative costs are not always reaped in practice (see section II.2).

In what follows, *returns to scale* refers to the combined effect on administrative and material costs of an increase in enterprise size.

In the capitalist market the hierarchy tries to influence enterprise behavior by direct intervention in the market only where, in its view, market coordination is failing. The more often this happens, the more it will spend resources on directing microeconomic activity. But market failure is more likely in concentrated industries, so that few large enterprises may be more likely to present it with problems than many smaller ones.[11] Thus the optimal hierarchy will be smaller and more efficient when the enterprises are many.

In market socialism the hierarchy acts as the board of directors of all enterprises, evaluating their work and participating in their investment decisions. But the number of problems which each enterprise poses is much smaller than in the centralized system. Furthermore, large enterprises and concentrated industries may here, too, require more attention than enterprises in splintered industries. Thus once again market socialism occupies the middle ground.

I.3. The Distributive Sector

The division of labor between the distributive sector and the productive sector may depend on the number of enterprises. Small enterprises may

10. R. H. Coase, "The Nature of the Firm," *Economica*, n.s. 4 (1937): 386–405. Reprinted in *Readings in Price Theory*, ed. Stigler and Boulding (Chicago: R. D. Irwin, 1952), pp. 331–51. I am grateful to Professor Balassa who has brought this article to my attention.

11. The other side of the coin is that in splintered industries the collection of information and the creation of lines of communication with enterprises is so difficult that the hierarchy may not have the stamina to deal with them.

have to buy from retail or wholesale outlets what larger enterprises buy directly from the producer. The large enterprise performs for itself some of the services which the smaller enterprise purchases. It may also have some real savings because it does not need to break large consignments into small orders; in a market economy it may have additional savings due to a better bargaining position. These different division lines between the sectors are taken into account if, in measuring returns to scale (section 1.4), all higher costs of distribution, except the last, are included among operating costs. In other words, the costs of distribution to enterprises of differing sizes are assumed to be included in the production costs of the productive sector as higher input costs. Since the other functions of the distributive sector do not seem to be related to the size and number of enterprises, that sector, as such, will be omitted from the model in the following section.

1.4. Numbers and Potential Output

The previous sections have shown that given the detail of the plan and the mode of its formation, the number of enterprises in an economy may have an effect on its production potential. It will be seen below that it can also affect actual performance, and in an opposite direction; but here we shall be concerned with potential only.

A simple mathematical exposition will summarize the point. The planner has an industry, with given endowments of labor (L) and capital (K) to plan. His problem is to find the optimal number of enterprises (n) to which these resources should be allotted, remembering that the amount of labor spent on the planning operation (P) depends, in part, on the number of enterprises. All enterprises are assumed to be subject to the same production function, characterized by diminishing returns and homogeneity of degree σ. Thus for any enterprise i, whose output is Q_i,

$$Q_i = F(K_i, L_i), \qquad F_K, F_L > 0, \qquad F_{KK} \text{ and } F_{LL} < 0,$$

where the subscripts denote partial derivatives, and, for $\alpha > 0$,

$$F(\alpha K_i, \alpha L_i) = \alpha^\sigma F(K_i, L_i).$$

The sameness of the production function and diminishing returns ensure that, to maximize output, all enterprises should be of identical scale, with the available supplies of labor and capital divided equally between them. Thus, for any enterprises i and j,

$$L_i = L_j, \qquad K_i = K_j, \qquad i, j = 1, \ldots, n,$$

or

$$K_i = \frac{K}{n} \quad \text{and} \quad L_i = \frac{L - P}{n}, \qquad i = 1, \ldots, n$$

where $n = 1, 2, \ldots$. The planner wishes to maximize the homogeneous output, Q:

$$Q = \sum_{i=1}^{n} Q_i = nF\left(\frac{K}{n}, \frac{L - P(n)}{n}\right) = n^{1-\sigma}F(K, L - P(n)).$$

The optimum number of enterprises is an integer. It can, nevertheless, be approximated. Differentiating Q partially with respect to n,

$$\frac{\partial Q}{\partial n} = \frac{1 - \sigma}{n}Q - n^{1-\sigma}F_L P'$$

where P', the derivative of planning costs P with respect to the number of enterprises, depends on the economic system.

When $P' = 0$,

$$\frac{\partial Q}{\partial n} \gtreqqless 0 \quad \text{as} \quad \sigma \lesseqqgtr 1$$

for any number of enterprises. Thus when $\sigma > 1$—when there are increasing returns to scale—the smallest number of enterprises ($n = 1$) gives the highest total output. When $\sigma < 1$—when there are decreasing returns to scale—the largest number of enterprises, or $n \to \infty$, is most efficient. The case of $\sigma = 1$ is the watershed; here, as always with constant returns to scale, the optimum scale is indeterminate.

When $P' > 0$, as in the centralized system, the second term of the partial derivative is negative, and for $\partial Q/\partial n$ to vanish the first term has to be positive. In other words, only in the case of $\sigma < 1$, that is, of diminishing returns to scale, can there be an optimum number of enterprises different from one. In general, unless cases of diminishing returns to scale abound, the number of enterprises should be as small as possible.

In section 1.2 it was argued that in the capitalist market it may be the case that $P' < 0$. If this is so, then when there are constant returns or even slightly increasing returns to scale it may be useful to limit the size of enterprises. The socialist market, being in between, may be the case where $P' = 0$ (see above), where the advantages and disadvantages of concentration, as they pertain to the pressure on the hierarchy, just balance out.

1.5. Numbers and Performance

The evaluation of an industry's probable performance will be carried out by examining motive, opportunity and control.

Motive. The objective function of the manager determines which parameters he will try to manipulate in his favor. The capitalist profit-maximizing manager has prices as an obvious target. The market-socialist manager may have profits or the profit/wage ratio to maximize; in either case his motive is similar to that of the capitalist manager. The manager in the traditional Soviet firm, on the other hand, is subject to a very complex incentive system. He is not a simple maximizer of any static success indicator because of the ratchet effect. His objective function (in simplified terms) is to attain a given level of, let us say, output, with a minimum expenditure of effort. Thus the quantity index is the obvious object for his manipulation.

Opportunity. An enterprise must not be in a position to change those parameters which it may be motivated to manipulate, lest it damage resource allocation. An enterprise in the ideal competitive market is unable to change prices because of competition. In other words, common terms of sale are established in the market, terms which both seller and buyer can enforce because of the existence of alternatives: an enterprise cannot raise prices because the potential buyer can always go to another seller.

Arrow has argued that this restriction does not exist (even in a normally competitive market) when the system is out of equilibrium. Thus, when demand exceeds supply, any seller can raise his price above his competitors' level because they will not satisfy any extra demand at the ruling price. There is no reason to believe that the rate of price change by different sellers will be uniform. Rather, it will depend on bargaining between the parties to each transaction. In other words, the market is splintered into many small, bilateral markets, until it is reconstituted as a single uniform market when equilibrium is reapproached.[12] In the centralized economy the enterprise is always in a fragmented market. The traditional centralized supply system does not provide the enterprise, either seller or buyer, with an alternative: the *kontingente* (in the GDR), the *fondy* (in the Soviet Union), tie the buyer to a specific seller for a given quantity of output to be transacted at a fixed price, and create a situation of bilateral monopoly. The remaining terms of the transaction, the determination of the exact specification of the goods and of the time pattern of their delivery, have to be ironed out in bargaining between these monopolists. The outcome depends on their relative power, which does not depend on size in relation to the market: usually the seller, even though small, is stronger. Consequently a centralized system, relying on centralized supply, has less to fear of small numbers of enterprises because competition and performance are not much improved when there are large numbers.

It is not in the conflicts between enterprises that large numbers of them play a beneficial role in a centralized system, but in their effect on the latent clashes of interest between the top of the hierarchy and the enterprises. The hierarchy requires information to produce a good plan. Much of this information is in the hands of enterprises. Enterprises are obliged to provide

12. Cf. K. J. Arrow, "Towards a Theory of Price Adjustment," in M. Abramovitz et al., *The Allocation of Economic Resources* (Stanford: Stanford University Press, 1959), p. 46 f.

the hierarchy with full information, but they are tempted to falsify the information so as to influence the hierarchy to produce a plan to their liking. When the number of enterprises is large, superiors can compare the technological data they receive from various enterprises and thus get a more reliable estimate of the true parameters. With single-enterprise industries the technological data will always be more suspect. This, however, seems to be a much less important source of efficiency of large numbers of enterprises.[13]

Control. The aim of control is to create situations where each transactor has to accept terms of trade dictated from outside. In this the government can help either directly or indirectly; directly, by itself enforcing the terms of trade; indirectly, by helping the market enforce them through competition. In the latter case it has to see to it that a sufficient number of transactors are actually or potentially participating in any market. This may require trust busting and maintaining conditions of free entry. If these means are too costly or infeasible, the government itself may set terms of exchange, particularly prices. This raises certain unsolved problems: on what should prices be based—average or marginal costs? short-term or long-term costs?

In the centralized economy there is no place for the indirect setting of terms of trade. The remaining, direct, route requires that there be certain predefined terms, and that arbitration be provided for cases where the bilateral monopolists disagree on the interpretation of the terms for a given transaction. Usually price terms are not open to dispute; quality is. Thus whereas the "parametric role of prices" for any given good is flouted in capitalism when a party has market power, here it is used to change the goods themselves.

I.6. Conclusion: Concentration and Performance

Section I.4 showed that to maximize potential output the number of enterprises should be smaller for a centralized economy than for a market economy. Section I.5 showed that a market economy produces closer to its potential as the concentration of its industries is lowered. Thus, to maximize *actual* performance, an even larger number of enterprises than would maximize potential is required. In a centralized economy there are no forces linking many enterprises to a better exploitation of potential. Hence, all other things being equal, the number of enterprises should be larger in market than in nonmarket economies.[14]

13. Cf. Michael Keren, "Central Allocation of Resources Under Uncertainty" (Ph.D. diss., Yale University, 1968), section 3.7.2 and appendix C.

14. The present model can explain, in addition, the narrower range of consumers' goods, and the lack of flexibility of centralized economies. An increase in the number of items produced is also costly to a burdened hierarchy; the costs of planning an additional item may offset the benefits due to greater variety, leading to a tendency to restrict the gamut of goods produced. Similarly, when the information on whose basis a plan has been prepared changes, it will be costly to change the plan; in other words, a centralized hierarchy may not be too flexible.

It would be entirely misleading to conclude that concentration alone leads to greater efficiency in a centralized economy. Much of the advantage of concentration may be in the creation of units which are capable of decision making at the bottom of the planning hierarchy. This opens the possibility of alleviating the burden on the top of the hierarchy by delegating decision-making competence to its lower rungs. The problem here is that decisions need coordination, and coordination, if not effected by superiors, has to be obtained by horizontal information flows among branches of the hierarchy (which have so far been excluded from consideration).

There is, however, no magic in horizontal links. They can help coordination only if the aims of the parties are reconcilable. For this a proper incentive system and a proper system of scarcity prices are essential; it is possible that a certain amount of slack is also a precondition. How the reformed incentive and price systems figured in the GDR's New Economic System, and the role of the slack plans in the success of the reform, are the subject of the second half of part II. The first half surveys the concentration process, whose rationale was the subject of part I.

II. GDR: Reformed Centralism

Criticism of the economic machinery of the GDR has never been lacking, but it was not allowed to amount to wholesale rejection of the centralized allocation system, as it was in some other economically advanced countries of Eastern Europe.[15] Dissatisfaction with the system in the early 1960s was nurtured by the poor performance of the economy, indicated by the drop in the growth of net material product from over 10 percent per annum in 1958 and 1959 to a total growth of 8 percent in the three years 1961–63, with a near standstill in 1962.[16] Though other factors than the allocation mechanism may have been at fault, the system took part of the blame.

Much of the criticism directed against the prereform system can be summed up by saying that the upper tiers of the economic hierarchy were too busy with day-to-day decisions to be able to properly coordinate their actions with one another, especially as far as longer range plans were concerned. Furthermore, incentives and the price system did not make it easy to delegate decisions to lower tiers, particularly to the enterprise level. An increase in

15. Critics of the system who were too outspoken were soon censured. Consider the case of Behrens and Benary, as reported in Gert Leptin, "Das 'Neue ökonomische System' Mitteldeutschlands" [The "New Economic System" of middle Germany], in *Wirtschaftsreformen in Osteuropa*, ed. K. C. Thalheim and H. H. Höhmann (Cologne: Verlag Wissenschaft und Politik 1968), p. 113 f, or that of Kohlmey, a decade later, in P. Mitzscherling, "Zunehmender Dirigismus oder Ausbau des neuen ökonomischen Systems?" [Growing *dirigisme* or extension of the New Economic System?], *Vierteljahreshefte zur Wirtschaftsforschung*, 1969, no. 2, p. 252.

16. *Statistisches Jahrbuch der DDR 1968* [Statistical yearbook of the GDR, 1968], p. 17, and *Statistisches Jahrbuch der DDR 1969*, p. 39 (East Berlin: Staatsverlag der DDR, 1968 and 1969).

the planning capacity of the hierarchy was not an available solution, if the claims of the previous section are correct. Consequently the essence of the reform had to be a reduction in planning drudgery and a shift of much of the remaining routine work to lower levels of the hierarchy, leaving only directive and supervisory tasks in the hands of the upper tiers. The price and incentive systems had to be overhauled to make any devolution of functions possible, and to make it worthwhile by harmonizing the interests of the lower tiers with those of the economy at large as perceived by the upper tiers. The heart of the allocation system—the centralized material supply mechanism—was to remain, though here too some of the daily drudgery was shifted down the hierarchical ladder.

II.1. Streamlining the Hierarchy

The modern history of the GDR industrial hierarchy starts with the 1958 reorganization. The pre-1958 structure had the State Planning Committee (SPC) at the top, industrial ministries as the middle tier, and enterprises at the bottom. The ministries were abolished in 1958. Their *Hauptverwaltungen* ("main administrations," the equivalents of the Soviet *glavki*), each of which was responsible for an industrial branch, were renamed *Vereinigungen Volkseigener Betriebe* ("associations of people's own enterprises" [VVBs]).[17] Their other departments, of which the supply and the sales departments were most important, were merged into the SPC.[18]

The principal change in the hierarchy was the formation of strong VVBs in 1958. The authority of the VVB has expanded since its inception. In 1958 the VVB was instructed to cooperate with locally directed enterprises of its branch. True to the spirit of 1957–58, this step was combined with the transfer of some 500 enterprises, including important gas and power works, to local administration. This step was reversed with a vengeance with the advent of the New Economic System (NES) in 1963–64 when all enterprises with more than local significance were placed under the tutelage of the central VVBs. The VVBs were also instructed to coordinate the work of *all* enterprises in their industries, regardless of formal jurisdiction. In other words, each VVB was granted a formal monopoly position in its branch.

The strengthening of the VVBs answered the need to increase the authority of those parts of the hierarchy which were nearest production. In the language of the present paper, the aim was to increase the competence of the lower rungs of the hierarchy so that less information and fewer problems needed

17. Cf. Keren, sections 2.1 and 2.2. The term *Volkseigener Betrieb* is translated as "nationally owned enterprise" in official publications.

18. The SPC-VVB-enterprise structure lasted only until 1961. In that year the *Volkswirt-schaftsrat*, the German *Sovnarkhoz*, was hived off the SPC and was made responsible for operating the current plan. The *Volkswirtschaftsrat* was split into industrial ministries in 1966.

to travel up. This was to be one way of reducing planning drudgery at the top and of making decisions where the information was not yet too coarse (see note 9, above). The concentration of like enterprises under one roof, the VVB, made coordination by the top easier and reduced the loss of information through aggregation.

An interesting further step was taken when the NES put the VVB on *Wirtschaftliche Rechnungsführung* ("economic accounting" or *Khozraschet*). The VVBs were told to act like socialist holding companies and their personnel were given the same incentive system as enterprise workers; the final aim, by now attained, was that profits should be the principal incentive.

The VVBs are, of course, not holding companies. The holding company under this system is ultimately the state, represented by the complete hierarchy of which they are but a part. The meaning of the change was rather that a tier of the hierarchy was provided with a distinct success criterion, instead of the amorphous, indefinite criteria against which the performance of a unit of a hierarchy is usually evaluated. Now any functionary in a VVB knows what target to follow, rather than having to aim at some diffuse commonweal. This makes delegation of authority to the VVBs possible, since the VVBs now know which criteria to use when making decisions and need address fewer problems to the top of the hierarchy.

The fate of the industrial administration rung under the Hungarian reforms was quite different. Those industrial directorates which survived the concentration drive (see section II.2 below) were abolished, and several of the merged enterprises—trusts—were split up. The reasons for doing away with this level of the hierarchy were two. First, severing the existing links between the enterprise and the top forced the enterprise to make independent decisions.[19] Second, there was the fear that directorates and trusts would be tempted to make use of their monopolistic positions to subvert the freer price system.

II.2. The Concentration Process: An Overall View

The number of industrial enterprises in the GDR has been shrinking since the mid-1950s, while industrial output and, to a lesser extent, employment, have been expanding. This is true particularly of socialist enterprises, as table 4.1 shows.[20] Over a 13 year span the number of socialist enterprises has declined by over 50 percent, but the rate of decline was uneven: before 1968 it exceeded 6 percent during only two years, 1960 and 1964. Since 1968 the rate has been accelerating; the GDR has launched a concentration drive, a drive of combinate formation. A comparison to the concentration drives

19. This point was made by Professor Portes at the Conference.

20. The coverage of the term "industry" in GDR statistics has changed from time to time, and there is no consistent series separating cooperatives from state-owned industry both before and after 1968. The concentration trend may have been faster in state-owned industry.

TABLE 4.1. Index Numbers and Rate of Change in Number of Industrial
Enterprises in the GDR, 1955–70 (Selected years)

	Index of Number of Enterprises		Average Annual Rate of Change of Number of Enterprises	
Year	All Industry	Socialist Industry	All Industry	Socialist Industry
1955	100	100		
			−1.0	0
1957	98	100		
			−2.0	−3.0
1959	94	94		
			−4.5	−6.0
1960	90	88		
			−2.0	−2.5
1963	84	81		
			−3.5	−8.5
1964	81	74		
			−2.5	−4.0
1967	75	65		
			−4.0	−7.5
1968	72	60		
			−5.0	−12.5
1970	65	46		

Source: Statistisches Jahrbuch der DDR 1971, p. 99.
Note: The definition of "industrial enterprises" has changed several times since 1955, and the latest series, which brings us up to 1970, has been given only in index form, rounded to full percentage points.

TABLE 4.2. Industrial Enterprises in Hungary, 1960–70
(Selected years)

Year	State Enterprises	Cooperatives	Total Socialist Enterprises
1960	1368	1251	2619
1962	1283	1092	2375
1963	894	993	1887
1965	840	811	1651
1967	807	784	1591
1968	811	792	1603
1970	813	821	1634

Sources: Hungary, Statistical Yearbook (Budapest: Hungarian Central Statistical Office) 1962, p. 121; 1963, pp. 104, 120; 1968, p. 101; 1969, pp. 89, 133, 149. Statistical Pocket Book of Hungary 1971 (Budapest: Statistical Publishing House), p. 93.

TABLE 4.3. Industrial Enterprises in Czechoslovakia, 1957–68
(Selected years)

Year	National Enterprises	Local Industry	Cooperatives	All Enterprises
1957	1445	247	575	2267
1958	935	210	544	1689
1959	923	163	508	1594
1961	818	196	399	1413
1965	715	183	338	1236
1967	713	183	331	1227
1968	743	185	338	1266

Sources: Statisticka Ročenka ČSSR (Prague: SNTL), 1958, p. 114; 1959, pp. 137, 139; 1960, pp. 129, 131; 1962, p. 158; 1966, pp. 187, 379; 1968, p. 216; 1969, pp. 119, 374.

of Hungary and Czechoslovakia may provide some perspective. In Hungary the number of state enterprises, which was nearly stable in the neighborhood of 1300 between 1959 and 1962, fell to under 900 in 1963 (see table 4.2). The number of centrally directed, or ministerial, enterprises fell even more sharply: from 840 at the end of 1962 to 495 at the beginning of 1964 and 435 in the middle of that year. This was a reduction of nearly 50 percent within a year and a half.[21] In Czechoslovakia (table 4.3) the number of national enterprises was slashed by some 35 percent within one year, 1957. The GDR concentration process was tame and deliberate by comparison.

The two East German drives, that of the early NES and that following 1967, had somewhat different aims. The former grouped together, in the main, similar enterprises. The post-1967 combinate drive (which is more fully discussed in the following section) merged vertically linked enterprises. The methodical manner by which combinates were set up is, however, relevant to this comparative context. Combinates grew out of the sub-VVB hierarchy, the *Erzeugnisgruppen* ("product groups") that VVBs were entitled to organize. These were formed on horizontal, vertical, or locational lines and had "leading enterprises" at their heads. Product groups were set up to encourage specialization and divide up product lines through joint planning of production (the Hungarian profile decree tried to accomplish the same end by giving ministries the authority to reserve production of goods to selected enterprises). The product groups were also used to co-ordinate interenterprise flows, then to regularize them and remove them from the "market place" by turning them into intraenterprise flows when the

21. *Partelet*, July 1964, pp. 14–21; Istvan Garamvolgyi, "Vita a vállalati vezetésröl és szervezésröl" [Dispute about the enterprise managing and organization], *Közgazdasági Szemle* 11, no. 9 (September 1964): 1109–18.

group, or some part of it, was merged. The VVBs were thus relieved of some of their coordination functions, and the number of problems which had to rise to this level was reduced; administrative efficiency was apparently improved.

I have so far found no complaints against the functioning of combinates in the GDR. On the contrary, one often reads their praises.[22] The Hungarian concentration drive was often criticized, and the fact that work on the reforms started soon after its completion is an indication that it was not considered a success. Why, then, did the similar drive in the GDR succeed? What are the main differences between the two?

One difference is the haste with which the Hungarian drive proceeded. The East Germans saw to it that new and stable patterns of enterprise inter- action and transaction were institutionalized before they became subject to intraenterprise decisions; thus the new managements inherited a going routine and were not faced within a short time with the tasks of both estab- lishing a new routine and running it. Furthermore, the Hungarian con- centration drive was carried out amid growing pressures on the economy.[23] In the GDR most of the reforms were carried out under slack plans; these were basic preconditions for the success of devolution (see section II.7).

It was claimed in part I that centralized economies are likely to benefit from a more concentrated industrial structure. Hungarian data (table 4.2) support this contention: even though the concentration drive of 1963–64 may have misfired, the number of enterprises continued to shrink until the reforms. The case of Czechoslovakia (table 4.3) is similar. It is only after the reforms that we find, in both countries, an increase in the number of enter- prises. As Dr. Levčík makes clear,[24] Hungarian (and Czechoslovak) industry is still far more concentrated than that of the GDR, so that there might be some objectively optimum concentration in between. Nonetheless, it is note- worthy that the trend of concentration tends to change with decentralization. The timing is suggestive.

The combinate drive was closely linked to an interesting experiment in priority planning, "planning by structure-determining task." Both deserve a few more comments.

II.3. Priority Planning and Combinate Formation

An important aim of the NES was to improve long-term planning, par- ticularly of investment. The combinate formation drive which started in

22. Cf. Gerhard Zimmermann, "Zulieferindustrie hat den Vorrang" [Supply industry has priority], *Neues Deutschland*, 21 January 1971; Erich Honecker, *Report of the Central Committee to the Eighth Congress of the SED* (Dresden: Verlag Zeit im Bild, 1971), pp. 38 f.

23. This point was made by Professor Portes at the Conference.

24. In his comments at the Conference.

mid-1967 is closely linked to this greater stress on perspective planning.[25]

Process and product are often conflicting principles of organization. The early NES gave process the greater weight. The industry (all industrial units working according to similar production processes) was made the cornerstone of industrial administration in the VVBs. But for planning the future, trends in the production and consumption of products are easier to analyze; so an attempt was made to put the product in the center of planning and organization. The new priority planning consists of identifying leading products rather than leading sectors. These *strukturbestimmende Erzeugnisse* ("structure-determining products") are to get the most attention from the planning hierarchy. Both investment and current planning are to be centered around these products, with the rest of the economy—so the conception goes—getting less attention than before. It should be clear that such a system can work only if "the rest" functions smoothly with little attention. In particular, the system will work only if "the rest" can get all its required inputs[26] for continuous supply at a customary, if not growing, level. This requires slack plans.

Product-centered planning leads to a stress on product-centered organization.[27] This is required both to facilitate coordination of planning and production, and for accountability. The obvious choice was to make the producer of the final product responsible for organizing all earlier stages of production. Main suppliers, or primary subcontractors, were amalgamated under the main producer in a *Kombinat*. Secondary but important contractors were organized in a *Kooperationsverband*, a cooperative union of independent enterprises led by the combinate.[28] Combinates were, in general, subordinated directly to a ministry; the neat horizontal grouping under industrial VVBs was breached.

Planning according to structure-determining tasks is meant to be long-term planning. Combinates and cooperative unions are therefore to co-ordinate not only current flows of production; the stress in their work is to be on long-term coordination of market research, technological research and development, and investment.

Vertical concentration has both advantages and disadvantages for the *potential* of the economy. By unifying supplier and buyer within the same

25. Dr. Levčik, in his criticism of the original version of this paper, has pointed to the relevance of priority planning to the latest *Kombinat* formation stage.

26. Roland Scheibler et al., *Die Planung nach strukturbestimmenden Erzeugnissen und Erzeugnissgruppen* [Planning according to structure-determining products and product groups] (East Berlin: Verlag Die Wirtschaft, 1969), p. 224 f.

27. Ibid., p. 53.

28. Cf. W. Burian, "Der Wirtschafsverband—eine neue Form sozialistischer Partnerschaft" [The economic union—a new form of socialist partnership], *Die Wirtschaft*, 1968, no. 30 (25 July), p. 9.

enterprise, many of the advantages and disadvantages due to uncertainty are internalized, as Coase has pointed out. This cannot be done by contracts because it is inconceivable that all possible future events should be spelled out and their effects on transactions between the parties specified.[29] Thus long-term coordination is facilitated by vertical concentration. However, by removing certain stages of production from the "market" and tying them directly to one another, it reduces flexibility. To put this technically, the rates of substitution between different producers of similar products may come to diverge, and the possibility of removing this divergence by exchange is all but eliminated. Furthermore, if in the future economies of scale are discovered to be theoretically possible in the production of some fused intermediates, they will be hard to realize (by putting up plants which will serve all consumers).[30]

The vertical merger has some influence on *actual* performance. It removes the confrontation of buyer and seller as bilateral monopolists that is typical of the centralized supply system (see the discussion of "Opportunity" in section 1.5). It also creates larger units, units which, with a fine enough classification of products, would often be monopolists. But it has already been claimed in section 1.5 that the damage a monopolist can inflict on performance in a centralized market is limited.

Whether the attempt to introduce long-term decision making will actually succeed is an open question. In addition to investment decisions, which are irreversible, decisions on future flows of supplies are to be embedded in contracts. Thus many flows in the material balances each year will be predetermined and will not be reexamined, unless some major bottleneck appears. If none appears, the planning routine will have been simplified, but at the cost of added inflexibility. Even if circumstances change it may be difficult to change predetermined flows, particularly those which have been institutionalized by merging the parties in a single combinate.

The success of the new priority planning is closely bound up with the existence of some slack in the economy. "Balance problems" and "defects in the planning and management of [the economy] become clearly evident when heavy loads appear,"[31] i.e. when the economy is run too tautly. And indeed, when shortages appeared during 1970—a year whose plan was taut —planning by structure-determining tasks was criticized for the disproportions and deemphasized, if not entirely given up.

29. Coase, "The Nature of the Firm."

30. It has been long observed that enterprises in Soviet-type economies try to produce their own inputs in order to avoid having to rely on outside suppliers. This tendency, which was usually not approved, is being made official policy in the combinate drives.

31. Gerhard Schürer, "Entscheidene Aufgabe—höhere Effektivität auf allen Gebieten" [Critical task—higher effectiveness in all spheres], *Neues Deuschland*, 15 December 1970.

II.4. Motive: The Incentive System

The development of the incentive system in the GDR since 1957 had several traits. There was a sharp reduction in the number of success criteria, with a growing trend toward profits as the leading criterion; the attainment of some plan targets as the main condition for a bonus was gradually abandoned; and there was a slight increase in the weight of the bonus in total income, though even now the bonus is surprisingly small. Finally, the funds for bonuses to managers were transferred from supervisory agencies to the general premium fund.

Success criteria. The principal criterion for payments into the enterprise bonus fund before the NES was the fulfillment of the production plan. The bonus fund resolution of 1964, one of the first enactments of the NES, made profits the preferred indicator for the formation of the enterprise and VVB bonus fund. Bonus fund decrees for the following years (with the notable exception of 1965) entrenched profits, or profitability, as the main yardstick for the bonus fund. For 1969 and 1970 profits become even more prominent, because what remains of them after a differentiated profit tax is retained in the enterprise, both in the bonus fund and in an investment fund. Payments into the bonus fund depend on both profits and the increase in profits. The size of the bonus fund did not depend on profits alone. Up to 30 to 40 percent of the planned bonus fund would be withheld if two or three additional conditions, such as the fulfillment of the exports or investments plan, total sales target or delivery contracts, were not fulfilled.

Target linkage. The pre-NES 1960 order ties payments to the bonus fund to the fulfillment and overfulfillment of the various plan indexes, though the exact calculation is by no means simple.[32] For 1964 an interesting overbidding scheme was devised. There is a table which relates the enterprise bonus fund to the main indicator, starting with 35 percent of planned bonuses for 90 percent fulfillment, and reaching 100 percent at 100 percent fulfillment, with additions for overfulfillment. But if the enterprise (or VVB) overbids the suggested target by proposing a higher target, an additional bonus is paid that exceeds the overfulfillment bonus.[33] This scheme, which

32. "Vierte Verordnung über den Betriebsprämienfonds sowie den Kultur- und Sozialfonds in den volkseigenen und ihnen gleichgestellten Betrieben" [Fourth decree on the enterprise premium fund, as well as the fund for cultural and social needs in the people's own and equally ranked enterprises], *Gesetzblatt der DDR*, 1960, pt. II, no. 12, p. 114, pars. 4 ff. (hereafter cited as "Bonus Decree, 1960").

33. "Beschluss über die Bildung und Verwendung des einheitlichen Prämienfonds in den volkseigenen und ihnen gleichgestellten Betrieben der Industrie und des Bauwesens und in den VVB im Jahre 1964" [Resolution on the formation and use of the unitary premium fund in the people's own and equally ranked enterprises in industry and construction, and in the VVB], *Gesetzblatt der DDR*, 1964, pt. II, no. 10 (31 January), p. 80, pars. II-5, 6 of supplement (hereafter cited as "Bonus Resolution, 1964").

blunts the conflict of interest between the target fixer and his subordinate, can still be found in 1968,[34] but not later. In 1966–70 we find a significant break with the past, with the bonus tied to actual profits and to their increase over the previous year.[35] For the first time there is no direct relation to the plan, except for the two side conditions mentioned above.

Weight of bonus. The normal bonus fund for 1960 was to be limited to 4.5 percent of the wage fund. This could increase up to 6.5 percent in case of overfulfillment and the fulfillment of special tasks (such as production out of waste material and "reserves").[36] Since the bonus fund is free of both the wage tax and social security contributions, it can account for less than 10 percent of net wages; this is not much. The 1964 bonus order allows the fund to rise up to 9 percent when there has been overbidding (see above). On the other hand, it cannot fall below 1.5 percent.[37] For 1969 and 1970 the basis is again the previous year's bonus fund (expressed as a percentage of profits), with an increase for 1970 dependent on the gain in profits in 1969. The maximum bonus fund per worker was to be 1,000 marks, and the minimum, 150 marks.[38] Since average monthly wages in 1968 were around 700 marks,[39] and bearing in mind the tax exemption, the average bonus could reach some 16–17 percent of net income, a substantial increase over the level permitted by the 1960 decree.

The manager's bonus. The changed position of the manager's bonus is perhaps most significant. The 1960 Bonus Decree, and earlier decrees, make no explicit mention of the manager as a recipient of premiums from the bonus fund. The Bonus Directive for 1967 introduces a change: the manager, and other leading personnel, will receive their bonus as an "end-of-the-year premium" from the general bonus fund. Special bonuses, including those from the VVB director's disposal fund, are to be paid into the general bonus

34. "Verordnung über die Bildung und Verwendung des Prämienfonds in den volkseigenen und ihnen gleichgestellten Betrieben und die VVB (Zentrale) für das Jahr 1968" [Decree on the formation and use of the premium fund in the people's own and equally ranked enterprises and the VVB (central) for the year 1968], *Gesetzblatt der DDR*, 1967, pt. II, no. 17 (28 February), p. 103, par. 2(3).

35. "Verordnung über die Bildung und Verwendung des Prämienfonds in den volkseigenen und ihnen gleichgestellten Betrieben, volkseigenen Kombinaten, den VVB (Zentrale) und Einrichtungen für die Jahre 1969 und 1970" [Decree on the formation and use of the premium fund in the people's own combinates, VVB (central), and organizations for 1969 and 1970], *Gesetzblatt der DDR*, 1968, pt. II, no. 67 (5 July), par. 2(5), (6) (hereafter cited as "Bonus Decree, 1969/70"). But see below; these additional criteria may be the most important ones for the manager.

36. "Bonus Decree, 1960," par. 10.

37. "Bonus Resolution, 1964," pars. II-2 and 9 of supplement.

38. "Bonus Decree, 1969/70," p. 491, par. 5.

39. *Statistisches Jahrbuch der DDR 1969*, p. 22.

fund.[40] The manager's bonus is, as always, to be determined by the VVB director, and to be dependent upon the fulfillment of "material tasks, contracts," etc.[41] But this is to be an individual variation imposed on the general premium which, basically within each firm, is to be an equal percentage for all.[42]

The important point is that whereas formerly the manager's income depended on the fulfillment of the output target alone, now it is subject to the general constraint imposed by the ratio of the profit-linked premium fund to the general wage fund, though within this ratio it will vary in accordance with the satisfaction of his superiors with his target fulfillment. Profits have become more important for him.

But have profits become important enough to make East German managers profit maximizers? The weight of the part of the bonus actually dependent on profits would hardly seem sufficient for that. Nevertheless, manager's careers depend on their superiors' perception of their success, on the way the performance of their enterprises is judged. A general declaration of the type that "the development of net profits" was to be the indicator of "effectiveness" (see note 34) may be quite important; it may mean that the authorities want profits to become the main success indicator. They are by no means the only one: all decrees point out that the performance of the leading cadres should be judged by their fulfillment of material tasks, and the commentary to the 1971 plan again stresses the authority of the plan.[43] When a serious conflict between material targets and profits arises there is little doubt that the targets will prove their primacy. This would be the case when plans are taut. But with slack plans, profits could exert an important influence on managers' decisions.

The importance of the profit motive is that it puts equal weight on inputs and outputs. It thus serves as a precondition for the delegation of responsibility and for coordination by direct contacts between enterprises, for which an output maximizing target, which gives no weight to input savings,

40. "Richtlinie für die Bildung und Verwendung des Prämienfonds in den volkseigenen und ihnen gleichgestellten Betrieben und den VVB der Industrie und des Bauwesens im Jahre 1967 sowie zur Übergangsregelung für das Jahr 1966" [Directive on the formation and use of the premium fund in the people's own and equally ranked enterprises and the VVB in industry and construction in the year 1967, as well as for the transition regulation for the year 1966], *Gesetzblatt der DDR*, 1966, pt. II, no. 40 (15 April), p. 252, III.4.c.

41. "Bonus Decree, 1969/70," p. 592, par. 9(5).

42. "Erste Durchfürungsbestimmung zur Verordnung über die Bildung und Verwendung des Prämienfonds in den volkseigenen und ihnen gleichgestellten Betrieben, volkseigenen Kombinaten, den VVB (Zentrale) und Einrichtungen für die Jahre 1969 and 1970" [First regulation under the "Bonus decree, 1969/70"], *Gesetzblatt der DDR*, 1968, pt. II, no. 96 (16 September), p. 777, par. 8(3).

43. Schürer.

would not do. When profits do not matter, it is likely that excess demand would persist in most markets and, without some price flexibility, inter-enterprise contacts would not be an efficient way of allocating resources. Another precondition for interenterprise contacts to work well is, again, some slack in the economy.

The questions that remain concern the possible abuse of delegated authority in order to increase measured effectiveness: in what way could enterprises (or VVBs) adjust prices, or the assortment of goods produced, to increase their profits? The first question, the possibility of taking advantage of the price system, is discussed in section II.5. Section II.6 looks at changes in the supply system and at the compatibility of profits and centralized supply.

II.5. Opportunity: The Evolution of the Price System

The 1964 industrial prices were, to a large extent, still based on 1944 prices: no comprehensive price reform had been undertaken before the NES. Consequently, prices were far out of line with their declared aim of equalling average costs. The foreseen devolution of many functions to enterprises and VVBs and the planned use of profits as the principal incentive made a price reform imperative. The reform[44] was preceded by a revaluation of fixed capital to serve as a basis for depreciation charges. It then proceeded in three stages: in the first, basic industrial raw materials had their prices raised by 70 percent on the average. In the second, prices of other intermediate products were raised by 40 percent, and in the third, prices of final products were raised by some 4 percent. With the price reform over, in 1967 total subsidies by the state could be halved, and of these about 50 percent were retained only because the consumer was to be insulated from the changes in industrial prices.[45] An important break with the past came with the production fund tax of 1967. This tax, which is levied on all fixed capital held by an economic unit, is to serve in lieu of an interest rate as a regulator of investment. Since it was levied *after* the reform, it could not be imposed on all enterprises alike. Consequently, rates varied between 1 and 6 percent per annum.[46] A uniform rate of 6 percent is to be introduced without raising prices (that is, when costs fall).

44. For an exposition of the price reform see M. Meltzer, "Preispolitik und Preisbildungs-probleme in der DDR" [Price policy and problems of price formation in the GDR], *Viertel-jahreshefte zur Wirtschaftsforschung*, 1969, no. 3, p. 313; H. Böhme, "Dynamische Preisbildung in der sozialistischen Planwirtschaft der DDR" [Dynamic price formation in the socialist planned economy of the GDR], in *Jahrbuch für Nationalökonomie und Statistik* 183, nos. 3–4 (Stuttgart: Gustav Fischer Verlag, 1969): idem, "East German Price Formation Under the NES," *Soviet Studies* 19, no. 3 (January 1968).

45. Meltzer, pp. 314–21.

46. "Produktionsfondabgabe" [Production Fund Tax], *Wörterbuch der Ökonomie: Sozialis-mus*, p. 642.

Another break with the past, one which is more important for our topic, is the institution of so-called dynamic prices—a continuous price reform. To obviate a succession of comprehensive price reforms, between which prices would encourage the misallocation of resources, price changes were to be regularized and prices were to be continuously equated to average costs plus a profit margin. The profit margin was to be proportional to the capital employed and not, as was previously customary, to costs. The mechanism of price reduction is very simple: upper and lower limits of profitability are fixed for each product or product group. When profitability reaches the upper limit, prices are reduced so that profitability equals the lower limit. It was assumed that dynamic prices will be falling prices: money costs, so it was thought, fall over time, and hence prices, once profitability rises to the upper limit, will start declining. If this assumption proves to be true (if labor and import costs do not rise and if inputs in natural resource intensive industries do not have to increase because of depletion),[47] the equality of prices and average costs can be attained without raising any prices. However, prices are not to be reduced where demand would come to exceed limited supply or where "wrong" price relations with substitutes would come into being.[48] In these cases prices of other products are to be reduced, so that the average profitability of the product group does not exceed the upper limit.

Two questions arise with relation to this dynamic price system: first, can it be exploited by enterprises and VVBs wishing to raise their profits? Who is responsible for its operation? Second, does it provide incentives for cost reductions, which is one of its avowed aims?

To take the latter point first: the provisions made to keep enterprises interested in cost reductions are quite interesting. First, the price guidelines make sure that enterprises and VVBs neither gain nor lose through price changes, for a *limited period of time*. Thus, if prices for output are reduced on, say, 1 January 1970, the price differential per unit marketed in 1970 is refunded to the enterprise out of the net profits tax. Likewise, cost reductions through price changes are added to the profits tax.[49] Similarly, the decree on calculated prices (prices fixed by enterprises for special orders—see below) sees to it that input savings which lead to reduced material norms are not passed on to the buyer in reduced prices in the year or 18 months following

47. As is happening with lignite: Meltzer, p. 318.

48. Ibid., pp. 338 ff.

49. Provided they exceed 3 percent of costs: "Richtlinie zur Einführung des fondbezogenen Industriepreises und für die planmässige Senkung von Industriepreisen in den Jahren 1969/1970" [Guidelines for the introduction of fund-based industrial prices and for the planned reduction of industrial prices in the years 1969/1970], *Gesetzblatt der DDR*, 1968, pt. II, no. 67, (5 July), (hereafter cited as "Price Guidelines"). For net profits tax see p. 143.

their introduction.[50] Thus the enterprise does make short-term gains through any technical progress. Hence, if the cost saving measure is painless and requires no effort, it will be made. However, the amount of effort which the manager will put into cost reductions depends on the length of time he will enjoy their fruits.

As for the opportunity of producers to influence prices: firstly, classes of calculated prices, to be fixed by the supplying enterprise, were created for products that are not generally traded. Second, the price-fixing authority of the VVBs was extended, and as many as 75 percent of all prices were in the hands of the VVBs in 1969.[51] The VVBs are also responsible for the initiation of dynamic price reductions (the continuous adjustment of prices to costs mentioned above).[52] This authority notwithstanding, the price-fixing VVB or enterprise is not free in its choice of price. There is strict regulation of price fixing, and the trading partner has full rights to check the price and its calculation.[53] Of course, this is not to say that the price fixer cannot cheat, and cheating is easier for a monopolist than for a firm with competitors, who is not the only possessor of information about price-determining costs. But cheating can be the exception, not the rule, and it is limited in its extent. Furthermore, the provisions for dynamic prices make the effects of cheating obvious by raising profits above the norm and thus necessitating price revisions. Consequently, we have here a device which, if it works, and if the proper margin for capital costs is used, would permanently keep prices very near average costs. If it is the case that variable costs are fixed, and this is the basis of all material norms, and if there are no economies of scale in labor and capital inputs, average costs equal long-run marginal costs. Thus, under conditions which may not be far from reality, prices, though perhaps not clearing markets in the short run, may approach long-run efficiency prices.

II.6. Opportunity and Control: Supply and the Contract System

Price-fixing functions were not the only ones delegated: many balancing functions were also decentralized. Table 4.4 shows that VVBs and enterprises together, which were in charge of 12–14 percent of all balances in 1959 and 1963, have in the late 1960s been responsible for over 90 percent

50. "Anordnung über die Bildung von Kalkulationspreisen in Industriebetrieben" [Decree on the formation of calculated prices in industrial enterprises], *Gesetzblatt der DDR*, 1966, pt. II, no. 148 (17 December), p. 984, pars. 4(3), 5.
51. H. Mann in a report to a symposium on prices, *Voprosy Ekonomiki*, 1969, no. 7, p. 160. The reference is apparently to industrial transfer prices. The remaining 25 percent were fixed by the State Committee on Prices. This information was kindly sent to me by Dr. F. Haffner of the Osteuropa Institut at the Free University of Berlin.
52. "Price Guidelines," p. 500, par. 3.3.
53. "Price Guidelines," p. 499, par. 2.1.4.

TABLE 4.4. Devolution of the Balancing Function in the GDR: Number of Balances (Figures in parentheses indicate number of plan positions)

	1959[a] (rounded)	1963[b]	1964[b]	1965	1966
SPCs and the *Volkswirtschaftsrats*	570 (560)	1,188 (816)	874 (719)	436 (329)	249 (175)
Other central organs and trade	2,000	3,366	2,173 (85)	679 (40)	333 (61)
Local organs	330	33	46	2	5
VVBs	370	507	2,192 (45)	4,886 (375)	4,803 (532)
Enterprises	n.a.[c]	98	168	350 (15)	646 (38)
Total	3,270[c] (560)	5,192 (816)	5,453 (849)	6,353 (759)	6,036 (806)

Sources: 1959—Balances: H. W. Hübner, "Aktuelle Probleme der Planung der Industrie-produktion," *Sozialistische Planwirtschaft*, 1960, no. 1, p. 8, table 1.—Plan positions: Frederic Pryor, *The Communist Foreign Trade System* (Cambridge: M.I.T. Press, 1963), p. 285. 1963–66—Rolf Keilacker, "Voraussetzungen, Bedingungen und Kriterien der Delegierung von Bilan-zierungsfunktionen auf Betriebe," *Wirtschaftswissenschaft*, 1966, no. 10, p. 1629.

[a] The two sources are not necessarily comparable in their definition of balances.

[b] Slightly different data appear in the guidelines of the NES, *Dokumente zum neuen Ökono-mischen System* (East Berlin: Dietz Verlag, 1963), p. 113.

[c] The source indicates that several balances were entrusted to large enterprises. These are additional to the total given.

of all balances and 70 percent of all state plan positions.[54] It is noteworthy that enterprises were entrusted with balancing only if they did in fact have monopoly standing.[55] The balancers are, however, highly circumscribed in the exercise of their function. The total output which they have to distribute is determined by a superior planning organ, a ministry or the State Planning Commission; the ministry for material supply is responsible for input norms. These, as well as long-term contracts, bind the balancer. Thus, all that remains is the necessary calculation of input requirements, and if the sum of capacity output and planned imports cannot cover them, the task of balancing

54. Territorial decentralization, as can clearly be seen from table 4.2, has been fatally reversed since its heyday in the late 1950s.

55. R. Keilacker, "Voraussetzungen, Bedingungen und Kriterien der Delegierung von Bilanzierungsfunktionen auf Betriebe," [Prerequisites, conditions and criteria for the delegation of balancing functions to enterprises], *Wirtschaftswissenschaft*, 1966, no. 10, p. 1631.

is shifted to a higher level in the hierarchy.[56] This is a very clear example of the spirit of the GDR reforms: an attempt is made to leave upper echelons free of decisions on detail, without letting go the reins of authority over those details. Furthermore, the balancing function is carried out *eigenverantwortlich*, ("with responsibility"): the law requires the balancer to indemnify the partners to those transactions which he regulates for any losses which result from operative intervention on his part.[57] This limited delegation can function only with slack plans. Taut plans mean overcommitted balances (which cannot be delegated) and many plan changes (which would overstrain the judicial authorities which have to indemnify enterprises suffering from plan and contract changes).

For balancing to be meaningful, planners have to be reasonably assured that the planned supplies in the balances will be forthcoming. This is why the success criterion of the fulfillment of the marketed output plan is such an important prop of the centralized supply system. How can centralized supply function when enterprises are led by the incentive system to produce what is profitable to them rather than what they have been ordered to?

The link between the two seems to be the strengthened contract system. In other words, all targeted output of an enterprise has to be contracted for sale to other producing or trading enterprises. If the enterprise wishes to reduce its output, or to change the mix of goods assigned to it, it will break some contract and be liable to pay profit-reducing indemnities. The higher the indemnities, the less likely is the enterprise to stray away from its plan. The contract law of 1965 has increased the indemnities, and has made excuses of force majeure very difficult to sustain.[58]

The strengthened contract system forces the contract court and the enterprises themselves to undertake the policing of plan fulfillment. This would have been too much of a burden if contract breaking were the rule rather than the exception because enterprises were forced to sign contracts which they were unlikely to be able to fulfill—in other words, if the supply plan on which the contracts were based was unbalanced or overly taut. That the system has apparently functioned till the end of 1969 is an indication that the GDR economy has been working with much more slack than before the New Economic System. This slack enabled profit maximization to coexist with centralized supply.

56. Ibid.

57. "Verordnung über die Aufgaben, Pflichten und Rechten der Betriebe, Staats-und Wirtschaftsorgane bei der Bilanzierung materialwirtschaftliche Prozesse" [Decree on the tasks, duties, and rights of enterprises, state and economic organs in balancing material supply processes], *Gesetzblatt der DDR*, 1968, pt. II, no. 67 (5 July), p. 484, par. 5(5) (hereafter cited as "Balancing Decree"). On the other hand, enterprises which place unjustified demands for material rations are to be fined (p. 485, par. 7[2]).

58. See O. Spitzner, *Der Wirtschaftsvertrag in der Praxis* [The economic contract in practice], vol. 3 (East Berlin: Staatsverlag der DDR, 1968), pp. 43–50.

II.7. Slack, the Precondition for Devolution

The terms "taut" and "slack," in the sense used several times in this paper, were first introduced by Holland Hunter: taut plans are plans that are difficult to fulfill, and are therefore likely to be underfulfilled. Slack plans are easy, and hence likely to be fulfilled or even overfulfilled.[59] The success or even feasibility of many of the measures of the NES depended on plans being slack. Slack plans, it was said, were the precondition for the devolution of balancing, for the functioning of the contract system, for the efficacy of an incentive system based on profits (with inflexible prices). Without slack plans concentration may not be beneficial and priority planning has no chance at all. Greater slack has indeed characterized the annual plans in the GDR until 1969. They mostly foresaw an annual growth rate of net material product of some 5 percent, and plan fulfillment was very near that mark.

One can learn of the success of a course of action as perceived by its enactors by their reaction to its results. Had the attempts at devolution of the start of the NES misfired, the regime could easily have recentralized. They did the opposite, and slowly extended the scope of devolution. Table 4.4, which shows the devolution of balancing, demonstrates this: the number of balances entrusted to lower organs expanded in each year for which we have data. Indeed, many of the reforms, such as the strengthened contract act and the price reform, were introduced only in 1967. Another indication of success was the steadiness of the growth of net material product at 5 percent annually, with hardly any increase of the labor force.

More evidence on the importance of slack plans to the system was the change of course in late 1970. For 1969 and 1970 taut plans were drawn up, plans which aimed at an accelerated growth. The return to an apparently slack plan for 1971 shows that the new tautness misfired.[60] But there were more signs of discontent; many of the measures of the NES were suppressed in 1971. This, to my mind, shows that these measures were not compatible with tautness.

It is too early to say that this suppression is temporary, to be reversed when the slack plans for 1971 and 1972 have cured the tensions in the economy. It may mean the end of the experiment with devolution amid centralized control.

59. "The Optimum Tautness in Developmental Planning," *Economic Development and Cultural Change* (July 1961).

60. This is substantiated in Schürer. Dr. G. Leptin of the Osteuropainstitut at the Free University of Berlin has suggested that the principal improvement in the East German economy has in fact been greater slack, which has enabled centralized supply to function with fewer breakdowns and operative interventions. He points out that all institutional reforms came too late to explain the successful performance of 1964–66, before many of the reforms came into force.

5

Foreign Trade in the East European Reforms

ALAN A. BROWN AND PAUL MARER

Economic reforms, as East European economists continually remind us, are closely linked with international economic considerations. Numerous direct and indirect ties connect reforms and trade, and any analysis of these relationships must take into account the traditional features of the centrally planned economy (CPE). In this paper we can only offer a few general observations about the role of foreign trade in a CPE.[1]

Perhaps the most accurate term for the foreign trade policy of small CPEs after World War II would be "attempted import substitution." The system's directors tried to replace imports of every kind with domestically produced substitutes. In the case of heavy industrial products, this was, of course, the essence of the development strategy; in the case of consumer goods, or low-priority goods in general, preservation of foreign exchange militated against imports;[2] and, in the case of raw materials, the unwillingness of bloc trading partners to provide scarce materials curtailed the flow of imports. But the overall trade aversion of small CPEs became self-defeating, as is increasingly recognized by East European economists themselves: "Sooner or later it has come to light that *industrialization based on import substitution does not reduce imports, it only transforms the composition of imports.* If previously the country was importing commodities that have been replaced with new domestic capacity, then afterwards the

The authors gratefully acknowledge the helpful comments of Michael Kaser and George J. Stolnitz and the support of the International Development Research Center of Indiana University.

1. A more detailed discussion can be found in Alan A. Brown and Paul Marer, "Foreign Trade in the Traditional Centrally Planned Economy," mimeographed, 17 pp., obtainable from the authors by request. For a detailed theoretical and empirical analysis of centrally planned foreign trade, we refer to the individual contributions in Alan A. Brown and Egon Neuberger, eds., *International Trade and Central Planning* (Berkeley: University of California Press, 1968).

2. CPEs' aversion to imported consumer goods was at least partly the result of mistaken identification with consumption; conversely, imported machinery and raw materials were identified with investment.

import requirements will consist of goods made necessary by the process of import substitution itself."[3]

Attempted import substitution should be distinguished from a meaningful policy of autarky, which is hardly a realistic alternative for any small country. Attempted import substitution has not been notably successful in protecting CPEs from the adverse economic influences of the outside world, but has deprived the small CPEs of some of the benefits of international specialization, including the stimulus of external competition. One East European economist remarked: "The artificial price system and the lack of any incentive for marketing formed a ring of protection around the economy, not only against the unfavorable effects of world markets, such as major fluctuations, but against any pressure for rationalization."[4] This emphasis on large indirect losses of protection stands in sharp contrast to recent western findings that the direct loss of tariff protection tends to be relatively small.

Efficiency in general, even the assessment of various alternatives, is largely ignored in the policymaking as well as in the organization of CPEs. To be sure, essential industrial imports were in most cases obtained by the small CPEs, but as the volume of imports increased rapidly relative to domestic production, the economic loss due to the neglect of both actual and prospective comparative advantage in determining the composition of trade increased also. This lack of attention to opportunity costs can be largely ascribed to the traditional institutional mechanisms not only within given CPEs but also in the Council for Mutual Economic Assistance (CEMA, also known as Comecon) as a whole. This has been increasingly recognized:

> The shortcomings of CEMA cooperation appeared approximately a decade ago. . . . Of these, the most important are the inadequacy of raw materials produced for exports relative to demand; the parallel production of manufactures, occasionally in excess supply and frequently technically inadequate; and the relative shortage of quality products by world market standards. . . . These shortcomings are linked not only to domestic causes, but to a significant extent also to

3. Béla Csikós-Nagy, *Általános és szocialista árelmélet* [General and socialist price theory] (Budapest: Kossuth, 1968), p. 250. The conclusion that *intended* import substitution may result in an increase of actual imports reminds us of the Keynesian paradox of thrift: an increase in intended savings may indirectly lead to a reduction of actual savings.

4. Iván Berend (Hungarian Academy of Sciences), "The Historical Background of the Recent Economic Reforms in East Europe," *East European Quarterly* 2, no. 4 (September 1969): 84–85. Czechoslovakia in 1964, for example, still had a system which forbade imports unless the domestic producer of the same commodity signed an affidavit that it was unable to meet the domestic demand. J. Pleva (Czechoslovakia), as translated in *The American Review of Soviet and East European Foreign Trade*, no. 12 (1964), p. 44.

inadequate specialization and cooperation within industrial branches and products.[5]

As this diagnosis suggests, to eliminate inefficiencies in foreign trade is at least a potential inducement for economic reforms in the smaller CPEs. The next section is devoted to an examination of certain reform pressures and of their connection to foreign trade.

I. Pressures for Reforms: A Comparative Analysis

Eastern and western economists seem to have reached an agreement that traditional CPEs neglect efficiency considerations in foreign trade and that individual CPEs' problems are compounded by inadequate cooperation within CEMA. As the volume of trade increases rapidly, the opportunity cost of this inefficiency also rises, and this leads to intensified reform pressures.

We may link economic reforms and foreign trade by comparing the degree of economic pressures in various East European countries and the type of reforms these pressures are likely to generate. As background for the reform movement of the mid-1960s, we focus on economic performance during the 1960–65 period. Two kinds of economic pressures are examined: those emanating from unsatisfactory growth performance and those caused by balance-of-payments problems.

Given these countries' continued preoccupation with rapid growth, probably the most important cause of economic reforms has been a relatively slow or declining rate of growth. The planners' concern with a slow or declining rate of growth tends to direct their attention to inefficiencies in foreign trade, particularly if the unsatisfactory growth performance is associated with slow technological progress *and* if trade is important. It will be of interest, therefore, to observe comparative growth rates as well as growth *sources* in Eastern Europe (referring to them in combination as growth performance). As to the importance of trade, since we are dealing chiefly with relatively small countries we may take it for granted; although we could also marshal readily available empirical evidence demonstrating the rapid increase of trade relative to output.

In addition to growth performance, another very important pressure for reforms emanates from balance-of-payments problems. East European statements confirm that this issue is uppermost in the minds of the system's directors when reform decisions are made.[6] If we attempt to identify the

---

5. Sándor Ausch, *A KGST-együttmüködés helyzete, mechanizmusa, távlatai* [The position, mechanism, and perspectives of CEMA cooperation] (Budapest: Közgazdasági és Jogi Könyvkiadó, 1969), p. 70.

6. See the statement by Rezsö Nyers cited on p. 171.

mechanism that links balance-of-payment pressures to reforms, it appears that (1) balance-of-payments deficits in intrabloc trade may not present the same kinds of problems as similar deficits in East–West trade, and (2) the response of a more developed country (MDC) in Eastern Europe to a balance-of-payments disequilibrium—with East or West—may not be the same as the response of a less developed country (LDC) to a similar problem. (In this context, we define East European MDCs as net exporters of manufactures, and LDCs as net exporters of primary products.)

Since a detailed examination of comparative growth performance and comparative balance of payments are outside the purview of this paper, in this section we shall only summarize our conclusions, discussed in greater detail elsewhere.[7]

Relative Growth Performance

On the basis of official statistics, we calculated two types of "reform-pressure indexes." The first compares average performance during a more recent period with performance during an earlier period in the same country (single-country dynamic hypothesis). The second compares performance in a given period with performance in other East European countries during the same period (cross-sectional dynamic hypothesis).[8] The assumption is that the higher the "index of reform pressure," and the more the various pressure indicators converge on a given country, the more likely that comprehensive reforms will be undertaken by the country so pressured.

Based on official statistics, our calculations show that between 1960 and 1965 the growth rates of both aggregate and net industrial output were below the average for the group as a whole in Czechoslovakia, East Germany, and Hungary. The reform orientation, as shown later, was also the strongest in these countries during the early 1960s, thus lending support to the cross-sectional dynamic hypothesis. The rate of growth in Hungary and Czechoslovakia was also below the group average in both preceding five-year periods.[9]

7. Selected statistical evidence is presented in appendices B and C. A more detailed discussion and additional data can be found in A. A. Brown and P. Marer, "A Comparison of Economic Reform-Pressure Indicators in East Europe," mimeographed, 30 pp., obtainable from the authors by request.

8. Source of official data: S. K. Falusné, *Létszám, termelékenység—gazdasági növekedés* [Labor force, productivity—economic growth] (Budapest: Kossuth Könyvkiadó, 1968), pp. 22, 31.

9. However, the third country whose growth rates were consistently below the group average in the 1950s but *not* between 1960 and 1965 was Poland rather than East Germany. This might be one reason why the pioneering Polish reform proposals in the 1950s failed to blossom into comprehensive reforms during the 1960s. Another explanation for the somewhat paradoxical

(continued on page 157)

It appears that the decline in the rate of growth over time was a general phenomenon during the first five years of the 1960s, as compared with 1955–60, except in Romania and Poland (if, in the latter country, we take industrial production only). These slowdowns were most pronounced in Czechoslovakia, East Germany, Bulgaria, and Hungary for national income; and in the same group of countries, except Hungary, for net industrial production.

Independent western estimates of the growth of GNP in Eastern Europe broadly confirm these findings. A comparison of the 1950–55 and 1960–67 average compound growth rate of per capita GNP of the six East Central European countries shows that (a) between 1960 and 1967 the growth rates were below the average for the group as a whole in Czechoslovakia, East Germany and Poland; (b) a decline was registered during 1960–67 as compared with 1955–60 for the group as a whole but not for Romania, Poland and Hungary; and (c) the slowdowns were the most pronounced in Czechoslovakia, East Germany and Bulgaria.[10]

Comparative sources of growth. If we analyze the rate of growth of output by means of the production-function approach, possible explanations for the slowdown are[11] a decline in the rate of growth of inputs, a decline

(continued from page 156)
Polish performance is given by Leon Smolinski ("Planning Reforms in Poland," *Kyklos* 21, no. 3 [1968]: 499): "A substantial improvement had been achieved during the thaw of the mid-fifties, by merely doing away with the most flagrant irrationalities. Poland ... was then benefiting from what Egon Neuberger calls 'positive legacies' of Stalinism, in particular from the delayed effects on output of the high rate of investment of the Stalinist period ... national income and consumption were growing rapidly with relatively low marginal capital-output ratios."

10. Thad P. Alton, "Economic Structure and Growth in Eastern Europe," U.S. Congress, Joint Economic Committee, *Economic Developments in Countries of Eastern Europe*, A Compendium of Papers (Washington, D.C.: U.S. Government Printing Office, 1970), p. 47. Alton's calculations show no change in Hungary's average rate of growth from 1955–60 to 1960–67 because the country's exceptionally good performance during 1965–67 pulls up the growth rate for the entire 1960–67 period. A comparison of 1955–60 with 1960–65 only would show, similarly to official statistics, a declining rate of growth over time.

11. Let us write the production function as $Y = A[f(K, L)]$. Differentiating the function logarithmically and dividing by the original function, we obtain:

$$G_Y = G_A + \eta_K G_K + \eta_L G_L$$

where

G_Y = rate of growth of output;

G_A = rate of growth of technological change, total factor productivity, or the "residual";

G_K and G_L = rates of growth of capital and labor;

η_K and η_L = elasticities, or imputed factor shares of capital and labor.

(continued on page 158)

in productivity, and increasing difficulty in substituting one factor for another.[12]

Our calculations show that the rate of growth of nonagricultural labor inputs declined steadily in Czechoslovakia, Hungary, and East Germany,[13] while Romania, Bulgaria, and the Soviet Union were able to maintain relatively stable rates of growth of labor input over the entire period. Relative to other countries, pressure was most intense in East Germany, Czechoslovakia, Poland, and Hungary. Capital has grown faster in the 1960s than during 1955–60 in every country except the Soviet Union (where there was a slight increase compared with the early 1950s). It is noteworthy that the fastest rate of growth of capital input occurred in the least developed countries.[14] In making cross-national comparisons, pressure appears to have been strongest in the same set of countries as indicated before. (It would be an interesting further analysis to explore the degree to which the more rapid rate of increase of capital, as compared with previous periods, was able to compensate for the slower rate of growth of labor.)

Combined factor productivity cannot be determined without estimating or assigning weights to each of the two factors. If, however, the productivity of each factor declines separately, their weighted average, total factor productivity, will also decline.[15] We find, on the basis of official data, that labor productivity (assuming a given structure of production) declined in every country except Romania, and that capital productivity declined even more drastically in every country (except in Romania, where the decline in the 1960s was slight). We may conclude, therefore, that in every East European country, except perhaps Romania, total factor productivity has declined, which means that pressure clearly must have been felt to seek out new

(continued from page 157)

We see that a decline of G_Y may result from (1) a decline of factor inputs (G_L or G_K); (2) a decline of technological change (G_A); or (3) a change in the respective elasticities of capital and labor (η_K and η_L). These hypotheses can be investigated by fitting a CES production function, but *not a Cobb–Douglas function,* since the latter, having implicitly assumed constant factor shares, ignores the possibility of the third alternative. For a more detailed theoretical analysis, see A. A. Brown and E. Neuberger, "Dynamic L-Shaped CES Functions in Eastern Europe," Windsor University Working Paper no. 4 (Windsor, Ont., 1971).

12. During the 1955–65 decade, capital had been growing faster than labor in all East European countries (see Brown and Marer, "Economic Reform-Pressure.") Although no comparable capital data are available for East Germany, the above statement is probably applicable since labor inputs in East Germany increased less than 1 percent per annum during this period (ibid.).

13. In East Germany, the decline occurred during the 1950s; the rate of growth was less than 1 percent per annum during the 1960s (ibid.).

14. No data are available for East Germany (cf. n. 12).

15. This proposition may be derived from the production function shown above (n. 11).

sources of productivity. It appears that the pressure was greatest in Czechoslovakia, Hungary, and Bulgaria; somewhat less in the USSR and East Germany; considerably less in Poland; and least in Romania.

As for the difficulty of substituting capital for labor,[16] we have extensive econometric evidence for Hungary, showing that the elasticity of substitution in the early 1960s, the crucial period for reforms, approached zero.[17] The misallocation of capital, often documented by East European sources, is at least a partial explanation for this finding.[18] Certain institutional features within the organization of CEMA may also help to explain these findings. Since in individual CPEs, producers and foreign trade enterprises (FTEs) have been administratively separated, the decision to import capital (as far as quality, type, and other specifications) often did not take into account the requirements of the user. The problem was exacerbated by the institutional shortcomings of CEMA, which fostered "commodity bilateralism,"[19] forcing net machinery exporters in the bloc to import machinery that they did not really want.

Indirect, dynamic effects were also numerous. For example, underutilization of capital led to difficulties in producing the exports necessary to pay for imports (including the raw materials needed to sustain uninterrupted production). Under taut planning, this led to bottlenecks, and therefore to further underutilization of capital. Falusné succinctly sums up this vicious circle: "Productivity depends partly upon raw material supplies, while raw material supplies depend, via exports, on productivity."[20]

Thus, due to the increasing difficulty of substituting capital for labor, strong reform pressures may have been felt by Hungary and probably also by other East European countries, particularly by those that must rely more

16. In technical terms, whether the elasticity of substitution is less than one.

17. This finding was tested by one of the authors and confirmed not only for national income as a whole and for aggregate industrial output, but also separately for more than a dozen industrial branches. See A. A. Brown, "CES Production Function Estimates in Postwar Hungary," mimeographed, available from the author by request.

18. Microeconomic inefficiencies were blamed in a comparison of growth and productivity in all East European countries: "There has been little or no improvement in the underutilization of machinery and equipment, undoubtedly an important cause of the lagging productivity. Enterprises have held on to productive capacity, whether needed or not, since it might yield them some benefit without cost. Elsewhere, naturally, this meant a shortage of investment. Thus, there has been inefficient utilization of equipment in one place, and loss of time due to unavailability of new equipment in another." This problem, too, was linked to foreign trade: "In the countries examined during the 1960s there has been insufficient response to either foreign or domestic demand" (Falusné, p. 163).

19. The concept and the implications of "commodity bilateralism" are discussed in our paper, "Foreign Trade in the Traditional Centrally Planned Economy."

20. Ibid., p. 164n.

and more on productivity increases rather than on input growth to maintain a desired rise of output.

Comparative income elasticities of trade. As a rough approximation, intended only to show comparative changes in the relative importance of trade over time, we have calculated income elasticities of trade in each country, and have computed indexes of reform pressure, assuming that relatively high (or rapidly increasing) elasticities present more problems than low elasticities.

We find that trade on the average has increased considerably faster than national income, and that the differential rates of growth have widened consistently in every country over time. The unweighted average income elasticity of trade for Eastern Europe as a whole increased from 1.54 in 1955–60 to 2.21 in 1960–65.[21] The three countries for which *both* indexes show strong pressure are Czechoslovakia, Hungary, and Bulgaria.

External Disequilibrium

East European countries do not publish balance-of-payments statistics. As an approximation, therefore, we use balance-of-trade figures.[22] A consistent trade deficit would seem to be an indicator of pressure on the deficit country. With low foreign exchange reserves and without long-term foreign credits, a small CPE must increase exports to pay for this deficit. But a regular trade surplus would also present problems since it signifies capital exports, unless the surplus is offset by invisible imports. Such a surplus may also indicate the difficulty of obtaining required imports. Thus neither type of disequilibrium appears to be desirable for small CPEs.

In order to link a disequilibrium in trade specifically to the reforms, we need to consider what steps would be taken by a CPE in response to such pressures. The response, however, will be different if (1) the disequilibrium is with socialist or with capitalist countries—and within the latter, whether with MDCs or LDCs (as traditionally defined, based on per capita income); (2) the trade pattern of a CPE is that of an MDC (net exporter of manu-

---

21. Statistical details in Brown and Marer, "Economic Reform-Pressure."

22. Peter Wiles has estimated, as a "general guess," that invisibles in the trade of East European countries are about 11 to 12 percent of their commodity trade. (See P. J. D. Wiles, *Communist International Economics* [New York: Praeger, 1969], p. 348.) Poland, however, is cited as an exception (due to geographical location and port facilities), having an estimated 20 percent transit earnings relative to commodity exports (ibid., p. 347). Wiles's estimates are supported by an authoritative Hungarian source: "90 percent of all revenue in our balance of payments derive from commodity exports; therefore, balance-of-payments equilibrium depends largely on the trade balance" (István Friss, *Reform of the Economic Mechanism in Hungary* [Budapest: Akadémiai Kiadó, 1969], p. 26).

factures), or that of an LDC (net exporter of primary products); and (3) the trade balance is positive or negative.[23]

Based on a theoretical framework incorporating these three variables, the hypotheses with respect to trade *with socialist countries* can be summed up as follows: For an MDC in the bloc, an import surplus represents pressure in the form of an uncertainty of raw material supplies because its LDC trade partners would probably not be willing to continue exporting primary products on credit. This pressure would force the MDC to produce goods that are more marketable both on bloc and Western markets, which would probably require fundamental reforms. An export surplus for an MDC points to selling on credit and may also indicate difficulty in obtaining needed imports. This fosters a desire to redirect exports to the West, which would, however, require more marketable goods as well as greater entrepreneurial initiative. Thus, for a net exporter of machinery, any continuous disequilibrium in its trade with socialist countries represents strong pressure to increase efficiency and points to reforms.

An LDC in the bloc in similar circumstances appears to be under less pressure to institute fundamental reforms because in either case it will have more attractive alternatives and will be in a better bargaining position. When it has an import surplus, it may sell substandard machinery at good prices or be content with an unrequited inflow of capital. When it has an export surplus, it may bargain harder to obtain needed imports or redirect trade to the West.

Turning now to a balance-of-trade disequilibrium *with capitalist countries*, strong pressure is generated by an import surplus that needs to be financed and eventually repaid. There appears to be more pressure for fundamental reforms in bloc MDCs because of their increasing difficulty in competing on Western manufactures markets. An overall surplus with the West may hide a deficit with MDCs and a large surplus with LDCs, in which case

23. The table below, on the balance of trade ratio of East European countries, illustrates the framework based on these variables.

Balance of Trade Ratio (BTR) (X/M) 100	Level of Development (or structure of trade)	
	MDC	LDC
Trade with East		
Import surplus	...	...
Export surplus	...	...
Trade with West		
Import surplus	...	...
Export surplus	...	...

Appendices B.1 and B.2 summarize the empirical evidence which could be interpreted within this framework.

strong reform pressures will again be felt. LDCs in the bloc are also less likely to feel pressures from a given deficit since they can more easily re-direct trade from East to West. This advantage, however, will be gradually lost as LDCs become more industrialized.[24]

We may offer an additional observation: LDCs, being able to reduce their pressure by redirecting exports from East to West, tend, in fact, to transmit their own pressures to bloc trading partners and to increase the overall raw materials shortage within the bloc.

Empirical evidence. We calculated balance-of-trade ratios for 1950–69 separately for each East European country.[25] It appears that regardless of the trade balance, bloc LDCs have been redirecting their trade to the West, while this is not the case for bloc MDCs. Trade has been redirected from CEMA to the West by the USSR, Bulgaria, Romania, and (earlier) by Poland; but no such shifts could be observed for Czechoslovakia, Hungary, and East Germany. These changes in the regional distribution of trade, combined with commodity bilateralism, have undoubtedly compounded internal economic pressures in the latter countries. Among the more de-veloped countries in the bloc, Hungary appears to have had the most critical balance-of-payments situation during the mid-1960s.

Considering trade with capitalist countries, we have found surprisingly large balance-of-trade deficits in the case of Romania and Bulgaria (par-ticularly with MDCs, during the 1960s). What they have imported, how they financed these deficits, and how they intend to pay for them are questions that need to be explored in more detail. Their large deficits may explain, in part, the redirection of their trade from CEMA to western countries, as indicated above. The necessity to pay eventually for these deficits has im-portant implications for the availability of "hard goods" from these countries to CEMA trade partners during the 1970s.

Pressures for Reforms: A Summary

If we compare the strengths of reform pressures generated by such im-portant economic considerations as growth rates and sources of growth as well as balance-of-payments disequilibria (as approximated by balances of trade), we can tentatively conclude that by the mid-1960s the strongest re-form pressures relative to other CEMA countries were probably felt by Czechoslovakia and Hungary, followed closely by East Germany, and then,

24. For further discussion of the hypotheses, see Brown and Marer, "Economic Reform-Pressure."

25. Balance-of-trade ratios with European CEMA, total West, and Western MDC groups of countries are presented in appendices B.1 and B.2, while appendix C shows the proportion of trade (average of exports and imports) with capitalist and European CEMA countries, respec-tively. Again, intrabloc trade and East–West trade are separately analyzed.

at a distance, by Bulgaria. Compared to these countries, there was less pressure in Poland, the USSR, and Romania. Considering that the relative importance of trade has been rapidly increasing in all of these countries, economic pressures should signal the planners not only to pay more attention to inefficiencies in the existing system of trade, but also to focus increasingly on the potential benefits of trade as a new source of growth.

II. PARTIAL REFORMS

Partial reforms may be defined as measures that do not change the essential features of the traditional CPE (detailed planning in quantitative terms and reliance on direct instruments of coordination and control); in contrast, a comprehensive reform may be defined as an attempt to introduce the market mechanism.

In small CPEs, partial reforms invariably stress prevailing inefficiencies of foreign trade. It does not take long, of course, until the difficulties of selling exports and obtaining imports (or, more broadly, the recurrent balance-of-payments pressures, deterioration of the terms of trade, and worsening domestic supply bottlenecks) become apparent to the system's directors. Conversely, there are also many promising opportunities in the foreign trade sector that the reformers would like to utilize. In contrast to the domestic economy, where alternatives to produce a given output tend to be limited by fixed input coefficients, "the 'production' of imports by exports vastly increases the scope of alternatives, [prices] indicating only the terms on which any export can 'produce' an import. . . . Thus, the presence of foreign trade, by greatly increasing the scope of economic choice, emphasizes the need for the development of rational decision-making procedure."[26] Reforms in foreign trade are also facilitated because it is relatively easy to quantify the objectives; for example, maximization of foreign exchange earnings and minimization of foreign currency expenditures. Nonetheless, fear of external instability may be an important reason why only partial rather than comprehensive reforms are introduced. "There is a simultaneous danger that shortage of foreign exchange will also cause the retention of central controls, thus holding back the impetus toward decentralization."[27]

26. Herbert S. Levine, "The Effects of Foreign Trade on Soviet Planning Practices," in Brown and Neuberger, *International Trade*, p. 274.

27. Gregory Grossman, "Foreign Trade of the USSR: A Summary Appraisal," in Brown and Neuberger, *International Trade*, p. 344. The same point is also emphasized by Neuberger with reference to Yugoslavia: "Despite the reforms of 1952, 1961, and 1965, strong elements of central control over foreign exchange still exist. . . . In the Yugoslav case, the foreign exchange system appears to have become one of the last bastions of strength for those elements who oppose decentralization" (ibid., p. 362).

We may identify three types of partial reform measures. First, there are reforms of prices and exchange rates (such as the calculation of profitability coefficients, leading eventually to the gradual linking of foreign and domestic markets by meaningful exchange rates); second, there is a reduction of the number of plan targets; and, third, there are reforms of the foreign trade monopoly. Some of these reforms may represent distinct improvements over the prereform era, while some may create new problems as they attempt to solve old ones. In any case, partial reform measures are of interest, since they may be considered stepping stones to comprehensive reforms.

The systemic changes introduced in Yugoslavia (1965) and in Hungary (1968) are comprehensive reforms; therefore, they are not discussed in this section. In contrast, the series of economic changes introduced in Czechoslovakia between 1965 and 1968 can be considered partial reforms, since the intended comprehensive reforms were aborted in August 1968.

Price and Exchange Rate Reforms

Forging a meaningful link between domestic and foreign prices[28] represents one of the crucial steps in both price reform and foreign-trade reform. In traditional CPEs, exchange rates tend to be arbitrary, their purpose being to isolate, rather than connect, domestic and foreign markets. Under reforms in Eastern Europe, the official exchange rate generally has not been affected; instead, shadow exchange rates have been introduced, which may euphemistically be called "adjustment coefficients." What differentiates partial from comprehensive reforms is not the calculation of such coefficients but their application. Countries with partial reforms have permitted the new rates to influence major export-import decisions at the *enterprise* level.

The calculation of profitability coefficients in foreign trade—the antecedent of shadow exchange rates—was among the earliest reform measures in Eastern Europe. The operational significance of these coefficients, however, remained limited. Their use required very great effort and, in spite of this, they were fairly unreliable indicators of economic efficiency. Domestic price structures, even after adjustments, neglected important cost elements (interest, rent, and realistic depreciation charges). Over time it became evident that a meaningful application of profitability indexes and shadow exchange rates by planners or by enterprises must be linked with domestic price reforms.[29]

28. A discussion of specific measures in individual East European countries appeared in United Nations, *Economic Bulletin for Europe* 20, no. 1 (Geneva, 1968): 43–54.

29. For a critical evaluation of the earlier shadow exchange rates, see A. A. Brown, "Centrally Planned Foreign Trade and Economic Efficiency," *The American Economist* 5, no. 2 (November 1961): 11–28.

With the exception of Romania, all East European countries have undertaken wholesale industrial price reforms during the last several years. These reforms attempted to bring prices closer to factor costs and they also tried to harmonize domestic prices, to some extent at least, with foreign prices. Such price reforms were introduced first in Hungary, then in Czechoslovakia and East Germany, and (to a much more limited extent) in Poland and Bulgaria. As domestic prices have become more closely attuned to scarcity prices, it has also become easier to calculate realistic shadow exchange rates.

Steps have been taken in almost every East European country to reform the old system of separate and automatic price adjustment for each commodity by a "uniformization" of the shadow exchange rates. This means that the rates, or adjustment coefficients, have been set at the same level for major commodity groups or for given trading areas. As a next reform step, the provision should follow that enterprises producing for export (or those purchasing imports) be paid at a foreign price equivalent rather than at a fixed domestic price. But if foreign trade taxes and subsidies are used to wipe out all enterprise profits or losses, this mechanism will not have a substantially different effect on enterprise decisions than automatic price equalization under the old system. As a temporary, second-best solution, taxes and subsidies might be fixed (in rate or amount) for specified periods of time.

Among CEMA countries, uniform (in fact, dual) shadow exchange rates and fixed tariff-cum-subsidy schemes have been introduced only in Hungary, a development to be analyzed below in discussing comprehensive reforms. At this point we will consider other East European countries where only partial reform measures have been introduced.[30]

Some important steps were taken in Czechoslovakia toward the implementation of an operational exchange rate. Actually, two separate *sets* of exchange rates were introduced for each commodity category (one set for capitalist and another set for socialist markets). In subsequent stages, Czechoslovakia had also planned to establish: (1) uniform exchange rates within each trading area (by 1969), and (2) partial or full convertibility (by the early 1970s).

In East Germany, export earnings of FTEs and of producing enterprises are calculated by the official exchange rates, adjusted by so-called currency-relation coefficients, which take into account bilateral price levels by countries or by groups of countries. Managerial bonuses are based on profitability but, in most cases, the enterprise's freedom of decision is limited to assortment selections. A similar system has also been introduced in

30. For bibliographic references see United Nations, *Economic Bulletin*, and Frederic L. Pryor, "Barriers to Market Socialism in Eastern Europe in the Mid-1960s" (paper presented to the American Marketing Association Convention, Cincinnati, August 1969).

Bulgaria, but with more emphasis on the specific adjustment coefficients than in East Germany.

In Poland, actual foreign exchange receipts in exports are converted into zlotys at one of three shadow exchange rates, applicable in trade with MDCs, LDCs, and socialist countries. To calculate profits on exports, domestic costs are adjusted for differences between domestic and world-market prices of inputs, trade margins, and the sales tax; finally, these adjusted costs are subtracted from export yields, calculated in domestic zlotys. But since foreign trade plans continue to be assigned, partly in physical and partly in value terms, enterprises have only limited flexibility to make assortment decisions on the basis of profitability considerations.

Thus, multiple shadow exchange rates have been introduced in all smaller East European countries except in Romania, where until 1970 a central government body determined the prices at which export goods were bought from, and import goods sold to, domestic firms; even in Romania, however, new shadow exchange rates are planned to be introduced in the future.[31]

Planning Reforms

In all CEMA countries there has been an unequivocal tendency to reduce the number of quantitative plan targets. Yet, except for Czechoslovakia (and, of course Hungary and Yugoslavia), material balancing and central supply allocation have remained essentially intact in CEMA countries. In fact, planning reforms in these countries have been more "administrative streamlining"[32] than a purposeful preparation for market socialism. It would be a mistake, however, to identify automatically a reduction in the number of plan targets with greater economic efficiency. As earlier Hungarian experience shows, *partial* reduction of compulsory targets may be worse than detailed, specific directives. We owe this insight to Ivan Berend:

> The enterprises still had no market and price incentives, while on the other hand, they were hindered in their operations by too few directives. Thus the enterprises were beset by difficulties in obtaining the necessary raw materials and in delivering the goods produced. . . . Even the foreign trade enterprises, always most interested in a more elastic system, now strove for a completely detailed plan for export. Otherwise, they would not have been assured of being adequately supplied by the producing firms.[33]

31. See Michael Kaser, "Rumania: Perfecting the Management and Planning of the National Economy," in Hochman, Kaser, and Thalheim, eds., *Changing Economic Systems in East Europe* (London: Allen and Unwin, 1972), pp. 23–24.

32. Pryor, p. 52.

33. Berend, p. 87.

Modifications of the Foreign Trade Monopoly

Every East European country has shown signs of recognition that the functional separation of foreign trade and domestic production is very inefficient and has undertaken reforms to deal with this problem. The issue of foreign trade monopoly was debated with great vigor by East European economists after 1955.[34] These debates led to various compromises between the need to decentralize and the desire to maintain the old framework of central control.

Direct trading rights were granted to selected industrial firms or associations in all East European countries by the mid-1960s. These rights were already important in the 1950s in certain branches of production, in some countries. In addition to Yugoslavia and Hungary, East Germany and Czechoslovakia have been pioneers in this field. There have been fewer direct trading arrangements in Romania, Poland, Bulgaria, and, particularly, the USSR.

In Czechoslovakia, producing enterprises, industrial associations, and cooperative bodies may participate (with central permission) in the operational work of their respective FTEs. In fact, some FTEs have been reorganized as joint-stock companies, with direct participation of producing enterprises in their management. But as the independent power of FTEs diminished, "much unnecessary duplication resulted," and the bureaucracy was forced to issue more and more directives, until ". . . there arose what one might call 'permanent planning'—more and more frequent adjustments to adapt the plan to the real situation."[35] In East Germany, a number of specialized FTEs have been set up in addition to the newly established joint domestic-foreign trading enterprises, under the aegis of industrial branch associations. The organizational forms of foreign trade have changed relatively little in the USSR, Romania, Poland, and Bulgaria. In Romania, some FTEs have been subordinated to production ministries (which is a rather small change considering the sweeping reform decisions of the Central Committee of the Party in December 1967),[36] and these now receive export sales targets instead of quantitative targets, as previously.[37]

Perhaps the most radical departure from a rigid concept of foreign trade monopoly is the industrial cooperation between enterprises in East and West. By 1969, there were approximately 400 such agreements in force. The most

34. For a summary of this debate and a bibliography, the reader is referred to a discussion of the foreign trade monopoly in A. A. Brown, "The Economics of Centrally Planned Foreign Trade: A Case Study of Hungary" (Ph.D. diss., Harvard University, 1965).

35. Pleva, p. 40.

36. "Foreign Trade Directive of the Central Committee of the Rumanian Communist Party," *The American Review of East–West Trade* 1, no. 1 (January 1968): 51–55.

37. Kaser, p. 24.

frequent trade partners in Eastern Europe were Yugoslavia, followed by Poland, Hungary, and Czechoslovakia (and more recently by Romania and Bulgaria).[38]

All of these modifications of the foreign trade monopoly, however, represent only ad hoc changes in the existing system. These new arrangements fail to provide the new set of basic organizational principles needed to regulate the relationship of producing enterprises with FTEs or with the central authorities. To find such principles we must turn to an examination of the comprehensive reforms.

Partial Reforms: A Summary

Setting aside for the moment both Hungary and Yugoslavia, where much more fundamental foreign trade reforms have been introduced, we can offer a brief summary of the relative progress of partial foreign trade reforms in various East European countries.

We have found reforms of industrial wholesale prices in all countries except Romania, some price flexibility in Czechoslovakia, and, to a much more limited extent, in Poland and Bulgaria. There has been some progress toward the introduction of operational exchange rates in Czechoslovakia and East Germany and, to a lesser extent, in Poland and Bulgaria. In all East European countries, there has been a movement away from hyper-centralization in foreign trade. The number of compulsory plan targets has been reduced and the old concept of foreign trade monopoly has been reinterpreted. As a result, vertical levers of control have to some extent given way to horizontal links between producing enterprises and outside markets. In this area, too, Czechoslovakia and East Germany have gone further than bloc LDCs.

It appears, therefore, that—leaving aside the comprehensive reforms in Hungary and Yugoslavia—the most extensive partial reforms have been introduced in Czechoslovakia and East Germany, while at the other end of the scale we find Romania and the USSR. The rank correlation between foreign trade reforms and the indexes of reform pressures is indeed very high.

III. Comprehensive Reforms

General Considerations

Comparative analysis of economic pressure indicators and of partial reforms has shown that unsatisfactory economic performance is associated

---

38. United Nations, *Economic Bulletin*, p. 80. The significance of the new institutional flexibility for East–West trade is discussed in A. A. Brown and P. Marer, "East–West Trade: Old Issues and New Prospects," U.S. Congress, Joint Economic Committee, *A Foreign Economic Policy for the 1970s* (Washington, D.C.: U.S. Government Printing Office, 1971), pt. 6, pp. 1211–26.

with foreign trade reforms. Although stronger pressures are generally correlated with greater willingness to institute reforms, this stimulus-response relationship is somewhat obscured by noneconomic factors as well as by lags and discontinuities. In particular, any transition from partial to comprehensive reforms is likely to be a discontinuous process. Partial reforms in any given area provide no benefit beyond a certain point without introducing coordinated reforms in other areas. Decentralization, for instance, requires proper individual incentives as well as rational evaluation criteria (prices and exchange rates). Therefore, as pressures accumulate, at a certain point the futility of further partial reforms tends to be recognized, and this prepares the ground to institute *simultaneously* a set of interrelated reform measures.[39]

Although the introduction of comprehensive reforms represents a discontinuity, a multifaceted break with past practices, there is also in the background a certain evolutionary process that deserves emphasis. Earlier partial reform measures in foreign trade help to create the building blocks of a subsequent comprehensive reform. Thus, for instance, compulsory plan targets may be first reduced in number, then abolished altogether; foreign trade licenses may be first granted to producing enterprises only in exceptional cases, then approved as a rule; domestic prices may be first tenuously connected to foreign prices by efficiency index calculations, then closely linked by operational exchange rates.

Empirical Evidence

The interrelationship between comprehensive reforms and foreign trade can be analyzed on empirical grounds only in Yugoslavia and Hungary, the two countries where such reforms have been introduced and are still moving forward. In Czechoslovakia, foreign trade has again come under the centralized direction of the Ministry of Foreign Trade,[40] and during 1969–70 an indeterminate system of "planning through agreements" was used. Yugoslavia is somewhat of a special case in Eastern Europe with respect to foreign trade. It is not a member of CEMA, it trades mainly with the West, it has received exceptionally large Western aid, and it permits substantial international mobility of both capital and labor. Therefore, one can apply the Hungarian experience much more meaningfully to the other East European

39. What is required, given the legacies of CPEs, is a radically different approach to economic issues—substitution of the concept of opportunity cost for the traditional priority ordering of major target goals. This issue is considered in Alan A. Brown and Richard Yin, "Communist Reforms vs. Orthodoxy," *Communist Affairs* 3, no. 1 (January–February 1965): 3–10, esp. p. 9n.

40. "Decree No. 164," *Sbirka zakonu CSSR 1969* [Collection of laws of Czechoslovakia 1969] (Prague: November 1969), p. 540.

countries with whom Hungary shares certain institutional and political limitations, including heavy dependence on CEMA trading partners.

Hungarian trade composition. Economic pressures for reform, chronicled in section I, appeared to be particularly strong in Hungary by the mid-1960s. Further evidence of reform pressure for Hungary can be gleaned from the country's statistics on trade with the East and West.[41] The average growth rate of raw materials imports (including semiprocessed goods) from the East was 12.4 percent between 1955 and 1960, 9.5 percent between 1960 and 1965, and 6.2 percent between 1965 and 1969. There have been innumerable complaints in Hungary about the scarce supply of raw materials. What can Hungary do about the declining rate of growth of raw material imports from socialist countries? One possible option is to reduce raw material exports to socialist countries, but this may lead to further repercussions due to commodity bilateralism. Another option might be to attempt further import substitution, but this has already been pushed to extremes in some areas (e.g. coal), while in other areas there are no domestic sources to tap. The third option might be to import more raw materials from the West (already comprising, along with semiprocessed goods, more than three-fifths of western imports), either at the expense of other commodity groups or by increasing exports.

Citing long-term and short-term comparative advantage, Hungarian economists have emphasized the desirability of substantially expanding machinery exports to the West to pay for imports. This, however, is becoming increasingly difficult, as shown by the declining annual rate of growth of machinery sales to the West: 21.5 percent between 1950 and 1955, 7.8 percent between 1955 and 1960, 5.2 percent between 1960 and 1965, and 0.1 percent between 1965 and 1969 (see appendix chart D.14). By the late 1960s, machinery exports (including spare parts) represented only 6 percent of sales to Western countries. Thus, Hungary has been selling more and more raw materials, semimanufactured goods, and agricultural products in order to import machinery and needed primary products.[42] Adverse trade composition and its deterioration over time, along with the previously emphasized balance-of-payments pressures, can be said to have contributed to the comprehensive reform decision.

From recognition to implementation. The awareness of Hungarian economists that partial reforms will not solve their basic problems is illustrated by the following statement: "The assumption that prominent faults of the planning machinery could be corrected by changing its cogwheels ... proved

41. Data on Hungarian trade by major commodity categories for 1950–69 and subperiods are presented in appendix D.

42. Compare appendix charts D.13 to D.20. Raw materials were the fastest growing exports (D.18) and the slowest growing imports (D.17).

wrong. This led to the recognition that instead of partial modifications, complete and far-reaching reforms were needed."[43]

The successful launching of a major reform requires that the economists' recommendations be harmonized with the thinking of the political leadership. In Hungary, this was achieved during the early 1960s. At a meeting of the Central Committee of the Hungarian (Communist) Party (May 1963), R. Nyers stressed that the major economic problems would have to be solved comprehensively rather than piecemeal. He emphasized the need to increase the rate of economic growth, to improve the balance of payments, to increase the standard of living, and to improve enterprise management.[44]

The political directive to introduce comprehensive economic reforms in Hungary was issued in May 1966. It placed particularly strong emphasis on foreign trade's new role in the Hungarian economy: "Faster rate of economic growth requires that we increase our participation in the international division of labor and make more extensive use of its advantages. Foreign markets must be allowed to have a stronger stimulus on our production. . . . Under the new economic mechanism, an organic link must be established between domestic and foreign markets. We must reduce the overprotection of domestic production, eliminate the laxness resulting from such overprotection. Foreign trade must be encouraged to play a role in speeding up specialization, and in the more rapid attainment of higher technological standards."[45]

The Plan and the New Market in Hungary

The most important aspect of Hungary's comprehensive economic reforms is the giving up of the detailed annual plan as the chief instrument of coordination and control, and the placing of the market mechanism, previously a peripheral instrument, at the center of the economic stage.[46] Accordingly: (1) the relationship between enterprises, as a general rule, is regulated by contracts, although the right of entry remains strictly controlled at the center; (2) the new prices introduced in 1968 are (with important exceptions) based on factor costs (some prices are fully flexible,

---

43. Berend, pp. 87–88.

44. Rezsö Nyers, *Gazdaságpolitikánk és a gazdasági mechanizmus reformja* [Our economic policy and the reform of the economic mechanism] (Budapest: Kossuth Könyvkiadó, 1968), p. 18.

45. As quoted in György Tallós, *A gazdaságirányitási reform a külkereskedelemben* [Reform of economic management in foreign trade] (Budapest: Közgazdasági és Jogi Könyvkiadó, 1968), p. 31. The resolution also contained the usual caveats about the preservation of central control, as well as a stress on gradual adjustment during the transitional period.

46. This paper is concerned with the relationship between foreign trade and economic reforms only; for a general assessment of the Hungarian New Economic Mechanism, see Bela Balassa, "The Economic Reform in Hungary," *Economica* 37, no. 145 (February 1970): 1–22.

others have limited or no flexibility); and (3) the new exchange rates link foreign and domestic markets operationally, that is, importers pay and producers receive the domestic equivalent of the actual foreign price. While the market is permitted to play an important role, the influence of market forces is still circumscribed by various direct and indirect instruments such as quotas, tariffs, foreign trade taxes and subsidies, licenses, and selective controls.

Foreign trade planning. Comprehensive, short-term planning has always been more of a myth than a reality in foreign trade. The idea that detailed, centrally determined commands can effectively coordinate short-term decisions in resource allocation has now been discarded. Only a few specific, short-term plan targets have been retained (in the quarterly and annual plans) because of institutional limitations and fear of domestic bottlenecks. The major institutional limitation is the system of bilateral agreements specifying the quantities of goods to be exported and imported. The retained plan instruments are central allocations[47] and forced contracts for production and distribution, supplemented by a large number of "market control instruments."[48]

The main planning emphasis has shifted to medium-term (five-year) plans. Under the new system, the medium-term plan includes projections of the volume and rate of growth of foreign trade, estimates of trade balances by principal foreign markets, and outlines of commodity composition. These plans consider not only existing capacity but also projected domestic input and foreign marketing developments, estimated by sophisticated micro- and macroeconomic models.

The chief instrument of long-term plan implementation is investment planning. Major investment decisions, those that determine the future "proportions" of the economy, are retained by the center. To insure that enterprise investments will also conform to plan projections, the market mechanism is centrally manipulated so as to permit the expansion of selected enterprises only.

The relationship between producing and foreign-trade enterprises. Before the reform, FTEs traded for their own account, independently of producing enterprises; since the reform, FTEs have become mainly agents for producing enterprises. FTEs trading for their own account handle mostly the products of local and cooperative industries.

Two types of contractual relationships are common between producing enterprises and FTEs: agency contracts and partnership contracts. There

47. In 1968, meat and grain belonged to this category.
48. For a detailed description of these new tools, see A. A. Brown and P. Marer, "Instruments of Trade Control in the Hungarian New Economic Mechanism," mimeographed, 12 pp., obtainable from the authors by request.

are variations within each type, but their names indicate the essentials of each arrangement. In general, producing and foreign trade enterprises are free to enter into different types of contracts although central authorities encourage partnerships, calling them "higher forms." Table 5.1 shows the proportion of trade conducted under the various contractual arrangements.[49]

TABLE 5.1. Share of Trade by Type of Trade Organization in 1968
(Percentage of total trade)

	Import		Export	
Organizational form	East	West	East	West
Enterprises with foreign trading rights	11.5	7.0	19.6	8.9
FTEs trading for own account	9.6	5.8	9.0	10.6
Various agency contracts	68.0	73.9	42.5	30.9
Partnership contracts	10.2	12.1	28.9	49.4
Other	0.7	1.2	0.0	0.2
Total	100.0	100.0	100.0	100.0

During 1968, and again in 1969, more producing enterprises have been given independent foreign trade rights, an arrangement that had been introduced in Hungary as far back as 1957.

The new price system. The new price system endeavors to set relative prices of industrial commodities (but not agricultural or retail trade prices) approximately proportional to costs, including a more realistic valuation of imported inputs. To link domestic and foreign prices, two new exchange rates were introduced, the so-called foreign trade price coefficients (FTCs). One of these is applicable to trade with the West, the other to trade with the East. Sales receipts of exporting enterprises are calculated from actual foreign exchange earnings, converted into domestic currency at the appropriate exchange rate; importing enterprises similarly pay the domestic equivalent of the actual import cost.

These "dual exchange rates" (one of which is designed to operate in CEMA markets where currencies are not convertible and bilateral agreements prevail) raise many interesting issues, to be explored in greater detail in the next section. At this point, we want to indicate how the authorities attempt to harmonize flexible foreign trade prices and controlled domestic prices within a viable market mechanism.

49. Sándor Czeitler, *Az új gazdasági mechanizmus bevezetésének tapasztalatai a külkereskedelemben* [Experiences of the New Economic Mechanism in foreign trade] (Budapest: Kossuth Könyvkiadó, 1969), p. 79.

There are four types of domestic prices: fixed, maximum, delimited, and completely free. During the first few years of the reforms, while the economy continues to be a sellers' market, maximum and delimited prices are usually "sticky" at the upper limit, so the issue of flexibility is between controlled prices on the one hand (fixed, maximum and delimited), and free prices on the other. Table 5.2 shows the proportion of controlled and free prices for some sectors in 1968.[50]

TABLE 5.2. Controlled and Free Prices after the 1968 Price Reform
(Percentage of production)

	Controlled Prices		
Product	All types	Fixed	Completely Free Prices
Raw materials			
Fuels	85	75	15
Other ind. raw materials	35	10	65
Semimanufactures			
Metallurgical products	85	0	15
Textile fibers	75	0	25
Manufactures			
Chemicals	45	10	55
Machinery	35	0	65
Textiles	10	0	90
Foodstuffs	15	5	85
Agricultural goods	88	59	12
Consumer goods	77	20	23
Food	87	31	13
Clothing	75	0	25

· Prices are controlled for fuels, most standard semimanufactured products, agricultural products, and a substantial portion of consumer goods. Prices are essentially free for nonfuel industrial raw materials and most manufactured products. But we note that controlled prices tend to set upper limits only (with the exception of fuels and agricultural goods) in order to give some play to market forces even in these areas while, at the same time, preventing inflation in an essentially protected, not yet competitive economy. The experience of Yugoslavia and Czechoslovakia with rapidly rising prices following their market reforms made the Hungarians cautious about their price reforms.

50. Sources: Béla Csikós-Nagy, "Az új magyar árrendszer" [The new Hungarian price system], *Közgazdasági szemle* 14, no. 3 (March 1968): 267; see also his article in Friss, *Economic Mechanism*, esp. pp. 49, 51.

Suppose prices on the world market rise above the domestic price. If the latter is controlled, will domestic producers now increase exports, even if it would mean supply bottlenecks, or will the state intervene? To guard against such problems, various measures were introduced as part of the price reform package. It was decided, for example, that domestic and import prices should generally be uniform for those products whose domestic price is fixed. This "uniformization of prices" would be centrally determined for some products; in other cases, the FTE or the wholesaler would calculate an average "accounting" price to remain fixed for a certain period of time. Subsequent deviations from this "accounting" price may be reflected in a new domestic price, or the state could step in with specific subsidies or taxes.

A number of additional measures were also taken to "harmonize" foreign and domestic prices at desired levels, such as a revised, three-column tariff schedule (introduced partly as an instrument of commercial policy, to facilitate negotiations for GATT membership), export and price subsidies, and various new taxes on exports and imports.[51]

How extensively should the central authorities delegate pricing decisions? Kaser formulated the dilemma concisely: "If they devolve too little authority for price setting to the production units, prices will not find their proper level and the ensuing shortages could induce a return to central direction. If, on the other hand, too much power is put into the hands of industrial enterprises, the latter may be tempted to act as a monopoly."[52] The latter possibility is a particularly clear danger in Hungary, where industrial concentration is generally greater than in other countries, East or West.[53] The Hungarian reforms during the 1968–70 transition period represent an attempt to escape between the horns of this pricing dilemma. Their solution is a temporary compromise that is to be periodically reassessed.

IV. THE ECONOMICS OF DISEQUILIBRIUM EXCHANGE RATES

Concept of the New Foreign Exchange Rate

An essential instrument of the market mechanism introduced by the Hungarian reforms is the new exchange rate. The old official exchange rate was not changed but two additional foreign trade price coefficients (FTCs) were introduced in 1968. The FTCs are quasi exchange rates; they serve as guides to resource allocation; hence, the two concepts are used interchangeably in this paper. Under the new system, all importers pay the domestic

51. These, and various other measures, are discussed in Brown and Marer, "Trade Control."

52. Michael Kaser, "The East European Economic Reforms and Foreign Trade," *The World Today* 23, no. 12 (December 1967): 518.

53. Bela Balassa, "The Firm in the New Economic Mechanism in Hungary," below, ch. 10, pp. 356–58; see also Pryor, pp. 8–9.

equivalent of the actual foreign trade price converted into forints at the respective FTCs (modified by import duties, various turnover taxes, and in a few cases by import subsidies); and, similarly, all exporters receive the domestic equivalent of the actual foreign trade price calculated at the FTCs (also modified by subsidies and special taxes).

Let us illustrate the concept and operation of the FTC, provisionally assuming that Hungary trades with only one country; consequently, there is only one FTC or exchange rate.

Method of calculation. The FTC attempts to indicate the cost of earning a unit of foreign exchange. The domestic cost of the export bill is divided by the estimated foreign exchange yield. Symbolically,

$$R = \frac{D}{F}. \tag{5.1}$$

There is some question as to the precise calculating procedure. Since both domestic prices and the exchange rate need to be adjusted, a set of simultaneous equations could theoretically provide a solution. Alternatively, successive approximations might be employed. In fact, it has been reported by Kornai that such calculations had been made;[54] however, according to other Hungarian sources, the mutual interdependence between the exchange rate and new domestic prices was not taken fully into account in the final calculations.[55]

In the numerator, estimated 1968 domestic prices included profit margins, as well as the foreign trade margin and all additional forint expenses connected with exports (transport, packaging, advertising, etc.); in the denominator, projected foreign exchange receipts were reduced by transport and other costs incurred in foreign currencies (f.o.b. exports).[56]

Alternatives considered. There was a long debate in Hungary concerning the methodology of establishing the correct level of FTC, particularly about whether the numerator in equation 5.1 should be based on average or on marginal costs. In opposing the average rate (which was actually chosen), the advocates of the marginal FTC wanted to consider the domestic cost of earning a unit of foreign exchange in the least economical 10 to 20 percent of exports that (for a given volume of imports) would still be necessary to

54. János Kornai, *Mathematical Planning of Structural Decisions* (Amsterdam: North-Holland Publishing Co., 1967), p. 302.

55. Different models of price and exchange rate adjustment yield surprisingly similar results, but it is not clear which model was actually used. New domestic prices introduced in 1968 are closer to factor costs than before the reforms, but significant deviations, especially in agriculture and food industry, remain. See Csikós-Nagy, "New Hungarian Price System," p. 267, table 3.

56. See Zsuzsa Esze, "A devizaárszorzó és az árrendszer" [The foreign exchange coefficients and the price system], *Közgazdasági szemle* 14, no. 6 (June 1968): 676–86, esp. p. 680; Friss, p. 183; and Czeitler, p. 30.

ensure an equilibrium in the balance of payments. The main opposition to the marginal rate centered around its potential inflationary effect.[57]

The most important consequence of using the average rather than the marginal rate is that, to encourage a volume of exports necessary to pay for a given volume of imports, additional instruments are required to equilibrate the balance of payments. Since the new FTC is based on average cost, the authorities have to grant huge subsidies to maintain a required volume of exports. They must also impose various taxes and other restrictions to reduce the effective demand for imports. These measures, of course, conflict with the main objective of the reform, efficiency.[58]

The dual exchange rate solution. Let us now remove the simplifying assumption that Hungary trades with only one country, and there is only one FTC. In fact, FTCs have been calculated separately for the two world markets. The exchange rate in trade with Western countries has been set at 60 domestic forints to the dollar; in trade with Eastern countries, the rate has been 40 domestic forints to the ruble. Symbolically,

$$R_w = \frac{D_w}{F_w} = \frac{\text{ft } 60}{\$1} \quad \text{and} \quad R_e = \frac{D_e}{F_e} = \frac{\text{ft } 40}{\text{r } 1} \tag{5.2}$$

where

R_w = calculated exchange rate in trade with the West;

R_e = calculated exchange rate in trade with the East;

D_w or D_e = domestic costs (in domestic forints, ft) of the export bill to West or East, respectively;

F_w or F_e = the foreign exchange yield of the two export bills (in dollars or accounting rubles, respectively).

Since, for purposes of reporting foreign trade transactions, all East European countries consider the accounting ruble to be 11 percent more valuable than the dollar (on the basis of the official exchange rate), we may bring the two FTCs to a common denominator in terms of dollars:[59]

$$R_w = \frac{D_w}{F_w} = \frac{\text{ft } 60}{\$1} \quad \text{and} \quad R_e = \frac{D_e}{F_e} = \frac{\text{ft } 36}{\$1} \tag{5.3}$$

57. E.g., Zs. Esze, "Foreign exchange coefficients," and Béla Sulyok, "A devizaárszorzó kérdéséhez" [On the question of the foreign exchange coefficient], *Közgazdasági szemle* 14, no. 9 (September 1968): 1102–7.

58. It would be interesting to integrate the Hungarian methodological debate on FTC calculations with the purchasing power parity doctrine in the West. Here we can only note that little attention has been paid to the choice of alternative bills of goods. Sulyok briefly mentions two alternatives to using the export package: national income excluding nontradables (i.e., both actual and potential exports), and consumer goods. (Sulyok, pp. 1102–03.)

59. Symbolically, if we substitute into $R_e = (\text{ft/r})40$ the official dollar value of one ruble (r 1 = \$1.11), we obtain $F_e = (\text{ft/\$})36$.

Thus, according to the new exchange rates introduced in 1968, the dollar is about 67 percent more valuable than the ruble in Hungarian export transactions. The implications and significance of this relative valuation of the two currencies are discussed in section v.

Consequences of Disequilibrium Exchange Rates

We may elucidate the meaning and economic consequences of using a disequilibrium exchange rate with a diagram. On the vertical axis in figure 5.1 is shown the price of securing a unit of foreign exchange, which is a ratio

Fig. 5.1. Supply of foreign exchange

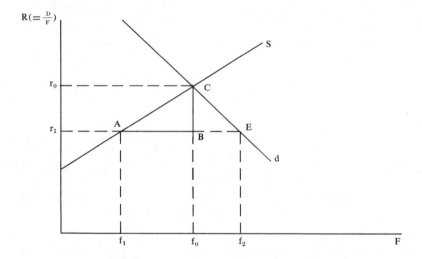

of domestic and foreign currencies. In the FTC calculations, the price is the cost of producing an export good worth an average unit of foreign exchange, which is, simply, the rate of exchange ($R = D/F$, where D is domestic currency and F is foreign exchange, dollars or rubles). Corresponding quantities of foreign exchange are measured along the horizontal axis (F, in terms of dollars or rubles). Let us now arrange, according to increasing domestic procurement cost, all export goods (or additional amounts of the same good), each yielding a specified amount of foreign exchange.[60] This enables us to calculate and plot the price of each additional unit or amount of foreign exchange. The locus of these points will be an upward-sloping curve (S), as

60. It should be noted that domestic costs include normal profits in the Marshallian sense, while foreign exchange yields are f.o.b. (i.e., excluding transportation and other expenses incurred in earning foreign exchange).

depicted in figure 5.1. This line will be called the supply curve of foreign exchange. (The simplifying assumption of linearity will be later modified.)

If a certain amount of foreign exchange, say f_0, is necessary to maintain equilibrium in the balance of payments (to pay for a given amount of imports), then the equilibrium exchange rate level will be r_0. Conversely, at a level below r_0, say r_1, we have a disequilibrium rate, since the corresponding amount of foreign exchange, f_1, is less than f_0.

The consequence of using a disequilibrium rate, such as r_1, is a deficit in the balance of payments, unless additional measures are introduced (e.g. subsidies to increase exports). The deficit is shown by the distance between f_0 and f_1, if imports are given at f_0; the deficit, however, will be larger (e.g. the distance between f_1 and f_2) if enterprises are free to buy abroad on the basis of price. The amount of required subsidy is shown by the area of the triangle ABC; if there is a downward-sloping demand curve (d), the amount of imports to be reduced through quotas, tariffs, and taxes is given by the triangle BCE. (In our subsequent analysis we assume that the demand for foreign exchange is given at a certain level, since the actual shape of the curve would be difficult to derive empirically on the basis of available information.)

Derivation of Hungary's foreign exchange supply curves. On the basis of scattered but reliable official data, we were able to construct the two Hungarian foreign exchange supply curves for 1968, separately for Eastern and Western trade (see appendix A). The supply curves of Hungary's exports to Western and Eastern countries are shown in figures 5.2a and 5.2b. The

Fig. 5.2a. Hungary's supply of foreign exchange (West)

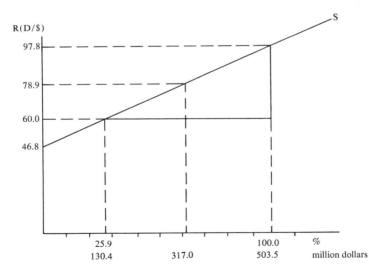

Fig. 5.2b.   Hungary's supply of foreign exchange (East)

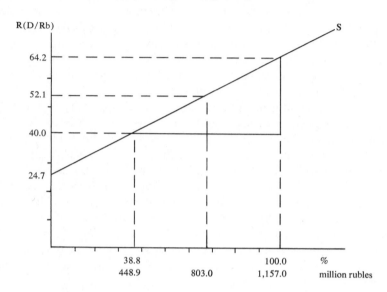

official FTCs, R_w and R_e (see equation 5.2), are 60 and 40, respectively, which are disequilibrium rates, like r_1 in figure 5.1. At these levels, the volume of exports that could be undertaken without subsidy is $130.4 million to the West (25.9 percent of Western exports), and 448.9 million rubles to the East (38.8 percent of Eastern exports). The fact that substantially more than half of the exports to both areas had to be subsidized indicates how much the actual FTCs were set below the intended average exchange rates. Applying Hungarian data to our diagrams, we have calculated the average FTCs as 72.3 and 44.4, respectively. In fact, these results are similar to ex post Hungarian calculations which show that "on the basis of 1968 structure, actual FTCs were on the average 70.5 and 44, respectively."[61]

Our calculated FTCs are based on linear supply curves. On the basis of Hungarian calculations, however, we know that there is a high degree of dispersion of the coefficients at both ends of the curve.[62] Thus, the curve is shaped as indicated by the broken line in figure 5.3. The rapid rise of the cost

61. Czeitler, p. 35. Actually, the estimates cited by this source range from (ft/$)69 to 72 and from (ft/r)43 to 45.

62. "Sector exchange rates" are given in Kornai, p. 302, where he states that calculations "on the product level reveal an even greater dispersion. The domestic delivery price of imports [per] dollar shows a dispersion between ft 10 and ft 470." The source of Kornai's calculations is a report of the Central Statistical Office.

Fig. 5.3.   Supply of foreign exchange: increasing versus constant costs

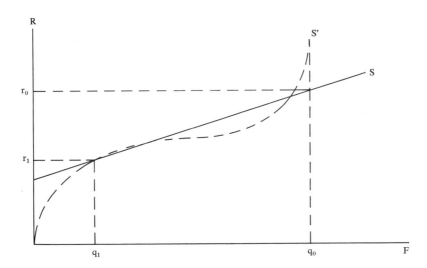

of foreign exchange at the right is of significance for the effectiveness of the reform. This will be apparent when we consider potential export substitution by producing enterprises that are currently not subsidized.

Efficiency considerations. The effectiveness of the foreign trade reforms is greatly reduced by the fact that central authorities have to subsidize a majority of the enterprises. Fixed subsidy rates or amounts, which essentially equalize domestic and export prices, create too much risklessness for enterprises and do not stimulate them to undertake technological improvements and reduce costs. The other problem is that subsidized enterprises may not be the most efficient ones.

It was an important innovation of the Hungarian New Economic Mechanism during its initial phase (1968–70) that subsidies were shifted from the FTEs to producing enterprises and that they were no longer to be granted automatically on each commodity. Instead, subsidies were set for individual enterprises on the basis of their entire export activity, and the subsidies were to remain fixed (in rate or amount) for three years. The expectation was that subsidized enterprises would try to increase efficiency not only by cost-cutting but also by changing the existing structure of their exports. As we have already mentioned in discussing partial reforms, such a modification signifies a radical break with the old system; although, it should be added, the scope of altering the commodity composition of exports remained limited to the export mix *within* individual enterprises. A corollary is that

potential exporters were discouraged from entering export trade, as long as
their unit costs exceeded the existing level of FTCs.[63]

Potential new exporters, to be sure, could be stimulated by administrative
methods; the reforms, however, have not been able to deal with the legacy
of bureaucratic risk-aversion. There has been, in fact, opposition to innovation at two different organizational levels. First, enterprises have
learned from long experience that it is safer to follow established routines
than to seek out new markets, which is a risky proposition. Entrepreneurial
spirit is hardly fostered if, in case of success, extraordinary profits are taxed
away and, in case of failure, subsidies are denied to the pioneers. Second, the
higher authorities are also reluctant to experiment with a new, would-be
exporter who may, after all, fail to live up to expectations. Even though the
requested subsidy may be smaller than some other subsidy already granted
to established exporters, the central authorities know that it is easy to mis-
calculate in foreign trade. Little justification is needed to maintain existing
subsidies; why, then, take a chance on some promising novice whose errors
may need lengthier explanations?

63. The supply curve of foreign exchange may be shown as an envelope curve of the cost
curves of exporting enterprises. The cost curve of an excluded, would-be exporter (C_0) appears
to the right of f_1.

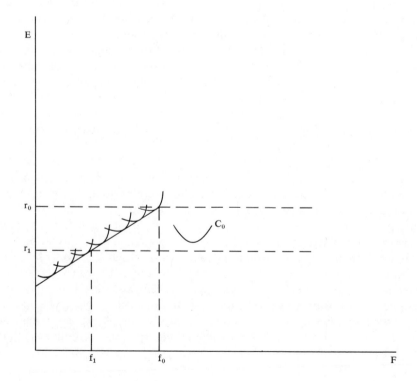

In response to these shortcomings, foreign trade subsidies differentiated by enterprises have been replaced, starting in 1971, by subsidies differentiated according to twelve industry groups.[64] The new subsidy schedules are fixed, identically for each firm within a branch, for five years (in declining rate or amount). This change represents a further movement toward "uniformization" of exchange rates; indeed, the National Planning Office expects that industrial subsidy levels will be uniform within a few years.[65] In the meantime, the task of improving the structure of exports among branches remains centralized, the chief instrument being the state's continued control over investments.

To conclude: keeping exchange rates much below marginal levels requires large subsidies. This is not only costly in the short run but it also freezes, to some extent, the prevailing inefficiencies of the export structure in the long run. Entrepreneurial spirit and potential competition are stifled as long as would-be exporters are discouraged. The present exchange rates also require continued administrative restriction of imports and provide no clear guidelines for enterprises to weigh the alternatives between exporting and import substitution. Therefore, average or below-average FTCs offer only suboptimization.

While the exchange rate can be adjusted to an equilibrium level over time, the institutional limitations of CEMA for a given East European country's foreign trade reforms appear more intractable. Hungary's close links with the CEMA market, where trade is conducted under bilateral agreements, are an important reason why various additional control mechanisms must still operate in her foreign trade, despite her attempt to use the market mechanism (e.g. exchange rates).[66]

V. Implications of Dual Markets

Interpretation of Dual Exchange Rates

In the previous section we reported that Hungary introduced two separate regional rates. It would be interesting to see why these two exchange rates differ (from equation 5.3, $R_w > R_e$), and why by such a large margin (60 versus 36). One possibility is that they are "incentive" exchange rates, designed to stimulate exports to, and restrict imports from, Western countries. On the basis of repeated assurances that this is not the case, and statements that the two FTCs were similarly calculated (see above), we may safely reject this explanation. Actually, there is evidence that the differential between the two exchange rates should be even greater.[67]

64. See Balassa, "The Firm," p. 369; also, T. Nagy (p. 4) in his comments on Balassa at the Conference.
65. Interview with O. Gadó in *Figyelö* 14, no. 44 (4 November 1970): 3.
66. See Brown and Marer, "Trade Control."
67. See n. 61.

Let us consider a representative bale (analogous to a Marshallian bale, in fact, a representative sample unit) of commodities exported to each of the two markets. This approach enables us to compare the domestic cost and foreign exchange yield not of the total export bills to the two trading areas, but the cost and yield of two representative units of exports. Let each of these export units (e.g. a jar of jam to the West and a radio tube to the East) be worth, say, one dollar at the going world market price (determined from price quotations on similar products in Western markets). Retaining our earlier notation, but now referring to representative units, we have from equation 5.3:

$$\frac{D_w}{F_w} > \frac{D_e}{F_e}. \tag{5.4}$$

This provides two possible explanations of the difference between the two FTCs. The inequality in equation 5.4 will hold if either $D_w > D_e$, or $F_w < F_e$, or both.

On the basis of direct evidence, we have grounds to reject the first possibility; that is, the average domestic cost of a dollar's worth of exports is not higher to the West than to the East.[68] *Therefore, $F_w < F_e$ must be true.*

By itself, this fact is not surprising. Western economists have long been aware of this possibility (even though adjustments similar to those we usually make for domestic prices in these countries have not been made for foreign trade prices). It is, however, of great significance that our analysis leads to the conclusion that all or a substantial share of the 67 percent divergence between the two exchange rates should be attributed to the disparity between the foreign trade price levels in the two markets.[69] Evidence is available that the results of similar calculations for other countries are not dissimilar.[70]

68. In eastern exports, manufactured goods dominate; in western exports, agricultural goods. Domestic prices of manufactured goods are generally above factor costs, while domestic prices of agricultural products are lower (cf. n. 55). Our detailed input-output calculations at the IDRC East European Project point to the same conclusion. For a thorough analysis of these results, see Douglas O. Walker, "Socialist Price Formation Models and Input-Output Analysis: A Study of Hungary, 1959–1964" (Ph.d. diss., University of Southern California, 1970). We have also considered the possibility that domestic costs (D_w and D_e in equation 5.4) could have been based not on projected 1968 prices (which are still distorted, as mentioned in n. 55) but on adjusted factor-cost prices. But in this case, the inequality $D_w > D_e$, would suggest that Hungary's exports to the East were more in accordance with comparative advantage than western exports. This fact, however, would seem to have been an important finding for the Hungarians to stress, but no discussion of it has come to our attention.

69. If we took into account the possible divergence between D_e and D_w suggested by Csikós-Nagy (see n. 55), this conclusion would be further strengthened.

70. "The production [through exports] of a unit of convertible currency requires approximately 50 percent more domestic resources in Hungary and in Czechoslovakia than the [production] of a unit of socialist currency" (Ausch, p. 115n).

A Conclusion for Foreign Trade Analysis

Before considering the implications of the dual exchange rates for the Hungarian reforms, we should point out the significance of this finding for future research in East European foreign trade. As a by-product of Hungarian, Czechoslovak, and other East European reforms' efforts to establish a market mechanism, what we suspected in the past with respect to foreign trade prices of CEMA countries now emerges with greater clarity. The price levels on the two markets are substantially different, suggesting that official East European foreign trade statistics should be adjusted.

Would East European sources substantiate our conclusions reached on the basis of Hungary's dual exchange rates? Supposing that the price level difference is indeed large, how much of this difference can be assigned to relatively high prices in intrabloc trade and how much to relatively low prices in East–West trade?

There is an important East European study containing the statistical findings of a group of CEMA experts on intrabloc foreign trade prices.[71] These findings, whose importance has not been widely recognized in the West, are consistent with our interpretation of Hungary's dual exchange rates. It enables us to estimate the level of intrabloc prices, relative to world market (*not* East–West trade) prices.[72] Using the CEMA price study as a point of departure, our calculations show that:

1. The average level of foreign trade prices in intra-CEMA trade (considering all member countries) appears to be substantially higher than world market prices. In 1963, this difference was in the neighborhood of 20 percent. If quality considerations could have been taken more fully into account, the actual difference would have probably been even greater.
2. The price level of manufactures in intrabloc trade is generally higher, while the price level of primary products is lower, than the average price level differential.[73]

Additional statistical studies, comparing the level of East–West prices to estimated world market prices, indicate that East European countries tend to export to the West below world prices. Accepting the range of these

71. S. Ausch and F. Bartha, "Az árak elméleti problémai a KGST-országok közötti kereskedelemben" [Theoretical problems of prices in trade among CEMA countries], *Közgazdasági szemle* 14, no. 3 (March 1967): 283–300.

72. For calculations, see P. Marer, *Postwar Pricing and Price Patterns in Socialist Foreign Trade (1946–1971)*, IDRC Report no. 1 (Bloomington: Indiana University, 1972).

73. For a suggested explanation of *relative* prices in intrabloc trade, see ibid. and P. Marer, "Foreign Trade Prices in the Soviet Bloc," *ASTE Bulletin* 10, no. 2 (Fall 1968): 6–9.

studies' findings, we estimate that manufactured goods are sold by East European exporters to the West at prices between 10 and 30 percent lower, and primary products between 5 and 20 percent lower, than prices obtained by Western exporters for similar products.[74] While the observed price differentials between eastern exports to the West and estimated world prices are, no doubt, influenced by the poorer quality of CEMA exports, as long as we can assume that the quality of Eastern goods sold to the West is not lower than the quality of goods exported by East European countries to each other, the two calculations (intra-CEMA and East–West prices) can be combined.

Thus, by combining export price levels of CEMA countries in their intrabloc and Western markets, it appears that Eastern export prices were substantially higher in CEMA trade than in East–West trade during the 1960s. These price differences were larger for manufactures in general, and for machinery in particular, than for primary products. Our previous examination of the dual exchange rates introduced in the Hungarian reforms has shown how substantial the average price difference may be in the case of Hungary.[75]

Dual Markets and Yugoslavia's Exchange Rate Reform

If a CPE introduces the market mechanism to implement decentralization, domestic and foreign markets must be meaningfully linked. Since there are substantial differences between price levels in the two world markets, this must be recognized, measured, and then reflected in the exchange rates. As we have seen, this has been done in Hungary; it will be of interest to consider the experience of Yugoslavia, where this has not been done. To be sure, most of Yugoslavia's trade is with the West, and the Yugoslav dinar is considered semihard currency by East European countries, but in some respects Yugoslavia's conduct of trade is similar to that of other East European countries.

As part of its foreign trade reform, Yugoslavia introduced a new exchange rate in 1965, without taking into account differences in East-West price levels. A sudden shift may be observed in Yugoslavia's balance of trade with the East in 1965, a shift that seems to be associated with the failure to use a dual set of exchange rates. Thus, from 1964 to 1965, the balance-of-trade ratio (exports divided by imports) with CEMA countries skyrocketed from 0.82 to 1.25.[76] A Yugoslav observer, Z. Mrkušić, states: "The adoption of a

74. See Marer, *Postwar Pricing and Price Patterns*, for further discussion. There is little evidence that import prices from the West are substantially different from world market prices.

75. An experimental adjustment of official Hungarian foreign trade statistics has been made in ibid.

76. See appendix B.1.

uniform exchange rate has only heightened an already existing tendency towards a rapid increase of exports through clearing rather than on the basis of convertible currency; this attended by the increased growth of imports on the basis of convertible currency rather than through clearing accounts. The reason seems to be that as a rule, trade through clearing involves prices somewhat higher than the 'world' prices, i.e., those prevailing on the convertible currency markets."[77]

Anatomy of Exchange Rate Failure in an Inconvertible Market

For Hungary, or for any East European country at the present time, even dual exchange rates represent an oversimplification. Not only are there differential exchange rates by industrial branches (between 1968 and 1970 by enterprises), but there are also various inconvertible currency submarkets in both eastern and western trading areas on which prices tend to differ. The problem might be solved by means of appropriate discounts and premiums, as long as bilateral price level differences can be calculated. Indeed, the Hungarians have used discounts in trading with western LDCs whose currency is not convertible. On the other hand, there is no clear evidence that similar discounts (or premiums) are also applied in trade with eastern countries, though both the problem and the potential solution are mentioned in the literature.[78]

What remains to be examined is whether Hungary can succeed in implementing its reforms even with realistic dual exchange rates (which may be further adjusted to take into account bilateral price level differences within a given regional market). How can this problem be solved in view of the continued problem of different commodity price *ratios* in the two major markets and the existing institutional limitations imposed by the inconvertibility of currencies within the CEMA trading area?

At this point we consider the problem of different commodity price ratios. We have seen, for example, that machinery prices are relatively more overpriced in the East than raw material prices. If enterprises could freely decide on exports and imports according to profitability criteria, they would attempt to export more machinery to the East, import more materials from the

77. Zarko Mrkušić, "Organization of Foreign Trade in Yugoslavia," *Slavic Papers* (Florida State University) 3 (1969): 30–31.

78. Thus, Imre Vajda writes: "Where our export prices are higher—for example, in trade with China—than elsewhere on the socialist market, there our import prices in general also exceed the average elsewhere." *Szocialista külkereskedelem* [Socialist foreign trade] (Budapest: Közgazdasági és Jogi Könyvkiadó, 1963), p. 87. We may also cite a statement by B. Csikós-Nagy: "Discounts are calculated primarily for non-socialist clearing currencies, but there is no problem conceptually to calculate discounts for the various clearing rubles also relative to the transferable ruble" (*Általános*, p. 359).

East, import more machinery from the West, and export more materials to the West. The consequences of these attempts can be separately analyzed.

As long as the exportation of relatively poor machinery is profitable, there is little incentive to improve technology. Given the availability of "softer" Eastern markets, Hungarian enterprises would not be forced to face Western competition, which has been considered a mainspring of technological progress by the architects of the reform. Thus, one major purpose of the reform would be negated.

Turning to Hungarian imports from the East, we may expect that increasing exportation of Hungarian machinery, as long as its quality is inferior to that of Western machinery, would lead to increased unwillingness by CEMA partners to supply Hungary with raw materials. The problem is that in the absence of comprehensive reforms in other countries, trade decisions there remain in the hands of central planners, whose preference for commodity bilateralism has been discussed above. (We have already noted that net exporters of raw materials are pushing most vigorously in this direction.) Once again, there would be a conflict between enterprise and state interest. The state, if it permitted the market to make foreign trade decisions, might have to countenance domestic bottlenecks in raw material supplies (or turn to the West, which is another problem), or intervene.

An increase of Hungary's demand for Western machinery would tend to increase total import demand, unless import demand for other goods declines. This seems unlikely. For instance, Hungarian import demand for Western primary products increased very rapidly in the crucial prereform period (see appendix charts D.17 and D.19) at least partly because Eastern trading partners were not anxious to continue supplying Hungary with raw materials in payment for Hungarian machinery. An overall upward shift of the import schedule would intensify the already strong balance-of-payments pressures, unless exports also increased. Thus relief from a crisis in the balance of payments would depend on Hungary's ability to increase exports to the West *pari passu* with the rise of imports. We now turn to this question.

Hungary's exports to the West, because of existing price ratios within CEMA, would be more profitable in raw materials and agricultural products than in machinery (an observation that also tends to hold for other CEMA countries). Domestic prices of materials and agricultural products have been relatively low in Hungary (and will remain low during the transitional period) as compared with either world markets or factor costs,[79] and the prices of most of these products are fixed on the domestic market (see table 5.2, p. 174). Thus, Hungarian enterprises would be motivated to sell

79. See n. 55.

primary products to the West, diverting them not only from eastern markets but also from domestic users. Without state intervention, this would lead to growing friction in bilateral CEMA trade relations, as well as to domestic bottlenecks.

A large variety of trade control instruments, designed specifically to deal with the problems outlined above, were introduced by Hungary as part of its comprehensive reforms. These instruments are simply variants of the familiar control measures that kept European trade in bondage during the 1930s. Thus, there are import and export quotas, bilateral registers, commercial policy funds, export license auctions, and various foreign trade subsidies and taxes;[80] in addition, central authorities have retained the right to use direct control measures at their discretion.

It has been recognized in other East European countries, too, that the interlocking problems of distorted price ratios, in each domestic economy as well as in CEMA trade, present a formidable obstacle that cannot be solved simply by setting an equilibrium exchange rate. For instance, a Polish economist suggested that realistic uniform exchange rates should link domestic and CEMA prices in every country, but then he added: "It may prove useful, nevertheless, to implement [uniform exchange rates] during the transition period with other measures such as supplemental payments and equalization grants."[81] Even more explicit, and pessimistic, are two Czechoslovak economists:

> The most difficult question is the renewal of the price function as an indicator of resources and requirements. The extraordinary complexity of this problem is due to the distortions of price relations of domestic prices in comparison with the relations as they developed on international markets. . . . As a result, the effectiveness of labor as well as the effectiveness of investments is highly variable. . . . This is a problem of price ratios, not one of currency exchange rates.[82]

In sum, existing differences in commodity price ratios in the two world markets necessitate continuous state intervention in Hungary, unless other East European countries also adopt comprehensive domestic reforms and

80. See Brown and Marer, "Trade Control." A bilateral register is a fund to compensate or to tax either the exporter or the importer when trading in a given bilateral relationship is not equally advantageous to both. The commercial policy fund is the source of special subsidies offered to fulfill bilateral obligations when the transaction would not otherwise be profitable.

81. Pawel Bozyk, "Domestic and Foreign Trade Prices in the Process of Integration in Comecon Countries," *Handel zagraniczny* (Warsaw) (November 1969), as translated in the *American Review of Soviet and East European Foreign Trade* 6, no. 2 (Summer 1970), p. 137.

82. V. Černiansky and J. Pleva, "On Theoretical Questions of Foreign Trade Management," *Hospodářské noviny* (Prague) (September 1965), as translated in ibid. 2, no. 1 (January–February 1966).

agree to a reform of the CEMA organization. As Michael Kaser correctly pointed out, bilateral trade agreements (and the related inconvertibility) may well be considered instruments for offsetting the shortcomings of CEMA's version of world market prices; nonetheless, all of these instruments ultimately limit the freedom of enterprises to make export and import decisions on the basis of profitability considerations. The formidable arsenal of trade control that has been introduced in Hungary along with the comprehensive reform presents not only actual problems but also a potential threat. As we have learned in the West, adroit use of various trade restrictions may very effectively overshadow the "rules of the game."

VI. Summary and Conclusions

Pressures for Reform

The strategy of extensive development has been blamed for the slowdown of economic growth in Eastern Europe. New sources of growth have been sought, including, prominently, more effective participation in international division of labor. The fact that trade in the region has grown faster than domestic production is not so much the result of planned development as of a rise in unintended imports and the corresponding exports necessary to pay for them.

Expanding trade flows of CPEs tend to be concentrated in the East trading area's sheltered market, where (as in each of the domestic sellers' markets) outdated producer goods and inferior consumer goods can be sold. Whatever advantage sheltered markets may provide during the takeoff period of industrialization, they eventually become a liability. One of the most serious undesirable consequences of a CPE is inefficiency in foreign trade. Absence of competition, lack of entrepreneurial initiative, parallel industrial structures, and slow technical progress interact to create "dependency traps" for the smaller countries in the region.

MDCs in East Europe, being exporters of machinery and importers of primary products, are the first to be caught in the dependency trap. Owing to parallel development strategies and lagging technical standards, many of their exports become "soft" goods and their imports "hard" goods—a distinction that has *not* been reflected in CEMA prices, because of institutional limitations. The adjustment has shifted from price to commodity composition, forcing MDCs to buy undesired manufactured products to secure raw materials and at the same time to increase their reliance on the Soviet Union to fill raw material deficits—a dependence viewed with ambivalence by both sides. Therefore, to tap new benefits from trade, MDCs wish to reduce their overdependence on Eastern suppliers and markets and to turn gradually to the West. Their ability to do so, however, is checked by a lack of suitable exports; they find it difficult to compete with Western manufactures in terms of quality, marketing, and service. This leads to a cul de sac within the traditional CPE. Recognition of this problem contributes significantly to a reexamination of the traditional system and this scrutiny may culminate, if economic and political conditions are propitious, in comprehensive economic reforms.

There tends to be a lesser need for fundamental reforms in LDCs, because primary-product exports can be sold more readily in Western markets, and because LDCs are in a relatively strong bargaining position in Eastern markets. To be sure, if dissatisfied with the rate of growth, LDCs might also become more receptive to efficiency considerations, but they are not likely to go beyond partial reforms as long as the old strategy of extensive development appears to be feasible. Thus, while certain partial reforms in foreign trade have been introduced in all CPEs in order to eliminate the most obvious inefficiencies of the traditional system, our indicators have registered the strongest reform pressures in MDCs.

Comprehensive Reforms in Theory and Practice

The touchstone of a comprehensive reform is the introduction of a viable market mechanism (i.e. guided market socialism or New Economic Mechanism). The architects of such reforms in Czechoslovakia (until 1968), Yugoslavia, and Hungary have stated that one of the prime purposes of the market is to provide large additional gains from trade; both directly, through more advantageous international specialization, and indirectly, through a more competitive environment, spurring initiative and technological progress.

Three essential elements of comprehensive reforms with respect to foreign trade have been the elimination of compulsory annual plan targets, the subordination of FTEs to producing enterprises, and the introduction of operational exchange rates. Partial reforms, though less than successful, have been important in preparing the ground for comprehensive reforms. Thus, the reduction in the number of plan targets foreshadowed the elimination of the compulsory annual plan; the selective granting of export and import licenses foreshadowed the subordination of FTEs to producing enterprises; and the calculation of foreign trade efficiency indexes foreshadowed the adoption of operational exchange rates.

Our empirical analysis of the achievements, limitations, and prospects of comprehensive reforms draws heavily on the experience of Hungary, the only country within CEMA where such reforms continue to be implemented. With respect to foreign trade, Yugoslavia is somewhat of a special case in Eastern Europe: its trade is concentrated with Western partners; it is not a member of CEMA, and thus is not bound by CEMA's institutional rules;

it permits substantial international factor mobility of both capital and labor; and it is in a somewhat stronger position than CEMA members to tolerate either inflation or unemployment. The Hungarians laid the cornerstone of a new, market-oriented foreign trade system in 1968. They abolished most compulsory plan targets, even in foreign trade; they also allowed producing (rather than foreign trade) enterprises to make decisions on the basis of market criteria—including, significantly, operational exchange rates. The forint has in effect been devalued, separately, vis-à-vis Western and Eastern trading areas.

One should also consider, of course, that along with market reforms, the Hungarians have introduced an assortment of direct and indirect control weapons. While some of these measures are needed to protect the "infant market" (using Michael Kaser's felicitous expression), as long as the new exchange rates are disequilibrium rates, external balance can be maintained, in any case, only by means of an elaborate tariff-cum-subsidy scheme.[83] Looking at the formidable array of trade restrictions and special incentives, one may justifiably wonder: Are the new market rules operationally meaningful, or are controls, restrictions, and exceptions decisive? At the present transitional stage, the answer can only be speculative.

Short-run versus Long-run Considerations

The stated goal of Hungarian foreign trade reforms is to substitute the competitive pressures of the market for direct and detailed state controls. Continued state intervention might be justifiable in the short run on the grounds that it is designed to effect a smooth transition to the new system. Adjustment lags must be taken into account, which may be particularly troublesome because of the experimental nature of the new rules and the untried response of participants to market signals. It has been emphasized, for example, that the huge foreign trade subsidies, which are necessary to maintain external balance (since exchange rates are below equilibrium levels), are expected to be reduced gradually over time. These subsidies could hardly be eliminated overnight without causing serious dislocations: bankruptcies and large-scale structural unemployment, for example. We, in the West, have had ample opportunity to learn that successful monetary and fiscal policies and the fine tuning of an economy are complex instruments, and that to master them takes time.

On the negative side, we may add that gradualism is not costless either. For example, periodic revisions of subsidies, whether frequent or infrequent, are counterproductive to efficiency. Short intervals between successive

83. For some further discussion of the Hungarian tariff-cum-subsidy scheme and for bibliographic references on the question of import duties and export subsidies in western economic literature, see Brown and Marer, "East–West Trade," p. 1213.

adjustments cause enterprises to bargain and simulate (as they did before the reforms); longer intervals tend to freeze prevailing inefficiencies in production and trade. As for imports, tariffs are "temporarily" too high, and other restrictions too stringent, to safeguard external equilibrium against pent-up demand (compounded by "Western-good fetishism"). This, of course, is not conducive to the introduction of effective competition from which many of the benefits of the reform have been expected. Such problems are familiar to us in the West. We should, therefore, not point to the dangers of passing between Scylla and Charybdis without acknowledging our own difficulties in devising optimal navigational guides for the policymaker.

One of the most serious shortcomings of the New Economic Mechanism in Hungary is that, much as before, investment and foreign trade decisions remain uncoordinated. In 1969, more than a year after the inauguration of the reforms, reportedly even the methodology to calculate the long-run effect of given investments on the balance of payments had not been worked out. Until this is done, little progress can be made toward implementing one of the stated objectives of the reform: to take comparative advantage into account in choosing among alternative investment projects.

External Limitations

Hungary has spared no effort in trying to mold its guided market into the existing CEMA framework. In addition to the old instruments of subsidy, licensing, and direct state intervention (on a stand-by basis), various new monetary and fiscal instruments have been introduced to ensure that bilateral obligations will be fulfilled. Gains from trade are likely to remain limited, however, as long as comprehensive reforms are confined to a single country that continues to be bound by the institutional constraints of CEMA. Traditional CPEs plan their export and import structure, including its direction, in great detail; the decentralized trading partner would prefer not to take on similar obligations. A CPE wants fixed prices; the essence of a decentralized market economy is that prices should be allowed to respond to changing demand and supply conditions.

Decentralized decision-making in foreign trade is incompatible with the existing CEMA mechanisms of bilateral trade, such as fixed prices, commodity bilateralism, and inconvertibility of balances. Problems of the CEMA foreign trade price system are also becoming more visible now that some countries are undertaking (or considering undertaking) comprehensive reforms. Differences in average price levels between Eastern and Western markets may be approximated by dual exchange rates, but differences in relative prices on the two markets, as well as differential bilateral price levels in submarkets, could become very troublesome if only one country (or a few countries) try to decentralize before these problems are solved. It is understandable, therefore, that the preparation of comprehensive reforms has been correlated in Eastern Europe with critical exposures of the irrationality of CEMA prices.

Having recognized these problems, the Hungarians have made concrete official recommendations to encourage a step-by-step transition to multilateral trade and payments with CEMA. A number of CEMA members seem to be in full or partial agreement with the Hungarian proposals, but progress is likely to be uncertain, at best, until comprehensive reforms are undertaken by a decided majority of member countries.

The difficulty of trying to develop a viable market mechanism under the existing constraints can scarcely be overestimated. As Viner observed many years ago: trade with CPEs requires direct trade controls even in Western market economies, where such trade is marginal. Much greater is the vulnerability of an incipient socialist market economy, where, owing to internal legacies and external constraints, the rules of the new game might be denied operational significance.

Appendix A

Calculation of Hungary's Foreign
Exchange Supply Curves

ALAN A. BROWN

We start with the total cost function of exports
$$C = f(Q)$$
where C = Total domestic cost of Q amount of exports or of foreign exchange (domestic cost includes enterprise profits), and
Q = Quantity of exports (measured in foreign exchange).

The supply function of foreign exchange is the marginal cost function, or the first derivative of the cost function with respect to Q,

$$M = dC/dQ = f'(Q).$$

From the cost function we can also calculate the average cost curve

$$A = C/Q = f(Q)/Q.$$

If we assume that the marginal and average cost curves are approximately linear, then the function of total cost can be represented by a general quadratic equation:

$$C = aQ^2 + bQ + c.$$

The corresponding marginal and average curves are

$$M = 2aQ + b \tag{5.5}$$

and

$$A = aQ + b. \tag{5.6}$$

We shall use the linear approximation, as shown in equation 5.5, to estimate Hungary's foreign exchange supply curves. We may note that there was lengthy debate in Hungary concerning the applicability of marginal versus average rates, and the new exchange rates introduced in 1968 were based on the average cost of earning a unit of foreign exchange (i.e., on equation 5.6 rather than on equation 5.5) in each of the two markets. Along with the new exchange rates, a tariff-cum-subsidy scheme was also instituted,

196 ALAN A. BROWN

which had the effect of a (further) devaluation. The use of the average exchange rates without this scheme would have led to a consistent deficit in the balance of payments.

On the basis of available official information, we can estimate the cost and foreign exchange supply functions for Hungary's trade with the West and with the East, respectively.

1. Western Trade

The parameters of a linear supply curve, as in equation 5.5, can be derived from two given points. According to Czeitler,[1] at the new exchange rate of 60 ft/$, 74.1 percent of Hungary's Western exports were subsidized in 1968; conversely, 25.9 percent of the exports were unsubsidized. Since the volume of total exports to the West was $503.5 million (i.e., 5,911.2 million devisa-forint [dft] at the official rate of 11.74 dft/$),[2] the volume of unsubsidized exports was $130.4 million. This ordered pair of M and Q (60 ft/$, $130.4) represents a point on the Western foreign exchange supply curve.

A second point on the curve can be obtained from the following data. The average rate of subsidy on exports to the West in 1968 was 18.90 ft/$.[3] By adding this average rate of subsidy to the new foreign exchange rate of 60 ft/$, the marginal cost of 78.90 ft/$ is obtained. Since we assumed that the marginal cost is rising at a constant rate (b), the marginal cost of 78.90 ft/$ corresponds to the midpoint of the section of the supply curve representing subsidized exports (see figure 5.2a on p. 179). To calculate this amount, we add one-half of the subsidized exports (half of $373.1 million) to the unsubsidized exports ($130.4 million), which gives $317.0 million. Thus the second ordered pair of M and Q, representing another point on the Western foreign exchange supply curve, is (78.90 ft/$, $317.0 million).

Next we calculate the parameters of the foreign exchange supply function a and b by solving the system of equations

$$QX = M$$

where

$$Q = \begin{pmatrix} 2q_1 & 1 \\ 2q_2 & 1 \end{pmatrix}; \qquad X = \begin{pmatrix} a \\ b \end{pmatrix}; \qquad M = \begin{pmatrix} m_1 \\ m_2 \end{pmatrix}.$$

The solution set is

$$X = (Q)^{-1}M$$

1. Czeitler, p. 34.
2. *Statisztikai Havi Közlemények* (Budapest: Központi Statisztikai Hivatal), 1969, no. 1, p. 48. The same figure is quoted by Czeitler, p. 17.
3. Czeitler, p. 34.

and for Hungary's Western trade we have

$$\binom{a}{b} = \begin{pmatrix} 260.8 & 1 \\ 634.0 & 1 \end{pmatrix}^{-1} \binom{60}{78.9} = \binom{0.05064}{46.79}.$$

This yields the supply function

$$M = 0.1013Q + 46.79;$$

the corresponding average cost curve is

$$A = 0.05064Q + 46.79.$$

From the average cost curve we can compute the average exchange rate, which is the average domestic cost of the given export bill.

$$E = A_t = 0.05064(503.5) + 46.79 = 72.3 \text{ ft/\$.}$$

Alternatively, the average exchange rate may also be derived by dividing total domestic cost by foreign exchange receipts. Assuming that there is no fixed cost, total domestic cost of Western exports is

$$C_t = 0.05064(503.5)^2 + 46.79(503.5) = 36,397 \text{ million ft.}$$

The average exchange rate is

$$E = C_t/Q_t = 36,397 \text{ million ft/\$503.5 million} = 72.3 \text{ ft/\$.}$$

We may calculate separately the cost of unsubsidized exports (C_u), and the cost of subsidized exports (C_s).

$$C_u = 0.05064(130.4)^2 + 46.79(130.4) = 6,963 \text{ million ft;}$$

$$C_s = C_t - C_u = 36,397 - 6,963 = 29,434 \text{ million ft.}$$

Finally, to calculate the cost of export subsidy (S) we multiply the average rate of subsidy $(\bar{s})$ by the domestic cost of subsidized exports (C_s):

$$S = \bar{s}C_s = (18.90)(373.1) = 7,052 \text{ million ft.}$$

2. Eastern Trade

We follow the same steps as in the case of Western trade. In 1968, Hungary exported 15,093.0 million dft to the Eastern trading area,[4] or 1,157.0 million rubles (r) at the official exchange rate. Out of this total, subsidized exports were 61.2 percent or 708.1 million r, and unsubsidized exports 38.8 percent or 448.9 million r.[5] Exports whose domestic cost was above the new official

4. *Statisztikai Havi Közlemények*, 1969, no. 1, p. 48.
5. Czeitler, p. 34.

exchange rate of 40 ft/r had to be subsidized. This information provides the first ordered pair of M and Q (40 ft/r, 448.9 million r).

To derive the second pair, the average rate of Eastern export subsidy, 12.10 ft/r, is added to the average exchange rate of 40 ft/r, yielding a marginal cost of 52.10 ft/r.[6] To calculate the corresponding volume of exports, we again add one-half of the subsidized exports (half of 708.1 million r) to the unsubsidized exports (448.9 million r), and obtain 803.0 million r (see figure 5.2b on p. 180). Thus, the second ordered pair of M and Q is (52.10 ft/r, 803.0 million r).

From this information we can estimate the parameters a and b:

$$\begin{pmatrix} a \\ b \end{pmatrix} = \begin{pmatrix} 897.8 & 1 \\ 1606.0 & 1 \end{pmatrix}^{-1} \begin{pmatrix} 40 \\ 52.1 \end{pmatrix} = \begin{pmatrix} 0.01709 \\ 24.66 \end{pmatrix};$$

therefore, Hungary's foreign exchange supply curve for Eastern trade is

$$M = 0.03418Q + 24.66.$$

The corresponding average cost curve is

$$A = 0.01709Q + 24.66,$$

and the average exchange rate

$$E = 0.01709(1,157.0) + 24.66 = 44.4 \text{ ft/r}.$$

Total domestic cost of Eastern exports was

$$C = 0.01709(1,157.0)^2 + 24.66(1,157.0) = 51,409 \text{ million ft}.$$

The cost of unsubsidized exports

$$C_u = 0.01709(448.9)^2 + 24.66(448.9) = 14,514 \text{ million ft},$$

and the cost of subsidized exports

$$C_s = C - C_u = 36,895 \text{ million ft}.$$

Out of this, the amount of subsidy was

$$S = \bar{s}C_s = (12.10)(708.1) = 8,568 \text{ million ft}.$$

3. *Summary*

The linear supply and average cost functions here calculated should be taken as rough approximations of the indicated functional relationships. In certain respects, the assumption of linearity is not unreasonable; for instance, our estimates of the average exchange rates are practically the same as

6. Ibid.

Hungarian calculations based on actual 1968 data. The Hungarians report the average range for Western trade was 69–72 ft/$,[7] while our estimate is 72.3 ft/$; for Eastern trade, Hungarian calculations show the range 43–45 ft/r,[8] while our calculations yield 44.4 ft/r.

There is some indication, however, that the marginal cost curves of Hungarian exports are not linear in the highest and lowest regions; they tend to increase at an increasing rate (see footnote 62, p. 180). Eventually, as additional data become available, we should be able to fit appropriate sets of nonlinear marginal cost curves.

The following table summarizes our calculations of costs, revenues, and average exchange rates in Hungary's 1968 exports to Eastern (socialist) and Western (nonsocialist) markets.

Hungary's 1968 Exports

	West	East
Domestic cost of:		
Unsubsidized exports (C_u)	6,963 mill. ft	14,514 mill. ft
Subsidized exports(C_s)	29,434 mill. ft	36,895 mill. ft
of which: Subsidy (S)	7,052 mill. ft	8,568 mill. ft
Total exports (C_t)	36,397 mill. ft	51,409 mill. ft
Foreign exchange revenue (given)		
Total exports (Q_t)	$503.5 mill.	1,157.0 mill. r
Average exchange rate		
(Domestic cost ÷ foreign		
exchange revenue) ($E = C_t/Q_t$)	72.3 ft/$	44.4 ft/r

7. Ibid., p. 35.
8. Ibid.

APPENDIX B.1

Balance of Trade Ratios of East European Countries with European CEMA Group, 1950–69

(Exports as percentage of imports)

Year	USSR	Bulgaria	Czech.	E. Germany	Hungary	Poland	Romania	Yugoslavia
1950	114.8	94.3	119.3	77.7	119.5	86.7	n.a.	No Trade
1951	109.2	n.a.	n.a.	125.0	105.4	79.3	n.a.	No Trade
1952	113.1	108.3	n.a.	98.9	101.8	87.4	n.a.	No Trade
1953	98.9	98.0	110.8	99.5	116.0	100.8	n.a.	No Trade
1954	97.2	114.7	103.1	120.4	109.1	91.6	n.a.	140.6
1955	107.2	93.6	107.0	112.7	137.1	93.8	n.a.	106.9
1956	96.8	127.4	112.3	106.5	102.8	80.0	n.a.	70.3
1957	132.4	115.0	85.1	116.7	60.8	70.9	n.a.	73.5
1958	103.8	100.4	107.3	120.3	97.0	77.6	88.7	63.5
1959	115.8	88.9	105.0	109.7	90.4	72.4	100.6	86.5
1960	110.0	90.5	105.6	104.0	86.2	83.8	107.0	86.1
1961	111.7	98.1	103.5	98.8	103.2	88.7	102.0	103.8
1962	110.6	96.0	108.3	98.7	96.8	83.0	89.2	88.6
1963	100.4	88.9	115.8	119.8	94.2	84.0	90.5	87.9
1964	101.1	96.3	104.8	115.2	95.6	102.6	85.4	81.6
1965	97.4	107.8	100.3	113.9	102.6	91.3	113.2	124.6
1966	105.2	94.2	99.8	101.8	106.8	84.5	103.6	90.3
1967	98.9	97.5	103.5	107.5	97.5	90.5	101.6	102.0
1968	99.9	93.1	92.8	111.5	101.9	100.6	103.2	89.3
1969	103.1	101.6	93.2	99.0	108.1	96.3	104.6	89.4

Source: Paul Marer, Soviet and East European Foreign Trade (1946–1969): Statistical Compendium and Guide (Bloomington: Indiana University Press for the International Development Research Center, 1972).

APPENDIX B.2

Balance of Trade Ratios of East European Countries with the West, 1950-69

(Exports as percentage of imports)

Year	USSR Overall	MDC	Bulgaria Overall	MDC	Czech. Overall	MDC	E. Germany Overall	MDC	Hungary Overall	MDC	Poland Overall	MDC	Romania Overall	MDC	Yugoslavia Overall	MDC
1950	92	116	51	48	126	121	114	112	82	80	105	106	75	n.a.	68	73
1951	104	113	n.a.	n.a.	94	n.a.	92	93	92	97	84	n.a.	n.a.	n.a.	47	48
1952	84	89	123	n.a.	96	n.a.	95	94	89	83	96	n.a.	n.a.	n.a.	66	70
1953	83	87	115	n.a.	117	113	88	86	79	69	120	n.a.	n.a.	n.a.	47	41
1954	77	81	130	n.a.	111	n.a.	98	94	78	70	102	n.a.	n.a.	n.a.	70	65
1955	109	125	92	85	123	116	100	96	78	72	104	113	101	n.a.	54	49
1956	101	102	88	83	124	96	99	98	98	91	118	115	98	n.a.	67	66
1957	97	102	92	n.a.	114	95	97	94	85	74	84	83	69	n.a.	56	53
1958	105	107	94	n.a.	112	97	89	88	107	103	86	76	112	108	64	60
1959	103	113	51	n.a.	106	100	96	96	103	96	93	92	111	104	64	22
1960	82	91	90	82	103	94	93	92	87	79	91	89	111	100	62	58
1961	100	98	107	n.a.	96	88	101	96	84	75	89	83	89	84	53	46
1962	112	87	101	97	105	92	102	101	88	82	96	93	84	71	75	60
1963	105	89	91	78	105	102	111	112	88	86	99	97	84	80	71	65
1964	95	74	77	70	101	91	100	99	78	75	97	95	84	71	62	58
1965	107	92	80	71	102	91	101	99	90	84	103	111	83	77	69	63
1966	112	99	68	58	101	88	90	83	92	94	98	98	87	81	72	67
1967	126	107	79	70	108	100	97	91	90	87	101	96	77	61	64	60
1968	115	96	83	74	102	88	106	103	89	90	96	95	76	64	63	70
1969	109	90	105	102	111	98	99	95	107	103	98	94	78	69	63	60

Source: Marer, Statistical Compendium.

APPENDIX C

Share of Trade of East European Countries with the West and European CEMA Countries, 1950–69
(Average of imports and exports)

Year	USSR West	USSR CEMA	Bulgaria West	Bulgaria CEMA	Czech. West	Czech. CEMA	E. Germany West	E. Germany CEMA[b]	Hungary West	Hungary CEMA	Poland West	Poland CEMA	Romania[a] West	Romania[a] CEMA	Yugoslavia West	Yugoslavia CEMA
1950	19.2	57.1	11.1	88.7	44.4	54.3	27.7	72.3	38.7	60.5	41.0	58.1	16.5	83.5[b]	98.5	0.0
1951	19.0	57.4	n.a.	n.a.	38.4	n.a.	23.8	76.2	32.7	60.8	42.5	54.3	n.a.	n.a.	99.4	0.0
1952	19.1	58.8	11.4	n.a.	28.6	n.a.	24.9	75.1	27.0	65.8	33.7	62.5	n.a.	n.a.	99.3	0.0
1953	16.9	58.8	14.1	n.a.	21.5	71.5	22.4	77.6	23.9	68.0	29.9	66.1	n.a.	n.a.	99.8	0.0
1954	20.5	54.6	12.9	n.a.	25.1	67.4	23.9	76.1	29.0	63.7	29.9	66.1	n.a.	n.a.	98.0	1.7
1955	20.7	53.0	10.5	86.7	29.7	63.5	27.9	72.1	39.1	53.2	36.1	59.1	18.2	81.8[b]	89.2	10.6
1956	24.3	49.2	15.6	81.3	34.2	58.5	26.9	73.1	37.5	53.5	37.4	56.4	39.2	n.a.	75.3	22.4
1957	26.4	52.9	15.6	80.9	32.4	59.8	26.7	73.3	29.8	61.1	39.3	54.5	32.3	n.a.	74.2	23.4
1958	26.3	51.7	14.2	81.3	29.5	60.7	26.0	74.0	28.4	59.6	41.6	50.2	22.3	71.5	70.1	28.0
1959	24.7	51.3	17.2	78.9	27.8	63.4	24.0	76.0	29.0	61.8	37.7	55.6	20.2	72.4	70.3	27.8
1960	26.8	52.5	16.0	80.2	28.2	63.4	25.4	74.6	29.1	62.3	36.9	56.3	27.0	66.7	70.5	28.8
1961	28.4	54.5	15.8	80.3	30.3	64.2	25.0	75.0	28.9	65.3	37.5	56.7	31.3	64.0	74.2	24.7
1962	29.8	56.0	17.4	78.4	25.8	69.4	21.0	79.0	27.4	68.4	35.5	59.5	32.1	65.0	76.6	22.7
1963	29.6	58.0	17.4	79.3	25.5	68.8	21.5	78.5	30.3	65.4	34.8	60.5	31.1	64.3	74.4	24.7
1964	30.3	58.0	22.3	74.4	26.8	67.7	23.6	76.4	31.1	65.1	36.3	59.1	31.6	64.6	68.5	30.9
1965	31.2	56.8	23.2	72.8	26.8	67.5	26.1	73.9	31.5	64.8	35.3	60.0	35.1	60.3	64.3	34.7
1966	33.6	54.7	27.0	68.2	29.7	63.5	26.9	73.1	33.4	62.5	37.0	57.7	40.4	54.1	65.2	33.6
1967	32.2	55.9	24.0	72.1	28.2	66.2	25.9	74.1	32.4	64.1	35.3	60.7	47.6	47.2	68.4	30.2
1968	32.6	56.5	22.3	73.6	28.5	65.5	23.9	76.1	29.8	66.5	34.9	61.0	44.8	48.8	68.4	30.7
1969	34.6	55.7	20.5	76.0	29.4	64.5	27.2	72.8	32.1	64.0	34.2	62.0	44.8	48.7	72.5	27.1

Source: Marer, Statistical Compendium.

Note: Table is based on official statistics aggregating trade with East and West regardless of substantial price level differences on the two markets. For a more detailed discussion of this problem and an experimental adjustment of one country's trade statistics, see Marer, Postwar Pricing and Price Patterns (cited above in n. 72).

[a] New series since 1958.
[b] Trade with all Socialist countries.

Appendix D
Hungarian Trade

The source for the following charts is the IDRC Foreign Trade Data Bank.

Total trade with Socialist and capitalist countries, 1950-69

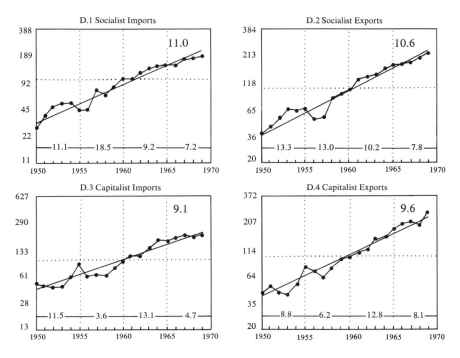

Trade in manufactures with Socialist countries, 1950-69

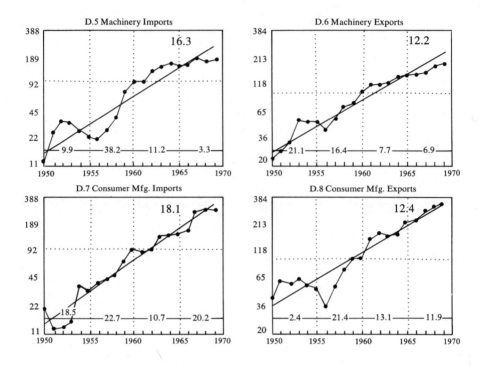

Trade in primary products with Socialist countries, 1950-69

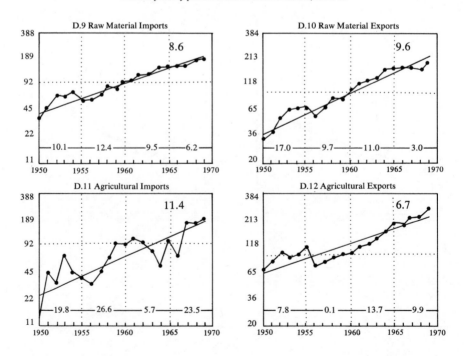

Trade in manufactures with capitalist countries, 1950-69

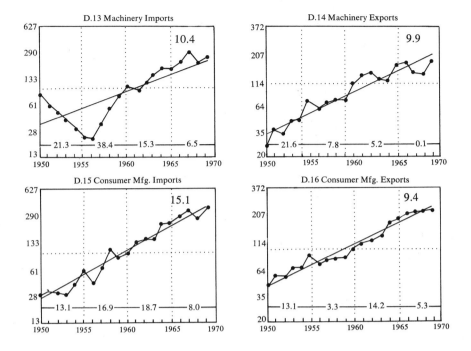

Trade in primary products with capitalist countries, 1950-69

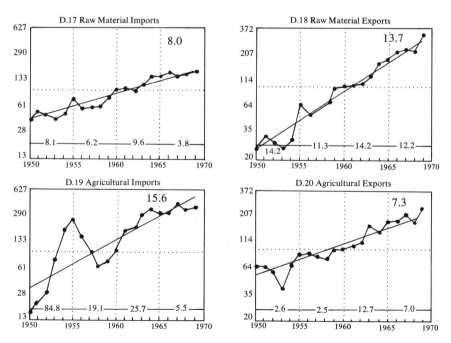

6

Agricultural Reform in Eastern Europe

JERZY F. KARCZ

The task of describing and analyzing agricultural reforms in Eastern Europe tends to be difficult for at least two reasons. We are accustomed to regard 1965 as the watershed of systemic reform,[1] and it is true that introduction of the New Economic Systems or New Economic Models gave added impetus to change in agriculture. Yet, it is also true that in Eastern Europe—as well as in the USSR—significant agricultural reforms began much earlier, while a number of important measures were enacted as recently as the spring of 1970. Hence, our subject demands a broader time horizon than the reforms in industry.

Furthermore, the increasingly diverse nations of "Eastern Europe" are an unruly aggregate for economic analysis, and standard taxonomic criteria are not altogether appropriate for an investigation of their agricultural problems and performance. This is apparent from a casual inspection of some economic indicators assembled in table 6.1. In Bulgaria and Romania, the least developed countries of the region, trends in agricultural output since 1954–56 have been similar. But trends in net product of agriculture, and manpower problems, have been very different indeed. East Germany and Czechoslovakia, the most developed countries, are dissimilar if only because of the very special problems faced by the Prague leadership in Slovakia. Finally, the Polish and the Yugoslav experiences with agricultural reform are drastically different, despite the fact that in both countries over 80 percent of agricultural land is owned and farmed by individual peasants.

Editor's note: Professor Karcz's untimely death prevented him from revising his paper for publication after the conference. This task was kindly undertaken by Miss Nancy Nimitz.

In the earlier version of this paper, Professor Karcz expressed gratitude to Radio Free Europe in Munich for assistance in gathering data, to Ivan Loncarević and Miklos Zilahy-Szabo for allowing him to consult the unpublished copies of their papers on the Yugoslav and the Hungarian reforms, and to the Institut für kontinentale Agrar- und Wirtschaftsforschung, Justus Liebig University, Giessen, for hospitality and assistance.

1. Gregory Grossman, "Economic Reforms: A Balance Sheet," *Problems of Communism* 15, no. 6 (November–December 1966): 43.

TABLE 6.1. Selected Performance Indicators for East European Agriculture

Indicator	Bulgaria	Czech.	E. Germany	Hungary	Poland	Romania	Yugoslavia
1. Agricultural output[a] (1954–56 = 100)							
1960–62	140	114	108	119	120	132	141
1965–67	184	126	130	142	145	162	166
1968	173	140	134	146	156	167	170
2. Per capita agricultural output (1954–56 = 100)							
1960–62	132	108	112	116	110	123	133
1965–67	168	116	136	137	125	146	147
1968	155	127	140	139	132	149	148
3. Net product in agriculture[b] (1954–56 = 100)							
1960–62	119	100	101	93	118	125	137
1965–67	107	89	119	118	132	136	158
1968	87	103	124	123	142	137	163
4. Per capita net product in agriculture (1954–56 = 100)							
1960–62	113	85	106	92	108	116	129
1965–67	97	82	125	114	114	123	140
1968	78	94	129	117	120	107	142
5. Per capita agricultural land			(hectares)				
1950	0.56	0.59	0.37	0.75	0.80	0.91	0.59
1965	0.59	0.50	0.37	0.68	0.63	0.77	0.56

6. Population active in agriculture

(thousands)

1950	2,982	2,250	2,069	2,121	7,113	6,914	—
1960	2,240	1,695	1,604	1,828	6,659	7,226	—
1968	1,825	1,383	1,257	1,498	6,223	6,457	—

7. Share of agriculture in total investment

(percentage)

1950–54	10.0	10.1	—	13.0	9.1	10.1	9.2
1960–64	12.6	15.6	13.2	19.1	12.6	20.4	10.7
1965–67	9.3	12.3	12.4	15.8	15.7	18.5	9.2

8. Arable land per tractor

(hectares)

1950	688	207	144	440	573	715	1,244
1960	179	72	72	139	258	234	233
1967	97	41	35	83	103	113	176

9. Application of mineral fertilizers

(kilograms per hectare of arable land)

1950	7.8	64.1	147	9.4	33.5	2.2	7.8
1960	33.8	94.6	188	29.4	45.9	7.9	33.0
1967	133.0	173.0	276	91.4	102.0	47.3	60.7

10. Cattle herds

(thousands)

1947/8–51/2	1,688	3,966	3,297	2,052	6,895	4,387	5,248
1960/61	1,452	4,387	4,675	1,957	9,168	4,530	5,297
1967/8	1,363	4,437	5,019	2,096	10,940	5,332	5,710

(*Continued*)

Table 6.1—Continued

Indicator	Bulgaria	Czech.	E. Germany	Hungary	Poland	Romania	Yugoslavia
				(thousands)			
11. Hog herds							
1947/8–51/2	998	3,612	4,361	4,006	7,439	2,110	4,295
1960/1	2,553	5,962	8,316	5,921	13,434	4,300	6,210
1967/8	2,314	5,544	8,878	5,799	13,911	5,365	6,985

Sources:

Rows 1–4: Recomputed from Lazarcik (cited below in n. 43), pp. 476–79, 488–89.

Row 5: W. Misiuna, "Stopniowa itensyfikacja rolnictwa w krajach **RWPG**" [Gradual intensification of agriculture in CEMA countries], *Zagadnienia Ekonomiki Rolnej*, 1969, no. 2, p. 71.

Row 6: Elias (cited below in n. 34), pp. 209–14.

Row 7: Lazarcik (cited below in n. 43), p. 517.

Row 8: *Statisticke prehledy*, 1969, no. 2, p. xvi (supplement to *Zemedelska ekonomika*, 1969, no. 3).

Row 9: Ibid, p. xv.

Rows 10–11: Ibid, 1970, no. 3, p. v (supplement to *Zemedelska ekonomika*, 1970, no. 3).

[a] Total crop and animal production less intermediate products utilized on farms (= output available for human consumption and industrial use).
[b] Agricultural output less current operating expenses and depreciation (= net value added by productive activity within the agricultural sector).

Such considerations argue that the best approach would be country by country, but space limitations forbid this. A compromise will therefore be attempted. We first consider briefly the pressures for agricultural reform in Eastern Europe in order to identify the key relationships or problem areas. We then describe recent institutional or systemic changes against the background of earlier partial reforms. A short section is devoted to the special, and in a sense the limiting, case of Yugoslavia after 1965. We conclude with some general remarks and a tentative appraisal.

A uniform English terminology will be used to render a variety of Eastern European expressions. Thus, we speak throughout of state farms and cooperative farms, instead of making a distinction between a "People's Own Farm" in Germany and a state farm in Bulgaria, or between a "Unified Agricultural Cooperative" in Czechoslovakia and a "Labor Agricultural Cooperative Farm" in Bulgaria. Similarly, we shall speak of provinces and districts to describe the Polish *wojewodztwo* and *powiat* or the Czechoslovak *kraj* and *okres*.

I. Pressures for Reform

In agriculture as well as elsewhere in the East European economies, pressures for economic reform can be traced to the fundamental decision to industrialize on the Soviet model. The main characteristics of the Soviet pattern are well known. Priority was given to industrial development, and within that sector to industries producing investment goods, and particularly to machinery. The emphasis was on capital-intensive technology, using large-scale methods of production. The necessary high rate of investment was sustained by forced savings. Agriculture, housing, and consumer goods industries were treated as shock-absorbing sectors, while the peculiar Soviet autarkic bias was translated in Eastern Europe into a more or less simultaneous development of virtually all branches of heavy industry in every country.

This is not the place to argue whether the peculiar set of Soviet institutions that emerged in the 1930s was a necessary component of the Soviet pattern of industrialization. The fact remains that, broadly speaking, all of the most important Soviet economic institutions were introduced in Eastern European economies, including the collectivization of agriculture. This proceeded more gradually, and without the initial shock of the Soviet "Big Collectivization Drive" of 1929–30. But with the exception of Yugoslavia and Poland (where decollectivization occurred in 1952 and 1956 respectively), the socialization drives were completed by 1962.

One consequence of these developments for agriculture was the emergence of "command farming," or a set of constraints imposed on the economic activity of agricultural enterprises. The various mechanisms of command farming have been described elsewhere,[2] and it will be sufficient to summarize here the impact of its main characteristics on the economic performance of socialized or private farms.

Most prominent was the concentration on government procurement of farm products, with the aim of guaranteeing supplies of food for the rapidly growing urban population, raw materials for domestic industries, and product for export. In order to extract savings from the agricultural sector and to limit its demand for consumer goods, governments paid very low prices for the bulk of the products procured. The extent to which terms of trade shifted against agriculture in the period of the massive industrialization drives prior to 1953 varied from one country to another. The case of Bulgaria illustrates perhaps the limit of what was achieved in this respect. Between 1945 and 1953, the indices of state retail prices for industrial consumer goods and of procurement prices for various groups of farm products changed as shown in table 6.2.

TABLE 6.2. Price Trends in Bulgaria, 1945–53
(1939 = 100)

| | | Procurement Prices of: | | |
Year	Prices of Industrial Consumer Goods	Grains	Vegetables and Potatoes	All Farm Products
1945	575.7	n.a.	n.a.	553.7
1949	697.4	821.4	703.0	654.6
1950	919.2	741.7	693.2	n.a.
1951	1,063.5	694.2	463.8	n.a.
1952	1,085.8	483.2	445.7	n.a.
1953	1,010.9	443.8	312.0	388.9

Source: G. Kostov, "Zakonut za stoinostta i tsenite na selskostopanskite proizvedeniia" [The law of value and prices for agricultural products], Trud i tseni, 1961, no. 6, pp. 43, 44, 45.

Since farms could not be expected to produce the desired assortment of marketings for token prices, governments took over planning functions down to minute details usually left to the discretion of low-level farm managerial personnel. Local agricultural agencies of the state planned for each farm the areas under various crops, the number and kinds of animals to be held or slaughtered, the timing of various farming operations, productivity targets, the use of farm equipment, and the like. Until 1955, each

2. See the various writings of Naum Jasny, Alec Nove, and Nancy Nimitz, and my "An Organizational Model of Command Farming," in Comparative Economic Systems: Models and Cases, rev. ed., ed. Morris Bornstein (Homewood, Ill.: Richard D. Irwin, 1969), pp. 278–99.

Bulgarian state farm was thus assigned 600 compulsory indicators, approved by the Council of Ministers itself.[3] (Similarly detailed planning extended to farms of individual peasants in East Germany and Czechoslovakia; it often happened that plans for production and procurement were not coordinated, with the result that more was scheduled for delivery to the state than could be produced on the approved area.)[4] Machine Tractor Stations, not farm management, controlled machinery inputs on cooperatives. Managerial freedom was reduced still further by the interference of local Party officials in even those decisions nominally reserved to farm management, such as income distribution. Though industrial enterprises also suffered interference (from administrative, rather than party, cadres), it can hardly have been so pervasive.

Production costs were not calculated on cooperative farms during the early period of command farming, largely because the results would have been embarrassing. For example, over the period 1952–55, Bulgarian procurement prices covered the following proportions of average cost (percent): wheat, 69; corn, 35; sunflower, 44; milk, 49.[5]

The impact of such pricing practices on farm incomes hardly needs elaboration. A considerable part of the cooperative farmer's effort was of sheer necessity devoted to his private household plot. In Czechoslovakia in 1958, 43 percent of the cooperative farmer's total income came from the plot; his cash and kind income from the cooperative was only half the average wage paid in the socialist sector of the economy.[6] In Bulgaria in 1953, average earnings from the cooperative were only 30 percent of the average wage in the national economy.[7]

Competition from private plots reduced the supply of labor to the socialized sector, while the low level of wages in agriculture accelerated the pace of migration from the village. Though movement to the cities was to some extent desirable, there are many indications that it occurred at too rapid a

3. E. V. Rudakov, S. A. Mellin, and V. I. Storozhev, *Ekonomicheskaia reforma v sel'skom khoziaistve sotsialisticheskikh stran* [Economic reform in agriculture of socialist countries] (Moscow: Ekonomika, 1968), p. 89.

4. Vladimír Vydra, *Úloha výkupů v ekonomickém svazku dělnické třídy a rolnictva* [The role of procurements in the economic alliance between the working class and agriculture] (Prague: 1963), p. 71.

5. Evgeni Rudakov, *Materialnoto stimulirane v selskoto stopanstvo na niakoi sotsialisticheski strani* [Material incentives in agriculture of some socialist states] (Sofia: 1970), p. 43.

6. J. Nikl et al., *Problémy vývoje a plánovitého řízení reprodukce v JZD* [Problems of development and planned management of reproduction in cooperative farms] (Prague: 1966), pp. 92, 97.

7. *Razvitie narodnogo khoziaistva Narodnoi Respubliki Bolgarii* [Development of the national economy of the People's Republic of Bulgaria] (Moscow: 1958), p. 146, and Akademiia Nauk SSSR, Institut ekonomiki mirovoi sotsialisticheskoi sistemy, *Sotsialisticheskoe preobrazovaniia v sel'skom khoziaistve evropeiskikh stran narodnoi demokratii* [Socialist transformations in agriculture of european countries of people's democracies] (Moscow: 1963), p. 199.

pace, and that departure of the young and the skilled distorted the structure of the agricultural labor force in a later period. This is a topic to which we shall return.

Some observers have concluded that the features of command farming as outlined here were essential to rapid industrialization. This, I submit, is a hasty judgment. There is, of course, no doubt that command farming did assist in the industrialization of Eastern Europe. But this is true of agricultural sectors in growing economies everywhere, and we must also consider the costs of command farming as a growth-fostering device. Some of its negative consequences on overall productivity have proved singularly resistant to various reform measures to this very day.

Farm efficiency matters particularly in industrialization along Soviet lines because of the high income elasticity of demand for food, which is largely due to such features of these systems as low rents, free or virtually free medical care and education, poor quality of industrial consumer goods, and the like. I have discussed this point elsewhere,[8] and it is reassuring to find similar conclusions expressed by a number of East European and Soviet writers. The problem is stated in a nutshell by three Soviet economists surveying the East European agricultural reforms: "Socialist production relationships promoted a rapid growth of productive forces and a considerable increase in the welfare of the members of socialist societies. One problem, however, appeared: the purchasing power of the population grew while not enough final output was produced."[9]

Part of the growing demand for food could have been met by imports if rapid industrialization had yielded a large increase in exports of industrial goods. Unfortunately, this did not happen, largely because the quality of industrial goods produced in Eastern Europe (and in the USSR too, for that matter) has been lower than that offered on the world market by other producers. At the same time, no large economy within the socialist bloc has been able to produce adequate surpluses of the most important farm products. Hence, what could not be done on the world market as a whole could not be done on the socialist world market either. As a result, farm products be-

8. J. F. Karcz, "Seven Years on the Farm: Retrospect and Prospects," in U.S. Congress, Joint Economic Committee, *New Directions in the Soviet Economy* (Washington, D.C.: Government Printing Office, 1966), pt. II-B, pp. 436–38.

9. Rudakov, Mellin, and Storozhev, *Ekonomicheskaia*, p. 6. For a different formulation of the same problem see Zygmunt Kozlowski and Marian Brzoska, "Ogólna charakterystyka rozwoju rolnictwa" [General characterization of the development of agriculture], *Zagadnienia Ekonomiki Rolnej*, 1966, supplement to no. 6, pp. 47–49. The average income elasticity of demand for meat in Poland was estimated at 0.9 by Stanislaw Rochna, "Próba oceny równowagi na rynku miesnym" [An attempt to estimate equilibrium at the meat market], ibid., p. 136. The income elasticity of demand for food in Poland was given as 0.7 in a commentary by Wiktor Herer in ibid., no. 5, p. 215.

came (and remain) hard goods in the socialist bloc, a fact best illustrated by Khrushchev's plea to a group of East European farm experts in January 1960: "We still do not have enough grain reserves to fully satisfy the growing demands of friendly socialist countries. . . . Therefore, we would like to ask you to consider our position and capabilities, and refrain from the stubborn insistence that you have shown on other occasions; don't make demands that we would be hard put to meet."[10]

Failure to specialize in farm production at the national level[11] has been matched by failure to specialize at the regional and farm level within nations. This too can be traced to certain features of command farming. So long as the prices paid for compulsory deliveries were far below cost, quota distributing agencies were inclined to spread the burden as widely as possible —mainly to "plan safely," but also out of a dim concern for equity. Therefore every farm had numerous quotas: even "specialized" farms might deliver 30 to 40 different products. The existence of two different prices for the same product (a very low one for the compulsory quotas, and a higher one for above-quota deliveries) also affected specialization perversely, sometimes encouraging production in the least favorable regions. For example, farms in the Slov mountains, where wheat and pork quotas were small or zero, were impelled by above-quota prices to switch from rye or oats to wheat, and from cattle to hogs, often fed on imported grain transported over considerable distances.[12]

10. N. S. Khrushchev, *Stroitel'stvo kommunizma v SSSR i razvitie sel'skogo khoziaistva* [Construction of communism in the USSR and the development of agriculture] vol. 4 (Moscow: 1963), p. 115.

11. Several recent studies of agricultural cooperation in the socialist bloc stress inadequate international specialization. See: V. I. Storozhev, ed., *Razvitie sel'skogo khoziaistva i sotrudnichestvo stran SEVa* [The development of agriculture and collaboration of CEMA countries] (Moscow: 1965); Julius Lipták, *Mezinárodní dělba práce v zemědělství zemí RVHP* [International division of labor in agriculture of CEMA countries] (Prague: 1965); G. Jaehne, *Landwirtschaft und landwirtschaftliche Zusammenarbeit im Rat für Gegenseitige Wirtschaftshilfe* (Wiesbaden: Otto Harrassowitz, 1968).

12. V. Vydra, pp. 121–22. For at least a decade East European economists have acknowledged that failure to specialize is traceable to various mechanisms of command farming. Thus Arturo Precioso comments: "The two-tier price system . . . obstructs specialization of individual areas in the products for which local soil and climate are best suited." *Proporce mezi průmyslem a zemědělstvím a její vytváření v Československu* [Proportions between industry and agriculture and their emergence in Czechoslovakia] (Prague: 1959), p. 191. And Anatol Brzoza, in his introduction to Zygmunt Kozłowski, *Obowiazkowe dostawy w planie sześcioletnim* [Compulsory deliveries in the Six-Year Plan] (Warsaw: 1960), writes that "Compulsory deliveries, intended to restrain a rise in farm prices, become simultaneously a source of inflationary pressures . . . . Compulsory delivery prices . . . become a factor restraining the growth [of output] and distorting its proportions. The increase in marketings is no longer accompanied by an increase in production. Animal husbandry develops but its feed base contracts. Forced surpluses of grain turn out to be insufficient. New differentiating processes appear as a function of the progressive system of obligations and of spontaneous compensatory processes" (p. 5).

As in the USSR, disregard of production costs led to planned distortions in land use. Czechoslovakia forced sugar beet production at what turns out to have been a monumental social cost for the economy as a whole.[13] A recent major study of regionalization in Bulgarian agriculture points to similar errors in that country, including the attempt to force production of cotton at the height of the Stalinist industrialization drive.[14] It is clear that restoration of more rational patterns of production will require major improvements in domestic feed supply and fairly drastic changes in the structure of farm prices.[15]

Throughout the region, of course, feed production has long been neglected. Total feed rations are well below recommended levels, and the deficiency in protein feed is particularly troublesome. Paradoxically enough (for a region afflicted with the "grain problem" ever since the beginnings of socialized agriculture), the distorted structure of feed rations has resulted in considerable overfeeding of grain: in Poland, for example, the amount of grain overfed to animals is estimated at 1.5–2.0 million tons (when annual grain output in 1965–67 was around 16.5 million tons).[16] And there are indications that even the current plans for feed production fail to recognize the fact that heavier animals (desirable for a variety of agro-technical reasons) simply require more feed.[17]

Capital intensity turned out to be another characteristic of command farming, largely because of the decision to collectivize livestock production. Gradual collectivization, which resulted in the formation of very small cooperative farms in the early stages, probably increased capital requirements. Every new cooperative tried to construct its own animal shelters, and these

13. Julius Lipták, *Medzinárodná del'ba práce v pol'nospodarstve* [The international division of labor in agriculture] (Bratislava: 1969), pp. 258–75. Lipták discusses the subject under the heading "The Blood-Draining Production of White Gold." For a discussion of other distortions in the structure of Czechoslovak output see ibid., pp. 237–56, 275–89.

14. Marko Lidzhi, Slobodan Amich and Krustiu Brusarski, "Problemite na raionirovaneto, spetsializatsiiata i kontsentratsiiata na selskoto stopanstvo v Bulgaria prez godinite na narodnata vlast" [Problems of regionalization, specialization and concentration of agriculture in Bulgaria in the years of people's government], *Ikonomika na selskoto stopanstvo* 7, no. 1: 37, and *Statisticheski godishnik Narodna Republika Bulgariia, 1966* [Statistical handbook of People's Republic of Bulgaria, 1966] (Sofia: 1966), p. 183.

15. J. Krilek, *Hlavní zásady plánovitého řízeni zemědělství* [The main principles of planned management of agriculture] (Prague: 1966), p. 11.

16. Rudakov, Mellin, and Storozhev, *Ekonomicheskaia*, p. 21. The unbalanced structure of rations raises the feed requirements for poultry by 100–200 percent (ibid., p. 22). For comparable figures describing the situation in Bulgaria see the remarks of Minister of Agriculture Palagachev in *Rabotnichesko delo*, 7 January 1968.

17. Eugeniusz Gorzelak, "Wstępna ocena wykonania planu pięcioletniego w rolnictwie (1966–70)" [A preliminary assessment of the fulfillment of the Five-Year Plan (1966–70) in agriculture], *Wieś Współczesna*, 1970, no. 7, pp. 41–42.

buildings were necessarily very small: in 1954, the average barn for young cattle constructed in Czechoslovak cooperatives had space for only 20 head.[18] In East Germany many cheap barns without individual stalls were built during the year of the massive collectivization drive. Later, expensive conversion was necessary because animals froze in these buildings during the winter.[19] In general, more than half of total agricultural investment in the region was devoted to the construction of farm buildings. Investment in structures accounted for 55 percent of total farm investment in Czechoslovakia in 1955 and 57 percent in 1960.[20] In Hungary, more than half of farm investment in 1959–63 was devoted to these purposes, while in Bulgaria 61.9 percent of all productive capital stock additions in 1952–62 (excluding investment in land improvement) consisted of structures.[21] Yet in the early 1960s in Bulgaria, 20 to 30 percent of productive livestock still lacked shelter.[22]

Much of this investment turned out to be obsolete either as a result of subsequent farm mergers or because of faulty design and poor construction. In 1963 in Bulgaria, investment in reconversion of structures was almost as large as new capital investment.[23] According to the Hungarian expert Martin Lovas, more than 40 percent of all Hungarian stables should be demolished, while only 30 percent of pig sties, 35 percent of cattle barns, and 50 percent of poultry houses are suitable for large scale production.[24]

Overinvestment in (the wrong) structures was accompanied by underinvestment in machinery and equipment. In part, this reflects underdevelopment of the farm machinery industry throughout the bloc. Because of intensive use and inadequate maintenance, machinery has worn out long before

18. Zygmunt Smoleński, "Procesy integracyjne w spółdzielniach produkcyjnych NRD i CSRS" [Integration processes in cooperative farms of East Germany and Czechoslovakia], *Zagadnienia Ekonomiki Rolnej*, 1969, no. 3, p. 96.

19. Ibid.

20. Władysław Misiuna, "Przemiany w rolnictwie Czechosłowacji" [Changes in Czechoslovak agriculture], *Zagadnienia Ekonomiki Rolnej*, 1970, no. 3, p. 104.

21. Imre Dimeny, "Za polozhenieto na ungarskoto selsko stopanstvo" [On the condition of Hungarian agriculture], *Novo vreme*, 1963, no. 12, p. 74, and Stefan Stoilov, "Fondoemkostta na selskostopanskata produksiia" [Capital-output ratios in agricultural production], ibid., 1964, no. 11, p. 83.

22. Data compiled by the Bulgarian Planning Commission and cited by Dimitur Kinov, *Effektivnost na proizvodstenite fondove v selskoto stopanstvo* [The effectiveness of productive capital in agriculture] (Sofia: 1965), p. 54.

23. Adakemiia na selskostopanskite nauki, Institut po ikonomika i organizatsiia na selskoto stopanstvo, *Vuprosi na materialnata baza, spetsializatsiiata i izdurzhkata na proizvodstvoto v TKZS* [Problems of material equipment, specialization and production costs in cooperative farms], (Sofia: 1965), p. 96. I visited some farms in Czechoslovakia where reconversion of buildings constructed earlier for small numbers of animals was an acute problem after the merger.

24. *Figyelo*, 29 April 1970, as cited by Radio Free Europe, "Hungarian Situation Report 20," 26 May 1970.

officially prescribed depreciation rates allow it to be retired. For example, until 1970, tractors in Bulgaria were supposed to last 10 years (compared with a realistic expectancy of 5 years). This goes far to explain "under-utilization" of the Bulgarian tractor inventory in 1964 by 42.3 percent.[25]

Machinery supply has been unsatisfactory in quality and assortment as well as overall quantity. In one Czechoslovak district in 1967–68, there were only 40 pieces of appropriate equipment for the available 69 RS-09 tractors, and some farms had no equipment at all for this type of tractor. On the other hand, some unwanted machines that farms were compelled to buy had to be written off and destroyed without ever having been used.[26] In 1960–64, only 5 percent of Bulgarian tractors were equipped with a complete set of the required accessories.[27] No wonder that a Polish economist was moved to comment in April 1966:

> I do not know why this country adopted the principle that agriculture must buy everything that industry "servicing agriculture" (or as non-farmers like to put it, "helping agriculture(?)") produces, whether this machinery is usable in agriculture or not. . . . Industry "must fulfill the plan," and agriculture "must pay for the bubbles," which are often found (later) in the weeds.[28]

According to a recent study by the Experimental Station for Farm and Forestry Machinery in Repy (Czechoslovakia), half of the farm machines currently produced perform inadequately.[29] The USSR continues to export the now-obsolete D-54 tractors and SK-4 combines.

An old difficulty is best illustrated by a recent (1970) comment in a Bulgarian newspaper: "The spare parts problem is *the* problem, which still awaits solution after many years." It is particularly acute with respect to imported parts.[30]

25. *Rabotnichesko delo*, 19 September 1970. A recommendation was then made to lower the expected useful life of tractors to 6–7 years. See also the statement of the Hungarian Deputy Minister of Agriculture and Food, Dr. Gábor Soos, in *Magyar Hirlap*, 10 March 1970, as reported in Radio Free Europe, "Hungarian Situation Report 11," 17 March 1970. On Bulgaria see Stefan Stoilov, "Tempove i effektivnost na selskostopansko proizvodstvo" [Rates of growth of effectiveness of agricultural production], *Novo Vreme*, 1966, no. 10, p. 72.

26. O. Doležal, "K problému přeinvestovanosti v zemědělství" [On the problem of over-investment in agriculture], *Zemědělská ekonomika*, 1969, nos. 9–10, p. 591.

27. Stoilov, p. 72.

28. Ryszard Manteuffel in *Zagadnienia Ekonomiki Rolnej*, 1966, no. 5, p. 212.

29. Doležal, p. 599.

30. *Večerbí noviny*, 9 May 1970. According to *Zemědělské noviny*, 18 December 1968, the USSR contracted to supply 1,757 types of spare parts in 1968. The contract was completely met for only 108 items, while 100 items were not supplied at all. East Germany failed to supply 24 promised items, while shipments of 117 items were below the contracted amounts. "These are the hard facts; the consequences are also severe."

Trends in machinery supplies and in the state of machinery inventories are important because the agricultural labor force has declined markedly (see table 6.1). In a region as varied as Eastern Europe, the severity of the manpower problem in agriculture is not, of course, uniform. Shortages are most pronounced in Bohemia and East Germany, but seasonal shortages appeared in the last decade in Bulgaria as well,[31] and Hungary is also beginning to feel the pinch.[32] Yet, acute seasonal shortages are accompanied by serious underutilization of labor (particularly low-paid crop workers) during the winter months. Unstable earnings for hard manual labor have impelled the young, especially, to leave agriculture.[33] "As in many other countries, agriculture in Eastern Europe is becoming an employer of the old, the unskilled, and of other persons generally unemployable elsewhere."[34]

Planners view these developments with a good deal of apprehension, partly because migration trends are generally recognized as spontaneous (that is, only slightly amenable to planned remedies) and also because the exodus of young and skilled agricultural personnel seems to be gaining momentum throughout the socialist bloc. In Bulgaria, the number of "steadily employed" cooperative farmers declined by 25.2 percent between 1963 and 1967. In 1963, the age group 16–36 accounted for 36 percent of the cooperative labor force. By 1969, this percentage had declined to 29.4, and it is now estimated that unless demographic trends are offset by economic incentives, it will drop to 18.5 percent by 1975.[35]

Manpower problems are particularly apparent on weaker farms, for here "the exodus of workers . . . was not the result of substitution of machinery for part of the labor force which could be freed for other branches of the economy, but rather the opposite. The lower level of production and the resulting low level of material incentives . . . reduced interest in agricultural work, especially on the part of the young."[36] And the proportion of weak

31. Minko Minkov, "Razvitie i sustav na rabotnata sila v selskoto stopanstvo" [Development and composition of labor force in agriculture], *Trud i tseni*, 1965, no. 3, p. 2.

32. *Kisalföld*, 4 February 1970, and *Szabad Föld*, 8 February 1970, as quoted in Radio Free Europe, "Hungarian Situation Report 7," 17 February 1970.

33. For example, only 4 out of 38 graduates of the general school located on the cooperative farm Nádasd, Vas province, Hungary, wished to make a career in agriculture. Of those who remain, very few want to work in general crop or animal production (see the experience of the Hungarian cooperative farm Nyalka described in *Kisalföld*, 4 February 1970).

34. Andrew Elias, "Magnitude and Distribution of the Labor Force in Eastern Europe," in U.S. Congress, Joint Economic Committee, *Economic Developments in Countries of Eastern Europe* (Washington, D.C.: Government Printing Office, 1970), p. 159.

35. Khristo Khristov, Marin Karadzhov, "Izmeneniia vuv vuzrastovata struktura na rabotnata sila v selskoto stopanstvo" [Changes in the age structure of labor force in agriculture], *Problemi na truda*, 1969, no. 2, p. 33 and *Rabotnichesko delo*, 28 July 1970.

36. *Efektivnost výroby v zemědělství* [The effectiveness of production in agriculture] (Prague: 1963), pp. 175–76.

farms in Eastern Europe is very considerable indeed. In Czechoslovakia a large part of even the state farm sector (mainly farms on territory formerly settled by the expelled Germans) falls in this category. In Hungary, 28 percent of all cooperatives are classified as weak; they hold 25 percent of all agricultural land and account for 33 percent of all cooperative farmers, including the retired. Incomes of farmers on these weak cooperatives are only 57 percent of the average for all cooperatives.[37] In Bulgaria, where the average income distributed per cooperative member in 1962 came to 601 new leva, the figures for farms in the Smoliani and Gabrovo provinces were 311 and 341 leva respectively. By 1965, the countrywide average rose to 790 leva per farmer, but there were still farms distributing 61 and 150 leva annually in return for 212 or 207 mandays worked.[38]

Weak farms continue to operate because the state cannot get along without their produce. At the same time, they absorb an inordinate share of available agricultural capital, the return on which would be considerably higher on more efficient farms elsewhere.[39]

The role of private production on the household plots of cooperative farmers, state farms workers, and other members of the rural population is closely related to issues of farm productivity and income. Interdependence of the private and the public sectors of socialized agriculture in the USSR has recently been investigated in detail by Karl-Eugen Waedekin.[40] Though the structure of private output is by no means identical in other socialist countries, its importance cannot be questioned. The private sector accounts for one-third of the gross output of Hungarian and Romanian agriculture, about 28 percent of output in Czechoslovakia, and over 25 percent in Bulgaria.[41] Even in Poland, household plots in 1965 yielded 46 percent of the total income of cooperative farmers and 21 percent of the income of

37. Radio Free Europe, "Research Report Hungary—14," 26 March 1970, citing data from *Statisztikai Időszaki Közlemenyek*, I/68.

38. Nikola V. Velikov, *Suvremenni tendentsii v razvitieto na TKZS* [Current trends in the development of cooperative farms] (Sofia: 1968), pp. 40, 97–98.

39. Cooperative farms located in the mountainous regions of Bulgaria produced 7.1 percent of output in 1966, but had 18.6 percent of the capital stock. Ibid., p. 43.

40. Karl-Eugen Waedekin, *Privatproduzenten in der sowjetischen Landwirtschaft* (Cologne: Verlag Wirtschaft und Wissenschaft, 1967), chapter 5.

41. Władysław Misiuna, "Przemiany w rolnictwie Wegier" [Changes in Hungarian agriculture], *Zagadnienia Ekonomiki Rolnej*, 1968, no. 5, p. 110; idem, "Przemiany w gospodarce rolnej Rumunii" [Changes in the agricultural economy of Romania], ibid., 1969, nos. 5–6, pp. 156–57; Rudakov, *Materialnoto*, p. 14; *Statisticheski Godishnik na Narodna Republika Bulgariia, 1966* [Statistical handbook of the People's Republic of Bulgaria, 1966], p. 173. In Hungary and Romania, privately owned livestock accounted for about half of total herds in the mid-1960s.

state farm workers.[42] Though still indispensable, the private sector is trouble-some on ideological grounds, and until the mid-1960s the terms of its survival within a socialized environment are best described by Waedekin's phase "uneasy coexistence."

That pressure for reform made itself felt at an early stage is evidenced both by the introduction of certain "New Course" policies after Stalin's death in 1953, and by the sluggish trend in output throughout the region. According to recent calculations of Gregor Lazarcik, agricultural output in 1954–56 surpassed the prewar (1934–38) level in only one country, Poland.[43]

In addition to the pressures from domestic demand to which we referred earlier, there is also a formidable balance-of-payments pressure for greater agricultural efficiency. Of the various East European countries we deal with here, East Germany and Czechoslovakia are net food importers, while all the others are net exporters of agricultural produce. In spite of major shifts in the structure of Bulgarian foreign trade, foodstuffs accounted for 37 per-cent of all Bulgarian exports in 1966–67. The share of farm products in exports of Hungary, Poland, Romania and Yugoslavia is smaller, but still critical in securing an export balance on current account.[44]

Thus various pressures make the achievement of greater efficiency in farm production important if not imperative. The areas of concern can be grouped conveniently under the following headings:

1. reform in planning and administration, with the aim of placing farm management in a position to manage farm production again in a meaningful sense of the word;[45]
2. replacement of command tools of control and coordination with market-type instruments which would make macro- as well as micro-economic efficiency attainable;
3. improvement of relative farm incomes.

We shall discuss the various efforts under these headings in the following section.

42. Ryszard Manteuffel, "Porównanie gospodarstw państwowych, spółdzielczych i rod-zinnych w Polsce z punktu widzenia technicznego i ekonomicznego" [A comparison of state, cooperative and family farms in Poland from the technical and economic standpoint], *Zagad-nienia Ekonomiki Rolnej*, 1969, no. 2, p. 22.

43. Gregor Lazarcik, "Growth of Output, Expenses and Gross and Net Product in East European Agriculture," in U.S. Congress, *Economic Developments*, pp. 476–77.

44. "Eastern European Communist Countries Foreign Trade Statistical Tables," ibid., pp. 556–57. The position of Yugoslavia has just shifted to that of a net exporter of agricultural products.

45. This includes efforts to strengthen the position of individual farms in their relations with government suppliers or procurement agencies.

II. Agricultural Reforms

Planning and Administration

The early reforms. It was the death of Stalin, and more specifically the emergence of reforms in the USSR, that opened the door to greater rationalization of planning in Eastern Europe. But developments in individual countries were by no means uniform, and belated introduction of command farming institutions occurred even as the Soviet model was beginning to change. For example, a carbon copy of the Soviet procurement system was introduced in Czechoslovakia only in 1953; it even included the milling tax in kind, which the USSR abandoned in that year.[46] On the other hand, Eastern Europe pioneered in some alterations of the procurement system. Bulgaria abolished compulsory deliveries from households a year before this occurred in the USSR. Hungary (impelled by the revolt) moved in late 1956 to abolish the lower-priced category of deliveries from cooperative farms,[47] and Romania followed the Hungarian example in 1957.

By and large, however, Khrushchev set the pace. All of Eastern Europe followed the USSR in 1955–56 in gestures toward replacing detailed output planning by procurement targets alone. Not until after the USSR abolished lower-priced deliveries in 1958 were similar moves made in Bulgaria, Czechoslovakia, and East Germany.[48] Similarly, the Soviet MTS reform of 1958 was generally copied in all East European countries, though most have retained some machine tractor stations to serve the weak farms referred to earlier.

Ministries of agriculture and unions of cooperative farms. In retrospect, many of the subsequent changes in agricultural administration may be interpreted as efforts to reduce the dominant position of ministries of agriculture in production planning, with the aim of shifting this function closer to the farm level. As I have explained elsewhere, the substitution of procurement planning for production planning in the mid-1950s was not very meaningful, since the large number of procurement quotas assigned to each farm effectively frustrated management attempts to alter output structure.[49]

An early attempt to change agricultural administration occurred in Romania in 1962, when the Ministry of Agriculture with its provincial and

46. Vydra, pp. 58–75.

47. Rudakov, *Materialnoto*, p. 34. There is little doubt that compulsory (lower-priced) deliveries were heartily disliked by all farmers, though it is possible that for many farms in the medium or above-average category the resulting tax burden was smaller than a ground tax would have been.

48. Ibid.

49. See my "Certain Aspects of New Economic Systems in Bulgaria and Czechoslovakia," in *Agrarian Policies in Communist Countries*, ed. W. A. D. Jackson (Seattle, Wash.: University of Washington Press, 1971). The point is that as soon as procurement targets for grain, meat, milk, and technical crops are determined, the sown area of a farm is also 90 percent or more determined.

regional departments was replaced by the Supreme Council of Agricultural Economy and its corresponding regional organs. (The system may well have been modeled on Soviet efforts in the same year to streamline agricultural administration by introducing territorial production administrations at the *raion* or inter-*raion* level.) The Romanian attempt failed: as a perceptive Polish observer noted, the Supreme Council simply took over the Ministry's functions, and there was no essential change in planning or administrative methods. Allegedly under pressure from below, a Central Union of Agricultural Cooperatives was formed at the end of 1965 to direct cooperative farm production. Again, there was little real change, since the Supreme Council of Agricultural Economy continued to distribute state investment funds and controlled the supply of basic means of production (machinery, fertilizers). It was only in 1966 that a special organization under the jurisdiction of the Union of Cooperatives was formed to take over the supply functions of the Supreme Council.[50] The Cooperative Council also took over the procurement of virtually all fruit and vegetables, was empowered to construct processing enterprises for these products and to conduct some foreign trade operations. Simultaneously, the number of directive indicators in the national plan for the cooperative sector was reduced until only 5 procurement targets remained in 1967 (wheat, corn, sunflower, sugar beet, and potatoes). Procurement of all other products was planned by the contract system.

A rather unusual and complex system of agricultural administration was introduced in East Germany in 1963 (and streamlined further at the 10th Peasant Congress in 1968). The Ministry of Agriculture was replaced by a Council for Agriculture and Food Industry, subordinated directly to the Council of Ministers. Corresponding agencies were set up at the province and the district level. In addition to many ex-officio members (including deputy ministers of economic ministries and high officials from other state agencies), the National Council includes members elected at the biannual Peasant Congress. Its executive controls committees for land improvement, farm equipment, state purchases and procurements, and forestry. The chairman of the provincial and the district council is the ex-officio head of the local production administration. Each of these levels of administration is also product oriented, in that *kombinaty* or special offices handle problems of production affecting grains, meat, poultry, and dairy production.[51]

50. Misiuna, "gospodarce rolnej Rumunii," pp. 161–62. See also Rudakov, Mellin, and Storozhev, *Ekonomicheskaia*, pp. 35–36, and Rudakov, *Materialnoto*, pp. 16–17, 37–38.

51. Cf. P. V. Grechishnikov, "Novoe v planirovanii i rukovodstve sel'skim khoziaistvom v evropeiskikh sotsialisticheskikh stranakh" [New developments in planning and managing agriculture in european socialist states], in Akademiia obshchestvennykh nauk pri TsK KPSS, *Nekotorye voprosy upravleniia sel'skokhoziaistvennom proizvodstvom* [Some problems of managing agricultural production] (Moscow: 1967), p. 305. For diagrams of the new administrative structure see Peter Friedheim, "Die agrarpolitische Konzeption der DDR," in *Beitraege*

(*continued on page 224*)

The Council's main task is to elaborate long-range plans, which are integrated into the economic plan at the national level by the State Planning Commission. The Council is also expected to control and enforce regulations on pricing, work norms, and other measures implementing government policies in agriculture. Its agencies prepare "optimal variants" of production and development plans, which are later used as a basis for the formulation of the national economic plans.[52] Regional bodies control state as well as cooperative farms in a given district or province, though a national agency for state farms also exists.

In Bulgaria, a National Union of Cooperative Farms, formed in March 1967, merged seven months later with the Central Union of (Rural) Co-operatives (mainly a trading organization with some procurement activities) to become the Central Union of Cooperatives, with corresponding provincial unions. These agencies absorbed most of the planning functions formerly performed by state administrative departments. This stripped the Ministry of Agriculture of most of its administrative functions and in 1968 it was merged with the Ministry of Food Industry, following a pattern now dominant in Eastern Europe as a whole.[53]

The Central Cooperative Union is supposed to handle "the basic economic and organizational problems" of cooperative farms, offering advice and recommendations on specialization, intensification, and concentration of production within the framework of the national economic plan. It submits one variant of the agricultural plan to the State Planning Commission (though another version is also submitted by the Ministry of Agriculture and Food Industry). The national as well as the provincial councils are empowered to set up processing enterprises for farm products, either on their own account or jointly with cooperative farms, which then hold "shares" in the new enterprise.[54]

(continued from page 223)

zur Entwicklung der Landwirtschaft der DDR, ed. Eberhardt Schinke and Heinz-Ulrich Thimm (Giessen: Foto-Druck Lenz, 1970), pp. 154–56; G. Jannermann, "The Close Links of Inter-action Between Centralized State Planning and Management of the Integrated Processes of Society and Independent Responsibility of the Co-operative Farmers for the Development of Agricultural Production and Social Life on the Countryside," in Papers Presented by the Agricultural Economy Group of the German Democratic Republic at the XIV International Conference of Agricultural Economists (the table of contents of this pamphlet, distributed in Minsk in August 1970, is dated February 1970), pp. 38, 41.

52. Jannermann, pp. 37–39. See also Rudakov, Materialnoto, pp. 15–16.
53. Władysław Misiuna, "Przemiany w gospodarce rolnej Bułgarii" [Changes in the agri-cultural economy of Bulgaria], Zagadnienia Ekonomiki Rolnej, 1969, no. 4, pp. 116–19; Rudakov, Mellin, and Storozhev, Ekonomicheskaia, pp. 37–38.
54. Misiuna, "gospodarce rolnej Bułgarii," p. 118; Rudakov, Mellin, and Storozhev, Ekonom-icheskaia, p. 45.

When the Council of Cooperatives was first set up, it was apparently intended to act—at least in part—as an agency of countervailing power, representing farm interests vis-à-vis the highly centralized procurement and processing agencies of the state. The latter were simultaneously converted into state economic associations, operating on a *khozraschet* basis, and able to exercise considerable monopoly pressure in setting contract terms for delivery of farm produce. Some of these agencies control the entire whole-sale trade or processing of given product groups: *Bulgarplod*, for example, conducts both foreign and domestic trade operations. *Bulgarplod* and similar associations were first subordinated to the Ministry of Foreign Trade; after 1968, all these associations again came under the umbrella of the Ministry of Agriculture and Food Industry.[55] It may well be that this reversal reflects second thoughts among the Party leadership on the advisability of creating countervailing powers of considerable magnitude. Certainly there was reluctance to extend the powers of the Central Cooperative Union: nothing came of early proposals that it absorb the remaining machine tractor station and repair enterprises and also assume guidance of the agricultural ma-chinery industry.[56] Political developments in Czechoslovakia in 1968 may have reinforced cautious attitudes. However, it is impossible to predict trends in Bulgaria before the impact of agro-industrial complexes (see below) is known.

In Hungary, the first Congress of Cooperative Farms met in April 1967, at which time the National Union of Cooperative Farms was formed and steps were taken to establish regional associations at provincial and lower levels. In one sense, the Hungarian development is unique: the National Union does not represent the apex of a pyramid of individual associations, but is instead a separate organization. Moreover, the establishment of regional associations was clearly represented, and understood, as a step designed to offer protection to individual cooperatives who faced powerful or monopolistic agencies and enterprises in the state sector.[57] What hap-pened subsequently may be indicative of the obstacles facing reform from the party bureaucracy: party committees at the province level decided on the number of associations to be set up within each province, and on the organizational procedures. Though farms were nominally free to join,

55. Rudakov, *Materialnoto*, p. 38.

56. Rudakov, Mellin, and Storozhev describe the proposals (*Ekonomicheskaia*, p. 39). Ruda-kov's later work does not mention them. See also Velikov, pp. 52–53.

57. Rudakov, Mellin, and Storozhev, *Ekonomicheskaia*, p. 39. On the reaction of cooperative farmers to the creation of regional associations see K. K., "A New Era in Hungarian Agriculture" (Radio Free Europe," Research Report, Hungary 3," 15 March 1968), citing various Hungarian sources. Thus, the decision to set up regional associations of cooperative farms is said to have "caused 'the greatest stir' among the ... peasantry" (*Társadalmi Szemle*, October 1968).

sufficient pressure was exercised to ensure virtually total participation in associations to which farms were assigned by the "steering committees."[58]

Besides acting as a buffer against state procurement agencies, regional associations are to supply technical information to farms and conduct market research on their behalf. The National Council may also propose legislation on matters affecting cooperative farms (and may bring proposals before the Council of Ministers even if the Ministry of Agriculture and Food Industry opposes them).[59]

In Czechoslovakia, the Ministry of Agriculture was merged with the Ministry of Food Industry and the Central Administration for Procurements of Farm Products and Supply of Off-Farm Inputs in the spring of 1967. The new measure, aimed at establishing an agro-industrial complex, called for the creation of *khozraschet* agricultural associations at the district level, uniting state and cooperative farms on a purely voluntary basis. By the beginning of 1968, 65 associations had been organized,[60] taking over most of the staffs of the disbanded district production administrations.[61]

A Union of Cooperative Farmers was created in Czechoslovakia in 1968, but the hopes entertained for this organization were dashed by the aftermath of the invasion. It is now charged that "reactionary circles" tried to create a national center for the district agricultural associations to act as an organization fully independent of the state.[62] It is, of course, true that during the "Prague spring," the leaders of cooperative farms demanded the transfer of procurement points and of various processing plants (including distilleries) to the jurisdiction of the district agricultural associations,[63] and that the creation of a real (and much needed) countervailing power was often advocated.

At this point it is rather immaterial whether this power would have devolved upon the Union of Cooperative Farmers or the associations. On 12 September 1969, the Presidium of the Central Committee approved temporary rules for the "stabilization" of district agricultural associations in an effort to "increase the influence of the state on the sphere of production."[64] At the National Conference of Chairmen and Managers of District Agricultural Associations held in Prague in May 1970, the director of the

58. K. K., pp. 114–19.
59. Ibid., pp. 120–21, citing *Magyar Mezőgazdaság*, 14 June 1967.
60. *Státní statky*, 1967, no. 9, p. 129.
61. *Zemědělské noviny*, 14 November 1967. As it turned out, the district agricultural associations lost one-third of their personnel by 1970 (ibid., 20 March 1970); it is difficult to say whether this represents the impact of purges, the departure of old-type administrators, or both.
62. *Zemědělské noviny*, 13 May 1970. The charge was made by J. Černý, the minister of agriculture and food.
63. Ibid., 27 March 1968.
64. Monitored broadcast, Radio Prague, 12 September 1969.

agricultural division of the Bureau of the Central Party Committee defined the future agenda of the Union of Cooperative Farmers as lying in the field of "social policy, recreation facilities for cooperative farmers, and problems related to pensions in agriculture. . . . Under no circumstances, however, will the Union encroach upon the economic management of cooperative farms."[65] The district associations will, however, be retained as the basic link in farm management at the district level.

As we have seen, administrative reorganization in Eastern Europe aimed at (among other things) strengthening the position of individual farms in their relations with state agencies, and it looked for a whole as if the trend was toward placing agriculture under the overall guidance of the newly created unions of cooperative farms. Besides events in Czechoslovakia, two recent developments suggest a possible reversal of this tendency.

The first is the reestablishment of the Ministry of Agriculture in Romania in October 1969, following bitter criticism by Nicolae Ceausescu of the activities of the Supreme Council of Agricultural Economy and of the National Union of Cooperative Farms.[66] The Ministry again took over responsibility for investment, supplies, procurements, and financial and accounting problems on farms, while the National Council of Cooperative Farms lost its leadership functions with respect to procurements of vegetables and fruit.[67] The Union of Cooperative Farms was henceforth to concentrate on problems of organization, the provision of legal assistance to farms, issues of pensions and recreation, etc. As is so often the case, however, this recentralization of administration occurred jointly with the introduction of measures increasing the autonomy of cooperative farms in some matters.[68]

The second development is the planned establishment of agro-industrial complexes in Bulgaria, highlighted in Zhivkov's speech at the April 1970 Plenum of the Central Committee of the Bulgarian Communist Party. Agro-industrial complexes, implemented through mergers of several farms "according to the branch principle, . . . are now emerging as the most suitable form of concentration in agriculture."[69] The complexes are to be

65. *Zemědělské noviny*, 13 May 1970.

66. The criticism was aimed in part at insufficient investment by cooperative farms, in part at the inefficient planning and activities of the central agencies.

67. *Biuletinul Official* no. 127 (13 November 1969), as reported in Radio Free Europe, "Rumanian Situation Report 107," 11 December 1969. The former chairman of the Supreme Council became the new minister of agriculture.

68. Thus each farm is to decide on its own internal organization and its own minimum number of man-days to be worked by members. Work norms are tightened, but minimum pay per normative man-day is guaranteed for the next two years. Cf. *Scanteia*, 25 December 1969, reporting on the Plenum of the Central Union of Cooperative Farms.

69. Zhivkov's speech and the Plenum decision are reproduced in *Rabotnichesko delo*, 29 and 30 April 1970.

set up on a voluntary basis, with farms retaining their independence (although perhaps only in the early stages);[70] they will aim at specialization of production and vertical integration, and may establish their own processing enterprises. The formation of what seems to have been pilot complexes has been going on for about a year, with the first one uniting five state farms in the Kurdzhali province (described as "farms unable to stabilize their economy") on a total area of 1,427 hectares. A number of other mergers were reported in the news media in the winter of 1969–70, undoubtedly as a preparation for the creation of complexes.[71] For the time being, the Bulgarian government has commendably refrained from imposing a uniform organizational structure on the complexes, but it is not clear how farms integrated vertically with processing enterprises can retain significant operational independence. Nor is it possible to predict the impact of complexes on the functions of the Union of Cooperatives.

Planning practices. In all East European countries much emphasis has recently been placed on long-range planning covering a period of 15–20 years. These plans have been elaborated with the active participation of academic economists and other scientists, and their scientific character has been stressed time and again.[72] It is this very stress that raises a tinge of doubt. Perhaps some earlier errors—for example, growth of animal herds without a corresponding increase in production or imports of feed—will be avoided. (According to French practitioners, the great virtue of perspective planning lies in identifying those actions that planners should not take.) But the literature creates the impression that perhaps too much faith is being placed in the correctness and appropriateness of long-range projections.[73]

Five-year and operational planning (more often 2-year rather than annual) has increasingly shifted to the use of economic policy instruments rather than the command tools of coordination and control. In line with this principle, the number of compulsory indicators has been considerably reduced since the early days of command farming, with the greatest progress visible in Hungary, Czechoslovakia, and East Germany, and the least in

70. Thus "cooperative and state farms will be retained initially as independent legal and economic units" (Mincho Georgiev, "Vuprosy na upravlenieto" [Problems of administration], *Partien zhivot*, 1970, no. 10, p. 7).

71. *Kooperativno selo*, 24 November 1968. According to ibid., 21 December 1968, two complexes were planned in the Vrachna district, one to encompass 42 villages. Radio Sofia, 14 January 1970, reported organization of a complex embracing 8 cooperative farms and 40 thousand hectares. Mergers were reported in Vidim, Russe, Plovdiv, and Stara Zagora districts.

72. Cf. Rudakov, Mellin, and Storozhev, *Ekonomicheskaia*, pp. 47–48.

73. Cf. Jannermann, passim. The full texts of the perspective plans have not been released, though references to their main conclusions or to individual aspects are frequently found in the literature. For Germany, see Friedheim, p. 145.

Poland. In Poland, compulsory deliveries have been retained for all the important farm products. In Bulgaria, compulsory state procurement targets remain for 8 products. We have already noted that Romanian co-operatives were given 5 compulsory procurement targets in 1966–70. In East Germany, procurement quotas apply only to grain and potatoes.[74] The Czechoslovak Five-Year Plan for 1966–70 included compulsory indicators for marketings of wheat, potatoes, sugar beets, meat, milk and eggs; by 1967, compulsory targets applied only to grain, and ostensibly only to district production administrations (in practice, however, farms were often assigned individual targets).[75] In Hungary after the introduction of the New Economic Model, the only compulsory indicator was the area sown to grains; its elimination was discussed in the summer of 1969.[76]

Much stress has been placed in East European literature on the contract delivery system as a means of decentralizing production decisions to the farm level. Rudakov's caveat should be borne in mind here: contracts are truly a decentralizing device only when they are signed *before* farms receive procurement targets, so that they serve as a basis for output planning at the farm level. This has been the case only in Hungary since 1966, and elsewhere with products for which no centralized procurement indicators are assigned.[77]

If the amount contracted for does not cover the state's minimum requirement, the short-run solution frequently sought by planners is to increase the real price, either through payment of cash premiums (see below) or through preferential allocations of scarce fertilizers, machinery items, and building materials. At this stage, therefore, something like the Walras *tatonnement* process ideally takes place, until planners are no longer able to raise the real price or until their demand is satisfied.

Farm bargaining power. Autonomy of the individual cooperative has unquestionably increased as a result of the measures discussed above. The old days when farms were virtually at the mercy of local procurement organizations are no more; for example, Bulgarian cooperatives may conclude contracts with a procurement organization anywhere in the country.[78] This is a step forward, even though specialization of procurement organizations by product places limits on this type of competition. In Hungary, where a

74. Ibid., p. 146.

75. *Věstník Ministerstva Zemědělství a Lesního Hospodářství* 13, no. 36 (24 September 1966): 214, and personal observations in Czechoslovakia in 1967.

76. K. K., p. 94, and Radio Budapest, 13 August 1969 (information supplied by Radio Free Europe).

77. Rudakov, Mellin, and Storozhev, *Ekonomicheskaia,* pp. 52–54.

78. Nikola Popov, "Izpolzuvaneto na ikonomicheskite kategorii v razvitieto na nasheto sotsialistochesko selsko stopanstvo" [The use of economic tools in the development of our socialist agriculture], *Ikonomika na selskoto stopanstvo,* 1969, no. 5, p. 65.

multichannel marketing system was introduced as part of the New Economic Mechanism, farms may sell to state procurement agencies, to institutions, or (with certain exceptions) directly to the consumer; the products that may not be sold directly are feed grains, slaughter cattle and hogs, raw wool, hides, and tobacco.

The ability of farms to bargain with procurement agencies was further strengthened by measures increasing the scope of subsidiary activities—processing, direct marketing, construction, and the like.[79] Governments promoted this kind of activity for a variety of reasons: to improve farmer incomes through the provision of year-round employment opportunities, to accelerate rural construction, and to increase supplies of food for the non-agricultural population.

The degree to which processing and direct marketing were legitimized varied from one country to another. In 1967, Czechoslovak farms were still forbidden to market eggs directly to consumers, or to operate their own dairies. In Germany, the number of interfarm subsidiary enterprises (including feed lots) rose from 733 to 1,565 between 1965 and 1969, and employment in these enterprises increased from 17.6 to 77.8 thousand. In Bulgaria, there were 31 fruit and vegetable canning plants operated by cooperative farms in 1968.[80]

Despite difficulties in obtaining building materials, subsidiary enterprises mushroomed in Hungary after the 1967 law permitting cooperatives to process their own output (except for tobacco and spirits).[81] By 1968, 94 percent of all cooperatives operated one or more subsidiary enterprises embracing 150 different lines of activity.[82] Many of these flourished, in part because they often undercut competing state or consumer cooperative enterprises.[83]

79. I still recall vividly the satisfied expression on the face of a Czechoslovak state farm director, whose grain elevator was about to be completed in 1967, when he exclaimed: "And then I sell to the procurement organization when I want to sell to them!"

80. *Statistisches Jahrbuch der Deutschen Demokratischen Republik 1970* (Berlin: 1970), p. 194, and Vladimir Radoikov, "Ikonomichesko reguliranie na vzaimootnosheniata mezhdu promishlennostta i selskoto stopanstvo" [Economic regulation of the interrelationships between industry and agriculture], *Ikonomicheska misul*, 1970, no. 2, p. 51. (In addition, 4 state farms operate canning plants, while 3 such plants have been set up by the Central Union of Cooperatives.)

81. K. K., p. 87.

82. *Népszabadság*, 26 January 1969, as cited in Radio Free Europe, "Hungarian Situation Report 47," 14 July 1969.

83. Thus the marketing office of cooperative farms in the vicinity of Budapest charges a commission of 1 percent to members and 2 percent to outsiders, while the Provincial Marketing Office of the Consumer Cooperatives charges a commission of 5 percent. Cf. *Magyar Hirlap*, 27 November 1968, as cited in Radio Free Europe, "Hungarian Situation Report 51," 5 August 1969.

It does appear, however, that the Hungarian government underestimated the entrepreneurial drive of its farmers. In 1968, only 25 percent of the income of cooperative subsidiary enterprises originated in processing or direct marketing of farm products.[84] A large proportion came from activities that had nothing to do with agriculture: one enterprising subsidiary built a small airport, while others set up TV-servicing and other repair shops.[85] Another subsidiary enterprise, tooled to produced poultry processing equipment for the USSR and faced with loss of market when the Russians changed their mind, shifted to subcontracting with industrial enterprises afflicted with labor shortage. It then proceeded to hire away skilled industrial workers from state enterprises (presumably at higher wages) and ended the year with a handsome profit of 1.6 million forints.[86]

Such zestful pursuit of profits wherever they may be found is anathema to the doctrinaires, some of whom are discomfited even by activities that are clearly within the law. For example, cooperative canning plants in Bulgaria were recently criticized as small, high-cost operations whose entire output could be produced by existing state canneries if the latter received the necessary fruit and vegetables. The implication was that farms divert produce to their own plants; the explicit conclusion was that ways must be found to halt "the attempt of every cooperative farm to have its own canning plant."[87]

One major problem area remains essentially untouched by reform: there has been little improvement in farm influence over the quantity and assortment of machinery and spare parts. "The slogan that we now sell rather than distribute does not alter the heart of the matter. If a farm finds on the market only one type of machine, and one that is not always appropriate for its particular conditions, if a farm has no choice, and cannot select another machine for a given purpose—then this state of affairs cannot be called a market, or trade."[88]

At this point it is hard to predict how effectively the various measures aimed at increasing farm bargaining power will function in the future. In Hungary, at the meeting of the National Council of Cooperative Farms in December 1969, there were complaints that the old system of distributing off-farm inputs (formally abolished in 1967) was still in effect, and the chairman of the Borsod province regional association stated unequivocally

84. *Népszabadság*, 12 July 1969, as cited in Radio Free Europe, "Hungarian Situation Research Paper Hungary 36," 23 July 1969, and *Népszabadság*, 14 November 1969.

85. *Dolgozók Lapja*, 2 July 1969, as cited in Radio Free Europe, "Hungarian Situation Report 47," 14 July 1969.

86. *Magyar Hirlap*, 1 July 1969 as cited in Radio Free Europe, "Hungarian Situation Report 47," 14 July 1969.

87. Radoikov, p. 52.

88. Doležal, p. 601.

that relations between farms and other enterprises had worsened.[89] Since the autonomy of industrial enterprises and of suppliers is also increasing under the reforms, difficulties such as these are perhaps inevitable, and need not imply a retreat in official policy.

Prices, Taxes

Farm prices and prices for inputs. The early reforms mainly involved changes in procurement procedures and the elimination of lower-priced ("compulsory") deliveries. A single-price system was introduced in Hungary in 1956, in Romania in 1957, in Bulgaria in 1959, in Czechoslovakia in 1960, and in East Germany in 1966 (crops) and 1969 (livestock products). Poland alone retains the old multiple-price system for state procurements.[90]

Though average farm prices rose with the introduction of single pricing, they did not always cover costs. In other words, prices continued to be a device for redistributing income between agriculture and the other sectors of the economy. Given the wide disparities in the level of "profitability" (calculated against costs), the resulting tax burden has been very unevenly distributed among individual products. Most livestock products were, and still are, produced at a loss throughout the area.

Analysis of trends in most countries confirms the view expressed in 1968 by Silar and Baca: increases in procurement prices have always been introduced reluctantly and ex post, as if they were a measure of last resort.[91] To a large extent, this grudging attitude stems from unwillingness to alter the existing level and structure of retail prices.[92] But it also reflects the hope that reforms in command farming would yield rapid cost reductions. Unfortunately, significant cost reductions in agriculture belong to the realm of what the Germans call *Zukunftmusik*.

89. *Népszabadság*, 16 December 1917; *Magyar Hirlap*, 16 December 1969, as cited in Radio Free Europe, "Hungarian Situation Report 1," 5 January 1970; Radio Budapest, 11 December 1969, as cited in Radio Free Europe, "Hungarian Situation Report 70," 16 December 1970.

90. Rudakov, *Materialnoto*, p. 34.

91. Jiří Silar and Jan Bača, "Téze ke koncepci ekonomické reformy řízení zemědělství" [An outline of the conception of the reform of management in agriculture], *Zemědělská ekonomika*, 1968, nos. 7–8, pp. 482–83. Procurement prices have risen as follows (1960 = 100): Bulgaria (1966), 146.4; Czechoslovakia (1967), 124.8; East Germany (1969), 135.3. See S. Khrustev, "Niakoi tendentsii na obmianata mezhdu promishlennostta i selskoto stopanstvo" [Some trends in the exchange between industry and agriculture], *Novo vreme*, 1968, no. 8, p. 44; *Statistická ročenka ČSSR 1970* [Statistical handbook of the Socialist Republic of Czechoslovakia, 1970] (Prague: 1970), p. 474; *Statistisches Jahrbuch 1970*, p. 341. The German index does not include premiums paid for increasing output, and therefore understates the price increase since 1960.

92. The disturbances that followed increases in retail prices in Poland in December 1970 show that apprehensions on this score are well founded. The increases were subsequently revoked with the aid of Soviet credits.

In retrospect, all the recent price reforms including the Czechoslovak (1967) and the Hungarian (1966–67) conform to the pattern described above. In Bulgaria, procurement prices of meat and milk rose considerably in 1968, but the level of profitability in livestock production was still expected to be only 3 percent.[93] In Hungary, the 1967 prices of livestock products still failed to cover costs, and they were accordingly raised again as of 1 January 1970 (retail prices of meat and milk remained unchanged).[94]

Price increases in off-farm inputs have gone far to cancel out trends in procurement prices. Thus in Hungary, the recent rise in meat and milk procurement prices will be achieved by eliminating a subsidy on repair of farm machinery.[95] In Czechoslovakia, the 1967 price reform that raised procurement prices by 11 percent simultaneously increased prices of off-farm inputs by 22 percent. Machinery prices in 1967 were about 50 percent above 1960.[96] Prices of imported machinery (about one-half of total sales in Czechoslovakia in 1967) rose further in 1969 by 25 to 30 percent, while farm prices remained unchanged.[97] As a result of these trends, farm demand for machinery in Czechoslovakia declined: the physical volume of sales in 1968 was below the 1966 level. As might be expected, cooperative farms were harder hit than state farms: their purchases of machinery in 1967 were 50 percent below those of 1960.[98]

Machinery is also very expensive in Bulgaria: sale prices to cooperatives exceed import prices by 100 to 190 percent, and are much higher (relative to procurement prices) than those paid by Soviet kolkhozes. A 1967 reduction in the very high prices for repair work in Bulgaria may not offset the effect of a 1966 increase in prices for spare parts (most of which are produced domestically).[99]

The present level of farm prices is very high compared either with international standards or with other domestic prices, and there is little doubt that questions about price relationships are being raised in party and government circles. Writing in *Figyelo* on 24 December 1969, Bela Csikós-

93. *Rabotnichesko delo*, 7 January 1968.

94. *Magyar Hirlap*, 5 December 1969, as cited in Radio Free Europe, "Hungarian Situation Report 69," 9 December 1969.

95. Ibid., and *Népszabadság*, 10 December 1968, as cited in Radio Free Europe, "Hungarian Situation Report 1," 10 January 1969.

96. Doležal, p. 600, and *Statistické přehledy*, 1969, no. 7, p. vii.

97. *Zemědělské noviny*, 28 November and 11 December 1968.

98. Doležal, p. 589.

99. Khristo Kuminev, "Kapitalnite vlozheniia i fondoemkostta na produktsiia v TKZS" [Investments and the capital-output ratio in cooperative farms], *Ikonomika na selskosto stopanstvo*, 1968, no. 8, pp. 36–39. The cost of the tractor DT-75 to a Soviet kolkhoz is 31 tons of wheat; for a Bulgarian cooperative it comes to 102 tons of wheat. Tractor DT-54 costs 26 tones of wheat in the USSR, 37 tons in Czechoslovakia and 81 tons in Bulgaria.

Nagy answered such critics by pointing out that farm prices have to be high because farm incomes must be high (or peasants will simply leave the countryside), and that machinery prices must also be considered in any analysis of farm prices. All of this suggests that price problems are still far from settled.

One likely direction for further change—and one consistent with the reform spirit as such—would be an increase in the number of uncontrolled prices. Most countries have at least decentralized price-setting procedures for some products. Prices for minor products fluctuate freely in Czechoslovakia. In Hungary about 10 percent of farm prices fluctuate freely, while another 10 percent are constrained by an upper limit only; 20 percent vary between upper and lower limits, while the remaining 60 percent (which cover all the important farm products) are fixed.[100]

One persistent difficulty relates to the level of subsidies for weak farms, an important issue so far as the allocative function of farm prices is concerned.[101] Some bolder reformers have suggested the abandonment of large-scale (read: socialized) farming in unsuitable areas, but there is little evidence that significant steps are contemplated in this direction.[102]

Taxes. Major changes occurred only in Czechoslovakia and Hungary. Czechoslovakia introduced a land tax as one component of the agricultural tax. For this purpose, all land is classified into 44 different classes according to natural conditions, and tax rates range from zero to 930 crowns per hectare (about 13 percent of gross income per hectare in the best group of farms in 1967). The rest of the agricultural tax is levied on gross income per worker. The tax is imposed on both state and on cooperative farms.[103]

A similar system was introduced in Hungary in 1968, though here the land tax on farms with very poor soils is less than zero—that is, they actually receive subsidies. The income tax is levied at a rate of 6 percent on income distributed to members (allocations to investment funds do not enter into

100. Dr. Miklos Zilahy-Szabo, "Wirtschaftsreform Ungarn—Landwirtschaft" (unpublished manuscript).

101. The share of the base farm price as such (net of all subsidies, premiums, etc.) in the total payment to the socialist sector in Czechoslovak agriculture was only 67.6 percent; the corresponding figure for all state farms was 57.7 percent. Cf. Gabriela Olmova, "Stanovisko k 'Tézím ke koncepci ekonomické reformy řízení v zemědělství'," [A view on "An outline of the conception of the reform of management in agriculture"], *Zemědělská ekonomika*, 1968, nos. 11–12, p. 639.

102. E.g., the vice president of the Hungarian Academy of Sciences, Ferenc Erdei, in *Közgadasági Szemle*, November 1968, as cited in Radio Free Europe, "Hungarian Situation Report 51," 26 August 1969. Some steps have been taken in Czechoslovakia to construct small inns (15–20 beds) in mountain areas or in the borderlands to be leased to operator families together with some 15–20 hectares of land. Cf. Julius Bezděk, "Horské usedlosti, nebezpečný experiment" [Mountain homesteads—a perilous experiment], *Doba*, 29 May 1969, pp. 5–6.

103. *Sbírka zákonů Československé Socialistické Republiky* [Colllection of laws of the Czechoslovak Socialist Republic], no. 47 (1966), pp. 593–98.

the tax base). Rates rise when the proportion allotted to investment falls below that of the preceding year.[104] According to Vagi, the new system resulted in a considerable increase in taxes paid by the more efficient farms. Per unit of net profit, taxes plus social insurance payments in 1968 rose over the 1967 level as follows: weak farms, zero; average farms, 16–18 percent; strong farms, 30–40 percent. Steps were to be taken in 1969 to correct this situation through changes in the rates of land tax.[105]

Farmer Incomes and the Private Sector

As we observed earlier, low incomes in agriculture during the period of rapid industrialization reduced interest in work in the public sector and contributed to the outflow of labor from agriculture. Since the mid-1950s, reduction of the differential between farm and nonfarm earnings has been a major goal of policy. By way of illustrating the trend, table 6.3 compares cooperative distributions and state farm wages with the average wage in

TABLE 6.3. Average Earnings in the National Economy, State Agriculture, and Cooperative Farms in Bulgaria, 1951–66
(New leva per year)

Year	Average Wage in the National Economy	Average Wage in State Agriculture	Average Distribution to Cooperative Farmers[a]
1951	n.a.	n.a.	347
1952	646	472	194
1953	695	525	250
1954	735	598	217
1955	754	623	306
1956	778	651	284
1957	815	691	404
1958	835	732	357
1959	864	844	421
1960	939	893	469
1961	993	886	476
1962	1,020	907	601
1963	1,051	930	641
1964	1,076	939	734
1965	1,109	987	790
1966	1,157	1,057	886

Source: Velikov (cited above in n. 38), p. 97.
[a] Including rental payments through 1958.

104. Rudakov, Materialnoto, pp. 60–61; Zilayi-Szabo.
105. Ibid., citing F. Vagi, "A termelöszövetkezetek adózása es az uj gazdasàgi mechanizmus" [Taxing the cooperative and the New Economic Model], Tudomany és mezögazdaság, 1968, no. 1. Dr. Zilahy-Szabo was unable to locate a reference to the actual change (if any) in land tax rates after 1968.

236   JERZY F. KARCZ

the national economy as a whole in Bulgaria. Between 1955 and 1966, the
average cooperative distribution almost trebled, while the increase in the
national economy average was 53 percent.

The Bulgarian case is admittedly extreme because of the exceptionally low
base level of cooperative farm payments. In East Germany over the same
period (1955–66) monthly incomes in agriculture doubled.[106] In Poland,
real income of peasants rose by 66 percent between 1955 and 1968.[107] The
average distribution in Hungarian cooperative farms in 1969 came to 1,562
forints per month, when the average wage in industry was 2,176 forints.[108]

These figures do not tell the whole story. On the one hand, dispersions from
country-wide averages are very large: 41 percent of Hungarian cooperative
farmers in 1969 received less than 1,000 forints a month, and reference has
already been made to the low wages on some Bulgarian cooperatives in
1965–66. On the other hand, total family incomes do not consist only of cash
and kind distributions of cooperative farms, and the average family includes
more than one wage earner. The average income of the Hungarian peasant
family in 1968 was a very respectable 40,500 forints—twice the amount
received in 1963, and a sum roughly on a par with the salary of an average
engineer. One-third of family income was derived from the private household plot, 54 percent came from the cooperative farm, and 13 percent was
from other employment or social insurance.[109] In Bulgaria, income per
person in families of cooperative farmers about caught up with per capita
income in families of industrial workers by 1965, and in 1969 there was no
difference between industrial wage earners and cooperative farmers in total
family incomes. Here, too, about 30 percent of farmers' family income was
obtained from the private plot.[110] In Czechoslovakia, the total income of the
cooperative farmer in 1960–63 was virtually identical with that of the worker
employed in state agriculture. Once more, 33 percent of this income was
supplied by the household plot.[111]

Thus, the private sector is still an important source of income for cooperative farmers. It is also an important source of food for both the urban

106. *Vorwaerts*, 11 September 1970.

107. Eugeniusz Gorzelak, p. 46.

108. *Szabad Föld*, 19 April 1970, as cited in Radio Free Europe, "Hungarian Situation
Report 16," 22 April 1970.

109. Zilahy-Szabo citing S. Belak, "A termelöszövetkezeti gazdaságokban dolgozók foly-
matos foglalkostatásának es kereseti lehetösegeinek javitasa" [The improvement of earning
opportunities for steadily employed workers in the productive sector of agricultural cooper-
atives], *Tudomany Es Mezogazdasag*, 1969, no. 3.

110. Atanas Dimitrov, "Vliianeto na niakoi faktori za formirane dokhodite na naseleniento"
[The impact of some factors on the formation of earnings of the population], *Finansi i kredit*,
1968, no. 5, p. 5, and *Zemedelsko zname*, 17 July 1970.

111. Nikl et al., pp. 92, 97.

and rural population. Given the difficulties facing expansion of output in the socialist sector (largely because of massive investment requirements), the further development of private farming activities can contribute much to the improvement of living standards and the morale of the population at this juncture of the economic reform.

This is a lesson that has been grasped fully only in Hungary, where a major effort to increase livestock output "through the household stable" has been going on since 1968. Interestingly enough, local initiative resulted in the granting of workday credits (counted toward the required minimum of work for the cooperative) for farmers contracting to sell their animals to the farm.[112] High officials of the Hungarian government repeatedly exhorted cooperative farms to render greater assistance to household plot farming, and between 1965 and 1968 the output of small tools and implements suitable for plot production tripled.[113] The number of private garden plots worked by the nonagricultural population increased significantly.

At the end of 1969, the government removed all earlier restrictions on the number of animals allowed per plot: now as many may be kept as can be maintained, provided that private livestock production does not interfere with the farmer's duties toward the public sector (a rather flexible limitation, indeed!).[114] A considerable subsidy has been granted for sales of small machinery items and tools for livestock production.

Special shops to supply private sector farming have by now been opened in some areas, and agronomists have been assigned to act as "private plot extension agents" by numerous cooperative farms and regional associations of farms. A proposal was also advanced (and publicly endorsed by the deputy prime minister, Lajos Feher) to double the existing upper limit on loans for the purpose of modernizing private plot operations.[115]

To anyone familiar with the traditional "uneasy coexistence" of private and public farming in socialized agricultures, the new Hungarian approach smacks of revolution. Apparently it is opposed by many influential party and government officials who believe that private farming can only be developed at the expense of the public sector; such views have been publicly rebutted by Feher and Imre Dimeny, the minister of agriculture and food.[116]

112. E.g. *Népszabadság*, 3 April 1968, as cited in Radio Free Europe, "Hungarian Situation Report 75," 11 November 1968. The formal decision of the Council of Ministers dates from 12 March 1970 (*Népszabadság*, 13 March 1970).

113. *Fehér Megyei Hirlap*, 17 October 1968, as cited in Radio Free Europe, "Hungarian Situation Report 77," 21 November 1968.

114. *Magyar Közlöny*, 31 December 1969, as cited in Radio Free Europe, "Research Paper Hungary 2," 14 January 1970.

115. Radio Free Europe, "Hungarian Situation Report 16," 28 April 1970. Feher's endorsement is in *Népszabadság*, 13 May 1970.

116. Radio Budapest, 14 May 1970 as cited by Radio Free Europe, "Hungarian Situation Report 19," 19 May 1970.

The results of this major campaign, which involved considerable effort and resources (including imports of small Czechoslovak tractors for work on the plots), were sufficiently mixed to prompt a major investigation by the People's Control Commission, which sent inspectors to about 900 cooperatives in 1970. An evaluation of the policy was also published by the Ministry of Food and Agriculture before the investigation of the People's Control Commission was completed.[117] The Ministry declared itself satisfied with progress in pig and poultry production, and noted that numbers of private cows declined at a smaller rate than in 1969. Among the reasons cited for the less satisfactory development of cattle production were lack of interest on the part of younger members of the cooperative population, decrease in the size of households where large dairy herds had previously been held, and new sanitary regulations that forbid construction of stables next to dwellings.[118] The first two reasons are probably the more significant, and it remains to be seen whether the Hungarian government is prepared to follow Bukharin's famous slogan "enrichissez-vous" to its logical conclusion in order to overcome lack of interest and unfavorable demographic trends.

In Bulgaria, following a decline in private livestock herds between 1965 and 1968, the Council of Ministers also enacted measures in February 1970 designed to increase private livestock holdings. Here, too, opposition is considerable: "Some leaders of national councils and of state and cooperative farms look with a jaundiced eye at private animal husbandry."[119] As in Hungary, an effort is being made to involve individuals who would not normally participate in economic activity because of age, disability or housework. Given the short period since this policy began, any evaluation would be premature, but the campaign is certainly far behind the massive Hungarian effort with respect to publicity and support of major officials.

A chillier attitude toward the private sector appears to prevail in Romania. Here labor inputs of collective farmers into the public sector are relatively small (only 146 man-days per year, or about the same as in Hungary). Since 1970, farmers who fail to work the required number of man-days have been subject to reduction of their household plots. Simultaneously, however, a payment of a minimum wage of 15 lei per "normative work-day" is envisaged for weak cooperatives.[120]

117. Radio Free Europe, "Hungarian Situation Report 22," 9 June 1970. The evaluation was to continue through September 1970. The Ministry's survey results were published in *Magyar Hirlap*, 11 August 1970.

118. Radio Free Europe, "Hungarian Situation Report 32," 18 August 1970.

119. *Otechestven front*, 13 June 1970. See also *Kooperativno selo*, 31 March 1970. The decision of the Politbureau on expansion of private livestock production was taken on 10 February 1970, and was referred to in *Rabotnichesko delo*, 23 and 28 March 1970.

120. *Lupta da Clasa*, 1970, no. 6, as translated in Radio Free Europe, "Rumanian Press Survey, No. 849," 13 August 1970.

Little has been said about Poland, largely because there is, for all practical purposes, no agricultural reform in that country. However, some recent developments have modified farm tenure in the private sector. Since 1963, members of the nonagricultural population have been barred from inheriting (or purchasing) farms of less than 8 hectares; draft of a new law for regulating problems in land tenure that may arise in this connection is now being prepared by the Ministry of Agriculture. Moreover, since 24 January 1968, owners of farms exceeding 5 hectares have been able to turn their farm over to the State Land Fund in return for a pension. Lack of funds has so far precluded the extension of this provision to owners of smaller farms.[121]

III. The Yugoslav Reform

The general aim of the 1965 Yugoslav reform was improvement in agriculture's terms of trade, leading to a rise in personal farm incomes, a substantial increase in agricultural investments, and an increase in farm exports. More specifically, it was expected that the rise in farm prices would amount to 33 percent in the socialized sector and 37 percent in the private, leading to a 30 percent increase in personal incomes. Production was to rise by 4.6 percent on the average and farm exports by 11.3 percent. The share of agriculture in total investment was to amount to 14 percent.[122]

In line with the general principles of the economic reform, these goals were to be achieved by the use of market instruments of economic control. While guaranteed and minimum prices were maintained for some products (wheat, sugar beets, tobacco, milk, and sunflower seed), other prices were free to vary with market conditions. Many restrictions on imports (as well as some export subsidies) were removed. Subsidies were retained only for the purchase of mineral fertilizers and for the production of milk, cotton, and pork. The share of subsidies in the value of market output of the socialized sector was to decline from 15.1 percent (the 1964 level) to 6.6 percent.[123]

At least through 1968, the results of the reform were mixed and many goals had not been attained. The initial increase in farm prices was greater than planned: 43 percent in 1965 and an additional 16 percent in 1966. There-

121. Stefan Ignar, "Niektore problemy rolnictwa w latach 1969–75" [Some problems of agriculture in 1969–75], *Wies Wspolczesna* 1969, no. 3, pp. 32, 34. About 25 percent of Polish peasant farm operators are over 60 years old.

122. *Prijedlog razvoja poljoprivrede do 1970 godine* [A proposal for the development of agriculture until 1970] (Zagreb: 1965), as cited in I. Loncarević, "Die Auswirkungen der Wirtschaftsreform von 1965 auf die Landwirtschaft Jugoslaviens" (unpublished manuscript).

123. "Poljoprivreda u reformi" [Agriculture in the reform], *Jugoslovenski pregled*, 1969, no. 4, p. 163.

after prices declined, by 2.5 percent in 1967 and 4 percent in 1968, and by 1969 were back at the 1966 level.[124]

Simultaneously, however, the prices of fertilizers, tools, machinery, and commercial feed rose substantially, as did interest rates, taxes, and fees paid to various government agencies. One calculation of changes in the terms of trade of the agricultural sector between 1964 and 1967 indicates that virtually all of the early gains (8.7 percent in 1965) were wiped out by 1967. Since prices of inputs as well as tax payments continued to rise in 1968 and 1969, it is clear that only a very minor improvement—if any—remained by 1969.[125]

The goals for increases in output were not achieved either (in part because of bad weather in 1967 and 1968). The socialized sector fared better in production, but not in efficiency. Here, too, farms were affected by changes in terms of trade, the tax on capital stock, etc. Financial losses of the socialist sector increased monotonically from 310 million dinars in 1964 to 867.8 million in 1968.[126] Indebtedness rose to the point where loan repayments absorbed three-quarters of available funds. The expected increase in the share of agriculture in total investments did not materialize, and the absolute volume of farm investments fell.[127]

The reform did, however, affect the structure of output, as farms shifted to more profitable lines of activity. Socialized farms increased their grain sowings and shifted away from livestock production, particularly in the more developed parts of the country. In the cooperative sector, livestock production (except for pedigreed stock) was said to have fallen apart because of "disloyal activities of market middlemen,"[128] as individual peasants (who expanded their animal husbandry) purchased increasing quantities of feed and concentrates. As was the case in Hungary, Yugoslav cooperatives often switched to more profitable activities, especially to marketing.

There was a noticeable decline in "cooperation" between socialized farms and individual peasants—that is, performance of various operations on private farms with socialized sector equipment in exchange for livestock

124. K. Džeba and M. Beslać, *Privredna reforma—što i zašto se mejenja* [The economic reform —what changes and why] (Zagreb: 1965), pp. 136 and 137; Alexsandar Raic and Adam Zaleski, "Ekonomiczne problemy integracji rolnictwa w Jugoslawii" [The economic problems of integration of agriculture in Yugoslavia], *Wiés Wspołczesna*, 1969, no. 6, p. 109.

125. Ibid., p. 110, and M. Radić, "Savremene tendencije u ekonomskom razvoju i položaju poljoprivrede SFRJ" [Current trends in economic development and the situation of agriculture], *Ekonomika poljoprivrede*, 1969, no. 6, p. 386.

126. "Poslovanje privrednikh organizacija u 1968 godini" [Business activity of economic organizations in 1968], *Jugoslovenski pregled*, 1968, no. 4, p. 179, as cited by Loncarević.

127. *Statistički godišnjak SFRJ 1969* [Statistical handbook of the Federal Socialist Republic of Yugoslavia, 1969] (Belgrade: 1969), p. 468.

128. Raic and Zaleski, p. 114.

deliveries. The number of private farmers cooperating in this fashion fell by 14 percent between 1964 and 1968.[129]

Government dissatisfaction with the results of the reform is made clear in the Draft Resolution of 14 July 1970. It calls for continued improvement of peasant incomes and more modernization of farm technology, to permit Yugoslav agriculture to compete on international markets. A new feature is the explicit acknowledgement of the very great regional differences in Yugoslav agriculture, and the expressed desire to foster development only in those parts of the country where suitable conditions for modern agriculture exist. This is perhaps the first recognition by any East European socialist government of the need to concentrate resources in areas where the returns are likely to be the greatest. While no details on implementation have as yet been spelled out, the decision may well turn out to be a landmark.[130]

Another (perhaps equally important) issue has not been resolved. The present Yugoslav laws on land tenure limit individual holdings to 10 hectares (though some larger private farms still exist). No increase in this maximum is contemplated at present; instead it is suggested that further socialization of agriculture proceed through cooperation with the socialist sector. Pensions and greater participation in agencies of self-management will now be granted to peasants.

IV. Concluding Remarks

Peter Wiles once remarked that although agriculture has often been called the Achilles' heel of the Soviet economy, Achilles managed to walk upon his heel for quite a few years. Various agricultural reforms, begun almost as soon as the transfer of command farming to Eastern Europe was completed, testify eloquently to the fact that East European governments have been treating their heels with increasing care. Recent measures convey a sense of special urgency, and it is clear that the progress achieved to date falls short of the requirements of East European societies.

One of the major reform goals has been greater efficiency, which ought to be reflected in reduced costs. Cost data tend to reach us with a considerable delay, but such evidence as is available does not lead to optimism. The trend has been steadily upward throughout the region, largely because of the continuing increase in material costs, but also because of high (and generally also rising) labor costs. Labor costs have risen both in Poland and in the

129. Ibid., p. 112 (data from official Yugoslav handbooks).
130. *Politika*, 15 July 1970. See also *Borba*, 22 July 1970.

first three years of reform in Czechoslovakia.[131] It used to take 2 crowns worth of capital goods to replace a crown of labor costs in Czechoslovak agriculture; by the spring of 1969 the ratio had risen to 3:1. In Bulgarian cooperatives, the ratio of labor and material costs to gross output rose steadily from 0.849 in 1966 to 0.904 in 1968, and no change in this trend was expected in 1969.[132]

What are the prospects for the future? Increase in factor productivity at this point requires a substantial increase in the supply of off-farm inputs. Machinery is clearly crucial, and it appears to be in a much worse state than outsiders have commonly realized. It is revealing that the amount of investment needed to modernize Hungarian agriculture is now estimated at some 120 billion forints, or nearly one-half of total investment under the Fourth Five-Year Plan. About three-quarters of the existing machinery inventory appears to be earmarked for scrapping within this period.[133] (It remains to be seen, of course, whether the investment plan will be realized.)

About half of the machinery inputs in Hungary, Czechoslovakia, and Poland are imported, and the proportion is probably even larger in Bulgaria and Romania. Anyone familiar with the present state of the agricultural machinery industry in the Soviet Union and Eastern Europe must have reservations about the gains from replacing old machines with new ones of obsolete design and poor quality. Thus it is not unfair to say that future cost reductions depend less on reform within agriculture than on the success of reform in the industrial sector.

Machinery supplies are closely related to the availability of skilled and trained personnel on farms. There is probably no quicker way to lose a specialist than to supply him with inadequate or outmoded equipment on the job.

Frequent reference has been made in this paper to labor problems in East European agricultures. The subject has not been studied sufficiently in the West to allow firm conclusions, but I suspect that it is the combination of labor problems with those of machinery supply that creates the impression of urgency mentioned earlier. Only the future will tell whether the socialist

131. V. Houška and J. Glaserová, "Vývoj nákladů v zemědělství v posledních letech" [The trends in costs in agriculture in recent years], Zemědělská ekonomika, 1969, nos. 9–10, p. 633, and Mirosław Pietrewicz, "Przychody ludnósci chłopskiej z produkcji rolnej w latach 1961–67" [The revenues of peasants from agricultural production in 1961–67], Wies Wspolczesna, 1969, no. 3, p. 62.

132. Ekonomika zemědělství, 1969, no. 2, p. 42, and Rudé právo, 26 March 1969. The figures for Bulgaria are from Zemedelsko zname, 19 February 1970.

133. Figyelö, 29 April 1970, as cited in Radio Free Europe, "Hungarian Situation Report 20," 26 May 1970, and a summary of discussion of the analysis of the Hungarian National Planning Board in Magyar Hirlap, 14 August 1970, as cited in Radio Free Europe, "Hungarian Situation Report 33," 25 August 1970.

governments in Eastern Europe are willing to pay wages in agriculture that may have to exceed industrial wages by very considerable amounts.

This raises an issue first identified by Gregory Grossman in his discussion of the economic reforms in general. There is no doubt that abandonment of the concept of the solidary society by the reformers is "the most fundamental ingredient in the philosophy of economic revisionism."[134] But the leadership's understanding of conflicts of interest is still quite primitive. (Here as elsewhere, Hungary is head and shoulders above the rest of the bloc, now that the Czechs have been reined in.) To paraphrase Silar and Baca: the leadership appears to be dragged into the reform movement ex post, by the harsh necessities of the situation. Will the reform forces be able to withstand opposition in any kind of serious economic difficulty?

Unquestionably, academic economists (or economic "scientists") have been one of the groups pressing for further implementation of the reform. In one sense, politicians were prepared to receive their proposals. For after all, were not the earlier difficulties due to incorrect understanding of *scientific* principles? The present stress on "optimality," on the scientific nature of long-range projections and specialization, can easily be reconciled with the "scientific" nature of Marxism by all but the most puritanical obscurantists.

At the risk of stressing the obvious, we must recall that many of these projections, which are based on prices that depart significantly from relative scarcities, and which require risky guesses about future developments in organization and technology, are likely to serve as the basis for considerable investment expenditures. For instance, the present emphasis on integrating agriculture and industry, including the creation of agro-industrial complexes, may have very high investment costs. I suspect that this course was selected on rather dubious logic: agro-business is productive in the West and agro-business is thus the answer to East European problems. But the fact that merely ordinary competition (not even the textbook variety) is a fundamental component of Western agro-business is probably not sufficiently appreciated at the highest levels in East European economies.

The ultimate problem may well boil down to this: the top decision makers in these economies are not used to taking the interest rate into account in their major decision making. This may well be the reason why so much of the discussion appears to focus on narrow, technological efficiency—and this may prolong efforts to raise yields on weak farms *coute que coute*.

Two final conclusions appear safe: the process of agricultural reform is by no means completed; and given the economic as well as the ideological constraints under which East European governments operate, further reforms are likely to be gradual.

134. Gregory Grossman, "Economic Reforms: The Interplay of Economics and Politics," in *The Future of Communism in Europe*, ed. Richard V. Burks (Detroit: Wayne State University Press, 1968), pp. 122–27. The quotation is from p. 125.

7

The Yugoslav Self-Managed Enterprise: A Systemic Approach

EGON NEUBERGER AND ESTELLE JAMES

I. A DECISION MODEL FOR ECONOMIC SYSTEMS ANALYSIS

In this paper we posit an organization which must make decisions about resource allocation. We set forth a conceptual framework for analyzing the organization's economic system—the set of procedures for making, co-ordinating, and implementing these decisions. Our central premise is that such a framework can provide meaningful insights into the behavior of all types of organizations—economic enterprises, nonprofit institutions, social clubs, etc.—as well as national economies, which have usually been associated with the term "economic system." Our purpose in this paper is twofold: to develop this framework for future use by ourselves and, we hope, other students of economic behavior, and to take the first step in this direction by analyzing the operations and efficiency of the Yugoslav self-managed enterprise.

The Organization and Its Decision Set

The organization[1] possesses a bundle of resources and a group of members. Which resources are said to "belong" to the organization, particularly where

The authors are grateful to Edward Ames, Alan A. Brown, Luigi Luzatti, and Paul Marer for their valuable comments on earlier versions of this paper; to Jan Vanek, whose comments led us to reconsider some parts of the paper; and to the many Yugoslav economists and sociologists who have helped us, especially Mitja Kamušić and Josip Županov. None of them can be held responsible for the use or misuse of their advice.

This paper includes material prepared by Egon Neuberger for a monograph on Yugoslav development and systemic change, sponsored by the International Development Research Center of Indiana University.

Estelle James has included material developed in connection with her National Science Foundation supported project on the economics of education and her work for the Urban Science and Engineering program at Stony Brook.

1. We use the term "organization" in a broad nontechnical sense. Although the literature contains frequent references to "organizations," we have been unable to find or develop any completely satisfactory criterion for locating the boundaries of the organization. We have

(continued on page 246)

property rights are fractured and parceled out among several parties, is in part an arbitrary matter. Similarly, we have found no generally applicable criterion for "membership" and must simply adopt a different but useful definition in each case.[2]

The current utilization and future level of the organization's resources will be determined by a set of potential decisions and by the economic system or procedures for making these decisions. Those decision makers who are also "members" of the organization are called internal actors and their decisions are internal decisions. Those who are not members of this organization are external actors, and their decisions are external decisions. We shall focus on the economic system for the internal decision set. If the sets of external actors and decisions are null sets we use a closed model for analyzing the decision process of this organization. As necessary but not sufficient conditions for an organization to be approximated by a closed model its activities must include both production and consumption, provision of inputs and outputs, and must exclude imports from or exports to other organizations. For example, an isolated primitive tribe or the entire earth would be studied by a closed model; the economy of the United States, while not fully independent of other economies, may for some purposes be approximated by a closed model.

If, however, the sets of external actors and decisions are not null sets, we use an open model for analyzing the decision process of this organization.

(continued from page 245)
consulted some colleagues in sociology and were assured that this problem is on the frontiers of their field, but were not supplied with any satisfying solutions. An organization could be defined by the existence of common objectives or customary relations among a group of people. Harvey Leibenstein uses this approach in *Economic Theory and Organizational Analysis* (New York: Harper, 1960). For our purposes, we find it most useful to identify the organization by its resources and members, so that we can talk about resource decisions and internal or external control.

2. One might, for example, include as members all those whose utility is affected by the organization, but this would make a large proportion of U.S. citizens "members" of, say, General Motors, hardly a useful concept for most purposes. (Admittedly, Ralph Nader might cogently argue to the contrary.) Or, one might include all those whose decisions influence the organization's resource allocation; the Treasury Department would then be a member of every U.S. firm. Alternatively, one might designate all suppliers of resources to the organization as its members, but this would make the state a member of every socialist enterprise and banks members of most capitalist enterprises. If the definition were restricted to suppliers of labor, stockholders in the U.S., who are both decision makers and beneficiaries, would not qualify. And, if a contractual relationship is the basis for membership, an automobile purchaser with a one-year guarantee or a consultant on a retainer would be included but a regular customer of a grocery store or a senior worker without tenure would be excluded; and so on. We finally decided that the only recourse was to adopt, for any particular institutional study, a definition of membership that seemed meaningful in that context. When a study cuts across several organizations, this ambiguity in membership concept must be borne in mind.

Internal decisions, then, do not completely determine the level and allocation of the organization's resources unless all external decisions are exogenously given. For example, in analyzing the decision process of an organization with a large international trade sector (for example, a firm or a city) without including all its trading partners as internal actors, we must use the open model; this holds, too, for a taxpaying firm or a national economy with external political connections which influence its resource allocations.

Clearly, every open model is embedded in some larger closed model. As we shall see below, the choice of a decision process within the open model immediately limits the kinds of decision processes available to the larger closed model, and vice versa.

When shifting from pure decision theory to welfare analysis we must also associate with each organization a group of beneficiaries—all those with whose utility the organization is or ought to be concerned. The beneficiaries can be positively or negatively affected by decision of actors; the organization provides "bads" as well as "goods" to its beneficiaries.

The selection of relevant beneficiaries allows us to construct a feasible utility space. Specifying the relative weights attached to each beneficiary yields a "social welfare function" and bliss point. The choice of beneficiaries and weights is clearly a subjective value judgment. In welfare theory, much of which is implicitly based on national economies, all inhabitants of a country are ordinarily included as beneficiaries. For other less inclusive organizations, such as factories and hospitals, the choice is far from obvious and poses significant normative and analytic problems; it must be made, however, to provide a vantage point from which to evaluate the organization's performance.

The Economic System in a Closed Model

For a given set of beneficiaries and their tastes, technology and resource stocks (i.e. land, initial fixed capital and inventories, population), we can conceptually derive the "technologically" feasible (ordinal) utility space for an organization represented by our closed model. We now impose on this closed model a (closed) economic system: a set of procedures for making allocation decisions within the technologically feasible space.[3] It is the system

---

3. Beneficiaries, tastes, technology, and resources are taken as fixed in deriving the technologically feasible utility space. Although this concept is generally taken to be value free, we may note that it already implies the choice of relevant beneficiaries, which is itself a value judgment.

When technology or resources change, the feasible utility space shifts and we may compare the new space with the old. If beneficiaries or their tastes change, however, the new and old

(continued on page 248)

which fixes, in determinate or probabilistic form, the final outcome, and thereby determines how well the given resources are combined to satisfy the preferences of the beneficiaries. Theoretical systems have been devised which would allow us to reach the technologically feasible frontier; however, no such ideal system has ever existed in the real world.

Our conceptual framework of the economic system defines it in terms of three sets of variables. We say that:

$S \equiv S(R, A, L)$ where:

S = the economic system;

R = a set of a priori restrictions or constraints on flows of resources and information, which partition the (internal) decision set into two mutually exclusive and jointly exhaustive subsets, the prohibited subset and the permissible subset;

A = a set of (internal) actors, each with his own objective function, who have decision-making power over the permissible subset of decisions;

L = a set of restrictions or prescriptions which define the locus of decision-making power among the actors, and the nature of the information network.

We have carefully avoided calling this an economic model, and used instead the term "conceptual framework," a much less ambitious construct.[4]

The a priori restrictions. These are fixed decisions which set the "rules of the game" and are not changeable by the actors within our system during the time period under consideration. As such, they limit the options available to the actors and rule out certain resource and information flows which would otherwise be possible (analogous to the limitations imposed by factor endowments and technology). Some of these fixed decisions were made by specific actors in the past; others are deeply embedded in the culture, difficult to tie to a specific decision maker, and much more difficult to change.

(continued from page 247)

utility spaces are, in general, noncomparable. For a discussion of a preference transformation where the new and old utility spaces are comparable see E. James and L. Nordell, "Preference Transformations and Welfare Theory," Stony Brook Working Paper No. 22A, December 1971. There exists, of course, a complex relationship between the long-run shift in the technologically feasible space and the economic system. That is, the system influences changes through time of technology, resources, and tastes, so that the latter, at any given point in time, are functions of past systems, while the final outcome depends on the technologically feasible space plus the present system.

4. Somewhat different, yet closely related, approaches to economic systems are provided in E. Neuberger and W. J. Duffy, *Comparative Economic Systems: A Decision-Theoretic Approach* (Allyn and Bacon, forthcoming), and in E. James, "The University as an Economic System," Stony Brook Working Paper No. 53, 1972.

These restrictions are generally of three types. (1) They may specify separabilities or nonseparabilities among resources or goods, such as the following: (*a*) certain inputs are always (never) used jointly; (*b*) certain outputs are always (never) produced or consumed together; (*c*) certain suppliers of inputs are always (never) tied together in production; (*d*) certain users of outputs always (never) consume the outputs together; (*e*) an individual's consumption of certain outputs is always (never) linked to his supply of certain inputs. (2) Closely related are nontransferabilities, which specify factor endowments or product mix and prohibit the organization from exchanging one kind of input or output for another. Or (3) the restrictions may set a floor or ceiling (i.e. lower or upper limit) to the employment, production or consumption of certain inputs or outputs by firms or individuals. When the floor and ceiling are identical this is equivalent to establishing a fixed amount to be employed, produced or consumed.

The content of the fixed decisions, when added to the technological constraints, defines the "technosystemically" feasible utility space, which is a subset of the technologically feasible space.[5] The final outcome point must lie within this technosystemically feasible space and depends on the variable decisions made by the actors.

Of course, as the time perspective becomes longer many fixed decisions become variable and endogenous to our model. New laws may be passed, the constitution may be amended, revolutions may occur, etc. Thus, for the very long run, the set of a priori restrictions becomes a null set and the technosystemically feasible utility space approaches the (ever-shifting) technologically feasible utility space.

The internal actors and their objective functions. The actors are the decision makers of the system, who determine its allocation of resources and information. To each permissible decision about resources and information is attached at least one actor who has the power to make that decision, and to each actor is attached at least one permissible decision over which he has control. In a polar (Robinson Crusoe) case, the system contains only one actor and his objective function may be considered the objective function of

5. This is similar but not identical to the utility feasibility locus described by P. Samuelson in "Evaluation of Real National Income," *Oxford Economic Papers* 2 (January 1950): 1–29. Leibenstein has also constructed a related model in which the production frontier is not reached because of the large exertion of effort which this requires. If we associate effort with disutility, this phenomenon has already been subsumed in the construction of our technologically feasible utility space. If, on the other hand, systemic characteristics have interfered with the optimal exertion of effort, this enters instead into our systemically feasible space and the choice of the final outcome point within it. See H. Leibenstein, "Allocative Efficiency versus X-Efficiency," *American Economic Review* 56 (June 1966): 392–416, and idem, "Organizational or Frictional Equilibrium, X-Efficiency and the Rate of Innovation," *Quarterly Journal of Economics* 83 (November 1969): 600–624.

the organization. In more interesting and realistic cases, however, there are multiple actors, each with his own objective function. The organization is not assumed to have its own objective function; its actions result from the coordination of the separate but interrelated decisions of all its actors.[6]

In many situations, the actors will also be a subset of the beneficiaries, but this is not always the case. For example, let us assume a university whose sole actors are the faculty. If we are interested in the welfare of the faculty only, the sets of actors and beneficiaries are equivalent. If, now, we completely shift our attention to the students, the actors and beneficiaries form two disjoint sets. On the other hand, if we are concerned with the utility of both faculty and students, the actors are a proper subset of the beneficiaries. And, if reforms should give the students some decision-making power but we are only considering the faculty's utility, the beneficiaries would be a proper subset of the actors.

The actors are assumed to make decisions purely on the basis of their own objective functions and the information available to them within the constraints imposed by technology and the a priori restrictions. We shall be interested in observing their impact on their own welfare and the welfare of the beneficiaries, particularly if the two groups do not coincide.

The initial set of actors is exogenously given but may be changed through time as discussed immediately below. The initial objective function of each actor is also exogenously given. Through time, however, these may be influenced by informational messages from other actors, or "indoctrination." If the actors are also beneficiaries, we get a new technologically feasible utility space which is, in general, noncomparable with the old.

The distribution of decision power and information. In the following discussion we distinguish between the *primal system*, which consists of all the exogenously-given locus variables, and the *augmented system*, which includes endogenously-determined components as well. We describe the primal system, but do not explain how or why it was chosen from among all the possible system options available. The augmented system, on the other hand, is the result of dynamic optimizing behavior within our framework, subject to the constraints imposed by the given primal system.

The primal holder of power over each resource is exogenously specified in our framework. His power may stem from property ownership, political or bureaucratic position, technical expertise or custom; the source of power is

---

6. Adherence to a common set of goals may be a criterion used in the selection of actors or members of the organization. Furthermore, indoctrination may take place among the actors, narrowing the range of individual differences. Therefore, in some cases we may be able to speak of a single objective function even for a complex organization. This homogeneity results, however, from the optimizing actions of (past and present) individuals, and not from some mythical organizational ethos.

likely to influence his objective function, the information at his disposal, and therefore the final outcome. He may make "final decisions" about resources or may delegate this power to another actor. In fact, the decision-making process may be viewed as a successive narrowing of options until only one outcome remains to be implemented.

The initial holder of each bit of information is somewhat different: he may be exogenously specified, he may generate the information endogenously in the course of his own maximizing activities, or he may stumble on the information naturally, as a consequence of his role in the economic process. In all cases, however, he must decide whether to forget, store, process, or transmit the message to a secondary holder, and in transmitting he may filter, bias, or otherwise manipulate the information. The delegation of authority and information is endogenous to the system and may be thought of as an "intermediate decision," akin to the production of materials which will eventually be used to produce final consumer goods.

Each decision of actor i can be mapped into a set of consequences, in deterministic or probability distribution form. This mapping depends on (1) the state of nature and (2) the decisions of other actors, past, present, and projected into the future; the latter are termed the incentive structure facing actor i. The incentive structure, thus, links together interdependent decisions of multiple actors. The further mapping from consequences to utility for actor i is called the objective function for actor i and has already been discussed in the preceding section.

The Economic System in an Open Model

We move on now to consider the economic system of our open model, that is, an open system. The first new problem encountered here is that choices made in an open system are functionally related to external choices. These must, consequently, constitute an additional informational input into the internal decision process. The second new problem is that whenever the decisions of an organization depend upon external actions, the resources at its disposal and the welfare of its beneficiaries probably do as well. Therefore, we cannot specify a pure internally-determined technologically feasible utility space for our open model. For example, the feasible utility space of an open model can be expanded by an inflow of capital or by a favorable shift in the terms of trade between its imports and exports, all of which depend partially upon external decisions.[7]

7. Note also that the opposite is true, and decisions of this organization may partially determine the resources and utility space of other organizations, so the relevant group of beneficiaries may be broader for an open than for a closed model.

(continued on page 252)

The latter may be fixed decisions, which are known with certainty and cannot be changed, except in the very long run. Or, they may be variable decisions which are known, at best, in probability distribution form. To investigate our open model, however, we take their actual or expected values as exogenously given. We may then define a "quasi-technologically" feasible utility space for an open economy as a function of its beneficiaries and their tastes, resource stocks, technology, and exogenous external decisions. The fixed internal decisions limit us further to a technosystemically feasible utility space.

In our open model we find it useful to redefine the concept of a priori restrictions to include two subsets—R_I, fixed internal decisions which determine the technosystemically feasible utility space, and R_E, fixed external decisions which affect the quasi-technological space as well. The final outcome within the technosystemic space depends, as before, on the previously defined variables A and L.

The effects of external decisions are thus explored in our open model. However, the rationale for these decisions and the patterns of interactions among external actors can only be explained in the context of the larger closed model which encompasses all interdependencies among decisions and utilities. Consequently, our approach is most useful if the internal decision set is large; the higher the proportion of external relative to internal decisions, the less interesting it becomes to study the internal economic system of an organization.

Implications and Questions

Several questions about the economic system of an organization emerge directly from our approach:

1. What is the impact of the a priori restrictions on the efficiency of the economy?

2. Do the various actors in the system have similar objective functions, what are the mechanisms for reconciling differences, and how does this affect the stability and optimality of the final outcome?

3. What is the relation between the formal and informal loci of control over decisions? If these differ, should this be viewed as deliberate delegation

(continued from page 251)

The external decisions influencing our organization may be of the floor-ceiling, separability-nonseparability or nontransferability (constraint) types, defined above, or they may be of the terms-of-trade (incentive) type. In a purely competitive economy all external decisions are presented to the firm in the form of prices or terms of trade between its imports and exports. On the other hand, in a completely centralized command economy all external decisions come down to the enterprise in the form of direct input supplies and output demands, a simultaneous floor and ceiling on imports and exports.

—i.e. as part of the augmented system—or simply as a breakdown of the primal system?

4. To what degree does information get biased or dysfunctionally screened in the process of transmission? What is the relation between the loci of control over resources and information? Do those who make decisions about resources also have (accurate) information?

5. How does the system coordinate the decisions of its many inter-dependent actors? What is the correspondence between the intent and effect of incentives and how close do they get us to the technosystemic utility frontier?

6. How autonomous is the organization? That is, what is the mix between the internal and external decisions which determine its resource allocation?

Many of these questions have been posed, usually on a rather ad hoc basis, in studies of national economies. They do not arise in traditional microeconomics, which conceives of the private firm as a monolithic entity with a single internal actor and objective function and perfect information. The more recent behavioral and informational schools of microeconomics deal with some of these issues and are closest in spirit to our approach.[8] This shift in theoretical emphasis may be particularly relevant for the ever-increasing sector of our economy which is endowed with special social privileges and responsibilities (e.g. state-supported or nonprofit insti-tutions). Our model of an economic system is one which, we believe, can be applied to the study of national economies as well as any complex organi-zation with multiple decision makers determining resource allocation.

The proof of the pudding is in the eating. A preliminary test of the value of our framework is provided by the remainder of this paper where we apply it to the Yugoslav enterprise, and address some but not all of the above-mentioned issues. A fuller test will be provided in other papers, currently in

8. Recent contributions to organization theory by Simon, March, Cyert, and Williamson come particularly to mind in this connection. See, for example, J. March and H. Simon, *Organi-zations* (New York: Wiley, 1958); R. Cyert and J. March, *A Behavioral Theory of the Firm* (Englewood Cliffs: Prentice Hall, 1963); O. Williamson, *The Economics of Discretionary Be-havior* (Chicago: Markham, 1967). The literature on information theory, such as the theory of teams, is also related, but these models have not as yet developed to the point where they can deal with multiple decision-makers who have conflicting objective functions. See, for example, K. Arrow and L. Hurwicz, "Decentralization and Computation in Resource Allocation," in *Essays in Economics and Econometrics: A Volume in Honor of H. Hotelling*, ed. K. Pfouts (Chapel Hill: University of North Carolina Press, 1960); J. Marschak and K. Mijasawa, "Economic Comparability of Information Systems," *International Economic Review* 9 (June 1968): 137–75; T. Marschak, "Computation in Organizations: Comparison of Price Mechanisms and Other Adjustment Processes," in *Risk and Uncertainty: Proceedings of Conference held by the Inter-national Economic Association*, ed. K. Borch and J. Mossin (New York: St. Martin's Press, 1968). We have attempted to integrate elements of modern organizations, information, decision, and utility theory into our models.

progress, where we apply it to a more diverse set of organizations including the American university and hospital.[9] The conceptual framework became considerably refined as we used it to analyze the open system of the Yugoslav enterprise and we expect that it will be further modified as we extend it to other types of organizations.

II. The Open Model of a Yugoslav Self-Managed Enterprise

Before engaging in a detailed discussion of the Yugoslav enterprise in terms of our variables R, A, and L, let us comment very briefly upon the reasons behind the introduction of self-management[10] and describe its key institutional features.

Yugoslav rulers were led to adopt self-management in the early 1950s by a desire to reap the politico-ideological gains from a new, more popular and more humane economic system in which workers could control their own destiny. This move toward economic democracy and the elimination of worker alienation provided domestic political support for the regime in its fight against Stalin and reinforced its ideological attack against the Soviet system where workers are dominated by state officials and managers. The slogan "factories to the workers" was the keyword. Of secondary importance was the hope of improving the performance of Yugoslav enterprises by providing workers with a motive for greater effort and efficiency.

The system, as it has evolved through the past two decades, is outlined below.

1. The initial quasi-technological space of the Yugoslav enterprise is determined by its founders, who provide the fixed and variable capital and recruit the management, professional experts and labor force needed to run the enterprise. Permissible founders are government units, social organizations, existing enterprises, or groups of individuals.

9. James, "The University as an Economic System."

10. Several terms have been used to identify the Yugoslav enterprise, such as "worker management," "worker self-management," "labor management," etc. We have selected the term "self-management" (*samoupravljanje*) as reflecting most faithfully the spirit of the Yugoslav experiment. It implies that the enterprise is "self-managed" by its members and that not all of the members are necessarily blue-collar workers.

An abundance of descriptions of the model of the Yugoslav self-managed enterprise exist. We have depended primarily on the following sources: Jaroslav Vanek, *The General Theory of Labor-Managed Market Economies* (Ithaca, New York: Cornell University Press, 1970); Jan Vanek, *The Behavior and Performance of Self-Governing Enterprises under Workers' Management: A Yugoslav Case Study*, Preliminary Draft, 1969; Benjamin Ward, *The Socialist Economy: A Study of Organizational Alternatives* (New York: Random House, 1967); Mitja Kamušić, "Economic Efficiency and Workers' Self-Management," in *Yugoslav Workers' Self-Management: Proceedings of a Symposium held in Amsterdam, 7-9 January 1970*, edited by M. J. Broekmeyer (Dordrecht, Holland: D. Riedel Publishing Company, 1970) pp. 76–116.

2. The managers, professional experts and workers—that is, all full-time employees of the enterprise—are commonly referred to as its "members." Once a sufficient number of members has been recruited, the founders must relinquish major control to them, and these full-time employees become the sole internal actors of the Yugoslav firm. The founders are primal holders of power during the founding process, and the members are primal power holders thereafter. A key a priori restriction to be discussed below is this forced separability between the founders and subsequent decision making.

3. In recent years, the decision set of the members has been greatly increased relative to that of external actors. Therefore, the Yugoslav enterprise has sufficient autonomy to justify a careful analysis of its internal decision process. However, the sets of external decisions and actors are by no means null sets since bankers, consumers, and officials of the federal government, republic or commune (the local government unit) still retain some power over resource allocation. Therefore, we use our open model to analyze the economic system of the Yugoslav enterprise.

4. The enterprise members face an important set of a priori restrictions. These cannot be changed by either internal or external actors except in the long run. They restrict the ways in which various resources can be combined and thereby limit the firm's technosystemic space. These restrictions are discussed in section III.

5. A key restriction is the requirement that all means of production be owned by society as a whole, rather than by private individuals or institutions.[11] Members of the enterprise enjoy collectively the usufruct of the assets associated with their firm and we shall consider these part of the firm's resources. Workers control the use of the assets, the distribution of the fruits of the assets' productivity, and the choice between maintaining or augmenting the stock of assets. However, when a member leaves the enterprise he loses all rights to the assets and the income derived from them.

6. Another restriction is the formal abolition of the category of "wage costs." Instead, wages and profits are both included in "residual income," the amount remaining after all material costs, interest payments, taxes, etc. have been subtracted from total revenues. The residual income is then divided into investment, reserve funds, collective consumption and personal income. The latter is shared by all members according to their labor contribution.

11. In this paper we shall not deal with the private sector in Yugoslavia. This does not mean that we consider it unimportant. The largest part of agriculture and handicrafts, and more limited parts of construction, catering, trade, and other service industries belong to the private sector. The private sector thus constitutes a significant part of the technosystemically feasible utility space in Yugoslavia, despite the systemic restrictions that no more than five people can be hired by the owner and that generally no more than ten hectares can be owned.

7. Each participant in the national labor force is free to choose and change his enterprise and the enterprises are free to add or not to add new members; it is less easy for the enterprise to dismiss a member. Barriers to labor mobility resulting from the system are discussed below.

8. As discussed above, the choice of relevant beneficiaries is both arbitrary and crucial for any welfare judgment. It is tempting to consider the workers as the sole beneficiaries of the Yugoslav firm, in which case the objective functions of internal actors and beneficiaries would coincide. The firm's consumers, the commune in which it is located, and the founders are additional contenders for this designation. Each of these groups, of course, has its own goals and will place a different index of success on the economic system of the self-managed enterprise.

In summary, it appears that self-management has expanded the techno-systemically feasible utility space of the enterprise by increasing the value of the participation component of members' objective functions and by motivating additional productive energies from the workers. Certain a priori restrictions on resource flows have, on the other hand, narrowed the feasible utility space. Which of these opposing forces dominates is difficult to assess. The optimality of the final outcome under self-management depends further on the distribution of decision power and information, and on the relation between the incentive structure and objective functions of its internal actors. In the following pages we analyze the economic system of the Yugoslav firm more fully in terms of this model.

III. The A Priori Restrictions

As discussed above, a priori restrictions on the feasible utility space fall into two major categories: fixed internal and fixed external decisions. In our generalized discussion of Yugoslav self-management we focus on fixed external decisions, which are common to all enterprises. A case study of specific enterprises would, of necessity, pay greater attention to fixed internal decisions, which vary from one firm to another. The a priori restrictions explored below, therefore, were generated externally and as such will affect the quasi-technological as well as the technosystemic utility space of the enterprise. The distinction between these two spaces becomes unimportant for our purpose.

Particularly significant in Yugoslav self-management are fixed decisions which prohibit the separation of certain inputs and outputs. The most crucial nonseparability is the assignment of virtually all entrepreneurial functions, and the benefits and costs deriving therefrom, to the suppliers of the labor input, i.e. the members of the enterprise. The second key non-separability consists of the assignment of these functions, benefits, and costs to the members collectively and not to each member individually. Other nonseparabilities tie the use of certain communal consumption outputs to (all) suppliers of the labor input of an enterprise. These will be discussed in the following section.

For purposes of analysis, we divide the "entrepreneurial function" into its major components: (1) founding the enterprise, (2) making basic decisions on product mix, factor proportions, innovations, and methods of management, (3) providing the necessary capital, (4) bearing the resultant risk, and (5) reinvesting or consuming the net revenues of the enterprise. The Yugoslav system is not unique in tying some of these functions to a specific factor of production. A priori restrictions creating such nonseparabilities are quite common and invariably limit the technosystemically feasible utility space. In the United States, for example, entrepreneurial functions are generally tied to the supplier of equity capital. One must examine in each case the extent of these nonseparabilities and the relative efficiency with which different resources can fulfill the entrepreneurial functions.[12]

Forced Separability Between Founders and Subsequent Decision-Makers

The most obvious carrier of the decision-making function, the founder of the enterprise, is prohibited from playing this role in a self-management system. As mentioned above, the founders, whether government units, firms, or individuals, must turn most decision-making power over to the members of the enterprise.

The analysis of this forced separability appears to be "virgin land"[13] despite the fact that it constitutes a key distinction between self-management

12. The parallelism between the nonseparability of labor and entrepreneurship in the Yugoslav enterprise and the nonseparability of equity capital and entrepreneurship in the capitalist firm is drawn explicitly by Dinko Dubravčić in "Prilog zasnivanju teorije jugoslovenskog poduzeća" [Contribution to the founding of the theory of the Yugoslav enterprise], *Ekonomska Analiza* 1968, nos. 1–2, pp. 120–26, as quoted in Jan Vanek. While it is true that equity capital is tied to many of the entrepreneurial functions in the United States, we would argue that the nonseparabilities are less restrictive than that between labor and entrepreneurship in Yugoslavia. For example, loan capital, which is freed from most entrepreneurial functions, is a readily available substitute for equity capital in the United States; there exists no such substitute for labor in Yugoslavia.

Jan Vanek, in his most interesting manuscript, quotes Max Weber as opposing emphatically the giving of any decision-making power to workers and arguing in favor of the expropriation of workers from all means of production. Weber felt that this was the only way to achieve rational economic behavior by the enterprise. However, he admitted that his approach introduced a contradiction between economic rationality and the more basic human values and aspirations. The Yugoslav system attempts to eliminate the contradiction. *The Theory of Social and Economic Organization*, ed. T. Parsons (New York, 1966), p. 248, quoted in Jan Vanek, p. 154.

13. Letter from Josip Županov, 7 September 1970.

and other economic systems. It imposes significant constraints on the willing-ness of individuals or groups to found new enterprises and raises the likeli-hood of conflicts between the objective functions and preferred actions of founders and members.[14]

The process of founding a new enterprise involves three primary tasks: the choice of what, where, and how to produce; recruitment of personnel; and provision of embodied capital. The decision options available to members of the enterprise, once power is turned over to them, are severely limited by these initial actions. The founders will have selected the product mix, the original director and his chief assistants, some of the technical and professional staff, and part of the labor force. Furthermore, they will have determined the physical location, the buildings, and the equipment, rather than merely providing the members with financial capital to use at their own discretion. In the short run these resources and products are nontransferable and tie the members to a particular quasi-technological space. Only over time can this space be altered by electing a different director, replacing the present staff, investing in new assets, changing the outputs, etc. In some cases, the members of Yugoslav enterprises inherited plants that, from their point of view, were built at the wrong place, with the wrong technology, and the wrong product mix; these usually resulted from political pressures on the government to provide employment and prestige to a certain geographical area, and are therefore called "political factories."[15]

Nonseparability Between Labor and Decision Making

This nonseparability involves two types of constraints: (1) most decision-making power is turned over to the full-time "employees" of the enterprise, whom we have defined as internal actors or members, and (2) all members have the same voting power regardless of their interest in or aptitude for decision making: the Yugoslav enterprise is formally a democracy. While the participation of workers in decision making may expand the feasible utility space, as outlined above, it may be a difficult system to implement

14. For a thorough discussion about founding new firms (the "entry problem"), see Jaroslav Vanek, *Labor Managed Market Economies*, and his article, "Decentralization under Workers' Management: A Theoretical Appraisal," *American Economic Review* 14 (December 1969): 1006–14; Stephen R. Sacks, "Entry of New Competitors in Yugoslav Market" in "Socialism," unpublished manuscript, as well as Evsey Domar's comments in "Market and Price Mechanism in Socialist Countries—Discussion," *American Economic Review* 15 (May 1970): 325.

15. Anto Barišič, "O čemu se sastoji ekonomska funkcija proizvodjača u samoupravnoj radnoj organizaciji?" [What is the content of the economic function of producers in the self-managed work organization?], comment on an article by Josip Županov, *Moderna Organizacija* 1969, no. 9, p. 722.

and may have offsetting negative impacts on the size of the feasible space or the final outcome within it.[16]

Utilizing Galbraith's historical analysis of the shift of decision-making power from land to capital to technostructure, Županov has argued that, in general, the scarcest factor has the power to dominate the decision-making process. Thus, he sees a contradiction between the scarcity of capital and technostructure in Yugoslavia and the systemic requirement that labor (the most abundant factor) serve as decision maker.[17]

One may question the conclusion that the scarcest resource must dominate. After all, no one has ever argued that state bureaucrats or party apparatchiks are the scarcest input in the Soviet system and yet they have maintained their control for over fifty years. The more interesting question, then, is not the ability of labor to hold decision-making power, but rather its ability to exercise that power wisely and well. In particular, do workers have the information and incentives to produce optimal decisions? This topic is discussed in section v.

Even if labor were the most efficient decision-making factor, the requirement that all members participate equally could lead to significant inefficiencies. The enterprise may not hire workers for a wage and exclude them from decision making (except for experts who can be hired as temporary consultants). Nor may it establish a formal division of labor between those members who do and do not have the desire and ability to act as decision makers.[18]

The impact of this restriction is strengthened by a preference for direct rather than indirect participation in decision making. Indirect decision making is clearly important in the Yugoslav enterprise, with workers' councils and management boards having considerable policy-making power and the director having great executive power. However, referenda are used

16. The designation of labor as the primal decision-maker could, alternatively, be considered part of the third set of variables in our system, the locus of decision power, which affects the final outcome rather than the feasible space. We have found it more convenient to discuss it at this point as an a priori restriction on resource flows.

17. John K. Galbraith, *The New Industrial State* (Boston: Houghton Mifflin, 1967), p. 56; Josip Županov, *Samoupravljanje i Društvena Moć* (Zagreb: Naše Teme, 1969), pp. 72–75.

18. As we shall show in the section on the locus of decision making, this restriction is not consistently honored in practice; all available evidence shows that some division of labor does, in fact, take place. An enterprise can effectively eliminate the decision-making power of a whole category of workers by contracting out a certain function to another enterprise. For example, the director of a clinic told one of the authors that the laundry and cleaning functions were handled on a contract basis, rather than by hiring people to do this work, partly in order to prevent a large group of unskilled workers from having major decision-making powers in the clinic.

for the most important decisions—on mergers, basic changes in commodity mix, and technological innovations. Furthermore, relatively autonomous units have been created within enterprises in order to make the decision-making units small enough to permit direct participation.[19] The potential problems introduced by the decentralization of decision-making power within the enterprise are beyond the scope of this paper.

Nonseparability Between Labor and Investment

The two constraints imposed on decision making have their counterparts in the other nonseparabilities we shall discuss, those dealing with investment, the taking of risk, and the distribution of residual income. Thus, much of the firm's investment funds comes from its own members, and all members must share in the costs of current investment and the returns to past investments proportionately to their labor contribution.

Some "equity" capital is available to firms from other enterprises, who are rewarded by a share of the profits, but these opportunities are severely restricted. Enterprises can, it is true, borrow from banks. However, the amount a bank is willing to lend is directly related to the amount the members themselves are providing, in the form of reinvested earnings. Consequently, loan and equity capital tend to be complementary rather than competitive and the workers supply almost all of the latter. The reliance on self-financing means that firms with relatively profitable investment opportunities may not be able to attract sufficient funds; possibilities are limited for equalizing marginal returns through capital mobility.

In order to fulfill the firm's investment goal, each individual member must contribute a fixed amount proportionate to his labor contribution; he cannot consult his personal preferences and increase or decrease his share. Furthermore, he loses all rights to past investments and their returns (positive or negative) as soon as he leaves the enterprise; principal plus returns are nonvested. As one might expect, this restriction has created considerable difficulties in the investment-consumption decision. Workers who are temporary or near retirement, those who have a high time preference or a low expectation about an investment's yield, would all opt for current

19. One of the best discussions of economic units, their history, their advantages and disadvantages may be found in two books by Dr. Gudrun Leman, a leading student of Yugoslav self-management. Dr. Leman also reports that referenda have been gaining in importance as a form of direct participation. See Gudrun Leman, *Ungeloste Fragen im jugoslawischen System der Arbeiterselbstverwaltung* [Unsolved questions in the Yugoslav system of worker self-management], Berichte des Bundesinstituts fur Ostwissenschaftliche und Internationale Studien (Koln: 37/1969); *Stellung und Aufgaben der ekonomischen Einheiten in den jugoslawischen Unternehmungen* [The position and tasks of the economic units in the Yugoslav enterprises] (Berlin: Duncker und Humblot, 1967).

consumption—but might be forced by the collective to save. Workers whose particular units are not scheduled to receive the new assets often fall into this category. On the other hand, workers who are optimistic, have a low time preference, or would personally benefit from a given project (e.g. it would make their work more pleasant or interesting) would prefer higher invest-ment—but might be prevented, by majority rule, from realizing their wishes. The only option open to such individuals is to place some of their income into personal savings bank accounts to earn a much lower rate of return than may be available through investment in their enterprise.

Furubotn and Pejovich examine the nonseparability between labor and investment contribution in the more usual context of property rights. They show that the nonvesting of property rights in investments discourages members from saving and requires a much higher rate of return on enterprise investment than on private bank accounts to make a worker indifferent be-tween the two.[20] They omit from their analysis some very important benefits of enterprise investment—in particular, the "leverage effect" (i.e., each dinar invested by a member increases the ability of the firm to borrow at interest rates which may be much lower than the marginal efficiency of investment) and the "employment security effect" (i.e., each dinar invested increases the firm's competitive strength and thereby serves to "insure" the worker's job). Despite these caveats, we agree fully with Furubotn and Pejovich's central argument that the prohibition on permanent property rights for members limits their willingness to invest, as well as reducing the allocative efficiency of the saving which does take place.

20. For example, if the member expects to stay with the firm for five years, the rate of return on enterprise investment would have to be 23 percent to make it as attractive as a personal savings account yielding 5 percent. See Eirick G. Furubotn and Svetozar A. Pejovich, "Property Rights and the Behavior of the Firm in a Socialist State," *Zeitschrift fur Nationalekonomie*, December 1970; idem, "Tax Policy and Investment Decisions of the Yugoslav Firm," unpub-lished paper; and Svetozar Pejovich's chapter in this volume.

Empirical studies do indeed show a significant response to the lack of vesting. The personal marginal propensity to save in Yugoslavia may be as high as 14 percent. Marijan Korošić, "Osnovne dileme daljeg razvoja samoupravljanja 2," *Moderna Organizacija* 1968, no. 2, p. 193. Deposits of private citizens in savings banks have been rising rapidly and steadily, from 651 million dinars in 1959, to 1,476 in 1962, 3,523 in 1965 and 9,597 in 1968 (Kamušić, p. 116). The preference for private savings over enterprise investment was evident in a survey of students in a school for workers and a construction school in Zagreb. The index of relative preference was 49 for private savings, 17 for investing in a new enterprise, and 15 for investing in their own enterprise (Županov, p. 68).

As a response to such widespread attitudes, there have been suggestions for "workers' shares," i.e. vested equity investments for workers, and some enterprises have experimented with internal loans from members, withdrawal pay for members leaving voluntarily, additional pension benefits for members retiring, etc. (Županov, pp. 68–69). One such scheme, based on vested bonuses, is proposed by Evsey Domar.

Nonseparability Between Labor and Risk

If members were to substitute savings bank deposits fully for enterprise investment, the total amount of resources available for investment in the economy would be unchanged. However, the availability of risk capital would decrease; banks are not known as providers of high-risk capital. This leads us to another major nonseparability, that between labor and risk taking.

Since the members must all participate in the costs and benefits of investment, they must also accept a proportionate share of its risk. Thus, risk taking is not delegated to a specialized "capitalist" group as in market economies, nor is it pooled by the state (and possibly reduced) as in centrally-planned socialist economies. Under Yugoslav self-management, individuals cannot choose among varying options, based on their preference for or aversion to risk. Instead, each worker must bear a fixed degree of risk, whether he wants to or not. Furthermore, his investment risk is positively correlated with his employment risk: negative returns to the former may result in the loss of his job.[21]

Yugoslav research shows that workers generally want stable and assured incomes rather than the fluctuations and insecurity which come with risk. Often, they do not even realize that they are, in fact, bearing the risk of the enterprise. A survey by Županov of worker attitudes toward risk is particularly interesting in this regard. When asked who *would* suffer the consequences of a drop in enterprise income, a large number of workers were unable or unwilling to answer; the majority of those responding felt that no one would have his personal income cut. When asked who *should* bear the risk, a large number again provided no answer and a majority of those responding felt that either no one should suffer or the loss should be borne by the executive and professional staff. This aversion toward risk was inversely correlated with status and was particularly characteristic of the blue-collar workers.[22] We may infer that significant differences in attitude exist among members of Yugoslav enterprises, but many of them clearly evince

21. Job loss may also occur from a highly successful investment as well, i.e. modernization, which substitutes capital for labor and results in job loss for the displaced workers but higher earnings for those remaining. The likelihood of job loss, of course, varies among workers, which helps to explain their differing attitudes toward investment and risk.

22. Županov, pp. 13–38. Županov's study covered 1,156 members of 10 enterprises in Croatia in 1966 and is a veritable gold mine of interesting data on the attitudes toward risk of various groups within the enterprise. A few additional samples are worth mentioning here. Most respondents were willing to punish individuals who were responsible for a drop in enterprise income, but were not willing to have anyone suffer for losses for which no one could be held responsible. They also believed that a worker should be paid according to his labor without regard to the success of his enterprise or economic unit. Most workers, especially at the lower rungs of the hierarchy, felt that even enterprises which continually operate at a loss should not

(continued on page 263)

the mentality of an employee rather than a risk-taking entrepreneur, a role which the system forces them all to assume.

Nonseparabilities Among Factor Incomes

The decisions on founding and operating the enterprise and on the amount of investment and risk undertaken determine the residual income available for allocation each year. The residual income includes, in undifferentiated form, payments for all labor services and all the entrepreneurial functions discussed above. It is used for enterprise investment, reserve funds, communal consumption, and personal income of the members. This nonseparability between factor incomes has several important consequences.

Problems in cost accounting. Under the Yugoslav system, it is not possible to calculate implicit wages or capital costs and compare them to each other or to material costs in order to determine a rational input mix. Neither is it possible to analyze the contributions of labor, management, risk taking, monopoly power, etc. to the "profitability" of various enterprises.[23] This

(continued from page 262)

be liquidated. When asked whether price controls should be abandoned and enterprises permitted to set their own prices, a majority replied in the negative. The negative attitude of many workers toward risk is also discussed by J. M. Montias, "Market and Price Mechanism in Socialist Countries—Discussion," *American Economic Review* 15 (May 1970): 322. Montias gives examples of risk aversion among workers in Germany and France where income and educational levels are higher than those that prevail in Yugoslavia.

23. The Yugoslav wage system is analyzed in Howard Wachtel, "Workers' Management and Wage Differentials in Yugoslavia" (Ph.D. diss., University of Michigan, 1969), pp. 86–109. Wachtel argues that the enterprises still differentiate informally between the fixed wage (payment for labor services) and the variable wage (payment for entrepreneurial services). However, we may note that the accounting and economic differentiations may not correspond. Wachtel calculates that, for the years 1956, 1959, and 1961, the proportion of nonwage member income ranged from 5.1 percent to 17.1 percent; it was much more important for white collar workers than for blue collar workers, and within each category, it was larger for those with higher educational or skill qualifications. The proportion rose from 1956 to 1959 and then fell in 1961.

Yugoslav economists, too, have addressed themselves to this question. A strong argument for operating with an artificial labor price, subject to social control and determining the resultant profitability of the enterprise, is presented by Lado Rupnik, "Društveno usmeravanje raspodele ličnih dohodaka" [Social direction over the distribution of personal incomes], *Moderna Organizacija* 1970, no. 1, pp. 51–70.

France Černe argues for establishing a category of accounting wages to permit rational resource allocation in "Raspodjela dohotka prema radu u teoriji i stvarnosti" [The distribution of income according to labor in theory and practice], *Ekonomist* 1968, no. 2, p. 299. Of course, if all enterprises could calculate the payoff accruing for each possible input bundle they could choose the optimal bundle without differentiating among factor incomes. However, the computations become much simpler if "shadow prices" for each resource are known.

The unwillingness to compensate members separately and directly for their entrepreneurial contributions is probably attributable to Marxist ideology, under which the only permissible income differentials are based on hours worked, natural and acquired skills, and differences in family status (Ibid., pp. 284–85).

situation obtains, of course, whenever two or more functions are combined in a system of income distribution; e.g., we cannot easily differentiate between pure profit, risk taking, and managerial wages in an American proprietary firm.

Entrepreneurial incentives. A member's share in the undifferentiated residual income of the enterprise is determined by an evaluation procedure that takes into account his skill, educational qualifications, and productivity.[24] However, little weight is placed on the worker's contribution to decision making in the enterprise. Thus, although active participation is formally a key feature of self-management, the incentive structure does not encourage such input and, in fact, discriminates against those who participate yet receive no return for their time and effort. This is akin to university salary and promotion practices whereby professors engaged in governance suffer in comparison to those devoting all their energies to research.

Similarly, no value is placed on differential amounts which the member may have contributed to the firm's capital stock through previous collective saving and investment. A new member with a small accumulation of contributions has exactly the same income rights as an old member with a much larger accumulation. Furthermore, a worker who leaves the enterprise voluntarily or because he is fired loses all such rights. These effects all stem, of course, from the prohibition on private ownership of enterprise capital, discussed above. They clearly discourage investment, growth, and probably labor mobility, and may be questioned on equity grounds as well.

Residual income and labor mobility. An important consequence of the system of income distribution is its impact on labor mobility. When there exists serious unemployment, as has been true in the Yugoslav economy, a potential employee cannot get a job by offering to work for less money—by taking a lower implicit wage, for example, or by surrendering his share of entrepreneurial income. The only way he can make himself more attractive is to accept a lower skill classification that carries with it a smaller proportion of total enterprise income. This would not only imply financial penalties,

24. For discussions of some of the rather sophisticated versions of these evaluation procedures, see Elvira Vulić, "Analiza distribucije osobnih dohodaka direktora" [Analysis of the distribution of personal incomes of directors], *Direktor u Samoupravnim Odnosima* [The director under self-management relations], ed. D. Gorupić and J. Brekić (Zagreb: Informator, 1967), pp. 301–15; Medjo Balaban, "Klasifikacija poslova po kriterijumu vrednosti uz primenu diskriminacione analize" [Classification of positions according to the criterion of value using discriminant analysis], *Moderna Organizacija* 1969, no. 2, pp. 125–33; and Anto Barišić, "O problemu procjene funkcija u našoj industriji" [About the problem of evaluating functions in our industry], *Moderna Organizacija* 1969, no. 1, pp. 3–21.

but also a diminution of his status. It would be extremely interesting to discover whether this type of reaction has occurred frequently in Yugoslavia, that is, whether market forces have reasserted themselves indirectly by manipulation of skill categories rather than directly through wage competition.

Just as it is difficult for an unemployed worker to make himself attractive to the enterprise, it is similarly difficult for an aspiring enterprise to attract a desirable employee. This is particularly important in the case of poorly functioning enterprises that need highly qualified professionals. The enterprise cannot offer these professionals superior wages except by placing them in arbitrarily high skill classifications. Even then the firm cannot guarantee fixed payments, but can only promise a share in its potential—and very uncertain—residual income. Such uncertainty can be avoided only by hiring professionals as "consultants" rather than as full-time employees, or by contracting out these functions—and thereby circumventing the entire self-management system.

As we shall discuss later, there exists in Yugoslavia a cultural "norm of egalitarianism" which limits income inequalities within enterprises and produces some of these serious distortions of entrepreneurial incentives and factor mobility. These problems may diminish, in time, as Yugoslav workers develop more of an entrepreneurial mentality. However, so long as individual differences remain in proclivities for decision making, risk taking, and investment, the a priori restrictions will prevent the broader Yugoslav closed system from operating on its technologically feasible utility frontier.

IV. The Actors and Their Objective Functions

How the self-managed enterprise operates within its technosystemically feasible space depends, in part, on the objective functions of its internal actors. This section constitutes a preliminary report on some of our ideas on this important topic.

Dynamic Optimization: Maximizing Consumption Over Time

Most Western theorists have used static models to analyze the Yugoslav self-management system. The usual assumption is that workers wish to maximize current residual income per member rather than total profits, as would be the case in a capitalist firm. This goal appears to result in inelasticities, instabilities, and inefficiencies. The static income-maximization hypothesis, however, has been less popular with Yugoslav economists, sociologists and management experts, who presumably are closer to the realities of the situation.[25]

The first and most obvious modification of the short-run maximization function would be to convert it into a dynamic function, in which each member is assumed to maximize the present discounted value of his lifetime consumption stream. Part of the residual income could then rationally be reinvested or held as reserves, an aspect of reality which is incongruous within the static model. These funds are then treated as providing future rather than current consumption.

In a dynamic model, it is crucial to use an appropriate social discount rate and risk premium, but Yugoslav capital markets are clearly too imperfect to give us an unambiguous choice. In the general literature on this subject a controversy has developed about whether the collective (enterprise) risk premium should be less than the private (personal) one, because of risk pooling; whether people want different discount rates to prevail for collective and private projects; and whether the subjective time preference or the productive rate of return constitutes the correct social discount rate, when the two diverge.[26] This entire theoretical issue is relevant to our present discussion.

25. The first serious theoretical treatment of the self-managed enterprise was Benjamin Ward's path-breaking article, "The Firm in Illyria: Market Syndicalism," *American Economic Review* 48 (September 1958): 566–89. This was followed many years later by Evsey Domar's extensions in "The Soviet Collective Farm," *American Economic Review* 56 (September 1966): 734–57. Ward expanded his ideas in his book, *The Socialist Economy*. This was reviewed and an alternative objective function suggested (i.e. that implicit wages are fixed and the total residual is maximized each year) by Branko Horvat, "Prilog zasnivanju teorije jugoslavenskog poduzeća" [A contribution to the founding of a theory of the Yugoslav enterprise], *Ekonomska Analiza* 1967, nos. 1–2, pp. 7–28. The most recent rigorous analysis in the same spirit is contained in Jaroslav Vanek, *Labor-Managed Market Economies*. An empirically-oriented International Labor Organization study of Yugoslav self-management, conducted by Jan Vanek, was published in the early sixties. In his recent unpublished manuscript, Vanek attacks the Ward model in general and the income-per-member maximization hypothesis in particular (pp. 159–250). He shows clearly that most Yugoslav experts, both inside and outside enterprises, stress other objectives. We shall draw heavily on Vanek's analysis of the objective-function problem.

26. The lengthy literature on the optimal social discount rate and risk premium includes: J. Hirshleifer, "On the Theory of Optimal Investment Decisions," *Journal of Political Economy* 66 (August 1958): 329–53; S. Marglin, "The Social Rate of Discount and the Optimal Rate of Investment," *Quarterly Journal of Economics* 77 (February 1963): 95–112; J. Hirshleifer, "Investment Decisions Under Uncertainty: Applications of the State Preference Approach," *Quarterly Journal of Economics* 80 (May 1966): 252–78; K. Arrow and R. Lind, "Uncertainty and the Evaluation of Public Investment Decisions," *American Economic Review* 60 (June 1970), 364–79; W. J. Baumol, "On the Social Rate of Discount," *American Economic Review* 58 (September 1968): 783–802; E. James, "On the Social Rate of Discount: Comment," *American Economic Review* 59 (December 1969): 912–17; E. James, "A Note on the Social Risk Premium," mimeographed (April 1970).

If, as we would argue, members will be discounting and making decisions according to their own subjective time preferences, it seems probable that a short-term time horizon will prevail.[27] It is also inevitable that significant differences among individuals and groups will appear. Some workers have a low time preference, are optimistic about the future, expect to remain with the firm for a long time, and will therefore place a high estimate on the present discounted value of an investment project; while for others the opposite is true. Thus, dynamizing our model also brings to the surface the inherent potential for conflict among members of the enterprise.

Stability of Employment

Even more important to Yugoslav workers than maximizing consumption is the stabilization of income and employment.[28] This should not surprise us when we consider the serious unemployment existing in Yugoslavia, the norm of egalitarianism which restricts wage differentials, and the distaste workers must have for firing their colleagues with whom they will continue to live as neighbors.

This aversion to job loss, and the resulting marginal rate of substitution between security and income, could be included as arguments in the members' objective functions. The purchase of job security would then be viewed as a form of communal consumption, i.e. elimination of psychic anxiety or insurance against the prospect of being dismissed or dismissing others, for which workers are willing to sacrifice other kinds of communal consumption or personal income.

Alternatively, we might say that the workers are trying to maximize (discounted) lifetime consumption, subject to a no-firing constraint.[29] Such

27. This is the general view. Jan Vanek is one of the few dissenters. He argues that the horizon of workers in the average Yugoslav firm may be as long as twenty years or more, as some would include their families, and would be considering their own advancement possibilities as a function of the enterprise's (and the community's) development (pp. 133–34). To the extent that labor mobility is low, e.g. because of a combination of a no-firing constraint (discussed immediately below in the text) and a difficulty in obtaining new jobs due to high unemployment levels, the members' time horizons will be lengthened.

28. This point was brought out very forcefully in a meeting on the self-managed enterprise in Opatija, 29–31 October 1969. "The participants in the discussion consider that economic relations in an enterprise must be based, first of all, on respect for the basic goal of the enterprise. This goal is stability in business operations and income, greater efficiency, social security, etc. It is considered that maximization of income and personal income is not the basic principle of business operation, but stability of income and personal income. It is thought that social security of the worker as a unit is very small and must be assured as much as possible." Bogdan Ilić, "Samoupravna organizacija preduzeća" [The self-management organization of the enterprise], Gledišta (December 1969), p. 1717.

29. A no-firing constraint is specifically suggested by Jan Vanek: "A non-negative outcome in regard to levels of employment is usually postulated as a major constraint, at least where levels of income are not tending towards a (partly subjectively determined) minimum" (p. 204).

a constraint would convert labor into a fixed cost, like capital, with voluntary withdrawals and retirements the counterpart of depreciation, which sets a floor to the rate at which (nontradable) capital assets will diminish. The irreversibility of the hiring decision would raise the optimal capital/labor ratio during a cyclical upswing and reduce it during a recession, in comparison to a variable labor model. It would, in effect, convert the "Illyrian firm" into the "Nipponese firm," since Japanese workers can usually count on keeping their jobs for life. The analogy to the tenure system at an American university is obvious.[30]

Finally, it is clear that workers with differing skills, seniority, and aggressive impulses will also differ in their trade-offs between income and security and their attitude toward a no-firing constraint.

Communal Consumption

It may be helpful at this point to divide the firm's activities into production (or revenue-raising activities), communal consumption (or revenue-using activities), and transfers (or revenue-distributing activities). The first covers all those activities, including investment, which yield revenue rather than direct satisfaction; from this set we can derive the maximum attainable net revenues of the firm. The second covers all those activities which use revenues to provide goods entering directly into members' objective functions. The third consists of disbursing the difference between maximum net revenues and communal consumption as personal incomes which may be consumed or saved by the members.

Production and transfer payments have received most systematic attention in Western microeconomic theory of the firm. Communal consumption is also found in capitalist firms, such as oligopolies, particularly when the profit constraint is not binding. The concept may be especially helpful in explaining the behavior of nonprofit institutions. We are interested in it here because of its quantitative importance to the self-managed enterprise, which provides services such as housing, vacation retreats, sports facilities, and improved working conditions to its members.

"Communal consumption" should not be confused with "collective goods," since the former need not be consumed jointly by all members; yet, they are financed jointly by all members out of the firm's residual income.[31] Consequently, we have another potential conflict in objectives, this time

---

30. For a fuller discussion of the implications of converting labor into a fixed asset in the context of the educational sector, see E. James, "Product Mix and Costs in Higher Education," Stony Brook Working Paper No. 52, 1972, and idem, "The University as an Economic System."

31. For a discussion of the various properties associated with collective goods and their implications for theory and policy, see E. James, "Joint Products, Collective Goods, and External Effects: Comment," *Journal of Political Economy* 79 (September 1971): 1129–36.

among members who will make differential use of and place different values on the communal consumption activities of the enterprise.

Participatory Democracy

Intangibles, such as participatory democracy, constitute a special case of communal goods, deserving particular attention. This is, after all, the raison d'être behind the Yugoslav self-management system. Worker participation in decision making may provide valuable psychic benefits to many members, well worth reduced efficiency in producing material commodities and pecuniary rewards. To other workers, particularly those with a temporary attachment to the enterprise, the need to engage in decision making may be an undesired obligation. Since different members attach different values to industrial democracy we can expect disagreement over the appropriate trade-offs with more tangible consumption goods and over the optimal amount of participation (within the limits imposed by the a priori restrictions of the system). Some evidence on worker attitudes toward participation will be presented in section v.

Conflicts on Objective Functions

In our model we do not conceive of the enterprise as having its own objective function. Instead, the firm's actions result from the separate objective functions and interacting decisions of its individual actors and harmony may be the exception rather than the rule.[32]

In an enterprise where workers dominate the decision-making process in practice as well as theory, we would argue that the maximization of lifetime (private plus communal) consumption, discounted at a relatively high rate, and subject to a no-firing constraint, is most likely to prevail. However, agreement is not likely among all members on the appropriate discount rate, the optimum value for the firm's investment and communal consumption activities, and trade-offs between job security and maximum income. Coalitions of workers are likely to evolve: the more educated and skilled

---

32. Some authorities disagree with this approach and believe that any enterprise, once it has existed for any length of time, develops a life and goals of its own. This is the position taken by Jan Vanek, who argues that "the prime object of our inquiry is the worker-managed enterprise or its workers' collectivity, rather than the workers themselves. Such enterprise or collectivity may take, as we shall see, most diverse shapes and forms but it cannot be defined as a mere collection or sum of the workers who belong to it. No doubt they also are, each one individually, economic subjects in their own rights; they form a constraint and a motivational background from the point of view of their own enterprise, but the latter alone has a full and distinct economic existence." It should be noted that Vanek identifies the worker collectivity and the enterprise, although they are not identical; the worker collectivity consists of the present members while the enterprise may be thought of as including legacies from previous members and taking into account future members. See Vanek, pp. 8, 9, 225.

in the middle-age brackets forming one group interested in long-run growth, communal consumption, and participatory democracy; those near retirement preferring short-run income maximization;[33] and the young unskilled workers concerned primarily with job security and equal income distribution. One may even speculate that probable voting patterns of prospective employees (rather than their productivity) might govern the hiring decision.

This heterogeneity is even greater when we compare the objective functions of workers and managers. While some directors and members of the technostructure may simply try to please their workers and emphasize maximization of (short-run) consumption, those who regard themselves as professionals are likely to favor growth and modernization (like their American counterparts)—even if this is at the expense of consumption for their members.[34] A successful growth policy will yield prestige to the director and his assistants and enable them to move on to larger enterprises or to prestigious positions in social or political organizations.

The commune, which may have founded the enterprise and has continuing influence over its activities, tends to be concerned primarily with maximizing employment and tax revenues.[35] This goal is complementary with rapid growth and a no-firing constraint. Those directors trying to gain favor with commune officials, for their own personal advancement or for the good of their enterprise, may opt for expansion using a labor-intensive technology. On the other hand, the commune's goals may conflict with those of directors

33. Workers nearing retirement have two reasons for favoring immediate personal incomes over investment: they will be retired before the investment pays off and their pension is based on their present incomes, so their pensions will actually be lower if funds are diverted from personal income distributions to investment. See Josip Županov, in "Osnovne dileme daljeg razvoja samoupravljanja" [Basic dilemmas in the further development of self-management], *Moderna Organizacija* 1968, no. 1, p. 12. As we show in section v, this group is not heavily represented in self-management organs.

34. One of many examples of the director's interest in investment and new technology and the workers' interest in higher immediate incomes is presented by Duško Vojvodić, the director of the enterprise ME-BE. He relates that his enterprise used to have two camps of opinion concerning the division of income. The director and his technical staff saw the need for new equipment, while the workers, viewing the rise in the cost of living and the customary standard of life, wanted the maximum percent distributed as personal incomes. This problem was partially solved when the investment decision was decentralized to the economic units, with each unit forced to cover its own investment needs; the percent of investment funds for the enterprise as a whole rose by more than 12 percent. "Direktor izmedju tehnologije i društvenih odnosa" [The director between technology and social relations], in Gorupić and Brekić, pp. 173–74.

35. Drago Gorupić, *Poslovna Politika Poduzeća* [The business policies of the enterprise] (Zagreb: Informator, 1963), pp. 219–20; G. Macesich, *Yugoslavia: The Theory and Practice of Development Planning* (Charlottesville: The University of Virginia Press, 1964), p. 87. Josip Županov, in a letter of 7 September 1970, argues that the total residual income of the enterprise is more important to the commune than its profitability (after subtracting implicit wages) because taxes are based primarily on the former rather than the latter.

who prefer capital-intensity, and with workers who wish to maximize short-run per capita income.

If the founder was another enterprise, it will expect a share in profits and may seek to obtain (sell) raw materials from (to) the new firm at favorable rates. This can easily produce conflicts with both director and workers of the new enterprise.

As some goals are met, they may decline in significance compared with others which have been neglected. Cyclical changes in the larger closed model, the Yugoslav economy, may also be reflected in the behavior of the open subsystems, the enterprises. For example, in a highly profitable enterprise during a boom period when both personal incomes and investments can be high, long-run objectives may control the enterprise's actions; in a less successful enterprise or during a recession, short-run income maximization and job security are likely to take precedence.[36]

Any organization will, of course, find heterogeneous preferences among its many members. Its actions depend upon the manner in which these disparate objectives are reconciled—on the voting or bargaining scheme for aggregating individual choices. The possibility of a dictatorial outcome, in which one group dominates, is discussed in the following section. If, however, decisions are democratic, we encounter the familiar welfare problem that the social ordering may not be transitive and a uniquely determinate solution may not exist.[37] In view of the multiplicity of decision makers and

36. Professor Miladin Korać has found a negative correlation between the absolute level of personal incomes in an economic sector and the percent of total residual revenues allocated to personal incomes. Thus, the more profitable enterprises can afford to invest more, thereby increasing future incomes as well. Miladin Korać et al., *Analiza ekonomskog položaja privrednih grupacija na bazi zakona vrednosti, 1962–1966* [The analysis of the economic position of economic branches on the basis of the law of value, 1962–1966] (Zagreb: Economic Institute, 1968), quoted in Županov, *Samoupravljanje*, p. 64. A similar conclusion was reached by Wachtel for the year 1966 (pp. 111–15), and was confirmed by a rank correlation we did on 1967 data. The correlation was significant at the 5 percent level for economic branches and for economic regions it was significant at the 0.1 percent level. *Statistički Bilten*, no. 552, *Industrijska Preduzeća 1967* [Industrial enterprises 1967] (December 1968), p. 23.

37. The extensive theoretical literature on this subject includes: K. Arrow, "A Difficulty in the Concept of Social Welfare," *Journal of Political Economy* 58 (August 1950): 328–46; Duncan Black, "On the Rationale of Group Decision Making," *Journal of Political Economy* 56 (February 1948): 23–34; Gordon Tullock, "Problems of Majority Voting," *Journal of Political Economy* 67 (December 1959): 571–79.

Some of the issues faced by the Yugoslav firm are likely to produce individual preferences which are not single peaked and, therefore, the possibility of an intransitive social ordering. For example, suppose the enterprise must choose among three strategies which stress, respectively, short-term income maximization (A), collective consumption (B), or long-term growth (C). Suppose further that the members are divided into three homogeneous groups each of equal size. The first group, consisting of the director and technostructure, orders these alternatives C B A. The second group, young untrained workers, orders them A C B. The third group, middle-aged skilled workers, orders them B A C. Since none of these alternatives gets a majority over both others, the order of voting will determine the outcome and we do not have a rational, consistent social ranking.

objective functions, the absence of a well-developed mechanism for conflict resolution may be counted as a serious deficiency of Yugoslav self-management and an area needing further exploration by economic reformers. We shall return to this problem in the following section.

V. Distribution of Decision-Making Power

We turn now to the third set of variables in our model of the Yugoslav enterprise, the decision-making and informational interrelationships among the actors, as they operate within the technosystemic space of our open system. This subject has been treated much more exhaustively in the Yugoslav and Western literature than the other variables in our model, the a priori restrictions and objective functions. Therefore, in order to keep this paper to a manageable size, we shall merely touch upon a few of the interesting aspects of the locus of control. We ignore the role of all external decision-makers as well as party and union officials who are members of the enterprise. Nor shall we deal with extremely important questions concerning the incentive structure and informational network in a self-managed system.[38] We focus instead on the ideal and actual distribution of power among the director, the workers' council, and the workers.

Self-Management Organs

As indicated in our discussion of the a priori restrictions, the formal and legitimate decision-making power rests with members of the enterprise, i.e. all full-time employees. The workers' council and management board are the elected instruments of the membership; ideally, this is a combination of direct and representative democracy.[39]

The role of director is a more ambiguous one, and has created a tremendous amount of discussion and concern in Yugoslavia. He is elected by the workers' council of the enterprise, but must maintain good relations with commune officials and other external actors. Thus, the director has a multiple mission—he must follow the wishes of the members of the enterprise, satisfy the leaders of the commune, and operate as a professional-technical manager

38. These two subjects will be treated in a forthcoming monograph written by Egon Neuberger as part of the Eastern Europe Project of the International Development Research Center at Indiana University. Similarly, other issues discussed in this paper will be dealt with at greater depth and breadth in that book.

39. In small enterprises, workers elect only a management board of 5 to 11 members, while in large enterprises, they elect workers' councils, consisting of anywhere from 15 to 120 members, as well as a management board. The workers' council is the basic policy-making unit of the enterprise, roughly comparable to the board of directors of a U.S. corporation. M. Dautović, *Osnovi Ekonomike i Organizacije Preduzeća* [The fundamentals of the economy and organization of the enterprise] (Belgrade: Savremena Administracija, 1965), pp. 68–72.

of the firm. This position, similar to that of a department chairman in many American universities, presents obvious difficulties.

In addition to these self-management organs at the enterprise level and their various commissions and committees, there exist in large enterprises one, two, or even three layers of self-management organs in the economic units.[40]

Power Distributions and the Yugoslav Ideal

The locus of decision-making power within an organization may be studied in many ways. One useful approach, developed by Tannenbaum and Kahn and applied by Yugoslav sociologists, differentiates between four types of distributions: (1) democratic, where the "masses" have more power than the "elite" (workers have more power than the director); (2) autocratic or oligarchic, which is just the opposite of democratic; (3) anarchic, where all groups exercise roughly equal power, but each has very little; and (4) polyarchic, where all groups exercise roughly equal and quite substantial power.[41]

This approach differs from the usual centralization-decentralization polarity since it takes into account the total control exercised by all actors jointly as well as the relative power position of each. If we consider decision making as not only determining a desired course of action, but also getting this action implemented, it becomes clear that the distribution of such power

40. The formation of economic units and subunits is a function primarily of the size of the enterprise. Of enterprises with 250–499 members, 50.6 percent had no economic units, 48.7 percent had one level of economic units, and 0.7 percent had two levels. When we move to the largest enterprises, those with over 1,000 members, we find that only 6.6 percent had no economic units, 79.1 percent had one level, 13.4 percent had two levels, and 0.9 percent even had three levels. *Statistički Bilten*, no. 492, *Samoupravljanje u Preduzećima sa 1000 i Više Članova Radne Zajednice u 1966* [Self-management in enterprises with 1000 and more members in the worker collective in 1966] (Belgrade, 1967), and *Statistički Bilten*, no. 564, *Samoupravljanje u Preduzećima sa 250–999 Članova Radne Zajednice u 1968* [Self-management in enterprises with 250–999 members in the worker collective in 1968] (Belgrade, 1969). The existence of such a large number of self-management organs at various levels indicates the seriousness of the attempt to decentralize decision-making power so that the individual worker can participate directly and can see a more immediate connection between his efforts and his income. It also raises very significant problems of coordination among the various self-management organs and potential conflicts over the degree of decentralization desired. See the two books by Gudrun Leman for a discussion of these issues.

41. The fourfold classification and the method of the control graph underlying this approach are presented in Arnold S. Tannenbaum, "Control Structure and Union Functions," in *Control in Organizations*, ed. A. S. Tannenbaum (New York: McGraw-Hill Book Co., 1968), pp. 32–33. In the control graph, various groups are placed along the horizontal axis and the amount of control exercised by each is shown on the vertical axis. The graph then indicates two distinct aspects of control: the shape of the curve shows the distribution of control, and the y-intercept the total amount of control.

is not necessarily a zero-sum game. In an anarchic situation everyone has an equal right to make decisions, but these may not be implemented if they conflict with other actors' decisions. In a polyarchic situation everyone still has equal rights, but the resulting decisions are coordinated and implemented, so that the effective power is much greater than under anarchy.

The distinction between democratic and oligarchic distributions is most helpful in analyzing questions of decentralization and participation. In an oligarchy the primal holders of power are a small group of people at the top of the pyramid who may, however, delegate some power to those below. They will do so if, and only if, they feel that this delegation will yield better results for them than centralization—and they will try to structure the available decision options and incentives so as to maximize their own objective functions. On the other hand, in democratic organizations the primal holders of power are the majority of the members, who may, in turn, delegate some power upward to an elite, if they feel this will maximize their objective functions. Worker participation in most Western countries may be viewed as an example of the former, Yugoslav self-management of the latter.[42]

It is helpful in our discussion of the Yugoslav firm to contrast the self-management subsystem (which deals with long-term broad-ranging "social" policies concerning personnel, residual income distribution, communal consumption, mergers, etc.) and the executive-managerial subsystem (which establishes "technical" policies in production, investment, and finance, and is responsible for all implementing actions).[43] The interrelationships and overlaps between these two subsystems are great. For example, personnel

42. These ideas are developed in Drago Gorupić, "Tendencije u razvoju radničkog samo-upravljanja u Jugoslaviji" [Tendencies in the development of worker self-management in Yugo-slavia], in Gorupić and Brekić, pp. 16–18, and Rudolf Bičanić, "O monocentričnom i poli-centričnom planiranju" [On monocentric and polycentric planning], Ekonomski Pregled, 1963, nos. 6–7. The distinction between systems in which the primal decision-making power rests with some central organ at the apex of a pyramid and those where it rests with primary economic units (households, workers, enterprises) was stressed by Aleksander Bajt in "Decentralized Decision-Making Structure in the Yugoslav Economy," Economics of Planning, 1967, no. 1, p. 73. The whole question of decentralization, as well as all the other issues involved in the systemic model will be dealt with in greater depth in Neuberger and Duffy.

43. The Yugoslav literature distinguishes between three decision categories: rukovodjenje ("execution"), upravljanje ("management"), and samoupravljanje ("self-management"). Žu-panov, Samoupravljanje, pp. 149–58; Vlado Arzenšek, "Analiza ankete o kadrovskoj politici" [Analysis of a survey about personnel policy], Moderna Organizacija 1968, no. 7, p. 557; Branko Horvat, "Yugoslav Economic Policy in the Postwar Period: Problems, Ideas, Institutional Development," American Economic Review, Supplement (June 1971), p. 102. We have compressed the first two into a single executive-managerial category. Our twofold classification is closely related to Županov's "representative" and "hierarchic" substructures. Županov, Samou-pravljanje, pp. 173–79, and Marijan Korošić, "Funkcija direktora s obzirom na tržište i cijene" [The function of the director with respect to the market and prices], Gorupić and Brekić, pp. 185–88.

decisions affect production, income distribution influences investment, and the practical import of any policy depends upon how it is interpreted and implemented on a day-to-day basis. Nevertheless, it appears that the Yugoslav enterprises are groping toward some division of labor along these lines.

Officially, the ideal distribution of power in the self-management subsystem is democratic, or at least polyarchic, with authority running from the members to the workers' council, the management board, and the director. There is less agreement about the executive-managerial subsystem, possibly because of the functional ambiguities discussed above. One can, however, argue that for these technical matters it is in the interests of the members, as the primal holders of power, to abdicate in favor of an oligarchic distribution. Authority would run from the director through his staff, the chiefs of economic units, foremen, and workers (with the workers retaining the right to review the actions of the managers, and dismiss them, if necessary). The fact that these two lines of authority go through the same individuals but in opposite directions has been, as one might imagine, a source of considerable organizational confusion in Yugoslavia.

Actual Power Distribution Between Workers and Managers

Županov summarizes the actual distribution of decision-making power in Yugoslavia as follows:

(1) All investigations up to this point, without any exception, show that the distribution of influence in the hierarchical substructure [executive-managerial subsystem] is oligarchic, which is, by the way, typical for economic organizations in capitalism and probably also in administrative socialism. The introduction of working (economic) units has not, it appears, significantly modified this traditional form of distribution. On the contrary, some investigations suggest that even in the economic units themselves the influence is distributed oligarchically. (2) An oligarchic distribution is found also in the representative substructure [self-management subsystem], although not always—in some investigations a polyarchic distribution was found. The democratic form was not found in any working organization. (3) It has been determined that different social groups have different degrees of influence on the work and decisions of workers' councils: the executives of the enterprises (and in some working organizations also the experts) have great influence, while workers have small influence.[44]

44. Županov, *Samoupravljanje*, pp. 103–04. Županov bases these conclusions on his own work, as well as that of V. Rus, I. Šiber, S. Kljaić, M. Magdić, B. Šverko, B. Kavčić, S. Možina, and J. Jerovšek. The same conclusions were reached by Kamušić and by outside observers—e.g. Gudrun Leman and Howard Wachtel.

These conclusions are supported by observations of outsiders as well as participants in self-managed enterprises. In one survey, a large number of Yugoslav management and technical personnel were asked to rank various groups within the enterprise according to their decision-making power. Using an index ranging from 1 to 5, the responses were as follows:

	Perception of Power	
Group	*By Directors*	*By Non-Directors*
Director	4.30	4.46
Other executives	3.77	3.72
Technical experts	3.38	3.30
Socio-political officials	2.71	2.68
Workers' council	3.42	3.57
Workers	2.64	2.31

Thus, a very high degree of decision power is perceived to be held by the director and a somewhat lesser amount by the technostructure and the workers' council. The low scores of the workers, the legitimate primal holders of control, is striking.[45]

45. This survey was described by Županov, *Samoupravljanje*, p. 252. The question was asked of 245 directors, upper and middle-level managers, and technical personnel participating in a symposium in April 1968. Very similar results were reported in another survey conducted in a "typical" enterprise:

	Index of Power	
Groups	*Actual (Perceived)*	*Ideal*
Top executives	4.36	4.06
Chiefs of economic units	3.29	4.01
Immediate supervisors	3.08	3.94
Workers	2.63	4.81
Members of management board	3.51	4.65
Members of workers' council	3.22	4.66

Stane Možina, "Interesi samoupravljača za odlučivanje" [The interest of self-managers in decision making], *Moderna Organizacija* 1968, no. 9, p. 714. In this survey, the actual distribution is perceived as oligarchic while the ideal is democratic, with an increase in decision-making power desired for all groups except the top executives.

   In evaluating these and other surveys, it is important to bear in mind the severe limitations facing the investigator. He is not measuring actual influence but must depend on perceptions, which often differ from reality. Only a small proportion of all Yugoslav workers have been surveyed, a scientific sampling process is generally not followed, and most surveys were conducted in the advanced regions of the country. In addition, it is well known that the precise wording of the questions can cause substantial differences in the responses. For example, the low index of power of the workers may be due to the fact that the respondents assumed the question to concern the relative power of a single worker, rather than the power of the worker collective as a whole.

Another survey indicated workers believe that rewards for positive contributions to the enterprise are directly correlated with status and punishments for damaging the enterprise are inversely correlated with status. The incentive structure, in other words, was believed to discourage participation by workers and encourage decision making by the more elite groups.[46]

Thus, it appears that the director and his staff often dominate the executive-managerial subsystem and perhaps the self-management subsystem as well. Yet, their informal power is not formally recognized; they must undergo the frustrations inherent in a role with ambiguous authority and status. Alternatively, they may try to pass responsibility to the workers' council, e.g. by asking the council to endorse their more difficult decisions.[47] The council, in response, has tried to develop expertise in many technical areas for which its members are hardly suited by education or experience.

Control over the information system is one of the key factors behind the director's decision-making power. Most of the information is generated by members of the technostructure who are under the direct control of the director, and other members of the enterprise are generally not able to interpret the information even when they get access to it. The attempt by workers' councils to gain greater direct control over the technical affairs of the enterprise has led to many difficulties. As Branko Horvat has pointed out, "The confusion between management and self-management generated tendencies to transfer more and more of formal coordination [i.e. decisions on technical matters] to bodies [i.e. the workers' councils] whose [ideal] task was social integration. As a consequence, satisfactory social integration was not achieved, while nonprofessional management meant lower efficiency."[48]

One of the key culprits in the piece is the management board, an elected body much smaller than the workers' council but of similar composition and qualifications. The director has been forced to deal with this body, as well as the workers' council and the *kolegij* containing key members of his staff. A reorganization of the management board was a major result of Amendment XV to the Yugoslav Constitution, adopted in 1969, which relaxed some of the externally imposed restrictions on enterprise governance.[49]

46. Županov, *Samoupravljanje*, pp. 190–200.
47. Duško Bilandžić, "Odnosi izmedju radničkog savjeta i direktora u poduzeću" [The relations between the workers' council and the director in the enterprise], in Gorupić and Brekić, pp. 87–91.
48. Horvat, "Yugoslav Economic Policy," p. 102.
49. Until the adoption of this amendment, each enterprise was required to have a workers' council and a management board, and their composition, method and term of election, and respective competencies were all externally imposed, thereby limiting the freedom of enterprise

(*continued on page 278*)

One possible solution is to make this board an expert body, capable of dealing with technical problems. Another is to abolish it completely and assign management to the director and his staff, subject to workers' council review. Either alternative would result in a division of labor, with workers' councils responsible for self-management and the director and his techno-structure dealing with executive-managerial problems.[50]

How Representative Are Self-Management Organs ?

The workers' council and management board are elected by the membership at large. Is their composition also representative of that membership?

One sophisticated statistical investigation used factor analysis to confirm the hypothesis that workers who participate in self-management organs constitute a different socio-psychological population from those who do not.[51] Men aged 30 through 45 with average or higher education and skill levels comprise a high proportion of these participants; while women, unskilled workers, the very young and very old are underrepresented.[52]

(continued from page 277)

decision-making. Amendment XV removed many of these restrictions and provided that "working people in work organizations shall determine the organs of management of their work organizations, specify their province of work and tenure, and shall lay down conditions for and the mode of their election and removal." Miodrag Trajković, "Yugoslav Self-Management and Constitutional Amendment XV," *Yugoslav Facts and Views* no. 68 (12 February 1970), p. 1.

50. Leman, *Ungeloste Fragen*, p. 36. An alternative proposal was made by Professor Drago Gorupić and the Economic Institute of Zagreb. They suggested that the executive and self-management functions not be separated, but instead a reorganized management board be given both functions. Under their system, the economic units would elect their chiefs on a democratic basis, but based on professional competence, and these unit chiefs, the director, and two of his assistants would form the new management board. Gorupić, "Tendencije u razvoju," pp. 33–38. This proposal would create certain problems, such as how to assure that the unit chiefs have sufficient technical competence as well as sufficient popularity to win an election, and the ambivalent position in which they would find themselves as representatives of the interests of their units and decision makers for the enterprise as a whole.

51. Josip Obradović, "Razlike u faktorskim strukturama nekih sociopsiholoških varijabili kod radnika i radnika-članova organa upravljanja" [Differences in factorial structures of some socio-psychological variables of workers and workers who are members of management organs], *Moderna Organizacija* 1969, no. 8, pp. 593–606.

52. For example, in 1968, workers under the age of 25 constituted only 8.3 percent of the membership of workers' councils, and those over 50 years of age only 5.5 percent. Semiskilled and unskilled workers and white collar workers with little education comprised only 25 percent of the membership of workers' councils and women of all ages and qualifications only 16 percent. These groups were represented in even smaller proportions on management boards. *Statistički Bilten*, no. 559, *Samoupravljanje u Privredi: Izbori i Sastav Organa Samoupravljanja 1968* [Self-management in the economy: elections and composition of self-management organs 1968] (Belgrade, 1969).

A study of management boards in enterprises in Zagreb in 1967 indicated that 25 percent of those elected were "leading persons," 19 percent were engineers and technicians, and 13 percent other administrative personnel. Only 43 percent were "direct producers" who accounted for 70 percent of the membership in these enterprises.[53] These results are reminiscent of the lack of active participation by American workers in their own trade unions.

Representation on workers' councils and management boards is not the only criterion of influence. At least as important is the degree of participation of various groups in the deliberations and decision-making process of these organs. In one enterprise studied during the period 1962–64 executives or well-educated members skipped few meetings of workers' councils, while members with low professional credentials missed them often. Similarly, the ratio of participation in discussion by highly qualified and semiqualified personnel was 39 to 1.[54]

The respective roles of director, technostructure, and various categories of workers in the self-management organs is a particularly crucial question in view of their disparate objective functions, discussed in the preceding section. The groups which do not participate in decision making may well find their "self-managed" enterprise pursuing goals and adopting policies very different from those which they would support. The existence of un-official "strikes" in Yugoslavia evidences such discontent as well as the absence of an institutional mechanism to deal with and channel the resulting conflicts between workers and management.[55]

---

53. Kamušić, p. 93.

54. Zorka Antonijević, "Položaj u procesu proizvodnje kao činilac samoupravljanja" [Position in the production process as a factor in self-management], *Gledišta*, 1968, pp. 179–85, quoted in Gudrun Leman, *Ungeloste Fragen*, p. 23.

55. A Yugoslav sociologist has made the interesting suggestion that in the United States conflict between workers and management can be both functional and dysfunctional, while in Yugoslavia it is always dysfunctional because of institutional deficiencies. Janez Jerovšek, "Konflikt izmedju menedžmenta i radnika u SAD i Jugoslaviji" [Conflict between management and workers in the United States and Yugoslavia], *Moderna Organizacija* 1968, no. 1, pp. 97–104. The number of strikes registered by the Federal Ministry of Interior rose from 106 in 1961 to a high of 291 in 1964 and then fell to 161 in 1966. Gudrun Leman, *Ungeloste Fragen*, p. 101. A recent study analyzed 513 strikes involving 73,000 people during the period 1966 to 1969. Over 60 percent of the strikes involved fewer than 100 workers, and only 11 percent involved over 300 workers. Similarly, 77 percent of the strikes lasted one day or less and only 5 percent lasted more than 4 days. Neca Jovanov, "Prilog razmatranju pojave štrajka u našem društvu" [A contribution to the study of the phenomenon of the strike in our society], *Naše Teme* 1970, no. 2, pp. 319–20. The strikes were generally over income distribution in the enterprise or other intraorganizational issues and workers conducted the strikes either against management or against "bureaucratic workers' councils." Leman, *Ungeloste Fragen*, p. 100.

Worker Attitudes Toward Self-Management

What kind of decision-making power do the workers really want?

A survey of two Slovenian enterprises showed that members were most interested in having some influence over working conditions, income distribution, and the hiring and firing of immediate superiors and workers in their own economic unit. A smaller proportion were concerned with production and sales policies and the selection of executives at the enterprise level. In almost all cases, they wanted an opportunity to present their views, rather than power to make the actual decision.[56]

In another survey members were asked to rank various conditions of employment in terms of their motivational importance. Participation in self-management was uniformly placed at the bottom of the list after such items as: interesting work, high earnings and promotional possibilities, congenial superiors and coworkers. Arzenšek points out that this result may imply that the workers already have considerable decision-making power, or, alternatively, that they do not want such power or consider it an unrealistic goal. Since the actual distribution of power seems to be oligarchic, he rejects the first explanation.[57] Other studies support the conclusion that workers believe the director and his professional staff should carry the greatest responsibility for the operation and development of the enterprise.[58]

It appears further that the desire of workers for decision-making power may have been decreasing and the demand for higher personal incomes increasing. Executive personnel, on the other hand, have become more insistent on obtaining greater legitimate power and professional autonomy.

56. Arzenšek, p. 560.
Similar results were reported in a survey of construction enterprises, where most respondents indicated they were interested in obtaining information and reviewing the decisions, but a much smaller number (and virtually none of the unskilled workers) wanted to make the actual decision. Možina, pp. 715–16.
57. Vladimir Arzenšek, "Samoupravljanje kao motiv i socijalna vrednost" [Self-management as a motive and social value], *Moderna Organizacija* 1969, no. 1, pp. 24–25. Arzenšek's conclusions are questioned by Mitja Kamušić, "Odjeci" [Echoes], *Moderna Organizacija* 1969, no. 8, pp. 628–29, who maintains that the other desires were even less well satisfied than the desire for self-management. Kamušić also questions the conclusions of Arzenšek, Županov and others about the oligarchic nature of the power distribution. Since the executives are democratically elected, he argues, the fact that they have the most power does not prove the absence of democracy.
58. For example, in a survey covering 2,109 workers in 15 enterprises, 69 percent of the respondents were willing to rely on the director and his professional staff for this purpose, 20 percent chose the workers' council or management board, 4 percent chose the members of the enterprise, and less than one percent selected the socio-political officials. "Troje tabela iz ankete o odgovornosti nosilaca samoupravnih funkcija u radnim organizacijama" [Three tables from a survey of the responsibility of the carriers of self-management functions in working organizations], *Moderna Organizacija* 1969, no. 1, p. 76.

Thus, the evolving desires of these two groups may be complementary and represent a movement from the existing normative models of self-management toward more conventional models of power distribution in enterprises.[59]

This leads us to a final set of questions about the locus of control. Are we observing the breakdown of the ideal system of self-management and a return to the division of labor between (producing) workers and (decision-making) managers which we find in virtually all other systems? Or are we simply witnessing an augmented self-managed system in which the workers have delegated some of their primal power to the director and his technical colleagues? We, of course, cannot supply a definitive answer, but we would guess that the Yugoslavs are trying to preserve the social, ethical and political values of self-management while improving its organizational efficiency.

VI. FINAL REMARKS

In this brief section we shall discuss two cultural and socio-political legacies which helped shape the Yugoslav experience with self-management—the norm of egalitarianism and the nationality problem. It is beyond the scope of this paper to explore fully the relationships between the norm of egalitarianism, the nationality problem and self-management, and we shall merely suggest a few of the more striking implications.

Norm of Egalitarianism

The "norm of egalitarianism" is an important cultural legacy, based on the peasant origin of many Yugoslavs and the egalitarian ethos of the communal organization in the traditional Yugoslav village.[60] Many of the systemic variables we have discussed in our paper represent an attempt to support this key social norm which enters as an important argument into the objective functions of most Yugoslavs. Consequent negative effects on efficiency must be weighed against the positive utility of egalitarianism to much of the Yugoslav population.

59. Veljko Rus, "Status stručnog i rukovodečeg kadra s obzirom na komuniciranje, moć i odgovornost" [The status of professional and executive personnel with respect to communication, power, and responsibility], *Moderna Organizacija* 1968, no. 5, p. 387.

60. Darinka Tadić and Josip Županov, "Ekonomske aspiracije i društvena norma egalitarnosti" [Economic aspirations and the social norm of egalitarianism], *Sociologija* 1969, no. 2, reprinted in Županov, *Samoupravljanje*, pp. 271–99. This norm of egalitarianism has been reported by many other observers of the Yugoslav scene; e.g. Vanek, as well as S. J. Rawin, "Social Values and the Managerial Structure: The Case of Yugoslavia and Poland," unpublished manuscript. Rawin's whole analysis of the differences between the Yugoslav and Polish experiences with managerial structures rests on the egalitarian nature of Yugoslav society and the elitist nature of Polish society.

In analyzing the norm of egalitarianism, Županov distinguishes between its applicability in issues concerning power distribution and income distribution. A democratic distribution of power and prestige is stressed by both official pronouncements and popular opinion although, as we have seen, it is hardly achieved in practice. The official policy and actual practice regarding income is to base payments on labor contribution; the majority of citizens, on the other hand, really believe in payment according to need.[61] The former coincides with Marx's view of socialist distribution and the latter with his definition of communism.

Inequalities in income distribution within and among enterprises are limited by the fear of external social sanctions (which have, at times, been applied).[62] The egalitarian norm also dampens the aspirations of workers for attaining very high incomes.[63] This is not to say that income differences between people with similar qualifications are absent in Yugoslavia. In fact, they are extremely great in some places, partially due to low labor mobility stemming from a priori restrictions. However, these differences are considered unfair and a major blemish on the self-management system.

We have observed earlier a positive correlation between the level of personal income in an economic sector and the proportion of residual revenues allocated to investment. It may be that the more profitable enterprises are prevented from distributing all their high incomes to their members by the likelihood of socio-political disapproval. While reducing current inequalities in personal incomes of workers, this practice will lead to ever-increasing future inequalities as these investments bear their fruits.

The Nationality Problem

Yugoslavia is characterized by tremendous regional differences in political history, cultural allegiance, religion, and economic development. It is likely

61. A survey of members of 10 enterprises illustrates this ambivalent attitude toward income distribution. When asked whether they were in favor of the "equal stomachs doctrine" (the unskilled worker's stomach is no smaller than the director's, so both should have the same income), a large majority, except for workers with the lowest qualifications, came out against this doctrine. However, all groups, except executives, felt that income differentials should be kept as small as possible. In choosing a range between minimum and maximum incomes, the great majority chose the narrowest one. Josip Županov, "Egalitarizam i industrijalizm" [Egalitarianism and industrialism], *Naše Teme* 1970, no. 2, pp. 259–62.

62. Županov, *Samoupravljanje*, pp. 70–71. At the end of 1967, the Yugoslav government placed administrative limits on the personal incomes of workers in the electric power industry, banks, foreign trade organizations, and others, because they were considerably higher than in other branches. The government actions were only the last step, following attacks in the media and general public opposition to such inequalities.

63. Tadić and Županov report on an interesting survey comparing actual and aspirational earnings, which shows that the higher the actual earnings the smaller is the proportionate difference between them and the aspirational earnings (p. 279).

that the nationality problem[64] played a significant role in the establishment of self-management. The various nationalities that had felt themselves to be under Serbian domination welcomed the move toward local autonomy implied by self-management. Furthermore, the political tug of war among the regions for investment funds during the late forties and early fifties had led to a disillusionment with central planning and a willingness to experiment with the more decentralized self-management system. The purge of nationalist elements in Croatia in 1971–72 shows the continued seriousness of this problem.

The nationality problem and the attendant regional parochialism do not directly affect the operation of the open subsystem, the enterprise. They do, however, pose significant difficulties for the larger closed system of the national economy. They may interfere with labor and capital mobility, thereby exacerbating two serious deficiencies of self-management (or, alternatively, absolving self-management from responsibility for the immobilities which would have existed anyway). In addition, they limit the potential for regional diversification in certain sectors (such as wholesale trade) where such diversification might be economically desirable.

These consequences—both positive and negative—for self-management would not exist in most other East European countries, since their populations are much more homogeneous than Yugoslavia's.

Relations Between the Open and Closed Systems

The choices of system options for the open model and the closed model in which it is imbedded are interdependent. Thus, the imposition of self-management at the enterprise level imposes severe restrictions on the permissible decision process at the national level.

Self-management, to be meaningful, requires a significant degree of autonomy for the enterprise. This immediately eliminates the possibility of Soviet-type or cybernetic central planning for the whole economy. The permissible set includes various decentralized mechanisms for coordinating enterprise decisions, e.g. the market, bargaining, or negotiation. Some Yugoslav and foreign experts feel that only a pure market system for the closed model is compatible while others argue that planned market systems (such as French indicative planning or the "visible hand" in Yugoslavia in the 1950s)[65] can coexist with self-management.

64. An excellent discussion of the nationality problem may be found in Richard V. Burks, "Nationalism and Communism in Yugoslavia: An Attempt at Synthesis," unpublished manuscript.

65. The reasons for the demise of this type of planned market system and the roles played in it by self-management and the "nationality problem" are discussed in Egon Neuberger, "The Yugoslav Visible Hand: Why Is It No More?" to appear in *The Economics of the Communist World*, ed. Janet G. Chapman and Shun-hsin Chou; Stony Brook Working Paper no. 23, December 1970; International Development Research Center, Working Paper no. 3, April 1971.

We would venture a guess that these systemic restrictions in the economic sphere, plus the danger that democracy in the enterprise may create pressures for democracy in the national political arena, have made self-management a bête noire of Soviet leaders. It comes as no surprise that Czechoslovak reformers attempted to introduce worker self-management as one of their last acts, only to have it annulled by Soviet orders. Thus, whatever the merits of self-management as an economic system—and this is still a wide-open question—it is potentially an excellent system in the socio-political sphere, if human dignity, democracy, and eliminating alienation are the goals.[66] However, so long as Soviet influence is significant, the introduction of real self-management will occur in Eastern Europe "when the shrimps learn to whistle."

66. This is by no means a purely East European problem. As we academics are all aware, it is a major current problem in universities in most of the world. It is even a problem in American industry. An executive of the Ford Motor Company, hardly a socialist enterprise, said of young secretaries in his department: "They want to participate. It's not so much what they make, if they don't feel they are participating." *New York Times*, 8 August 1970, p. 10.

8

The Banking System and the Investment Behavior of the Yugoslav Firm

SVETOZAR PEJOVICH

The premise of this paper is that a powerful and possibly the most effective approach to the analysis of various economic systems and countries should be based on the following simple analytical framework : (1) economics studies the behavior of people in resolving conflicts of interest that arise because of one inevitable fact—scarcity; (2) a valid core of economic theory *does* exist and is applicable to all economic systems and countries; and (3) the scope and content of property rights structures affect the way people behave in a world of scarcity. Thus, a generalization of the standard economic theory of production and exchange, using the property rights approach, could explain a number of activities which take place outside the classical market framework, and serve a useful purpose in the area of comparative economic studies.

In the context of this paper, property rights are defined as the behavioral relations *among men which arise from the existence, and pertain to the use, of things*. They specify the norms of behavior with respect to things which each and every person in his daily interaction with other persons must observe. The prevailing system of property rights in the community is then the sum of economic and social relations with respect to scarce resources in which individual members stand to each other. At this point we only mention the often-forgotten fact that both trade and production are contractual arrangements, not so much to exchange goods and services, but to exchange bundles of property rights to do things with those goods and services. The value of goods that are exchanged and terms of trade then depend on the bundle of property rights in things that are exchanged.[1] For example, the value of a house to me will increase and I will pay more for it if the bundle of

A number of analytical concepts discussed in sections III and IV were developed jointly by Professor E. Furubotn and the author and published in various papers. Professor M. Lovenstein read the entire manuscript and his comments were extremely helpful. The financial assistance of the Earhart Foundation and the National Science Foundation is also gratefully acknowledged.

1. H. Demsetz, "Towards a Theory of Property Rights," *American Economic Review* 57 (May 1965): 247–59, and R. McKean, "Products Liability: Implications of Some Changing Property Rights," *Quarterly Journal of Economics* 84 (November 1970): 611–26.

property rights I acquire contains the right to exclude gasoline stations, chemical plants, etc. from the immediate area.

It follows that the possession of various property rights in resources enters into the utility function of individuals. Thus, a change in the system of property relations affects the way people behave and, through this effect on their behavior, property rights assignments affect the allocation of resources, composition of output, distribution of income, etc. To quote Alchian: "In essence, economics is the study of property rights over scarce resources. . . . The allocation of scarce resources in a society is the assignment of rights to uses of resources . . . for the question of economics, or of how prices should be determined, is the question of how property rights should be defined and exchanged, and on what terms."[2]

The right of ownership (private and state) of an asset consists of the right to use it, to change its form and substance, and to transfer all (e.g. sell) or some (e.g. rent) rights in that asset to others. However, even though this definition suggests that the right of ownership is an *exclusive* right, it is not— and could hardly be expected to be—an *unrestricted* right. The right of ownership is an *exclusive* right in that it is limited *only* by those restrictions which are explicitly stated in the law. It is important to recognize that the attenuation of private (or state) property rights in an asset by various restrictive measures affects the owner's expectations about things he can do with that asset, the asset's value to the owner, to others, and, consequently, the terms of trade. For this reason we shall use the term "attenuation" to signify the degree of restriction on the owner's rights to change the form or substance of an asset and to transfer all right in it to others at a mutually agreed-upon price.

Since a comprehensive, all-inclusive discussion of the Yugoslav economy cannot and perhaps should not be attempted in a single study, the analysis in this paper will be limited to (1) the behavior of the Yugoslav firm, (2) the role of the banking system, and (3) the rate of investment determination. The paper begins with a brief discussion of the history of economic changes in Yugoslavia and some basic institutional arrangements in that country. Then, in section II, consideration is given to the variables that determine the macrorate of investment. An analysis of the investment, output and employment behavior of the firm in Yugoslavia is presented in section III. Section IV deals with the role of the banking system in the Yugoslav economy.

I. GENERAL BACKGROUND

The organization of the Yugoslav economy during the period of administrative planning (1946–52) was quite similar to that of the Soviet economic

2. A. Alchian, *Pricing and Society*, Occasional Paper No. 17 (London: Institute of Economic Affairs, 1967), p. 6.

system. The state determined production quotas for the economy as a whole, for each industry, and for each firm. All product and factor prices (with some insignificant exceptions) were set administratively. Each firm's revenue and production expenses were budgeted (planned) in advance by the state authorities. The government allocated new capital goods to enterprises, transferred the existing ones from one firm to another, and determined the use of depreciation funds.

The achievements of the policy of administrative planning were extremely disappointing, and in the years 1950–52 the Yugoslav economy actually retrogressed.[3] In addition to the damaging effects of the Cominform blockade, the two most frequently mentioned reasons for the poor showing of the economy are (1) the lack of information at the center, and (2) the tendency toward bureaucratic transformation of the Yugoslav society.

The basic objective of the Yugoslav government during the period of partial decentralization (1952–64) was to create a workable economic system consistent with the following general conditions: (1) public ownership of the nonhuman means of production; (2) organization of production activity in accordance with the overall economic plan; (3) relaxation of direct administrative controls over firms; and (4) maintenance of a strong positive correlation between workers' productivity and their earnings.[4]

On the macrolevel, the annual economic plan was supposed to determine the minimum utilization of capacity in each industry, the size and distribution of the General Investment Fund,[5] the aggregate wage fund, the rate of accumulation to be achieved by each industry, and the allocation of funds to be paid into and distributed from the state budgets. The new system of planning left it up to the individual firms to determine the quality and quantity of their respective outputs.[6]

To guide economic activities at the microlevel, the Yugoslav government introduced some far-reaching institutional changes. It proclaimed that the right of management should be in the hands of the employees of each firm.[7] The organizational structure was specified: the managing organs of the

3. The social product (in 1956 prices) fell from 1,391 billion dinars in 1949 to 1,258 and 1,165 billion dinars in 1950 and 1952, respectively. See S. Pejovich, *The Market-Planned Economy of Yugoslavia* (Minneapolis: University of Minnesota Press, 1966), chapter 3.

4. M. Vujosević, "Karakteristike Privrednog Sistema" [The characteristics of the Yugoslav economic system], in *Privredni Sistem i Ekonomska Politika Jugoslavije* [The Yugoslav economic system and economic policy] (Belgrade: Rad, 1962), p. 8.

5. The size of the General Investment Fund was determined every year by the plan. Sources of this fund were interest on the value of fixed and working capital held by firms, a percentage of the profit tax, etc.

6. See *Službeni List* [Official Bulletin], 30 December 1951.

7. See *Službeni List*, 5 July 1950.

firm would be the Workers' Council, elected by the firm's employees; The Executive board, elected by the Workers' Council; and the director, elected by a commission appointed by the government and the Workers' Council.

In order to implement the principle of self-management, the state had to link the employees' self-interest to the efficient functioning of their respective firms. That was done by a change in the content of property rights in both the means of production and the income derived from capital goods.

The Law on Management of Fixed Capital by Enterprises[8] transferred some specific property rights in the means of production from the state to the firm. This law gave the Workers' Council the *right of use* over the means of production held by the firm. The firm was allowed to sell its fixed assets to other firms, to buy capital goods from other firms (the purchase agreement gives the buying firm the right of use and not the right of ownership), and to produce the means of production for its own use. On the other hand, the firm had to maintain the book value of its assets if they were diminished by depreciation or other means; for example, if the firm sold assets for less than their book value the difference had to be deducted from the firm's profit and reinvested. The firm was also required to pay interest to the state on the value of its capital. In addition to asserting the state's ownership rights, the purpose of this interest payment was to induce the firm to use capital goods efficiently, and to provide funds for the General Investment Fund. In short, the firm obtained the freedom to control both the composition and the rate of growth of its physical assets.

Moreover, the collective was granted the right of ownership in the firm's net income (profit) which tied the workers' incomes to the firm's profit. However, the Law on Distribution of Total Revenue of Firms,[9] as well as some other legal and administrative acts of the Yugoslav government, regulated the distribution of net profits between the Wage Fund and the Business Fund[10] of the firm. In other words, the government restricted the collective's right of ownership in the firm's profit.

The 1961 scheme of revenue distribution was of special interest because it ruled that wages were to be paid from the profit residual. The scheme of revenue distribution after 1961 is summarized in figure 8.1.

The solution of the interaction of politically administered macromeasures and market-oriented microdecisions was entrusted to the banking system.

8. *Službeni List*, 26 December 1953.
9. *Službeni List*, 27 December 1953.
10. Retained profits are allocated to the Business Fund, Collective Consumption Fund and Reserve Fund. For simplicity we assume throughout this paper that all retained earnings are allocated to the Business Fund and used for investment.

Fig. 8.1.   Distribution of total revenue of the Yugoslav firm before 1965.

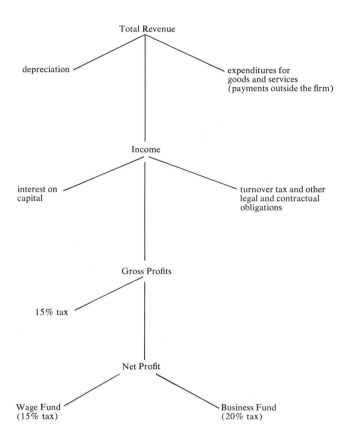

Source: Službeni List (Official Bulletin), 2 March 1961 and 12 April 1961.

The government expected the banks to distribute administratively-determined investment funds within each industry in accordance with the criterion of profitability. The result was the growing importance of monetary institutions in Yugoslavia.

The period of partial decentralization saw the Yugoslav economy grow at a respectable real rate of over 8 percent.[11] Nevertheless, the economy was plagued by a number of problems such as inflation of about 6 percent per

11. S. Pejovich, p. 59.

annum,[12] a relatively high rate of unemployment,[13] a balance of payments deficit,[14] and the rise of "political factories."

To deal with these and similar problems the Federal Assembly adopted "The Resolution on the Basic Guidelines for Further Development of the Economic System" in 1964.[15] This resolution and the subsequent legal acts have since been referred to as the 1965 reform. The basic objective of the 1965 reform was to create an improved institutional environment that would allow more scope for individual initiative and promote economic efficiency.

At the macrolevel the Yugoslav government abolished the General Investment Fund, and transferred to the banking system the responsibility for controlling both the pattern and rate of investment activity. Each year, the Federal Assembly issues a resolution on the aims of monetary and credit policy. The National Bank of Yugoslavia then has the responsibility of regulating credit policy in accordance with the objectives stated in the Assembly document.[16] Moreover, the 1965 reform allowed the banks to open branches in all parts of Yugoslavia, and permitted depositors and borrowers to choose a bank in accordance with their own judgment of the economic advantage present.[17] Finally, the incomes of bank employees, excluding only those employed by the National Bank, were linked to the profits earned by their respective banks.[18] These changes suggest that the allocation of investable funds in postreform Yugoslavia is likely to be governed, at least to a considerable extent, by economic criteria.[19]

The abolition of official guidelines for the allocation of profit represents a major change at the microlevel. The Yugoslav firm is now allegedly free to determine the allocation of its profits between the Wage Fund and the Business Fund. The scheme of revenue distribution after 1965 is summarized in figure 8.2.

The system of administrative planning from the center seems to have come to an end in Yugoslavia in the late 1960s. In spite of the continued presence

12. M. Vucković, "Development of Money and Banking Systems of Yugoslavia," *Journal of Political Economy* 71, no. 4 (August 1963): 368; S. Pejovich, "The Problem of Rising Prices in a Planned Economy," *Western Economic Journal* 3, no. 3 (September 1965): 301–6.

13. S. Pejovich, *Market-Planned Economy*, p. 76.

14. *Yugoslavia Between the Seventh and Eighth Congress of the League of Communists of Yugoslavia* (Belgrade: Federal Institute of Statistics, 1964), pp. 59–60.

15. For the English text of this resolution see *Yugoslav Survey*, April–June 1964.

16. *Credit and Banking System of Yugoslavia* (Belgrade: Association of Banks of Yugoslavia, 1968), p. 5.

17. See E. Furubotn and S. Pejovich, "The Role of the Banking System in Yugoslav Economic Planning, 1946–1969," *Revue Internationale D'Historie de la Banque* 4 (May 1971): 83.

18. *Credit and Banking System of Yugoslavia*, p. 20.

19. Some vestiges of administrative control of the economy are still present in Yugoslavia, such as administrative investments in less developed areas, price controls, various informal channels of administrative interference, etc.

Fig. 8.2.   Distribution of total revenue of the Yugoslav firm after 1965.

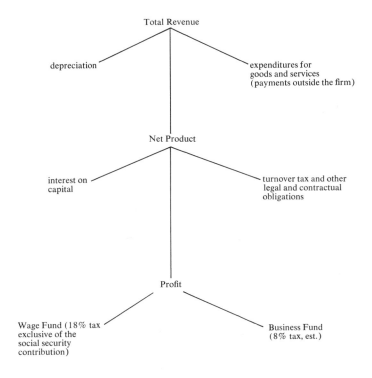

Source: Nove Mere za Sprovodjenje Privredne Reforme [New measures for the implementation of economic reforms] (Belgrade: Književne Novine, 1968).

of some vestiges of administrative planning, such as the budgetary allocation of investment funds to less developed regions, administrative price
controls, and relatively strict governmental control over foreign trade, the
allocation as well as utilization of scarce resources in Yugoslavia today
appears reasonably free from direct administrative interferences. In short,
the system of planning in Yugoslavia has shifted from *current operational
plans* to long-range development plans which, in Yugoslavia as well as anywhere else, are no more than a hazy vision of things it would be nice to have;
something for the government to shoot at and for the planners to shout
about. A result of this slow, uneven, and yet persistent substitution of
economic criteria for administrative measures has been the growing importance of monetary and fiscal policies in Yugoslavia.

The history of economic changes in Yugoslavia suggests a constant search for a set of laws and institutions which would induce microunits to carry out the state's macroobjectives willingly and with efficient use of the available resources in an environment where capital goods cannot be privately owned.[20] It follows that understanding the working and performance of the Yugoslav economy requires a full comprehension of the effects which some key institutions are expected to have on the pattern of behavior of microunits. The most significant features of the Yugoslav economy today are: (1) the growing importance of the banking system as a major supplier of investment funds and the primary source of short-term credits; (2) the worker's right of ownership in the earnings of his firm; and (3) the state's (attenuated) right of ownership in capital goods.

II. The Macrorate of Investment

The purpose of this section is to discuss some important factors and relationships that are likely to contribute to a difference in the rate of income *voluntarily* diverted to gross investment in a private property community and in a Yugoslav-type economy. The investment model used in this section was originally developed by Clower[21] and Witte,[22] and subsequently expanded by this author[23] to incorporate the effects of four different types of property rights assignments on the community's choice between present consumption and investment.

Briefly, the properties of the model are as follows: Let the line SS in figure 8.3a represent the stock of capital goods in the community. The demand curves DD relate the demand for capital goods to hold to the price of capital. The latter is determined in the capital market where the rate of interest is equated to the percentage return from the capital stock. Conventionally, the price of capital is defined as the present value of the flow of expected net returns discounted at the relevant rate of interest ($r_0 < r_1$).

Should the community's time preference change in favor of current income the price of both the stock of physical assets and bonds would fall and the rate of return would rise. The demand curve for capital goods to hold would then shift downward (from $D_0 D_0$ to $D_1 D_1$) and the rate of interest implicit

20. The Yugoslav citizen can own and operate some private ventures such as taxi businesses, small restaurants, artisan shops, etc. However, the nature and extent of his right of ownership in the means of production in contemporary Yugoslavia are still quite limited.

21. R. Clower, "An Investigation into the Dynamics of Investment," *American Economic Review* 44 (March 1954): 64–81.

22. J. Witte, "The Microfoundations of the Social Investment Function," *Journal of Political Economy* 71 (October 1963): 441–56

23. S. Pejovich, "Towards a General Theory of Property Rights," *Zeitschrift fur National-okonomie* 31 (spring 1971).

Fig. 8.3.   Short-run equilibrium in the capital market

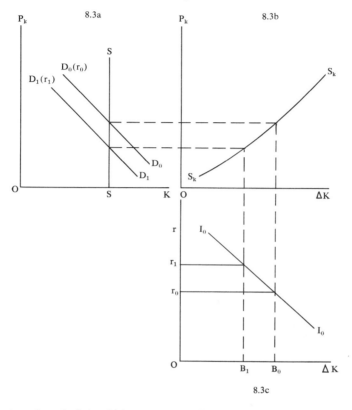

in the price of capital would increase. In other words, all the various rates of interest would be brought into equality by switching activity among markets.

The schedule $S_k S_k$ in figure 8.3b is the supply curve of *additional* capital goods.[24] Assuming a competitive environment, this schedule relates the rate of production of new capital goods to each given price of capital on the vertical axis. Since the purpose of our discussion here is primarily to draw some inferences about various comparative situations we can unrealistically but conveniently simplify the exposition by assuming that the flow of new capital goods adds such a small quantity to the stock of capital that the rate of return is unaffected. That is, we assume that the supply of new capital can be sold at the going price.

Figure 8.3c relates the output of new capital goods (gross investment) to the rate of interest. The investment schedule $I_0 I_0$ is a market equilibrium curve and not a demand curve for investment; the rate of interest and the

24. The scales on the horizontal axes in figures 8.3a and 8.3b are different.

marginal efficiency of investment are equal at each given point on the schedule $I_0 I_0$.

The rate of interest r_0 is the equilibrium rate of interest because it brings into equality, through switching activity among the various markets, the rate of net productivity of investment, the community's valuation of future income relative to current consumption, the return on monetary assets (bonds, loans, etc.), and the interest rate implicit in the relative prices of capital goods. Accordingly, saving and investment in the schedule sense are equated by the lending-borrowing market, the capital goods market, and production-activity market.

Let us now apply this model to the investment determination in Yugoslavia. The set of choices which are available to those Yugoslavs who are not employed by business firms is generally limited to (1) savings deposits, and (2) investment in human capital.[25] The rate of accumulation of nonhuman wealth by this group can then be taken as perfectly inelastic *above* the regulated rate of interest paid on savings accounts. The employees of a Yugoslav firm, on the other hand, can increase their wealth by earmarking a part of the enterprise's profit for investment in additional physical assets. Their incentives to invest in the physical assets of the firm are subject to the following constraints: (1) when a worker leaves the firm, he loses all his claims to the future earnings of that firm despite the fact that his earlier sacrifice of current consumption helped the firm to finance the enlarged stock of capital; (2) the workers' decision to accept lower current wages (i.e. to save by investing in physical assets) is irreversible. Given the firm's legal obligation to maintain indefinitely the value of its capital stock, the employees cannot recover the market value of their original investment at some later date.

It follows that those Yugoslavs who are employed by business firms have two major wealth-increasing alternatives: investment in physical assets by retained profits, and investment in owned assets such as savings accounts, human capital, cash, etc. These two investment alternatives can be compared, and a common denominator for their comparison will be discussed later. At this time, it should suffice to assert that one important behavioral implication of the prevailing property relations with respect to physical assets in Yugoslavia must clearly be a shortened time horizon of the employees (which obviously depends on the expected length of their employment by *that* firm) and consequently a higher time preference rate than that which would prevail if the workers were granted the right of ownership over the assets acquired by the firm during the period of their employment. Thus, the logic of economics suggests that a change in the content of property rights in capital goods from the right of private ownership to the Yugoslav variant of attenuated state ownership should shift the demand curve for capital goods downward to, say, $D_1 D_1$ in figure 8.3a and reduce the rate of

25. See n. 20.

income diverted to gross investment. It is important to note that the curve D_1D_1 is the curve D_0D_0 *adjusted* for the behavioral effects of a change in property rights structures, all other things remaining the same.

The new equilibrium rate of interest r_1 clearly brings into equality the rate of net productivity of investment and the interest rate implicit in the relative prices of capital goods. It also brings into equality with those rates the community's valuation of current consumption relative to future income because: (1) the saving schedule of those who are not employed by business firms is perfectly inelastic above the rate of interest paid on savings accounts; and (2) the adjustment in the firm's employees' valuation of current consumption relative to future income from investment in capital goods (see figure 8.6) shows that each given rate of savings requires a higher rate of interest. Thus, the community's savings schedule shifts upward and, in the process, it brings the community's valuation of present consumption relative to future income into equality with other rates.

The discussion of the behavioral effects of the prevailing property-rights structures in Yugoslavia on the rate of investment suggests that the *voluntary* allocation of resources between present and future consumption tends to favor current consumption relative to what it would be if capital goods were privately owned, other things in the community remaining the same. It follows that better understanding of the investment problem in Yugoslavia requires an analysis of the behavior of Yugoslav firms and the role of the banking system in that country.

III. The Investment Behavior of the Yugoslav Firm

The 1965 economic reform supposedly abolished administrative guidelines for the distribution of profits between the Wage Fund and the Business Fund. It would, of course, make little sense for the government to do away with guidelines for the division of profit unless it had some confidence that the typical Yugoslav firm would continue to distribute some of its profits to the Business Fund. That is precisely what firms have done: they have continued to allocate some of their earnings to the Business Fund. This phenomenon of continued self-financing of investment activity in Yugoslavia raises three related questions: (1) Why is the Yugoslav firm willing to allocate part of its profit to the Business Fund when according to the strict logic of the wage-maximization hypothesis the collective should opt for zero net investment from its own sources?[26] (2) What are the factors which determine the

26. There is a lack of consensus on the behavioral goal of the socialist firm. See E. Domar, "The Soviet Collective Firm," *American Economic Review* 56 (September 1966); P. Pelikan and R. Kocanda, "The Socialist Enterprise as a Participant in the Market," *Czechoslovak Economic Papers*, 1967, no. 9; J. Vanek, *Labor-Managed Market Economies* (Ithaca, N.Y.: Cornell University Press, 1970); and B. Ward, "The Firm in Illyria: Market Syndicalism," *American Economic Review* 48 (September 1958).

allocation of the firm's profit between the Wage Fund (W) and the Business Fund (B)? And (3) what are the effects of profit allocation between W and B on the firm's employment and output policies?

Let us consider a hypothetical firm in Yugoslavia which, assuming that information is available at zero cost, faces the situation depicted in figure 8.4.[27] If the object of the collective is to maximize the income per worker (i.e. $B = 0$), the equilibrium labor input will be L_1, while the output will then be determined by the firm's production function. If the collective allocates I_0 to the Business Fund the optimal employment will change to L_2.

Fig. 8.4. Allocation of profit and the level of employment

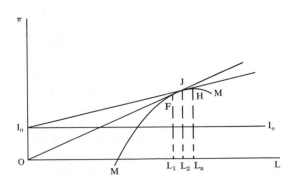

If the objective is to maximize the allocation to the Business Fund ($W = 0$ is clearly the limiting case) the equilibrium labor input will be L_n. Assuming that tradeoffs between the Wage Fund and the Business Fund can proceed *continuously*, the effective area of employment, investment and output choices (given the firm's production function) is given by the *FJH* segment of the firm's profit function. In the absence of direct outside interference, the firm's ultimate decision will depend on the pattern of behavior of both the firm's director and the working collective.

The director. The director of the firm in Yugoslavia occupies a middle ground between the firm's employees and the government. On the one hand, his immediate job security as well as his current income depend on his popularity with the Workers' Council and the size of the Wage Fund. On the other hand, the director's long-term career is likely to be influenced by the degree to which his management of the firm contributes to the realization of what the state defines as national goals. Since a high rate of economic growth is certainly one of the most important economic objectives of the Yugoslav

27. For a more comprehensive analysis see E. Furubotn and S. Pejovich, "Property Rights and the Behavior of the Firm in a Socialist State," *Zeitschrift fur Nationalokonomie* 30 (winter 1970). It is also assumed that the Yugoslav firm can sell all it wants to sell at the going price.

government, the picture of his firm as a vigorous and growing firm must seem essential to the director.[28] These conflicting motivations of the director can then be expressed by a simple preference function:

$$U = f(w, B)$$

where the investment magnitude B is taken as a proxy for the long-term advantages and w is the average wage W/L. These alternatives are substitutable and a set of indifference curves $(U_1, U_2, \ldots, U_n)$ can be used to explain the director's choice of the allocation of profit between W and B.

The director is, in addition to routine management, responsible for the formulation of the set of opportunity choices which are available to the firm as well as for the development (search) of new alternatives. The members of the Workers' Council have neither the resources nor the skill necessary to engage in doing the director's job. After all, that is the job for an expert, and the director is the Council's expert. Thus, the director's job in Yugoslavia is to formulate the alternatives and develop new ideas, while the Workers' Council's job is to make the final choices for the firm, to "encourage" the director to seek new ideas, and to fire him if the Workers' Council decides that the director has failed to do his job. To stress the role of the Yugoslav director is not to describe a "desired" substitution of power between the Workers' Council and its director. They have two different tasks to perform. Yet, the director's evaluations (and method of presentation) of the available alternatives must have some considerable influence on the Workers' Council policy decisions.

Returning to our hypothetical firm, the position of segment FJH in figure 8.4 limits the relevant area of discretion to L_1–L_n employment levels and the associated volumes of profit and output. Let us consider only three possible alternatives, L_1, L_2, and L_n. If total profit in each case is allocated wholly to the Wage Fund, the corresponding *average* wage rates w_1, w_2, and w_n can be calculated and located on the vertical axis in figure 8.5. Conversely, if total profit is allocated wholly to the Business Fund, B_1, B_2, and B_n can be located on the horizontal axis. The lines w_1B_1, w_2B_2, and w_nB_n represent the possible tradeoffs between the *average* wage rates and the total allocation to the Business Fund at each given level of employment, given the background data.

It follows that the average wage falls as the allocation to the Business Fund is increased. However, a point of considerable importance is that *the rate of decline in the average wage rate can be reduced as the employment level is changed* (along the curve w_1B_n in figure 8.5).

---

28. This point was frequently mentioned during the author's visit to Yugoslavia in the summer of 1970.

How far the director can go in inducing the collective to depart from the pure wage maximization policy w_1 is an empirical question. Let us assume that he sees w^* and B^* as the minimum average wage and the minimum retained profits that will be acceptable to both the collective and outside authorities, respectively. Then, given the constraints w^*w^*, B^*B^*, and $w_1 B_n$ and his preference map (U_1, U_2, U_3), the director will try to induce the Workers' Council to select a point such as D in figure 8.5. That solution would yield the average wage rate w_d, the rate of investment B_d and, via the production function, the firm's output.

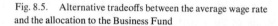

Fig. 8.5.   Alternative tradeoffs between the average wage rate
and the allocation to the Business Fund

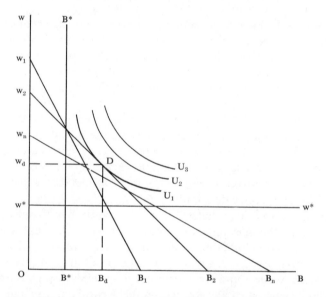

The workers. The employees of the Yugoslav firm have two major wealth-increasing alternatives: *joint* investment in physical assets of the firm through retained profits, and *individual* investment in other assets. In Yugoslavia, those individual investment alternatives are restricted to monetary assets, human capital, and some limited types of physical assets such as small real estate holdings, taxis, artisan shops, jewelry, etc., where the right of ownership does not necessarily and obviously violate the principle of workers' management of business establishments. We shall take the rate of interest on savings accounts to represent the highest return available to the employees from taking the entire profit π^o out as wages and investing it individually.[29]

29. The problem of rising prices in Yugoslavia tends to reduce the importance of savings relative to other alternatives such as investment in land, gold, foreign currency, etc.

To explicitly consider other alternatives would only complicate the analysis without affecting the basic analytic argument which rests on the existence of two fundamentally different types of wealth-increasing alternatives in Yugoslavia. The analysis will also abstract from the effects of the differences in risk level and liquidity.

Let us assume that the employees of our firm have identical time preferences as well as a common time horizon (the expected length of employment by that firm). Given a time horizon n, the employee who saves one dollar out of his current wages acquires, in effect, a stream of income equal to

$$a = \frac{i_1(1 + i_1)^n}{(1 + i_1)^n - 1} \tag{8.1}$$

where i_1 is the rate of interest on savings accounts. The employee will then prefer to take a reduction in his current pay so that the firm can purchase new capital goods only if he can expect to receive over a period of n years, through higher wages, a stream of income at least equal to a. Given the firm's obligation to maintain the value of fixed assets indefinitely the *rate* of return from investment in fixed assets which would generate the stream of income equal to a is

$$r_1 = \frac{i_1(1 + i_1)^n}{(1 + i_1)^n - 1}. \tag{8.2}$$

For example, if $n = 10$ years and $i_1 = 10$ percent, the annual return from investment in physical assets which would just be equal to the annuity from saving one dinar is 16 para (that is, the present value of 16 para a year for 10 years discounted at 10 percent is about one dinar). Given the firm's obligation to maintain the value of its capital assets indefinitely, the rate of return which makes investment in physical assets *equal* to saving deposits at 10 percent is 16 percent (for a ten-year time horizon). Obviously, the factors affecting the average length of employment expected by the employees of the firm are quite important. The longer the time horizon the smaller is the gap between the two rates of return. However, the important point is that the rates i_1 and r_1 are equal from the point of view of the firm's employees, given the background data.[30] The "equalizing" differential between the two rates should be attributed to the behavioral effects which arise from the differences in the content of property rights between savings accounts which are privately owned and capital goods which are not. To quote Professor Vanek: "The confusion and inefficiency that this [differential between the rate of interest and the rate of return on internal investment] will generate ...

30. See S. Pejovich, "The Firm, Monetary Policy and Property Rights in a Planned Economy," *Western Economic Journal* 7 (September 1969).

will be easily recognized by anyone with even a rudimentary training in economics."[31]

Given the labor input L_1 in figure 8.4, the collective's savings function, and the firm's schedule of investment opportunities for the use of additional capital goods, a rate of return r^* can be estimated at which the equilibrium condition $S = I$ is satisfied. If this rate of return r^* is greater or equal to r_1 in equation 8.2, where r_1 is the rate of return on investment in physical assets that is equivalent to the rate of interest i_1 paid on savings accounts, the workers will want to allocate a specific amount of the firm's profit to the Business Fund. Given the level of employment, the rate and productivity of investment and the firm's production function, the expected stream of output and income can then be estimated. For a different level of employment such as L_2 in figure 8.4 the investment schedule would shift upward,[32] and so most likely would the saving schedule because of a reduction in the wage rate and modal income. The process could, of course, be repeated for all the different levels of employment in the $L_1 - L_n$ range in figure 8.4. The highest present value of all the possible income streams would then suggest the firm's optimal level of employment, investment and output. It follows that the behavior of the Yugoslav firm is likely to diverge from the pure wage-maximization hypothesis. The workers as well as the director might find it to their advantage to allocate a part of the firm's profit to the Business Fund.

If individual employees have different time preferences and expected lengths of employment with the firm, the firm's decision with respect to its employment, output and allocation of profit will emerge from a political process and contain substantial compromises. Yet, the analysis presented above *explains* the pattern of behavior of individual workers which necessitates a "compromise" solution. Moreover, the differences in the workers' utility functions is likely to result in (1) the emergence of intrafirm coalitions, and (2) some resistance to hiring additional workers. The last point is especially important for understanding the relationship between the time horizon of the Yugoslav collective on the one hand, and the mobility of labor and the level of employment on the other. New workers could eventually change the planning horizon of a firm as well as its objectives, and consequently place the welfare of the original labor force in jeopardy. Moreover, all workers are eligible to share in the firm's profits, but the new employees have not participated in financing additional capital. Thus, the marginal product of the labor increment must be substantial and possibly in excess of the average product of labor if the increase in the labor force is

31. J. Vanek, "Some Fundamental Considerations of Financing and the Right of Property under Labor Management," unpublished manuscript.

32. Assuming that the production function is homogeneous of degree one, the rate of return r from each given I will vary directly with L.

to be acceptable to the original group. It follows that the low mobility of labor (averaging about 1 percent of the labor force per annum),[33] high unemployment rate, and the firms' preference for capital-intensive production techniques have a solid rational explanation and are, at least in part, generated by the structure of the postreform economic system in Yugoslavia.

To the "official" level of unemployment of about 315,000 in 1969,[34] one should perhaps add some 500,000 Yugoslavs who left the country looking for jobs in the capitalist West, for a majority of them would, in case of a recession in Western Europe, return to Yugoslavia and increase the "official" number of unemployed workers. It is also significant to note that the level of employment was just about the same in 1969 as in 1964 (3.7 million), while the official unemployment rate rose from 228,000 to about 315,000.

Finally, the workers' preference for investment in physical assets is likely to be negatively affected by the fact that compared to savings accounts those assets are more risky and certainly less liquid. The collective might, therefore, be expected to reduce the rate of profit allocated to the Business Fund below the solution discussed above and summarized in equations 8.1 and 8.2.

A rigorous test of our assertions—and traditional wisdom suggests that they are more than assertions—will require extensive and detailed empirical work. At this time we shall only cite a few examples that are consistent with our deductions.

The 1965 reform gave the working collective the right to determine the allocation of the firm's profit between the Wage Fund and other internal funds. Table 8.1, which begins with the prereform year of 1964, shows that business firms have increased the share of profit allocated to the Wage Fund.

TABLE 8.1. Allocation of Profits
(Percentages)

	Wages Fund (Gross of Taxes)	Other Funds
1964	69	31
1965	70	30
1966	72	28
1967	76	27
1968	77	23
1969	81	19
1970[a]	80	20

Sources: Podatci Završnih Računa Privrednih Organizacija, 1964–68, and Statistički Godišnjak Jugoslavije, 1970.

[a] Estimated from Statistički Bilten SDK, 1972, no. 2.

33. As calculated from Statistički Godišnjak Jugoslavije, 1970 [Statistical Yearbook of Yugoslavia, 1970] (Belgrade: Savezni Zavod Za Statistiku, 1970), pp. 87–99.

34. Ibid., p. 97.

Since 1965, a strong tendency in Yugoslavia has been for firms to substitute bank credit for self-financed investment (see table 8.2). The worsening of the

TABLE 8.2. Sources of Gross Investment in Fixed Assets
(Percentages)

	1964	1965	1966	1967	1968	1969	1970	1971
Business firms	26	28.9	39.3	32.7	31.2	28.4	27.1	26.7
Banks (including investment in housing)	31	36.6	38.9	44.9	47.1	49.3	51.1	50.9
Government	36.5	26.6	15.2	17.7	15.7	15.7	15.5	15.1
Others	6	7.0	6.6	4.7	6.0	6.6	6.3	7.3

Sources: Statistički Bilten SDK, 1970, nos. 6 and 8; 1972, no. 2.

position of business firms in financing investment is further indicated by the percentage of their total allocation to the Business Fund earmarked for repayment of investment loans (principal only).[35] This percentage changed from 48.8 percent of the allocation to the Business Fund in 1965 to 53.4, 81.5 and 110.9 percent in 1966, 1967 and 1968, respectively.[36] Also, the firms' interest payments to banks amounted to 5.8 percent of their total net product in 1969.[37]

An often-mentioned objective of the 1965 reform was to enlarge the share of the net product (value added) left to business firms from about 50 percent in 1964 to about 70 percent. Table 8.3 shows the distribution of the net

TABLE 8.3. Distribution of Net Product
(Percentages)

	Firms	Other Claimants
1964	50	50
1965	55	45
1966	60	40
1967	57	43
1968	56.5	43.5
1969	54.4	45.6
1970	53.5	46.5
1971	54.9	45.1

Source: D. Vojnić, Aktuelni Problemi Ekonomske Politike i Privrednog Sistema Jugoslavije (Zagreb: Informator, 1970), p. 64, and Statistički Bilten SDK, 1972, no. 2.

35. Interest payments are treated as production expenditures (i.e. contractual obligations).
36. D. Vojnić, "Investiciona Politika i Sistem Proširene Reprodukcije," Ekonomist 22 (December 1969): 857.
37. See Statistički Godišnjak Jugoslavije, 1970, p. 123; and Informativni Bilten (Belgrade) 8 (July–August 1970): 24.

product of Yugoslav firms. "Other" claimants are all the different levels of government, various social funds, banks, social security administration, insurance companies, chambers, etc. Their claims are satisfied by the turnover tax, interest payments, income tax, fees, social security contributions, and other legal and contractual obligations. The trend in the share of the net product left to business firms has yet to conform to the 1965 reform expectations.

The analysis of the Yugoslav firm presented in this section shows the dependence of the equilibrium solution on the extant property-rights structures. Moreover, it incorporates into the model the mutual interdependence of output, employment and net investment decisions of the firm. Finally, the analysis of the investment behavior of the Yugoslav firm supports our earlier discussion about the voluntary allocation of real income between present and future consumption, and points to the importance of the banking system in freeing investment from the limitations imposed by the rate of voluntary savings.

IV. THE ROLE OF THE YUGOSLAV BANKING SYSTEM

The Law on the National Bank of Yugoslavia[38] and the Law on Banks and Credit Operations[39] established the role and the structure of the Yugoslav banking system in the postreform years.

Investment, commercial, and mixed banks are formed by working organizations (enterprises) and sociopolitical communities. The founders contribute to the credit fund of the proposed bank (the credit fund of a bank is its own capital which is formed from contributions made by the founders of the bank and from allocations made from the bank's income); they are represented in the bank assembly (the bank's highest management body), and are free to sell their property rights in the credit fund to other enterprises and sociopolitical communities.

The revenue of the National Bank comes from various fees. However, a part of interest earnings, which are treated as state revenue, is returned to the National Bank to cover some of its operating expenses. Investment, commercial, and mixed banks receive their revenues from interest charges and various fees. The bank's earnings (revenue minus operating costs and interest paid to its creditors) are allocated by the bank assembly among (1) additions to the bank's own credit fund, (2) payments to working organizations and sociopolitical communities which have contributed to the bank's credit fund, and (3) the bank's net income, which is then divided between the wage fund and other internal funds in the manner of other Yugoslav firms.

38. *Zbirka Propisa o Bankama i o Kreditnim i Drugim Bankarskim Poslovima* [The Collection of Laws on Banks and Credit] (Belgrade: Sluzbeni List, 1966), pp. 181–214.

39. Ibid., pp. 7–187.

The three major functions of the National Bank are: (1) the issuance of money; (2) the control of money stock through the minimum reserve requirements[40] and the volume of credit granted by the National Bank to other banks; and (3) the control of external payments. The investment banks are primarily responsible for financing investments in fixed assets, although they are allowed to extend short-term credit as well. Commercial banks concentrate on the extension of short-term credit. However, they are also allowed to invest in housing and communal services. Finally, the investment-commercial (mixed) banks can extend both short-term and long-term credits.[41] It is quite likely, however, that this distinction between investment, commercial, and mixed banks will disappear in the near future.

The important point is that before 1965 the banks were responsible for the placement of "social investment funds" in accordance with the basic prop-ositions of the economic plan, while after the 1965 reform the banks are expected to mobilize and place investment funds at their own risk. It is likely that the 1965 reform has affected the mobility of capital and the allocation of resources in Yugoslavia through (1) the remuneration scheme that tied employees' incomes to bank earnings and (2) the abolishment of territorial limitations on bank activity. One observable accomplishment of this dual provision has been the decline in the total number of banks from 112 in 1966 to 67 in 1969, and the concentration of deposits in some of the most aggressive banks. The 15 largest banks accounted for about 62 percent of all short-term credits and 67 percent of demand deposits and savings in 1968.[42]

The supply of money in Yugoslavia consists of currency in circulation, demand deposits, and balances in clearing. One peculiarity of the monetary system is that cash balances are held mainly by individuals (personal check-ing accounts are yet to be introduced in Yugoslavia) while demand deposits are held by firms, government agencies, and other organizations. Thus, a change in the ratio of demand deposits to the money supply could easily indicate a change in the liquidity position of business firms. In 1968 and 1969, the currency in circulation and the cash holdings of individuals stood at 33–34 percent of the stock of money.[43] For practical as well as analytical purposes, the composition of the money stock in Yugoslavia is as important as its total volume.

40. The minimum reserve requirement is currently set at 35 percent of demand deposits, time deposits that can be withdrawn in less than a year, and some other bank obligations maturing in less than a year.
41. For a detailed analysis of the Yugoslav banking system see E. Furubotn and S. Pejovich, "The Banking System in Yugoslav Economic Planning."
42. *Credit and Banking System of Yugoslavia*, pp. 9–10.
43. See *Statistički Bilten SDK*, no. 8 (August 1969), pp. 13 and 26.

Short-term credits are granted from demand deposits held by banks and from credits they obtain from the National Bank. The short-term credit is, therefore, a primary instrument of money creation in Yugoslavia. Short-term credits are granted to firms mainly for financing inventories, accounts receivable, and accounts payable. Investment credits are granted from the banks' own resources and from time deposits that cannot be withdrawn in less than a year, the proceeds from issues of bank securities, credits received from domestic and foreign lenders, etc.[44] (See figure 8.6.)

The effects of bank investment credit on the allocation of profit. The curves $S_1 S_1$ and $S_2 S_2$ convey the information contained in equations 8.1 and 8.2. $S_1 S_1$ shows the amount of total income the collective is willing to divert from current consumption to accumulation of savings deposits for the various rates of growth of wealth. The portion of $S_1 S_1$ lying above the maximum allowable rate of interest on savings accounts (i_1) does not come into effective play. $S_2 S_2$ shows the required equalizing differential between incremental wages resulting from the workers' joint investment in fixed assets of the firm and the highest-valued investment alternative available to them individually. $S_2 S_2$ is the curve $S_1 S_1$ adjusted for the behavioral effects of a change in property rights from owned savings accounts to the right of use in capital goods.[45] *II* reflects the opportunities a given firm possesses for the use of additional capital and is based on the firm's initial position, current prices and labor input, and the characteristics of the existing production function. If the intersection of $S_2 S_2$ and *II* yields a rate of return greater than or equal to r_1, the workers will find it advantageous to use some of the firm's profit for investment in additional capital goods. In this case, the collective will allocate the amount *B* to the Business Fund.

Let us now assume that the firm obtains a loan of *LL* dinars. The *adjusted* savings schedule will shift to the right by the amount of the loan. Thus, the collective will invest more than *B* but it will, also, reduce the amount of profit allocated to the Business Fund. That is, *each additional dinar borrowed from the bank will increase the firm's investment in capital goods by less than one dinar because the collective will increase the share of profit allocated to the Wage Fund.* Tables 8.1 and 8.2 are not inconsistent with this assertion.

Given the rate of interest on investment loans i_2, the firm's demand for credit is *F* in figure 8.6. The amount of credit the firm can actually get depends on bank reserves and the investment schedules of other enterprises. Suppose the firm does better than *LL* and gets a loan in excess of *C* but less than *F*. The firm's demand for investment funds will appear insatiable, while at the same time its entire profit will be allocated to the Wage Fund. The conclusion is: given the behavioral effects of the prevailing property rights

44. *Credit and Banking System of Yugoslavia*, p. 6.
45. For a detailed analysis, see S. Pejovich, "Property Rights in a Planned Economy."

Fig. 8.6.   Bank credit and the investment behavior of the Yugoslav firm

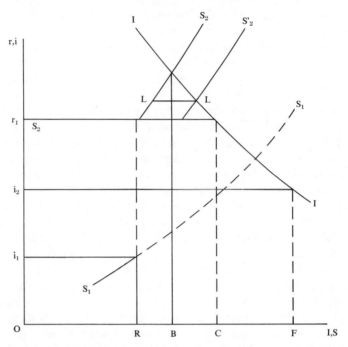

structures in Yugoslavia, the banking system can increase the rate of investment beyond the limitations imposed by the rate of voluntary savings at the price of making the allocation of profits even more biased in favor of current consumption. This conclusion explains why some people in Yugoslavia are currently discussing an arrangement which would, in effect, revive the Law on Commercial Investment Loans of July 1956, which required the firm to assure the bank that it intended to participate with its own funds in financing the investment project.

The analysis of the effects of investment loans on the allocation of profit by business firms suggests—and the Yugoslav experience does not refute—that: (1) bank credit for investment tends to enlarge the share of profit allocated to the Wage Fund relative to that which would otherwise prevail; (2) as long as the rate of interest charged by banks is fixed by the state, profit-oriented banks might be in a position to use criteria other than price competition in order to ration their available funds;[46] and (3) the govern-

46. Several studies have suggested that the rate of return from investment in capital goods is in excess of 10 percent. See for example I. Turcić, "Effikasnost Uloženih Sredstava Industrije po Područjima Jugoslavije" [The effectiveness of regional investments by industry in Yugoslavia in 1964 and 1967], *Ekonomski Pregled* 20 (January 1969): 66–90, and D. Vojnić, *Investicije i Fiksni Fondovi Jugoslavije* [Investment and fixed assets of Yugoslavia] (Zagreb: Ekonomski Institut, 1970), pp. 94–102.

ment could use fiscal policy to increase the rate of voluntary as well as forced savings.

The implications of (1) are simple: a decrease in the share of profit which the firms allocate to the Business Fund (see table 8.1) must, especially because of larger investment outlays, raise the firm's demand for short-term credits. Since these credits are a primary source of money creation in Yugoslavia, the supply of money will tend to increase. The term "tend" is used here because the effects of (2) on the money supply might just be the opposite. The paper now turns to those effects.

Monetary assets. Monetary assets in Yugoslavia can be classified as: (1) money, (2) quasi money, (3) semimonetary assets, and (4) nonliquid monetary assets. The "quasi money" category includes individual savings and certain sight deposits. The "semiliquid" assets include such items as demand deposits earmarked for specific uses and time deposits that can be withdrawn within a year. The "nonliquid" category includes such items as time deposits that cannot be withdrawn in less than a year, frozen demand deposits, foreign deposits at the National Bank, etc.[47]

Any switching of monetary assets from true money to other categories causes a reduction in the money supply, and vice versa. Some of the shifting of balances among the various monetary forms is brought about by the normal ebb and flow of economic life and by government policies of freezing and unfreezing particular demand deposits.[48] More importantly, however, the indications are that the banks have been doing precisely the same thing. Thus, changes in the composition of monetary assets are, in addition to short-term bank credit, a major factor affecting the money supply in Yugoslavia.

The value of total monetary assets of firms increased by 22.7 percent in the first 6 months of 1969 over the same period of 1968. Yet the money holdings of business firms fell from 26.1 percent of the value of their monetary assets to about 20 percent over the same period of time.[49] Also, the money holdings of business firms fell from 35 percent of the money supply in 1965 to 31.3 percent, 26 percent and 24.3 percent in 1966, 1967, and 1968 respectively, and to 20.3 percent in the first 6 months of 1969.[50] At the same time,

47. I. Perišin, *Monetarno-Kreditna Politika* [Monetary and credit policy] (Zagreb: Informator, 1968), pp. 47–54.

48. For example, bank credit increased by 4.8 and 1.2 billion dinars in 1965 and 1966, while the money supply rose by only 0.9 billion in 1965 and 1.04 billion in 1966. The reason for this divergence between credit creation and changes in the money supply was the increase in value of other monetary assets. Ibid., p. 55.

49. A. Šokman, "Sektorski Raspored Novčane Mase Kao Komponenta Likvidnosti Privrede," [Sectoral distribution of the money supply as a component of liquidity], *Ekonomist* 22 (December 1969): 903. The data for 1969 are the average monthly figures.

50. Ibid., pp. 898–900.

short-term credits to business firms increased by about 15 percent in 1969.[51] It might sound unusual that an increase in short-term credits to business firms, the growing value of their monetary assets, and a relatively high average rate of increase in the money supply of about 10 percent in the 1965–69 period could have led to a serious liquidity crisis in Yugoslavia. The reason for that crisis is, however, quite simple.

The behavior of the Yugoslav banks suggests that they prefer investment loans to short-term loans.[52] Investment loans yield higher interest,[53] the funds from which investment loans are granted are not subject to the 35 percent reserve requirement, and the bank can always use investment loans as a vehicle for inducing the borrower to transfer his other accounts to *that* bank. It follows that as long as the demand for investment funds exceeds the available supply of loanable funds at the regulated rate of interest i_2, the Yugoslav banks should be expected to prefer time deposits to demand deposits. Given the firms' lack of resources for financing investment activity, the bank can be expected to try to persuade them not only to transfer the funds to that bank but to switch their funds from demand deposits to time deposits as well. The resulting change in the composition of monetary assets affects the money supply, provides the banking system with resources for granting additional investment credits, contributes to inflationary pressures in the economy, and, most importantly, creates a serious liquidity problem for Yugoslav firms. This liquidity crisis is, in this author's judgment, the central problem of the Yugoslav economy today. Firms find their transaction balances seriously depleted and are, frequently, unable to meet their financial obligations, even though the value of their monetary assets has been constantly rising. For example, about 36 percent of the firms in Yugoslavia failed to meet their contractual obligations in 1968. The number of court rulings in that year ordering firms to fulfill their contractual obligations was 582,707; the amount of indebtedness involved in those court orders stood at over 9 billion dinars or about 9 percent of the net national product in that year.[54] Table 8.4 shows the magnitude of the liquidity crisis in Croatia.

The value of monetary assets held by households increased by 27.8 percent in the first 6 months of 1969 over the same period in 1968. The money holdings of households amounted to over 44 percent of their total monetary

51. *Informativni Bilten* 8 (July–August 1970): 8.

52. This point is derived *directly* from my interviews in Yugoslavia, *analytically* from the expected behavior of profit-oriented banks, and *indirectly* from the repeated requests by the association of banks to allow the banks to make investment loans from demand deposits.

53. P. Mihailović, "Tržište Finansijskih Sredstava Jugoslavije" [The Yugoslav financial markets], *Ekonomist* 22 (January 1969): 127.

54. L. Sirotković, "Monetarno Kreditna Politika i Likvidnost Privrede" [Monetary and credit policy and the problem of liquidity], *Ekonomist* 22 (December 1969): 883.

TABLE 8.4. Economic Courts' Decisions in Croatia

	No. of Decisions	Failure to Comply	Value of Decisions in Dinars	Failure to Comply in Dinars
January–March 1969	38,226	9,453	620,073,000	234,196,000
January–March 1970	47,774	14,440	776,462,000	307,492,000

Source: B. Cota, "Likvidnost Privrede," Ekonomski Pregled, 1970, nos. 6–7, p. 426.

assets, while savings deposits stood at 47 percent in 1969.[55] The liquidity crisis in Yugoslavia is, therefore, limited to business firms.

The role of the banking system in Yugoslavia can briefly be summarized as follows: Given the effects of the prevailing property-rights structure in Yugoslavia on the pattern of behavior of business firms, bank credit for investment reduces the allocation of profit to the Business Fund. This, in turn, forces the firms to increase their demand for short-term credit, which is a primary source of money creation in Yugoslavia. The banks then find it advantageous to induce business firms to transform this increase in the money flow into other forms of monetary assets. And this process generates additional investment funds as well as additional demand for short-term credits which is supplied by borrowing from the National Bank. It follows that the banking system has, in the process of freeing the rate of investment (and the potential growth rate) from the limitations imposed by the rate of voluntary savings, helped to create a liquidity crisis for the Yugoslav firm and to generate inflationary pressures in the Yugoslav economy as a whole.[56]

Fiscal policy. The Yugoslav government has been continuously using fiscal policy for the purpose of affecting the allocation of profit. The 1965 reform did away with the 15 percent general profit tax and set a tax rate of 18 percent (exclusive of social security contributions) on the firm's profit allocated to the Wage Fund, and a tax rate of 8 percent (estimated) on the amount allocated to the Business Fund. It follows that the firm's tax payments out of its profits depend on the allocation of profits between the Wage Fund and Business Fund. Moreover, tax payments can be changed by reducing the allocation to the Wage Fund. The implications of this point were analyzed in some detail and summarized as follows in a recent paper.

> With t_w greater than t_i, there is clearly tax incentive for the Workers' Council to limit the size of the Wage Fund. . . . Ceteris paribus, the existence of differential tax rates ($t_w > t_i$) pushes the collective in the

55. Šokman, p. 907.
56. From 1967 to 1969, the cost of living index increased at an average annual rate of 6 percent. See Statistički Godišnjak Jugoslavije, 1970, p. 259.

direction of greater acquisition of *non-owned* assets and greater total saving than would otherwise occur.

. . . the Yugoslav government appears to have some understanding of the incentive effects just described. For, if the government were primarily concerned with raising a given amount of tax revenue and felt essentially neutral relative to the distribution of profits between current wages and investment, it could employ the proportional profits tax. The adoption of the discriminatory tax ($t_w > t_i$) constitutes prima-facie evidence that the authorities are interested in inducing enterprises to increase the share of profits earmarked for the Internal Fund.

. . . the Yugoslav government is attempting to use the discriminatory profits tax as a means for influencing the savings behavior of Yugoslav workers; the objective seems to be to make savings behavior come closer to the pattern it would take if individuals were allowed to own capital goods. Moreover, this new strategy is followed without any direct controls designed to change the workers' basic attitudes toward present and future consumption.[57]

V. Concluding Remarks

The paper suggests that no satisfactory theory of the working of the Yugoslav economy can be developed without explicit reference to the prevailing property rights structures in that country. True, the analysis rests on some highly simplified assumptions—the model could (and should) include some additional variables and relationships; some further research about the relevant discount rate of the Yugoslav collective is also certainly necessary. Yet, the analysis does point the way to deeper and fuller understanding of the allocation problem in Yugoslavia.

The paper also suggests that the current liquidity crisis, unemployment, and inflation could be attributed to the very structure of the Yugoslav economy after 1965, that is, to the pattern of behavior it generates. Given the seriousness of such a conclusion, we prefer to state it as a strong assertion that awaits additional empirical and analytical work.

The analysis lends some support, quite inadvertently and probably for different reasons, to the position of those Yugoslavs who are wary about the fast expansion of the market mechanism. The proponents of economic reforms in Yugoslavia seem to expect the operation of market forces to yield the same results in Yugoslavia and in the West, and they are caught by surprise when the results appear to be different. Moreover, their position with the ruling elite in Yugoslavia is then weakened, while the position of the so-called "centralists" gets stronger. Yet, the fact is that the market

57. See E. Furubotn and S. Pejovich, "Tax Policy and Investment Decisions of the Yugoslav Firm," *National Tax Journal* 22 (September 1970), pp. 347–48.

mechanism works precisely the way it is supposed to. The only problem is that the proponents of economic reforms have failed to incorporate the behavioral effects of property relations and some other key institutions in Yugoslavia into the standard economic theory of production and exchange.

This study has tried to do precisely that. The analysis in this paper has shown that the prevailing property rights structures in Yugoslavia affect the behavior of microunits in a *specific* and *predictable* way, that this pattern of behavior of microunits in Yugoslavia *differs* from that in the capitalist West, and that, accordingly, the operation of market forces in that country *should and does yield different but by no means analytically unexpected results.*

9

Planning and the Market in the Czechoslovak Reform

VÁCLAV HOLEŠOVSKÝ

As was to be expected, the Soviet invasion of Czechoslovakia in August 1968 had an important effect upon the course of the economic reform started a year-and-a-half earlier. However, the effect was delayed by some seven or eight months, and it did not quite correspond to a simple scrapping of what had been accomplished before. To set the chronology of the reform straight, it should be noted that between 21 August 1968 and about March/April 1969 the reform movement gathered momentum and proceeded, at a feverish pace, in the spirit imparted by the period known as the Czechoslovak Spring. As Lenin once explained, the maximalist tone of early revolutionary decrees was due to the desire to lay down, in haste, all the basic principles in the expectation of certain defeat. Similarly, the reformers and the entire Czechoslovak nation seemed determined to push the movement as far as it would go before the internal totalitarian restoration gained the upper hand. This finally happened in April 1969. There followed a period of uncertainty as to the basic policy attitude of the post-Dubcek leadership toward the issues of system change. It took until January 1970 for the Central Committee of the Party to issue a fundamental directive according to which the reform work was, in a certain sense, to be resumed.

The direction of this resumption was indicated in the assignment given the appropriate administrative organs "to elaborate a new steering system so as to strengthen and rehabilitate the role of the plan and to utilize the positive aspects of the economic reform introduced from 1965 until 1969."[1] As we shall see in the concluding section, this phrase calls for a good deal of interpretation before its meaning can be pinned down—*if* it can. However, as far as could be judged in late 1970, there is no question of going back to the status quo ante, the centralized command planning of the years 1962–64, into which the system relapsed after the decentralizing episode of 1959–61.

The author wishes to acknowledge his debt to Arthur Wright for his criticism and help in improving the manuscript. No guilt by association is implied.

1. *Hospodářské noviny*, 1970, no. 18, p. 5.

At the same time, there is no question of continuing the reform in the direction taken in 1968–69.

The reform process was in a state of crisis from the very start (1967). The spirit of 1968 engendered methods of dealing with this crisis which became unacceptable in the atmosphere of a totalitarian restoration. The resumption of reform in 1970, therefore, signals at the same time a thorough frustration of the methods of 1968.

The nature of the crisis will be explained in the second part of this paper. In the third part we shall outline the 1968–69 attempt to deal with the crisis in a fundamentally revolutionary way. The reason one can currently speak of resumption is that the design of the 1967 measures allowed for different possibilities in the subsequent implementation and development of the reform. Which of these latent alternatives was to be ultimately realized depended, I believe, on noneconomic, i.e. political and social, parameters. One such alternative was a "participatory reform" movement, heavily determined by the spontaneous behavior of people in their different economic roles. This was the direction of the movement during the years 1968–69. Another alternative was a tame, well-behaved reform, carefully kept in hand by administrative authorities, bringing into play the familiar set of taxation valves and incentive propellants. This tame and well-behaved alternative, promoted with the twin formula of "binding nature of the plan" and "utilization of commodity-monetary relationships," is the aim of the current, post-1969 stage.

Economic systems and their transformations are to actual economic processes and policies what form is to content. The examination of one naturally leads to questions about the other. It is entirely legitimate to ask what has been happening to the real substance of the economy throughout those years of hopes and frustrations, centering on changes of the institutional, systemic shell. How far did the men in charge—enterprise managers, administrators, agents of the financial system—succeed in shifting investment resources toward renewal of overaged and overused branches of the economy; in fostering an intensive search for lines in which the economy either had true comparative advantage, or could attain it at relatively low expense; in deciding what production structure was worth pursuing in the long run; in adapting the supply of consumer goods and services more closely to the structure of consumer demand; and so on. As important as all of these substantive questions are, they will remain on the periphery of the present inquiry, which focuses on systemic aspects.

I. 1967 MEASURES: A RECAPITULATION

A proper summary of the Czechoslovak economic reform is difficult because only its beginning is known more or less precisely: the package of measures introduced in 1967, intended as the first act of an open-ended process, the eventual outcome of which was defined only in the most general terms. The reform work was conceived as a succession of measures subject to permanent review, each new generation of measures correcting and amplifying the preceding one. The ultimate shape of the "target solution" was to be a synergetic combination of autoregulation at the microlevel with macroeconomic plan forecasts of a reality-constrained, "geneticist," not "teleological," not voluntarist, not subjectivist, nature. Aided by a systematic application of market-research techniques, the productive apparatus was to cater to an autonomously determined final demand. Progressive rationalization of the price system was expected to reveal true domestic cost relationships, and the structure of exports and imports was to be slowly adapted to the hitherto unknown relations of comparative advantage—i.e. integrated into the world market.

The literature dealing with the economic model of the future in the years between 1963 and 1968 had a ring of doctrinaire proselytism; it was the product of recent converts to the competitive-equilibrium creed. Nevertheless, in the domestic context, this was more than refreshing, and from the point of view of Western unwitting theoretical mentors, encouraging. On the other hand, for the immediate purpose of devising practical measures that would facilitate the transition to the new system, theoretical insights into the logic of the market mechanism and forecasting were not sufficient. Besides, theoreticians of the reform did not have free rein, and the initial set of reform measures was the result of bargaining and consultation with practical planners and political agents whose idiosyncrasies and resistances had to be taken into account. Thus, a summary of the measures adopted for 1967 should be read with the understanding that they were a torso, put together by many hands and then abandoned, or rather altered by important elements of administrative planning which they were originally intended to supplant.

The detailed description of measures constituting the initial reform package has been given more or less adequately elsewhere.[2] This permits us to select those features which are useful for the purpose of general characterization, and refer the reader to other sources for details. The features discussed here will be (1) the determination of output by firms; (2) the

2. See Václav Holešovský, "Financial Aspects of the Czechoslovak Reform," in *Money and Plan*, ed. G. Grossman (Berkeley: University of California Press, 1968), pp. 84–99; George Staller, "Czechoslovakia: The New Model of Planning and Management," *American Economic Review* 58, no. 2 (May 1968): pp. 559–67; George R. Feiwel, *New Economic Patterns in Czechoslovakia* (New York: Frederick A. Praeger, 1968), pp. 274–318; K. Paul Hensel und Mitarbeiter, *Die sozialistische Marktwirtschaft in der Tschechoslowakei* (Stuttgart: Gustav Fischer Verlag, 1968).

objectives to be maximized and the incentive role of tax charges; (3) the strategy of price rationalization; (4) the sources of investment finance and investment criteria; and (5) the status of enterprises in the general framework of economic administration.

1. *Determination of output by firms.* The overnight disappearance, with very few exceptions, of quantitative output targets made production planning the responsibility of enterprise managements. Production plans were to be geared to anticipated sales, and the order book was to become the principal guide in production decisions. The choice of suppliers was to be freed. As for customers, it was not particularly stressed—perhaps because it was so obvious—that the priority of certain exports and domestic deliveries would be secured by continued imposition of production obligations and their supervision by the center.

2. *The economic maximand and incentive taxation.* The parameter to be maximized by enterprise managements, as implied by the full set of new prescriptions and rules, was to be net disposable revenue after taxes, attainable by maximizing revenues from sales and minimizing production costs. The major tax was to be a type of value-added tax, called the gross-revenue tax (gross because of the inclusion of the wage bill, not because of depreciation charges). Wage rates were to be determined, as before, by central wage tariffs. To counteract a possible tendency of managers to give in to wage demands too easily or to enlarge the number of their workers, a type of incremental payroll tax was introduced. In order to discourage uneconomical use or enlargement of capital stock, a tax or charge on capital was imposed. And in order to prevent enterprises from economizing on the wrong type of capital, hygienic and pollution-control devices were excluded from the base of the capital charge. Thus, the value-added tax, being proportional to the net product of an enterprise, was expected to remove taxation impediments to the expansion of the national product. Supplementary charges were to nudge the managements to economize on the use of basic categories of inputs.

3. *Wholesale-price revision.* To make the financial measures of economic performance effective, the wholesale-price system was revised in one single ambitious operation undertaken in the course of 1966. The basic feature of the recomputation of wholesale prices was the introduction of what was then believed to be an economically meaningful and consistent rate of profit markup—an error which will be examined in the next section. The system of retail prices was to remain untouched, for the time being, pending a later progressive equalization of turnover tax rates on articles sold in retail trade. In this manner, the structure of consumer demand remained temporarily untouched. Insofar as the 1967 price revision affected allocation of commodities, it remained circumscribed to intermediate sales of inputs.

4. *Investment allocation*. Allocation of investment funds was to be progressively shifted from nonreturnable budgetary capital grants to long-term repayable bank loans. The economic logic of the shift was the desire to link investments tightly with anticipated current production decisions, and to make enterprises financially responsible for the actual results. Bureaus of the State Bank were to screen applications for investment credit by applying commercial criteria of success—the soundness of profit expectations—and by considering repercussions on import needs and export possibilities. In the first two years of the reform, there were voices demanding greater articulation and liberalization in the area of capital markets.

5. *Status of enterprises*. Enterprises entered the era of reforms as part of horizontally integrated administrative groupings, with jurisdiction severely circumscribed by the executive organs, the "general boards of directors," of these groupings. The effect of financial measures of economic performance and incentives was distorted by their authority to determine financial transfers between individual enterprises, to impose supplementary charges or grant subsidies, to participate heavily in investment decisions, to formulate incentive schemes for enterprise managerial personnel, etc. Autonomy of enterprises versus tutelage by their superior organs remained a burning issue throughout the period of reforms.

It should be apparent, from this quick survey, that the 1967 reform was in many respects a step in the intended direction, but in other respects suffered from legacies of the past, or ill-conceived innovations (which will be examined shortly). The planning machinery continued to operate and to issue figures for the sake of orientation, not as mandatory targets. Forecasting as the major tool and form of the new type of planning remained in a preparatory and experimental stage, consisting mainly of the construction of a model of the Czechoslovak economy. At the same time, an economic research group charged with the analysis of short-run "business conditions [*konjunktura*]" was set up and began operating in 1968.

The Czechoslovak economic system was clearly moving in the direction of a model inspired by the example of planning in West European mixed economies, customarily described as a combination of market and planning. Without going too deeply into taxonomic problems let us note in passing that in this conception the terms "market" and "planning" have been losing their antithetical character of mutually exclusive modes of allocation. Indeed, because of their traditional connotations as antithetical types of economic organization, these terms are beginning to outlive their usefulness. It seems more appropriate to think of "markets" as merely one type of planning—a system of decentralized plans by firms, characterized by phenomena of nonconvergence of plans, cumulative movements away from equilibrium, imperfect accounting for externalities, and inadequate methods of communicating and asserting social preferences with respect to public goods and services. If the concept of markets is thus redefined in terms of decentralized plans, planning in the usual sense becomes an economic service, supplying a special set of information and decision making, which plays the role of complementary activity correcting for market failures. The relationship between market and planning may be seen not as one of opposition, or of hierarchical interference, but of articulation of executive functions within an integrated economic system. What we have been used to calling "market" may then cease to be viewed as a survival of the preplan era but, instead, as a deliberately conserved and nurtured component of planning.

II. Crisis of the Reform

The particularities of the Czechoslovak case make it necessary to pay attention to the historical sequence of events. In this case, the chronological framework is also the staging ground for a drama of which we are now witnessing the third act. We have been referring to a "reform *process*," in order to indicate that we are neither dealing with a reform introduced all at once and then "unfolding," as seems to have been the case in Hungary, nor with one degenerating into stagnation because of internal contradictions in the inherited system and piecemeal innovations, as in the Soviet Union. The mention of drama in connection with this reform process is not due to an intention of artificially injecting effects of suspense into what otherwise would be a cut-and-dried economic story. The reform in Czechoslovakia did not proceed as a smooth sequence of corrections and improvements, the kind of learning-by-doing anticipated by the reformers, but indeed as the result of dramatic conflicts between political and social forces.

Blunders of 1967

The era of reforms opened disappointingly with a crisis of the new arrangements of 1967. If the economy performed acceptably well, it was perhaps due to its own momentum, or to some unintended effects of the new measures, such as the high liquidity position of enterprises and the stimulating effects of inflation, but not to the expected working of the new measures, because they did not work as expected.

The reform of wholesale prices, pushed and rushed in the course of 1966 so that the new prices would be ready for use from the very start of 1967, was correctly identified as one major cause of the crisis in question. However, an equal if not greater responsibility should be placed on the category of "gross revenue" which was to play a central part in the definition of enterprise finances, taxation, and incentives—or, more exactly, to a little-noticed but crucially important deviation in the actual application of the gross-revenue category from the "intent of the legislator." For all practical purposes, these two elements nullified the effects which the reformers counted on. Compared to the decisive negative influence of these two factors, the new system of taxation and industrial organization, with their deficiencies, can be said to have contributed to the disappointing opening stage only secondarily.

Price Reform: New Disorder for Old

The ill effects of the price reform lay both in the new pattern of relative wholesale prices and in their new absolute level. We shall discuss these two aspects in turn, and then make some observations concerning the sequence of steps—actual and desirable—used in attempts to cure sick price systems.

The whole drift of the discussion preceding the 1967 reform led us to expect that the price reform would represent a first rough adjustment of existing price relations in the general direction of efficiency prices. This is the only conception that would make sense. Many writers stated that self-regulation of the enterprise sector by means of financial returns, earned through a successful catering to market demand, presupposed a set of prices providing room for generating positive financial returns related to efficiency in the use of enterprise resources. Therefore, it came as a shocking surprise when, at the time the mathematical framework for the recomputation of prices was set up, a clear notion of what constitutes enterprise resources, and how financial returns are supposed to be related to them, appeared to be missing.

The poverty of Czechoslovak price theory was revealed primarily in the choice of the so-called "double-channel price type" according to which the average price level of some 416 commodity groups was changed. This price recomputation can be criticized on a number of counts: it operated in terms of average-cost-plus-average-profit rather than of marginal-cost-plus-zero-profit; it relied for basic cost data on enterprises vitally interested in providing biased information; it used excessively aggregated capital values measured in prices based on capital censuses riddled with arbitrariness; it used several inadequately justified coefficients in adjusting the census values of components of the capital stock for inflationary price-level changes. While shortcomings of this sort were to some extent unavoidable, the choice of the price formula was entirely at the discretion of the men in charge once the recomputation procedure was decided upon. Thus, it was entirely possible to avoid the disparate pattern of rates of return insofar as this pattern related to the choice of price formula.

The efficiency rate of return, as usually understood, indicates the magnitude of net revenue produced in the various lines of production, relative to the values invested in the stock of corresponding productive assets. In the dimensions of an enterprise, these assets are represented by the depreciated value of fixed capital and the average value of working capital, including liquid balances needed to span the normal time lag between the flow of revenues and outlays, as well as to meet contingencies. In more general terms, it is the average value tied up in a productive operation during a given period, due to the noncoincidence of cost outlays, and revenues from sales of output. Among all the possible "price types" usually discussed in the East European and Soviet literature, it is the "production price," relating profit rates to the value of fixed capital and inventories, which comes closest to the notion of the price incorporating a rate of return on productive investment.[3]

The "double-channel" price type dispenses with the notion of a rate of return on value invested in productive operations and defines profit as composed of two distinct elements: one part proportional to the value of "production funds" (fixed capital and stock of inventories—with a different proportionality factor, or percentage, used for each), and another part proportional to the wage bill. It should be immediately apparent that the rate of return (or rentability) on investment will vary, under this double-channel price formula, according to the relative capital-labor intensities of production processes in different industrial branches. Let us call the two proportionality factors a and b, the stock of capital K, and the wage bill W. The value of r, the rate of return on investment (approximated by K), will tend to approach the value of a as the capital intensity of a given production line increases, and will move in the direction of infinity as the production line becomes more labor intensive, as is evident from the formula

$$r = \frac{aK + bW}{K}.$$

In principle, there is no reason why rates of return on investment should vary according to the technical characteristics of production processes. (Especially if one factor is represented by a *stock*, and the other by a *flow* value.) It is conceivable, in a situation of general equilibrium, to find the same rates of return on investment at both extremes (fully automated, and labor-only branches), provided the time pattern and magnitudes of the expenditure and revenue flows are the same in both cases, or yield identical discounted values.

One may doubt whether there was much theoretical reasoning behind the

3. It is interesting to note that Professor Šik changed his definition of the "socialist production price" from the one referred to in the text, to one which identifies it with the double-channel price. Compare passages in *K problematice socialistických zbožnich vztahů* [On the problem of socialist commodity relationships] (Prague, 1965), pp. 146–47, with the later English version, *Plan and Market under Socialism* (White Plains, N.Y.: IASP Press, 1967), p. 247 (footnote).

choice of this formula.[4] It seems that it was intended to have a close relationship to the new charges imposed on enterprise revenues. Thus, the construction of business taxes interfered with the construction of the basic price formula. The idea was apparently that the price had to be constructed, and the values of coefficients a and b set, so as to enable enterprises to pay the new charges and be left with an incentive residual. However that may be, the result was a wild pattern of rentability rates, acting, in important cases, at cross purposes with the proclaimed objectives of promoting certain hitherto neglected branches. According to one fairly recent survey, rentability has varied between sub-branches of industry from minus 0.19 to 27.21 percent.[5] It is probably impossible to determine the range of variation of individual products. However, considering that relative prices of individual products *within* commodity groups were not changed, but merely shifted up or down according to the new average price levels of commodity groups, and considering that many products included in the calculation of prices were dropped from production soon afterward, there can be little doubt that the result of the price reform was a new price chaos.[6]

4. For a more thorough treatment of the theoretical rationale of this formula see Václav Holešovský, "The Double-Channel Aberration in East European Price Formulas," in *Jahrbuch der Wirtschaft Osteuropas*, ed. Franz-Lothar Altmann, vol. 2 (Munich: Gunter Olzog Verlag, 1971), pp. 329–42. (Contrary to an erroneous statement made by me on p. 332 of the *Jahrbuch*, Hungary, too, used the double-channel formula in its price reform. See István Friss, ed., *Reform of the Economic Mechanism in Hungary* [Budapest: Akadémiai Kiadó, 1969] p. 136.) Readers familiar with the price-type discussions in East European countries will recognize in the double-channel formula an uneasy compromise between the "production price" and "labor value" approaches. Cf. Morris Bornstein, "Soviet Price Theory and Policy," in U.S., Congress, Joint Economic Committee, *New Directions in the Soviet Economy* (Washington, 1966), pp. 70–73.

5. *Hospodářské noviny*, 1970, no. 17, p. 4—aggregated by branches, the variation ranged from 4.32 to 17.32 percent.

6. Professor Alec Nove amplified these points in the subsequent discussion by the following remark: "When I was in Prague in the spring of 1966, and discussed their intended price reform with economists at the research institute, I argued that it could not work. My strongest argument, it seemed to me, was related to *excessive aggregation* of the prices themselves. When there are over a million actual prices, how can 400 aggregated price groups be administered? Suppose that there are 2,000 kinds of agricultural machines produced, what is 'the price of agricultural machinery?' In the end, someone must decide the price of each actual machine. This, as well as the reasons given in the paper, provided for too much room for maneuvre and distortion.

"It is correct to say that many prices need to be freed from control at an early stage of reform, if only to make possible a more flexible system of price-fixing for the items still to be price-controlled.

"We ought not to aim at an unattainable perfection. We have in the West a much 'less than perfect equilibrating price-setting procedure,' to quote one participant's words. Reference should be made to Silberston's excellent article in the *Economic Journal*, September 1970.... This being so in the West, we cannot ascribe the inadequacies and failures of the Czech price reform of 1967 primarily to their non-conformity to standards of economic perfection. The essential problem was *excess demand*. Over-taut planning, planners' tension, causes excess demand of a kind hardly correctible by price manipulation, since the 'traditional' central plan is mandatory on everyone, including financial institutions."

Turning to the change in the absolute level of wholesale prices emerging from the price recomputation, we are faced with another source of crisis. The original expectation was that the price reform would raise the general level of wholesale prices by about 19 percent. Certain key decisions concerning the level of fiscal charges, prices of imported commodities, revaluation of stocks, etc., had been made on the basis of this expectation. Actually, the recomputation resulted in a raising of the general wholesale-price level by about 29–30 percent.[7] At the same time, actual production-cost levels turned out to be lower than those on which the price recomputation was based.

The combined effect of these unforeseen shifts in price levels was a generous cash flow, only partially drained by the new fiscal charges, going to the enterprise sector as a whole. The original scheme was intended to put enterprises on a financial starvation diet at the start. They were expected to depend, at first, almost entirely on bank credit for their liquidity requirements. This would have strengthened the will of management to build up its own interest-free liquidity positions, a goal attainable only by earning disposable revenue through sales. However, the new price-cost relationship reduced the need for such a strategy. In the aggregate, no particularly aggressive sales drive was necessary to keep enterprises well supplied with cash. Some individual enterprises suffered from liquidity shortages because of the effect of the price and tax reform upon their relative rentability and disposable-revenue positions; their predicament merely served as a legitimate basis for claiming subsidies and short-term credit. Thus, a generous cash flow to high-rentability firms and a hard-to-refuse subsidy and credit supply to low-rentability firms combined to form a source of inflationary spending on wage and salary increases, inventory financing, and self-financed investments. (This does not, however, represent a full enumeration of the sources of the post-1967 inflation.) Under these conditions, disposable net revenue could never fulfill the kingpin role assigned to it in the new incentive system. The theoretical problems of "the firm in Illyria," eagerly discussed in journal articles, did not develop for real Czechoslovak enterprises.

The new price chaos could only undermine the value of newly introduced investment criteria and selection procedures as well. All investment projects above a certain value, including those provided through autofinancing, had to pass through a screening procedure administered by the State Bank and checked by a number of other administrative organs. Investment projects approved for the years 1968 and 1969 were ranked according to their expected efficiency, measured with the aid of an ill-conceived "index of rentability of investments" (*ukazatel výnosnosti investičních prostředků*),

7. *Cenový zpravodaj*, supplement to *Finance a úvěr*, 1967, p. 1.

that is, a ratio of the sum of *discounted* gross profits to the sum of *compounded* investment outlays.[8] Quantitative criteria applied to project proposals envisaged for 1970 and later were more numerous—seven in all—and in part also more refined.[9] Unfortunately, the values inserted in the formulas of these efficiency indicators were based on existing prices, if not, indeed, on their optimistic adaptations on the part of the applicants for investment funds. Since the quality of these formulas could hardly make up for the inferior ingredients fed into them, the results of the new project selection methods would not have been good even if all other circumstances had been ideal.

Similarly, the new disorder in domestic prices had a devastating effect upon the serious intentions of foreign-trade organizations to apply efficiency criteria in their policy of export stimulation. Starting in 1967, prices of export articles were adapted by means of an elaborate system of subsidies or "surcharges," and financial imposts or "deductions." This may be interpreted as equivalent to the establishment of multiple individualized foreign-exchange rates. Insofar as this superstructure of subsidies and imposts rested on the new wholesale prices, it is difficult to see how the corrections could have resulted in a substantially improved pattern of export prices.[10]

"Gross Revenue Produced": Another Déjà Vu

A second principal cause of the reform crisis was a crucially important deviation from the intent of the legislator in the application of the gross-revenue category. Gross revenue (equivalent to net value added, augmented by other enterprise revenues, price surcharges or rebates, and subsidies) and net disposable revenue after the deduction of financial charges, were the categories expected to be maximized in the original scheme of things. This feature is the one which really makes an economic reform, so important are its effects as a source of incentive payments and as a visible signal of success in the satisfaction of demand and the application of production methods that keep costs at competitive levels.

What a disappointment, then, to find out that

> for practical reasons (simpler monitoring) one employs the method of the so-called gross revenue *produced* [*vytvořený hrubý důchod*] which

8. Cf. Vladimír Kyzlink's critical examination of this indicator in *Finance a úvěr*, 1969, no. 11, pp. 685–86.

9. See special supplement to *Hospodářské noviny*, 1969, no. 15, prepared by Ing. Josef Votava.

10. Cf. "Hospodářská směrnice vlády na rok 1969" [Economic guideline of the government for the year 1969], *Hospodářské noviny*, 1968, no. 32, pp. 1 and 8–11; also Jaromír Kubálek, "Konkretizace hospodářské politiky v oblasti vnějších ekonomických vztahů [Practical implementation of economic policy in economic relations with foreign countries], supplement to *Hospodářské noviny*, 1968, no. 32.

records all performance (output) of the enterprise, irrespective of whether it was realized (verified by the market). It relates performance to cost outlays; however, gross revenue produced does not represent disposable means of the enterprise because it comprises also the increment of unfinished production and finished products. Because of difficulties connected with the monitoring of wages, material costs and depreciation imputable to realization, use is not being made, for the time being, of the method of the so-called gross revenue *realized*, which is net of unfinished production and unsold finished products. [Emphasis added.][11]

Thus, one of the most offensive aspects of the old gross value of output was reproduced in a financial form. It is difficult not to conclude that this feature places the Czechoslovak reform of 1967, widely accepted as the most far-reaching and radical of all East European reforms, behind the Soviet reforms of 1965, in which *realizacia* became the basis of other derived success indicators (unless, of course, Soviet application has deviated from the letter of the *ukaz* as much as in Czechoslovakia).

The most telling evidence of the deleterious effect of "gross revenue produced" has been the movement of inventory accumulation. During the years 1964 and 1965, in the wake of the recession of 1962–63, stocks of inventories were first reduced and then moderately replenished. With the start of the reform, inventory accumulation first returned to, and then phenomenally exceeded, recorded prerecession rates. This is dramatically shown in the following tabulation (in billion crowns).[12]

	1964	1965	1966	1967	1968
Increase in inventories	−0.7	0.2	6.0	9.1	10.5
Increase in unfinished investments	−4.0	1.0	4.1	8.3	12.8
Increase in national income (Cz. defin.)	−3.4	4.0	18.8	41.2	21.4

Even though other factors would have to be considered in a full explanation (disorganization in the supply of materials, for example), one can hardly dispute explanations which blame the working of the incentive system in the microsphere, under which "the steep increase in inventories has not been hurting anybody."[13]

Fiscal Charges and Net-Rentability Patterns

If the price reform, through the pattern of relative prices, created a large degree of variation in rentability of individual enterprises, the 1967 system

11. Supplement to *Hospodářské noviny*, 1968, no. 12, p. 7.
12. Data from *Plánované hospodářství*, 1970, no. 3, p. 13.
13. *Hospodářské noviny*, 1970, no. 19, p. 9. Cf. also *Finance a úvěr*, 1968, nos. 9–10, p. 591.

of fiscal charges pushed this variation further by leaving some enterprises with a negative net disposable revenue and in need of subsidy. This result is traceable to the fact that the *source* of tax payments (net revenue) was not identical with the *tax base* (capital stock, value added, wage-bill increments), so that the total of charges due may easily have exceeded the sources available. Again, this phenomenon carried its share of responsibility for the anti-efficiency results of the reform: by arbitrarily creating rich and bigger enterprises, it smudged the line between the effects of managerial efficiency (or inefficiency), and the results of the interplay of artificially produced profit markups and tax charges. The result was that enterprises became dependent for aid on the organs of supraenterprise organizations, the "economic production units" (*výrobně hospodářské jednotky*). Thus there arose a new "jumble of helter-skelter redistributions and subsidies, blunting the points of possible social conflicts, but undercutting at the same time the spirit of entrepreneurship."[14]

Always sure of being able to turn to their trusts as money sources in the last resort, enterprises did not have to worry much about the various taxes originally intended to make them use labor and capital economically. The two main charges, the capital charge and the labor-force-stabilization charge, were designed on the simple principle of active incentive taxation according to which, as in Old England, if the government taxes the size and number of windows, windows will tend to be small and few. However, if the source of payment is an arbitrarily generous cash flow or deficit-plugging subsidy, then incentive taxation (which is what the Czechs seemed to mean by the expression *kriteriální odvody*) cannot bite. Another aspect of the superseded system, which cannot be properly classified as a legacy, was thus recreated.

A Better Timetable of Reform Measures

It is very likely that the aspects of the 1967 reform discussed so far could have been avoided, to a large extent, by a more careful design. The effects of the financial gimmickry raise the issue of the proper sequence of innovations in economic reforms of the East European type.

Changes in the incentive and information system oriented toward improved satisfaction of demand presuppose a live demand-and-supply nexus of relationships and transactions. It would, therefore, seem reasonable to first concentrate on everything capable of stimulating lateral relationships such as are characteristic of the Hayekian universe of intimate knowledge of the most specific circumstances in a firm's markets, and of sensitive responses to change. Although correction of the terms of exchange—the price system

14. *Rudé právo*, 22 January 1969, p. 5.

—is exceedingly important, for it to have salutary effects it has to be introduced into a situation where business instincts have been revitalized. This
requires some intervention other than setting up an obstacle course of
taxation gimmicks on the oversimplified assumption that every participant
in the economic process will start racing madly after a slice of the net disposable revenue.

In practical terms, the autonomy of enterprises should be established first,
and with it a managerial appointment policy that secures the best available
talent for positions where marketing and production decisions are made.

At the same time, the apparatus of macroeconomic control should be put
in place to be ready to deal with the global effects of microeconomic adjustments. Simplifying the sake of argument, all that is needed is enforcing some
elementary principles in the management of money supply and the manipulation of aggregate demand. There is no immediate need to create elaborate
new instruments; the control of credit volume and credit rationing, together
with a Lernerian attitude toward fiscal policies, should not be too difficult
to implement (with no analogue of the U.S. Senate around), provided the
principles of stabilization policies are clear.[15]

Only if these reform elements have been secured should adjustments in
the price system be considered. The crux of the decision concerns its method.
Should one start with a dry-run recomputation "from the drawing board,"
a drawing board provided with a computer? The apparent need to solve all
interconnected price relations simultaneously, in order to avoid chaos,
seems to recommend this path. However, on the basis of the Czechoslovak
experience, one may question whether, given the limitations of data ingredients, computational techniques are in a position to bring order into chaos.
The distrust of spontaneous price-adjustment processes may be unfounded.
In Czechoslovakia, a large proportion of prices were in any case subject to
spontaneous determination and adjustment on the part of enterprises,
entirely outside the official categories of fixed, ceiling, and free prices. It
might, therefore, be reasonable to leave price formation entirely to enterprises and to let market transactions take care of the iterations through a
real process—in short, to let the terms of trade be determined by trading.

It is clear that the public would have to be told that a period of price
movements was to be endured. Retail trade would have to be allowed to
participate actively in price determination, so that market relations would
not be confined to transactions in intermediate goods (which is what the
reform restricted to *wholesale* prices effectively was). The turnover tax
would have to come out of hiding and be shown on sales slips for consumers

15. In retrospect, it appears that the hopeful insights into monetary-policy problems noted
by this author a few years ago were the privilege of only a few Czechoslovak economists. Cf.
Holešovský, "Czechoslovak Reform," pp. 99–105.

to be able to witness the reasons for retail price adjustments. As an alternative, firms might be instructed to use a cost-plus price formula whereby the "plus" would be set so as to comprise, in the aggregate, the full amount of financial accumulation (profits and turnover tax), and taxation simplified to a single business profit tax. Fiscal revenues might have to be regulated by stopgap measures like borrowing, and one would have to relax considerably about the dangers and ills of inflation. This need not be too difficult as long as the internal price level remained insulated from foreign prices by controls of foreign trade flows and prices, or, if the country were free to modify its foreign exchange rate (as Yugoslavia was), until some equilibrium were reached. A certain amount of inflation should not be regarded as too high a price for getting the economy moving under its own steam.

It goes without saying that this brief improvisation should not be mistaken for a synopsis of an alternative scenario of integrated policy measures. It is merely to suggest an order of priorities that seems economically more logical and promising than that followed in the Czechoslovak reform.

III. FLIGHT FORWARD

It should not be concluded from the preceding discussion, however, that the economy was entirely inert as far as lateral producer-customer relationships were concerned. One of the early examples of a successful adaptation to sudden changes in market demand was the often-cited case of a large enterprise (VHJ Zbrojovka Brno) which experienced a sudden, unexpected collapse of demand for tractors.[16] Its successful solution consisted in finding new customers in the capitalist West.

The mere fact that the economy has operated, since 1966, without any binding annual plans under purely "indicative" economic guidelines in which the "plan was degraded to a mere wanton (*nezávazný*) hypothesis,"[17] is a sufficient proof, if not of the vitality of self-regulated demand-and-supply relations, then at least of the automaticity in the elementary exchange nexus.[18]

In addition to automatic market stimuli, Czechoslovak citizens have claimed to notice clear signs of what amounts to Harvey Leibenstein's "X-efficiency" emerging during the period of the Czechoslovak Spring: improved working morale attributed to the political climate, a spirit of

16. *Hospodářské noviny*, 1967, no. 42, p. 9.

17. Ibid., 1970, no. 18, p. 5.

18. It has been pointed out that a number of centralist practices in the allocation of commodities survived, sub rosa, from the prereform era. This was interpreted by some writers, including the present one, as one of the ominous legacies of centralism. See V. Holešovský, "Planning reforms in Czechoslovakia," *Soviet Studies* 19, no. 4 (April 1968): 549. However, one might regard this as a mere aid to enterprises trying to use former channels for marketing certain commodities during a transitional period when crutches are still useful.

initiative, a decrease of indifference, etc. These "psychological" effects, as well as the seemingly undisturbed economic routine during the early months following the Soviet invasion, testify to the ability of the economy to perform basic functions in a self-regulatory manner.

However, given the haphazard framework created by the 1967 measures, it was difficult to go much beyond preservation of the previously achieved level of economic functioning. (Indeed, routine and insensitivity to financial signals may have kept the misallocative effects of the new price and rentability relations within bounds.) Furthermore, an orderly pursuit of the announced or implied objectives of the economic reform was blocked by several other factors: (1) inertia ("legacy") in investment policies led to a cumulation of expansive investment expenditures, beyond and above the autofinanced wave mentioned earlier;[19] (2) the lack of a clear and definite concept of desirable structural shifts in production led to a perpetuation of the earlier set of priorities; (3) inflation, originating in excess monetary demand for investments and in wage pressures, was dealt with by means of a succession of administrative stop orders (starting with wage limits which were to prevent wage increases without productivity increases, in individual enterprises, in mid-1967) and supplementary business taxes; (4) the social and political upheavals of 1968 did not get a chance to work themselves out toward the establishment of a new source of political authority. Without this, the government was unable to exercise a reformist "economic statesmanship," that is, making interventions of what might be called the synergetic-planning type (broad shifts in investment allocation, restructuring of foreign trade, technological renovation and innovation, etc.).

While administrative organs tried to control the problem of inflationary disequilibrium by means of administrative roadblocks, they were also preparing corrections of certain major errors contained in the 1967 measures, in particular in matters of enterprise taxation (a profit tax and a tax on the value of total enterprise assets were to replace the levy on gross revenue and the set of capital and inventory charges). Further, the Ministry of Finance was proceeding in the direction of progressively introducing turnover taxation at a uniform rate, making the tax proportional to wholesale prices.

In the meantime, the momentum of the reform process shifted from administrative offices and the written output of economists and planners to the social arena at the "working economy" level. It was the turn of social forces, of spontaneity, to try to restructure existing authority patterns. Economic reform, which until then had been moving at the level of formal

19. Thus in 1968, for instance, state authorities approved additional investments (above the originally planned ceiling) amounting to 6 billion crowns—20 percent of the 1967 value of new fixed capital; cf. *Hospodářské noviny*, 1970, no. 7, p. 7.

financial rules, was to be provided with something much more basic: fresh social dynamism in the forms of management, industrial organization, and labor relations. This decidedly revolutionary process continued, and was intensified, after the Soviet invasion, culminating in the first two or three months of 1969. It was then thwarted by the increasing pressures of the totalitarian restoration.

This new dynamic movement attempted (a) to establish enterprise autonomy under the authority of a variant of "workers' councils"; (b) to create industrial associations of enterprises, research institutions, and export organs under the impetus of interested enterprises themselves; and (c) to proclaim and consolidate the autonomy of trade unions, conceived as authentic representatives of the economic interests of their membership, independent of the state and of management. This striving of major social-interest blocs to constitute themselves as autonomous organized forces represented a decisive breakup of the totalitarian mold of economic organization, and it is this feature of the process which gives it its revolutionary character. It represents the most basic social prerequisite for developing the self-regulating economic lateral relationships and dynamic processes typical of market economies, and it is indispensable for the synthesis of market and synergetic planning.

Workers' Councils

The demand that the decision-making competence of enterprise managers be enlarged was not new. It had been understood to be a necessary part of reform objectives, at least by the intellectual promoters of the economic reform. They kept pointing out the incongruence between the philosophy (or rather, the economics) of the reform on the one hand, and the subjection of individual enterprises to their trusts and associations (i.e. the VHJs [výrobně hospodářské jednotky], "economic production units"). Competitive behavior was deemed incompatible with the existence of "administrative monopolies" which confined enterprises to production programs imposed from above, supervised their investment plans, handled the disposition of their revenues, manipulated the compensation schemes of their executives, etc. Tied to the decision-making independence of enterprises was the problem of the professional competence of managers. The selection of managers has involved powerful vested interests on the part of the government and Party bureaucracies, and threatened many executives who survived as a social "legacy" of the prereform days.[20]

20. Symptomatically, in anticipation of personnel changes expected with the introduction of workers' councils, "there occurred sporadic suicides, more often resignations, transfers to inferior positions, and retirements." *Podniková organisace*, 1968, no. 12, p. 501.

As in many other social activity areas, the government and the Party sanctioned ex post a development which originated with various groups of society throwing off the organizational shackles of the totalitarian system. It would be erroneous to speak of some new, deliberately adopted Party line introducing changes from above as they were begun over the years, say, in Yugoslavia. The initiative, as a rule, originated with social-interest groups or individuals. Thus, one workers' strike concerned itself with matters of production programs and organizational affiliation, issues falling under the competence of managerial decision-making.[21] A general model of labor participation in management, supplying an intellectual framework for the spontaneous movement, was ready in the form of the idea of "workers' councils." As early as 1966 one could find statements proposing some form of labor participation in management as a desirable corollary to economic reform.[22] The spontaneous upsurge of the spring of 1968 received its official sanction and formal guidelines on 6 June 1968 ("Interim general principles for the establishment and testing of the activity of collective organs of democratic management and entrepreneurial organs in enterprises"). After the invasion, the wave of "experiments" was contained by the broad governmental hint of 24 October 1968, which suggested that their extension would not be serving any useful purpose. At the same time, existing workers' councils (podnikové rady pracujících) were engaged in vigorous activity: a regional conference was organized in Ostrava on 19 November 1968; a consultation of several workers' councils was held in Plzen on 6 December; an attempt was made to establish an information exchange on the activities of existing workers' councils; and finally, as a culmination, the workers' council in the Skoda enterprises in Plzen proceeded to elect, in a conspicuous manner, a new enterprise director of their own. As pointed out in an important survey article,[23] such actions were formally extralegal since old

21. The strike in question occurred on 26 March 1968 in a factory producing electric instruments. The strikers demanded (a) the retention of a certain production line in which the labor team of the factory had gained proficiency, and which was to be moved to another establishment; and (b) the constitution of the plant as an independent enterprise. A series of such cases were reported side by side with applications unaccompanied by strikes. "This movement," commented Práce on 27 March 1968, "is exploding the dikes between administrative conglomerations of plants and enterprises created according to obsolete directives of the center. The editors agree with those economists who advocate a natural concentration of production according to plant and enterprise interests."

22. Thus, for example, we read: "Enterprise collectives will have, under the new system, material incentive as well as responsibility for the results of business. Their right to make decisions, through their organs, in basic matters of plans, management personnel, distribution of gross revenue or profit, follows both from [the principle of] social ownership, as well as from their material interest and responsibility." Pavel Vranovský in Práce, 12 August 1966.

23. Hospodářské noviny, 1969, no. 3, p. 5.

laws charging governmental organs with the appointment of managerial personnel had not been abolished. Indeed, the advocates of workers' councils were not unaware of the revolutionary intent of such activities. ("One cannot wait to establish councils until the law is passed or until everything is theoretically clear!")[24]

The government, for its part, drafted new statutes concerning socialist enterprises, incorporating the idea of workers' councils in a blunted form. For a few months, a battle royal raged in the press on the theoretical and practical merits of different conceptions of workers' councils. Essentially it reduced to an argument over whether workers' councils should act as "organs of social control" (the government's conception), which would have been a mere consultative function while managers would have been appointed, as before, by governmental organs from above; or whether they should act as an "entrepreneurial organ," electing executives from a roster of candidates screened by means of competitive examinations, and making basic decisions in matters of enterprise policy. On 13 February 1969 the Czechoslovak government mounted a collective managerial demonstration in support of its own conception, spelled out in draft legislation, by calling a public meeting of directors, which the defenders of the "entrepreneurial" conception interpreted as a provocative attack upon themselves. In March, the Premier still expected passage of the bill by the end of the month. After the political changes of the following month, the bill was shelved and workers' councils were slowly dismantled.

Data on the composition and activities of experimental workers' councils point to a pronounced tendency to conceive of them as professional organs of competent management. They seem to have been staffed overwhelmingly by persons belonging to intermediate-level technical cadres, the group which had been credited with running the economy and protecting it from the worst under the regime of incompetent political appointees to the top management posts. Specialists in ideology had a field day discussing the merits of the two variants of socialist ownership—"collective ownership" exercised through the state machinery, and "group ownership" exercised through self-governing organs of enterprise employees. However, in enterprises, the practical issue of professional qualification remained in the foreground. In some of the strongest statements, the establishment of workers' councils, with an absolute separation of the state and enterprise spheres, was declared the necessary condition of the realization of economic reform,[25]

24. *Práce*, 12 December 1968.

25. "Without democratically constituted management organs, it is not possible to revive the initiative of enterprises and their employees, and to make the economic reform a reality." *Práce*, 18 February 1969.

while the government's conception was criticized for intending to perpetuate the basic mechanism of the bureaucratic-administrative system of management.[26]

Cartelization from Below?

Parallel to this spontaneous process of restructuring the internal lines of managerial authority of enterprises, and irrespective of the stage of this process in individual cases, there arose a movement on the part of managerial groups to change the nature of industrial associations or trusts (the so-called economic production units mentioned previously) from administrative supervisory organs to voluntary associations of participating enterprises.

The organizational form of administrative enterprise conglomerations had been a subject of controversy ever since they were introduced as part of the preparation of the economic reform. They were seen as incompatible with the decentralization tendencies of the reform; responding and adjusting to market forces presupposes enterprise autonomy. Strong executive organs of enterprise associations, the so-called branch directorates (*oborová ředitelství*), appeared to contradict this requirement.

In answer to such criticisms, the relationship between branch directorates and their subordinate enterprises was interpreted in semiofficial commentaries as one of a functional division of tasks, securing a happy combination of autonomy and judicious guidance. Branch directorates were given the task of providing a long-range conception of the development of the branch and adjusting the development of individual enterprise units to that conception. Enterprise management was to take care of the year-by-year planning of its operations.

The long-term management of the branch associations was to comprise tasks of the following sort: (a) establishment, liquidation, or merger of enterprises, and determination of their output programs; (b) design of the organizational structure and management systems of subordinate enterprises, presumably in the interests of the standardization required by modern management methods; (c) elaboration of the long-range expansion prospects of the branch; (d) research and development; (e) investment plan elaboration, as well as review and approval of applications for investment credit by enterprises; and (f) modification and differentiation of the new economic

26. Ing. Rudolf Slánský, "Workers' Councils, or Directors' Councils?" *Práce*, 18 February 1969.

This criticism was based not only on deductions but on actual observation. "Some councils found out from their own experience, that in the case of competitive examinations [for managers] all kind of winds were felt to be blowing—from above as well as from the side. [Play on words: "side" and "Party" are homonyms in Czech.] And that these winds were in no case favorable to candidates with the best professional competence." *Odborář*, 1969, no. 3, p. 1.

instruments (rates of financial charges, subsidies, allocations to various enterprise funds) as a means of implementing the general conception of the branch development.[27]

From this enumeration it is clear that the autonomy of individual enterprises foreseen by this organizational scheme was to be very circumscribed indeed, and the feared contradiction with the new economic principles a real one. (It should be noted that the branch directorates did not get much chance to exercise these prerogatives, their attention being fully absorbed by dealing with the financial chaos that arose as a consequence of the 1967 measures.)[28]

The voluntary regrouping of enterprises and revision of the nature of industrial associations that got under way in the fall of 1968 was diametrically opposed to the existing administrative scheme. The first such contractual integration took place among eighteen enterprises of the engineering sector on 5 December 1968. The new formation called itself an industrial entrepreneurial group (*průmyslová podnikatelská skupina*). The integration contract was signed by the interested production units, and by related marketing organizations, the engineering supply organization, and two research institutes as well. Furthermore, the foreign trade organization became part of the new integrated group because a majority of its shares—it was organized as a shareholding corporation—were held by enterprises who were parties to the agreement. Another case, which received somewhat less attention in the press, was the founding of a voluntary organization of the cotton and silk industry.

The remarkable innovation of these regroupings—besides their voluntary aspect—was the democratization of the top executive organs of the new associations. The role of the supreme organ was given to a Board of Administration (*správní výbor*) composed of representatives of the associated enterprises. Symptomatically, a similar shift of authority occurred within economic production units consisting of a single large enterprise, such as the trust Zbrojovka, Brno, where a Board of Administration that had previously acted in a purely advisory role, adjunct to the director general, acquired executive powers at the end of 1968.[29]

The trend toward self-determination was undoubtedly facilitated by a wave of important changes in the governmental organization, consisting of

27. Jaroslav Kobr, *Organisace průmyslu a průmyslových podniků v nové soustavě řízení* [Organization of industry and industrial enterprises in the New System of Management], 1965, pp. 40–46 and passim. Also "Zásady pro regulaci ekonomických a finančních vztahů uvnitř výrobních hospodářských jednotek" [Principles for the regulation of economic and financial relations within economic production units], *Sbírka zákonů*, 1966, no. 64.

28. *Plánované hospodářství*, 1970, no. 4, p. 6.

29. *Hospodářské noviny*, 1968, nos. 48/50, p. 4. (Some of these innovations seem to have been rescinded toward the end of 1969.)

the establishment of new functional ministries in April 1968 (Economic Planning; Technology; and a State Price Office of ministerial rank), and the elimination of several industrial-branch ministries (Mining; Power; Heavy Industry; Chemicals; and Consumer Goods) at the time of the enactment of federalization between Slovakia and the Czech part of the country at the end of 1969. In the course of this organizational flux one could observe a progressive shrinking of the executive functions of governmental economic organs and their reorientation toward concerns with long-term issues of development, at least in the mind of experts working on the final form of the governmental organization.[30] During the confused period of transition it would apparently have been hard to find an organ able to check the initiatives from below, even if the will to do so had been stronger.

Trade Unions to the Trade Unionists

In the sphere of spontaneous developments, the emergence of authentic trade-unionism from within the chrysalis of totalitarian pseudounions may have been the most significant event for the developing character of the reform and the economy. It is noteworthy that resuscitating this particular institutional component of the market economy had not been part of any of the original conceptions of economic reform, either during the preliminary reformist theorizing or during the stage of implementation.[31]

The wage/work rate of exchange derives its particular characteristics from the special nature of the object of the transaction. For one thing, suppliers of labor services suffer a disadvantage in this process of determination because they have few alternatives to immediate sale at the place of their residence. Because they supply goods of instantaneous perishability—services—which cannot be withheld by being stocked, they are limited in their movement not only by the cost of displacement, but also by the psychological and social requirements of reasonable residential stability. The price of labor services is the source of their livelihood, and individual household supply functions of labor tend to be negatively sloped not only at high but

30. Cf. the highly informative interview with the head of the section for management and organization at the former Ministry of Heavy Industry in ibid., p. 3.

31. Cf. a comment by Paul Barton: "It is a fact that Communist economists, no matter how great their reformist zeal, have been incapable of imagining changes that would not make the worker bear the cost of the fraud for which the *aparatchiki* alone have been responsible. Even while criticizing the communist management of the economy and preaching profound reforms, they remain victims of propaganda.... They are convinced that in Western countries the economy depends on a blind play of supply and demand.... Quite spontaneously they consider all effects injurious to workers as something regrettable but necessary, infatuated as they are with the idea of the free play of market forces." [French original.] *Le Contrat Social* 12, nos. 2–3 (April–September 1968): 100.

also at low wage-rate levels. Furthermore, the wage contract is a special case of a renting or leasing transaction; and as such it requires methods of determining the quantity of service supplied that take account not only of time worked but also of the intensity of work and of working conditions in general. Hence, the need for a legal delimitation of the employers' power to impose their own private legislation in the workshop is implied. This is the economic rationale for protective public labor legislation, as well as for on-the-spot bargaining and grievance procedures, conceived as a continuous process under conditions of never-ending technological change.

The necessity or desirability of authentic union-type organizations of labor can be further argued on the grounds of their influence upon the supply of housing, professional training and retraining, effective insurance against costs of obsolescence of skills due to technical progress (technological unemployment), insurance against unemployment due to structural changes and economic fluctuations, and possibly upon the process of substituting capital for labor in consequence of wage pressures.

In the Czechoslovak case, the defense of labor against the injurious effects of the economic reform was among the most immediate motives behind the revival of unionism. Well before 1968, this revival took place informally within the framework of the official trade-union organization, whose officers were being pushed by local circumstances into the role of defenders of workers' interests. From 1966 on it happened more and more frequently, particularly during attempts to close inefficient plants, but also as protests kept mounting against the fairly general disregard of various stipulations of the Labor Code in matters of safety, hygiene, and working conditions. It was realized with increasing clarity that the strength of managerial incentives might bring managerial interests into conflict with workers' interests. As one specialist in labor law put it, "a consistent application of the improved system of management would further intensify the tendency toward attainment of favorable economic results at the expense of the observation of workers' rights, on the part of the leading personnel of organizations and their collectives."[32] It was suggested by the same author that the dilemmas of the trade-union organization, torn between workers' interests and production tasks, be alleviated by the establishment of organs of state inspection and control that would restrain managers in their efficiency drive.

The only step taken in the direction of protective labor legislation was the granting of unemployment benefits in August 1967; it was a step long overdue and in some respects a caricature of unemployment insurance. According to the decree, laid-off workers would receive an allowance amounting to 60 percent of their past average net pay, up to 1,800 crowns. However, the

32. Prof. Karel Witz of the Law School of Charles University, *Rudé právo*, 9 August 1967.

payment of benefits could be granted only if the labor section of the local administration could offer them absolutely no job of any kind. According to paragraph 6 of the decree, "The allowance will not be granted, or will be revoked, if the employee refuses, without serious reasons, to enter appropriate employment compatible with his health and abilities, and as far as possible with his [professional] qualifications, or to participate in work assistance organized by the national committee for agricultural peak, seasonal, or similar operations."[33] Even if one should hesitate to infer from this stipulation the idea of forced-labor assignments, the arrangement is obviously too uncertain to be satisfactory from the point of view of laid-off workers.

The revolutionary process of the reconquest of trade-union organs by their memberships got underway in spring 1968, first by personnel changes at the top of the confederate executive (*Ústřední rada odborů*), and later by local removal of officers at the enterprise level and their replacement by men commanding the confidence of the members. The movement toward trade-union autonomy found its pragmatic reflection in the demand that individual trade-union federations be established as organizations independent of the central trade-union council (of which they had been mere implementing organs), and that this central organ be turned into a true confederate representation, chosen by and subordinate to the executives of individual federations.[34] As a point of central symbolic as well as practical significance, declarations of the legitimacy of strikes were obtained from trade union, state, and Party officials.

This trend reached its peak during the fall and winter months after the Soviet invasion. The federalization of Czechoslovakia (the constitution of Slovakia and the Czech provinces into two federated states), became the occasion—or pretext—for a basic overhaul of the organizational structure of the trade unions. Parallel to other organs and organizations, trade unions were to be split into Czech and Slovak portions, and then recombined, at the top executive level, into a state-wide organ. Although this step seemed to represent a weakening of the trade-union organization, it intended to strengthen the members' influence upon the executive organs of individual federations and thereby increase their power. Preliminary congresses of individual federations, held in the winter of 1968–69, offered members and their delegates an opportunity to change the personal composition of the executive organs of federations and to vote resolutions consonant with members' interests. This process was then continued at the next tier, at all-union

33. *Sbírka zákonů*, no. 86, 24 August 1967, pp. 321–24.
34. Cf. Reports on the national consultative conference of delegates of basic trade union organizations, *Práce*, 19 and 20 June 1968.

congresses of these federations, which elected new confederation organs according to new principles and adopted new statutes.[35]

Clearly, these new arrangements did not have a chance to be implemented under the conservative backlash. Removals of elected officers followed, the resolutions of the winter congresses were being annulled, and the charter of the trade-union movement was reinterpreted according to the principles of "democratic centralism."[36]

An important side development of the years 1968–69 was the attempt of one category of workers—railroad engineers—to constitute themselves as an entirely new autonomous organization, the Federation of Locomotive Teams. The remarkable tenacity of these men, determined to organize themselves without any assistance whatsoever, encountered massive resistance from the State and Party, as well as superior trade-union organs, and might have been obstructed further even if the totalitarian restoration had not taken place.

The existence of labor unions as representatives of labor interests poses a problem with respect to the institution of workers' councils as organs of labor participation in management. Considering workers' councils by themselves, there is, on the face of it, a danger of organizational schizophrenia: how should they act when workers' interests in their role as workers conflict with their role as entrepreneurs, that is, as their own employers? The doctrinal answer to this dilemma given by Czechoslovak writers of "unionist persuasion" was essentially the same one expressed in a simple and cogent way during the Hungarian revolution in an article of the trade-union daily, justifying the right to strike under a regime of workers' councils:

Not even the most perfect and most democratic decree concerning the workers' councils will ensure the right to strike for the simple reason that the right question [sic] is not connected with the workers' councils. The workers' councils fill the role of the enterprises' business management. The right to strike, on the other hand, is the peculiar form of the protection of interests, a trade-union activity . . . .

We want the workers, through the workers' councils, to be masters of the enterprises, in actual practice . . . . The world, however, has never seen a master who has assured the right to strike—whether a capitalist master or any kind. However, it is important that the master, the owner of the enterprise, even if it be the workers themselves, be

35. Cf. texts of resolutions adopted at the congress of Czech federations on 23 January 1969 in *Odborář*, 1969, no. 3, pp. 13–19, and the text of the new charter of the all-state trade union organization published as a supplement to *Práce*, 13 March 1969.

36. See the Resolution of the Fourth Plenary Session of the Central Council of the Czechoslovak Trade Unions of 25 and 26 November 1969 in *Odborář*, 1969, no. 25, pp. 2–7.

controlled by an organ whose primary task is to protect the workers' interest. This is the mission of the trade union.[37]

Translated into academic terms, this solution amounts to the advocacy of a functional differentiation of organizational forms according to identifiable interests within one social group, particularly if they are potentially conflicting, as is likely to be the case of interests related to different roles played by the same people in the economic process. It is assumed that the solution of conflicts arising from such divergent interests is facilitated by explicit organizational specialization between organs of management, even workers' management, and organs representing the interests of workers as employees; it is made more difficult if reconciliation is attempted through a single multipurpose body, or takes place under conditions of bogus differentiation, as in the case of totalitarian pseudounions.[38]

IV. FRUSTRATION-RESUMPTION OF THE REFORM

The dividing line between the upsurge of social and political energies after the Soviet invasion, and the eventual reinstatement of totalitarian structures and methods of government, is usually placed at the April 1969 Plenum of the Central Committee of the Party which replaced Alexander Dubček in his post of First Secretary with Gustav Husák. However, as far as the economic reform is concerned, there seems to have set in an interregnum characterized by perplexity about the future and some factual analyses of achievements and failures, as well as by a certain amount of official opprobrium of the major protagonists of the reform. The evanescent spirit of the intense and desperate activism of 1968 and 1969 lingered for a while. Thus, "even by mid-year, i.e., after the April Plenum, the Federal Ministry of Planning was preparing a bill on planning which was actually meant to abolish, by law, unified planning, to tear asunder enterprise planning and state planning, and to give the state economic plan a character of information free to be disregarded."[39] At the working-economy level the spirit of activism translated itself in phenomena of "X-inefficiency." During the transition from revolt to resignation, it was reported that workers engaged in deliberate slowdowns, with the particular intent of sabotaging exports to

37. *Nepakarat*, 24 November 1956, cited by Paul Barton, "The Workers' Demands in the Hungarian Revolution," *Saturn* (Monthly Review of the International Commission Against Concentration Camp Practices) 2, no. 5 (December 1956): 35–36.

38. Cf. Paul Barton, "Le Contrôle ouvrier," *Saturne* 3, no. 15 (October–November 1957), pp. 27–51. For recent Czechoslovak statements in the same sense, see, for example, Ing. Jiří Klenkner, "Odborová organizace a rada pracujících [The trade union organization and the workers' council), *Rudé právo*, 29 January 1969, p. 3.

39. *Nová mysl*, 1969, no. 11, p. 1371.

the Soviet Union (e.g. in loading and unloading railway wagons passing through Cierna).[40]

Recentralization or Only Governmental Controls?

As a counterpoint to the social effervescence of 1968–69, interpreted in the present context as a way of driving the reform process forward, governmental organs were simultaneously adopting administrative measures which may be characterized, if one wants to be generous, as temporary stop-gap wage and price controls, used by authorities panicking in the face of inflationary pressures; or, less generously, as backsliding toward recentralized administrative manipulation of the economy. We have already alluded to the interdiction of payments of profit-share advances in enterprises where productivity lagged behind wages (see p. 328). There followed soon after "special guidelines of the government concerning the regulation of wage trends"[41] which, according to an official of the Ministry of Planning, was "undoubtedly the worst measure of all . . . making wages dependent on the labor-productivity indicator measured by gross output, which meant a breach of the principles of the new model."[42] It goes without saying that foreign trade tasks determined by trade agreements with the Soviet Union and other "countries of the socialist camp," and output referred to cryptically as "special production," retained their priority status under the new "reform" conditions.

It was this incipient tendency toward backsliding that was carried on by the government in 1969–70. Thus, three sets of measures were elaborated in that spirit during the "restoration period": (1) In June 1969 it was decided to make the executive organs of industrial associations (VHJs) conclude "agreements" with the government, according to which they would accept the obligation to secure from their subordinate enterprises requisite deliveries of commodities for export and for the domestic market, in that sequence.[43] The same procedure was repeated in the form of "protocols" intended to provide the figures of the "implementation plan for 1970" with the character of mandatory tasks.[44] (2) The development of wages was subject to a definitive regulation introducing an obligatory stable share of wage payments in the gross value of sales. Organs of economic management were expected to set the rate of shares in a differentiated fashion, and supplement the indicator of "gross value of sales" with other indicators capable of

40. Cf. traces of this phenomenon in *Rudé právo*, 26 July 1969, and elsewhere.

41. *Hospodářské noviny*, 1967, no. 39, p. 5, and the daily press of 19 September 1967.

42. Vladimír Šiba in *Plánované hospodářstyí*, 1969, no. 2, p. 3 (footnote).

43. *Rudé právo*, 25 June 1969; *Práce*, 1 July 1969; *Rudé právo*, 12 July 1969; *Hospodářské noviny*, 1969, no. 34, pp. 1 and 6.

44. Ibid., pp. 1 and 4.

preventing enterprises from circumventing the intent of the measure by various manipulations.[45] (3) A general price freeze, called a "price moratorium," was imposed at the end of 1969, which cancelled the earlier categories of fixed, limited, and free prices.[46] In the background of these measures loomed the wish to endow the production figures of neocentralist annual plans—successors to the earlier "orientation guidelines" issued in lieu of plans from 1966 on—with the authority of must-targets.

Rehabilitation of the Plan: What Kind of Plan?

However, the situation has proved more complex and contradictory than an enumeration of administrative measures suggests. Not only is there a considerable amount of irreversibility in both the state of the economy and attitudes emerging from the period of 1968 and early 1969, but the leading organs of the "decontaminated" Communist party and government themselves were not united about the proper course for the implementation of the Central Committee guideline, which called for the rehabilitation of the authority of the plan while exploiting positive experiences of the reform at home.[47]

In a sense, we are witnessing a reenactment of the economic debate, and symptoms of behind-the-scene infighting which preceded the adoption of the principles of economic reform in 1965 and 1966. "Contemporary conditions" were characterized, at the beginning of 1970, as a "combination of, oscillation between, as well as haggling about command planning and the utilization of indirect methods."[48] The strength of political forces sponsoring the two alternative conceptions has apparently been sufficiently equal to check any clear-cut progress in either direction. During this temporary stalemate, major issues of the economic reform, and the related place and meaning of planning, were reopened to debate in the pages of economic periodicals, mostly with new sponsors but to some extent under unrepenting old ones.

The official line stresses the need to increase the binding character (závaznost) of plans while assuring that "this does not mean a return to outlived methods."[49] Despite this verbal assurance, a tendency to return to "outlived methods," or to press for their resurrection, must have been rather strong in order to justify warnings and exhortations "to block current campaigns of people calculating, in a one-sided fashion, how many command

---

45. The survey of pertinent prescriptions is to be found in two supplements to *Hospodářské noviny*, 1970, nos. 10 and 14.
46. Ibid., no. 10, pp. 1 and 4.
47. Ibid., no. 18, p. 5.
48. Dr. Pavol Steiner of the State Bank, in ibid., no. 4, p. 3.
49. *Plánované hospodářství*, 1970, no. 4, p. 5.

indicators will be reintroduced" and to criticize the identification of the increased role of the plan with "a simple declaration of the obligatory character of planned figures and their disaggregation (through obligatory tasks, ceilings, and priorities)."[50] Official declarations of principle aside, the practical attitude of the government has been to reintroduce obligatory tasks and priorities, or at least "to consider the fulfillment of export tasks as one of the decisive criteria for the evaluation of the work results . . . of responsible economic management employees."[51]

In contrast with this practical bias in favor of command methods, official declarations on the future nature of Czechoslovak planning still have the ring of pious intentions: the enhanced authority of plans is to derive not from *direktivnost* but from their improved quality; their quality is to improve through the application of "modern methods of plan construction," continuous structural prognosis, economic-structural and material balances, methods of successive approximation, efficiency comparison of plan variants, and mathematical methods.[52] Subjectivism and voluntarism in planning are to remain buried forever: planning will be approached as "primarily predetermined and constrained by objective problems of the economy."[53] Beyond these generalities little has transpired concerning concrete intentions, even though work on the elaboration of a new five-year plan (1971–75) has apparently been in full swing. It is not clear what relationship there is between activities which are under way in governmental offices and discussions via the printed page. The latter tend to evoke a picture of thoroughly unsettled goals and methods of economic policy.

Topics in Search of Solutions

Articles by new authors have appeared in economic journals which reexamine the nature of the planning function under conditions that are not those of a command economy. It would be tempting to review, for instance, the refreshingly caustic analysis of planning issues undertaken by Vítězslav Kazda, whose subtlety and conceptual discrimination is in itself an eloquent denunciation of the revival of the past in high places.[54] We shall resist this temptation to "talk ideas" and will limit ourselves to a selective enumeration of topics which have dominated the present stage of the economic debate, conducted mostly in the absence of the well-known names of the era of reforms.

50. Ibid., 1970, no. 1, p. 59.
51. *Hospodářské noviny*, 1970, no. 5, p. 4.
52. Ibid., p. 5.
53. Ibid., no. 3, p. 3.
54. Vítězslav Kazda, "Úloha plánu v systému řízení ekonomiky" [The role of plan in the system of management of the economy], *Plánované hospodářství*, 1970, no. 1, pp. 55–69.

1. *Concentration on research and development, and a deliberate strategy of technological rejuvenation.* In the course of the first discussions of reform, it was assumed that the revival of incentives and dynamics on the microlevel could be expected to stimulate technological innovation. Technological innovation was not, however, the hub of economic policies; economic instruments were not coordinated with this objective in mind. It seems that a shift in emphasis has recently been taking place.[55] This shift—or progress—is from reformist theorizing, which was all too often framed in terms of simple allocative models of individual commodities and factors, toward policy-oriented conceptions which intend to deal with large blocks of decisions involving entire technological processes (with the full complex of individual inputs and outputs which they comprise) and making decisions in terms of broad national technological strategies.[56] Such an approach had occasionally been recommended much earlier; in 1964, for instance, Otakar Turek formulated the simple but profound principle that "output growth will be achieved by concentrating on *conditions* of growth rather than on the *results* of growth, i.e., production volume."[57]

2. *Promoting vertical integration.* In contrast to the denunciation of horizontal integration (or what the Czechs refer to as "administrative monopoly" exercised by "economic production units") in favor of autonomy and independence of individual enterprises, the new tendency is to denounce both in favor of vertical integration. The breakup of integrated firms, and their regrouping into homogeneous administrative conglomerates, which took place after 1950, was meant to facilitate the disaggregation of plan figures into individual plant-output assignments.[58] The tendency to "organize the economy from the bottom up in a uniform and simple fashion,"[59] reflecting the perfectionist compulsiveness of the totalitarian mentality (more of geometric than economic inspiration), also played a part. With the rejection of detailed quantitative command planning, and with new attention paid to the necessity of making economic decisions in terms of large technological and structural "blocks," horizontal integration continues in disfavor. Whereas during the Šik era the stress was on the mutual adjustment of economic units, the current stress on vertical integration implies as a major objective the internalization of planning problems within large integrated

55. See, for example, A. Mrazek and J. Kubik, "Výsledky a perspektivy státní vědeckotechnické politiky" [Results and perspectives of the state scientific-technological policy], *Hospodářské noviny*, 1970, no. 19, pp. 8–9.
56. Cf. the informative survey by Robert Gilpin, "Technological Strategies and National Purpose," *Science* 1969, no. 3944: 441–48.
57. *Hospodářské noviny*, 1964, no. 15, p. 3.
58. Ibid., 1970, no. 18, p. 14.
59. Ibid., no. 5, p. 7.

units.[60] A corollary drive in favor of greater subcontracting with small satellite enterprises serving the large units has also remained alive, but has lost the force of urgency it had earlier under the influence of Evžen Loebl and others.

3. *Specialization.* Throughout the first stage of the reform, tendencies in two different directions were noticeable: (*a*) toward greater freedom of diversification, breaking out of the administratively imposed production lines and finding new, more efficient patterns of output, better adapted to local conditions, and thus toward fostering domestic competition; and (*b*) toward greater specialization, away from excessively diversified short production runs, in order to improve Czechoslovak chances in international competition. Currently the stress has been more and more on the latter.[61]

4. *Attention to the quality of basic data.* This manifests itself mainly through outspoken criticism of the existing state of economic information. The tendency toward understatement of the inflationary movement of wholesale prices in official statistics has become known.[62] It is only recently that the extent of this understatement and its effect upon figures of capital accumulation were revealed: "In 1967, relative to 1955, the rate of distortion in basic machinery stocks amounts to 27 percent, and in deliveries of machinery and installations for investments to 41 percent."[63] This confirms the complaints of the authors of an econometric model of the economy, bequeathed by Šik's Economic Institute to the new regime,[64] about the low quality of the basic data with which they had to work.

Similarly, accounting methods have been criticized for not providing sufficient insight into cost relationships, and not offering basic data for plans. Moreover, governmental organs seem to have lost track of the state of development in important areas, e.g. the value of investments under construction. (On the other hand, inquiries of a specialized nature, such as one concerning the age composition and state of fixed capital stock, have been completed or are being undertaken.)

5. *Miscellaneous.* The following is in the nature of an unsystematic sampling of additional facts and themes whose significance may emerge in the course of time. A system of price regulation, intended to carry forward

60. A recent book by Miroslav Rosický, *Společnost hospodářských možností* [Society of economic possibilities] (Prague: Svoboda, 1970), which tries to promote these ideas, received a very favorable review. *Hospodářsté noviny*, 1970, no. 18, p. 14.

61. Ibid., no. 5, p. 9.

62. Cf. Rolf Grünwald, "Pohyb cen pracovních předmětů a úkoly statistiky" [Movement of prices of means of production and statistical tasks], *Statistika*, 1967, no. 12, pp. 535–39.

63. *Plánované hospodářství*, 1970, no. 1, p. 71. (I was unable to determine the precise meaning of this "distortion.")

64. Jiří Beck et al., *Model optimálního střednědobého plánu* [A model of the optimal medium-term plan], 2 vols. (Prague, 1968–69).

the adjustment of relative prices and to enforce consistent rules in the pricing of new products, has been announced.[65] The need to preserve and increase elbowroom for the initiative of enterprises has been stressed again.[66] Market research and production planning using modern quantitative methods have proceeded within various large establishments.[67] Lines of administrative authority have been confused, parallel to the confusion of accounting and planning data.[68] Demands are being voiced to implement the set of priorities in investments proclaimed in 1968, favoring chemicals, consumer goods, and food industries.[69] Trade-union organs are attempting to safeguard a certain amount of autonomy, as can be gathered from their insistence on constructing an independent statistical index of living costs, despite protests on the part of the established institutions of statistical reporting.[70]

Market, Planning, and the Philosophy of Power

Throughout this paper it has proved impossible to discuss the problems posed by the market-planning relationship without reference to the modalities and distribution of noneconomic power. The types of solutions to the market-planning issue, proposed or advocated, contested or implemented, have been clearly correlated with political ideas and with the political constellation. Might one suggest the hypothesis that intellectual insights into the Czechoslovak economic problem, in particular the problem of the economic system, are incompatible with the totalitarian system of authority, in a way analogous to the conflict and incompatibility of past discoveries in natural science with the continued power of religious authority?

The current state of economic discussion and the number of unsettled issues of practical policy in Czechoslovakia indicate that a struggle between two antagonistic conceptions of planning and power continues to be waged, in repressed and subdued forms, close to the surface. It is the conflict between what we might call the "synergetic" and authoritarian types of planning, two opposing philosophies of intervention in the economic process.

65. *Hospodářské noviny*, 1970, no. 17, p. 4.
66. That X-efficiency again: "A man feels entirely different if he finds opportunities for applying his capabilities and living a full life in his work in society. The system of management has to create that necessary room for him." Ibid., 1970, no. 5, p. 9.
67. Ibid., no. 6, p. 7.
68. Ibid., no. 4, p. 3.
69. "We succeeded in discovering that central organs of economic management had not worked out resolutions into the state of concreteness required . . . . The center still lacks a global conception." Ibid., no. 7, p. 7.
70. *Hospodářské noviny*, 1970.

On one side, there is belief in the "Manichaean antagonism"[71] between market and plan; the distrust of all social self-regulation, spontaneity, and autonomy; the compulsion to control through prescription, command, and interdiction; the conviction that no control is possible unless exercised through heavy instruments in direct contact with the decision makers in the production process, and with the application of sanctions based ultimately on power. On the other side, there is confidence in a process of spontaneous activism which merely needs to be helped by rational insight and supplementary instruments, aiding the system to achieve its intrinsic objectives.[72] The contrast between the underlying moral and political values is evident. While the synergetic methods have perhaps not been tested long enough, or elaborated fully, and their ultimate success is far from guaranteed, human progress certainly lies in their direction. Unfortunately, nothing less Delphic can be said of the Czechoslovak situation as of this moment.

71. Cf. Philipp Herder-Dornreich, *Der Markt und seine Alternativen in der freien Gesellschaft* (Hanover: J. H. W. Dietz; Vienna/Freiburg: Herder, 1968), pp. 28, 97 and 106. (The author explains: Manichaeism: Religious doctrine characterized by a radical dualism between a god and an evil principle." Ibid., p. 97.)

72. Compare this with a similar opposition between "authentic planners" and "soft planners" in France. See Vera Lutz, *Central Planning for the Market Economy* (London and Harlow: Longmans, Green, and Co., 1969), p. 166 ff.

10

The Firm in the New Economic Mechanism in Hungary

BELA BALASSA

I. Guidelines for the Economic Reform

In the system of centralized planning practiced in Hungary until the introduction of the economic reform, firms' activities were regulated by central directives communicated to them by the supervisory ministries. The directives concerned the production plan of the firm, its product composition, material allocation, manpower and wage targets, as well as practically all its investments, including the replacement of existing facilities. Within the constraints these directives imposed on the firm, managers aimed at obtaining bonuses to provide a supplement to their salary.

More precisely, the managers' objective was to obtain bonuses as large as permitted by the constraints imposed on the firm but not so large as to result in a subsequent tightening of the conditions for their attainment by the supervising ministry. Because the principal condition for receiving bonuses was the firm's success in fulfilling and overfulfilling the production plan, managers tried both to reduce the plan target through bargaining with the ministry and to increase output by using legal as well as extralegal means. The latter included changes in product composition toward higher-value commodities, disguised price increases, quality deterioration, obtaining materials outside official distribution channels, and increasing output without regard to costs.

Some of the firm's activities aimed at obtaining bonuses—such as efforts made to increase output with given inputs—were beneficial to the national

For helpful discussions of the issues treated in this paper, I am indebted to Hungarian officials, firm managers, and economists, especially to Andrea Deák and András Nagy. My greatest debt, however, is to Joseph Bognár, whose invitation first provided me the opportunity to study the Hungarian economic reform and who has given me the benefit of detailed comments on an earlier version of this paper. I alone am responsible for any remaining errors and inaccuracies in facts and interpretations.

economy; others, such as price increases, were neutral; others again, including undesirable changes in product composition, quality deterioration, and increases in production costs, had adverse effects. Various features of the system of centralized planning practiced in Hungary made it possible for the firm to act to the detriment of the national economy.[1]

Firms had a certain latitude in fulfilling the targets communicated to them by the supervisory authorities; these targets were often contradictory and conflicts among them increased with changes in underlying conditions during the plan period. At the same time, as users generally had no choice among suppliers, they had to accept low-quality items or commodities which did not fully correspond to their needs. Nor was the firm penalized for the accumulation of unsalable products, since the evaluation of its performance was based on production rather than on sales. Cost increases incurred in fulfilling the production plan did not affect the evaluation of the firm's performance either.

The introduction of profits as one of the conditions for obtaining bonuses reduced but little the adverse effects of the incentive system.[2] Not only did the fulfillment of the production plan continue to loom large in the bonus scheme, but the prices at which profits were calculated had purely an accounting function and did not express resource scarcities. Prices did not include an allowance for the use of capital and land; did not equate domestic demand and supply; and were divorced from world market price relations. Exporters received, and importers paid, the prices set domestically; the differences between domestic and world market prices were paid into, or financed from, an equalization fund whose importance grew over time.

Planning methods were simplified somewhat during the early 1960s; the number of plan indicators communicated to the firm was reduced and greater contact developed between suppliers and users. But the basic character of the planning system did not change; the firm's productive activities were still largely circumscribed by the supervising ministry, and its performance was evaluated on the basis of plan fulfillment.

While centralized decision making may have been conducive to growth at an earlier stage of development of the Hungarian economy, its shortcomings became increasingly apparent as the industrial structure has become more sophisticated, labor shortages have appeared, and foreign trade has assumed greater importance. The realization of these shortcomings contributed to the adoption of the economic reform, customarily called the New Economic

1. The paper will not consider conflicts between sectoral and national economic interests, in the presence of which the fulfillment of sectoral targets presented by the supervising ministry does not ensure that the firm's activities serve the interests of the national economy.

2. On the "joint" maximization of production and profits, see my "La théorie de la firme socialiste," *Economie Appliquée*, July–December 1959, pp. 535–70.

Mechanism, which was introduced on 1 January 1968. The reform replaces the central allocation of most materials and products by market relations among firms; it provides incentives for profit maximization at prices increasingly reflecting valuation by the market; and it greatly increases the freedom of action of the firm in undertaking new investments. Government preferences are expressed chiefly by the use of indirect rather than direct measures.[3]

The Hungarian reform resembles the Lange–Lerner model of market socialism, which would ensure efficient resource allocation through the competition of socialist firms. But whereas the Lange–Lerner model is that of a closed economy, foreign trade is of great importance in Hungary; moreover, instead of price setting by a central authority à la Lange, price formation is to be increasingly left to market forces.

The purpose of this paper is to consider the role of the firm in the New Economic Mechanism. First, I examine the process of short-term decision making, the extent of domestic competition, and the limitations on the firm's activities. This is followed by a discussion of the process of long-term decision making, including investments financed by the firm itself, by the banking system, and by the state. Further consideration is given to export incentives, and the choice between exporting and producing for the domestic market. Finally, I describe the major achievements of the New Economic Mechanism, and note some of the problems and difficulties observable since its introduction.

II. Short-Term Decision Making

The Managerial Incentive System

Three questions need to be raised in connection with the managerial incentive system under the New Economic Mechanism: (1) Is the incentive system conducive to the maximization of profits? (2) Do managers consider profit maximization to be their main objective? And (3) Is profit maximization by the firm in the interests of the national economy? I will take up these questions in turn. To answer the first, regulations on the distribution of profits and their tax treatment need to be considered.

After statutory allowances for reserves, the firm's profits are divided between the distribution fund and the investment fund, which are taxed at different rates. This division is effected on the basis of the relative importance of wages and the gross value of assets in the individual firm, with upward

3. Various aspects of the reform are described in *Reform of the Economic Mechanism in Hungary*, ed. István Friss (Budapest: Akadémiai Kiadó, 1969). For a brief appraisal, see my "The Economic Reform in Hungary," *Economica*, February 1970, pp. 1–22.

adjustments made in the amount of wages on an industry-by-industry basis.[4]

Increases in average wages above the wage norm set for the firm by the supervisory ministry are financed from the distribution fund; the remainder is used to pay bonuses, and cultural, social, and educational expenses as well. The fund is subject to progressive taxation, based on its ratio to the amount of wages payable in accordance with the wage norm. Marginal tax rates vary between 0 and 70 percent; in contrast, a flat tax of 60 percent applies to the investment fund.

There has been considerable discussion in Hungary as to the incentives provided for the firm's activities by the regulations on the distribution and taxation of profits. Some have suggested that firms will aim at maximizing the per-capita incomes of workers which, for a given wage norm, would entail the maximization of the ratio of the aftertax distribution fund to the "allowed" amount of wages.[5] According to one author, this objective could be reached by maximizing the ratio of the total profit to the allowed amount of wages.[6] Subsequently, however, it has been shown that, under the regulations in effect, maximizing the per-capita incomes of workers involves maximizing the ratio of total profits to the sum of the allowed wages and the value of assets.[7] Should this objective be pursued, production will be less

4. The relevant formulas, applicable after allowance for reserves, are the following:

$$N_r = N \frac{sB}{sB + E} \quad \text{and} \quad N_f = N \frac{E}{sB + E}$$

when N is total profit, N_r and N_f are the pretax distribution and investment funds, B the amount of wages, s a factor of multiplication pertaining to wages, and E the value of assets. For the average firm, $s = 2$; the large number of upward deviations in the value of s granted in 1968 were reduced in the following year. In 1968, B had been determined by multiplying the wage norm set for the firm by the number of workers; in subsequent years B was taken to equal the amount of wages actually paid. The formulas cited below pertain to the situation existing in 1968.

5. In symbols, maximizing $(B + R)/L$ involves the maximization of R/B when R refers to the aftertax distribution fund, L is the number of workers, and B equals the number of workers multiplied by the wage norm. Thus B, the allowed amount of wages, changes in proportion with the number of workers, the proportionality factor being the wage norm.

6. Endre Megyeri, "Vállalati nyereségérdekeltség és termelési optimum" [Profit incentives in the enterprise and the optimum of production], Közgazdasagi Szemle, 1967, nos. 7–8, pp. 872–84. Megyeri's argument closely resembles that of Ward a decade earlier (Benjamin Ward, "The Firm in Illyria: Market Syndicalism," American Economic Review, September 1958, pp. 566–89).

7. In symbols, maximizing R/B requires the maximization of $N/(B + E/s)$. The conclusion follows since the relative size of the aftertax distribution fund depends on the ratio of the pretax distribution fund to the allowed amount of wages. This can be written as

$$\frac{N_r}{B} = \frac{N[sB/(sB + E)]}{B} = \frac{N}{B + E/s}.$$

Gábor Révész, "Nyereségszabályozás és vállalati érdekeltség" [Regulation of profits and the interests of the firm], Közgazdasagi Szemle, 1968, no. 1, pp. 38–53.

than under profit maximization, since the ratio in question will decline before profits reach their maximum, although with labor as the only variable factor it will be greater than if the ratio of profits to the allowed amount of wages were maximized.[8]

The described maximization principle is, however, of a short-term character. It further assumes that managers act in accordance with the desires of the average worker and it considers the welfare of the workers the firm has at the time the decision is taken to the exclusion of those to be hired subsequently. While these assumptions may be fulfilled in a labor-managed system, such as that applied in Yugoslavia, they did not appear to be realistic in Hungary, where workers' councils have not been established. Thus, although pressure from labor unions may provide a lower limit to increases in individual incomes, managers will also take account of increases in the investment fund in making decisions.

It may be suggested, then, that managers aim at maximizing the discounted value of aftertax profits, subject to the constraint that the average income of the workers rises at a certain rate.[9] It should be added, however, that the tendency toward profit maximization is tempered by a reluctance to show overly large profits for fear of social pressure or intervention by the supervisory ministry. This will be especially true for monopolistic firms.

With these qualifications, and neglecting differences in tax rates on the distribution and investment funds, the managers' objectives would be compatible with the maximization of the discounted value of pretax profits. This would be relevant from the point of view of the national economy, were it not for the rule that increases in average wages above the norm are payable from the distribution fund.

In 1968 the distribution fund—but not the allowed amount of wages— was taxable, so that the maximization of aftertax profits, excluding wage payments, and that of pretax profits did not coincide. Aftertax profits net of wages could be increased by hiring low-wage labor that simultaneously increased costs (reduced pretax profits) and reduced average wages (increased aftertax profits net of wage payments).[10] More generally, the

8. In symbols, for a given E, maximizing N/B will give a smaller production value than maximizing $N/(B + E/s)$ which, in turn, is less than the value obtained if N is maximized.

9. One author assumes this rate to equal zero and considers the constraint to be that of keeping average incomes unchanged. István Antal, "Vállalati érdekeltség és létszámstruktura" [The interests of the firm and the structure of employment], *Közgazdasagi Szemle*, 1968, nos. 7–8, pp. 925–35, and idem, "Vállalati érdekeltség és munkaerögazdálkodás" [The interests of the firm and manpower management], *Közgazdasagi Szemle*, 1968, no. 9, pp. 1072–86.

10. Take, for example, the case of a firm with (in millions) a production value of 100 forints and costs of 85 forints. If two-thirds of the profit of 15 forints is allotted to the investment fund and one-third to the distribution fund, with the former subject to a 60 percent tax and the latter

(continued on page 352)

incentive system strongly favored expansion by increasing the firm's labor force over measures such as upgrading the labor force or rewarding workers for productivity improvements, which would have entailed an increase in average wages.[11] The described tendencies were further strengthened by the absolute limitation of increases in average wages to 4 percent over the wage norm prescribed for the firm, which was often smaller than the average wage of the previous year.

On the firm level, actions taken in response to these incentives led to the creation—or maintenance—of disguised unemployment, the avoidance of quality improvements in the working force, and the practical exclusion of wage incentive schemes aiming at productivity increases. On the national economy level, the result was simultaneous labor surpluses in some firms and shortages in others. But, as firms competed for labor, in 1968 the gross movement of labor (total inflow and outflow combined) increased by one-fourth; firms on the average had to hire 700 workers in order to increase their labor force by 100. The incentives provided for "hoarding" rather than saving labor also contributed to a slowdown in the growth of productivity; in 1968 labor productivity measured in terms of product per man rose only 1.5 percent as compared to 5 percent in previous years. While the increase was 5 percent in terms of output per hour, this again was below anticipations since reductions in labor hours tend to raise the rate of growth of output per hour.[12]

(continued from page 351)
to an average 40 percent tax, the aftertax contributions to these funds are, respectively, 4 and 3 forints. Assume now that, out of the distribution fund, 2 forints are paid in the form of increases in average wages, leaving 1 forint. The firm could, however, avoid the penalty for exceeding the wage norm by hiring low-wage workers for, say, 1 forint. Costs would now be raised to 86 forints, pretax profits reduced to 14 forints and, assuming a marginal tax of 60 percent on the decrease in the distribution fund, the aftertax investment and distribution funds would be, respectively, 3.7 and 2.9 forints. Accordingly, the sum of the investment fund and the nonwage portion of the distribution fund would rise from 5 to 6.6 forints while the change in the latter, taken by itself, would be from 1 to 2.9 forints.

It is apparent from the example that the lower the valuation managers put on the investment fund as compared to the distribution fund, the greater are the incentives for such manipulations.

11. In the previous example, one-third of profits is allocated to the distribution fund, which is subject to a marginal tax of 60 percent. Accordingly, a one-forint increase in the wage bill due to a rise in average wages would have required an increase in pretax profits of 2.50 forints (1/0.40) to maintain aftertax profits constant, and an increase in pretax profits of 7.50 forints (1/0.33 × 0.40) to avoid a reduction in the aftertax distribution fund. If, instead, the increase in the wage bill was due to higher employment with average wages unchanged, no increase in pretax profits would be needed to maintain aftertax profits, including the aftertax distribution fund, constant.

12. J. Rózsa, "A létszámgazdálkodás és szabályozása az uj mechanizmus elsó két évében" [Labor management and regulations in the first two years of the new mechanism], *Közgazdasagi Szemle*, 1970, no. 1, pp. 13–25.

Further evidence about these consequences of the incentive system is provided by the findings of a sample survey conducted by the Research Institute for Industrial Economics of the Academy of Science under the direction of Zoltán Román. The system of incentives in effect in 1968 caused firms to hire labor unnecessarily according to 47 percent of the respondents, and 57 percent said it gave rise to labor shortages. The respondents regarded labor shortages as the single most important obstacle to the expansion of their activities.[13]

To reduce the adverse consequences of the incentive system, in 1969 the actual average wage replaced the wage norm for the purpose of calculating the share of the distribution fund in total profits, and the 4 percent ceiling on wage increases was abolished. But, as wage increases were still calculated on the basis of the 1968 wage norm, and increases undertaken both in 1968 and 1969 were deducted from the distribution fund for 1969, the adverse effects of the incentive system hardly diminished. This may explain why the gross movement of labor increased further while labor productivity stagnated.[14]

In 1970, increases in the working force also became taxable, with varying proportions of the increase in total wages burdening the distribution fund, depending on whether this represented a rise in average wages or in employment. Three-tenths of increases in average wages up to 4 percent compared to the 1970 level can be accounted for among costs while the remainder, as well as increases exceeding 4 percent and wage increases undertaken in 1968 and 1969, are financed from the distribution fund. Furthermore, one-third of the increase in total wages due to a rise in employment increases the tax obligation of the firm and reduces the distribution fund, and conversely for a decrease in total wages.

The rules introduced in 1970 reduced the differences in the tax treatment of the rise in total wages due to higher average wages or to larger employment. For the period 1971–75, the regulations will change again. Only increases in average wages compared to the previous year will be subject to tax, with a rate of 50 percent applying to increases not exceeding three-tenths of the percentage rise in the sum of profits and wages per worker and progressively increasing thereafter. The new rules will provide inducements for improving labor productivity, and thus for reducing the working force of the firm, although on balance expansion through increases in employment will continue to be favored.

Modifications in the incentives for managers should also be noted. After complaints that the bonus scheme introduced in 1968 treated workers as

13. "A vállalati magatartás és a vállalat helyzetének megitélése" [Firm behavior and appraisal of the firm's situation], *Ipargazdasági Tájékoztató*, May 1969, pp. 80 and 72.

14. J. Rózsa. In 1969, the ratio of the gross movement of labor to net increases rose to 15.

second-class citizens by limiting their bonuses to 15 percent of the basic wage while for managers the maximum rate was 80 percent, the scheme has been changed to avoid such apparent inequalities. As of 1970, the maximum was set at 25 percent for all categories of employees, but the managers' salaries were raised and they can also get additional bonuses on the basis of formulas determined by the supervising ministry that reward increases in profits and penalize increases in average wages. The ministry can modify the formula in particular cases and may even provide bonuses to the managers of firms which incur losses.

While changes in the regulations do not seem to have affected the average incomes of managers, the inclusion of wages among the indicators on the basis of which bonuses are paid represents a step away from regarding profits as the sole success criterion for the firm. Also, as we will see, the new incentive system increases the power of the ministries vis-à-vis the firm.

The Managers' Objective Function

I have suggested that managers aim at maximizing the firm's aftertax profit, subject to the constraint that the average income of the workers rises at a certain rate. The question arises, however, if managers indeed behave this way or whether they have a different objective function. This question is not specific to the socialist firm; it has been repeatedly raised in regard to the corporate enterprise in capitalist economies. Thus, according to various surveys, increases in output, consumer satisfaction, etc. figure along with profits among the managers' objectives in U.S. firms.[15]

The sample survey conducted by the Research Institute for Industrial Economics of the Academy of Science inquired into the relative importance of six objectives in decision making by managers of Hungarian firms. According to its findings, in 1968 the average of the weights managers assigned to these objectives were: increases in profits, 27 percent; increases in profits per worker, 15 percent; increases in output, 13 percent; satisfaction of needs, 23 percent; utilization of capacity, 14 percent; utilization of the firm's labor force, 7 percent; other, 1 percent.[16]

The findings point to a turnabout in the managers' objectives following the reform. The increase in production has apparently lost its preeminence and increases in profits have become the single major objective. Some of the other motivating factors listed also bear on profits, while the satisfaction of needs might have been given excessive weight because managers did not want to appear to put their interests above the interests of the community.

15. For a critical appraisal of the evidence, see Fritz Machlup, "Theories of the Firm: Marginalist, Behavioral, Managerial," *American Economic Review*, March 1967.

16. Román, p. 78.

Increases in profits also appear as the principal objective in the short-term and medium-term plans prepared by the firms.[17]

Maximization of any kind of objective function would require making calculations on costs and returns. Two-thirds of the firms reportedly base their production decisions on such calculations and, whenever calculations are made, these have a dominant role in decision making in 56 out of 100 cases.[18] Also, several firms have begun using mathematical methods to optimize their product composition.[19]

The objective of profit maximization, however, often does not carry over to intrafirm relations. Available information indicates that, since the introduction of the New Economic Mechanism, changes in the system of decision making in intrafirm units have been relatively small. Firms that have made the transition from acting on the basis of central directives to increasingly operating in a market context have frequently continued to conduct various activities within the firm as they had done beforehand. Thus, lower-level managers responsible for particular activities of the firm often continue to receive plan targets and their performance is evaluated on the basis of the fulfillment of production targets rather than on their contribution to the firm's profit.

Part of the problem lies in accounting procedures which do not always make it possible to allocate costs appropriately among various operations. It is also said that there is a shortage of skilled personnel to make such calculations on a consistent basis. But apart from these practical problems we find the continuing existence of equalizing tendencies within the firm, as lower-level managers in like positions often receive more or less the same remuneration irrespective of their performance. This is accomplished by allocating the distribution fund available to the firm among the various units in proportion to total wages paid by each, or by setting accounting prices in intrafirm relations so as to equalize profit rates. Equalizing tendencies also appear in the allocation of the investment fund within the firm.

However, profit maximization on the firm level would require that intrafirm units also act on this basis and that their managers' remuneration be based on it. Apart from improvements in accounting procedures, this will necessitate changes in the process of decision making and in performance criteria for lower-level managers. Progress in this direction is expected as

17. This is the conclusion of a large survey carried out by the Institute of Business Economics at the Karl Marx University of Economic Science on the firms' one-year plans. Cf. Sándor Varga et al., *A gazdasági funkciók valamint a vállalaton belüli termelö-egységek irányítási rendszerének helyzete az iparvállalatoknál* [The economic functions and the system of intrafirm decision making in industrial firms] (Budapest, 1970), pp. 23–33.

18. Román, p. 78.

19. Varga, p. 27.

such questions receive increasing attention from the government as well as from economists.[20] But continuing difficulties will be experienced, in part because of paternalistic attitudes on the part of higher-level managers and in part because of interventions by other organizations, to be discussed below.

The Extent of Competition

I come now to the question if profitability to the firm and social profitability may come into conflict in Hungary. As is well known, there will be no conflict if prices appropriately express resource scarcities, competition ensures that all firms are price takers, and there are no appreciable external effects (pollution is an often-mentioned example) emanating from the firm's activities. As external effects can be taken care of by appropriate tax-subsidy measures, I will limit my attention in this paper to problems relating to prices and competition.

Efficient resource allocation in a small country requires conforming to world-market price relations. Hungary, however, faces different sets of prices in ruble trade and in dollar trade and, despite the progress made since the introduction of the reform, domestic prices are often not related to either. Moreover, about one-third of the firms receive subsidies, many for exporting. In such circumstances, existing price relations often do not ensure that profit maximization by the firm would be in the interest of the national economy.

The choice of appropriate price relations in the Hungarian economy will be examined in section IV, and I will deal with the issue of competition here. It should be noted, however, that the two are interrelated since, under decentralized decision making, the adoption of a particular set of prices will not ensure efficient resource allocation in the absence of competition, nor will competition suffice to attain this objective if there are distortions in prices.

In the early 1960s, Hungary's industrial structure was transformed by combining firms, often located in different parts of the country, thereby greatly reducing the number of firms in each industry and increasing the number of plants per firm. There is only one firm each engaged in processing poultry as well as in manufacturing sugar, chocolate products, beer, cigarettes, vegetable oils, silk products, glass, paper, and asbestos. Furthermore, an average firm has 15 plants in the food processing industry and 10 plants in the textile industry.[21]

20. Intrafirm relations were the subject of the May 1970 meeting of the Hungarian Economic Association.

21. Central Statistical Office, *Az ipar koncentrációja* [The concentration of industry] (Budapest, 1967), pp. 17–19.

In the major branches of manufacturing, the degree of industrial concentration is much greater in Hungary than in the more developed Western industrial countries.[22] The number of firms is relatively small even in broadly defined industries and, when several firms coexist, specialization agreements have reduced overlapping in their product composition.

The reorganization of the industrial structure responded to the desire of the industrial ministries to reduce the number of firms under their supervision. It is doubtful, however, that this reorganization has contributed to greater efficiency, in part because of the difficulties involved in directing a number of plants located far from each other, and in part because the establishment of so-called horizontal firms combining several firms producing identical or similar products led to the breakup of vertical producing-relationships that had certain economic advantages. At the same time, due to increased administrative requirements, the number of not-directly-productive employees as a proportion of the number of physical workers rose by 14 percent.[23]

Apart from the higher costs associated with the transformation of the Hungarian industrial structure, the reduction in the number of firms means that there is often little domestic competition under the New Economic Mechanism. Thus, according to the results of the sample survey cited above, in 1968, 40 percent of the firms did not experience any competition from domestic firms, 48 percent experienced some competition, and only 12 percent experienced strong competition. The share of the latter group was 3 percent in the machine-building industry, 10 percent in the chemical and food-processing industries, and 23 percent in textiles, clothing, and shoes production.[24]

In response to the questionnaires, firms also provided information on the extent of import competition: 46 percent of the respondents did not experience any import competition, 37 percent felt the existence of some competition from imports, and 17 percent had much foreign competition. Foreign competition appears to be strongest in the machinery industry and weakest in the food industries. Still, nearly one-third of the firms in the machinery industry reported that they had neither domestic nor foreign competition.[25]

These figures are likely to overstate the extent of domestic competition in Hungary, since managers speak of competition even if there are only two or three firms in an industry. In such instances, firms might have reached agreements or implicit understandings that tend to further limit competition.

22. Ibid., chapter 5.
23. Ibid., p. 20.
24. Román, pp. 76–77.
25. Ibid., pp. 74–77.

And even in the absence of such agreements, with few exceptions we can speak of oligopolistic rather than pure competition.

Continuing excessive aggregate demand has also reduced the extent of competition. An extreme case is that of the construction industry, where there is no competition among state enterprises, and competition from building cooperatives is limited to relatively small construction projects. On the other hand, rapidly rising imports of producer as well as consumer goods have increased the extent of import competition since 1968. Moreover, as of 1 January 1971 several large horizontal firms were broken up into smaller units.

If there is not sufficient competition, firms have a certain latitude in increasing profits by raising prices, reducing product quality, and changing product variety, so that private and social profitability do not coincide. These differences between the theoretical model of competitive socialism and the actual situation in Hungary explain in part some of the limitations imposed on the firm's activities. But such limitations have also stemmed from other considerations, such as the desire to avoid inflation, the objective of maintaining employment in individual regions and firms, and the fear that giving unfettered freedom to the firm will have undesirable consequences in one form or another.

Limitations on the Firm's Activities

At the time of the introduction of the New Economic Mechanism, setting a ceiling on increases in average wages and maintaining controls on the prices and allocation of a variety of commodities had as their main purpose the avoidance of inflation. As Hungary has succeeded in maintaining price stability, the wage ceiling has been abolished and the scope of price and allocation controls reduced.

In 1968, prices paid to producers were freed for about 12 percent of agricultural goods, 28 percent of domestically produced materials and intermediate products, and 78 percent of industrial end-products. However, with the prices of most consumer goods as well as wholesale and retail margins being fixed, the last-mentioned figure overestimates the scope of free price determination for industrial end-products to a considerable extent.

In 1969 and 1970, the scope of price fixing was reduced for all three groups of products. But the Materials and Price Board retains its veto power over price increases on commodities accounting for about 5–10 percent of industrial production, and the rise of prices is restrained by limitations on profits whenever price determination required the agreement of the buyer and the seller.

In 1968, a number of materials and semimanufactures remained subject to quotas in one form or another. The scope of quota allocation was reduced in the following year; the value of the products subject to some kind of quota declined by 22 percent compared to 1968, and accounted for only 4–5 percent of all materials used in Hungary. Apart from meat, cereals, and fodder (which were centrally allocated), there were purchase quotas for 13 products in 1969, import quotas for 18 products (the two groups in part overlapped), sale quotas for 8 products, and export quotas for 10 products. Moreover, commercial monopolies handled the purchase or sale of 20 products.

Further liberalization took place in 1970. The central allocation of cereals and fodder was discontinued; the number of products to which purchase quotas applied was reduced to 4 (iron ore, copper and copper products, newsprint, and buses), and only 5 products (electric energy, passenger automobiles, coking coal, fertilizers, and fodder) were subject to import quotas. The scope of quota allocation will be again reduced and, with the exceptions of meat and scrap metal, commercial monopolies abolished, in the period 1971–75.

Limitations on the firm's activity also originate from nongovernmental organizations such as trade unions and the Communist party (The Hungarian Socialist Workers' Party). Trade unions have assumed an increasing role since the introduction of the reform. But while their declared purpose is to defend the workers' interests, they often take a short-term view, opposing reductions in employment even though this would lead to cost reductions.

The Central Committee of the Hungarian Socialist Workers' (Communist) Party was instrumental in designing and implementing the New Economic Mechanism. However, some local Party organizations have found it difficult to adjust to changes in the decision-making process and, together with the trade unions, local governmental authorities exert pressure on management to retain workers who might have become superfluous. There is also evidence of regional tendencies; local organizations may oppose the reallocation of production that would benefit one region at the expense of another even though such reallocations might take place within a single firm. Finally, trade unions and regional organizations often object to increased income inequalities that result from the application of the incentive system.

These tendencies are hardly surprising; they are found in one form or another practically everywhere in the world. They nevertheless interfere with the proper functioning of the New Economic Mechanism in Hungary. Most important, opposition to the firing of workers who have become superfluous exacerbates conditions on the labor market, with some firms having disguised overemployment and others suffering from labor shortages.

The role of the supervising ministries is a further consideration. The 1968 reform divested the ministries of their operational-directive function, but they continue to have legal authority over the firm in certain domains: the supervisory ministry determines the sphere of activity of the firm, nominates its director and deputy director, and can intervene if the firm is not acting in the "national interest." The legal situation is rather loose as the regulations on the ministry's functions leave much room for interpretation.

In the first year following the introduction of the New Economic Mechanism, the supervising ministries intervened relatively little in the affairs of individual firms, but they stepped up their activities afterwards. This change reflects an uncertainty on the part of the ministries about their role in the New Economic Mechanism at the time of its introduction, followed by the reassertion of some of their earlier rights and privileges; it also conforms to Parkinson's Law. Furthermore, some officials might have shared the views of those according to whom the adoption of the reform would automatically ensure that social and private profitability coincide, thus leaving little room for intervention. As it became manifest that under Hungary's present industrial structure this is not the case, the ministries have considered it their duty to intervene in order to redress the situation.

It should be added that, starting in 1970, the supervising ministry determined the conditions for bonus payments to managers over and above the 25 percent maximum payable to all employees. It can also increase or reduce the bonuses of managers depending on its evaluation of their work, and, in special cases, it can provide bonuses even though the firm has made no profit. But while this change in the bonus system will mean a strengthening of the ministry's power vis-à-vis the firms under its supervision, the increased freedom of firms to alter their product composition acts in the opposite direction.

There is no simple way to express the power relations between the ministries and the firms they supervise. This relationship is determined by a variety of factors whose importance varies from case to case. Personalities and personal connections are as important as the size of the firm, the source of its investment funds, and its success in exportation. A large firm such as the Aluminium Trust maintains direct contact with the Planning Office which decides on the financing of the Trust's major investments and has little to expect—or to fear—from the supervising ministry. By contrast, the ministry continues to play a major role in the construction and construction materials industry, which has been the least affected by the introduction of the New Economic Mechanism because it does not have sufficient capacity to fulfill the demands made on it.

III. Investment Decisions

Investments by the Firm

Prior to 1968, with few and unimportant exceptions, investment decisions were made by the central authorities rather than by firm managers. It was planned that in 1968 firms would have authority, on the average, over 40 percent of investments while the remainder was to come under governmental or local jurisdiction. Decisions taken by the firm were to have greater importance in manufacturing, since central or local authorities generally decide investments in mining, the production and distribution of energy, afforestation, transport, research institutes, education, housing, and tourism. Still, the government retained authority over manufacturing investments that would involve increases in capacity exceeding 25–30 percent of production in a particular branch of activity or in its major products, an expansion necessitating substantial imports, or the establishment of new factories.

In fact, as profits exceeded expectations by about one-fifth, the share of investments under the firm's decision-making authority exceeded the planned figure and approached 50 percent as early as 1968. Further increases are foreseen during the period 1971–75, with this proportion reaching 55 percent in all investments taken together and 69 percent in manufacturing investments. However, there is a need for increased social and infrastructural investments by the state.

Investments by the firm are financed from its own funds (which combine the profits allocated to the investment fund and three-fifths of depreciation), as well as from banks and from budgetary credits. We may again cite the findings of a sample survey which show that the firms' own funds do not permit (*a*) the maintenance of present levels of output (for 6 percent of the firms); (*b*) the modernization of production (for 36 percent); or (*c*) the expansion of production (for 33 percent). The lack of sufficient financing from its own sources is most prevalent in the case of the chemical industry, whose investment requirements are the largest.[26]

There are two major banks in Hungary; the National Bank and the Investment Bank. The former combines the role of a central bank with the normal functions of commercial banks. In its latter functions, the National Bank provides short-term credits to firms for financing accounts receivable and inventories. These credits are of considerable importance since allotments for such purposes were often set rather low at the time of the introduction of the New Economic Mechanism.

It was expected that, through its monopoly on short-term credits, the National Bank would play a powerful role in controlling the firms' financial

26. Ibid., p. 78.

behavior. In practice, this has not happened, and firms have been given short-term credits more or less automatically. This might have been considered equitable, as some firms received plenty of financing in 1968 and have not needed short-term credits. But a more important consideration has been to safeguard the operations of existing firms—a question to which I shall return later.

Medium-term and long-term investment credits are provided by the Investment Bank for purposes specified in the guidelines of credit policy. The former are given for up to 3 years and the latter for 5 years at an interest rate of 8 percent. Credits for longer periods are made available only for preferential uses. They include loans of 10 years' duration with an interest rate of 6 percent for the purpose of regional development, the exploitation of gas and oil deposits, bakeries, the production of certain steel-based materials, food processing, and various services. Also, loans are given for ten years at an interest rate of 7 percent to finance agricultural inventories, investments in intrafirm transportation, packaging, research institutes, mass-produced clothing, and the construction industry. Finally, agricultural establishments can receive loans for up to 15 years and pay an interest rate of 5 percent, and low-interest loans are provided for the purchase of machinery from socialist countries.

The Investment Bank supplies about 20 percent, and the government budget (chiefly for investments started before 1968) less than 5 percent, of the investment funds available to firms in Hungary. However, these credits have thus far mostly supplemented the funds of individual firms and have not resulted in an appreciable reallocation of new investments.

Investment Criteria

When the firm decides on the investments to be undertaken, the decision is generally based on rate-of-return calculations. The sample survey cited above reveals that this is the case in three-fourths of the firms, and the calculations have a dominant role in making decisions in one-half of the cases. The proportions are considerably higher than average in the food processing industries and in industries producing nondurable consumer goods, and lower in the machinery and the chemical industry.[27] The observed discrepancies reflect the fact that in the latter-mentioned industries non-economic considerations play a greater role.

According to the same survey, the objective of cost reductions dominates in one-third of the cases—a lower proportion than that reported in regard to production decisions. Nevertheless, the objectives of increasing production (one-third) and introducing new products (one-fourth) are also

27. Ibid., pp. 78–79.

often associated with increases in profits since firms are reluctant to expand nonprofitable activities that would reduce bonus payments.[28] Note further that, according to the findings of a more recent survey of twenty-two large and medium-size firms, in the majority of cases the firms' long-term plans envisage the maximization of profits or the distribution fund.[29]

In credit requests submitted to the Investment Bank, the minimum rate of return is 7 percent, but in most cases the expected rate of return reaches 20–30 percent. In such circumstances the Investment Bank necessarily has a rationing function. This is accomplished by ranking investments according to the geometrical average of the reciprocal of the rate of return and the repayment period.

The preferential treatment given to investments of a short repayment period is an imperfect substitute for the time structure of interest rates, and it has several disadvantages from which the latter is free. To begin with, as the repayment period is generally shorter than the period of recoupment, the rule applied by the Investment Bank favors firms that can effect repayment from the investment fund they generate in excess of that derived from the new investment.[30] The advantages of firms with their own resources restricts the possibilities of the Investment Bank to reallocate investment resources, and to finance new activities and the rapid expansion of old ones, although market conditions may warrant them.[31] Moreover, among firms of equal profitability, those with a lower asset value/wages ratio are at a disadvantage.

Factor Costs and Factor Demands

Since 1968 there has been much discussion in Hungary on the distorting effects of the existing pattern of relative factor costs on factor demands. It has been noted, for example, that the cost of social security in the

28. Ibid., p. 80.

29. György Varga, "Távlati tervezés a magyar vállalatoknál" [Long-term planning by Hungarian firms], *Közgazdasagi Szemle*, 1970, no. 5, pp. 565–80. A dissenting view on profits as long-term objectives is expressed in László Horváth, "Az optimális vállalati müködés feltételei és problémái hosszu távon" [Conditions and problems of the optimum functioning of the firm in the long run], *Közgazdasagi Szemle*, 1969, nos. 7–8, pp. 878–94.

30. Assume that the repayment period is 5 years and the interest rate 6 percent, the rate of profit on the new investment is 15 percent of which 30 percent is allotted to the investment fund, the rate of depreciation is 4 percent a year, and 60 percent of depreciation is credited to the investment fund; the firm will then have to finance over three-fourths of its annual repayment and interest obligations from profits other than that derived from the new investment financed by the loan. Cf. Gabor Havas, "Gondolatok a beruházási hitelrendszer továbbfejlesztéséről" [Suggestions for the further development of the investment credit system], *Pénzügyi Szemle*, 1970, no. 5, pp. 388–400.

31. A detailed discussion of the deficiencies of the rule applied for ranking investments by the Investment Bank is given in Mihály Gálik, "A hosszulejáratu fejlesztési hitelek rangsorolásáról" [On the ranking of investment credits], *Pénzügyi Szemle*, 1969, no. 4, pp. 299–310.

government budget is one-and-a-half times as large as the proceeds of the social security contributions paid by the firms, which amount to 17 percent of total wages. And while the 8 percent wage tax, also paid by the firms, provides for the excess of social security expenditures, other budgetary expenditures relating to labor, such as education, training, and miscellaneous benefits, are financed from the general budget. These may amount to another 10–15 percent of total wages.[32]

These results are hardly affected if account is taken of income taxes paid by workers since such taxes are of little importance in Hungary. By contrast, in Western countries taxes on workers' incomes not only cover all labor-related costs not financed by social security contributions but also finance some general budgetary expenditures.

The fact that the firm does not pay the entire cost of labor to the national economy tends to discourage economizing with labor, thereby exacerbating the tightness of the labor market. Also, incentives are provided for capital-widening as against capital-deepening investments, and these have apparently contributed to the observed excess demand for construction.

Attention should further be given to the appraisal of projects that come under the decision-making authority of the Planning Bureau. In such instances, rate-of-return calculations are made in world market prices under the assumption that if profitability is attained at such prices, the investment will also be appropriate for supplying domestic or socialist markets. The adoption of this principle reflects the fact that Hungary considers participation in the international division of labor to be of first priority.

IV. EXPORT INCENTIVES

Foreign Trade Before the Reform

In the early postwar period, Hungary intended to follow the Soviet pattern in replacing imports by domestic production. Import replacement extended to manufactured goods as well as to some agricultural products, of which cotton was an extreme example. The idea of comparative costs did not appear in discussions on the scope of foreign trade; rather, the declared objective was "to procure, through import, those producer goods and consumer goods which are not produced and not available in necessary quantity at home."[33] Exports in turn served the purpose of paying for the necessary imports.

While autarky is a feasible goal and may be attained without excessive

32. Tamás Szira, "Pénzügyi szabályozásunk sajátosságai a nemzetközi összehasonlitásban" [Peculiarities of our fiscal regulations: an international comparison], *Közgazdasagi Szemle*, 1970, no. 5, pp. 582–601.

33. E. Illyés, "A külkereskedelem szerepe és tervezésének jelenlegi feladatai" [The role of foreign trade and the present tasks in its planning], *Tarsadalami Szemle*, 1954, no. 5, p. 96.

costs in the Soviet Union, which has a large internal market and varied resource endowment, in Hungary both the smallness of the home market and the poor domestic raw material base call for participation in the international division of labor. In effect, policies aiming at autarky together with efforts to expand heavy industry led to increases in imports of materials and machinery, and also necessitated imports of foodstuffs the then disfavored agricultural sector could not provide. After a temporary decline, the share of imports in Hungary's national income rose substantially, thereby creating the need for a commensurate increase in exports.[34]

The need for higher exports, in turn, called for applying the economic calculus so as to minimize their cost to the national economy. This explains why it was Hungarian economists who pioneered in making calculations of export efficiency.[35] But such calculations were mostly limited to the choice among exports and—whatever adjustments were subsequently made—domestic "accounting" prices served as their starting point.

The prices exporters received domestically were not related to the prices obtained abroad; nor were the domestic prices of imports linked to foreign prices. The firm managers' actions (aimed at maximizing bonuses based on the fulfillment of the plan expressed in domestic prices) were thus unrelated to the national objective of minimizing the domestic cost of exports through the choice of appropriate export commodities. Moreover, attempts to make firms financially interested in exporting related incentives to the volume of exports rather than to their cost.

The incentive system did not provide the proper inducements to trading firms either.[36] Until the late 1950s, in line with the quantitative orientation of the system of centralized planning, each trading firm's plan was given in terms of export quantities, thus providing an incentive to increase exports by charging lower prices abroad. Foreign demand for Hungarian exports being elastic, trading firms continued to have an incentive for reducing selling prices, although to a lesser extent, when their plan was given in terms of foreign currency earnings after 1960.

34. The combined share of exports and imports declined from 28 percent in 1938 to 23 percent in 1951 but increased again afterwards, reaching 41 percent in 1955. Cf. T. Kiss, "A nemzeti jövedelem és a külkereskedelem összefuggései hazánkban" [The interrelationships of national income and foreign trade in our country], *Közgazdasagi Szemle*, 1957, no. 6, p. 645.

35. For example, T. Liska and A. Máriás, "A gazdaságosság és a nemzetközi munkamegosztás [Efficiency and the international division of labor], *Közgazdasagi Szemle*, 1954, no. 10, pp. 82–93. For an abbreviated English translation, see United Nations, *Economic Survey for Europe in 1954* (Geneva, 1955), pp. 131–35.

36. These firms were interposed between the producer and foreign buyers and for a time carried out virtually all exporting activities. At a later stage, some large producers received the right to export directly, but until 1968 trading firms remained responsible for over 90 percent of exports.

While considerations as to the behavior of producers were applicable to exports to all destinations prior to 1968, the described behavior of trading firms pertained principally to trade with the West since prices in trade with socialist countries were mostly set in advance. In the mid-1960s, the Soviet Union, the other socialist nations, and Western countries, each accounted for about one-third of Hungarian exports. The commodity pattern of exports, however, differed greatly among the groups. In particular, while machinery and transport equipment accounted for 43 percent of Hungarian exports to socialist countries, the share of these commodities in exports to Western developed countries was only 4 percent.[37] Hungarian exports to the latter group of countries continued to be dominated by foodstuffs and by simple manufactures.

Differences in the commodity composition of trade are largely explained by the higher technical requirements and technical level of Western industry. These differences are in turn related to the incentive system. While domestic as well as foreign competition induces firms to improve products and technology in the Western developed countries, under centralized decision making the socialist firm's interest in plan fulfillment is often not conducive to such improvements.[38]

Nor did Hungarian firms have much interest in making technical improvements in order to be able to export to Western developed countries, as they had ready markets for their products in the other socialist countries, if not at home. Demand for Hungarian machinery and equipment on the part of socialist countries continued strong throughout the postwar period, in part because of projected high rates of growth that required new machinery over and above their machine-building capacity, and in part because, for several of them, Hungarian machinery was of advanced design.

The Reform of the Foreign Trade System

One of the principal reasons for the introduction of the New Economic Mechanism was to increase the benefits Hungary derived from foreign trade and to reduce undue reliance on production for domestic markets. This was to be accomplished by linking domestic prices to foreign prices and by transforming the incentive system so as to favor efficient exporting and import substitution.

37. Imre Vajda, "External Equilibrium, Neo-techniques and Economic Reform," *Acta Oeconomica*, 1967, no. 4, p. 299. Machinery and transport equipment accounted for one-third of exports to developing countries (7 percent of the total); the commodity composition of this trade is, however, determined in bilateral agreements.

38. The conclusions pertaining to centrally-planned socialist economies also apply to developing countries following inward-looking policies. For a detailed discussion, see my "Growth Strategies in Semi-Industrial Countries," *Quarterly Journal of Economics*, February 1970, pp. 24–47.

A major conclusion of international trade theory is that a small country —which can affect the price of neither exports nor imports—will maximize national income by trading at world market prices which are translated into domestic prices at a uniform exchange rate. Under competitive conditions, profit maximization will ensure efficient exporting and import substitution since domestic production is not undertaken if the cost of production exceeds the world market price converted into domestic values at the equilibrium exchange rate.

Hungary does not face uniform world market prices since trade with the socialist countries (for short, ruble trade) is carried out at prices different from dollar trade.[39] And although dollars can be used in ruble trade, Hungary cannot utilize its balances in rubles to purchase in the West. Accordingly, the foreign exchange conversion ratios used to convert prices expressed in foreign currency into domestic values have to be set separately for trade with the two areas; these conversion ratios should ideally balance trade with both.[40]

One would expect that, apart from the special case when the domestic equivalents of foreign prices from the two sources (socialist and Western) are equal, Hungary will buy a particular product from one area or sell it to one area. For various reasons, this has not been the case. Owing to the existence of long-term agreements with the socialist countries, the limitations on supply availabilities in these countries, and the desire for bilateral balancing with them, imports often come from several sources. Particular commodities are also sold in several markets since some of them are subject to quota limitations abroad while others are differentiated products and hence increases in their sale in any given market would necessitate reductions in prices.

In such circumstances, one would have to devise a system of pricing goods and foreign exchange that would maximize Hungary's gain from trade while maintaining balance-of-payments equilibrium in dollar trade as well as in ruble trade with the individual socialist countries. Since dollar prices vary little with the quantities Hungary supplies to, or buys from, Western countries, application of the marginal principle would require adopting these prices domestically also for commodities traded both with the East and the West. At the same time, identical foreign exchange conversion ratios should be set in ruble trade as well as in dollar trade, with additional

39. It is customary to include in the latter trade with developing countries since, apart from long-term contracts specifying prices and quantities, both exports and imports are valued at world market prices.

40. There is a further complication in that ruble proceeds are practically not transferable among socialist countries, so that these countries aim at balancing their bilateral trade among themselves.

subsidies and taxes in cases when trade with particular socialist countries is unbalanced.

In actual practice, however, foreign exchange conversion ratios do not apply uniformly to all firms. Rather, firms where the cost of exports exceeds the foreign exchange conversion ratio (60 forints per dollar and 40 forints per ruble) receive a supplement. As this supplement (in effect, an export subsidy) is set on the basis of the average cost of export to the firm, it amounts to applying a different foreign exchange conversion ratio to individual firms. In 1968, about two-thirds of exporting firms received subsidies (had foreign exchange conversion ratios in excess of the basic ratio) averaging 29 percent in ruble trade and 33 percent in dollar trade. Export subsidies amount to 17 and 21 percent, respectively, of the total value of ruble and dollar exports.[41]

I have discussed the disadvantages of this arrangement in my earlier paper on the Hungarian reform.[42] At this point, it may be sufficient to note that while firms have incentives to alter the composition of their exports toward lower-cost products and may also be prompted to reduce the cost of their exports by planned reductions in export subsidies, the foreign trade regulations in effect do not provide sufficient inducements either for discontinuing high-cost exports or expanding low-cost exports in firms that do not require subsidies. Since export subsidies include an allowance for profit at the same rate as observed in domestic operations, profit considerations do not favor firms exporting at low costs over those exporting at high costs.

Tariffs and quantitative restrictions provide the counterpart of export subsidies on the import side. Relatively high tariffs on machinery (an average of over 30 percent as against 2 percent on raw materials in 1968) and prepayment requirements on machinery imports from the West further distorted relative prices. While tariffs were low on materials, many of these were subject to quotas in 1968.

These regulations create differences between domestic and foreign prices. The differences are even greater if we relate incentives to value added in the production process. Firms receiving export subsidies that use imported materials are in an especially advantageous position since low foreign exchange conversion ratios and tariffs apply to such imports. However, no effort has been made to estimate the extent of net subsidy (or net protection) to value added and, with one outstanding exception,[43] this problem has

41. Imre Vincze, "A külkereskedelmi árak és a belföldi árak közötti pénzügyi hidakról [Foreign trade prices and their relationship with domestic prices], *Pénzügyi Szemle*, 1969, no. 11, pp. 881–93.

42. "The Economic Reform in Hungary," pp. 15–17.

43. Ferenc Bartha, "Az exportösztönzési vitahoz" [A contribution to the controversy on export incentives], *Közgazdasagi Szemle*, 1969, no. 11, pp. 1357–65.

received no attention in Hungary.[44] Yet as in some cases, such as tractors and certain types of machinery, subsidies reach 60–70 percent on product value, subsidies on value added may easily exceed 100 percent and can even involve negative value added at world market prices (i.e. the world market value of material inputs exceeds that of output).

Despite high subsidies to exports, in 1968 incentives for import substitution were generally greater than for exports of finished commodities. Thus, according to the results of the sample survey cited above, cost-price considerations, as well as the technological and quality requirements of buyers, made exports to the West less advantageous than sales to socialist countries, with domestic sales being generally the most advantageous.[45]

Export Incentives and Export Performance

The shortcomings of the export incentive system notwithstanding, this represents an important advance over that applied prior to 1968. Domestic prices have been brought more into line with foreign prices; incentives to export relative to import substitutes have been improved, and both producers and trading firms have become directly interested in increasing profits from exporting. Furthermore, since export subsidies are set on the firm level rather than for individual products, producers can increase their profits by changing the product composition of their exports.

Changes in foreign trade regulations after 1968 have aimed at further improving the system of incentives. Tariffs on machinery imports have been reduced, as has the extent of prepayment requirements (they will be abolished in the near future). By contrast, tariffs on raw materials have been raised somewhat, and the scope of duty exemptions reduced.

Measures have also been taken to reduce the apparent advantages of ruble exports over the dollar trade which have contributed to surpluses in the former and have retarded the expansion of exports in the latter. A variety of exports to socialist countries have been made subject to quotas which are allocated by way of competitive bidding to firms where the domestic cost of earning foreign exchange is lower. In turn, dollar exports receive a variety of additional subsidies in the form of rebates of duties and profit taxes, bonuses, and credit preferences.

Most important, the foreign exchange conversion ratios set for individual

44. Net subsidy (to exports) and net protection (of import substitution) on value added are given expression by the so-called effective rate of protection. Cf. my *The Structure of Protection in Developing Countries* (Baltimore: Johns Hopkins University Press, 1971), chapter 1.

45. Román, p. 32. In some industries, however, exports to socialist countries are more advantageous than domestic sales. Cf. Imre Fenyo, "A fogyasztási cikkek belsö piacának egyensulya és a szabályozó rendszer hatása" [Domestic market equilibrium for consumer goods and the effects of the system of regulations], *Közgazdasagi Szemle*, 1969, no. 10, pp. 1143–47.

firms will be replaced by uniform conversion ratios for twelve industry groups. Apart from abolishing interfirm differences in these ratios within a given industry group, this change will also entail increasing conversion ratios for firms that have so far received the basic ratio only. Firms that show profits in dollar exports will receive additional bonuses.

The favorable results of the export incentive system became apparent in 1969, in part because of the delayed effects of the measures introduced in 1968, and in part because of the actions taken in 1969. Between 1968 and 1969, exports in dollar trade grew by about one-third and in ruble trade by roughly one-tenth. While sales to the West have been helped by favorable business conditions in the importing countries, export incentives have contributed to the increased export volume and prices. In particular, the interest of producers and trading firms in obtaining higher prices helps to explain that, within particular commodity categories, prices rose more for exported than for imported varieties.[46]

In trade with the West, increases have been the largest in agricultural exports, especially of labor-intensive fruits and vegetables, which have received remunerative prices since the introduction of the New Economic Mechanism. Increases are also shown in textile exports, with a shift toward products that incorporate more domestic value added. Machinery exports in dollar trade have not yet risen much, but cooperation agreements with foreign firms on the production of parts and components for assembly abroad augur well for future increases. As noted in my earlier paper, such agreements are of considerable importance for Hungary since they provide assured markets as well as technical knowhow.[47]

Between 1964 and 1967 altogether 25 cooperation agreements (including licensing arrangements) had been reached with Western firms. Their number increased by 26 in 1968 and by 42 in 1969, in large part in the machinery and chemical industries. This increase reflects the fact that the initiative has passed from the government to the firms that receive certain incentives for participating in such arrangements.

V. THE HUNGARIAN ECONOMIC REFORM: ACHIEVEMENTS AND PROSPECTS

The balance sheet of the New Economic Mechanism in Hungary is basically positive. Central directives have been by-and-large abolished; domestic prices increasingly reflect relative scarcities and are increasingly linked to foreign prices; and firms have shifted from an emphasis on output to an emphasis on profits. The profit motive also tends to induce firms to reduce production costs, although the imperfections of competition have given rise

46. Sándor Czeitler, "Népgazdaságunk külső és belső egyensulya" [The internal and external balance of our national economy], Közgazdasagi Szemle, 1970, no. 3, pp. 261–71.
47. "The Economic Reform in Hungary," p. 22.

to divergences between the interests of the firm and the national economy. These divergences, in turn, have led to diametrically opposed recommendations. There are some who call for increased intervention in the firm's activities, while others wish to create the conditions for the identity of the interests of the firm and the national economy by increasing the extent of domestic and foreign competition.

The loosening of controls on product allocation and prices, as well as changes in regulations on wages since 1968, indicate the desire of the policy makers to diminish the extent of intervention in the firms' activities. Nevertheless, the continuing existence of the supervising ministries creates a danger of increasing interventions. However good are the intentions of the ministries, such interventions may create further inefficiencies in the economic system and provide disincentives to the optimal operation of firms. By contrast, competition can assure that profit maximization by the firm conforms to the national interest.

Information on the existing degree of industrial concentration indicates that there are possibilities for increasing the degree of domestic competition in Hungary. On the one hand, horizontal firms could be broken up into their constituent parts; on the other, competition in individual commodities would increase if firms were given greater freedom in changing their product composition.

In a large segment of Hungarian industry and in particular in the most dynamic branches of manufacturing, however, the need for large-scale operations would hardly permit competition among domestic firms; in a number of instances, the size of the Hungarian market would not even be sufficient to support a single firm of optimum size. Foreign competition is necessary, therefore, in order to avoid the maintenance of monopoly positions. But increased foreign competition is desirable in other industries as well, both to provide inducements for technological progress and to align domestic prices with foreign price relations, the need for which was noted above. The adoption of unified foreign exchange conversion ratios, the lowering of tariffs, and the narrowing of scope of import quotas would serve this objective and would also tend to equalize incentives for all exports.

Furthermore, changes appear necessary in factor prices so as to remove existing incentives favoring the use of labor. This purpose would also be served by changes in the regulations on the allocation of profits that presently encourage labor use and penalize improvements in productivity accompanied by wage increases.

Increased competition and improvements in the structure of relative prices would permit lessening reliance on intervention in the firms' activities by the ministries. Also, to avoid the adverse effects of such interventions, it would be desirable to separate the regulatory and the supervisory-ownership functions of the ministries. One possible solution is to combine the industrial ministries into a single ministry and to transfer their supervisory responsibilities to a board of directors in which representatives of the state, the management, and the workers participate.

The suggested changes would also reduce the reliance of the firms on financial support by the government and redirect the activities of managers aimed at obtaining such support toward productive uses. Inefficient firms, then, would show losses; this did not occur in a single case in 1968 because of the granting of a variety of governmental support measures.[48] Consideration should then be given to furthering the reallocation of resources to more efficient firms by improving the credit system, creating capital markets, and liquidating inefficient firms.

48. Miklós Simán, "Termelésünk müszaki szinvonala és a gazdaságirányitás reformja" [The technical level of our production and the reform of the direction of the economy], *Közgazdasagi Szemle*, 1970, no. 3, pp. 272–85. However, a few unprofitable firms have been absorbed by other enterprises. Cf. Egon Kemenes, "The Enterprise and the National Economy," *New Hungarian Quarterly*, winter 1968, pp. 61–76.

11

The Political Implications of Economic Reform

R. V. BURKS

Viewed from the standpoint of politics, the programs of economic reform which are now such a prominent feature of East European government have resulted from a change in the basic relationship between the rulers and the ruled. In the days of Stalin, Communist leaders regarded their populations very largely as resources to be exploited; uncooperative elements were dealt with by the security police. But during the Khrushchev era the systematic use of terror as an instrument of governance was abandoned. This meant that the regimes had to place greater reliance on material rewards and to concern themselves with their public image, and even with the question of their own legitimacy. Since, in other words, men could no longer be driven to work, they had to be provided with a reasonable return for their labor and this meant that the regimes, if they wished to maintain high rates of growth, had to improve the unsatisfactory living standards of their populations.

THE POLITICS OF ECONOMIC REFORM

It is probable that to begin with the leaders did not think of this as a serious problem. They believed not only in the moral superiority of Communist society but also in its greater economic efficiency in the long run. Khrushchev himself proclaimed in 1959 that by 1975 the USSR would surpass the USA in per-capita production, thus guaranteeing the Soviet people the highest living standard in the world.[1] But in the years that followed, Communist

1. N. S. Khrushchev, *Target Figures for the Economic Development of the Soviet Union 1959–65: Report to the Special 21st Congress of the Communist Party of the Soviet Union, 27 January 1959 and Reply to Discussion* (London: Soviet Booklet no. 47, 1959), pp. 48–49. Khrushchev also said: "Bourgeois economists contend that at a certain point the industrial development rates in the USSR are bound to 'slacken.' What they are trying to do is to apply the capitalist economic yardstick to Socialism. Capitalism does indeed erect insuperable barriers to the development of the productive forces and its rates of industrial growth do begin to drop off. Socialism, on the other hand, creates every condition for a continuous expansion of the productive forces." Ibid., p. 48. Or again: "High rates of growth are a general objective law of

(*continued on page 374*)

leaders have had to face severe disappointments in the functioning of their economic system.

They have had to learn, for one thing, that the centrally planned economy (CPE), no matter what its advantages in securing rapid industrialization, is not especially well adapted to the requirements of mass consumption. They also have had to face the fact that their system, in comparison with the capitalist economies of Western Europe, has undergone a significant loss of factor efficiency. This is most easily demonstrable in the case of the two parts of Germany. A study of the Central Intelligence Agency suggests that, in 1961, factor productivity in East German industry was only 67 percent of that in the Federal Republic; an analysis of the West German *Deutsches Institut für Wirtschaftsforschung* indicates that, in 1968, the corresponding percentage was 63. But comparable losses in factor productivity in industry probably have taken place throughout the area—for example, Poland as compared with Italy, Bulgaria as compared with Greece.[2]

(continued from page 373)

Socialism, now confirmed by the experience of all the countries of the Socialist camp." Ibid., p. 50.

2. Agency analysts have produced the following table dealing with factor productivity in industry in selected East and West European countries. The year is 1961 and West Germany = 100.

	Productivity of Capital	Productivity of Labor	Factor Productivity
Czechoslovakia	57	65	62
East Germany	71	65	67
Hungary	74	40	45
Poland	58	56	56
Belgium	71	88	83
France	100	88	91
West Germany	100	100	100
Italy	81	69	72

Cf. Edwin M. Snell, "Economic Efficiency in Eastern Europe," *Economic Development in Countries of Eastern Europe: A Compendium of Papers Submitted to the Subcommittee on Foreign Economic Policy of the Joint Economic Committee, Congress of the United States* (Washington, D.C.: U.S. Government Printing Office, 1970), p. 270. See also "Arbeitsproduktivität in der Industrie der DDR und der Bundesrepublik—ein Vergleich," *Wochenbericht des deutschen Instituts für Wirtschaftsforschung 20/70*, 14 May 1970, pp. 137–44. According to a United Nations study, the rates of return to investment in terms of national income appear to show a widespread tendency toward decline throughout Eastern Europe, as can be seen from the following calculations of incremental capital-output ratios comparing national income increases with total investment. *(continued on page 375)*

The same proposition can be put in another way. The manufactures of Eastern Europe can be sold in Western markets only at substantial discounts. East German and Czechoslovak wares, for example, command on the average in the European Economic Community (EEC) only half the prices obtained by corresponding goods produced in the European Free Trade Association (EFTA).[3]

The problem of the East European leaders is compounded by the fact that the populations they rule regard themselves as European and fail to understand why they, in the long run, should put up with substantially lower living standards than West Europeans.[4] The gross national product of the

(continued from page 374)

	USSR	Bulgaria	Czecho-slovakia	E. Germany	Hungary	Poland
1950–55	1.77	1.86	2.61	1.28	4.04	2.75
1955–60	2.53	1.92	3.14	2.70	2.84	3.68
1960–65	3.83	3.89	14.28	6.02	5.65	4.62

Cf. Economic Commission for Europe, "A Fifteen-Year Review of Investment and Output in Eastern Europe and the Soviet Union," *Economic Bulletin for Europe* 18, no. 1, November 1966: 39.

3. Snell, p. 273. As of 1970, only 6 percent of East Germany's exports to the industrial countries of the West was made up of machinery; for Czechoslovakia the percentage was five, for Poland and Hungary three, and for Bulgaria one. Ibid., p. 255. The following Czech calculation shows prices obtained for Czech goods sold in EEC countries expressed as a percentage of the price obtained by EFTA countries in the same market.

Item	Czech Sales Price as percentage of EFTA Sales Price 1964
Tractors (1960)	62.4
Bearings	59.2
Passenger cars	49.0
Sewing machines	44.4
Metal-working machines	43.7
Excavation machinery and excavators	40.4
Generators and electric motors	38.2
Sorting and crushing machines	32.2

Cf. "Prices in Czechoslovakia's Trade with the EEC," *Politicka Ekonomie*, 1967, nos. 7–8, pp. 613–29, as translated in *Foreign Press Digest* (Washington, D.C.), 28 September 1967.

4. "The rapid development of technology in highly developed capitalist countries—and they are our main competitors—our failure to keep up with them in certain areas, creates doubts in the minds of some people as to whether we are capable of catching up with these countries in everyday confrontation." Statement of M. F. Rakowski, editor-in-chief of *Polityka* (Warsaw) to the Ideological Commission of the Polish Central Committee, *Nowe Drogi*, March 1970, as translated in *Radio Free Europe Research: East Europe: Press Survey: Poland*, 8 April 1970.

EEC grew for some years at a rate of six or seven percent per annum,[5] despite the out-and-out capitalist nature of that organization, and living standards in some EEC countries have reached unprecedentedly high levels. Indeed, the EEC is now in the process of expanding its membership to include four members of EFTA, and notably Great Britain. But what countries, in Europe or elsewhere, have been pressing for membership in the EEC's East European competitor, the Council for Mutual Economic Assistance (Comecon, also known as CEMA)?

The sharp contrast between living standards in the two parts of Europe, together with the likelihood that the difference will not diminish in the foreseeable future, is one of the major factors making for regime instability. The political landslide which took place in Czechoslovakia in 1968 was in part the consequence of the decision of the ruling party to abandon the CPE because its relative inefficiency was threatening an already stagnant living standard. In the Communist half of Europe the spectre of political landslide must haunt many leaderships. The need for increased economic efficiency remains clear and urgent, and helps explain the universality of economic reform.

THE TRADING RELATIONSHIP BETWEEN EASTERN EUROPE AND THE USSR

The relative inefficiency of the East European CPEs, however, is not alone the result of a new political situation; it is compounded by the trading relationship between the small states of Eastern Europe and the gigantic Union of Socialist Soviet Republics. We are not speaking of the terms of trade in the traditional sense of prices; indeed, it is not clear how much meaning prices have in intra-Comecon trade.[6] We have in mind rather the

---

5. "Der konjunkturelle Boom in der EWG. Quartalsbericht der Brüsseler Kommission," *Neue Zürcher Zeitung. Fernausgabe* (hereinafter cited as *NZZ*), 4 January 1970, p. 15. The projected rate for 1972, however, was 2.5 to 3 percent. B-t, "Die Wirtschaftslage in der EWG. Gedämpfte Prognosen der Brüsseler Kommission," *NZZ*, 17 January 1972, p. 13.

6. Holzman has disposed of the traditional notion that the Soviet Union exploits the East European populations by means of price discrimination. He has shown that whereas the USSR typically sells the same product at one price to a socialist partner and at a lesser price to a Western purchaser, the same is true, for example, of Bulgaria, which charges the Soviet Union more than a Western purchaser for the same goods. Holzman argues that one reason for this price differential is the poor quality of goods the socialist traders have to offer, in turn a reflection of the relative inefficiency of their system. Cf. Franklyn D. Holzman, "Soviet Foreign Trade Pricing and the Question of Discrimination," *Review of Economics and Statistics* 44 (1962): 134–47; Horst Mendershausen, "Mutual Price Discrimination in Bloc Trade," ibid., pp. 493–96; Holzman, "Soviet Bloc Mutual Discrimination: Comment," ibid., pp. 496–99; Mendershausen, "A Final Comment," ibid., p. 499; Holzman, "More on Soviet Bloc Trade Discrimination," *Soviet Studies* (Glasgow) 17 (1966): 44–65.

product mix; what is shipped to the USSR and what is received in exchange, and the advantages, or disadvantages, of this exchange to the East Europeans, in comparison with the advantages and disadvantages of the product mix which would obtain if Eastern Europe traded primarily with Western Europe.

Prior to 1938, the trade of the East European states with the Soviet Union and with each other was minimal. In 1936, for example, only twelve percent of Czechoslovakia's foreign trade went to the countries which are now socialist.[7] Today, with the exception of Yugoslavia, each of the East European states exchanges between two-thirds and three-fourths of its total foreign trade with its socialist neighbors, more particularly with the USSR. Speaking broadly, the exchange is one of East European manufactures for Soviet energy supplies and raw materials.[8] From Moscow's point of view, Eastern Europe provides an important increment to Soviet manufacturing capacity.

This new trade was made possible by the rapid industrialization of the East European countries under the aegis of communism through the instrument of central planning. In the case of those few countries which were already industrialized, Communist rule has meant a basic reorientation of output. Before the war, the population of what is today East Germany, for example, specialized in the production of optical goods, chemicals, musical instruments, and toys. Such raw materials as had to be imported in support of this production came mainly from the western part of the Reich. But today the German Democratic Republic (GDR) manufactures virtually every type of product, particularly in the producer goods line. This country of 17 million inhabitants now possesses a major iron and steel industry, a shipbuilding industry, an automotive industry, and many more. There are a variety of reasons for this kind of across-the-board development, but one of the more important was the need of a devastated Soviet Union for manufactures of all kinds in the early postwar years. What is true of East German industry is, of course, largely true of the industry of the other East European states. This contributes to their economic inefficiency, since runs are short

7. Calculations of Hanus Hajek, Director of Czechoslovak Research, Radio Free Europe (Munich), based on *Statistická Ročenka RSČ, 1938*, p. 138, as presented in H. Hajek to R. V. Burks, 4 January 1971. The sections of Germany now belonging to Poland and the Soviet Union, as well as the territory of the GDR, are excluded from the calculation, but the territories of Poland and Romania since annexed by the USSR are included.

8. According to a Soviet source, the share of Soviet deliveries in the raw material imports of the other members of the Comecon is two-thirds in the case of coal, nearly 100 percent of oil, three-fourths of oil products, one-half of coke, 85 percent of iron ore, nearly 100 percent of cast iron, 83 percent of steel alloys, 61 percent of rolled steel, and 60 percent of cotton. G. Sorokin, "Mezhdunarodnoe razdelenie truda—vazhnyi faktor ekonomicheskogo rosta," *Voprosy ekonomiki*, 1970, no. 2, p. 114.

and unit costs high. In addition, such a diffuse industrial effort militates against the research concentration which is usually associated with a high rate of technological innovation.

The high degree of dependence on Soviet raw materials also works to the disadvantage of the East Europeans. Before the war, for example, Czechoslovakia imported two million tons of iron ore a year. This she got by waterway from Sweden, where ore runs 61–65 percent iron. Today, Czechoslovakia imports more than 10 million tons per annum, but now the ore comes overland by rail from the USSR and contains only 54–56 percent iron. The processing of the poorer-quality Soviet ore requires more coke.[9] Dependence on Soviet fuels and raw materials also helps to widen the technological gap. In Eastern Europe, solid fuels provide between two-thirds and nine-tenths of the energy supply, while even in the coal-rich countries of Belgium and Germany solid fuels account for only one-half of gross consumption. This means that the East must rely more heavily on outdated processes, such as carbide chemistry, must depend primarily on railroads for transportation, and lags behind in the production of synthetics.[10]

Unfortunately for the East Europeans, Soviet raw material extraction costs run significantly above the raw material prices prevailing in the free market. According to Soviet sources, the Soviet miner produced 1.90 tons of coal per shift in 1967. But in the same year the French miner produced 2.24 tons per shift, the British 2.86, the West German 3.26, and the American more than 13 tons.[11] In these circumstances, Moscow has put pressure on the East European regimes to invest directly in Soviet extractive industries. When bilateral arrangements to this end proved insufficient, Moscow insisted on the establishment (April 1969) of an International Investment Bank to facilitate multilateral financing of Soviet raw material output. Moscow would also prefer to abandon the current Comecon practice of employing, for any plan period, the average free market prices of the preceding quinquenium. The Russians argue that in consequence of this practice, primary products are too cheap in Comecon, and capital goods too dear. Instead there should be created a set of Comecon prices based on average production

9. M. Brozik, "The Truth about Czechoslovak Trade in Raw Materials," *Rudé právo*, 17.23.10 [*sic*] and 11 November 1969, as translated in *Radio Free Europe Research: East Europe: Press Survey: Czechoslovakia*, 26 November 1969.

10. Snell, pp. 247–48.

11. O. Bogomolov, "Aktual'nye problemy ekonomicheskogo sotrudnichestva sotsialisticheskikh stran," *Mirovaya ekonomika i mezhdunarodnye otnosheniya*, 1966, no. 5, pp. 15–27; O. Bogomolov and V. Terekhov, "Lenin i razvitiemirovogo sotsialisticheskogo sodruzhestva," *Voprosy ekonomiki*, 1970, no. 2, pp. 3–15; L. E. Grafov, "Nekotorye itogi razvitiya ugol'noi promyshlennosti SSSR za 1959–1967 gg." *Ugol'*, 1968, no. 11, p. 8; *Wochenbericht, Institut für Wirtschaftsforschung*, 22 May 1969, pp. 137–38.

costs within the socialist commonwealth.[12] The matter is made more urgent by the fact that both East European and Soviet demand is growing more rapidly than Soviet output. Apparently oil and gas present the most difficult problem.[13]

Naturally, the East Europeans resist the Soviet demands as best they may. They are already unable to compete with manufactured goods in western markets, and if they must pay more for their raw materials they will be forced to reduce still further the rate at which they replace their obsolescent machinery, itself a prime reason for their inability to compete. The question as to whether the very close trading relationship with the USSR does not constitute a major barrier to improved economic efficiency and higher living standards must have often arisen in the minds of East European leaders. Intra-Comecon trade has in recent years risen at a rate substantially lower than either Comecon trade with the free world, Comecon industrial production, or intra-EEC trade.[14] Do not, therefore, greater economic efficiency

12. Secretariat of the Economic Commission for Europe, *Economic Survey of Europe in 1968: The European Economy in 1968* (New York: United Nations, 1969), p. 173, n. 187; Günter Reimann, "Entwicklungstendenzen im Comecon," *NZZ*, 28 December 1969, p. 15; review of V. N. Zhukov and Yu. Ya. Olsevich, *Theoretical and Methodological Problems of the Improvement of Price Formation on the Comecon Market*, in *Voprosy ekonomiki*, 1970, no. 6, pp. 133–36; Sorokin, p. 118.

13. *Vilaggazdasag* (Budapest) in its issue of 21 April 1970 asserted that the production of crude oil in the USSR will probably amount to 600–620 million tons in 1980, but that the percentage of crude oil exports in gross production will decrease because of rapidly increasing Soviet domestic demand. The Comecon countries would therefore have to look to the oil-producing Arab states, since the crude oil demands of the Comecon countries would double between 1970 and 1980. Cited in "Imports of Soviet Oil will Not Meet Demand in the 1980s," *Radio Free Europe Research: East Europe: Situation Report: Hungary*, 12 May 1970. The Situation Report is a regularly appearing chronicle of events. It is to be distinguished, on the one hand, from the Press Survey, which provides translations of important articles appearing in the five East European countries to which Radio Free Europe broadcasts, and the Background Report, in which the analyst presents an interpretation of events.

14. The following table is provided by J. Soldaczuk and J. Giezgała, "Economic Integration of Comecon Countries and the Means and Methods of Hastening It," *Gospodarka Planowa*, November 1968, as translated in *Radio Free Europe Research: East Europe: Press Survey: Poland*, 16 January 1969. (Professor Soldaczuk is Director of the Economic Institute attached to the Polish Ministry of Foreign Trade; Director of the Institute of Foreign Trade at the Polish Academy of Sciences; and Ordinarius for International Economic Relations in the Main School of Planning and Statistics, Warsaw.) The table shows average annual percentages for growth in Comecon and the EEC, for 1961–66.

Trading Area	National Income	Industrial Production	Total Exports	Total Exports within Comecon/EEC
Comecon, incl. USSR	6.1	8.3	8.1	7.0
All EEC	4.5	6.0	10.2	14.3

(continued on page 380)

and increased political stability lie in the direction of increased trade with
the markets of capitalism and of greater industrial specialization? And
can such a change in trading patterns be achieved without first reforming
the economic system?

ALTERNATIVE REFORM PROGRAMS

Most of the reforms adopted or under way in Eastern Europe are attempts
to improve the efficiency of the CPE. In only two countries, Yugoslavia and
Hungary, does the reform program envision abolition of central management in favor of reliance on market forces manipulated by the government,
which would retain ownership of industry. (The occupation of Czechoslovakia by the armies of the Warsaw Pact brought about the abandonment
of market reform in that country.)

So far, experience with improved central planning has not proved promising. The first regime to adopt this kind of reform, or any reform for that
matter, was the GDR, which overhauled its system in 1963. Since East
Germany is unusually well endowed with skilled administrators and industrial managers, the chances for success should have been better than
average. Yet, as we have already noted, factor efficiency in East German
industry has continued to remain stagnant or decline in comparison with
that of the Federal Republic, and the gap in living standards between the
two states has remained as large as ever. More recently, the leadership in
Pankow has announced a wide-ranging program of industrial specialization
within the framework of Comecon, with emphasis on chemicals, electronics
and electrical engineering. What effect the new policy may have remains to
be seen.

There seems reason to believe that, in conditions of competition with the
EEC and without recourse to terror, system improvement is not enough;

(continued from page 379)

The trend indicated in the table has continued since 1966. The rate of growth of intra-Comecon
trade in 1969 was less than that in 1967, whereas exports to the rest of the world grew 9.5 percent
in 1969, 9.1 percent in 1968, and 9.0 percent in 1967. "Verlangsamtes Wirtschaftswachstum in
Osteuropa: Ein Bericht der europäischen Wirtschaftskommission," *NZZ*, 31 March 1970,
p. 15. The Deutsches Institut für Wirtschaftsforschung states that Soviet trade with the other
Comecon countries increased at a rate of 11.3 percent in 1961–65 over 1956–60, but only at a
rate of 6.2 percent for 1966–70 over 1961–65. On the other hand, the plan figures called for an
increase of 8.9 percent for 1971–75 over the preceding quinquenium. Cf. "Die Entwicklung des
sowjetischen Aussenhandels mit den RGW–Ländern in den Jahren 1971–1975," *Wochenbericht
des deutschen Instituts für Wirtschaftsforschung 48/70*, 26 November 1970, p. 344. For a perceptive analysis of the trading relationship between the USSR and Czechoslovakia, as well as
its exploitative character, see Václav Holešovský, "Die Wirtschaftsreform und ihre Bedeutung,"
Prag 1968—Analyse, ed. Peter Sager and Christian Brügger (Bern: Verlag SOI, 1968), pp. 124–33.
The standard work on the Comecon is Michael Kaser, *Comecon: Integration Problems of the
Planned Economies* (London: Oxford University Press, 1965).

rather, system change is required. For one thing, it seems difficult to maintain a high rate of technological innovation in a centrally allocative system, especially in conditions of industrial maturity. The core of innovation appears to be the taking of great risks by individuals, but this does not occur where the rewards are totally inadequate.[15] Actually, a CPE would function best in a technologically static environment.

Centrally determined prices, furthermore, whatever their value in influencing the direction and pace of growth in an early stage, do not, in industrial maturity, provide an accurate enough rendition of alternative scarcities to permit economic allocation of costly resources. Such prices spread the wrong signals throughout the system. Only bargaining in the marketplace appears to provide a calculus joining together the great number of variables involved.

There is also the problem created by the voluntarism which is embedded in Communist-style totalitarianism. In the economic realm as in others, Communists persist in confusing what is needed with what is true. This fact is illustrated by the Stalinist dictum that "cadres decide everything."

THE POLITICAL COSTS OF MARKET REFORM

In the interests of improved economic efficiency, higher living standards, and increased political stability, the Communist leaders of Eastern Europe should have revealed a strong preference for market reform. In fact, as we have already pointed out, they have not. The reason for their reluctance seems obvious: economic reform tends to spill over into political reform, and marketization has a tendency to produce runaway political change.

Philosophically, Communist regimes are based on what Gregory Grossman has aptly called the "solidary conception" of society. In this conception, state and society are declared to be coterminous, the interests of government, social group, and individual being defined as identical. In the solidary society there is no room for particular interests or the conflict thereof. The business firm has no right to profit and its losses are covered by the state. Competition between firms is outlawed because it leads to the splintering of society. What constitutes the general interest is determined by the party leadership on the basis of its unique understanding of the Marxist–Leninist holy writ. The solidary is a sacred society which has its very specific Russian roots in the religious orthodoxy of tsarism.

Even very limited economic reform tends to breach the artificially satin surface of the solidary society. Changing the supreme objective of the

15. For a discussion of the institutional obstacles which central planning places in the way of high rates of technological innovation, see R. V. Burks, "Technology and Political Change in Eastern Europe," in *Change in Communist Systems*, ed. Chalmers Johnson (Stanford: Stanford University Press, 1970), pp. 265–312.

individual enterprise from gross value of product to profit based on actual sales has the psychological effect of authorizing management to openly defend its own interests, rather than those of the state. Any degree of decentralization represents some degree of pluralization (witness the resurgence of localism which accompanied Khrushchev's establishment of *sovnarchozy* in 1957), and involves some activity on the part of higher authority which the Western political scientist would recognize as interest aggregation. Because of the nature of the solidary conception, moreover, any formally recognized exception to it tends to breed other exceptions.[16]

In the long run, that is to say, it would be difficult to grant autonomy to industrial managers so that they might turn market situations to profitable account without granting to the unions a comparable autonomy, the right of defending worker interests against profit-minded managers by collective bargaining, including the right to strike. And how could the workers defend their actions and explain their point of view to the authorities and the public if they did not have access to an uncensored press? Between the solidary and the competitive societies there yawns a qualitative chasm.

In the short run, to be sure, economic reform need not necessarily entail political reform. As a group, industrial managers are not especially noted for their political liberalism, even in Western textbooks. In Eastern Europe, where authoritarianism has a long history, an autonomous managerial class might very well prefer a strong government, so as to keep the unions in line and wages depressed. In addition to the natural conservatism of management, there would be the obstacle of what might be called the clear and present national danger. Each of the states in our area tends to be confronted by such a danger, and to find its political elbow room limited in consequence. To give an example, Yugoslavia is faced with a difficult nationalities problem, a fact which may prevent for a long period any restoration in that country of the multiparty system, for fear that political parties might become identified with individual nationalities and thus pave the way for head-on collision.

In actual practice, however, it has proved difficult to separate economic from political reform, even in the short run. Throughout the socialist camp, in fact, the revisionists have insisted upon this association. Rightly they see that economic inefficiency is the Achilles' heel of Communist totalitarianism, because such inefficiency erodes the moral claim of communism and

---

16. This and the preceding paragraph lean heavily on Gregory Grossman, "The Solidary Society: a Philosophical Issue in Communist Economic Reform," in *Essays in Socialism and Planning in Honor of Carl Landauer*, ed. Gregory Grossman (Englewood Cliffs, N.J.: Prentice-Hall, 1970), pp. 184–211. The concept of the solidary society owes its importance to the fact that it restates the notion of totalitarianism in such a way as to allow for devolution of the system.

therefore undermines the morale of the Communists themselves. That the most influential revisionists were once devout Stalinists is almost a political maxim. The revisionists wish to utilize a necessary economic reform to ensure political changes which, they fear, would not be forthcoming otherwise and without which, in their view, socialism might not survive.

Having remained Marxists, moreover, if not Leninists, the reformers continue to believe that any change in the economic substructure will result in a corresponding shift in the political superstructure. In fact, the revisionists have worked out a specific theory of the immediate and necessary relationship between the two varieties of reform.

They argue that socialism stands at a crossroads. Its early successes, they assert, were due to what they call extensive industrialization, which they define as rapid growth through huge quantities of factor inputs; for this phase the central planning system was entirely appropriate. Now, however, in the second half of the twentieth century, the world faces the onset of a second industrial, or scientific-technical, revolution in which economic growth will be intensive in character. It will be the product of constant improvement in the quality of inputs. In the epoch of the scientific-technical revolution, industry will be the handmaiden of technology, and technology the servant of science. Economic growth will depend on releasing the creative energy of an ever-more-numerous intelligentsia, and on the granting of wide-ranging autonomy to enterprises functioning in a market situation. The intelligentsia will create an ever-more-powerful technology, while the managerial class will apply this technology to the productive process. To this end, both intelligentsia and managers will have to be given autonomy within the system, grants openly referred to by the revisionists as "further democratization."

There is no time to be lost, if the second industrial revolution is not to pass socialism by and become a monopoly of the capitalists.

There exists today a pressing need to undertake a series of measures leading to the further democratization of the social life of our country. This need arises in part from the close connection between problems of technical and economic development and of scientific methods of administration, on the one hand, and questions of freedom of information, publicity, and competition on the other.... We emphasize in addition that democratization cannot, in and of itself, resolve all economic problems; it can only create a more favorable basis for their resolution. But without the creation of this basis our economic and technical problems cannot be solved.[17]

17. "Sacharows Brief an die sowjetische Führungsspitze," NZZ, 22 April 1970, p. 13, and 24 April 1970, pp. 13 and 14.

These are the words of three prominent Soviet scientists, addressed to Brezhnev, Kosygin, and Podgorny in the spring of 1970, and generally known as the Sacharov letter. But the most systematic and detailed expression of these ideas is to be found in a volume entitled, significantly enough, *Civilization at the Crossroads*, which was published in Prague in 1964 as the collective work of some fifty Czech and Slovak academicians and professors.[18]

That the conservatives recognize the tactical association of political with economic reform is revealed by their continuing effort to limit reform to the planning process. They understand that marketization constitutes a change of economic system, and they have reason to fear a corresponding change in polity with unpredictable consequences. The political counterpart of marketization is not necessarily, or only, the establishment of something we might call one-party democracy, more or less along Titoist lines. The socialist market is also fully compatible with the introduction of a multi-party system. Perhaps the most grievous of the errors committed by the Czech and Slovak revisionists was their failure to formulate clearly the degree of political pluralization they had in mind. The Prague reformers were undertaking not only the aggregation of interests; they also showed signs of moving toward reconstitution of a loyal opposition. Sooner or later such policies could result not merely in a diminution of the power of the Communist party, but in its loss of power altogether.

For the sake of clarity, the set of relationships obtaining among the various types and degrees of reform is shown in diagram 11.1. The urgent

Diagram 11.1

ECONOMY	POLITY
Command	Totalitarian
Improved Central Planning	Authoritarian
Socialist Market	One-Party Democracy . . . . Multi-Party Democracy

18. Radovan Richta et al., *Civilization at the Crossroads: Social and Human Implications of the Scientific and Technological Revolution*, mimeographed (Prague, 1967). I am indebted to William E. Griffith for a copy of this translation. The original appeared in Prague in 1964 as *Civilizace na Rozčestí: Spoločenská a Lidske Souvislosti Vedeckotecknické Revoluce*. An English translation was published in New York in 1969.

political need for improved economic efficiency presents the regimes with a terrible dilemma. If they marketize they run the risk of losing control. If they limit reform to the improvement of central planning they must face the dangers of continuing instability. The pressure for political reform and the need for greater economic efficiency appear to have the same source: the evident inability of the Communist regimes to compete with their capitalist and democratic counterparts in Western Europe.

THE ROLE OF SYSTEMIC INTERDEPENDENCE

We have already referred to the occupation of Czechoslovakia by the armed forces of the Warsaw Pact. A military assault on one socialist state by its fellows betokens a situation of utmost gravity. The strategic blunder of the Prague revisionists was their stubborn refusal to recognize that the changes they had in hand threatened the fabric of the socialist common-wealth itself. There is direct evidence that Ulbricht believed his regime could not survive unless the Prague reform was not only stopped, but reversed. The Gomulka leadership in Warsaw also manifested distinct signs of nervousness. In Sofia, the leadership de facto abandoned economic reform in July 1968, apparently convinced they were facing a political landslide.[19] But even Piotr Shelest', First Party Secretary in Kiev, gave vent to a public utterance in that same July which suggests that he regarded the security of the Ukrainian republic to be placed in jeopardy.[20]

Among the regimes loyal to Moscow, only Hungary persists at present in the course of market reform and one-party democracy. Analysis of the output of Hungarian media at the time of Czech crisis would show that there was great concern in Hungary, both within the regime and among the population at large, that the occupation of Czechoslovakia, in which Hungarian units participated, would bring down a Soviet veto of Hungarian reform. Nothing of the sort appears to have happened; the implementation of reform has been continued in Hungary, gradually and without fanfare, as in the past.

Nevertheless, the occupation of her northern neighbor has presented Hungary with something of a dilemma. It is no longer feasible for her to think in terms of massive, long-term credits from the West; Prague's secret

19. R. V. Burks, "The Politics of Economic Reform in Bulgaria and Romania," (Paper Sub-mitted to the Research Conference on Economic Reform in Eastern Europe at the University of Michigan, 16–18 November 1970). See particularly pp. 39–46.

20. Grey Hodnett and Peter J. Potichnyj, The Ukraine and the Czechoslovak Crisis, Occa-sional Paper No. 6 (Canberra, Australia: Australian National University, 1970), 154 pp. See particularly "Report by Shelest, First Secretary of the Ukrainian Communist Party Central Committee," 6 July 1968, in Foreign Broadcast Information Service, USSR, no. 135, 11 July 1968, especially pp. B-12–B-15.

negotiations with Bonn on this point evidently had been one of the many reasons for armed intervention. Yet, improvement in factor productivity requires, among other things, the replacement of Hungary's outmoded machine park with the most advanced technology available. Unfortunately, such machinery and equipment are for the most part available only in the West, in exchange for hard currency. But Hungarian manufactures are not competitive in the West—the realization of this fact was the starting point of economic reform—and, given the rapid pace of industrialization and urbanization, it is difficult for Budapest to increase the share of foodstuffs sold abroad.

Massive Western long-term credit is politically unavailable for a very good reason. If debt payments are to be met, the debtor socialist economy must increase the share of trade which it conducts with the West, and reduce the share carried on with Comecon. To bring about such a shift, socialist policy makers must introduce a series of changes. They must reduce the number of different manufactures produced in order to specialize in those in which their country enjoys a comparative advantage. They must reorganize their own economy so as to make their enterprises sensitive to the requirements of the Western market. Such reorganization would normally include opening up the socialist economy to the competition of Western goods; otherwise socialist products will not be competitive, since in most cases they are turned out by firms enjoying a domestic monopoly. If policy makers are successful in making these changes, they will discover that they have balance-of-payments surpluses in the East, where technical standards are lower, and balance-of-payments deficits in the West, where they are still learning to compete. The reforming economy will thus tend to be dragged back toward its old trading relationship, a tendency gladly furthered by the Stalinist opposition. To offset this pull, the reformers will have to reduce still further their trade with the East. They will have discovered the qualitative chasm between the command and the competitive systems mentioned earlier, but in a new form: a socialist market economy must end up trading primarily with other socialist markets. In order to change systems, the reformers must also change trading partners.

At any rate, this has been the experience of Titoist Yugoslavia. In 1948, approximately three-fourths of Belgrade's foreign trade was carried on with the socialist camp, whereas today three-fourths is exchanged with the free world, primarily Western Europe. The shift did not take place overnight. It began with the embargo on socialist trade with Yugoslavia laid down by Stalin in 1949, but the final decision was not taken until 1966, when Tito's heir apparent, Aleksandar Ranković, was removed from public life, and the security police which he controlled were downgraded. Ranković and his security police had been blocking the implementation of reform measures, adopted in 1965, for marketizing the economy. There were a number of reasons for Tito's decision to remove his heir, but apparently among the more important was the fear that without market reform the Yugoslav economy might gradually be pulled into the Comecon orbit. The Yugoslav Marshall had begun with the assumption that his country could trade equally with East and West, occupying an uncommitted position in between. When he found that such a halfway house was untenable, he opted for the West, on the grounds that there was less risk to Yugoslav sovereignty in that direction.[21]

While publicly reassuring the Hungarian people that economic and political reform will continue, Kádár and his associates have hewed to the line in foreign trade. They have not entered into unseemly negotiations with any Western capital, and the Five-Year Plan figures for 1971–75 call for no significant increase in the ratio of trade with the West.[22]

How, then, do the Hungarians propose to reconcile, over the longer term, their foreign trade ratios with their marketization policy? The answer has not been long in coming. In January 1969, five months after the occupation of Czechoslovakia, Resö Nyers, the politburo member and Central Committee Secretary in charge of the reform, publicly proposed that the Comecon itself be converted from an institution of planned foreign trade to a regulated market. Member countries would coordinate in advance basic questions of the international division of labor. A partially convertible common currency with respect to which each national currency would have a rate of exchange should be established. Prices of selected commodities would be allowed to vary according to supply and demand, while enterprises would be permitted to deal directly with each other insofar as these selected commodities were concerned. Through realistic and coordinated rates of foreign exchange, an organic connection between domestic and foreign

21. For a general discussion of the foreign policy aspects of the economic reform of 1966, see Alvin Z. Rubinstein, "Reforms, Nonalignment and Pluralism," *Problems of Communism* 17 (March–April 1968): 31–40. Cf. also R. V. Burks, "The Removal of Ranković: an Early Interpretation of the July Yugoslav Party Plenum," Rand Memorandum 5132 PR (Santa Monica), August 1966.

22. On 12 June 1970, Imre Pardi, Chairman of the National Planning Bureau, gave a press conference in Budapest on the main directives of the Fourth Five-Year Plan. In the ruble area a yearly export increase of 7–7.5 percent is planned, and an 8–8.5 percent increase in imports. In the dollar area, the corresponding figures are 6–6.5 and 5–6 percent. The planned increase in imports of Soviet raw materials is remarkable. Crude oil imports, for example, will rise from the 4.0 million tons of 1970 to 6.5 million tons. If Hungary increases her industrial output in the next five years by the planned figure of 32–35 percent, she may be able to improve somewhat the ratio of trade with developed Western countries. But it is clear that no decisive shift in trade ratios is in the offing. "Protocol of the 1971–1975 Hungarian–Soviet Plan Coordination Agreement Signed," *Radio Free Europe Research: East Europe: Situation Report: Hungary*, 22 September 1970. Sixty-seven percent of Hungary's trade is carried on with the Socialist countries.

prices within Comecon would be created gradually. Conditions for multi-lateral clearing of foreign trade accounts in extraquota trade would be made possible by means of convertibility. In special cases, there would be mutual investment in joint enterprises and even the flow of manpower across national frontiers. Thus, Nyers was proposing that the first steps should be taken toward merging the national economies of the Comecon, not on the basis of plan coordination, as Khrushchev had proposed in 1963, but on the basis of market principles.[23]

Clearly the Nyers proposal could not succeed unless the other socialist countries, and especially the USSR, also undertook steps in the direction of market reform. Free trade in any given set of commodities would not be possible as long as these commodities were centrally allocated by all or most of Hungary's trading partners. The Hungarians were in fact proposing that all their fellow socialist states move toward marketization; in this way Hungary would save her own reform without escaping to the West. Inter-estingly enough, the Nyers proposal did not remain unsung. It found support not only in marketizing Yugoslavia, but also in Poland, at long last resolved on structural reform herself, and, though the voices are muffled, in Czecho-slovakia also.[24] The USSR, the GDR, and Bulgaria were openly opposed. Like the Czechoslovak, the Hungarian case brings into sharp relief the interlocking character of system change within the socialist commonwealth, including—primarily, it may be argued—the USSR.

STRUCTURAL REFORM AND THE SOVIET UNION

The population of the USSR is twice that of all the East European states combined, and her area seventeen times greater. The question of whether system change by peaceful evolution of the commonwealth is possible reduces itself, in this writer's view, to the question of structural change in the Soviet Union. Unless Moscow marketizes, it seems doubtful that she will permit her Comecon partners to do so. On the other hand, a Muscovite decision in favor of structural reform probably would bring such reform to all the countries of Eastern Europe, with the possible exception of the GDR.

23. R. Nyers, "Questions of Principle and Practice in Socialist Economic Integration," *Nepszabadsag*, 23 January 1969, as translated in *Radio Free Europe Research: East Europe: Press Survey: Hungary*, 3 February 1969. See also B. Csikos-Nagy, "Forint Convertibility," *Figyelo*, 12 February 1969, as translated in ibid., 2 April 1969. For a summary of a lecture along these lines, delivered by a leading Hungarian planner to a joint session of the Comecon and the Soviet Academy of Sciences, see "Difficulties in Comecon Integration," *Radio Free Europe Research: East Europe: Situation Report: Hungary*, 9 June 1970.

24. See, for example, L. Rusmick, "Currency Without Frontiers," *Tvorba*, 1970, no. 40, as translated in *Radio Free Europe: East Europe: Press Survey: Czechoslovakia*, 6 November 1970.

To address ourselves to the highly speculative, though important, question of Soviet structural reform, let us assume for the sake of argument the coming to power of a Soviet leadership determined and able to carry through a market reform, and then ask ourselves what impact such an eventuality might have on the Soviet regime and its East European satellites. This approach requires, of course, the making of other assumptions which are not necessarily defensible, such as the ability of this new leadership to carry out structural reform without producing a political landslide. By making such assumptions we free ourselves to cast up the passive side of the balance, so as to get some notion of the specific Soviet problems Muscovite reformers would face.

To begin with, market reform in the USSR probably would lower the rate of increase in the output of raw materials and fuels. Under market or semimarket circumstances it would be difficult to persuade the East Europeans to continue investing in Soviet extractive industry. On the contrary, as East European manufactures became more sophisticated, their producers would ask for greater quantities of raw materials in exchange. At the same time, Moscow, without a CPE, would herself experience difficulty in maintaining present rates of investment. The wage bill in extractive industry would go up because workers would be freer to seek alternative employment in less unattractive areas; and construction and transportation costs would continue to rise as older extractive sites were exhausted or abandoned and new ones developed to the north and east. The capital intensity of the Soviet extractive industry appears to be about three times that of East European manufacturing industry, and 40 percent of all Soviet investment goes to the former at present.[25]

Because the Soviet economy is already pressing on its fuel and raw material supplies, lowering the rate of growth of the production of the Soviet extractive industry would have at least a temporary adverse effect on the gross national product and on the USSR's ability to earn hard currency. Within the Comecon it would have the effect of improving the bargaining position of the East European states (or at least of their northern tier) where there is a high concentration of skilled labor, managerial know-how, and a better location relative to Western Europe. Within the Comecon, Soviet gold and hard currency would tend to flow toward the smaller, more advanced partners, enabling them in turn to increase their imports of the latest Western technology and to widen still further the technological gap

25. N. Mel'nikov, M. Agoshkov, and B. Laskorin, "Zapasam nedr nuzhen schet," *Pravda*, 27 January 1970, p. 2; P. Alamniev, "Kniga ob aktual'nykh problemakh mezhdunarodnogo sotsialisticheskogo razdeleniya truda," *Voprosy ekonomiki*, 1968, no. 10, pp. 139–40.

between themselves and the USSR.[26] Furthermore, East European dependence on Soviet fuels and raw materials would decrease, as the East Europeans increased their imports of these substances from third-world sources.

With the partial restoration of consumer sovereignty, the production of consumer goods could be expected to spurt forward. The automotive industry would no doubt experience phenomenal growth, as would housing construction and, to a lesser extent, the chemical industry. Agricultural and food prices would be likely to rise steeply. Life in the villages would show marked improvement and Moscow might have difficulty in preventing decollectivization (under some pretext such as the link system), even though this action would constitute a serious moral blow to the regime. The tourist trade would probably receive much greater emphasis, bringing with it a more relaxed atmosphere and improvement in the service industries.

But these developments would not be proportionately distributed among the various economic regions of the USSR. Stalin's industrialization policies not only gave priority to heavy industry but its location was influenced by military considerations; the reconstruction of industry after the Nazi invasion was governed primarily by the time factor. With the dismantling of the CPE, the natural advantages of the peripheral areas in the west and south would come to the fore: in some instances greater ease of access to the outside world; in others, superior reserves of skill and know-how; in still others, more favorable climatic conditions. Thus, in agriculture, dairy farming would grow most rapidly in the Baltics and cereal production would become more heavily concentrated in the Ukraine and the Kuban, whereas the Caucasus and Central Asia would produce a still-larger proportion of the fruits and vegetables. The newer industries, such as electronics, computers, and chemicals, would tend to concentrate in the Leningrad area and along the Baltic frontier, or even outside the Soviet frontier, in the GDR and in Czechoslovakia. Furthermore, the rate of population growth would decline in central Russia and in Siberia, whereas it would increase along the

26. An extreme example of this gap is provided by the relative application of synthetic fertilizer (kilograms per hectare).

	Potassium Fertilizers	Phosphoric Fertilizers	Nitrogenous Fertilizers
GDR	97.0	62.0	54.2
Czechoslovakia	55.2	39.0	35.9
Poland	33.3	25.9	20.6
Hungary	17.2	34.2	22.9
USSR	3.9	5.7	4.6

Cf. *Statistisches Jahrbuch der DDR 1969: Anhang I: Länder des Rates für gegenseitige Wirtschaftshilfe*, p. 11, as cited in E. L., "Das Aufholbemühen der sowjetischen Chemiewirtschaft. Spät erkannte Erneuerungs- und Erweiterungsbedürfnisse," *NZZ*, 13 December 1970, p. 19.

peripheries, partly due to higher net birth rates, but also as the consequence of internal migration.[27]

The fact that the abandonment of the CPE would benefit the southern and western peripheries to the disadvantage of the Muscovite center is not incidental, for these peripheries are inhabited by non-Great Russian populations. Economic decentralization would, therefore, very probably bring about a resurfacing of the nationality issue within the USSR itself; at least the repeated efforts at economic reform in Yugoslavia have had this effect. In the Yugoslav case, the Communist party itself has become a federation of national and regional subparties, with the result that today the country is governed by a process of negotiation between eight autonomous party leaderships.[28]

Despite their great differences in size and natural resources, the political and ethnic analogies between the USSR and Yugoslavia are rather striking and provide us with important clues as to the impact of the structural reform on the Soviet system. Both states are ruled by indigenous Communist regimes, centered around parties which literally fought their way to power in the course of a cruel and bloody civil war. Both have to contend with grave ethnic problems, made more difficult by wide regional differences in natural endowments. The conflict between Great Russian and Ukrainian resembles in some ways the struggle between Serb and Croat. (It is well to remind ourselves that Great Russians comprise 49 percent, Serbs 43 percent of the total population of their respective states.) Both Soviet and Yugoslav populations are preponderantly Slav, and the Orthodox-Byzantine heritage looms large for each. Both states are unevenly developed. Compared with Western Europe, both have low levels of skill and literacy, while each faces difficult problems of egress to the outer world. Consequently, Soviet structural reform would probably mean replacement of the present spurious federalism of the USSR with some genuine variety, and the de facto dissolution of the CPSU into a number of national parties, each with extensive autonomy in its own republic.

27. After having drafted the lines concerning internal migration, I discovered that, according to the 1970 Soviet census, migration to the southern periphery had already set in. Between 1959 and 1967, Siberia and the Urals, together with the Volga-Vyatski, Central Black Earth, and Belorussian regions had a negative migratory balance, whereas a strip of territories in the south, stretching from Moldavia through the southern Ukraine, the northern Caucasus, and Transcaucasia to Central Asia and Kazakstan, had a net migratory gain. The share of Siberia in the total Soviet population has already declined. V. Perevedentsev, "Migratsiya naseleniya i ispol'zovanie trudovykh resursov," *Voprosy ekonomiki*, 1970, no. 9, pp. 40–41. This change in migratory currents is, I think, largely the result of the ending of police terror. The liberalization attendant on structural reform would very probably accentuate these trends.

28. R. V. Burks, "The National Problem and the Future of Yugoslavia," (Santa Monica: RAND Corporation, 1972).

Indeed, existing regional differences in the Soviet Union, if the Yugoslav analogy held, would be accentuated rather than diminished by economic reform, although the degree of pluralization would probably vary from republic to republic. Revisionism would tend to be strong in the minority republics and those further west, while conservatism would find its stronghold eastward, particularly among the Great Russians. Just as conditions would improve more rapidly on the periphery, so also would the out-migration from the center and from Siberia earlier referred to grow in volume and perhaps release xenophobic reactions in the peripheral republics, or create pressure for migration to the Common Market, or even to the New World. It would be especially difficult to prevent the bulk of the Jewish population, with its greatly-needed reserves of skill and knowledge, from escaping to Israel or the United States (not to mention the return of the Tatars to the Crimea, etc.).

These decentralizing trends would, of course, apply with equal or greater force to the East European regimes, which presumably would be proceeding for the most part on the path of structural reform at a faster pace than their Soviet mentor. As we have indicated already, the tendency of Eastern Europe would be to shift the bulk of its trade westward as reforms took hold and its competitive capacity grew. There might also be a tendency for the East European states to form a special relationship with the (enlarged?) Common Market, while continuing close ties with the USSR as well. The Soviet Union would still be able to give some considerable protection to its interests in Eastern Europe because of the mutual self-support necessary among the regimes, in the political and ideological as well as the economic realms, and because of its military preponderance in the area. The regimes would be more beholden to Moscow than the Finnish state is, for example, and they would not have shared the Yugoslav experience of expulsion. On the other hand, East European industry would no longer serve as a supplement to Soviet industrial capacity; and the institutional differentiation among regimes would be greater than at present. Perhaps one could speak of condominium, with Moscow enjoying a military and political overlordship, while Brussels would have the upper hand in matters economic. Europe no longer would be divided sharply into Communist and capitalist halves, but would present a series of gradients running from less regulated markets in the West to more highly regulated markets as one moved East.

Thus, the CPE turns out to be the prime element of rigid Muscovite control in Eastern Europe, and of highly centralized control of the USSR by the Soviet Communist party. While it has been one of the chief instruments of control since the coming of the Communists to power, the CPE's importance has been enhanced in recent years by the reduction in the role of the security police throughout the socialist commonwealth and by the decline in the leading role of the Party in some countries. If it is improbable that the CPE can be abandoned in Eastern Europe without its first being given up in the USSR, it is also true that dismantling the Soviet CPE would necessarily bring a diminution in the role and influence of that enormous bureaucracy which has been the central feature of the Russian state for the last several centuries. In addition, the huge Soviet military establishment, at least its more traditional services, would also be faced with drastic budget cuts; this would be a sina qua non for the success of the reform. In foreign affairs generally, the Soviets would have to show a lower profile, and in negotiations with the West rely more heavily on the art of compromise. It would be tautological to assert that structural reform would lead to the transformation of the Soviet regime and its satellite states. Whether Soviet interest in reform will ever become so compelling is consequently the central question for any forecast.

THE GENERATION GAP

We shall discuss later in what circumstances, if any, the game might be worth the candle. Now we shall consider two additional elements of vital importance to that judgment, the generation gap within the Communist elites, and the possible impact of the new Eastern policy of the German Federal Republic (FRG). Let us deal first with the generation gap.

Structural reform, we have said, involves a downgrading of the bureaucracy. In Communist states the decision-making element in that bureaucracy is provided by the Party apparatus. It is not only that all basic decisions are taken by the Party leadership; it is also that under central planning the local Party apparatchik performs a vital interstitial function. By using his Party connections, he compensates for the failings and inefficiencies of the CPE. If a factory in his district cannot procure delivery of the necessary raw materials from a supplier in another area, he uses his Party connections to obtain them.

The devolution of managerial authority from ministries and other central bodies to the directors of trusts and enterprises naturally reduces the scope of the decisions taken by Party leaders. It also tends to deprive our apparatchik of his interstitial function, since economic decision-making now remains within the economic subsystem. In Hungary, for example, responsibility for the *nomenklatura* (power of appointment in the enterprise) has been taken from the Party representative and given to the enterprise director.[29]

29. Matyas Tot, "O rabote s kadrami," *Partinaya zhizn'*, 1968, no. 20, p. 76; "The Party and the Manager: a New Relationship?", *Radio Free Europe Research: East Europe: Situation Report: Hungary*, 14 November 1970.

In view of these considerations it is not surprising that the intransigent opposition of the apparatus was perhaps the most important reason for the abandonment of economic reform in Bulgaria. Such opposition has not been lacking even in countries where revisionism has got the upper hand. In these, the leadership has sought to ease the path of reform by banishing to the provinces the more dogmatic of the apparatchiki, assignments in agriculture being given preference. This helps explain the curious struggle which Budapest has waged with its own collective farm chairmen over the rights of the private plots.

Closely associated with the Party bureaucracy in its attitude toward structural reform is the security police, whose interests are adversely affected by any trend toward pluralization, because it brings with it an increased emphasis on socialist legality and even, in the Yugoslav case, has spawned a semiindependent judiciary. The East European policemen always seem to enjoy a special relationship with their Soviet colleagues, a fact which appears to reinforce their natural conservatism. In Yugoslavia, as we have already pointed out, the security police became in the end the major obstacle to market reform. Once the conservatives had lost control of the Party apparatus, as a consequence of its disintegration into its republican components, the police service became a refuge for semiliterate Partisan veterans, mainly Serb and Montenegrin, who had lost their positions in the apparatus or the state bureaucracy. At the last, the conservatives were making use of the police cells in government offices and major enterprises to block the implementation of the reform legislation of 1965. The removal of Ranković was followed by the purge of his followers in the police; it, in turn, was divided into two separate services. One service was to concentrate on the danger of foreign subversion and was permitted to work with the old methods. The other was assigned to security problems of domestic origin and was required to function under the supervision of the courts. In this instance there proved to be a direct tie between market reform and socialist legality.[30]

The state bureaucracy, in the narrow sense of that term, is also adversely affected by reform, even if reform is limited to in-system improvement, for it involves massive transfers of bureaucrats from ministries and state committees to trusts and collective farms. In Romania, reluctance to accept transfer has proved to be a major obstacle to the implementation of even limited reform. In Hungary, the central economic bureaucracy has undergone personnel reductions on the order of 30 to 40 percent.[31]

---

30. Burks, "The Removal of Ranković."

31. Tot, p. 76. The *nomenklatura* of the Central Committee, for example, was reduced by 40 percent.

On the whole, the key positions in the apparatus, the police, and the bureaucracy tend to be held by men in their fifties and sixties. In the Soviet case they are men who came forward in the great Stalinist purges, whether those of the 1930s or those of the 1940s. In Eastern Europe the key positions are held by men who joined the Party before World War II, or served in the Resistance, or climbed on the bandwagon in the first days of Communist power. For the most part, these men do not possess great talent or much formal education. In the more or less typical Bulgarian province of Vratsa, for example, only 9 percent of Party members have had any university education, while 70 percent have not even completed secondary school;[32] the proportion of well-educated men in the Party apparatus itself probably is still lower. The Czech reformers have furnished more complete figures. As of the early 1960s, only 3.7 percent of those employed in research and development in Czechoslovakia were scientifically trained, while just 25 percent of the directors and leading technicians in industrial enterprises had appropriate university training. The educational level of cooperative farm chairmen was below that of the population as a whole. A mere 29 percent of department chiefs in the state bureaucracy, and only 40 percent of the national leadership, had more than an elementary or lower vocational education.[33] Under central planning, more training is not desirable. The system emphasizes loyalty, compliance and ideological orthodoxy. Sergeants, not captains, of industry are required.[34]

Yet, Communism has been long enough in power to provide for a new generation of elites, of technicians, engineers, architects, and scientists. Judging by the numbers sent to school since 1950, nearly as many people

32. Michael Costello, "Expertise and Partiinost', a Question of Priorities," *Radio Free Europe Research: East Europe: Background Report: Bulgaria*, 21 November 1969.

33. Richta et al., p. 36 (footnote).

34. The characterization of the apparatchik by Lewis S. Feuer, "The Intelligentsia in Opposition," *Problems of Communism* 19 (November–December 1970): p. 2, is among the more perceptive I have run across: "For the Party apparatus is, above all, the ambitious mediocrity of all fields, drawn from all classes and social institutions, and endowed with dictatorial power. It would be a mistake to think of it as primarily a coalition of interest groups articulating, according to their respective numbers, the aims of the technical managers, the workers, the collective farms, the army. For while the apparatus recruits and coopts its members from all of these classes, its criterion of choice is primarily a psychological one: a mediocratic simplicism, an absence of brilliance, a colorless anonymity, an absence of any impulse to dissent from a decision handed down from above. Pareto thought that the challenging elite, the foxes, the speculators, would be marked by vigorous intellectual powers and initiative. The remarkable characteristic of the Stalinist apparatus which terrorized the Soviet scientists was that its members were intellectually inferior to those whom they destroyed; their bond was a mediocratic union and a thirst for power unrestrained by any moral consideration." Insofar as this description implies that factionalism does not exist within the apparatus, however, I would disagree.

with secondary education and at least as many with higher education are at work in East European as in comparable West European countries. In the 1950s, every East European country possessed more engineers per thousand nonagricultural workers than did leading countries in the West.[35] There has been, if anything, an overproduction of professionals under Communism; the new generation is pushing for place and perquisites, and is not slow to realize that pluralization of the society would put a premium on talent and training, to the disadvantage of the now-aging revolutionary generation. At the same time, the leadership hesitates to abandon the ineffective tried and true for younger cadres who are often politically apathetic or even disaffected.[36] The shadow of political landslide looms plain. Yet time, and the pressures of economic inefficiency, are on the side of the postrevolutionary generation.

DIE NEUE OSTPOLITIK

We have already mentioned the great interest of the reformers in Prague and Budapest in long-term Western credits. Such credits, had they been granted, would have involved substantial subsidies, since Western banks would not extend them on a commercial basis, but would have required governmental guarantees. That the need of Prague and Budapest is real is suggested by the experience of Belgrade, which has reached the socialist market only after a series of reforms; during much of this period Yugoslav experimentation was buttressed by an American subsidy (two and one-half billion dollars in gifts and grants between 1950 and 1965) which in effect covered the country's deficit in hard currency. Despite the effectiveness of the CPE in forcing up the rate of savings, all the socialist countries are short of capital, given their need to compete with their Western counterparts, in military power and in living standards as well. Despite her great size, her enormous natural resources, and her rather astonishing success with forced industrialization, the Soviet Union is short of investment funds. The investment problems of her extractive industry are one case in point, but the risks of structural reform, i.e. of a change in system, would be more easily borne if foreign capital were available on the right terms and in substantial amounts.

---

35. Snell, p. 272.

36. The East German Party, on the other hand, has been able to absorb many of the younger generation of technicians and experts into the apparatus and to politicize them. At the enterprise level the Party element is already made up of technological intelligentsia to the extent of 35 percent, and some high Party officials (politburo member Günther Mittag, for example) pursued careers exclusively in industrial management until called to positions in the Party leadership. Peter Ludz, *Parteielite im Wandel: Funktionsaufbau, Sozialstruktur und Ideologie der SED Führung: Eine empirische-systematische Untersuchung: Zweite, unveränderte Auflage* (Cologne: Westdeutscher Verlag, 1968). The East German case is the exception which proves the rule.

Such a subsidy is now being offered to the Soviet leaders by the Federal Republic of Germany. Suggestive of what Bonn is willing to do is a two-phase cooperation agreement concluded late in 1969. Under the terms of this arrangement, West Germany will supply some two million tons of outsized pipe on long-term credit. The Soviets have been trying without success to produce such pipe for themselves since 1960, when NATO forbade the West Germans to supply it on military grounds. The pipe will now be used to open up the Tyumen natural gas fields in northwestern Siberia, and to build a line to the Federal Republic for the delivery of payment in the form of methane gas (over a period of 20 years, beginning in 1973). The Tyumen fields contain 56 percent of known Soviet reserves in natural gas, and the interest rate granted by the Germans is substantially below that normally obtainable by the Soviets in West European transactions.[37] But the Tyumen agreement could be only a beginning.

Actually, the Soviet economy already is subsidized in some degree by the Federal Republic. This subsidy is a by-product of the so-called interzonal trade, i.e. trade between the two German states, which takes place on terms exceptionally favorable to the GDR. In accordance with the provisions of the Treaty of Rome (1956), interzonal trade is treated as trade within the Common Market, so that East German goods are liable to none of the tariff duties levied by the EEC on foreign imports. Further, the Federal Republic permits the GDR a sizeable standing swing credit, which amounts to a long-term loan. More important still, interzonal trade is not carried on in marks but in *Verrechnungseinheiten*, a device for treating the ostmark as equivalent to the Deutschemark, although the purchasing power of the two is by no means equal. As a consequence, East German industrial exports earn hard currency at standard prices in the West German market, whereas they must be discounted substantially elsewhere in the EEC. The FRG treasury makes up the difference. At present, East German industry works mainly on Soviet account, and it imports advanced technology from West Germany while exporting primarily machinery and equipment to the East. The extent of the indirect subsidy to the USSR could be substantially increased by a larger volume of interzonal trade, which amounts at present to

37. H. R., "Oestliches Erdgas gegen ·westliche Rohren," *NZZ*, 18 December 1969, pp. 17 and 18. The second article is a summary of a public lecture given by Dr. Margrethe Ottillinger, an officer of the Austrian Oil Products Administration (Oesterreichische Mineralölverwaltung, AG) after an official visit to the Soviet Union. Soviet authorities provided Frau Ottillinger with a quantitative table of their known gas reserves. According to R. R. Gill, "Brezhnev on Comecon Trade Policy," *Radio Free Europe Research: Communist Area: Background Report: USSR*, 30 October 1969, quoting *Handelsblatt*, 17 September 1969, the USSR is asking 20 percent less for its gas than the Dutch price now being charged to Germany (0.53 pfennigs per 1,000 thermal units instead of 0.616).

a mere 10 percent of total East German foreign trade.[38] The rulers in Pankow have so far limited the extent of the exchange out of fear of political dependency on Bonn, but conceivably they would reverse themselves on Soviet advice.

The new German Eastern policy goes further, however, than the offer of increased economic subsidy. The FRG has agreed in treaty form or in principle to accept the territorial arrangements resulting from the defeat of the Nazis: the new western frontier of Poland along the Oder-Neisse; the division of Germany itself along the Elbe-Werra line; and the expulsion of the German population from Czechoslovakia's Sudetenland. Bonn would retain only its right to pursue German reunification by peaceful means, and to refuse formal recognition of the GDR until such time as the regime there is more representative of the popular will. At the same time, Bonn made ratification of all these agreements and understandings with the Eastern Bloc dependent on the creation of a set of institutionalized guarantees for West Berlin.

As everyone should understand, Bonn's generosity is not without *Hintergedanken*. A part of the German population is held captive by 20 Soviet divisions and forced to exchange the product of its labor with the Soviet population under disadvantageous conditions. (Something comparable could be said about most of the other populations living under socialism.) Bonn is naturally concerned by the living standard of the captive Germans, and by their political helplessness, not least for fear that one day these deprivations will produce a flash rising involving major elements of the East German army and an urgent appeal to Bonn for help. It is also true that Bonn sees no way to the ultimate reunification of Germany other than that of promoting the peaceful evolution of the socialist commonwealth in the direction of social democracy.

The thrust of the FRG's new Eastern policy, therefore, is the promotion of the evolution of the commonwealth. By providing economic subsidies (*Verrechnungseinheiten*, Tyumen gas piping) Bonn hopes to improve living standards, raise growth rates, and increase the options open to the regimes. To put it crudely, Bonn is willing to offer Moscow a bribe bigger than the amount Moscow can extract from the captive East Germans. By guaranteeing contentious frontiers, Bonn hopes to deprive hard-liners of the nourishment they derive from the threat of German revanchism; a standard response

38. The GDR supplies the USSR with 27 percent of its imports of machinery and equipment and receives in return, according to the calculation of the World Economic Archive (Hamburg), 90 percent of its total raw material and energy needs. Fifty-eight percent of East German deliveries to the USSR consist of machinery and 60 percent of East German exports go to the USSR. Carlo Mötteli, "Deutschlands Funktion im Ost-West Handel," *NZZ*, 12 April 1970, p. 17.

to revisionist advance has been the raising of the Nazi bogeyman. Officially, the occupation of Czechoslovakia was undertaken to protect the Czech frontier against West German designs. Again, to resort to brutal language, Bonn is prepared to accept a separate East Germany for the foreseeable future in the hope that by so doing she will be giving pledges to the forces of Communist reform.[39]

Thus the FRG is offering both economic subsidies and political guarantees in the hope of pushing the Soviet regime toward a policy of pluralization.

The Soviet Dilemma

Just as East European politics is in part determined by the need to be competitive with Western Europe, so one of the determining conditions of Soviet politics is the Big Competition with the United States, a vast struggle for power, prestige, and leadership in the world.

In this competition the Soviet leaders are presently confronted, to paraphrase Alec Nove, with a dangerous multiplication of priorities. They have to face nuclear rivalry with the U.S. and, as well, the Chinese threat. They must import advanced Western technology at a more rapid rate and develop a series of new industries, such as serial manufacture of computers, while at the same time finding a sizable additional investment for their extractive industries. They must modernize agriculture and fill out the infrastructure. Finally, and perhaps most importantly, they must keep living standards rising. To say that the Soviet leaders are faced with a multiplication of priorities is to assert that, for reasons of competition, they have more to do than their resources will allow them to accomplish. Either they must change their system in order to utilize existing resources more efficiently, or they must resort again to the practice of increasing inputs by the use of force and terror. In 1969, industrial labor productivity in the USSR rose by 4.8 percent, whereas in West Germany and in France the increase ranged

---

39. It should be noted that the rioting of December 1970, which caused the overthrow of Gomulka, broke out in the port area of Gdansk-Gdynia-Sopot and spread to the port area of Szczeczin; there were no serious disturbances inland. The port towns were not only those in which the population was more aware of West European living standards—sharp increases in food prices touched off the riots—but they had also been, for the most part, German prior to 1944. The West-German–Polish treaty in which Bonn renounced all claims to such territory had been formally initialled in Warsaw by the German chancellor only a couple of weeks before, thus relieving the present inhabitants of these territories of the fear that action against their own government might somehow advance the German claim. For details of the rioting see "Swedish Reporter Says 300 Died in Week of Rioting at Gdansk," New York Times, 22 December 1970, p. 8; James Feron, "Poland Is Calm, Reports Indicated; Warsaw Normal," New York Times, 20 December 1970, pp. 1 and 14; "Poland Ends State of Emergency as Work Resumes," New York Times, 23 December 1970, pp. 1 and 4.

between 7 and 8 percent.[40] This is a statistical statement of the crucial Soviet problem; despite the great accomplishments of central planning, the USSR has not as yet been able to equal or surpass the Western rate of increased mastery over the forces of nature.

But neither of the available alternatives, system change or reversion to Stalinism, must appear very attractive to the Soviet leaders. System change would mean abandonment of the practice of perpetual mobilization and a downgrading of the traditional military and bureaucratic establishments, both of which actions would run directly counter to a deep-laid Soviet fear of renewed foreign aggression. System change also would mean a massive influx of foreign capital, in order to charm the twin demons of raw material extraction and technological innovation, and an opening up of a semi-closed society to the evil influences of capitalism. Perhaps most important of all, system change probably would bring with it an end to the hegemony of the Great Russian people, not only over the traditional Eastern Europe outside the Soviet frontier, but as well over the "Eastern Europe" inside. This would bring with it, at least to begin with, a marked degeneration in the economic status and political standing of the Great Russians. During the changeover, moreover, the danger of political landslide would be ever present.

Reversion to Stalinism probably would be viewed by the Soviet leaders as having the immediate advantage of reinforced control of present positions. Control over outer Eastern Europe, for example, could be reasserted through bilateral coordination of national plans, a process already under way insofar as Bulgaria and the GDR are concerned. But the costs of reversion are well known to the leadership. Terror, once systematically employed, has a tendency to get out of hand and destroy those who wield it. To bring about its reimposition on a more sophisticated and therefore doubly reluctant population would require the generation of an atmosphere of constant international crisis, not to mention Jew-baiting, with a consequent sharp rise in the danger of nuclear escalation. Above all, there would be serious question whether a forcible increase of inputs into the economy would bring the USSR abreast of the U.S. in substantially more fields than is now the

40. Secretariat of the Economic Commission for Europe, *Economic Survey of Europe in 1969: Part II* (Prepublication text) (New York: United Nations, 1970), chapter 1, p. 22, chapter 2, p. 10. The economic reform introduced by Chairman of the Council of Ministers Alexei Kosygin in October 1965, was limited to improvement of the central planning system. For an account see Eugène Zaleski, *Planning Reforms in the Soviet Union 1962–1968: An Analysis of Recent Trends in Economic Organization and Management*, trans. Marie-Christine MacAndrew and G. Warren Nutter (Chapel Hill: University of North Carolina Press, 1967). Without system change, the Sacharov letter asserts, "Our country . . . will fall behind the capitalist states during the course of the second industrial revolution and step by step become a second-class provincial power." "Sacharows Brief," 24 April 1970, p. 13.

case. For the miniaturization of electrical components, for example, the whip is a reasonably ineffective motivation. As Soviet physicist A. D. Sacharov phrased it in his letter to Brezhnev, Kosygin, and Podgorny, "a swing to the right, i.e., the victory of the tendency toward a harsher administrative rule, toward a 'turning of the screw', cannot solve these problems and would only multiply them in the extreme and lead our country into a tragic blind alley."[41]

Perhaps the dilemma will come into sharper relief if we think of the Soviet Union as that part of the developing world which had industrialized enough, and become powerful enough, to be able to capture a group of small, relatively defenseless, but on the whole more advanced Western populations. These peoples it holds captive as compensation for Western aggression, occupation and destruction directed against the USSR itself; it employs them as a security belt against renewed aggression; and it exploits them on behalf of its own economic progress.

The captive populations, however, are restless and discontented. They resent the imposition of an alien system and they feel deprived of their Western (European) birthright in both living standards and governmental practice. Their sense of deprivation is magnified by the astonishing successes of the Common Market. In a period of de-Stalinization, the captive peoples exert an increasing pressure toward reshaping the alien system in their own interests: toward integration with Western Europe through the creation of market socialism, for example, and toward the parallel development of one-party democracy. Because of systemic interdependence, such partial integration probably is not possible in the long run unless the Soviet regime itself is prepared to assume the risks and accept the costs of structural reform in the USSR. These risks and costs include not only massive dependence on Western (particularly German) capital and the setting up of a condominium over Eastern Europe, but especially the ethnic pluralization of the Soviet regime and a diminution of the role played in it by the Great Russians themselves.

It would appear that the CPE is not capable of coping with the industrialization-modernization problem at the level of industrial maturity—that it can put a developing country through the "first," but not the "second" industrial revolution. If this is so, then the choice before Moscow is gradual integration with the Atlantic community at the price of dilution of the regime itself and the downgrading of its carrier people, the Great Russians; or the retention of the regime and of Great Russian hegemony at the cost of reversion to Stalinism and declining influence as a superpower. The present Soviet leadership appears incapable of making a clear-cut decision;

41. Ibid., p. 14.

it very probably harbors great fear of political landslide and will no doubt continue to straddle the issue. Whether the new generation will be prepared for bolder action when it takes over leadership in the next decade or so, only the future can reveal.

Contributors

Bela A. Balassa	Professor of Economics, The Johns Hopkins University
Morris Bornstein	Professor of Economics, The University of Michigan
Alan A. Brown	Professor of Economics, University of Windsor (Canada)
R. V. Burks	Professor of History, Wayne State University
Václav Holešovský	Professor of Economics, University of Massachusetts
Estelle James	Associate Professor of Economics, State University of New York, Stony Brook
Jerzy F. Karcz	Late Professor of Economics, University of California, Santa Barbara
Michael Keren	Lecturer in Economics, The Hebrew University (Jerusalem)
Paul Marer	Visiting Associate Professor of Economics, Indiana University
Thomas A. Marschak	Professor, School of Business Administration, University of California, Berkeley
John Michael Montias	Professor of Economics, Yale University
Egon Neuberger	Professor of Economics, State University of New York, Stony Brook
Svetozar Pejovich	Professor of Economics, Ohio University

Index

Accounting wages, 263n23

Action(s), 36, 39, 40, 42, 43, 43n22

Actors: internal, in Yugoslav enterprise, 246, 255; external, in Yugoslav enterprise, 246, 255; internal, and their objective functions, 249, 250, 250n6, 265–72; internal, as beneficiaries, 250; indoctrination of internal, 250

Adjustment processes, 36, 41, 42

Aggregation: prices, 73n7, 89–97 passim; and decentralization, 89–97; partial, 94–97, 98, 103n32

Agricultural reforms, 16, 17, 207–43; pressures for, 211, 221; balance of payments pressure toward reform, 221; planning and administration, 222–32; successive, in Romania, 1962, 222–23; in East Germany, 223–24; in Bulgaria, 224–25; in Hungary 225–26, 227–28; in Czechoslovakia, 226–27; reversals, Romania, 227; changes in compulsory deliveries, 228–29; lower price for compulsory deliveries eliminated, 232; prices and taxes, 232–35; income and private sector, 235–39; in Yugoslavia, 237–41

Agriculture: collectivization, 3, 211, 216–17; command farming, 16; performance indicators, 207–10; procurement of farm products, 212; procurement prices, 212; procurement prices in Bulgaria, 212–13; consequences of compulsory quotas and prices, 215; supply of spare parts, 218, 231; contract delivery system, 223, 229; concentration, 227–28; planning practices, 228; cash premiums, etc., to increase supply, 229; prices and costs, 232–34; concentration of resources on better land, 241; investment, 242; machinery industry, 242. *See also* Farming

Agro-industrial complexes, 243; in Bulgaria, 225, 227–28

Albania, 3, 10

Allocation: mechanism, 47; disaggregation process, 86–87; system in East Germany, 136; framework for decisions, 245–54; decisions in closed model, 247–51

Annual economic plan in Yugoslavia: function in partial reform, 287

A priori restrictions of economic systems, 249; fixed internal in Yugoslav firm, 256; fixed external in Yugoslav firm, 256–65

Arrow, K. J., 133

Aspirational earnings in Yugoslavia, 282n63

Associations of enterprises, 9; in Czechoslovakia, 325, 329, 332, 333, 339

Autarky, 154, 211; and Hungary, 365

Authority: delegation of, 12, 13; relationships, 36–39

Autonomy: of enterprises, 8–9; of enterprise in Yugoslavia, 17, 255; of managers, consequences for solidary society, 282, 283

Balance of payments: disequilibrium with East and West, 160–62; disequilibrium and pressure for reform, 160–62; pressure for reform in agriculture, 221; deficit in Yugoslavia, before 1964, 290

Balance-of-trade ratios, 162, 200, 201

Balancing functions of enterprises in East Germany, 148, 149

Balassa, Bela, 14, 15, 20

Bank credit: as substitute for self-financing in Yugoslavia, 302; and investment in Hungary, 361

Bank funds: use of, 9

405